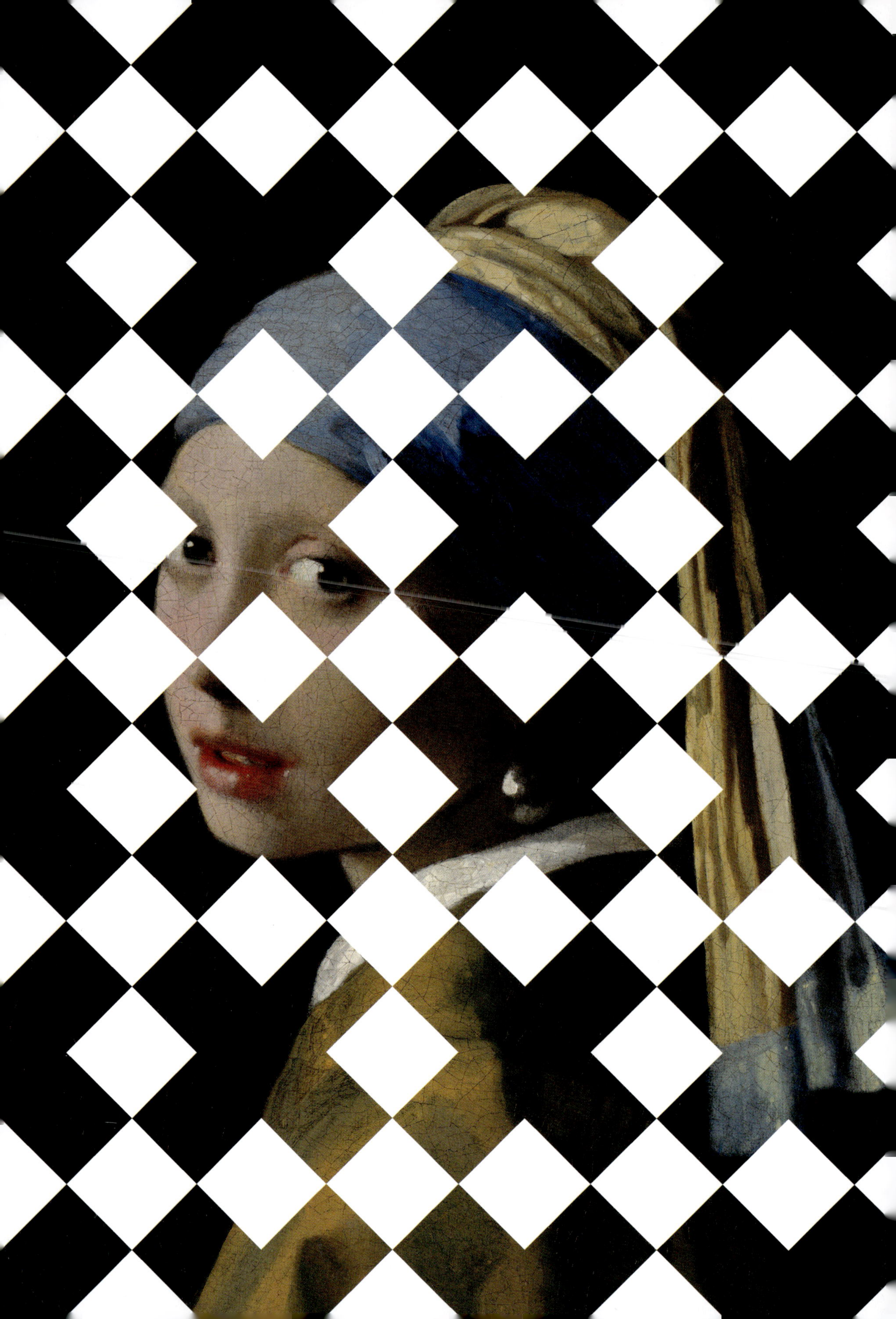

Vermeer's Afterlives

Ruth Bernard Yeazell

PRINCETON UNIVERSITY PRESS

PRINCETON & OXFORD

Published by Princeton University Press
41 William Street, Princeton, New Jersey 08540
99 Banbury Road, Oxford OX2 6JX

press.princeton.edu

GPSR Authorized Representative: Easy Access System Europe
Mustamäe tee 50, 10621 Tallinn, Estonia, gpsr.requests@easproject.com

ISBN 9780691277820
ISBN (epub) 9780691287812
ISBN (PDF) 9780691277912

Library of Congress Control Number: 2025949854

British Library Cataloging-in-Publication Data is available

Editorial: Anne Savarese and Emma Wagh
Production Editorial: Terri O'Prey
Text and Jacket Design: Chris Ferrante
Production: Steven Sears
Publicity: Jodi Price
Copyeditor: Francis Eaves

Frontispiece: detail from fig. 4.1 (*Girl with a Pearl Earring*); page XII: detail from fig. 3.1 (*Girl Reading a Letter at an Open Window*); page 90: detail from fig. 3.13 (*The Art of Painting*); page 200: detail from fig. 5.16 (*A Lady Writing*).

Jacket art: (Front) George Deem, *Extended Vermeer* (2000). Oil on canvas. 101.6 × 91.4 cm. Private Collection, Hartford, CT. © Artists Rights Society (ARS), NY. Image © Archives of American Art, Smithsonian Institution, Washington, DC. (Back) Johannes Vermeer, *Lady Writing a Letter with Her Maid* (ca. 1670–71). Oil on canvas. 72.2 × 59.5 cm. National Gallery of Ireland, Dublin. Image © National Gallery of Ireland.

This book has been composed in Signifier and The Future

Printed in China

10 9 8 7 6 5 4 3 2 1

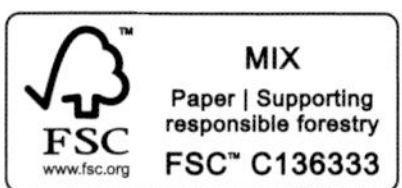

Contents

Preface

Johannes Vermeer was born in 1632 and reborn as an international phenomenon more than two hundred years later. Much admired by a small circle in his native Delft during his lifetime, the artist had virtually disappeared from collective consciousness by the mid-nineteenth century, only to undergo a revival so dramatic that he would become, in our lifetimes, one of the most admired painters in the world. A major exhibition of 1995–96 that originated in the National Gallery of Art in Washington, DC, before traveling to The Hague drew such large crowds to its winter opening that people lined up in the cold for as much as twelve hours to view it; when a government shutdown threatened to deprive them of the experience, a huge outcry ensued, and the exhibition reopened with the support of private donors, while the rest of the museum and the government itself remained closed.[1] The opening of a show on "Vermeer and the Masters of Dutch Genre Painting" in the spring of 2017 so overwhelmed the Louvre's capacities that it briefly triggered a staff strike.[2] Six years later, the Rijksmuseum in Amsterdam gathered twenty-eight paintings by the artist for a blockbuster exhibition that sold out within days and even prompted a temporary suspension of museum memberships, lest the total numbers prove unmanageable.

Vermeer's fame rests on a very small number of paintings. Even today, much remains unknown about his career and its immediate aftermath, but scholars generally agree that the thirty-five to thirty-seven works currently attributed to him represent the bulk of his output—a number that is all the more striking when compared to the hundreds of pictures turned out by many of his contemporaries. (After a very controversial process of winnowing, the official Rembrandt corpus, for instance, is still over three hundred.)[3] Just why Vermeer painted so little is a matter of speculation, though modern researchers have helped to sketch in some possible answers. The story of their discoveries is part of the artist's afterlife and thus part of my story as well. But this book is more concerned with the effects of Vermeer's art on later imaginations than with the history of its making or the visual culture in which it originated. Whatever the cause of Vermeer's slight production, for example, the idea of something "rare"—understood both as a measure of quantity and a term of value—has attached itself to his paintings ever since they began to resurface in the nineteenth century. And so too as regards the enigmatic aura that initially obscured the facts of his career and that soon appeared to emanate from the work as well: an aura that continues to surround the artist's name even after a century and a half of determined scholarship. Like other aspects of Vermeer's modern reception, including the very idea of him *as* "modern," the mysterious Vermeer is at once a product of the man who lived and died in seventeenth-century Delft and of those who later responded to him with visions of their own.

The facts of history still matter, of course, if only to understand how such visions differ from the views of Vermeer's contemporaries, and this book is deeply indebted to the many scholars who have made such understanding possible. But I also believe that art has a life—or lives—beyond its historical context and that its afterlives can prove illuminating, both for what they reveal about subsequent viewers and for what they disclose in the original. "In many cases even the errors in the reception of a poet can be traced back to genuine features of her texts," the classicist Glenn Most has observed about the afterlife of another elusive artist, the ancient singer we know as Sappho; and for all the differences between an archaic Greek poet and a seventeenth-century Dutch painter, his words still resonate for Vermeer's afterlife as well.[4] Not that error as such predominates among the works examined here, though the artist who emerges from contemporary scholarship certainly differs from the one reconstructed by his earliest champions, and the twentieth-century boom in Vermeer forgeries would have been impossible without the errors of many expert eyes. Most of the figures in this book see partially rather than wrongly, and by seeing partially—in both senses of the word—they focus attention on what others may have overlooked, even as they succeed in making new art from old. Vermeer's afterlives include works by other painters, as well as filmmakers, novelists, poets, and art historians, and while much of this work takes creative liberties with the original, the divide between the artists and the scholars is less sharp than one might think. That is partly because Vermeer has proved an appealing subject for writers who themselves cross the divide: poet/critics such as Jean-Louis Vaudoyer, for example, whose seminal articles on the Delft master in a French newspaper of 1921 strongly influenced Marcel Proust, or painter/critics such as the British portraitist and landscape artist Lawrence Gowing, whose monograph of 1952 still remains one of the most cited studies of Vermeer's work. Among the most useful of current resources on the artist is a website—www.essentialvermeer.com—curated by a contemporary painter, the American-born Jonathan Janson.

But even those who make no pretense to scholarship can scarcely help being affected, however subtly, by the discoveries of the historians. Unlike other world-famous painters—Leonardo da Vinci, or Rembrandt, for instance—Vermeer only entered public consciousness with the rise of art history as a discipline, and the coincidence of the two phenomena has continued to shape his reception ever since. Novelists credit scholars in their acknowledgments; visual artists and filmmakers invoke them in interviews; poets attach epigraphs from the documentary record or weave allusions to information derived from museum labels and catalogues into their poems. In a statement of 2002, one contemporary painter spoke of reading "nearly everything" on Vermeer published in the past decade, including fiction as well as history; another, who works primarily with collage, calls a 1981 study of the painter her "Bible."[5] The late George Deem, who produced some of the most inventive variations on his seventeenth-century predecessor, incorporated an extract from Gowing's book in a painting entitled "Gowing's Vermeer: Page One."

By the time Gowing published that book in 1952, he seems to have concluded that Vermeer's moment had passed. "Taste, with the painting it follows, has turned another way," he observed with a touch of melancholy in the closing pages of his introductory essay.[6] This book is premised on the belief that in this, at least, he was mistaken. Painting itself has been pronounced dead more than once since Gowing delivered his verdict, but an age of appropriation and pastiche has found new uses for old masters, only some of which involve the further creation of still images. Painters may no longer choose to emulate Vermeer's compositions as directly as they did at the turn of the twentieth century, and we seem unlikely to witness another spate of forgeries to rival the frauds perpetrated by Han van Meegeren around the time of the Second World War, but the very stylistic habits that enabled a clever artist like Van Meegeren to imitate Vermeer so effectively continue to make him peculiarly susceptible to various forms of artistic recycling. Proust's great novel excepted, most of the literature inspired by his art only began to appear in the second half of the twentieth century, with novels and poems alike multiplying in the aftermath of the 1995–96 show. Though his influence on film has arguably been more diffuse—he's been called the world's "first cinematographer"[7]—films explicitly connected to his life and work have also increased in recent decades. Among the viewing public more generally, Vermeer's popularity just seems to grow with each blockbuster exhibition and imaginative spin-off. One poll taken in the Netherlands even showed him surpassing Rembrandt as the nation's favorite painter, a result that would have been inconceivable two centuries earlier, when

Rembrandt was already famous and the Delft artist's name would scarcely have been recognized by most of his countrymen.[8]

That same reversal, of course, should make us wary of predicting the future. The history of taste is filled with salutary warnings about the impermanence of aesthetic judgment, and there's no guarantee that Vermeer's appeal will continue to register so strongly on viewers two hundred years hence. Though my own love of his work should be clear, the pages that follow are less concerned with justifying that love than with examining the various responses Vermeer's art has elicited since it was first restored to a broad public in the middle of the nineteenth century. As subsequent chapters will show, the very features of his art that some might characterize as limitations also prove to be among those that stimulate the work of others, especially when writers are tempted to fill in his silences or to narrate the stories his paintings leave untold. These are the particular temptations of novelists and poets, but even art historians are not immune, if only because they, too, inevitably deal in words.

Vermeer's afterlives don't always sort along obvious lines, and the argument of this book proceeds accordingly. Though the first part focuses on criticism and scholarship, the second on visual images, and the third on works of literature, some genres—and even media—figure in more than one place, and so too do certain recurrent modes of responding to Vermeer's art. His tendency to inspire pastiche, for example—by which I mean art produced by extracting and recombining motifs, sometimes from multiple canvases—shows up not only in the work of painters and other visual artists such as filmmakers (not to mention forgers!), but in the imaginary "Vermeers" of novelists and poets as well. By referring to the original paintings as "fragments of the same world," Proust memorably evoked the aspect of Vermeer's style that lends itself to this practice, though Proust himself did not engage in it.[9] Nor did he proceed, like novelists after him, to turn the paintings into narrative, or to imagine the turmoil on which the artist turned his back in order to paint them. On the contrary: for Proust the seeming autonomy of Vermeer's work from his life constituted part of its appeal. *À la recherche du temps perdu* remains the greatest novel to engage with Vermeer, and the present book therefore treats it not only along with other fictions in chapter 9 below, "Stories Not Told," but also in sections devoted to art history and criticism, especially chapter 2, concerned, as its title announces, with "How Vermeer Became Modern." Yet even as many in Proust's generation found the work of the seventeenth-century painter surprisingly prescient, that painter continued to retain the aura of mystery that had originally attached to his seeming disappearance from the historical record. Proust dubbed him, in a lovely turn of phrase, "ce maître inouï," the words playing on the double meaning of *inouï* as both unheard of and extraordinary.[10] A century later, that extraordinary master continues to tease the imagination of his admirers, but the sense in which he remains unknown has changed utterly. It is to the beginning of that transformation that I now turn.

Vermeer's Afterlives

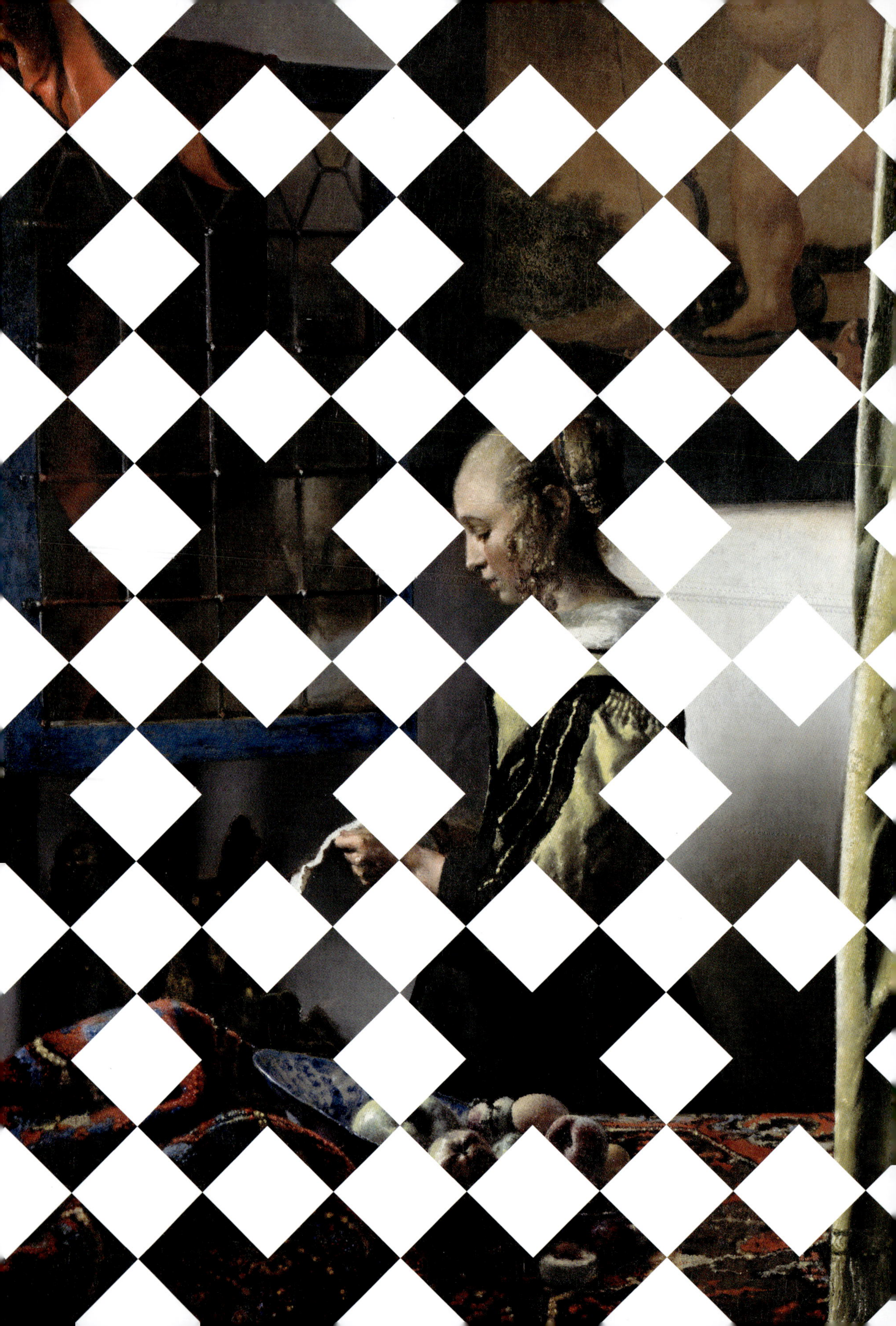

I

Mystery and Recovery

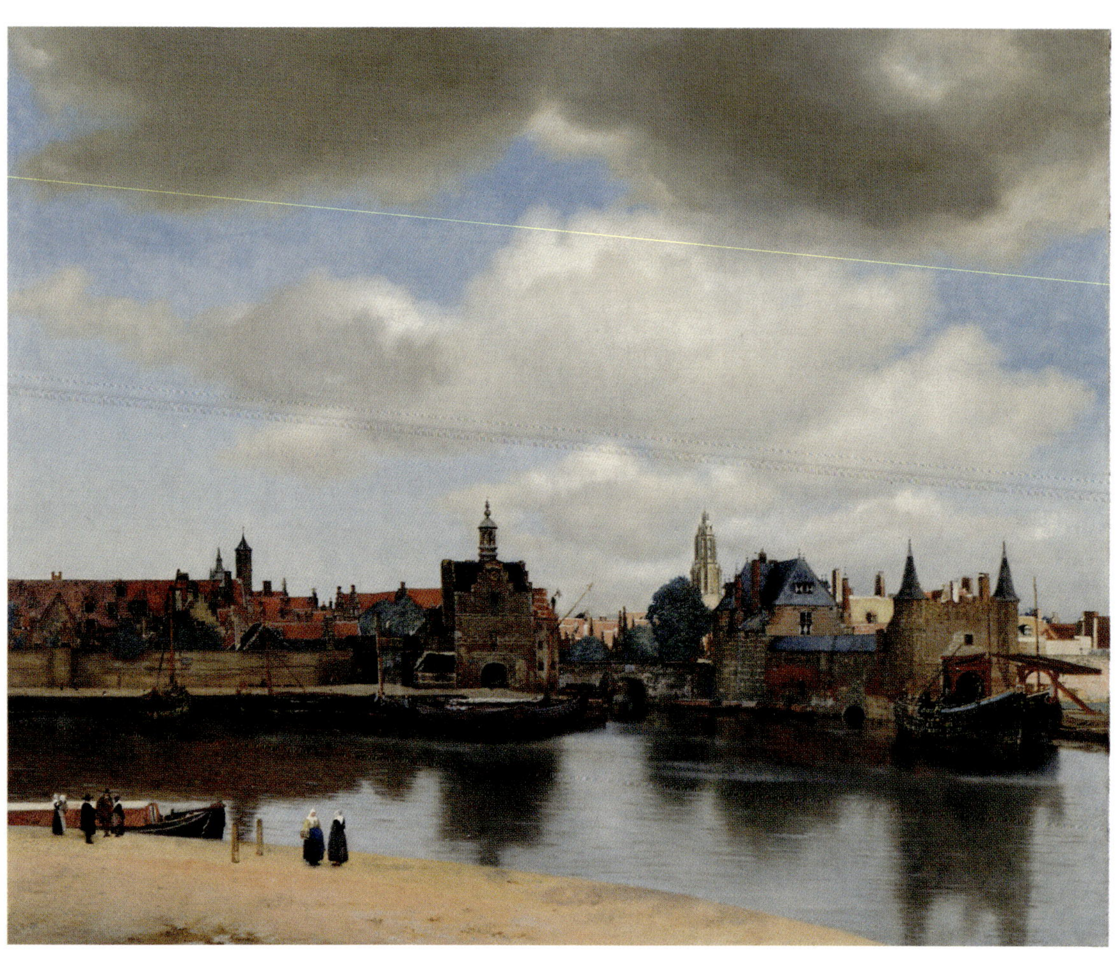

Fig. 1.1. Johannes Vermeer, *View of Delft* (ca. 1660–63). Oil on canvas. 96.5 × 115.7 cm. Mauritshuis, The Hague

1

Questions for the Sphinx

This Vermeer has driven us crazy. But we have revived him.
—THÉOPHILE THORÉ TO BARTHOLD SUERMONDT (1867)

"In the museum at The Hague, a superb and very singular landscape arrests all visitors and vividly impresses artists and connoisseurs." So opens perhaps the most influential account of Vermeer ever written, a three-part article by the radical journalist and art critic Théophile Thoré in the *Gazette des beaux-arts* of 1866 that is widely credited with rescuing the painter from the oblivion—Thoré's term was *l'oubli*—into which he had fallen. The landscape in question was of course the *View of Delft* (fig. 1.1), and after a brief description of its principal features, including the brilliance of its light, the intensity of its color, and the thick impasto of certain passages, Thoré quickly turned to his original encounter with the painting more than two decades earlier. "When I visited the museums of Holland for the first time in 1842," he wrote,

> this strange painting surprised me as much as *The Anatomy Lesson* and the other very curious Rembrandts in the museum at The Hague. Not knowing to whom to attribute it, I consulted the catalogue: "*View of the City of Delft*, from the canal side, by Jan van der Meer of Delft." Oh! Here's someone we don't know in France, and who very much deserves to be known!

"Even after having seen the *Night Watch*, the *Syndics,* and the other wonders of the museum in Amsterdam," he continued, "I carried back to Paris the indelible memory of this masterpiece."[1]

Thoré's enthusiasm for Vermeer is unmistakable, and I suspect there are few viewers these days who would find his admiration for the *View of Delft* overstated. But there is also a bit of mythmaking in his narrative, a myth that has in turn become an integral part of Vermeer's afterlife. While Thoré may well have been struck by his initial encounter with this work by an artist hitherto unknown to him, sixteen years would elapse before he commented on the experience in print; and when he finally did so, his verdict on the painting was rather more equivocal.

Eight years before his groundbreaking article on Vermeer, Thoré had published the first of two volumes on the museums of Holland under the pseudonym of W. Bürger—a pseudonym he had adopted after his exile from France for political activity in 1849, and which he would continue to employ for the remainder of his writing career. (*Bürger* of course means "citizen" or "freeman" in German.) Here is his entry on the *View of Delft* in that volume:

> In the painting at The Hague, *View of the Town of Delft, from the Canal Side*, he has pushed the impasto to a state of exaggeration that one sometimes encounters today in the work of M. Decamps. One could say that he wanted to build his town with a trowel, and his walls are real mortar. Too much is too much. Rembrandt never fell into these excesses [. . .].
>
> [D]espite this masonry, the *View of Delft* is nonetheless a masterful painting and altogether surprising for art lovers to whom Van der Meer is unfamiliar.

This passage is immediately preceded by a brief account of Vermeer as "a great painter" about whom little is known, as well as short descriptions of two other works by "this strange artist" that Thoré had seen on subsequent visits to Holland: *The Milkmaid* (see fig. 3.7) and *The Little Street* (fig. 1.2), both then in the collection of the Six family in Amsterdam.[2] But it wasn't until the second volume of the book appeared two years later that signs of what Thoré would eventually term his "mania" for the Delft artist were really in evidence.[3]

In the interval, he had been invited to catalogue a collection belonging to the Duke of Arenberg in Brussels, where he encountered yet another painting by this "incomparable original": the head of a young woman whose mysterious appeal he would later compare to that of the *Mona Lisa*. Though the current fame of the *Girl with a Pearl Earring* might lead us to imagine that hers was the picture in question, the Arenberg painting was in fact another so-called *tronie* (or anonymous head) by Vermeer—the *Study of a Young Woman* that now hangs in the Metropolitan Museum of New York (fig. 1.3). "How has this portrait, with its magisterial strangeness, never attracted much attention?" Thoré wondered. But the mystery on which he most began to dwell was that of the artist himself. The critic had thus far seen only four works identified with this "*Delfsche* van der Meer," though the very difficulty of distinguishing that name—and its

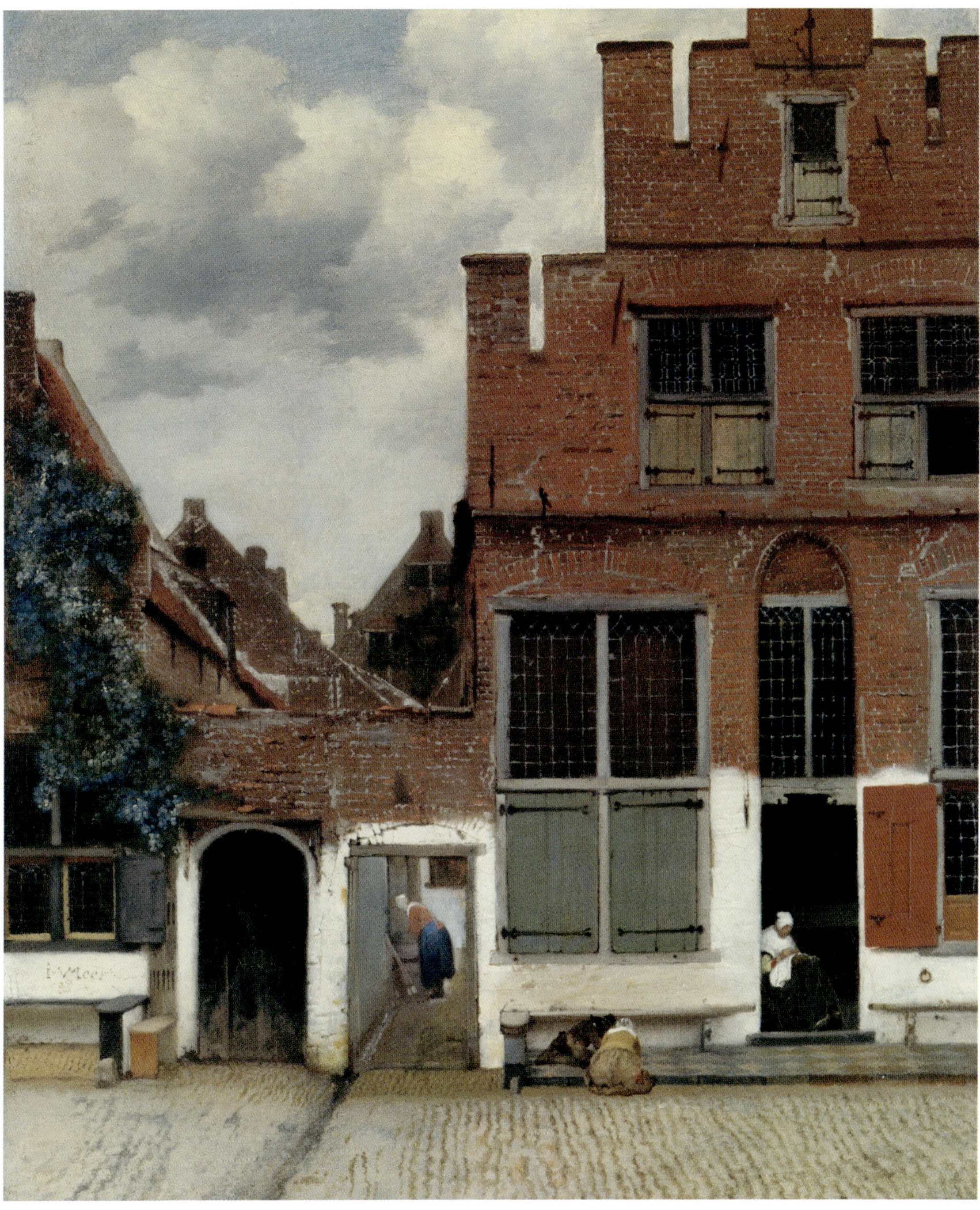

signature—from its many variants was already proving part of the puzzle. What else did this Van der Meer paint, if anything, and where were those paintings to be found? Who had trained him? How long had he lived? Why, for that matter, did other authorities have so little to say about his work? Such were the questions posed by the figure Thoré began to call "this so provocative sphinx."[4]

Fig. 1.2. Johannes Vermeer, *The Little Street* (ca. 1657–61). Oil on canvas. 54.3 × 44 cm. Rijksmuseum, Amsterdam

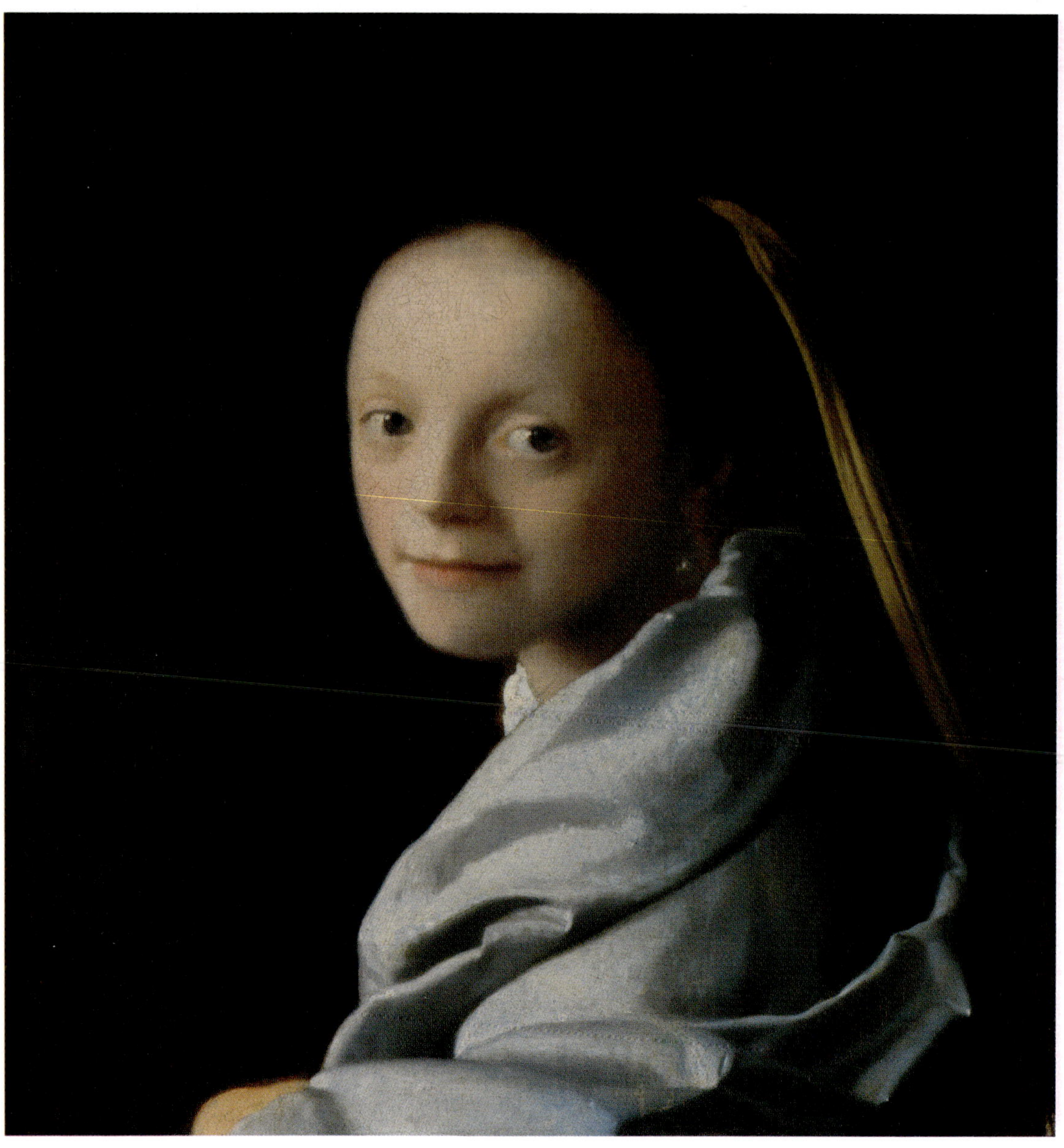

Fig. 1.3. Johannes Vermeer, *Study of a Young Woman* (ca. 1665–74). Oil on canvas. 44.5 × 40 cm. Gift of Mr. and Mrs. Charles Wrightsman, in memory of Theodore Rousseau Jr., 1979. Metropolitan Museum of Art, New York

Thoré continued to ask such questions—and to answer them—for the rest of his life. By the time the second volume of his *Musées de la Hollande* appeared two years later, his count of the surviving paintings had expanded fourfold, and he was already well on his way to tracking down more. The lengthy article on Vermeer for which he is now best known was the culmination of this process: both a glowing tribute to the art of the Delft master and a record of its author's obsession with what he still liked to call "my sphinx."[5] If he'd also managed to convince himself by that point that he had fallen in love with the *View of Delft* at first sight a quarter century earlier, such wishful backdating of his enthusiasm is surely forgivable.[6]

Thoré was not alone in his original ambivalence toward Vermeer's cityscape, a fact to which I shall return shortly. But what I want to emphasize here is neither his initial uneasiness at the painting's "excesses," nor his subsequent change of heart, but the power of his narrative to set the terms for those who came after him—even, or perhaps especially, when his rhetoric slightly exceeded the demonstrable facts.[7] Thoré's account of his first reaction to the *View of Delft* may not have been strictly accurate, but his "indelible memory" of his encounter with the painting made for a memorable opening to his study of the painter, as well as a template for later writers to follow on their own pilgrimages to the Hague.[8] Marcel Proust, who would make one such pilgrimage in 1902, later declared the *View of Delft* "the painting that I most admired in Holland," though it might be more accurate to translate his verb (*aimer*) as "loved" or "adored."[9] Whether or not Proust read Thoré himself, he certainly read those who read him, and it's also hard not to sense the reverberations of the critic's memorable introduction to Vermeer in the famous scene of *À la recherche du temps perdu* in which the writer Bergotte confronts the painting again at an exhibition in Paris—a painting "he remembered as more striking, more different than anything else he knew."[10] Proust's companion on the museum visit in 1921 that inspired this scene was Jean-Louis Vaudoyer, the poet and critic whose three-part article on Vermeer in a Parisian newspaper had originally prompted the ailing novelist to leave his sickbed for a final view of his beloved painting. "Once you have beheld the original," Vaudoyer had written of the *View of Delft*, "the remembrance that you keep of it transfigures any reproduction, and a feast of colors, light, and space immediately floods your memory."[11]

Like virtually everyone who wrote about Vermeer in the half-century after Thoré, Vaudoyer credited him with rescuing the artist "from oblivion," even as he continued to dwell on how much remained unknown about the painter.[12] (His article was entitled "Le mystérieux Vermeer.") Indeed, the image of the Delft artist as "an unknown of genius" may be among the most enduring legacies of Thoré's work, as well as the best example of how the genuine excitement of Vermeer's nineteenth-century revival inevitably became colored by some degree of mythmaking.[13] For if there is no question that the artist's name had fallen into obscurity by the time that Thoré consulted his catalogue in order to learn who had painted the *View of Delft*, it was hardly the case that Vermeer had disappeared from view altogether. The very fact that the catalogue correctly identified him argues otherwise, and so, of course, does the fact that the canvas was hanging in a public museum in the first place. The Royal Cabinet of Paintings at the Mauritshuis, in The Hague, had actually acquired the *View of Delft* in 1822—twenty years before Thoré's initial visit—and it did not come cheap. The price was 2,900 guilders, with the sellers' catalogue at the time of purchase calling it "the most famous painting of this master whose works seldom occur." The "way of painting," the description continued, "is the most audacious, powerful, and masterly one can imagine."[14]

Nor was this the only sign that Vermeer's work had continued to be admired in some quarters long after his death, as recent scholars have demonstrated.[15] Yet much of the evidence they have cited to question the myth of his total disappearance also helps to explain why Thoré could be said, with only slight exaggeration, to have rescued him from obscurity. The allusion to "this master whose works seldom occur" in the advertisement for the *View of Delft* is one such clue, since even as it celebrates Vermeer's achievement it reminds us that the sheer rarity of his paintings in circulation made it all too easy for that achievement to fade from public consciousness.[16] (Recall that Thoré had seen only three other works attributed to him before encountering the picture in the Arenberg collection.) Though we can't be certain why Vermeer produced so little by comparison to his contemporaries, the evidence strongly suggests that he was a slow and contemplative painter, much given to revision, who was partly shielded from the pressures of the market by his acquisition of a wealthy mother-in-law, and still more by a rich patron willing to pay high prices for the finished canvases. The fact that so many of the paintings had already disappeared into a single collection in the artist's lifetime clearly limited their capacity to circulate, though the death of the man who had inherited that collection in 1696—twenty-one years after the artist's own death—produced an auction catalogue that still provides the most authoritative documentation of Vermeer's work from the century in which he flourished. (That catalogue lists twenty-one paintings attributed to him, at least two of which have never been located.)[17]

Vermeer's name had also figured in a description of Delft published in 1667, where a commemorative poem on the premature death of Carel Fabritius—best known today for his marvelous *Goldfinch*—represents the dead artist as a phoenix from whose fires a magisterial Vermeer had arisen.[18] Despite that heady image, however, the standard accounts of Dutch painting in the century that followed scarcely registered his existence. One scholar has plausibly speculated that the damage was done when the earliest and most influential of these accounts, Arnold Houbraken's *Great Theater of Dutch Painting* (1718–21), accidentally skipped the crucial verse praising the artist risen from Fabritius's ashes, since it appears on a separate page from the rest of the poem.[19] Whatever the cause, Houbraken merely named Vermeer in passing, and subsequent authorities managed not to do even that. Nor did reproductive prints after his work help to stimulate the collective memory, as they did for many other Netherlandish artists of the period. The result was a vacuum of knowledge that effectively swallowed up the occasional mentions of Vermeer's art that nonetheless did surface from time to time over the following century, such as Joshua Reynolds's record of a painting he had seen on his journey to Holland in 1781: "A WOMAN pouring milk from one vessel to another" that Reynolds attributed to an artist named "D. Vandermeer."[20]

Even the few who singled Vermeer out for praise tended to imply that no one else had heard of him. In 1792 the French art dealer Jean Baptiste Lebrun

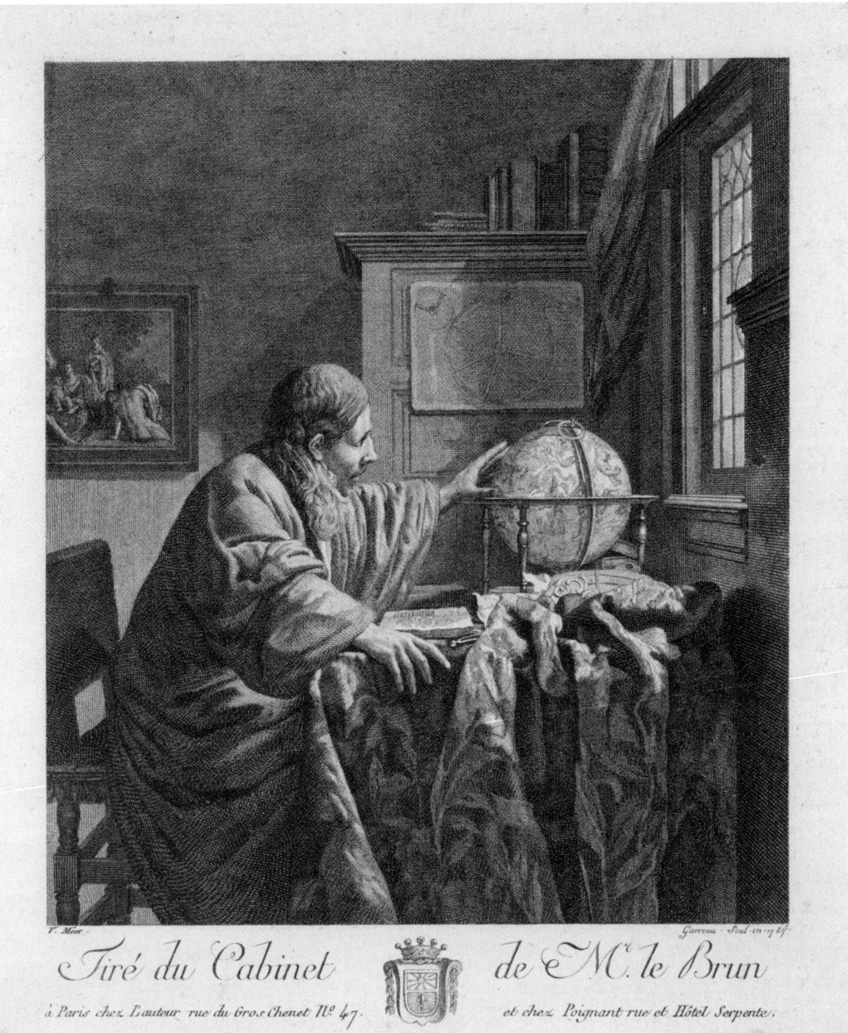

Fig. 1.4. Louis Garreau after Johannes Vermeer, *The Astronomer* (1784). Etching and engraving, as published in Jean Baptiste Pierre Lebrun, *Galerie des peintres flamands, hollandais et allemands [. . .]* (Paris, 1792). © The Trustees of the British Museum

set the pattern for such commentary when he published a brief entry on the artist, together with a rare print after his work—a 1784 engraving of *The Astronomer* (fig. 1.4)—in his so-called *Galerie* of Flemish, Dutch, and German painters. "This Vander Meer, of whom historians have not spoken at all, deserves particular attention," Lebrun observed, before going on to characterize him as "a very great painter in the manner of Metsu" and noting his special skill at rendering the effects of light.[21]

Nearly a quarter century later, a pair of Dutchmen published a biographical dictionary of Netherlandish artists that did "speak of" Vermeer and singled out the same three paintings—*The Milkmaid*, *The Little Street*, and the *View of Delft*—with which Thoré would later begin. "It goes without saying," the authors wrote, "that the works of the so-called Delft Ver Meer deserve a place in the most prestigious art collections."[22] Six years after they delivered this verdict, the state would acquire the *View of Delft* for the Mauritshuis. But perhaps because Dutch texts circulated less widely than French or German ones, the dictionary's pronouncement seems to have had little immediate impact outside the Netherlands. In 1833 the British picture dealer John Smith began his own brief commentary on the artist, whom he also associated with Metsu, by remarking, "Writers appear to have been entirely ignorant of the works of this excellent artist."[23] Thoré may not have been literally the first to break the silence, in other words, but that was only because the continuing silence had itself been one of the few things his predecessors knew about this "unknown of genius."[24]

And that genius had ironically remained unknown even when viewers were face to face with his work. Indeed, it's possible to argue that Thoré's greatest contribution to Vermeer's afterlife depended not so much on the capacity to see, as on the power to name: rather than observe the beauty of paintings no one had noticed before, what Thoré succeeded in doing was identifying them *as* Vermeer's. The *View of Delft* was not in fact the first of the artist's works to be displayed in a museum, nor was *The Astronomer* the first to be reproduced as a print; they were only the first to attain those forms of publicity under the name of their creator. A print of the *Girl Reading a Letter* (fig. 1.5) had appeared a year before *The Astronomer* engraving, but the painting it reproduced was then attributed to Govaert Flinck:[25] one of at least three artists, including Rembrandt and Pieter de Hooch, who were credited with the work before it was securely assigned to Vermeer.

The Music Lesson, meanwhile, (see fig. 3.10) has been in the Royal Collection at Windsor since the mid-eighteenth century, but was originally acquired as a Frans van Mieris; both the *Officer and Laughing Girl* (see fig. 1.14) in the Frick in New York and *The Art of Painting* (see fig. 3.13) in the Kunsthistoriches Museum in Vienna were once attributed to de Hooch; the *Young Woman with a Water Pitcher* (see fig. 3.8), now in the Metropolitan Museum in New York, twice changed hands in the late 1870s as a Gabriel Metsu; and the *Diana and Her Companions* (see fig. 2.1) at the Rijksmuseum was not officially identified as a Vermeer until the end of the nineteenth century, when curators determined that the signature of Nicholas Maes was a forgery.[26] And this is only a partial list—a fact all the more significant, of course, because the oeuvre was so limited in the first place.

One prominent scholar has sought to question the received narrative about the nineteenth-century recovery of Vermeer by arguing that a number of his canvases had long been admired under other names. But that's precisely the point: not until the oeuvre had been reassembled and identified as his did the artist we now celebrate emerge from obscurity.[27] The project was further complicated by a number of painters with similar names who also flourished in the seventeenth century, as Thoré noted with a mixture of bemusement and despair. There appeared to be a Jan van der Meer of Utrecht, for instance, who did make it into Houbraken's *Great Theater* and who specialized in large figure

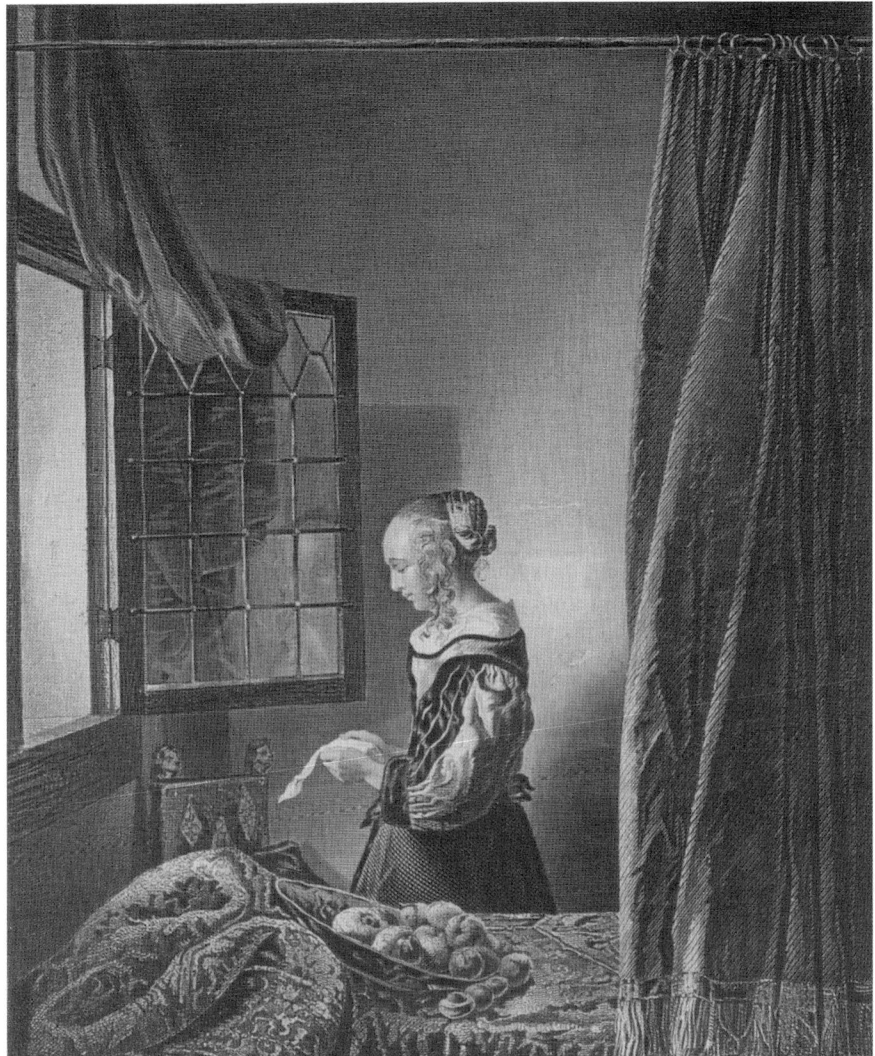

Fig. 1.5. A. H. Riedel Jr. after Govaert Flinck [Johannes Vermeer], *Girl Reading a Letter* (1783). Engraving

paintings; a father and son of the same name, both of Haarlem, who produced landscapes and animal pictures; and a B. van der Meer, listed as the painter of a large still life in the catalogue of the museum at Vienna, as well as a history painter recorded as H. van der Meer in a sales catalogue from Amsterdam—unless either or both of these initials, Thoré speculated, might simply prove to be typographical errors.[28] Hence his obsession with identifying the artist's signature: an exercise he charmingly sought to reproduce in his article (fig. 1.6). Only some of these signatures, incidentally, are now viewed as authentic, but the effort to reconstruct Vermeer's hand, in more than one sense, was key to solving the riddles posed by Thoré's "sphinx."

The surplus of artistic Van der Meers in the period was not the only source of potential confusion. Part of the puzzle, as Thoré saw it, arose from differences

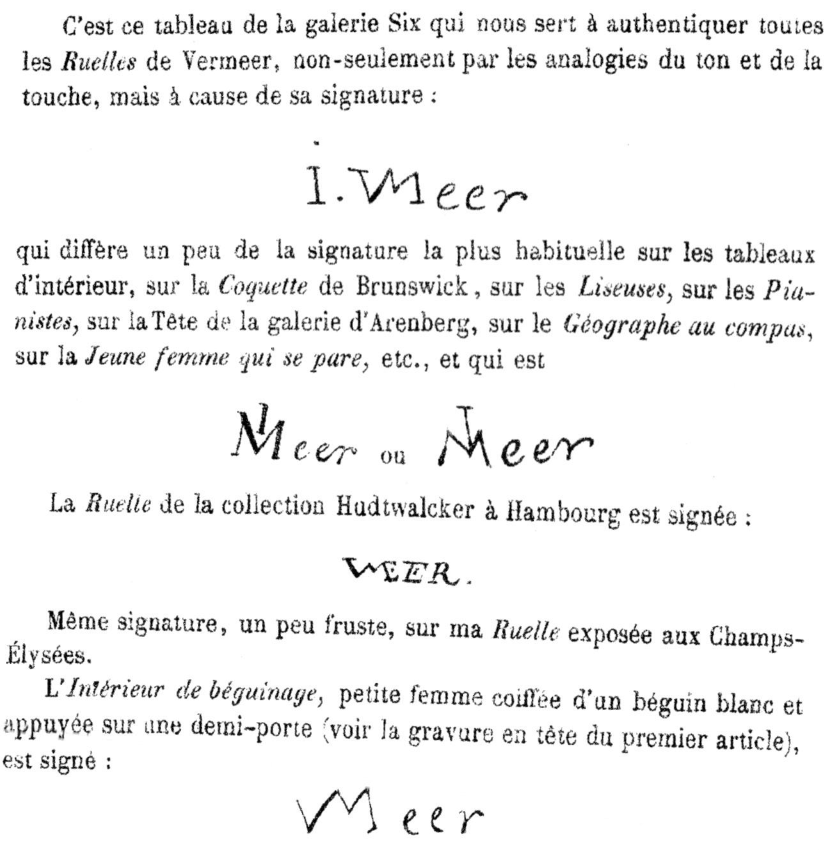

Fig. 1.6. Page from W. Bürger [Théophile Thoré], "Van der Meer de Delft," *Gazette des beaux-arts* (1866)

C'est ce tableau de la galerie Six qui nous sert à authentiquer toutes les *Ruelles* de Vermeer, non-seulement par les analogies du ton et de la touche, mais à cause de sa signature :

I. Meer

qui diffère un peu de la signature la plus habituelle sur les tableaux d'intérieur, sur la *Coquette* de Brunswick, sur les *Liseuses*, sur les *Pianistes*, sur la Tête de la galerie d'Arenberg, sur le *Géographe au compas*, sur la *Jeune femme qui se pare*, etc., et qui est

Meer ou Meer

La *Ruelle* de la collection Hudtwalcker à Hambourg est signée :

MEER.

Même signature, un peu fruste, sur ma *Ruelle* exposée aux Champs-Élysées.

L'*Intérieur de béguinage*, petite femme coiffée d'un béguin blanc et appuyée sur une demi-porte (voir la gravure en tête du premier article), est signé :

Meer

internal to Vermeer himself: differences first of all in his handling of the brush, but also in the kind of picture he set out to paint. By the time the second volume of *Musées de la Hollande* appeared in 1860, Thoré was beginning to wrestle with the problem. Having initially been struck by the thick impasto of the *View of Delft*, for instance (see fig. 1.1), he didn't quite know what to make of the thinly painted *Woman in Blue Reading a Letter* (see fig. 2.4) that he'd recently seen on a visit to Amsterdam, nor how to reconcile its "very delicate" execution with "the firmness of drawing and modeling" in *The Milkmaid* (see fig. 3.7), another of the paintings that had helped form his early impression of the artist more than a decade before. The *Girl with a Wine Glass* at Brunswick (fig. 1.7)—which, like the *Woman in Blue*, was a recent addition to his list—only seemed to compound the problem, since this "charming" scene apparently resembled the others neither in technique nor subject matter:

> I don't know a more delicious genre painting from the whole seventeenth-century Dutch school, including Terborch, Metsu, Jan Steen, and the best of them. Here, Van der Meer is no longer the brusque painter of his landscape in The Hague; what he seeks is no longer the firmness and character of *The Milkmaid* in the Six collection; it is the supreme elegance of this coquette

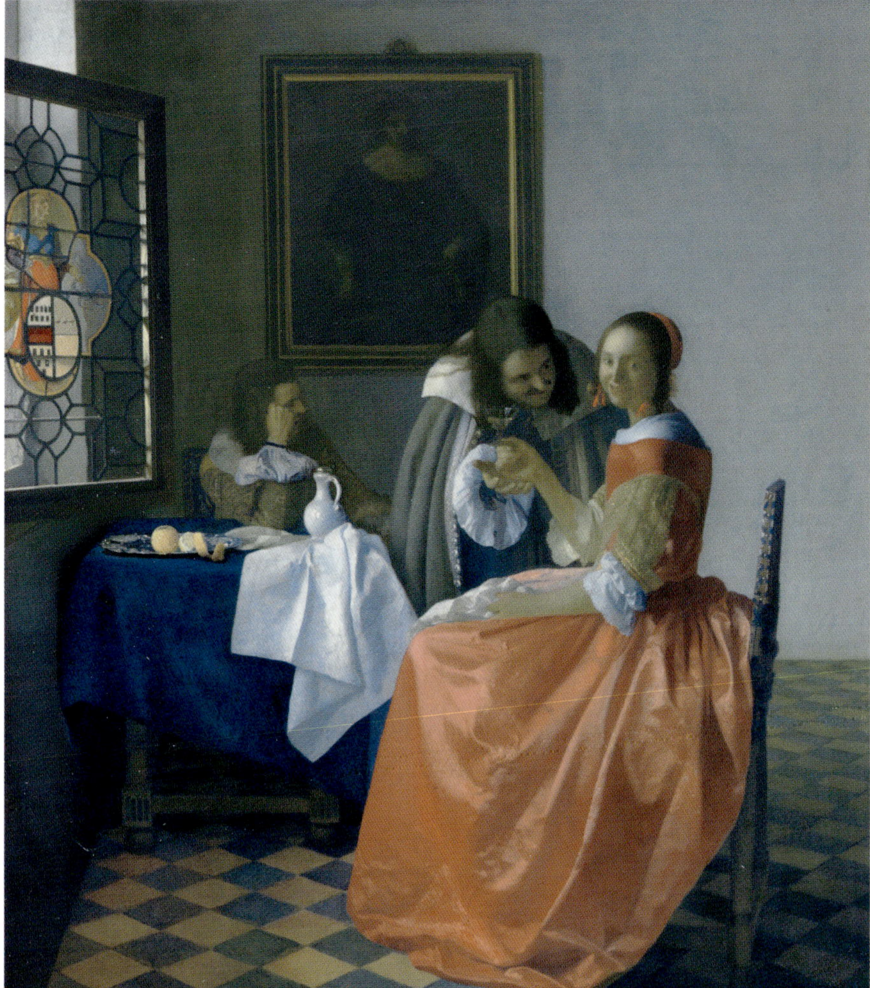

Fig. 1.7. Johannes Vermeer, *Girl with a Wine Glass* (ca. 1659–60). Oil on canvas. 71 × 67 cm. Herzog Anton Ulrich-Museum, Braunschweig, Germany. Photo: C. Cordes. bpk Bildagentur / Art Resource, NY

> with the fine and elongated figure, the appealing, sensuous, and witty face. The execution is sober, sharp, without impasto [. . .]. Terborch does not handle his brush and colors more lightly.[29]

"This devil of an artist no doubt had various styles," he observed wryly after describing his bafflement at the *Woman in Blue*, and his sense of that variety only intensified as his account of the oeuvre expanded.[30] The last installment of Thoré's article on the painter six years later consisted of a catalogue with seventy-three entries, loosely divided among figure paintings, cityscapes, and landscapes, including one for still life, and a final number for several further possibilities labeled simply "divers" (various)—the word he'd also used to characterize the style as a whole in the previous discussion. Thoré hadn't seen all of these canvases himself, and he frankly acknowledged that some of the identifications were tentative or dubious: despite his effort to distinguish one Van der

Meer from another, he also acknowledged that a small galaxy of artists by the same name might still be clustered in his catalogue. "Enough! and perhaps too much," he ruefully exclaimed as he neared his conclusion. But Thoré remained an enthusiast, and even as he signed off with this endearing concession, he immediately followed up by encouraging others to continue his quest—especially, he emphasized, the quest for more paintings.[31] He might only have uncovered a few facts about the artist's biography, he'd observed earlier, "but by means of the works, of which I know a great number, I hope almost to recreate the personality of Van der Meer. Don't people say that we know the worker by the work? The painting reveals the painter."[32]

As should be obvious by now, the painter potentially revealed by this exercise is only in part the Vermeer generally recognized by modern scholarship. In his eagerness to track down lost work, Thoré had allowed his wishes to outrun the facts, with the result that less than a quarter of the paintings listed in his catalogue are still attributed to the artist. The problem is partly endemic to connoisseurship, especially as it was practiced in an era before technological advances allowed at least some puzzles to be solved scientifically: witness the long-standing debate about the scope of Rembrandt's oeuvre. But Thoré's uncertainties were also fueled, I think, by the sequence in which he encountered the paintings, and by his early surprise at the *Woman in Blue*'s apparent departure from the style he first identified with Vermeer's art. Consider what to our eyes might seem the baffling number of street scenes and landscapes—over twenty—that Thoré listed in his catalogue. While we've grown accustomed to thinking of Vermeer as primarily a figure painter, the *View of Delft* and *The Little Street* were two of the first three Vermeers that Thoré saw, and in 1859 he found—or so he imagined—another: "a sort of landscape" that belonged to a wealthy German collector named Barthold Suermondt and that Thoré immediately christened *The Rustic Cottage* (fig. 1.8). At one time attributed to Hobbema and at another to Ruisdael, the picture had recently been ascribed to the Dutch landscape painter Philip Koninck by the director of the Gemäldegalerie in Berlin, Gustav Waagen, who had just completed a catalogue of Suermondt's collection. But for Thoré, whose prior experience had convinced him that one of Vermeer's "specialties" was to paint houses, both the picture's subject—"the *portrait* of a house, full-face view, and almost filling the canvas!"—and "the magic" of its light clearly pointed to the creator of *The Little Street* and the *View of Delft*. Drawing on comparisons to both pictures, Thoré devoted more than five pages of an essay accompanying Waagen's catalogue to making his case. *The Rustic Cottage,* he announced, "is incontestably a work—a masterpiece—of Jan van der Meer of Delft, and M. Suermondt has come round to my opinion."[33]

Scholars now attribute the picture to Dirk Jan van der Laan, a minor Dutch painter who flourished more than a century after Vermeer. But having convinced himself of its authenticity at an early stage of his "mania," Thoré inevitably

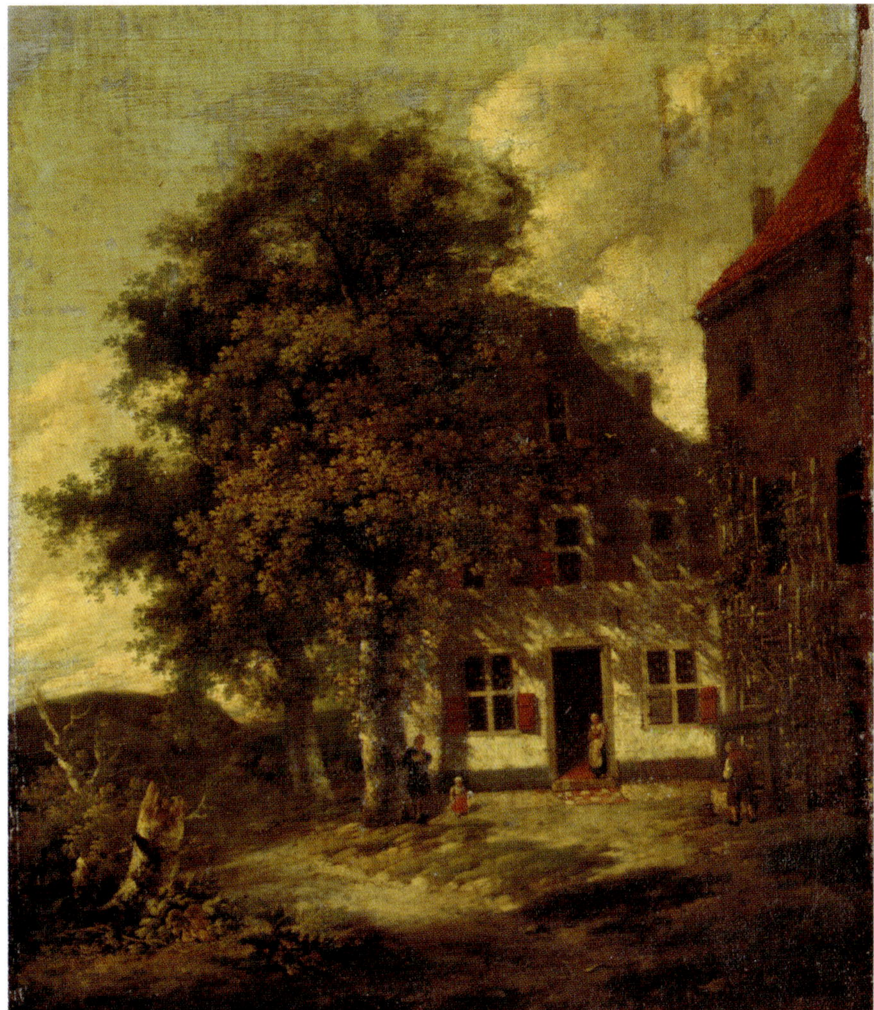

Fig. 1.8. Dirk Jan van der Laan, *The Rustic Cottage* (late 18th/early 19th century). Oil on canvas. 49.5 × 41.4 cm. Photo Jörg P. Anders. Gemädelgalerie, Staatliche Museen, Berlin. bpk Bildagentur / Art Resource, NY

looked for others like it, and it became part of the foundation on which his idea of the artist was constructed.[34] From the late 1850s until his death in 1869, Thoré increasingly acted both as an informal advisor to wealthy collectors like Suermondt and as a small collector in his own right, whose treasured acquisitions would include several authentic Vermeers, as well as more than one "little street" he mistakenly ascribed to the artist. (Among his other prized paintings was Fabritius's *Goldfinch*.) In 1866, a few months before the first installment of "Van der Meer de Delft" was due to appear in the *Gazette des beaux-arts*, Thoré deliberately set out to gin up publicity for his beloved painter by arranging for eleven works attributed to him to be included in a so-called *Exposition rétrospective* attached to the Paris Salon. The effort succeeded—"our Vermeer is on his way," he wrote triumphantly to Suermondt the following year[35]—even if this was another occasion on which Thoré's enthusiasm outran his knowledge: only four of the canvases, including two from his own collection, are now viewed as

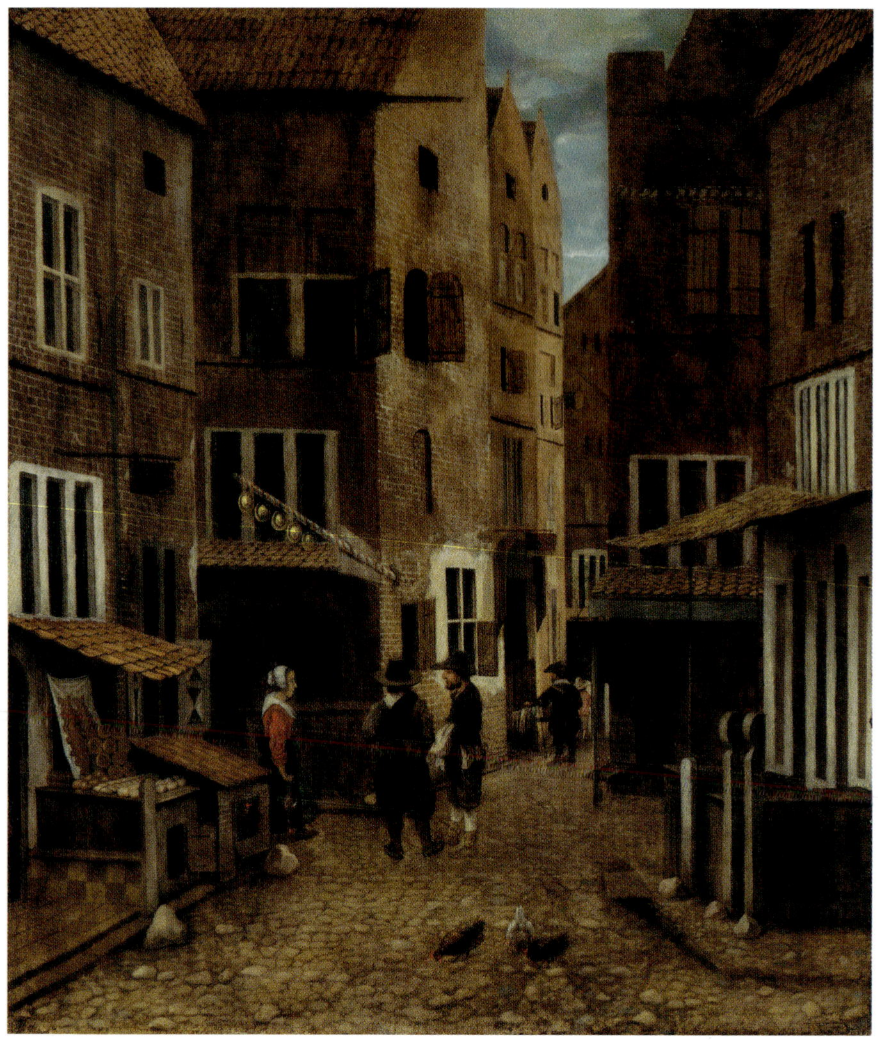

Fig. 1.9. Jacobus Vrel, *Street Scene* (ca. 1654–62). Oil on panel. 41.3 × 34 cm. The J. Paul Getty Museum, Los Angeles

genuine. *The Rustic Cottage*, ironically, was a crowd favorite, as was another landscape from the Suermondt collection, a *View of Dunes* signed "J. v. Meer" that turns out to have been painted by one of the master's lesser namesakes, Dirk Jan van der Meer. Critics were especially taken by the "harmony" and "poetry" of a *Street Scene* (fig. 1.9) that belonged to Thoré himself: one of two such "Vermeers" in his possession that would later be recognized as the work of Jacobus Vrel.[36]

Thoré, to his credit, increasingly began to question his attribution of those paintings, though he never abandoned his belief in *The Rustic Cottage*.[37] It didn't take long, however, for others to cast doubt on that picture too. As early as 1882 the young Dutch art historian Abraham Bredius published a short article entitled "A Pseudo-Vermeer in the Berlin Gallery," in which he attributed the painting to Van Laan, while scornfully dismissing those who had managed to confuse the Delft master with an artist who lived more than a century later.[38] But the particular association of Vermeer with the art of landscape lingered in some quarters well after Bredius's demolition work. "Every bend in the road shows a fresh picture such as Vermeer alone of masters might have hoped to paint," one American travel writer gushed of a visit to Holland in 1912.[39] In a climactic scene of *The Outcry*, a relatively little-known novel by Henry James published in 1911, a young British connoisseur named Hugh Crimble outsmarts a wealthy American collector, loosely modeled on J. P. Morgan, by identifying a "small landscape" that the collector has "rapidly studied and denounced." The landscape belongs to an impecunious aristocrat whose collection of paintings the American, Breckenridge Bender, is hoping to plunder and ship off to the United States. "For what do you take that little picture?" inquires the aristocrat's daughter, who has heard about Bender's quick dismissal of the landscape as a "bogus Cuyp":

> Hugh Crimble went over and looked. "Why, don't you know? It's a jolly little Vandermeer of Delft."
> "It's not a base imitation?"
> He looked again, but appeared at a loss. "An imitation of Vandermeer?"
> "Mr. Bender thinks of Cuyp."
> It made the young man ring out: "Then Mr. Bender's doubly dangerous!"[40]

Hugh's final triumph will ride on his identification of another rare painting, but it's his eye for the "little Vandermeer" that first certifies him both to the reader and to the young woman he will eventually marry. James, who seems to have known little about Vermeer apart from his new prominence among the cognoscenti, was almost certainly unaware of the historical irony that attends his hero's demonstration of critical prowess. Bredius had not only contested the authenticity of *The Rustic Cottage*: he had reassigned it to a painter who was in fact a Vermeer imitator.[41]

Some of the riddles posed by Thoré's "sphinx" were clearly of the critic's own making. But retrospective smugness about such errors is rarely warranted, especially regarding an artist whose paintings had long been assigned to others and whose oeuvre remains partly in dispute even today.[42] Bredius himself, for that matter, would later fall victim to one of Han van Meegeren's most spectacular forgeries. Though scholars sometimes question whether Thoré's role in Vermeer's recovery has been exaggerated, both the doggedness of his research and the power of his rhetoric surely made him the preeminent agent of the artist's revival.[43] But Thoré, of course, did not act alone, and the very fact that he could rely on the infrastructure of a nascent art world to take up and amplify his work was crucial to the success of his enterprise. Indeed, many of the same conditions that helped to make a career like his possible also help to explain how and why there was a public ripe for his discoveries. If Vermeer's virtual disappearance in the eighteenth century was partly the result of accident, the timing of his reemergence, by contrast, seems overdetermined.

As Thoré himself acknowledged, he was not the only writer to notice Vermeer at mid-century. Between 1858, when the first volume of *Museés de la Hollande* appeared, and 1866, when "Van der Meer de Delft" was published, a number of colleagues in France and Germany likewise commented on the artist's work—often, but not always, in direct response to one another. Thoré accompanied his own early account of the *View of Delft* by citing previous remarks on the painting by two contemporary writers—Maxime DuCamp and Théophile Gautier—the former of whom, at least, seems also to have been struck by Vermeer's liberal use of impasto. (DuCamp called Vermeer "a rugged painter, who proceeds by flat colors, broadly applied"; Gautier praised his "incredible force, precision, and fidelity of tone.")[44] In his *Histoires des peintres de toutes les écoles* of 1861, the art critic Charles Blanc recalled his own initial distaste at the painting's execution, which he'd found "coarse, with a brutal impasto and a monotonous appearance," before describing how he'd been pleasantly surprised by the "marvelous" light of *The Milkmaid,* among other Vermeers "of rare merit" that had recently been restored to the public's attention. Blanc, who now deemed Vermeer an artist "of the first strength," duly credited Thoré for much of this recovery work, though he couldn't resist a slight dig at the obsessive character of the quest: "Entirely devoted to his love [. . .] for this excellent painter that he's brought to light, M. Bürger now sees the *Delftsche* a little bit everywhere."[45]

Vermeer, as Ben Broos has observed, was clearly "in the air" around 1860.[46] In an article of that year the critic Paul Mantz singled out *The Geographer* (fig. 1.10) as "the capital piece" in the Dumont collection at Cambrai, even as he begged pardon for describing this latest find before Thoré himself, "whose patient studies of this master, recently famous—thanks to him—would naturally assign him the honor of speaking about it first."[47]

It's less clear whether Edmond de Goncourt had been reading Thoré when he recorded his own first impression of the *View of Delft* in his journal of 1861, though his suggestion that its "astonishing" creator was the unacknowledged precursor of the French Romantic painter Alexandre-Gabriel Decamps (1803–1860) echoes Thoré's reference to the same artist in his first comments on the picture. (*The Milkmaid*, by contrast, prompted Goncourt to thoughts of his beloved Chardin.)[48] On at least one occasion, however, Thoré left no doubt as to who was reading whom, since the second volume of the *Musées* (1860) explicitly credited a catalogue compiled two years earlier by Gustav Waagen with identifying the *Girl Reading a Letter at an Open Window* in Dresden (fig. 1.11)—a painting that had hitherto been ascribed to de Hooch, but which Waagen had recognized as the work of that "'so excellent and rare master, whom the Dutch call the Delftsche Van der Meer.'" This was the same Waagen who'd supposedly been so wrong about *The Rustic Cottage*, but in this case Thoré was happy to pronounce him right.[49]

Even more happily from Thoré's perspective, the report of the Dresden picture had prompted him to visit the museum himself, where he not only

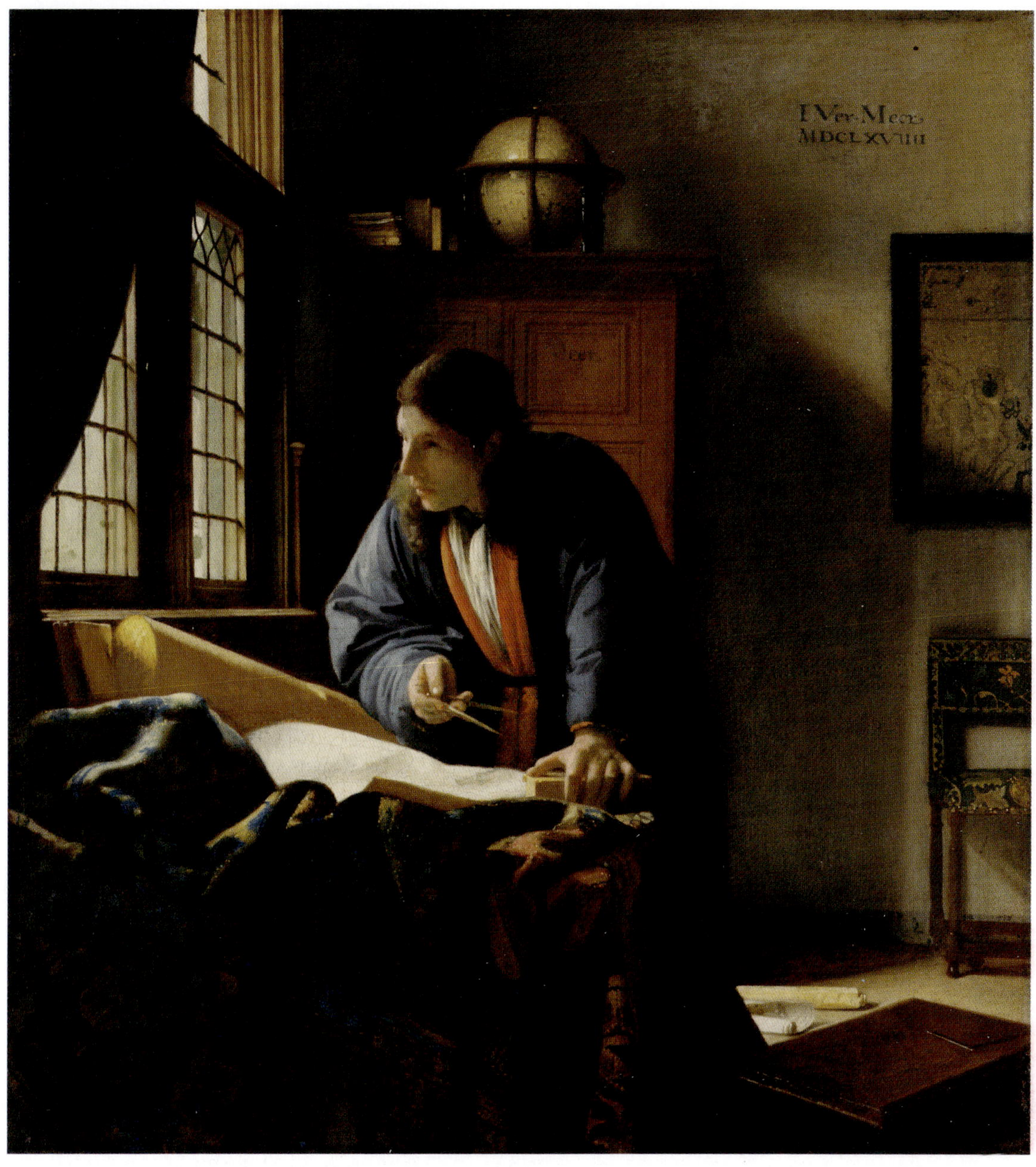

Fig. 1.10. Johannes Vermeer, *The Geographer* (1669). Oil on canvas. 53 × 46.6 cm. Städelsches Kunstinstitut, Frankfurt. bpk Bildagentur / Art Resource, NY

confirmed Waagen's attribution but made a discovery of his own—another large Vermeer hanging in plain view and serendipitously placed, as Thoré saw it, "right above one of the most precious paintings in the entire collection, the portrait of 'Rembrandt holding his wife Saskia on his lap!'" The painting, now known as *The Procuress* (fig. 1.12), was then ascribed to Jacob van der Meer of Utrecht, but Thoré, who'd persuaded museum officials to let him mount a ladder for a closer look, succeeded in spotting not just the anticipated signature, but a date—1656—under the name: the first such record of which he was

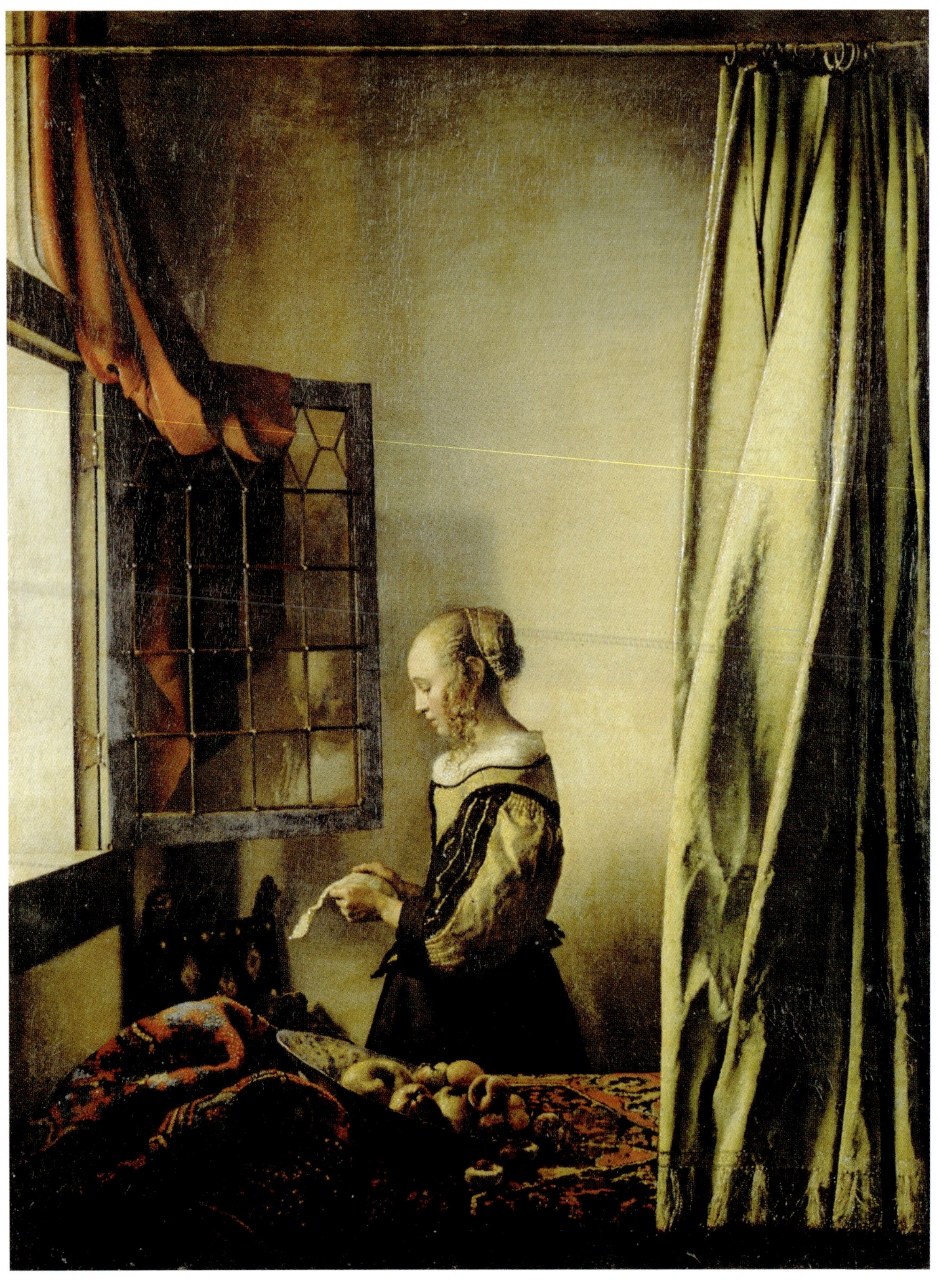

Fig. 1.11. Johannes Vermeer, *Girl Reading a Letter at an Open Window* (ca. 1657–59), before restoration. Oil on canvas. 83 × 64.5 cm. Gemäldegalerie Alte Meister, Dresden. Erich Lessing / Art Resource, NY

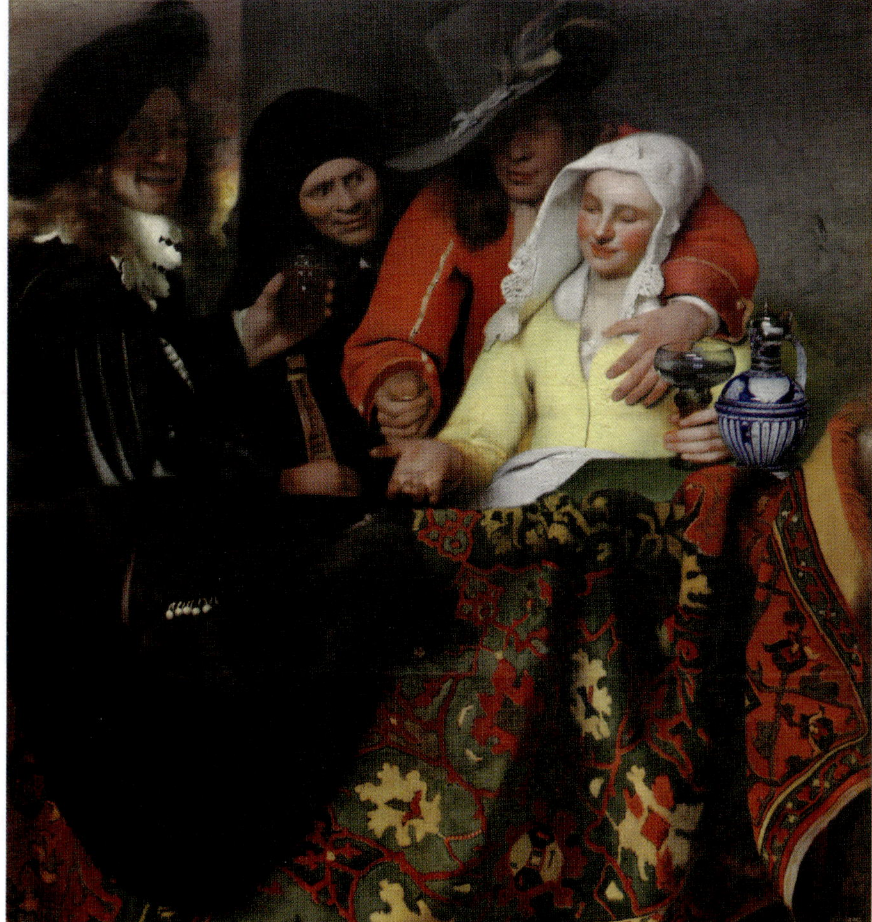

Fig. 1.12. Johannes Vermeer, *The Procuress* (1656). Oil on canvas. 143 × 130 cm. Gemäldegalerie Alte Meister, Dresden. bpk Bildagentur / Art Resource, NY

aware, and one of only four that are recognized today. (The others are the *Saint Praxedis* [1655], *The Astronomer* [1668], and *The Geographer* [1669].) For Thoré, the discovery did more than fill in a crucial bit of Vermeer's biography, though having previously known only the artist's birthdate, he had reason enough to be excited by that. Both the coincidental placing of the picture and the evidence that it was painted around the time when similar artists were thought to have been working in Rembrandt's studio reinforced Thoré's conviction that Vermeer, too, had been a pupil of Rembrandt.[50] That conviction would prove almost certainly mistaken, but Thoré had a profound investment in the image of the artist it created: an image quite removed, as we shall see, from the Vermeer soon to be championed as a proto-modernist.[51]

In all this back-and-forth, it can sometimes be hard to judge who spotted what first. As early as 1859, for instance, Thoré had publicly speculated that *The Art of Painting* in Vienna—a work he knew only from a printed description—was "an authentic Vermeer" rather than the work of de Hooch, though he admitted that he had yet to see the canvas for himself.[52] Official credit for the attribution therefore belongs to Waagen, whose *Handbook of the Dutch and Netherlandish Schools of Painting*, published three years later, characterized it as "one of the most beautiful works of the master from his mature period."[53] Waagen claimed that he had made the identification in 1860, which prompted an apparently injured Thoré to note in his catalogue of 1866 that he'd already anticipated his German colleague—a bit of exaggeration for which he's been tacitly scolded by a modern scholar.[54] But such squabbles are finally far less consequential for the story I tell here than the very conditions that made them possible. Art historical research of the kind that Thoré and the others practiced was a comparatively new phenomenon in the mid-nineteenth century, and it is very hard to imagine Vermeer's recovery without the overlapping networks of publication and exhibition that undergirded their efforts—as well, of course, as the burgeoning art market, whose wealthiest participants would also prove critical to the artist's reputation in subsequent decades.

The initial encounter with the *View of Delft* that Thoré would later transform into an "indelible memory" was itself a consequence of such institutional change, since he had only traveled to Holland because of his involvement in a new arts organization—dubbed the "Alliance des Arts"—that he had cofounded with another French journalist, Paul Lacroix.[55] Dedicated to cataloguing and analyzing—rather than merely listing—works of art, the organization would not endure for very long, but the technical experience it afforded Thoré would remain a permanent part of his arsenal. Lacroix in turn went on to inaugurate the first professional arts journal in France, the *Revue universelle des arts*, in 1855; three years later it would publish Thoré's initial account of that "unknown of genius," Jan van der Meer of Delft. The *Gazette des beaux-arts* had only been around for seven years when it ran his major article on the painter, though it would remain one of the most influential sources for connoisseurship and art history for over a century. The *Gazette des beaux-arts* was also the venue Paul Mantz had chosen for his earlier report on Vermeer's *Geographer*, issued a year after the journal's founding: one more sign of how closely entwined was the artist's rebirth with this nascent infrastructure for circulating such news.[56]

Compared to commentators on the Continent, where a French critic named Henry Havard would follow up his own articles in the same journal by publishing a short book on Vermeer in 1888, the British were relatively slow to devote whole monographs to the artist. But from 1867, when the *Art-Journal* offered a brief account of Thoré's findings, until the early months of 1901, when reports of a newly discovered painting by the artist at a London dealer's first appeared in periodicals and newspapers, scarcely a year passed without multiple invocations of what the *Saturday Review* would call in 1886 "the magic name of Vermeer of Delft."[57] (The painting discovered in 1901 was *Christ in the House of Martha and Mary* [fig. 1.13]). Many of these contributions remained anonymous, as was then common journalistic practice, but a number were initialed or signed, and the authors of others have since been identified, as in the case of

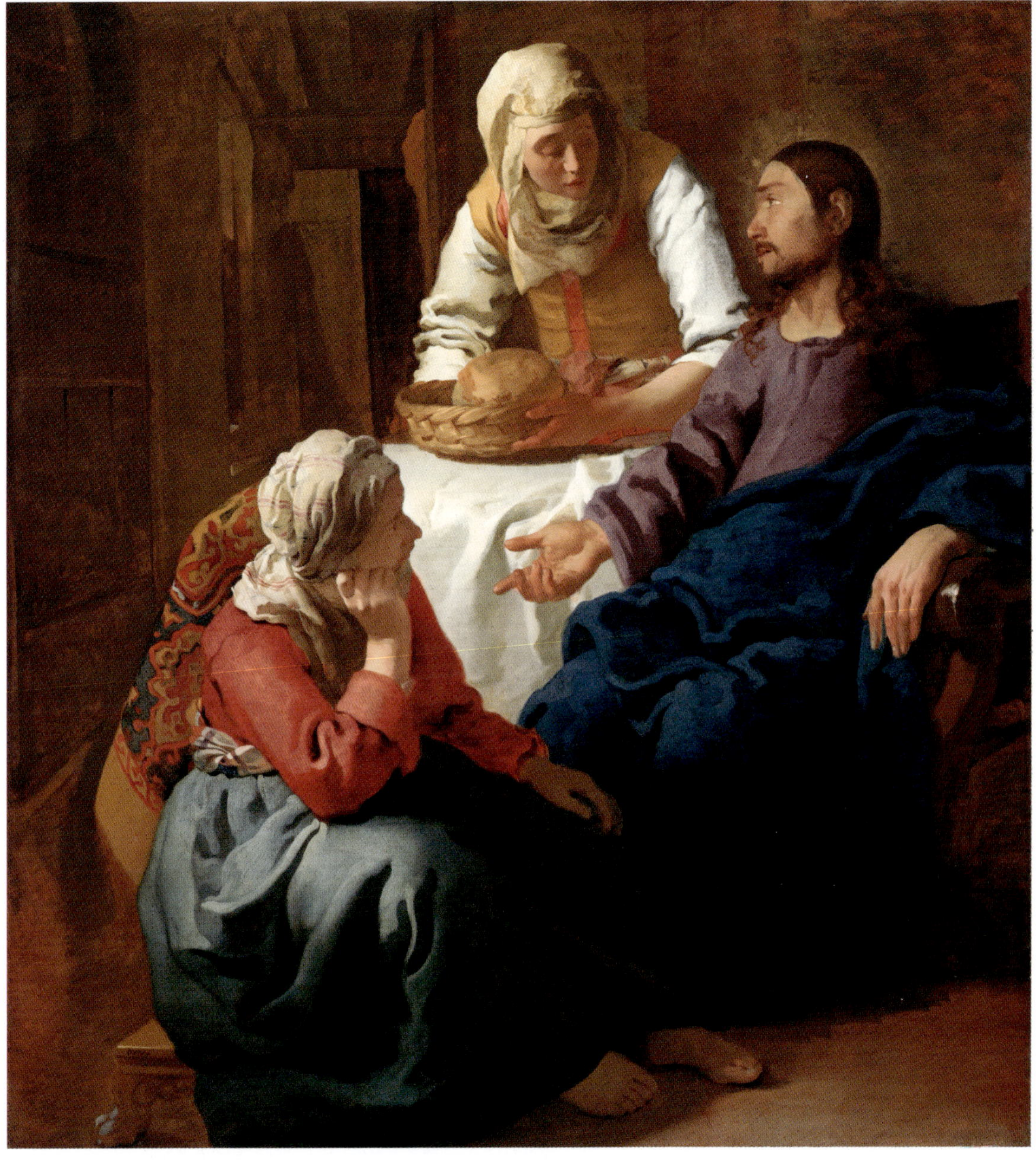

Fig. 1.13. Johannes Vermeer, *Christ in the House of Martha and Mary* (ca. 1654–56). Oil on canvas. 160 × 142 cm. National Gallery of Scotland, Edinburgh. © National Galleries of Scotland, Dist. RMN-Grand Palais / Art Resource, NY

"The New National Gallery at Amsterdam" published by *Macmillan's* in 1885, that turns out to have been written by Mary Augusta ("Mrs. Humphry") Ward, the woman soon to become famous for the bestselling novel *Robert Elsmere* (1888). Certain names, however, appear again and again, and all would figure prominently in the institutionalization of the late Victorian art world: the critic and novelist Frederick Wedmore, whose *Masters of Genre Painting*, published in 1880, may have been the first book in English to include an extended discussion of Vermeer; Sidney Colvin, Slade Professor of Fine Art and the first director of the Fitzwilliam Museum at Cambridge, as well as for many years the keeper of prints and drawings at the British Museum; Claude Phillips, who would become the first keeper of the Wallace Collection when it opened in 1900, and his successor, the Scottish watercolorist, art critic, and former keeper of the Tate, Dugald Sutherland MacColl; the newspaper critic Walter Armstrong, who served from 1892 until 1914 as director of the National Gallery of Ireland; and—perhaps most intriguingly—the Pre-Raphaelite painter Henry Wallis, best known then and now for his 1856 canvas *The Death of Chatterton*. "Such is his fascination," Wallis would write of the Delft painter in 1877, "that having seen a picture of his one becomes his fervid admirer."[58]

In both Europe and America, of course, the Vermeer revival was part of a larger shift of taste toward the painting of everyday life, a taste in turn driven by the increasing democratization of the viewing public in a bourgeois century. Thoré, whose very pseudonym (Bürger: "citizen") made his allegiances clear, had preceded his pioneering article on the Delft master with two volumes on the museums of Holland that spoke explicitly for such preferences, by contrasting the progressive "art for man" created by the freedom-loving Dutch with the backward-looking work he associated with the popes and princes of Renaissance Italy.[59] Paradoxically, however, his revival of Vermeer came at a moment when the kind of humanism he championed was about to be partly eclipsed by artistic developments that would make the work of his beloved "sphinx" feel all the more timely.[60] Vermeer was obviously not an Impressionist, but the recovery of his intensely optical paintings, with their striking color harmonies and close attention to the behavior of light, can seem exquisitely calibrated to the decade in which it took place. Nor was such proto-impressionism the only ground that the contemporary art world began to find for identifying with the Delft master. The word "modern" doesn't figure in Thoré's account of Vermeer, but, as we shall see, it didn't take long for it to enter the lexicon.

Vermeer's revival didn't depend on words alone, of course, though it's not the least of the ironies that attend his reception that the painter who had been among the most unliterary of his seventeenth-century peers—this "painter's painter," as he would come to be called—should owe much of his second life to acts of writing.[61] As many commentators have noted, Vermeer reemerged at a time when a new mechanism for producing images seemed to many eyes like the fulfillment of techniques he'd perfected. But if the rise of photography in the period is yet another reason why the nineteenth-century revival of Vermeer feels overdetermined, the verbal analogy between his light-obsessed work and the new medium seems to have circulated before reproductive technologies made it feasible to accompany printed texts with photographs of the paintings themselves. In a journal entry of 1861 Edmond de Goncourt already made the analogy explicit, by describing the painter of *The Little Street* (see fig. 1.2) as "the only master who has made of the brick house of that country a daguerreotype brought to life."[62] Writing for the *British Journal of Photography* in

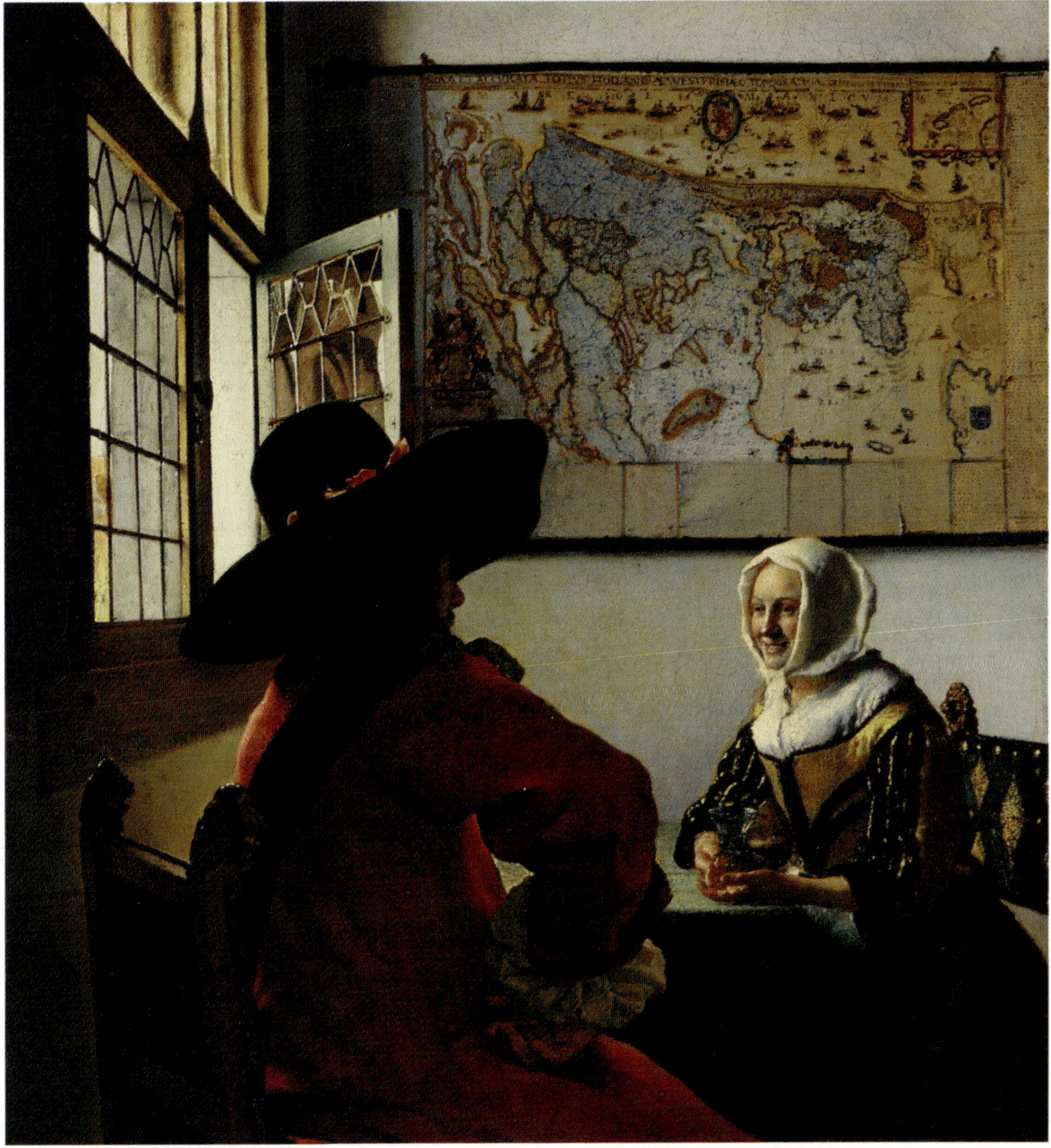

1891, the American printmaker—and future biographer of Whistler—Joseph Pennell apparently inaugurated the still persistent obsession with the artist's own possible use of the camera obscura, when he registered what he called the "photographic scale" of objects in the *Officer and Laughing Girl* (fig. 1.14).[63]

Fig. 1.14. Johannes Vermeer, *Officer and Laughing Girl* (ca. 1655–60). Oil on canvas. 50.5 × 46 cm. Frick Collection, New York. Image © Frick Collection

As best I can tell, however, the earliest photographically illustrated study of Vermeer didn't appear until the following century: a 1908 book by the Belgian novelist, playwright, and art critic Gustave Vanzype, whose reproductions would in turn serve Proust as a sort of aide-mémoire after his visit to the exhibition that partly inspired his novel's famous scene with the *View of*

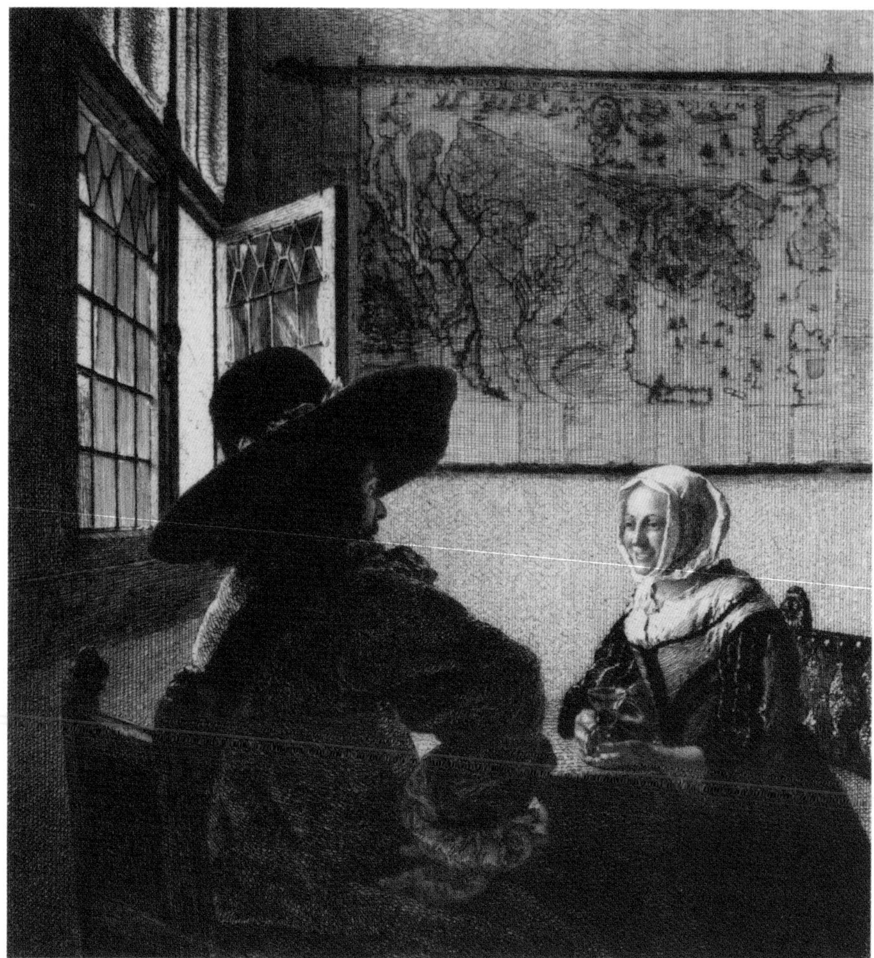

Fig. 1.15. Jules Jacquemart after Johannes Vermeer, *Officer and Laughing Girl* (1866). Etching. Gift of Theodore De Witt, 1923. Metropolitan Museum of Art, New York

Delft.[64] Though Thoré confessed to spending extravagantly on photographs of Vermeer's work, he had to fall back on older technologies for his article, which was illustrated with four woodcuts, one lithograph, and three etchings, as well as an additional woodcut for the title.[65] Unfortunately, fewer than half of these reproduced paintings are now attributed to the artist, though one etching, Jules Jacquemart's version of the *Officer and Laughing Girl* (fig. 1.15), drew repeated praise over the years. By the time the same journal published Havard's study seventeen years later, both the reliability and the quality of the images had much improved: there were still only seven illustrations, but they were all etchings, and only one reproduced a work no longer ascribed to Vermeer—an image that in turn would be eliminated when Havard's study appeared between hard covers in 1888.

That the *View of Delft* was on display in the first place also speaks to conditions that would increasingly shape Vermeer's afterlife. When the Mauritshuis acquired the painting in 1822, it was only the second work by the artist to enter a public museum—and the first to do so under his name. (The *Girl with a Wine*

Glass had been on exhibit in Brunswick since the mid-eighteenth century, but until the late 1850s it appeared in the catalogue as a "Jacob" van der Meer.)[66] By the turn of the twentieth century, a dozen Vermeers had entered museums in Europe and America: still a small number, admittedly, but a full third of the corpus now identified with the artist. The change was precipitated by his growing fame, but also by the rapid expansion of public museums themselves, which, like the boom in art publishing, was largely a nineteenth-century phenomenon. Among the museums that now hold one or more Vermeers, the vast majority opened their doors after 1800: a list that includes some of the most prominent venues for viewing his work, such as the Gemäldegalerie in Berlin (1830), the Metropolitan Museum of Art in New York (1870), the Rijksmuseum in Amsterdam (1885), and the National Gallery of Art in Washington, DC (1941). As this chronology suggests, Vermeer was reborn into an art world ever more dominated by museum culture.

When Thoré first set out on his quest, most of the artist's work remained in private hands, but that was soon to change—not least because of the market the critic himself helped to create. "This will be propaganda for our beloved Vermeer, whose works all the museums will rightly be forced to acquire," he wrote to Suermondt in 1868, when the *Woman with a Pearl Necklace* (see fig. 2.5), which had briefly been in his possession, was purchased by a dealer at auction and offered to the museum in Frankfurt.[67] Not that the transition was always seamless: partly at Thoré's urging, for instance, Suermondt intervened to buy the painting himself, and it was from his collection that the Gemäldegalerie in Berlin acquired it several years later. As early as 1864 Charles Eastlake, the first director of the National Gallery in London, had begun consulting Thoré about possible Vermeers for his institution, though the result of his dithering, ironically, was that the gallery would not acquire its first painting by the artist until almost seventy years after its founding, when it bought the *Young Woman Standing at a Virginal* (see fig. 3.3) from Thoré's estate in 1892. The irony was compounded by the fact that the picture was among three by Vermeer that Eastlake himself had hesitated to buy, the others being the *Woman with a Pearl Necklace* and the *Mistress and Maid* (fig. 1.16), now at the Frick.[68] Prices that had remained relatively modest during Thoré's lifetime shot up rapidly in the decades after his death: the National Gallery paid 50,000 francs for the *Young Woman Standing at a Virginal*, for example—a hundred times the amount for which he had purchased it three decades earlier.[69] *The Lacemaker* (see fig. 3.16) appreciated even more swiftly, going from 565 francs in 1851 to 6,000 in 1870, when it became the first of the artist's paintings to enter the Louvre.[70]

Given this market, it's hardly surprising that so many Vermeers should have passed through the hands of Gilded Age Americans on their way to becoming museum pieces. Initially driven by the period's appetite for old masters and further fueled by a growing perception of Vermeer's rarity—not to mention a contemporary "mania" for all things Dutch—the American buying frenzy

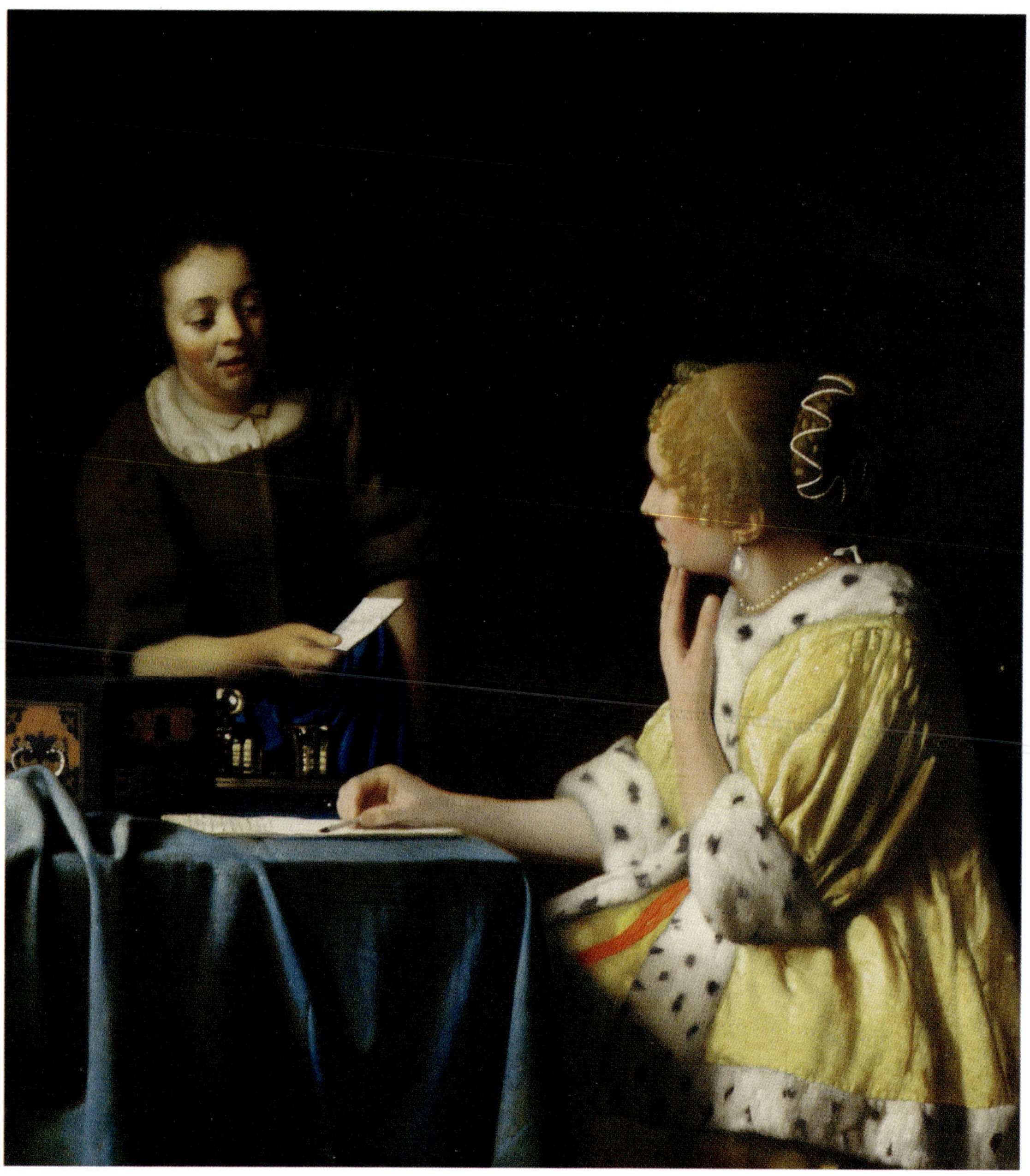

Fig. 1.16. Johannes Vermeer, *Mistress and Maid* (ca. 1666–68). Oil on canvas. 90.2 × 78.7 cm. Frick Collection, New York. Image © Frick Collection

eventually led to a third of the artist's oeuvre crossing the Atlantic.[71] Before buying *Mistress and Maid*, for example, the steel magnate Henry Clay Frick had also acquired both *Girl Interrupted at Her Music* (see fig. 3.6) and *Officer and Laughing Girl*; and all three paintings would be put on public display when his private collection was turned into a museum after the owner's death. *The Concert* (fig. 1.17), purchased from Thoré's estate by the Boston heiress Isabella Stewart Gardner in 1892, likewise ended up in a house museum before it was stolen by unidentified thieves in 1990.

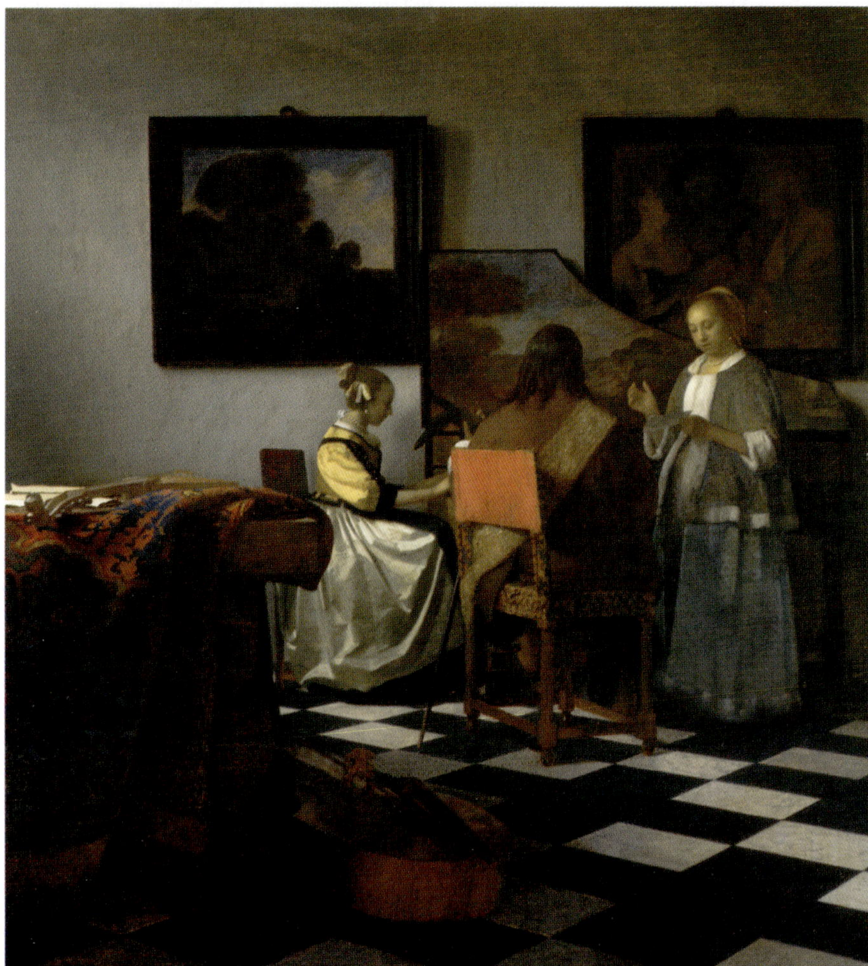

Fig. 1.17. Johannes Vermeer, *The Concert* (ca. 1663–66). Oil on canvas. 72.5 × 64.7 cm. Isabella Stewart Gardner Museum, Boston, MA

In other cases, individual paintings were donated to established institutions by wealthy benefactors such as Henry Marquand, the financier who gave the *Young Woman with a Water Pitcher* to the Metropolitan in 1889, or Collis P. Huntington, the railroad magnate who bequeathed the *Young Woman with a Lute* (fig. 1.18) to the same museum in 1900. The process continued, if at a slower pace, well into the twentieth century: the *Study of a Young Woman* that had first entranced Thoré when he saw it in the Arenberg collection, for instance, only arrived at the Met in 1979, having been donated to the museum by a pair of wealthy collectors, Charles and Jayne Wrightsman, who had originally made their money in oil.

Though the last Vermeer to enter a public museum didn't do so until 1993, the unusual circumstances of its arrival further underscore the increasingly intimate tie between such institutions and the artist's afterlife.[72] The painting in question was the *Lady Writing a Letter with Her Maid* (fig. 1.19), which had been bequeathed to the National Gallery of Ireland by its former owner, Sir

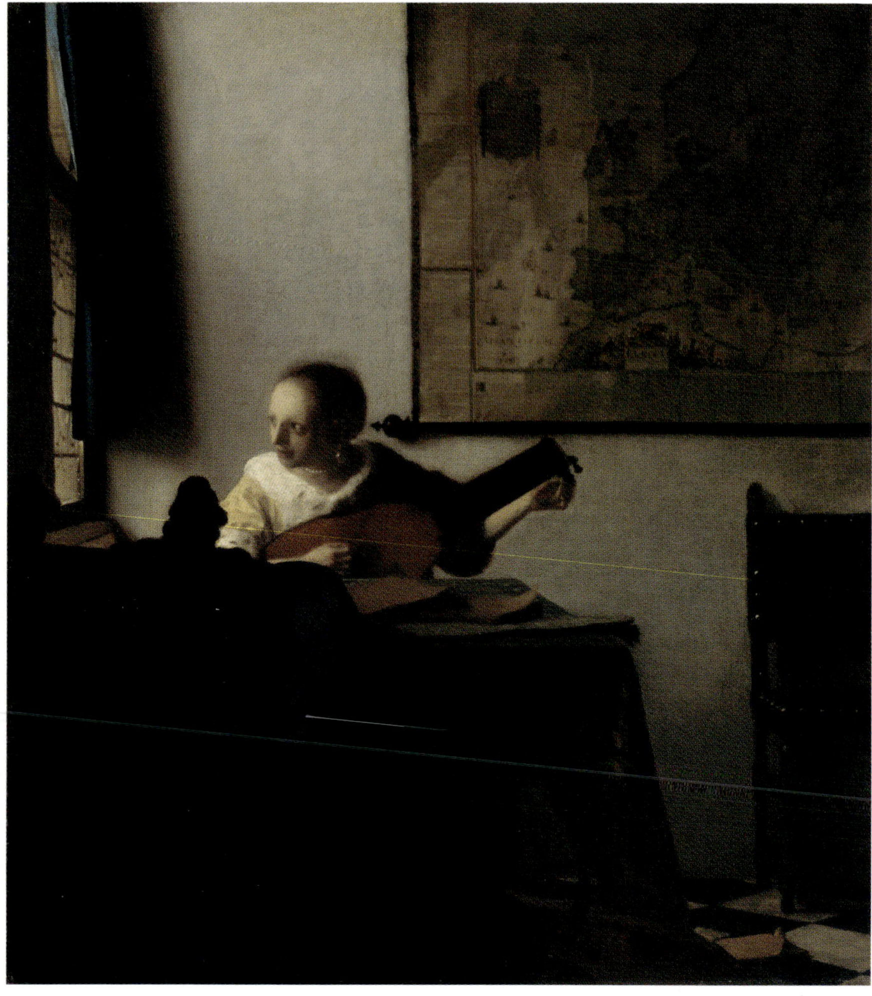

Fig. 1.18. Johannes Vermeer, *Young Woman with a Lute* (ca. 1662–63). Oil on canvas. 51.4 × 45.7 cm. Bequest of Collis P. Huntington, 1900. Metropolitan Museum of Art, New York

Alfred Beit, in 1987, at a moment when the work itself was no longer in his possession, having been stolen from his private collection the previous year. This was actually the second theft of Beit's painting, since it had previously been taken and held for ransom by an IRA sympathizer in 1974, but unlike that crime, which had been swiftly solved, this case dragged on for seven years, though the work itself never left the thieves' hands. As Beit observed at the time—and as the thieves apparently discovered—the problem with stealing such a famous painting was that it was too famous to sell. The rarer the work, and the more highly prized, the more it belongs in a museum.[73] And with the partial exception of the *Young Woman Seated at the Virginals* in the Leiden Collection (fig. 1.20) and *The Music Lesson* at Windsor, which is only sometimes on public display, it is indeed in a museum that every known painting by the artist currently resides.

To see Vermeer now—to see the paintings themselves, at least—is to visit a museum. The point is implicitly underscored by a Japanese biologist named

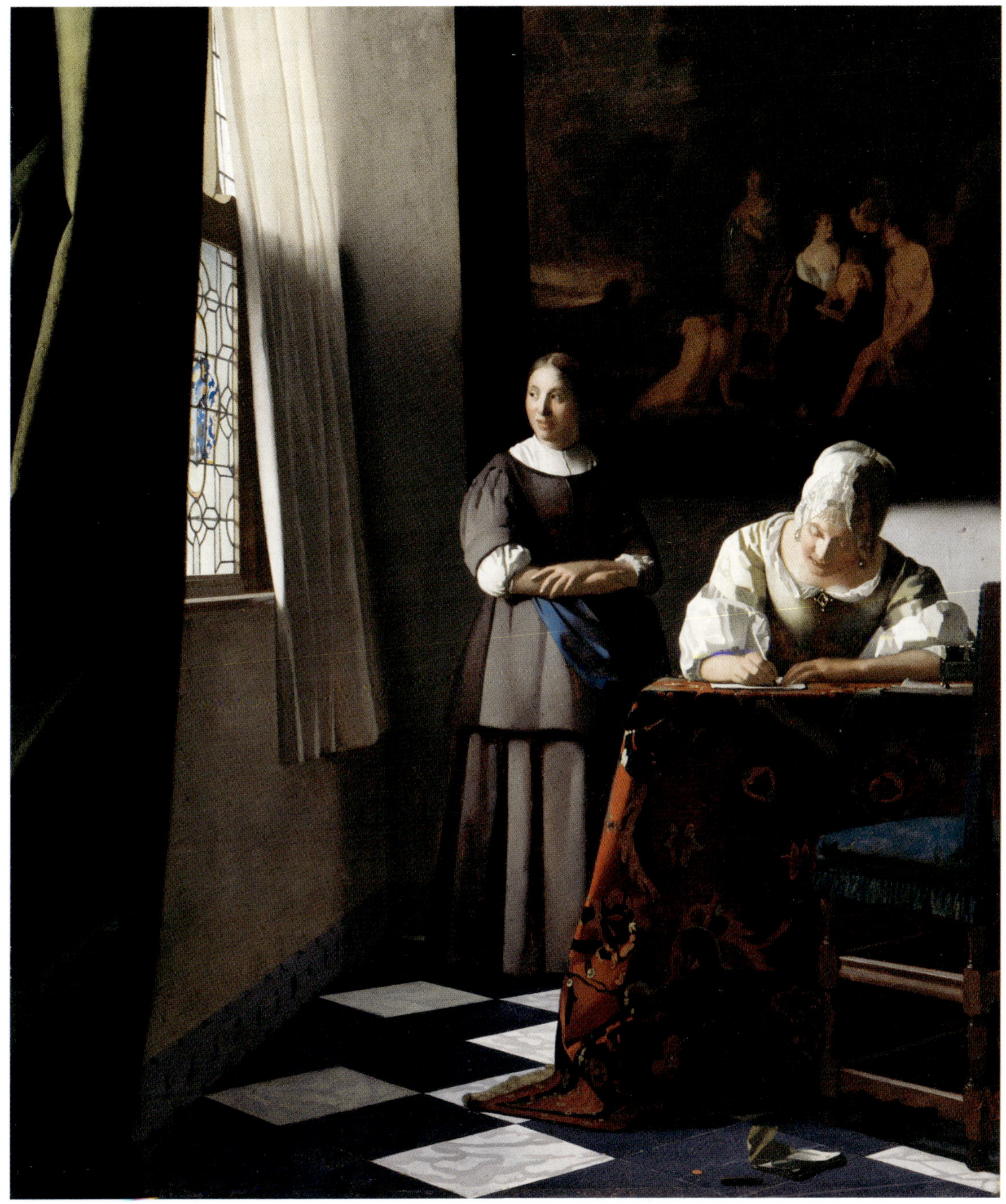

Fig. 1.19. Johannes Vermeer, *Lady Writing a Letter with Her Maid* (ca. 1670–71). Oil on canvas. 72.2 × 59.5 cm. National Gallery of Ireland, Dublin. Bridgeman-Giraudon / Art Resource, NY

Shin-Ichi Fukuoka, whose recent account of his "four-year journey to see all the existing paintings of Johannes Vermeer" manages to invert contemporary critiques of the institution's tendency to uproot and decontextualize works of art by repeatedly stressing the importance of visiting the Vermeers in "their permanent homes": homes Fukuoka approaches with almost as much reverence as the paintings themselves.[74] Thoré never fulfilled his hope of seeing

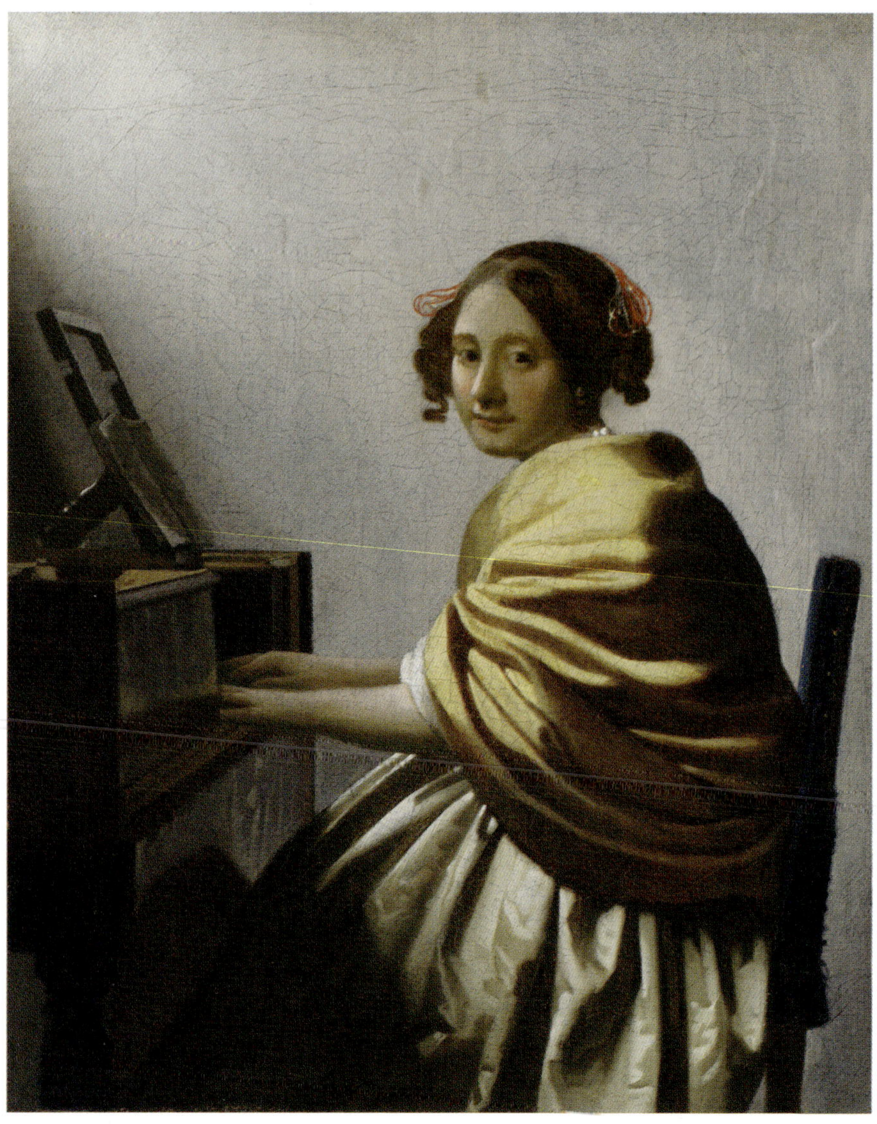

Fig. 1.20. Johannes Vermeer, *Young Woman Seated at a Virginal* (ca. 1670). Oil on canvas. 25.5 × 20.1 cm. The Leiden Collection, New York. HIP / Art Resource, NY

every Vermeer for himself, but as Fukuoka demonstrates, the combination of the oeuvre's limited size and its present setting means that the project is now within the scope of any viewer with a sufficient travel budget. "Seeing All the Vermeers"—the title of a 1999 poem by Alfred Corn about his own effort to see every one of them—even threatens to become the premise of a small literary genre.[75] "So you're a writer, eh?" inquires a guard at Buckingham Palace in the second decade of our century, as he spots the pen carried by a different poet on his way to see *The Music Lesson*: "Traveling the world, seeing the Vermeers, and writing a book about it, are you?" Michael White, the writer in question, is taken aback. "How did he know?" he wonders.[76] White would go on to publish two books based on his journey: one a collection of poems, the other a travelogue and memoir. The palace guard is clearly onto something.

2

How Vermeer Became Modern

We go to him because a sort of mysterious prescience made him see as we see.

—GUSTAVE VANZYPE (1908)

In 1925 the British painter George Clausen confidently summed up the prevailing consensus on the art of Johannes Vermeer. "Although he lived about 250 years ago, it is remarkable how modern his work is," Clausen declared, "and it is a strong testimony to its worth that today [. . .] artists of the most extreme and divergent views are united in their admiration before it."[1] A Royal Academician known especially for his landscapes and peasants, the seventy-three-year-old Clausen was scarcely venturing into radical territory by delivering this verdict. As early as 1876—a mere decade after Thoré's pioneering article—an anonymous critic in the *Saturday Review* had registered the "modernness" of Vermeer by comparison with his contemporary Gerard ter Borch; and by the time Clausen published his lecture on "Vermeer of Delft and Modern Painting" that conjunction had become something of a commonplace in writing on the artist.[2] Especially in the first decades of the twentieth century, everyone seemed ready to pronounce Vermeer, as a 1909 book called *The Story of Dutch Painting* put it, "a modern among moderns."[3]

The author of that *Story* was himself somewhat ambivalent about the modern cult of Vermeer, which he feared testified to a valuation of technique above all, but he had no doubt that "the artist of to-day, if he is alive to the modern spirit, works with the same motive and in the same way" as his seventeenth-century predecessor.[4] Four years later the American painter Philip Leslie Hale effectively confirmed that judgment when he opened his book on Vermeer by

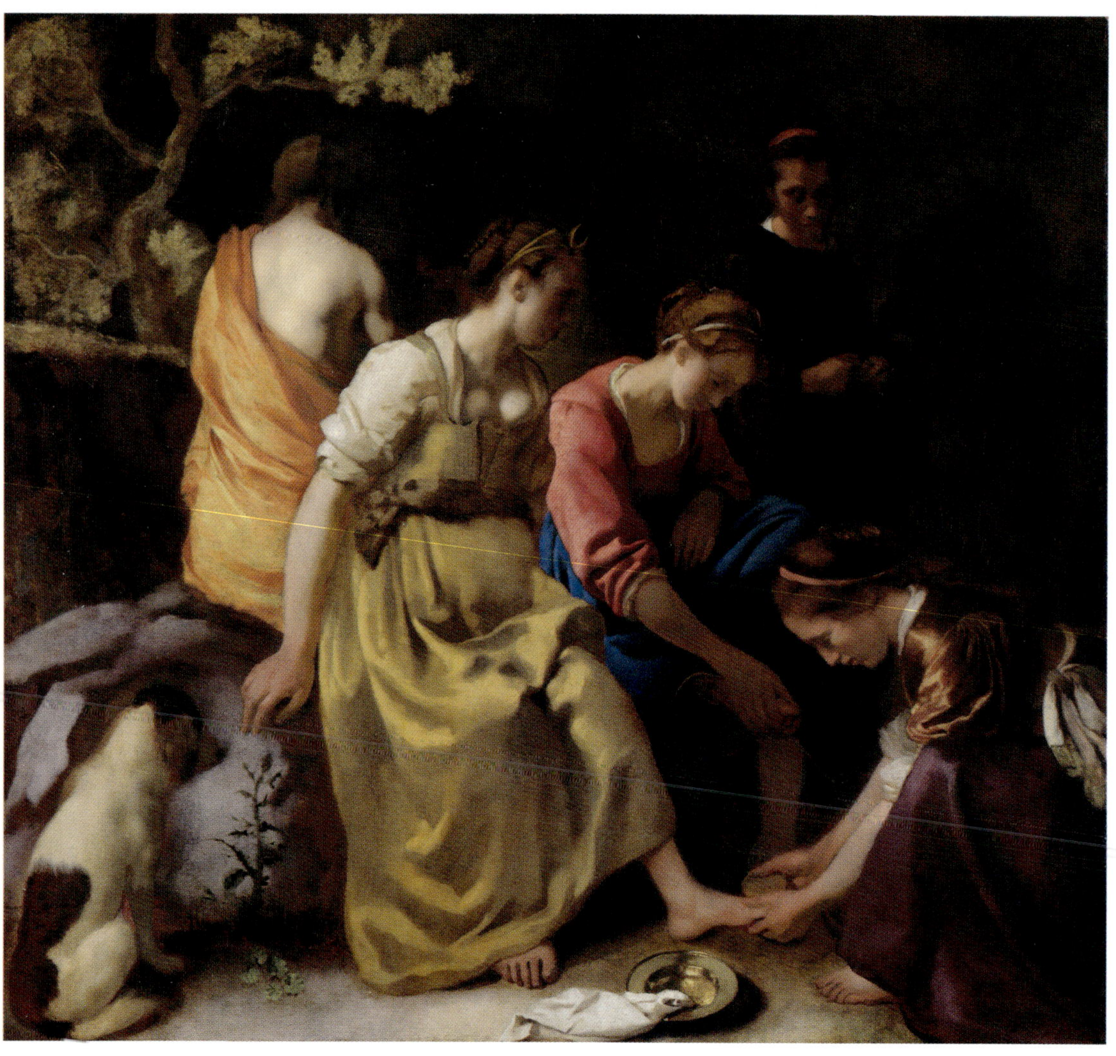

Fig. 2.1. Johannes Vermeer, *Diana and Her Companions* (ca. 1653–56). Oil on canvas. 97.8 × 104.6 cm. Mauritshuis, The Hague

baldly declaring him "the greatest painter who has ever lived"—an assessment he immediately went on to elucidate from what he termed "our ultra-modern point of view." Hale, who devoted the culminating chapter of his book to the subject of "Vermeer and Modern Painting," was among a group of visual artists at the turn of the century who specifically looked to the example of the Delft master.[5] But the modern Vermeer was not only a creation of other painters. "We go to him because a sort of mysterious prescience made him see as we see, made him discern, divine, anticipate a sensibility that would not develop until two centuries after him," the Belgian novelist, playwright, and art critic Gustave Vanzype declared in his own book on Vermeer, published in 1908.[6] "It is a picture of modern feeling, divinatory, marvelous," the French poet and critic Jean-Louis Vaudoyer observed of the artist's *Diana and Her Companions* in 1921 (fig. 2.1).[7] Only Vaudoyer's singling out Vermeer's one mythological picture for this accolade is in any way surprising.

What did all these observers see in Vermeer to identify him so intensely with their own ways of seeing? As with other aspects of the painter's afterlife, this "modern among moderns" is himself the product of multiple causes, some of which drove the revival of other previously undervalued artists as well.[8] In a recent study of the phenomenon in Britain, Elizabeth Prettejohn has shown how the Pre-Raphaelites and their successors responded to the rise of museum culture and the development of art-historical scholarship by excitedly imitating their newfound ancestors, thereby helping to create an expanded canon of old masters still celebrated today. Prettejohn's paradigm is the nineteenth century's "rediscovery" of Botticelli, but it is another of her examples—the revaluation of Velázquez—that seems most pertinent, since the Spanish artist was also thought to have anticipated modern ways of seeing.[9] A man of the seventeenth century who nonetheless managed to cope with what the Scottish painter and critic R.A.M. Stevenson termed "the most difficult problems of modern impressionism," this Velázquez "became," in Stevenson's phrase, "the prophet of the new schools": a title that, for all their differences, might equally have been accorded Vermeer too.[10] Indeed, as early as 1884, Stevenson's younger contemporary John Singer Sargent was already instructing Vernon Lee in the new pantheon: "Some day you must assert that the only *painters* were Velasquez, Frans Hals, Rembrandt, and Van der Meer of Delft, a tremendous man."[11]

But if in one sense Vermeer only became modern at the close of the nineteenth century, in another sense he had rarely been anything else. Like other seventeenth-century painters, the Vermeer who chose to focus his attention on scenes of contemporary life was already producing what would have been identified as modern pictures, as opposed to the biblical, mythological, and historical subjects that were classified as "antique."[12] This is presumably the sense of "modern" that Gerard ter Borch senior had in mind when he offered his son and namesake some artistic advice in a letter of 1635: "And if you want to paint, then first paint something of the modern kind of figurative group."[13] The pictures that resulted clearly bore out the wisdom of that advice, while offering templates that apparently inspired Vermeer as well. Compare, for instance, Ter Borch's *Young Woman at Her Toilet with a Maid* (fig. 2.2) with Vermeer's *Woman with a Pearl Necklace* (see fig. 2.5), as a recent exhibition on "inspiration and rivalry" among Vermeer and his contemporaries invited us to do.[14]

From the perspective of neoclassical theory, however, the decision to specialize in this modern kind of painting still threatened to consign its practitioners to an inferior branch of the profession. According to an influential treatise of 1707 by the painter and theorist Gerard de Lairesse, such pictures necessarily remained less noble than their antique counterparts, since changing fashions in dress and behavior would always render them ephemeral—an anxiety that continued to haunt subsequent theorists such as Joshua Reynolds as well.[15] Not until the early decades of the nineteenth century would official opinion begin to catch up with popular taste, as representations of everyday

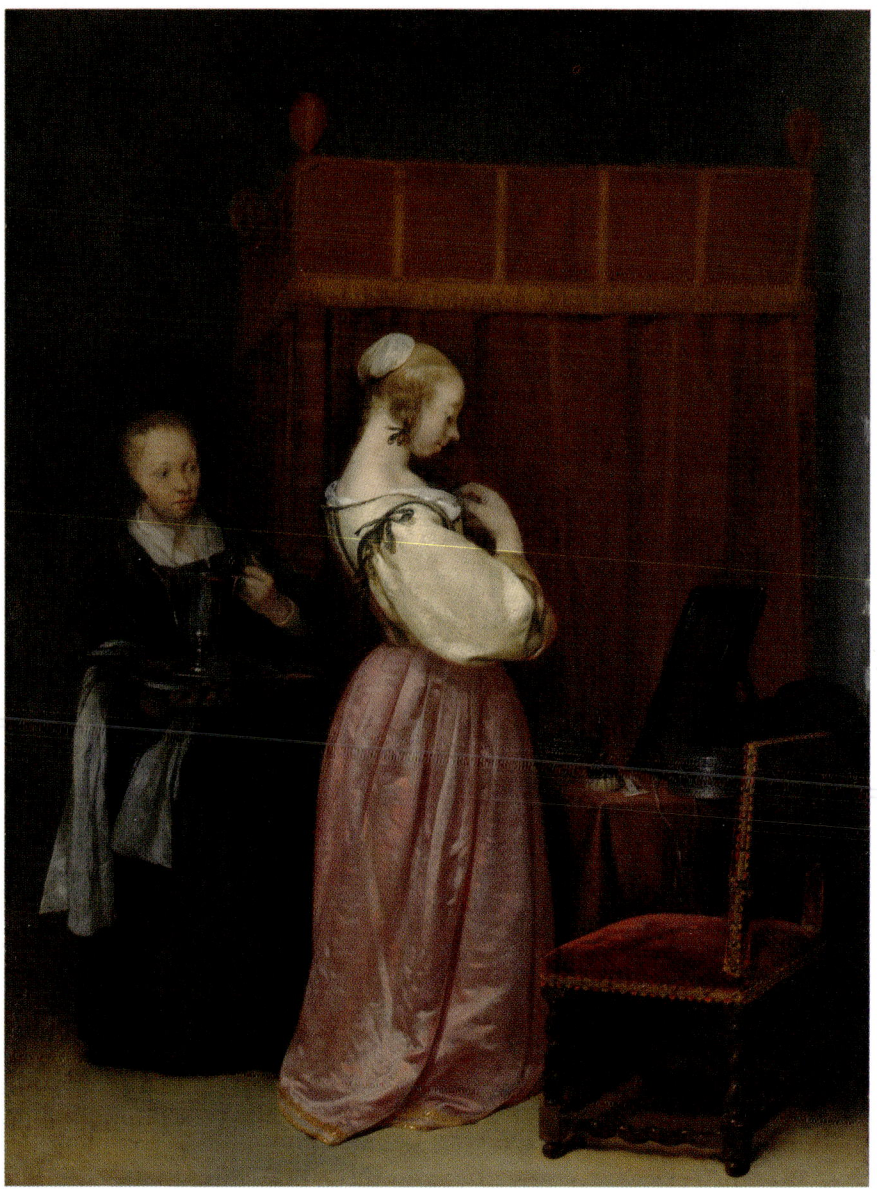

Fig. 2.2. Gerard ter Borch, *A Young Woman at her Toilet with a Maid* (ca. 1650–51). Oil on panel. 47.6 × 34.6 cm. Gift of J. Pierpont Morgan, 1917. Metropolitan Museum of Art, New York

life increasingly dominated the practice of painters in Europe and America alike. In the United States especially, the appetite for Dutch art was further fueled by the association between Holland's struggle for independence and the American Revolution in John Lothrop Motley's bestselling *The Rise of the Dutch Republic* (1855) and *The United Netherlands* (1860–67), volumes that also clearly resonated with democratic sympathizers in Europe.[16] Thoré, who actively promoted both kinds of modern painting—the art of the seventeenth-century Dutch as well as that of contemporaries such as Gustave Courbet and Edouard Manet—was thus very much a man of his time, even as he was himself an agent of changing tastes.[17]

Vermeer's reception as a modern artist in this sense also depended, at least in part, on the order in which his work was recovered. The comparative fame of the *View of Delft* before Thoré even began his research meant that its creator first came to public attention in the nineteenth century as a painter of landscape: not a "modern kind of figurative group," to be sure, but another kind of picture that had likewise long occupied an inferior status in the generic hierarchy and whose new rise to prominence would itself signal the advent of a modern approach to painting—one more attuned to the artist's rendering of familiar things than to the visual transcription of historical narratives from classical myth or the bible.[18] Most scholars now concur that Vermeer actually began with experiments in both kinds of historical picture—mythological with *Diana and Her Companions* and biblical with *Christ in the House of Martha and Mary*—but neither of these was securely attributed to Vermeer until the turn of the century, when the appearance of the *Christ* at a London dealer's in 1901 first enabled observers to remark the stylistic affinities between the two paintings and thus confirm a recently uncovered signature on the *Diana*.[19] (Compare figs. 2.1 and 1.13.) A more recent addition to the early works of a *Saint Praxedis* (fig. 2.3), modeled on an Italian painting of the same subject by Felice Ficherelli, initially proved controversial, but if this, too, is a Vermeer, it didn't enter discussions of the artist until 1969, long after he was first reborn as a modern.[20]

The only exception to the rule—and it's a partial one—is a painting listed by Thoré as "Seated Woman, Personifying the New Testament" and now known as *Allegory of the Catholic Faith* (see fig. 3.12): a work of whose existence Thoré was only aware from earlier sales catalogues and that did not publicly surface again until Bredius, then the director of The Hague's Mauritshuis, identified it as a Vermeer in 1899.[21] Having never seen the canvas himself, Thoré had nothing to say about it, and it was easily eclipsed by the seventy-two other entries in his catalogue. Many of those works, as we now know, were misattributed, but the artist they constructed was clearly a painter of modern subjects; and apart from a brief interlude in the 1930s and 1940s, when the forgeries of Han van Meegeren temporarily altered the context, it is with such subjects that the public has come to identify the art of Vermeer. Though scholars continue to study the historical paintings, and some have even tried to make a case for the widely disliked *Allegory*, the Vermeer who has entered the popular imagination, like the Vermeer who inspires contemporary artists and writers, is above all a painter of ordinary figures in domestic settings, and the creator of the *View of Delft*.

The artist recovered by Thoré, however, was not yet the artist he would become when later observers began to approach him from what Hale called "our ultra-modern point of view."[22] For all his democratic enthusiasms, Thoré's own sympathy for the more advanced work of his day occasionally betrayed its limits: he once protested Manet's apparent indifference to the relative importance of a basket of flowers and a woman's face, for instance, and it is clear

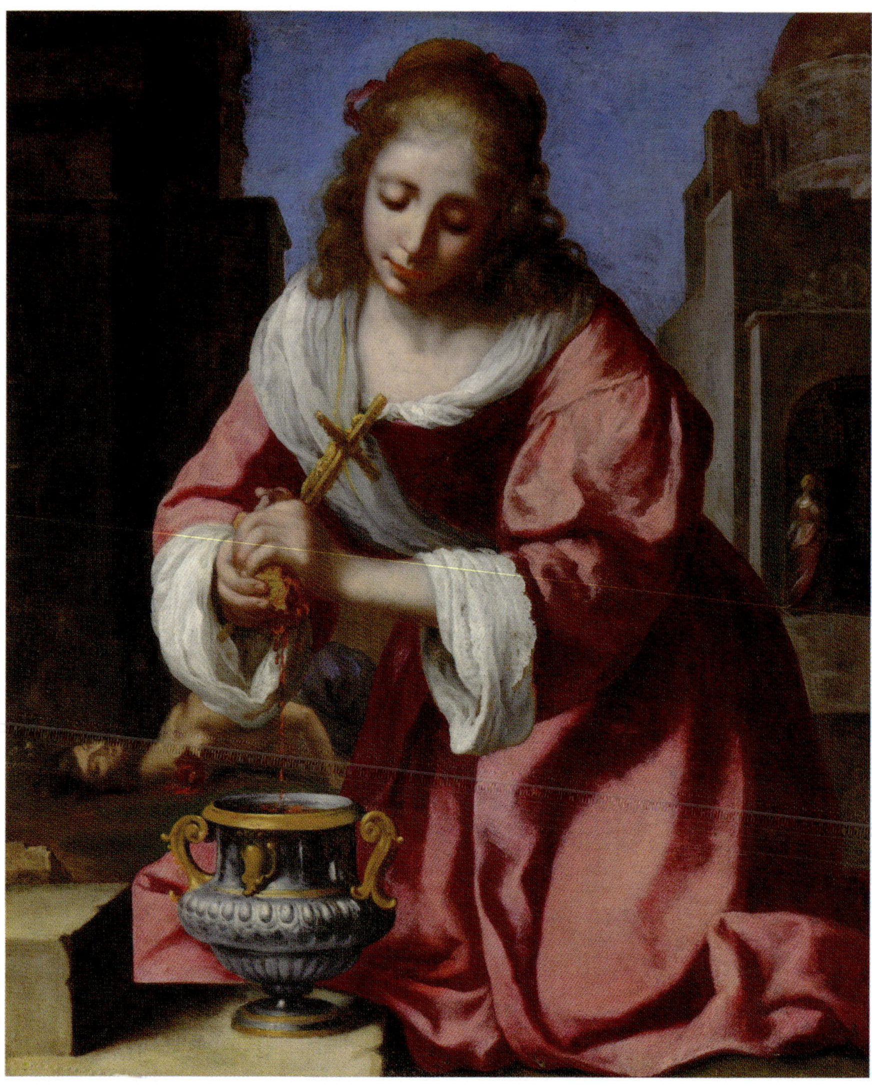

Fig. 2.3. Johannes Vermeer (?), *Saint Praxedis* (1655). Oil on canvas. 101.6 × 82.6 cm. National Museum of Western Art, Tokyo. Christie's Images / Bridgeman Images

from his writing as a whole that he would have been even more resistant to the spirit of art for art's sake in which subsequent generations of critics and painters would continue his advocacy of the Delft master. The very humanism that drew him to the seventeenth-century Dutch in general, and to Rembrandt in particular, inclined him to see a Vermeer quite different from the one celebrated for his anticipation of modern art at the turn of the twentieth century.[23]

As we shall see, it was one sign of Vermeer's modernity for such observers that he played down, almost to the point of disappearance, any narrative potential in his paintings; but it is characteristic of Thoré's approach to his beloved "sphinx" that he couldn't resist imagining the human relations he thought were suggested by Vermeer's images. So he responded to the *Mistress and Maid* and the *Woman in Blue Reading a Letter* (fig. 2.4), for example, by recounting "the small drama expressed by these physiognomies":

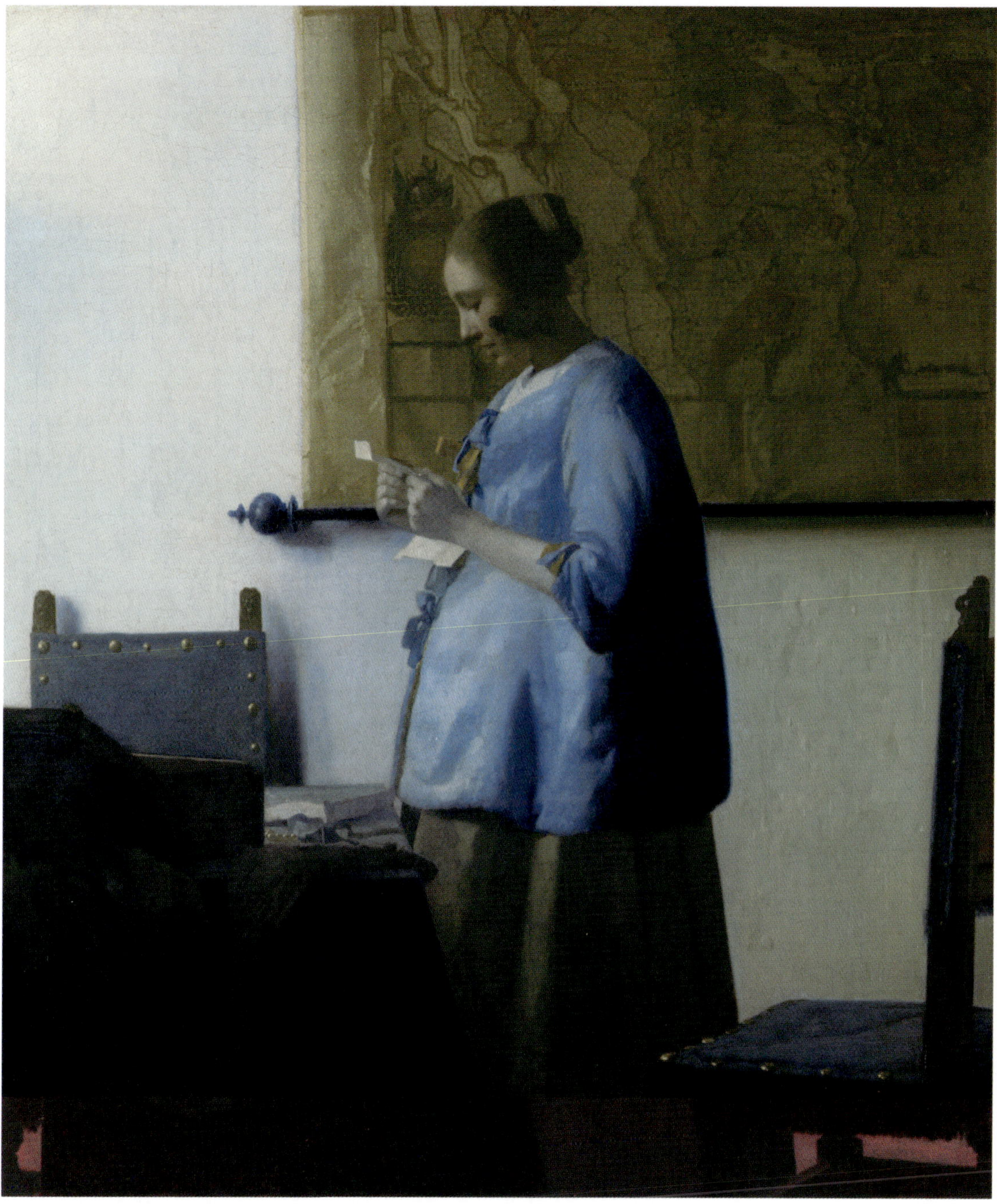

Fig. 2.4. Johannes Vermeer, *Woman in Blue Reading a Letter* (ca. 1662–65). Oil on canvas. 46.5 × 39 cm. Rijksmuseum, Amsterdam

The Reader in the Hoop Museum is disappointed by bad news: is it that her lover writes her that he is leaving for the Great Indies? In the painting in the Dufour collection, one seems to hear the woman saying to her servant in handing her the letter:—"You understand . . . it's for that young man . . . the blond . . . Don't mistake the address."[24]

Such an appetite for the stories that may be spun from Vermeer's images has an afterlife of its own, but it is far removed from the "ultra-modern point of view" that observers such as Hale would bring to the painter's art.[25] Indeed, it is a small irony of Vermeer's reception history, as Francis Haskell has noted, that the one time Thoré did approach such a view of his beloved painter, the canvas in question was not in fact a Vermeer at all, but the work of an eighteenth-century imitator of the Dutch Golden Age: *The Rustic Cottage*, now generally attributed to Dirk van der Laan (see fig. 1.8).[26] Thoré's account of that painting nonetheless significantly anticipated the terms on which Vermeer himself would soon become modern. "For Van der Meer," Thoré declared, "light itself is the subject; all the rest is nothing but a pretext or an accessory, even the human figure. When he has his light effect, the painting is done."[27]

Thoré wrote these words at the start of a crucial decade in the history of modern art, when a self-conscious avant-garde was beginning to make its own experiments with the painting of light. Though Vermeer himself was not of course an impressionist, some scholars have argued that his style approximated the early work of the group, and Camille Pissarro, at least, seems to have agreed, once singling out "the *View of Delft* by Vermeer," together with the paintings of Hals, as "masterpieces akin to the works of the impressionists."[28] Both the advent of impressionism and the development of photography in the nineteenth century have long been understood as helping to create the conditions for Vermeer's revival, but it's equally important to see how in doing so they also helped to create him as modern. That the artist cared more for his optical effects than he did for his subject matter became central to the cult of the modern Vermeer, as did an emphasis—often admiring, but also at times skeptical—on the technical means by which his effects were achieved. For the mid-twentieth century that would partly take the form of an obsession with his use of the camera obscura, but earlier commentators more typically focused on his color arrangements and his handling of paint itself. Marcel Proust's homage to "the little patch of yellow wall" in the *View of Delft* is probably the best-known example, but well before the climactic scene in which Proust's fictional novelist measures his own style against that patch and finds it wanting, the painter who could be celebrated in such terms had become a staple figure of modern commentary.[29]

Already in 1883, Thoré's principal successor in France was approaching Vermeer as if his representational content barely signified. For Henry Havard, it was not so much the treatment of light that distinguished the Delft artist from his peers as the complete subordination of any human action to the tonal arrangement of his canvases. "Not only does the drama of life not appear in his familiar scenes, but it is severely banished," Havard wrote, "and his personages, all peaceful and calm, make scarcely more noise than the multiple accessories that surround them. Vermeer, above all, is a silent painter." One could even remove the people from certain "small compositions," Havard suggested, without their losing interest entirely, since many "only figure there, in reality, as felicitous marks"—the phrase in French is "taches heureuses"—whose combined effect Havard then tellingly compared to a work of music. They are "agreeable notes," as he put it, "in a delightful concert of fine tonalities," and "if they play an important role in this melodious symphony, it is by the mark that they make and not by the idea that they express."[30]

Though Havard had little patience for Thoré's efforts to connect Vermeer with Rembrandt, he did agree with his predecessor about the artist's close resemblance to Pieter de Hooch—so much so, in fact, that his praise of "this melodious symphony" appears to be speaking of both men when it paradoxically evokes their "singular privilege" of producing such musical effects.[31] This practice of yoking the two artists was routine in the early years of Vermeer's revival, and there remain good reasons for pursuing the comparison, as the 2017 exhibition on "inspiration and rivalry" among Dutch genre painters demonstrated.[32] But the Vermeer who emerged in the first decades of the twentieth century increasingly did so as a distinctive figure, one whose anticipation of later developments seemingly outweighed any artistic twinship with De Hooch. Charged with introducing the catalogue for a major exhibition of Dutch painting in 1909 at the Metropolitan Museum in New York, the German-born art historian Wilhelm Valentiner, for instance, simultaneously classed Vermeer among "the greatest Dutch masters" and characterized his style as "more progressive" than his contemporaries: a group in which he specifically included De Hooch, as well as Ter Borch and Meindert Hobbema. Valentiner was by no means the most unequivocal of Vermeer's champions in those years, but the very terms in which he qualified his praise—by comparison with the "deep spirituality" of Rembrandt, Vermeer's "perfection" was "purely aesthetic"—help to explain why he too identified this particular seventeenth-century painter with "the modern spirit."[33]

As Valentiner went on to explain, "his whole power is concentrated in obtaining a perfection of surface, which hitherto, through absorption in the matter portrayed, had not received this close attention." In a variation of Havard's observation about the "silence" of Vermeer's figures, Valentiner remarked their "almost expressionless" character, while focusing his own attention on "the wonderful play of light" and "the perfect arrangement of the few colors" the artist employed. "He is unique, too," Valentiner added, "in his rejection of all the detail in which contemporary genre painters delighted. Compared with their work, his canvases with their few large surfaces seem empty, but the little there depicted presents in its exquisite proportions an absolutely harmonious whole."[34]

This association between the emptying out of Vermeer's subject matter, both human and material, and the formal perfection of his canvases would prove central to the perception of his modernity. "It would be hard in the whole range of painting to find a painter less dramatic than he," Hale would observe in his extended study of Vermeer four years later. "His composition, when it is successful, is always so from the aesthetic standpoint, never from the dramatic." Later in the same book, Hale made the connection between such a view of the artist's achievement and his modernity explicit: "One particularly modern thing about Vermeer's art," he wrote, "is his avoidance of story-telling." Though he went on to acknowledge that "a thin thread of anecdote" inevitably remained in most of the pictures—*The Art of Painting*, which he called *The Studio*, was a notable exception—Hale was convinced that the painter's true interest lay elsewhere. "Vermeer came as near to having his little figures do nothing at all as one well could unless they sat with folded hands," according to Hale, because their creator had his eye on other things: "the design, the colour scheme and the rendering were the elements that most engaged his attention."[35]

As a practicing painter, Hale devoted considerable portions of his book to such elements. One chapter focused on Vermeer's "technique," by which Hale meant such matters as the "square touch" of the artist's brush, his use of *pointillé* highlights, and his handling of the edges between objects, for instance, while others offered extended discussions of his treatment of values (both light and dark and relations of color) and of composition and design—the latter of which Hale suggestively compared to that of Japanese prints. Insisting that Vermeer was above all an "impersonal" painter and that this too made him modern, Hale prompted at least one contemporary reviewer to protest that the resulting portrait was at best a "half truth." Vermeer's technique is "the symbol of his dearest emotions," the American art critic Frank Jewett Mather Jr. contended, and "we must rather look to some rare lyrical sentiment in the artist's soul" to account for the power of his paintings. Yet even Mather agreed that "drama or narrative is not of their essence" and that Vermeer had become a favorite of modern artists in part because he had "anticipated many of the technical researches of the '60s and '70s." Indeed, rather than scholarship and criticism, it was primarily "the movement of modern art," Mather argued, that was responsible for Vermeer's revival.[36]

The response to Vermeer's perceived modernity was not only verbal, of course. Embracing him as their precursor, a number of artists, Hale among them, self-consciously adopted his work as a model, producing paintings that deliberately imitated his compositions and techniques. A subsequent chapter of this book will take up some of the results, as part of a broader inquiry into Vermeer's visual afterlives in the wake of his recovery. But the artistic company into which the Delft master was welcomed was not limited to those who set out to imitate him directly. Though commentators continued to compare him to other Golden Age painters such as Ter Borch and De Hooch, they also frequently drew analogies to more recent artists, a feature of Vermeer criticism that has persisted to this day. Hale himself offered a running comparison to James McNeill Whistler, remarking both men's affinities of pattern and design—the source in turn of Hale's speculation that the seventeenth-century painter, like the nineteenth-century one, might have been inspired by Japanese prints—and the ways in which Vermeer anticipated Whistler's "colour symphonies," a connection perhaps also implied by the musical language in which Havard had characterized Vermeer's tonal arrangements. Hale acknowledged that there was no evidence that the later artist had actually been influenced by the earlier one, even repeating a joke that appeared to invert the chronology: "as a jesting artist once said, Vermeer seemed to imitate Whistler a good deal."[37] But the point, of course, was to make an argument less about influence than about prescience: Vermeer's affinities with Whistler were simply further grounds for hailing him as a modern.

Two years later, the young protagonist of W. Somerset Maugham's *Of Human Bondage* (1915) would attempt to show off his recent immersion in the Parisian art scene by likewise identifying Vermeer with a modern painter. For Philip Carey, the touchstone is not Whistler, but Edouard Manet, and the work that immediately inspires his comparison is Manet's *Olympia* (1863). "I would give all the old masters except Velasquez, Rembrandt and Vermeer for that one picture," he announces; and when he discovers that his companion has never heard of Vermeer, he is predictably horrified. "He's the one old master who painted like a modern," he explains, before dragging his unenlightened friend off to the Louvre in order to drive home the comparison. Dismissing the other's desire to see the *Mona Lisa* on the grounds that "it's only literature," Philip leads him instead to *The Lacemaker*, which he pronounces both "the best picture" in the museum and "exactly like a Manet."[38] Though Maugham's relentless irony makes it doubtful that he shared in this judgment, he was clearly more up to date in this respect than the author of *The Outcry* (1911), whose fictional connoisseur was still engaged in distinguishing Vermeer from Albert Cuyp.

Other recent artists were also marshaled in support of the argument. Hale invoked an admiring letter from that "ultra-modern [. . .] type" Vincent van Gogh on the color scheme of the *Woman in Blue*, for example, and Mather duly echoed the allusion. Mather also spoke loosely of how "the generation represented by Degas" had anointed Vermeer as their predecessor and compared his flat modeling to that of Paul Cézanne.[39] The analogy to Cézanne would reappear in an interpretive essay on Vermeer's art published in 1948 by the chief curator of paintings and drawings at the Louvre, René Huyghe, who suggestively compared the earlier artist's method of negotiating between "the matter of the real and that of painting" to the later one's adjudication between the "solidity of traditional forms" and "the vibration of the impressionists' color." Huyghe, it perhaps goes without saying, also associated Vermeer with "the moderns," a classification which in his account extended to Velázquez as well. Unlike some of his more extravagant predecessors, Huyghe acknowledged that such artists could still aspire to give "a pictorial equivalent" of nature, but what made them modern, he implied, was their attentiveness to their medium itself. In Vermeer, he wrote evocatively, "Painting has just discovered its autonomous powers."[40]

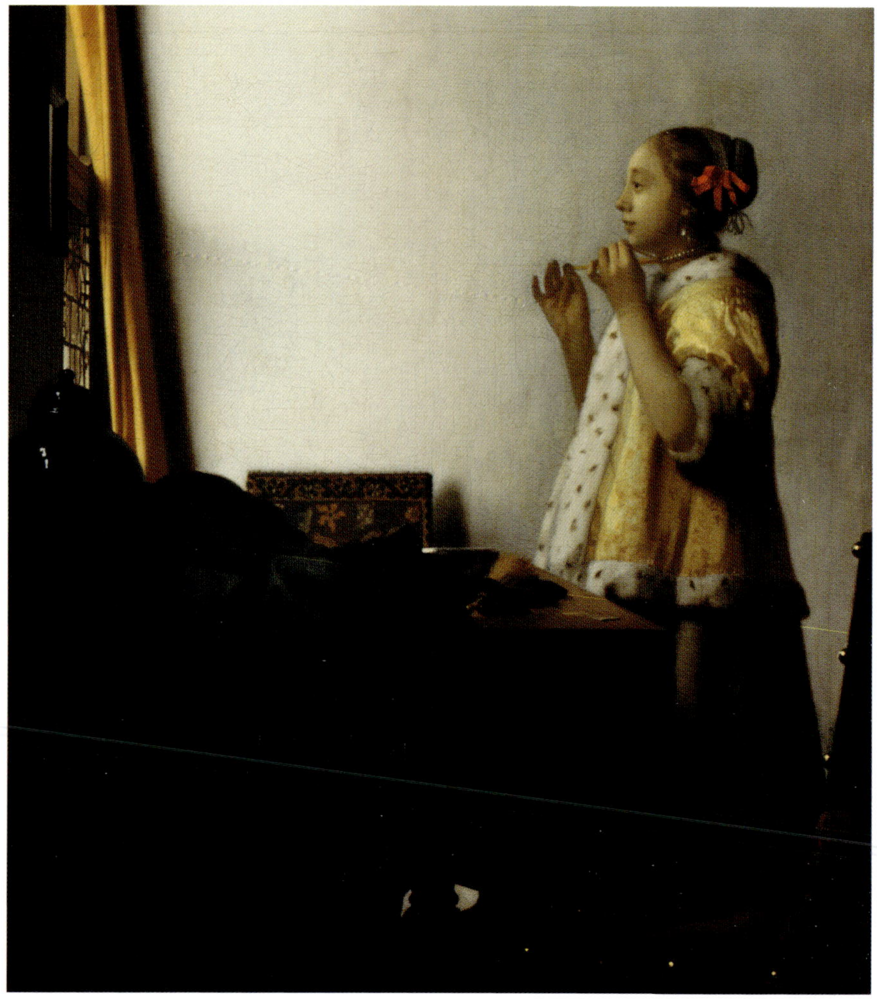

Fig. 2.5. Johannes Vermeer, *Woman with a Pearl Necklace* (ca. 1662–65). Oil on canvas. 55 × 45 cm. Gemäldegalerie, Staatliche Museen, Berlin. Photo: Christoph Schmidt. bpk Bildagentur / Art Resource, NY

Svetlana Alpers, who responded to the 1995 exhibition of Vermeer's work in the National Gallery of Art in Washington, DC, by comparing his feeling for abstract design to that of Piet Mondrian, credited Proust with inaugurating the critical emphasis on Vermeer's "painted mark."[41] But as we have already seen, the impulse to isolate areas of Vermeer's paint in this way goes back at least to the 1880s, when Henri Havard suggested that one might even remove the figures from the artist's canvases and concentrate only on his "felicitous marks."[42] Indeed, it might be truer to say that the modern Vermeer did not so much begin with Proust as reach his apotheosis in the decades when *À la recherche du temps perdu* was published (1913–27). It was in 1913, after all, that Hale had excitedly declared of Vermeer, "If ever a man believed in art for art's sake it was he": a claim whose very anachronism testified to the spirit in which the recovery—or creation—of the modern Vermeer had proceeded.[43] And it was in 1922 that the British poet, novelist, and essayist E. V. Lucas paid tribute to the *Woman with a Pearl Necklace* (fig. 2.5) by dwelling not on the woman

Fig. 2.6. Kazimir Malevich, *Suprematist Composition: White on White* (1918). Oil on canvas. 79.4 × 79.4 cm. Museum of Modern Art, New York. 1935 Acquisition confirmed in 1999 by agreement with the estate of Kazemir Malevich and made possible with funds from Mrs. John Hay Whitney Bequest (by exchange). Digital Image © The Museum of Modern Art / Licensed by SCALA / Art Resource, NY

herself, but on the white wall behind her, "beautiful beyond the power of words to express," while fantasizing about extracting from the canvas what amounted to an incipient piece of abstract art. "It is so wonderful," Lucas wrote, "that if one were to cut out a few square inches of this wall alone and frame them one would have a joy for ever."[44] Call it, perhaps, Vermeer's anticipation of Kazimir Malevich's *Suprematist Composition* of 1918, better known by its subtitle: *White on White* (fig. 2.6).

By comparison to this imaginary bit of abstract painting, Proust's "little patch of yellow wall" retains its representational status, but the very fact that much critical ink has been spilled over just which patch of wall—or even roof—in the *View of Delft* Proust had in mind (see fig. 1.1) confirms that representation signifies far less in his account than the area of paint itself.[45] In a three-part article on the artist from which Proust's novel borrowed some of its language, Vaudoyer had written of "those brick houses, painted in a material so precious, so heavy, so full, that *if you isolate a small surface of it, forgetting the subject*, you believe you have ceramic before your eyes as much as paint" (emphasis mine).[46] Proust likewise focused attention less on the wall itself than on the layers of paint that make up its surface, and by the time the dying Bergotte has shifted his gaze from "some small figures in blue" to "the precious substance of the tiny patch of yellow wall," both the imaginary novelist and his creator are well on their way to forgetting the subject too. "That's how I ought to have written," Bergotte concludes. "My last books are too dry, I ought to have gone over them with a few layers of colour, made my language precious in itself, like this little patch of yellow wall."[47] Bergotte's aspiration has nothing to do with mimesis: it is wholly a matter of style, of perfecting his medium. He wishes, in other words, to become the writerly equivalent of "a painter's painter"—the accolade that an admiring Lucas, just a year earlier, had accorded the creator of the *View of Delft*.[48] It was on such terms, as I have been arguing, that Vermeer became modern.

To say that this Vermeer reached his apotheosis in the 1920s is not to say that he disappeared in the decades that followed.[49] Something like Huyghe's capitalized "Painting" continues to haunt more recent accounts of Vermeer's work, whether in comparisons to the abstract grids of Mondrian—Alpers is not alone in this[50]—or in the argument, most influentially advanced by Arthur K. Wheelock Jr., that the artist's style developed toward increasing abstraction over the course of his lifetime. Commenting on *The Guitar Player* (fig. 2.7) and the *Lady Writing a Letter with Her Maid*, for instance, Wheelock almost produces a diachronic version of Huyghe's account, as he remarks how in such works the artist was beginning to free himself from the need to subordinate paint to the forms or textures his pictures represented. "Paint, however expressively applied, remained first and foremost paint," Wheelock observes of both canvases.[51] Unlike his turn-of-the century predecessors, however, Wheelock does not expressly characterize Vermeer as "modern."

As we shall see in the next chapter, the anachronism of postulating a seventeenth-century painter wholly devoted to art for art's sake increasingly troubled historically minded scholars, who were more concerned to place Vermeer in his own context than to claim him as their contemporary. For such scholars and the general public alike, it has rarely proved possible to forget the subject of his pictures altogether, however wonderfully their painted surfaces might respond to the exercise. Yet it is a central fact of Vermeer's afterlife that the same artist who has been celebrated as one who paints only for painting's sake has also been hailed for his illusionism, and in this, too, his work has sometimes been viewed as prescient. Beginning in the 1960s and 1970s, when some art historians began to argue that his paintings bore signs of having been produced with the aid of a camera obscura, the question of Vermeer's relation to various forms of visual technology has remained a live topic not just in the scholarship, but in popular culture too. The story of this Vermeer properly belongs to another chapter, after I take up several different strands in his reception that run counter to the narratives first advanced in the decades that followed his recovery. Like these other counter-histories, as I call them, the association of Vermeer with the mechanical manipulation of light

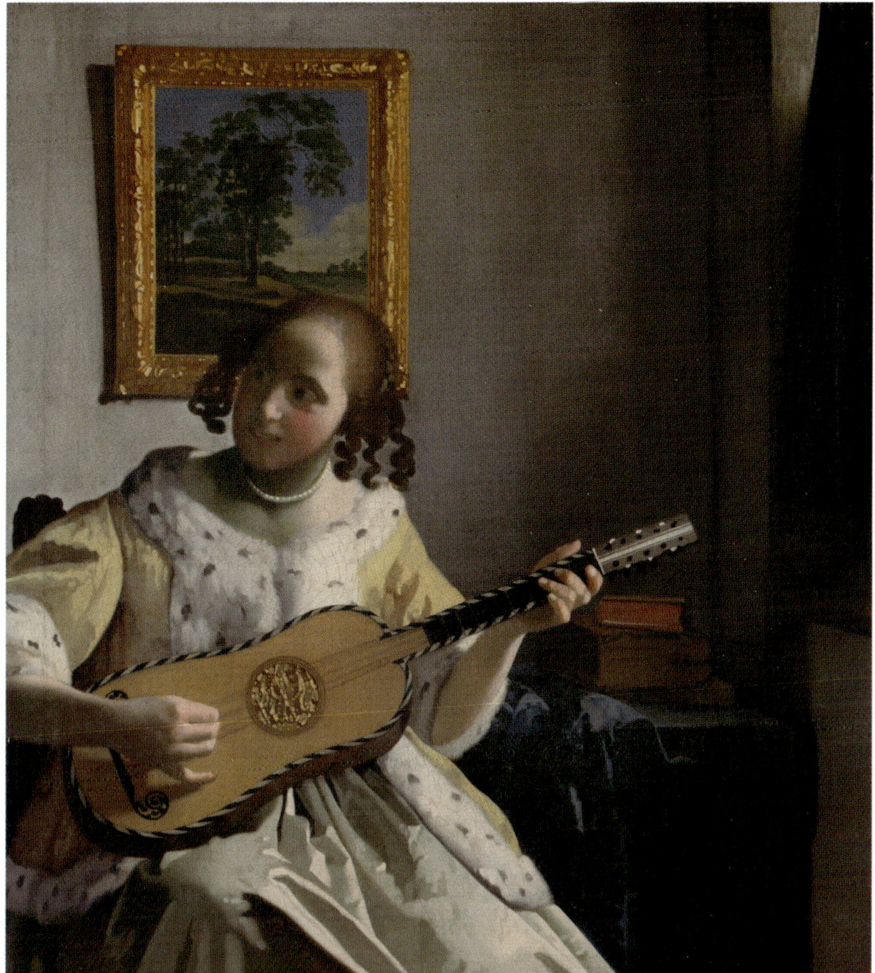

Fig. 2.7. *The Guitar Player* (ca. 1670–73). Oil on canvas. 53 × 46.3 cm. Kenwood House, English Heritage as Trustees of the Iveagh Bequest, London. HIP / Art Resource, NY

begins with speculation about the past. But it also shares with the writing we have looked at here a distinct tendency to identify him as a precursor of recent developments: not a painter's painter, in this case, but a proto-photographer or cinematographer—even, perhaps, a software designer. This Vermeer, too, in other words, looks like a modern among moderns.

3

Counter-Histories

Dead at an early age, in 1675, he remained a man of the seventeenth century.

—ALBERT BLANKERT (1995)

In May of 2019 the Gemäldegalerie in Dresden issued a press release whose eye-catching headline—"A 'New' Vermeer in Dresden"—quickly circulated through the art world.[1] As the accompanying story made clear, the museum was announcing not a new acquisition, but the restoration of an old one: a Vermeer that had remained effectively hidden from view despite having been on public display for over two centuries—longer, in fact, than any other work by the artist.[2] The painting in question, the *Girl Reading a Letter at an Open Window*, is by general agreement both one of Vermeer's earliest works and the first to establish the format for which he would become widely famous: a solitary young woman absorbed in a silent activity, her figure illuminated by the window of a domestic interior (see fig. 1.11). It was also generally thought to have initiated his practice of posing such a figure before a white wall, whose surface further diffused the windowed light. In his influential 1952 study Lawrence Gowing, for instance, called the Dresden picture "the first work in which we see [Vermeer's] mature simplicity," before going on to associate that simplicity with the way "a plain wall catches the light."[3] As we have seen, others before Gowing had already been drawn to this recurrent feature of the painter's style. When E. V. Lucas fantasized about cutting out a small piece of the *Woman with a Pearl Necklace* and framing it (see fig. 2.5), what he wished to extract for himself was a fragment of another such luminous wall—a fragment that would have been transformed by his gesture into a purely abstract epitome of Vermeer's

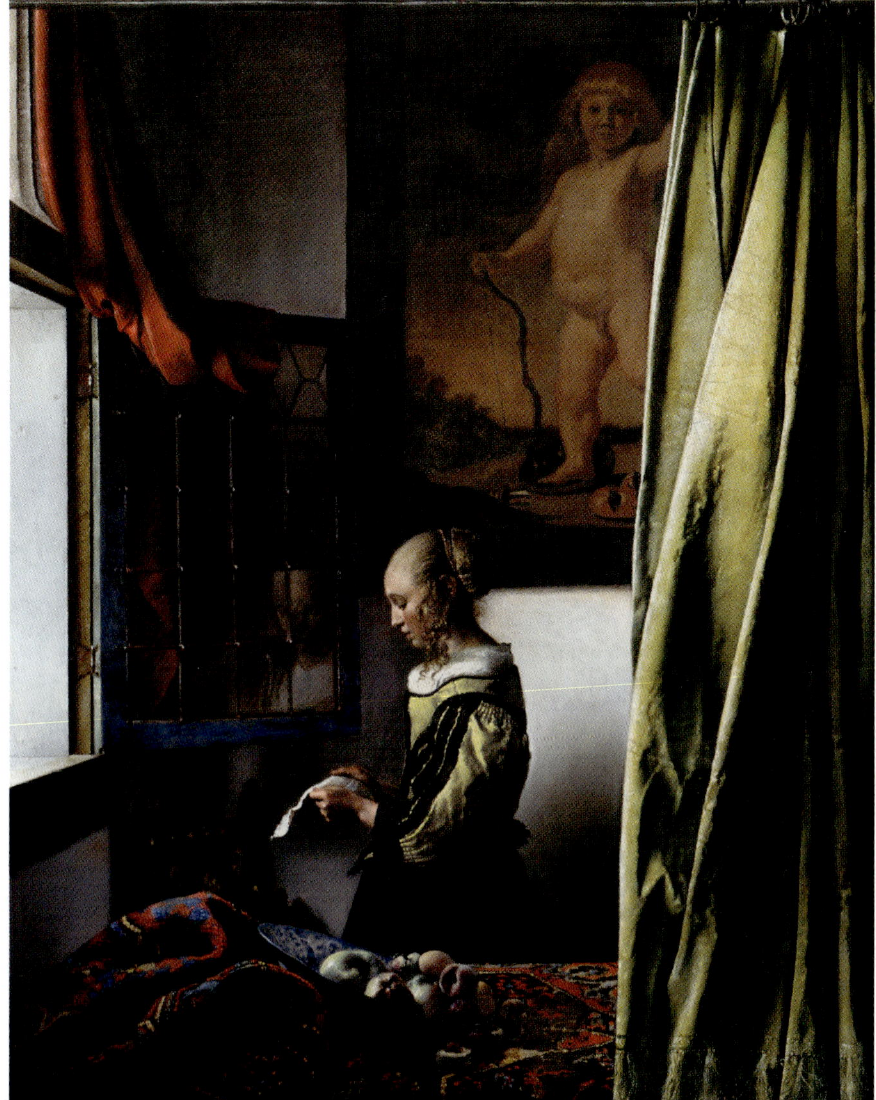

Fig. 3.1. Johannes Vermeer, *Girl Reading a Letter at an Open Window* (ca. 1657–59), restored. Oil on canvas. 83 × 64.5 cm. Gemäldegalerie Alte Meister, Dresden. bpk Bildagentur / Art Resource, NY

art. Before the Dresden museum's announcement, in other words, the blank wall of the *Girl Reading a Letter at an Open Window* had long been viewed as an early sign of how Vermeer became modern.[4]

What the Gemäldegalerie now reported, however, inevitably unsettled that account. According to the museum's restorers, the blank wall of the Dresden painting should in fact be ascribed not to Vermeer, but to a subsequent hand, which had covered over the large picture of a naked Cupid that originally hung in the background (fig. 3.1). Though the existence of this picture-within-the-picture had been known to scholars since 1979, when it was detected by X-ray, the prevailing assumption had been that the artist himself had painted it out, as he had other pentimenti first made visible by twentieth-century technology.[5]

Indeed, the story of how Vermeer eliminated such detail had itself become part of the argument for his modernity. Unlike his contemporaries, by this account, Vermeer sought not only to simplify his visual images but to remove the narrative and iconographic cues that characteristically help to stabilize meaning, thus progressively turning himself into an artist who painted more for art's sake than to tell a story or to moralize. The museum's discovery that the overpainting of the Dresden Cupid postdated the rest of the picture by several decades—and thus must have taken place after Vermeer died in 1675—now called that account into question.[6] The artist who juxtaposed his young letter reader against a large Cupid appeared to have been more engaged with his culture's conventions of meaning-making than had once been thought. In more than one sense, the decision to restore the painting to its original state entailed a return to historical context.

The case of the Dresden painting might easily appear an exception to the rule that has hitherto governed its creator's afterlife. Though the discovery has prompted calls to reevaluate other Vermeer paintings in which pentimenti have been exposed,[7] most commentators have tended to attribute the resulting changes in such cases to the artist's own hand and to take them as documenting a practice of careful—and sometimes protracted—revision. No one has yet questioned, for instance, that it was Vermeer himself who removed a man formerly visible through the doorway of another early painting, *A Maid Asleep* (fig. 3.2), or who substituted the chair in the foreground for a dog originally looking at the man—changes that are typically said to render the picture's narrative implications more ambiguous, while intensifying its poetic effect.[8]

Other such revisions have been confirmed in a number of canvases, from further acts of elimination, such as the removal of a small female figure seated at the entrance to the alley in *The Little Street* and of a chair from the left foreground of *Young Woman with a Water Pitcher*, or the overpainting of maps on the walls of both *The Milkmaid* and the *Woman with a Pearl Necklace*, to subtle modifications of posture and gesture: an adjustment of the woman's hands in the latter picture, for example, so that she holds the ribbons of the necklace stretched out before her rather than tying them, or an increase of the distance that separates the couple in *The Music Lesson*.[9] Though these and similar alterations of Vermeer's work have only been made visible with the aid of modern technology, they testify to acts performed in his lifetime, and the scholarship focused on them thus also belongs to what I term counter-histories: writing that seeks to return the artist to the period in which he flourished. When the conservator at the Mauritshuis, Jørgen Wadum, remarked that "a true understanding of Vermeer's painting cannot be achieved without technical data," he was chiefly concerned with the artist's method of establishing perspective; but looking for evidence of pinholes involves another return to history, and so, too, at least in part, do the heated arguments that arose in the middle of the last century over Vermeer's use of the camera obscura.[10]

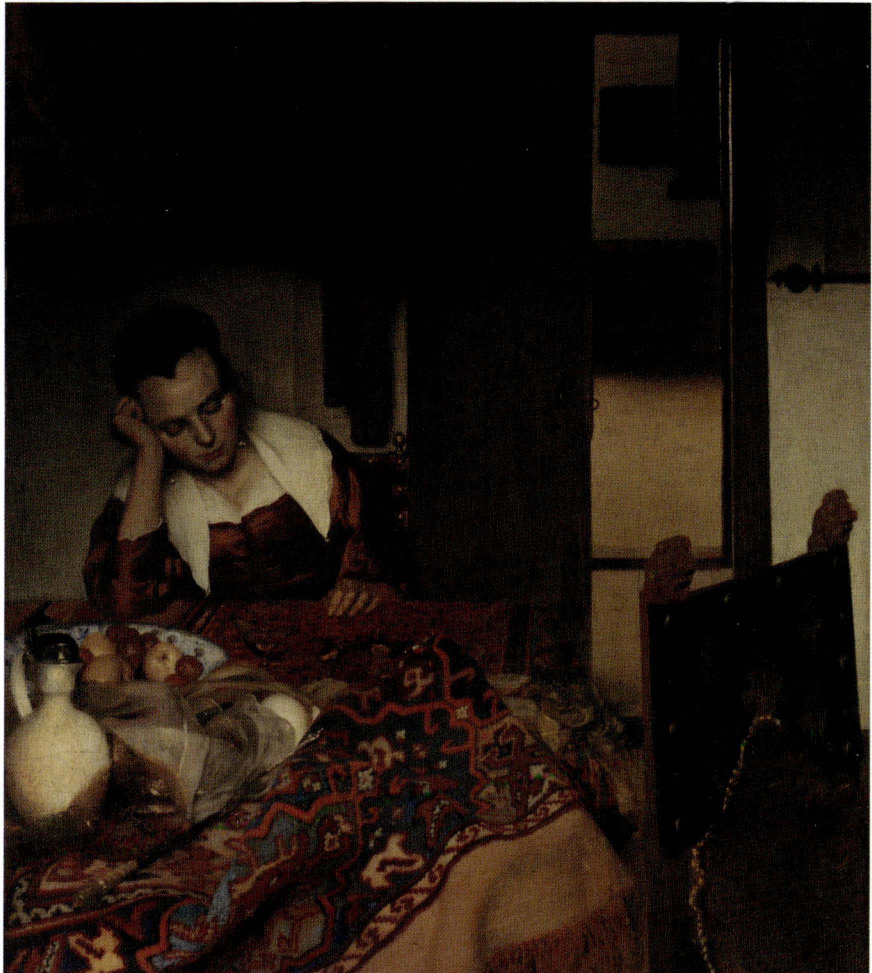

Fig. 3.2. Johannes Vermeer, *A Maid Asleep* (ca. 1656–57). Oil on canvas. 87.6 × 76.5 cm. Bequest of Benjamin Altman, 1913. Metropolitan Museum of Art, New York

As an event that took place after the artist's death, the overpainting of the Dresden canvas belongs to a different kind of history: one concerned with the reception of the work, rather than its creation. But the reappearance of the Cupid will only strengthen the case of those who have sought to counter the argument for Vermeer's modernity. In his analysis of perspective, Wadum had specifically noted how the vanishing point in the *Girl Reading a Letter* would have led our eyes to the Cupid and thus encouraged us to associate him with the woman herself: an effect Wadum presumed Vermeer had destroyed when he chose to replace the picture-within-the-picture by a blank wall.[11] Now, presumably, Wadum's initial observation will have renewed force—all the more so, in fact, because the Dresden Cupid is only one of several such images in Vermeer's oeuvre. And well before this particular Cupid surfaced, commentators on the artist had approached these and other pictures-within-the-pictures as important keys to meaning.

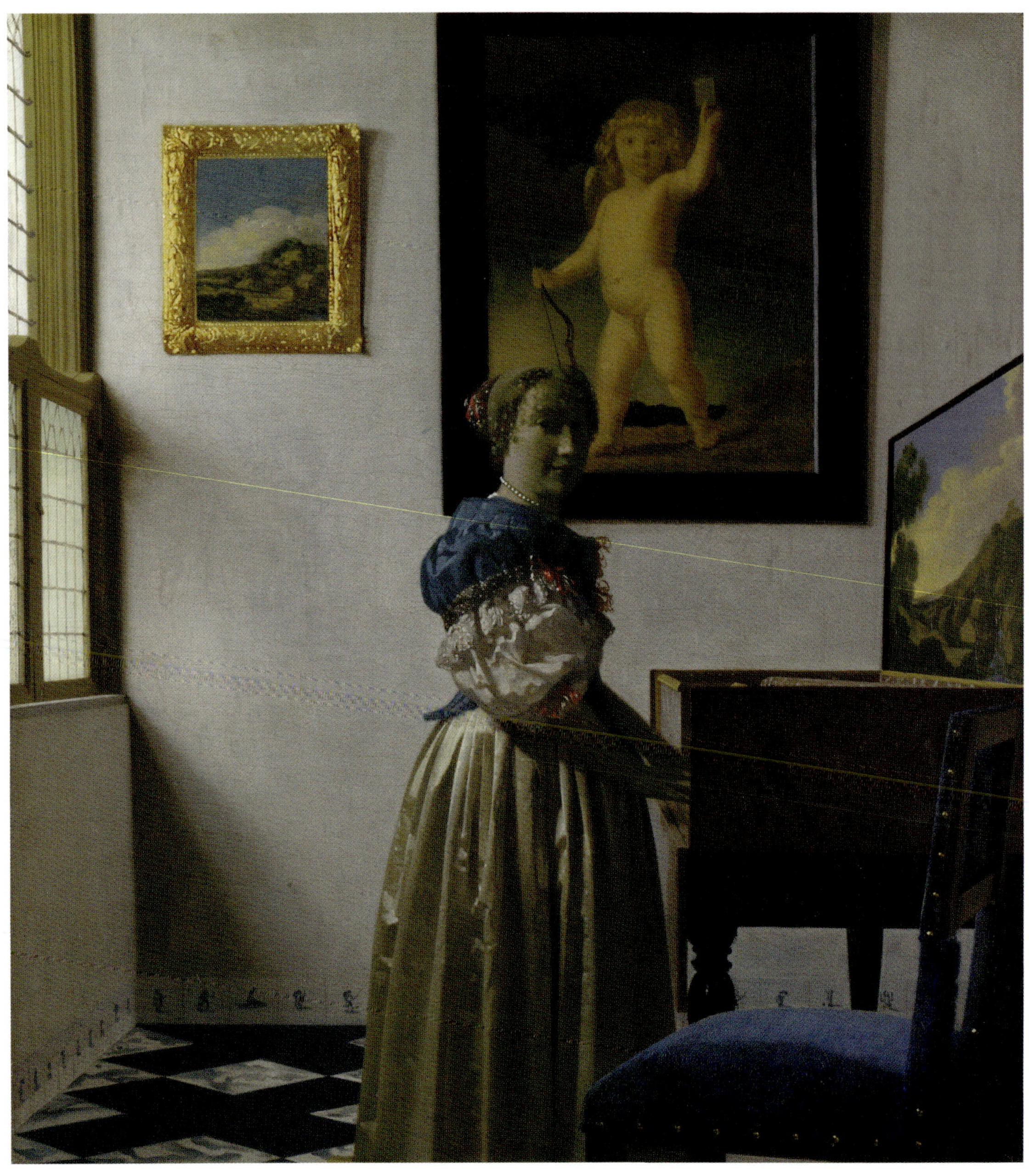

Fig. 3.3. Johannes Vermeer, *A Young Woman Standing at a Virginal* (ca. 1670–74). Oil on canvas. 51.7 × 45.2 cm. National Gallery, London. © National Gallery, London / Art Resource, NY

Among those most inclined to such iconographical interpretations of Vermeer's art has been the Dutch scholar Eddy de Jongh. In a prominent 1967 study, for instance, he sought to connect the Cupid on the wall of the *Young Woman Standing at a Virginal* (fig. 3.3) to a similarly posed image from a seventeenth-century emblem book by Otto van Veen, whose accompanying motto—"A lover ought to love only one"—is presumably illustrated by the numbered card in the figure's hand (fig. 3.4). Unlike the emblem, Vermeer's picture shows the god holding a blank, but that did not prevent De Jongh from

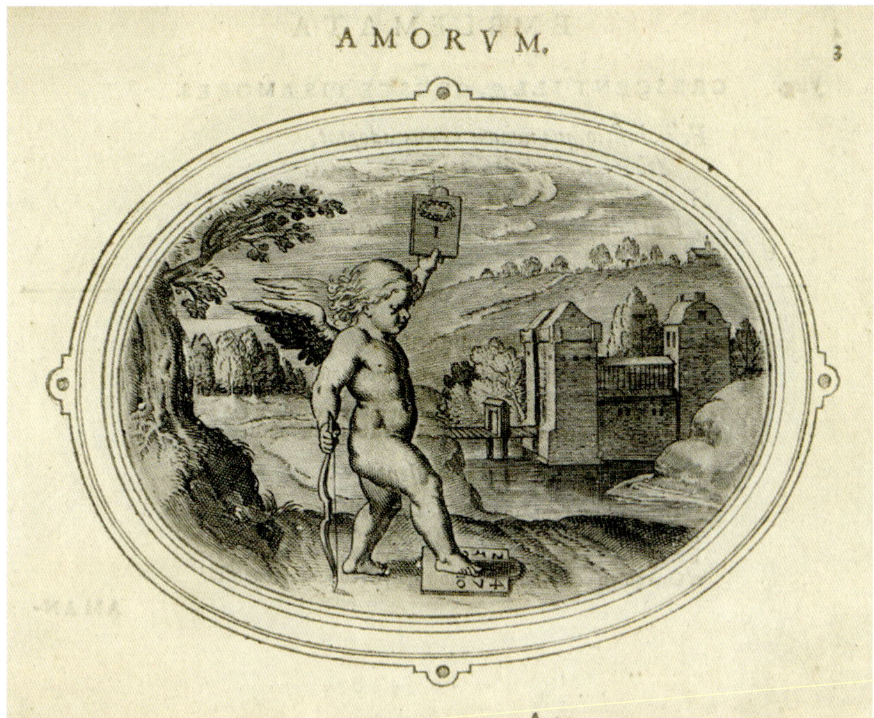

Fig. 3.4. "A Lover Ought to Love Only One," from Otto van Veen, *Amorum Emblemata* (Antwerp, 1609)

assuming that they convey the same message: an interpretation that was in turn adopted by the catalogue for the blockbuster exhibition of the artist's work almost three decades later.[12]

Building on De Jongh's observations, others have argued that Vermeer meant the picture to be paired with his *Young Woman Seated at a Virginal* (ca. 1670–75)—a work of nearly identical size, also now at the National Gallery in London—and that they were intended to represent opposed ideas of love, with the literally upright woman posed against the implied lasciviousness of the seated one. The fact that the latter has its own picture-within-the-picture, and that it can be identified as a painting by Dirck van Baburen called *The Procuress* (1622), adds to this argument, as does the comparative darkness in which the seated woman is cast and what one commentator calls "the rumpled disorder of her blue drapery" (fig. 3.5).[13]

Meanwhile, De Jongh himself had begun to qualify his initial reading. While still convinced that Vermeer meant to invoke the emblem, he was now less certain how that allusion signified: was the Cupid on the wall of the *Young Woman Standing* a sign of the young woman's devotion, or a critique of her faithlessness? Was she in fact the object of the warning, or was the implicit moral directed instead at the painting's viewers? De Jongh's tentative solution—that Vermeer intended the allusion to set such questions going while leaving the answer open—has become a common approach to interpreting his pictures, even when a specific emblem or other moralizing device is not in evidence.

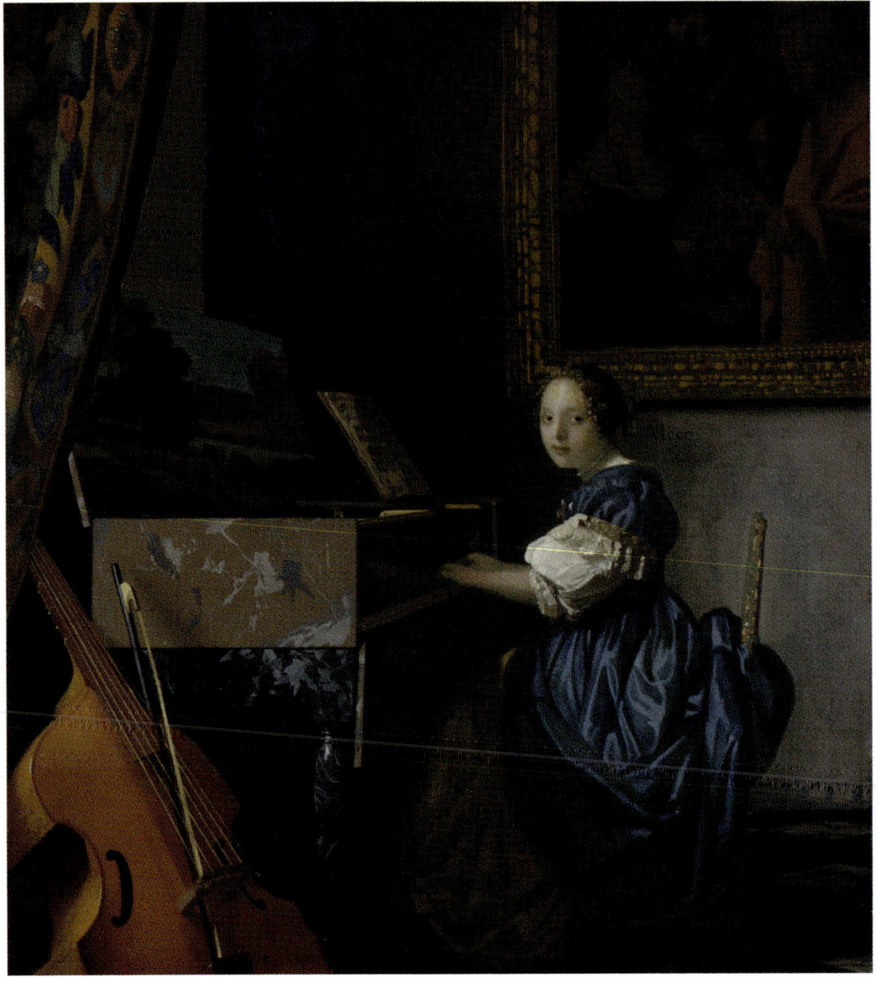

Fig. 3.5. Johannes Vermeer, *A Young Woman Seated at a Virginal* (ca. 1670–75). Oil on canvas. 51.5 × 45.5 cm. National Gallery, London. © National Gallery, London / Art Resource, NY

Though some scholars view such openness to interpretation as part of what distinguishes Vermeer from his contemporaries, that was not the thrust of De Jongh's argument. Quoting the famous author of other seventeenth-century emblem books, Jacob Cats, on the rhetorical effects of hiding meaning rather than revealing it, De Jongh contended that Vermeer's "pleasing obscurity" was itself very much a historical phenomenon.[14]

Other versions of the Cupid image in Vermeer's work have inspired further iconographical speculation. One commentator, for example, proposed that the mask lying at the figure's feet in the partly obscured Cupid of the *Maid Asleep* (see fig. 3.2) implies amorous disillusionment, while a second—contrarily—identified it with the liberatory unmasking of erotic fantasy made possible by sleep.[15] (Both these accounts may be called into question now that two masks have been uncovered at the feet of the Dresden Cupid and tentatively linked to a different emblem by Van Veen in which faithful love opposes the deception implied by the mask.)[16] The picture-within-the-picture of *Girl Interrupted at*

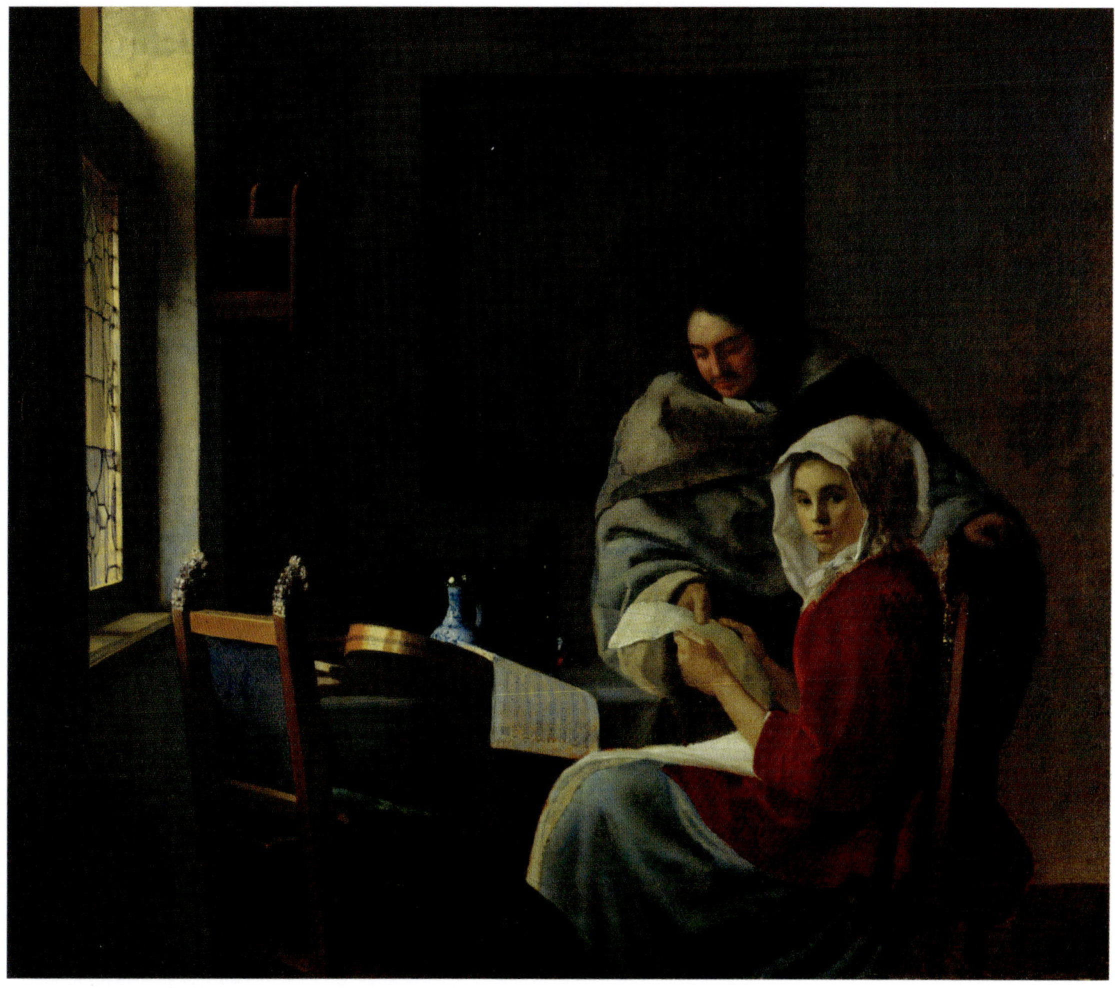

Fig. 3.6. Johannes Vermeer, *Girl Interrupted at Her Music* (ca. 1658–61). Oil on canvas. 39.3 × 44.4 cm. Frick Collection, New York. Image © Frick Collection

Her Music (fig. 3.6) has also prompted conflicting interpretations, depending in part on how closely it is linked to Van Veen's emblem.[17]

As it happens, the Cupid in this picture, like the Dresden one, only came to light after some overpainting was removed by restorers shortly before Henry Clay Frick purchased the picture in 1901. The Frick's Cupid had been concealed by a violon rather than a blank wall, and while commentators are generally agreed that the instrument was added by a later hand, there has been little speculation as to whether a modernizing taste was at work in the substitution.[18] But it seems worth noting that the fervent admirer of the white wall in the *Woman with a Pearl Necklace*, E. V. Lucas, didn't have much use for the large Cupid that obscures a similar stretch of wall in the *Young Woman Standing at a Virginal*. He even managed to convince himself that its inclusion could be blamed on a patron: left to himself, Lucas thought, Vermeer would have painted a map.[19]

Modernizers such as Lucas were still less interested, of course, in the artist's history paintings. As I have already suggested, this was partly a function of the sequence in which Vermeer's work was recovered: with the ambiguous exception of the *Allegory of the Catholic Faith*, which appeared (under a different title) as an entry in Thoré's catalogue, the religious and mythological pictures only surfaced after the artist's image as a painter of modern subjects had already begun to take hold in the collective consciousness. The relatively small proportion of history painting in the oeuvre as a whole also made—and still makes—an obvious difference, even with the recent addition of the *Saint Praxedis* to the total.[20] But the preference for Vermeer's modern subjects was clearly also a matter of taste; and apart from a brief interlude in the 1930s and 1940s when Van Meegeren's forgeries prompted a new interest in the historical pictures, the Vermeer who entered the popular imagination remained virtually identical to the one celebrated at the turn of the twentieth century. And not only in the popular imagination: as late as 1950 the Dutch art historian P.T.A. Swillens chose to exclude both *Diana and Her Companions* and *Christ in the House of Martha and Mary* from the canon, on the grounds that such pictures "had nothing in common with [Vermeer's] art."[21] Though the completion of Swillens's monograph had been delayed by the Second World War, he had in fact been working on the painter since 1914, and it may well be that his judgment was inevitably shaped by the generation that had first welcomed Vermeer as a modern.[22] If so, however, he was hardly the last to feel that the essence of the artist's genius had little to do with the traditional aims of history painting.

Yet the serious attention twentieth- and twenty-first-century scholars have accorded the religious and mythological work is also part of Vermeer's afterlife, and such attention clearly belongs among the counter-histories we have been examining.[23] Accounting for this work means turning to history in a double sense: both as the record of the artist's development and as evidence of his own investment in historical subject matter. We take for granted that a contemporary catalogue raisonné will arrange its images chronologically, but the absence of dates on all except four of Vermeer's canvases has made the establishment of such a sequence particularly challenging in his case; and it wasn't until both the *Diana and Her Companions* and *Christ in the House of Martha and Mary* were securely attributed to his hand that scholars began to think of Vermeer as an artist who first entertained ambitions as a history painter.[24] The *Diana* had hung in the Mauritshuis for nearly a decade before evidence of a Vermeer signature was discovered beneath that of Nicolaes Maes, and the question of which Vermeer was at issue remained unsettled until the turn of the century. (Though the official who had purchased the painting thought it the work of the Delft master, the institution officially attributed it to Vermeer of Utrecht.)[25] As we have seen, it was only when a clearly signed *Christ in the House of Martha and Mary* surfaced at a London sale in 1901 that the stylistic affinities between the two works led most commentators to group them together as early works by Vermeer of Delft.

Especially when viewed in conjunction with the first of the dated paintings, the *Procuress*, these works also prompted scholars to speculate that the young Vermeer may well have been influenced by the so-called Utrecht Caravaggisti: artists who in turn had studied in Italy, and whose Roman Catholicism may help to explain how someone born to Reformed Protestants acquired the connections that later enabled him to marry into a Catholic family. Dirck van Baburen (1595–1624), whose own *Procuress* figures on the wall of both the *Young Woman Seated at a Virginal* and *The Concert*, was a Utrecht artist; and the painting itself, or a copy, apparently belonged to Vermeer's mother-in-law (see figs. 3.5 and 1.17). Though the question of where Vermeer received his training remains a mystery, his most knowledgeable biographer, John Michael Montias, thinks a likely candidate for the artist's teacher was another Utrecht painter named Abraham Bloemaert (1566–1651), whom Montias discovered to have been distantly related to Vermeer's mother-in-law. An alternative candidate, Leonaert Bramer (1596–1674), came from Delft, though he too was Catholic and had spent time in Italy. As Montias and others have noted, Bramer's style has little in common with Vermeer's, but he does seem to have known the family, and the fact that he began his career with religious and mythological pictures makes for a suggestive parallel with the story most scholars now tell about the younger artist's development.[26] The *Procuress* is signed and dated 1656, while the current consensus places the undated history paintings even earlier in Vermeer's career, with estimates ranging from 1653 to 1656. Whether *Christ in the House of Martha and Mary* preceded the *Diana*, as the majority appear to think, or whether the order should be reversed, as Walter Liedtke has argued, there is widespread agreement that Vermeer soon abandoned his ambitions as a history painter for the representation of modern life.[27]

Just how much he still intended that representation to convey verbalizable meaning is far less settled, however. By comparison with other paintings I shall consider here, the problems posed by *The Milkmaid* are relatively simple, yet even this seemingly straightforward image has proved more ambiguous than might at first appear. Consider, for example, the question of how to interpret—if at all—the tiny Cupid that appears on the tile next to the footwarmer in the righthand corner (fig. 3.7). The presence of this small figure (or figures, since some have thought there are two) has prompted speculation that Vermeer intended a comment on the amorous implications of his subject, especially given the presence of the footwarmer, whose heat had already been associated with Eros in a popular emblem book of the period. Both the improbability of decorating a kitchen with Cupids and the fact that Vermeer apparently chose to substitute the footwarmer for a basket of peat originally painted in its place has suggested to some scholars that these details are meaningful, but how exactly to construe that meaning has proved a challenge even for those tempted by iconographical readings. Does the conjunction of Cupid and footwarmer signify "constant attention and caring," as Arthur K. Wheelock Jr. first hypothesized,

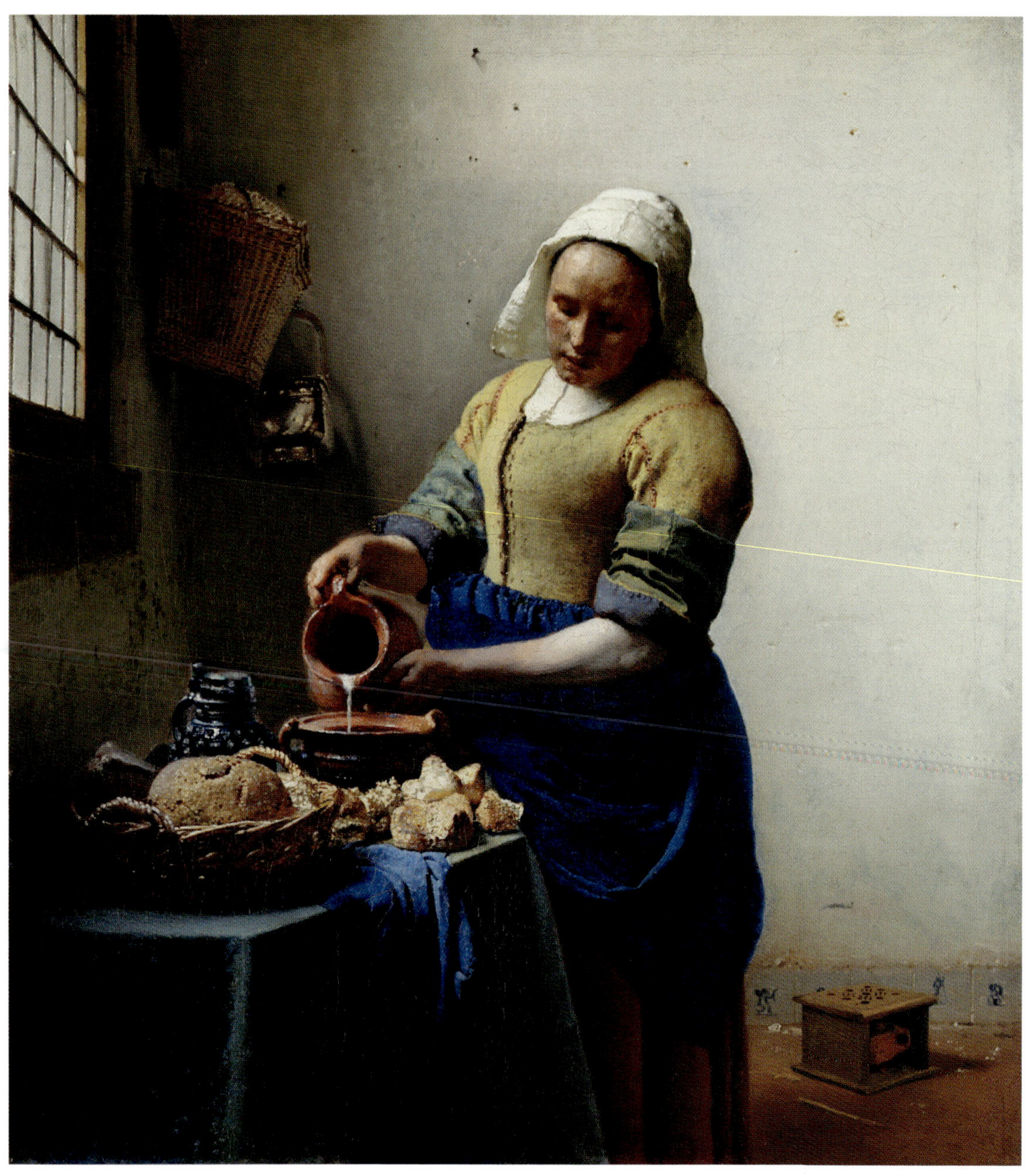

Fig. 3.7. Johannes Vermeer, *The Milkmaid* (ca. 1657–61). Oil on canvas. 45.5 × 41 cm. Rijksmuseum, Amsterdam

or is that to underplay the amorous suggestiveness of the motif? And if that motif is indeed meant to suggest erotic desire, does it "point to the maid's own proclivities," or is it rather intended "to solicit them from the viewer"? (The question appears to take for granted that the viewer at issue is male.)[28] For Walter Liedtke, who adheres to the latter position, the open-mouthed jug the woman holds in her hands only serves to confirm that she is "meant to be seen [. . .] as a discreet object of desire." Liedtke characteristically invokes several images of jug-wielding young women by the artist's contemporaries in support of his claim, which he further buttresses with reference to a popular tradition of more overtly pornographic carvings and prints.[29]

Observing that Vermeer's milkmaid turns away from the footwarmer—and that the object itself is apparently cold—others have speculated that he meant, on the contrary, to distinguish her dignified figure from her more lascivious counterparts in the work of his peers. At least two scholars who advance this argument also hedge their bets, however, by cautioning that "some foot-warmers in Dutch genre paintings are just foot-warmers" (H. Perry Chapman), or that "a broken window pane may be just a broken window pane" (Blaise Ducos)—this last a reference to another potentially suggestive sign that some have spotted in *The Milkmaid*.[30] While such adaptations of Freud's apocryphal maxim might well apply to any Dutch genre painting, the visual elusiveness with which Vermeer often renders iconographic details only intensifies the interpretive problem. As Irene Netta observes of *The Milkmaid*, "the very small cupids on the tiles can hardly be recognized as such with the naked eye"—one reason among several, in her view, for preferring to leave the question of the artist's iconographic intentions unsettled. As we shall see, she is hardly alone among recent scholars of Vermeer in drawing attention to what she calls, in a nicely paradoxical phrase, "this explicit elusiveness of iconographic meaning."[31]

Just where on the continuum a particular commentary falls can depend as much on the painting at issue as on the commentator's own assumptions about the culture of the seventeenth-century Netherlands. Both the *Young Woman with a Water Pitcher* (fig. 3.8) and *Woman Holding a Balance* (fig. 3.9), for example, come from what is generally thought to be Vermeer's middle period; and both represent the kind of painting for which he is now best known: a solitary young woman in a domestic interior, her figure illuminated by light from a left-hand window, as she stands absorbed in a silent activity. But while most treatments of the former painting offer little by way of iconographical analysis, apart from generalized allusions to the pitcher and basin as "objects imbued with the notion of cleansing and purification," in the words of one art historian, or "as time-honoured symbols of purity and innocence," in the words of another, the *Woman Holding a Balance* has been the subject of considerable interpretive controversy.[32] The juxtaposition of a picture representing the Last Judgment on the wall behind her with the activity of the woman herself has long seemed to suggest some form of moral or spiritual commentary, but what, exactly, the whole is "saying" has proved more elusive than scholars once thought.

First understood as a Vanitas, in which the worldly act of weighing gold or pearls was posed against the divine weighing of souls, the painting appeared to shift its meaning when a microscopic examination of its surface revealed that the scales in the woman's hand were actually empty. Rather than take the picture-within-the-picture as condemning her activity, scholars now began to see her, too, as engaged in a spiritual exercise: an interpretation more consistent, one might note, with the serenity and poise of the woman herself.[33]

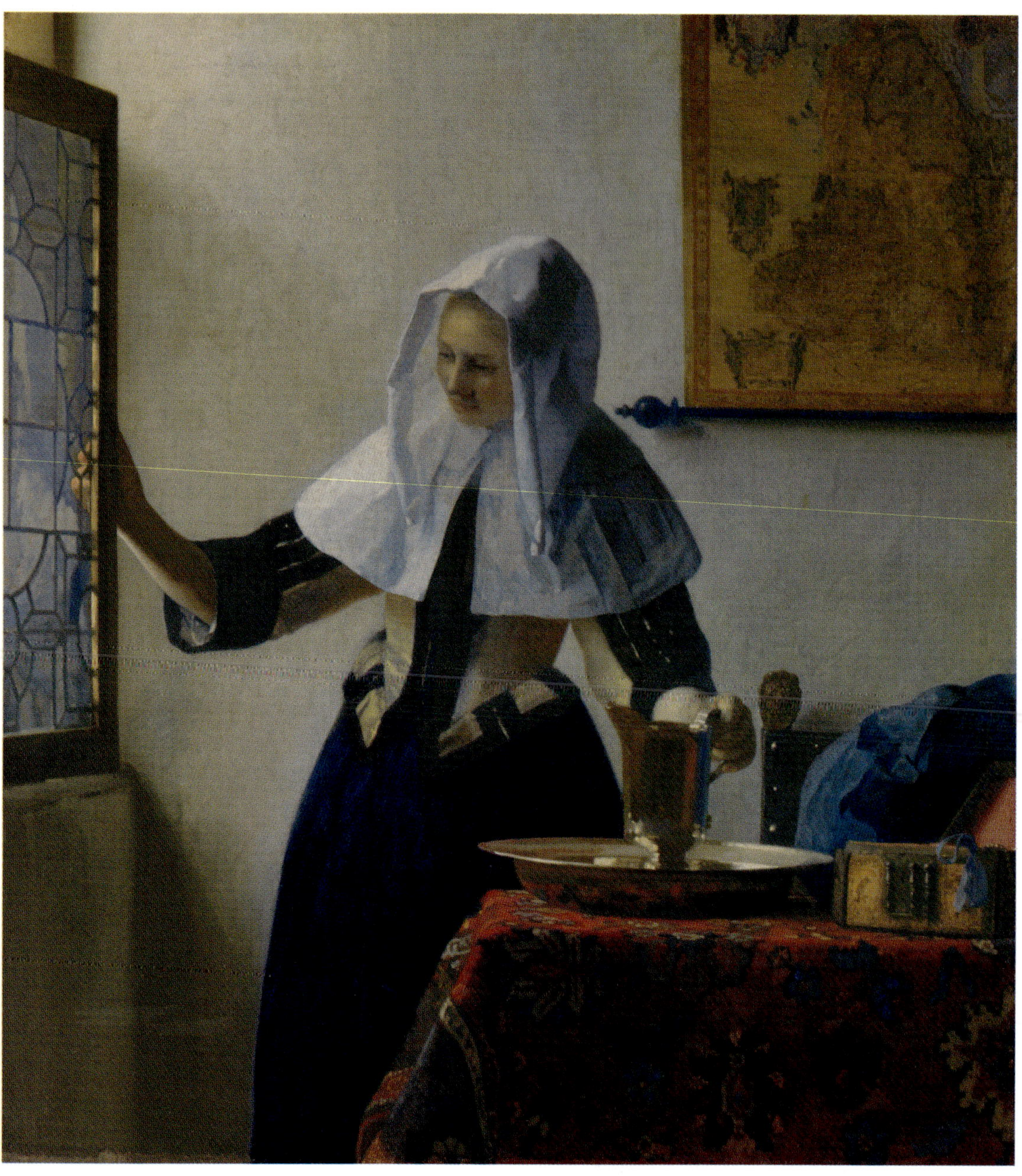

Fig. 3.8. Johannes Vermeer, *Young Woman with a Water Pitcher* (ca. 1662). Oil on canvas. 45.7 × 40.6 cm. Marquand Collection. Gift of Henry G. Marquand, 1889. Metropolitan Museum of Art, New York

Attempts to pin down the precise character of her act have reached no consensus, however, with interpreters searching for clues in a variety of external sources, ranging from yet more emblem books to printed allegories and devotional texts such as the *Spiritual Exercises* of Saint Ignatius of Loyola (1522–24). For Wheelock, who quotes from the latter work as well as the text of 1 Corinthians, the painting conveys "a message that one should lead a life of temperance and balanced judgment," while Eddy de Jongh also draws on Saint Ignatius, among other sources, in order to suggest that the woman might be viewed as

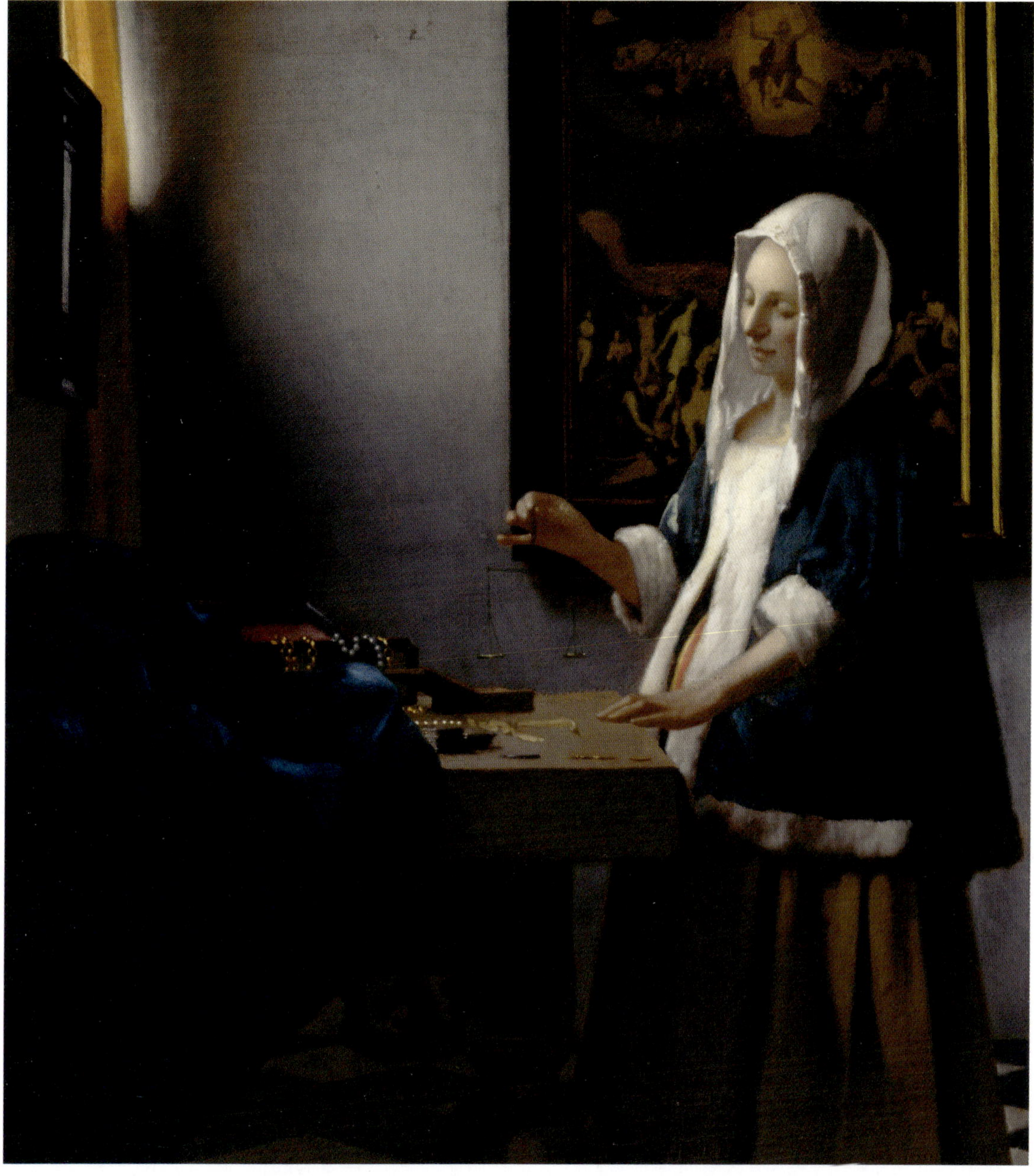

Fig. 3.9. Johannes Vermeer, *Woman Holding a Balance* (ca. 1662–65). Oil on canvas. 42.5. × 38 cm. Widener Collection, National Gallery of Art, Washington, DC

a personification of conscience. Ivan Gaskell identifies as the relevant key an emblem from Cesare Ripa's *Iconologia* (1593–1603), in which a woman holding a balance and a mirror serves as a figure of Truth, and Albert Blankert cites an engraved allegory in which another woman holding a balance against the backdrop of a painting of the Last Judgment is said to represent "the triumph of Truth over terrestrial forces."[34] Focusing more on the woman's apparent pregnancy, Nanette Salomon argues that she is weighing the destiny of her future child: an act itself illuminated by documents appearing to confirm that Vermeer had converted to Catholicism in order to marry his wife, since the salvation or damnation of an unborn soul would have remained open for Catholics, as presumably would not be the case for their Calvinist brethren. Though some scholars have questioned whether the woman in the painting is in fact pregnant, Salomon points to the way the light illuminates her rounded abdomen and invokes the precedent of the annunciate Mary.[35] It is an evocative comparison, even if it places Vermeer's painting at the farthest remove from the admonitory image that Thoré thought he saw more than a century earlier. "Ah! You are weighing jewels?" he inquired of the picture. "You will be weighed and judged in your turn!"[36]

Woman Holding a Balance is something of a limit case in Vermeer's oeuvre. Unlike a number of his solitary figures—the *Young Woman with a Water Pitcher*, say, or *The Milkmaid*—it cannot be easily assimilated to the "purely pictorial vision" for which Swillens, among others, once celebrated him, and thus would appear to cry out for the kind of explanation that I have been calling counter-history.[37] A work that appears—almost literally—pregnant with meaning, it is also, however, a painting that continues to elude definitive interpretation. Nor is it exactly another instance of Wadum's dictum that "a true understanding of Vermeer's painting cannot be achieved without technical data," despite the way in which modern technology, as with the Dresden picture, has exposed aspects of the canvas that had previously gone unperceived.[38] While the discovery of the Cupid in the *Girl Reading a Letter at an Open Window* may appear to narrow, however minimally, the possible meaning of the image, the revelation that there is nothing material in the woman's scales has only served to ambiguate a painting whose moral had once seemed comparatively obvious. There is also the further problem, as Daniel Arasse has shrewdly noted, that the emptiness of those scales is not really visible to the naked eye: a fact that at least calls into question the idea that what has been revealed with the aid of a high-powered microscope is the painting as it would have been understood by Vermeer's contemporaries.[39]

Consider another painting that would seem at first glance to invite—indeed to spell out—verbalizable meaning. Uncharacteristically for Vermeer, *The Music Lesson* includes not only a picture-within-the-picture but a textual gloss, in the form of a Latin motto inscribed on the open lid of the virginal: "MVSICA LETITIAE CO[MES] MEDICINA DOLOR[VM]" (Music, companion of joy, balm for sorrow) (fig. 3.10). The one such instrument in Vermeer to be decorated with words rather than a pastoral landscape, the virginal appears to offer the painted equivalent of the printed motto that would typically accompany an image in an emblem book and, in so doing, to sum up the scene before us.

Almost seventy-five years ago, however, Lawrence Gowing proposed a more elaborate account of the painting, by tracing the implications of the picture-within-the-picture that hangs on the right. Though only part of the picture is visible, it appears to represent the subject known as Roman Charity: the story of a loving daughter who offers to breastfeed her imprisoned father in

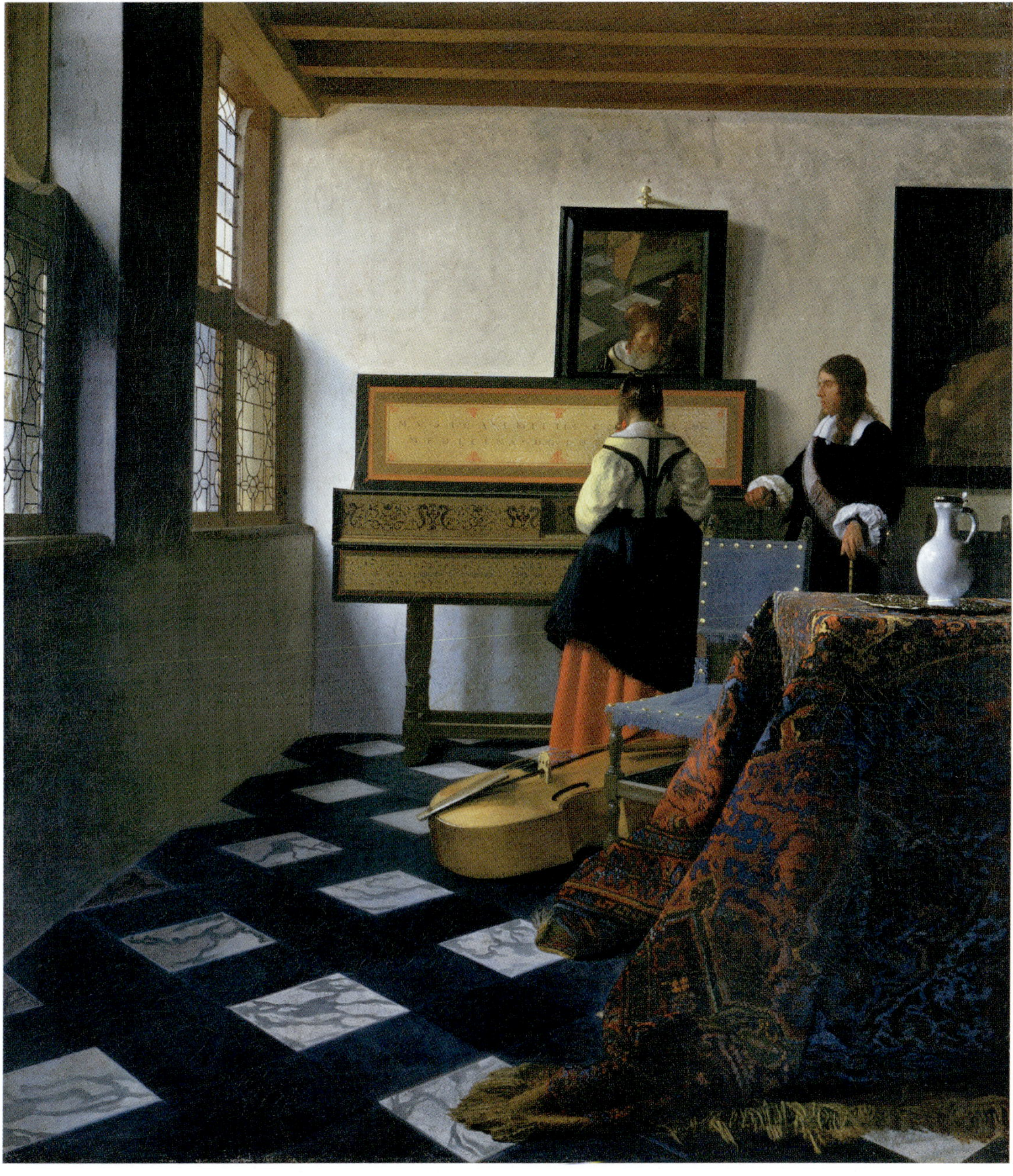

order to save him from starvation. Remote as the subject might seem from the musical couple, Gowing linked the father's situation to "the rapt look of the gentleman" in front of the picture—a look he in turn associated with the "abject dependence of man upon woman" that he saw as fundamental to Vermeer's work as a whole. For Gowing, the fact that the legend of the daughter's sacrifice first appears in an ancient ekphrasis of another painting only reinforced the connection with Vermeer himself, and so, too, did the coincidence that the

Fig. 3.10. Johannes Vermeer, *A Lady at the Virginal with a Gentleman* (*The Music Lesson*) (ca. 1662–64). Oil on canvas. 73.3 × 64.5 cm. Royal Collection, London. HIP / Art Resource, NY

father's name—Cimon—is that of "the ancient Greek painter supposed to have discovered perspective art."[40]

The interpretive ingenuity of Gowing's account is considerable, and others have since echoed it, by suggesting, for example, that "music and milk, each in its way, assuage the pains of captivity," or by observing that Vermeer discreetly places his own signature where it almost abuts the figures of both men.[41] Yet if this is indeed the associative chain Vermeer intended to weave, the very erudition required to unravel it, not to mention the more obvious difficulty of discerning the figure of Cimon in the radically cropped picture, means that its significance will probably be lost on most viewers, even as it is likely to have remained hidden from the majority of Vermeer's contemporaries. Emblems are usually public affairs, but the picture-within-this-picture yields something closer to what Arasse calls a "private" allegory.[42] Though *The Music Lesson* is a rare case in which Vermeer appears to multiply interpretive glosses rather than pare them down, most contemporary scholars continue to find something mysterious in the painting, not least, as we shall see, because of the enigmas posed by its formal arrangements.

The assumption that Vermeer intended the pictures within his pictures as emblematic guides to the whole is further complicated by his practice of reusing them from painting to painting, sometimes to quite different effect. Like other elements of Vermeer's pictorial world, in fact—the yellow jacket trimmed with fur, for example, or the leather chairs with their lion-head finials—the pictures that hang in his painted interiors almost certainly correspond to objects in his family's possession, and their reappearance from one work to another may have as much to do with Vermeer's sense of design as with his manipulation of meaning.[43] Having learned that *The Astronomer*'s book opens on a passage identifying "our ancestors the patriarchs" as "the first observers and investigators of [. . .] the stars," we may think we understand why *The Finding of Moses* appears on the wall behind the figure of the astronomer (fig. 3.11); but what, then, should we make of the same picture when it shows up with different dimensions behind the head of the mistress in the *Lady Writing a Letter with Her Maid* (see fig. 1.19)?[44] And if the *Procuress* on the wall of the *Young Woman Seated at a Virginal* is indeed a comment on the lasciviousness of the woman herself—an interpretation that not everyone accepts—how should we understand the appearance of the same picture in *The Concert*, where it hangs alongside a painted landscape?[45] Though some have concluded that the concert must be taking place in an elegant brothel, others have argued to the contrary that we are being invited to draw an implicit contrast between the figures in Baburen's picture and Vermeer's own refined scene, even if the same argument isn't usually extended to the relation between that scene and the landscape, which tends to be read as harmonizing with the concert (see fig. 1.17).[46] (Like all Vermeer's inset landscapes, the one in *The Concert* has been loosely linked to writing of the period that associates the natural world with themes of love and courtship).[47]

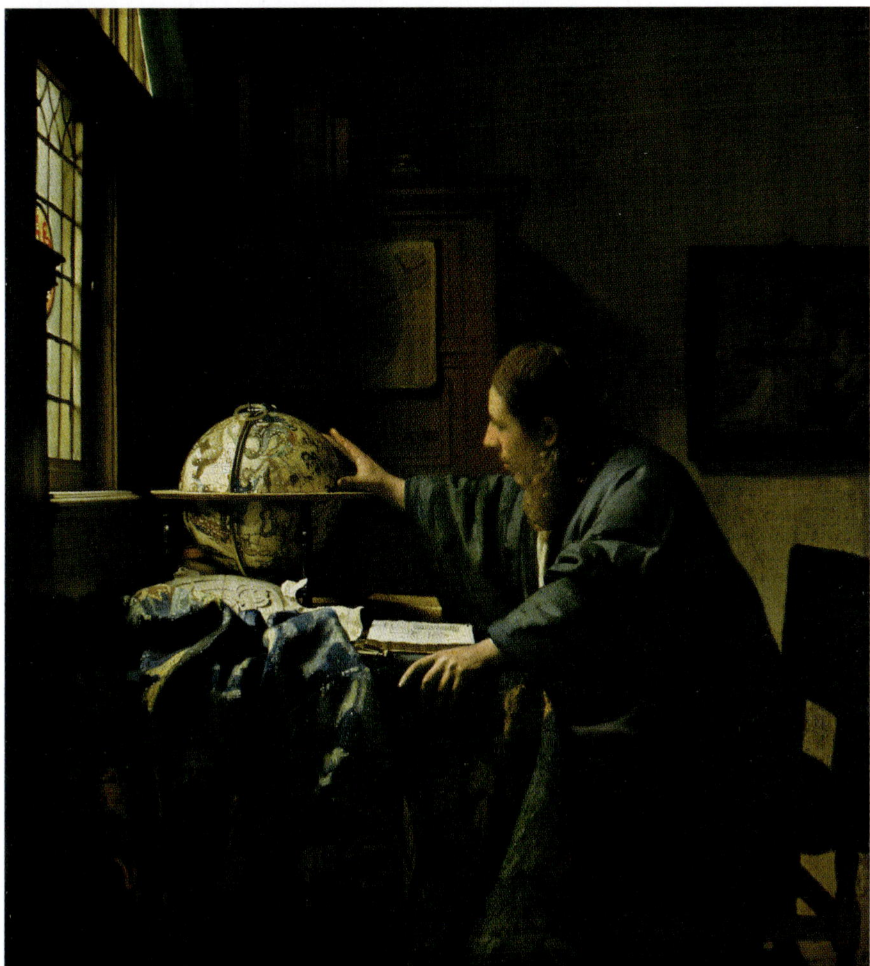

Fig. 3.11. Johannes Vermeer, *The Astronomer* (1668). Oil on canvas. 51 × 45 cm. Musée du Louvre, Paris. RMN-Grand Palais / Art Resource, NY

As for the *Finding of Moses* that accompanies Vermeer's mistress and maid: one scholar has speculated that it may be intended to convey an aura of divine protection for the beloved recipient of the letter, while another has proposed typological comparisons among the women, with Pharaoh's daughter prefiguring the nobility of the mistress and Moses's sister anticipating the maid's service as messenger.[48] Perhaps understandably, however, neither account is offered with much assurance. As yet another scholar sums up the problem: "One senses an analogy along the lines of the sending and receiving of something (a baby, a letter) of great value, but Vermeer's precise intent remains customarily obscure."[49]

The spirit of that conclusion—or lack of one—is widespread among recent commentators on Vermeer's art. Even as they offer alternative accounts of individual paintings, many historically minded scholars seem inclined to agree with Daniel Arasse when he argues that Vermeer deploys such iconographical cues not so much to enable interpretation as to elude it—or at least to multiply potential readings rather than stabilize them.[50] Arasse argues that Vermeer deliberately sets out "to hold meaning in suspense, to make the 'reading' of what is visible indeterminate," and Harry Berger Jr. reaches for similar language when he concludes an extended meditation on the *Woman Holding a Balance* with a question that generalizes the interpretative problems the image poses. "I want to know how to respond to her," he writes, "and I experience a curiosity which can only be called anecdotal. But Christ's judgment, the woman's judgment, and my judgment are called forth only to be held in abeyance. Should the painting, should all of Vermeer's paintings, be entitled *Suspended Judgment*?"[51] Not every scholar of Vermeer would subscribe to that hypothetical title, but the aura of suspended judgment nonetheless continues to hover over attempts to articulate the meaning of his art, even—or especially—when historical research appears to provide the keys to decode it.

Perhaps the principal exception to this rule, not surprisingly, is also the painting that has often been seen as Vermeer's most anomalous: the large canvas that the Metropolitan Museum of Art in New York currently titles *Allegory of the Catholic Faith* (fig. 3.12). Unlike the majority of his work, this is a painting that resists the impulse to explain its details as a credible representation of ordinary life and thus overtly demands to be read as allegory. Sometimes a footwarmer is just a footwarmer, in other words, especially when located in a domestic space that might well prove chilly; but a bloody snake crushed by a heavy stone doesn't typically sprawl on the tile floor of a Dutch interior, nor does the well-dressed mistress of such a household usually pose with one foot on a large globe, while directing her gaze toward a glass sphere suspended from the ceiling. Of all Vermeer's paintings, the *Allegory* is also the work that has proved least appealing to modern viewers. Though Philip Hale judged it "technically [. . .] among the most accomplished" of the artist's works, he thought "the mere fact that it was supposed to mean something [. . . had] paralysed Vermeer's energies." Among the picture's weak spots, Hale particularly singled out "the invention of the globe as a footstool"—"as puerile a thing as one has seen in art, though it should be noted at the same time that it is very well painted"—and the female figure, whose deficiencies were apparently still more total: "stupidly posed," with "a ridiculous expression," and "ill done into the bargain."[52] Lucas was less overtly critical, but he seems to have shared Hale's distaste for the painting—"it does not give me pleasure except in its tapestry curtain"—while speculating, as many later would do, that it was not Vermeer himself who had chosen the subject.[53] Indeed, the assumption that the *Allegory* must have been commissioned is now widely shared in the scholarly literature, with most attributing the request to a private Catholic patron rather than, as previously thought, a neighboring order of Jesuits.[54]

Resistance to Vermeer's "personification of Faith [. . . as] a fat, female figure with large feet and hands, and a head like an Easter egg" hardly died out with his first modern admirers, as the description just quoted from a 1967 catalogue by the Austrian-born art historian and publisher Ludwig Goldscheider may

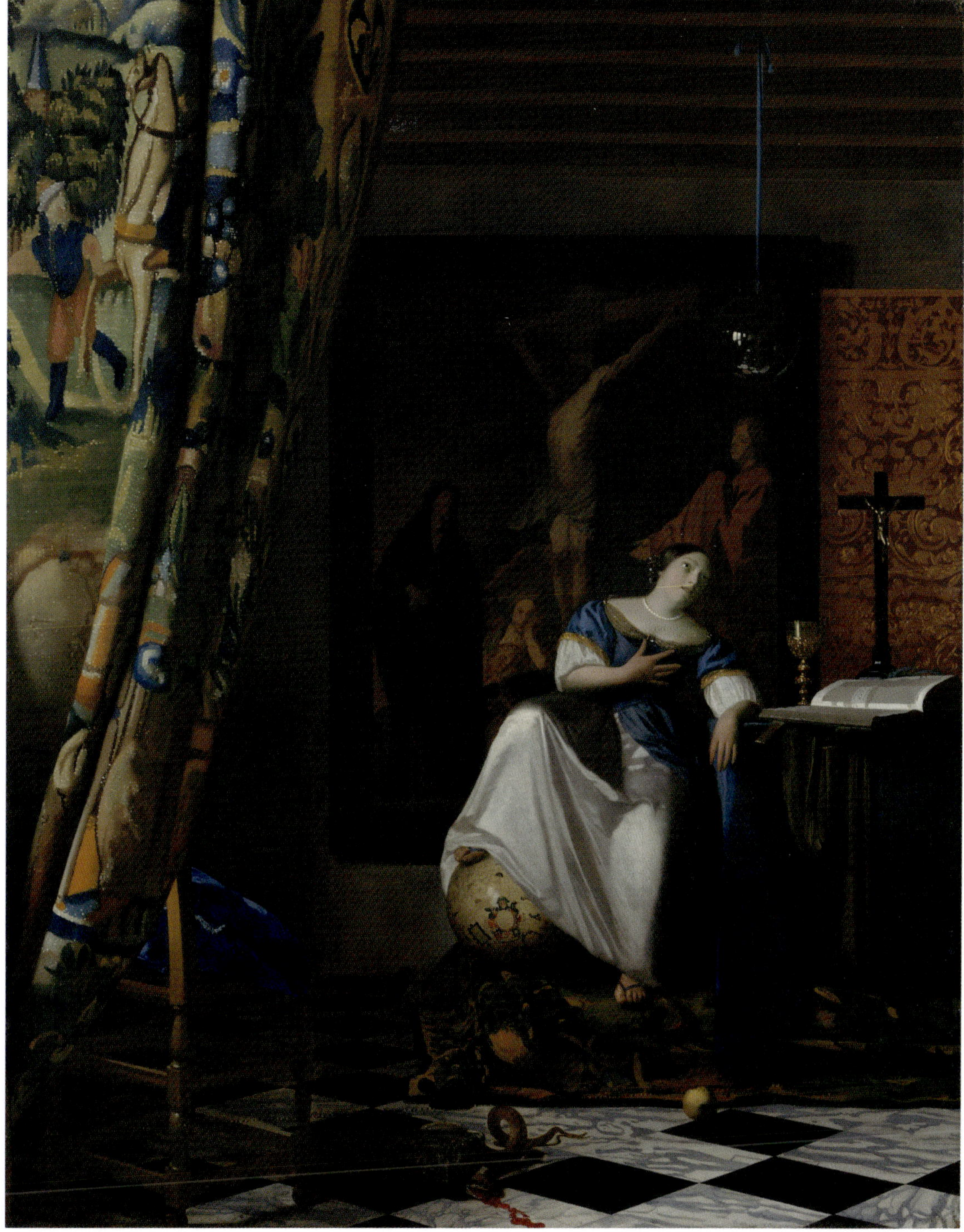

Fig. 3.12. Johannes Vermeer, *Allegory of the Catholic Faith* (ca. 1670–72). Oil on canvas. 114.3 × 88.9 cm. The Friedsam Collection. Bequest of Michael Friedsam, 1931. Metropolitan Museum of Art, New York

attest. (Goldscheider also characterized the woman's pose as "almost indecent.")[55] Writing in 1948 Ary Bob de Vries, the director of the Mauritshuis, had summarily dismissed the picture as a work of "circumstance," a command the artist had fulfilled "without love."[56] Some three decades later, the Dutch art historian Albert Blankert remarked the incongruity between the painting's symbolic program and its domestic setting, while likewise attributing "the peculiarities of the subject" to its having been "dictated by someone other than Vermeer himself."[57] For Arthur Wheelock, such explanations were finally beside the point: whatever the work's origins, he argued in 1981, the *Allegory* was a "silly and contrived" image that represented the one occasion on which the artist badly misjudged his own limits. Acknowledging that "it is [. . .] beautifully painted, with a fascinating iconography," Wheelock nonetheless baldly declared that "as a work of art it is a failure."[58]

Hale may have attributed the *Allegory*'s weaknesses to the fact that it was supposed "to mean something," but neither he nor Lucas, predictably, attempted to decode it.[59] Only a year after Hale wrote, however, a scholar had already provided the basis for interpreting the picture by tracing its symbolic program to instructions for representing faith—specifically the Catholic faith—in Ripa's *Iconologia*.[60] When De Jongh in turn expanded on that article in the 1970s, he was immediately concerned to explain aspects of the image that his predecessor had found puzzling, such as the substitution of the *Crucifixion* in the background for the *Sacrifice of Isaac* recommended by Ripa, or details that the earlier account had overlooked altogether, especially the glass sphere that hangs from the picture's ceiling and the pearl necklace that adorns its personification of Faith. The presence of the *Crucifixion* (by Jacob Jordaens) could easily be accounted for by the subsequent discovery that it had belonged to Vermeer himself and by the typological connection between the sacrifice it depicted and that originally prescribed by Ripa. The significance of the sphere proved more obscure, but De Jongh solved the problem to his satisfaction by locating a similar conjunction of cross and sphere in another emblem book and by tracing related allusions in the Jesuit literature, where it served as a figure for Heaven contemplated by the mind of Faith. De Jongh's chief aim, however, was not so much to provide a definitive account of the *Allegory* as to use the conundrum posed especially by the woman's pearls to explore a larger problem of iconographical interpretation, and the bulk of his article was devoted to a study of the multivalent significance of jewels in seventeenth-century culture, from emblems of faith and chastity to signs of vanity or worse.[61] To the degree that coming to terms with the *Allegory of the Catholic Faith* necessarily entails situating the painting in historical context like this, it is has clearly become a key document in the reevaluation of Vermeer's art that I have been calling counter-history.[62] But the very anomaly of the painting in the oeuvre as a whole has also meant that it has figured relatively little in the wider reception of his work. Though some recent scholars have sought not just to interpret the image

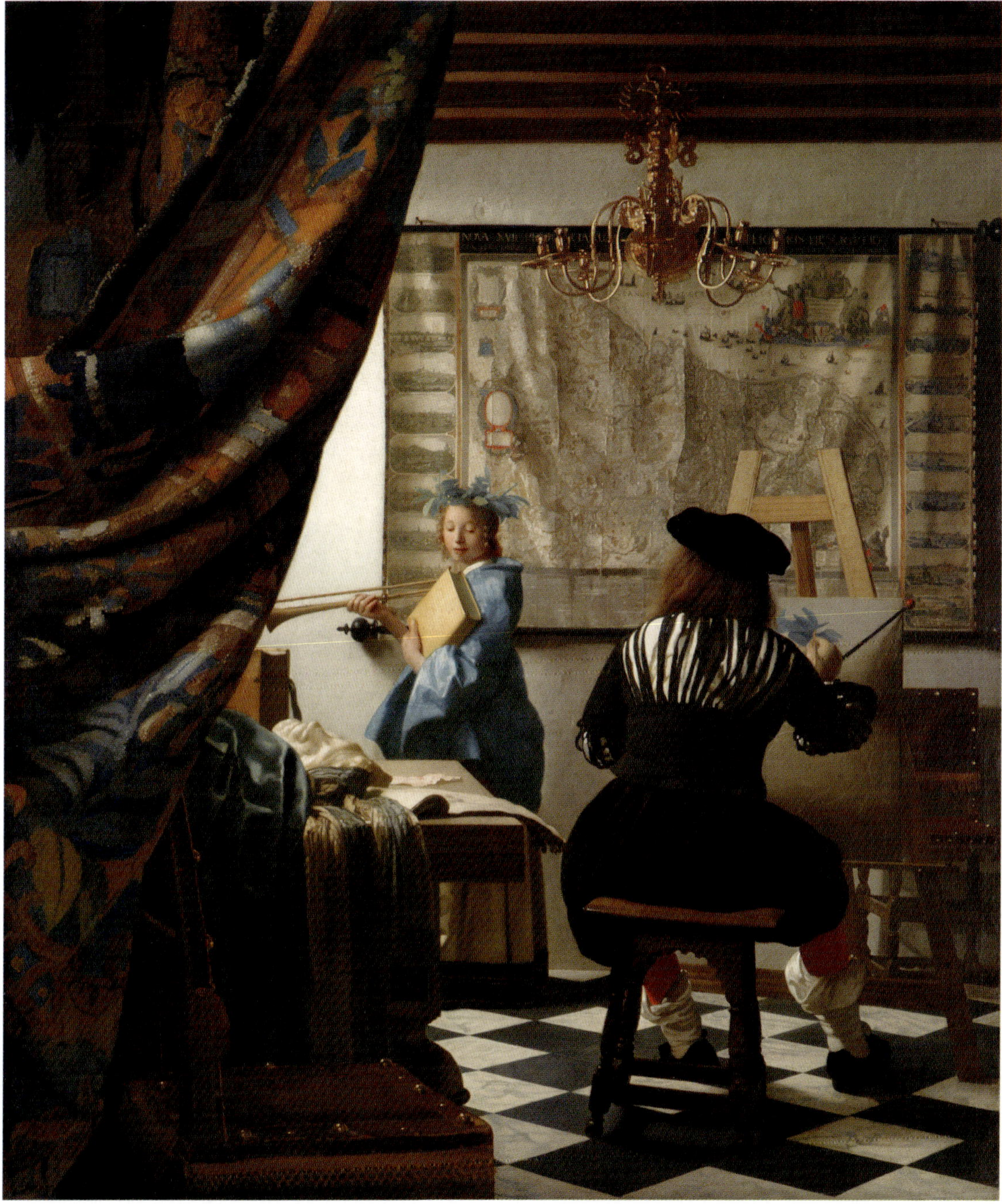

Fig. 3.13. Johannes Vermeer, *The Art of Painting* (ca. 1662–68). Oil on canvas. 120 × 100 cm. Kunsthistorisches Museum, Vienna. © KHM-Museumsverband

but to assimilate it to a more general reappraisal of Baroque art, the Vermeer who has continued to inspire other artists, writers, and filmmakers is not the man who painted the *Allegory of the Catholic Faith*.

The same is emphatically not true, however, of his only other surviving allegory: the work generally known as *The Art of Painting* (fig. 3.13).[63] Unusually for Vermeer, this is a title that has some claim to authority, since it was by the Dutch equivalent ("de Schilderconst") that his widow referred to the painting in a notarized document a few months after his death. Though the title clearly hints at the work's allegorical character, the document in question wasn't published until 1910;[64] and unlike the *Allegory of the Catholic Faith*, it wasn't always obvious to those who first rediscovered Vermeer that this, too, was a picture in need of decoding. Often called simply *The Painter's Studio*, it was sometimes approached as a kind of self-portrait, though one in which the artist had tantalizingly chosen to turn his back on us. (Thoré, who charmingly acknowledged the challenge this posed, nonetheless guessed that the figure was about thirty and that the painting should therefore be dated around 1665—exactly midway, as it happens, between the dates tentatively assigned to it by current scholarship.)[65] Even those who viewed it as a realistic image of a studio nonetheless recognized, however, that the artist it depicted was himself engaged in painting some kind of allegory. Thoré thought the young woman represented Fame, or perhaps Victory, while modern commentators usually associate her with Clio, the Muse of History, whose laurels, trumpet, and book can be traced, yet again, to Ripa's *Iconologia*. Though it was initially assumed that Vermeer was thus paying tribute to history painting's traditional place at the summit of the generic hierarchy, most recent scholars have concluded that the history in question is the future record of the painter's achievement rather than his subject matter: his own honor and fame, in other words—much as Thoré had first intuited.[66] Some scholars have also invoked the iconography of Pictura, whose traditional mask lies on the table to the left, in order to suggest that the young woman combines both figures, or even to contend, as Benjamin Binstock has done, that she represents Painting, pure and simple, and that this was what Vermeer's widow meant when she spoke of the artist as depicting "de Schilderconst."[67]

Most scholars would no longer agree with P.T.A. Swillens's claim that one reason the picture acquired a new title so quickly is that it fails as an allegory.[68] But general agreement as to the importance of decoding its allegorical intent clearly does not guarantee a consensus as to what exactly is being communicated, even among highly trained specialists. By comparison with the *Allegory of the Catholic Faith*, which relies on a widely recognized cluster of signs, *The Art of Painting* represents a scene whose details have proved far more ambiguous—both in the sense that they are susceptible to multiple interpretations and in the sense that it isn't always clear whether they signify at all. Is the painter's costume meant to appear anachronistic, for example, and if so, does it implicitly identify him with illustrious predecessors such as Rembrandt, or is the effect faintly mocking, as others have felt, especially when they focus their attention on those baggy stockings?[69] Or should the antiquated garb—if it *is* that—rather be understood as contributing to the deliberate unreality of the scene, together with the luxurious chandelier that implausibly hangs from the studio ceiling?[70] Does Vermeer wish us to see a version of himself in this image of the artist at work, or are we meant to distinguish between the creator of *The Art of Painting* and the artist within it, who begins, as many have noted, with the sort of preparatory drawing that his maker appears never to have employed for his own canvases?[71] And is that difference a sign of Vermeer's respect for artistic tradition, or further evidence of his gentle irony toward his painted avatar?

Related questions of historical meaning have also been raised about other components of the scene, notably the map on the wall, whose representation of a united Netherlands was likewise an anachronism at the time the work was painted. Does that fact signify, and if so, how? Answers have ranged from the argument that this, too, is a tribute to history painting, or that Vermeer was thus indulging a nostalgic vision of the nation's past, to the suggestion that the map serves rather to emphasize the artist's capacity to bring honor and fame to the homeland.[72] And then there are those who notice how a crease on its surface roughly corresponds to the division between the Protestant north and the Catholic south that was officially instituted in 1648, and wonder if this also should be read symbolically, or if it simply registers Vermeer's close observation of the original document: a map that—like others he painted—has been identified as one actually published in the seventeenth century.[73]

For Daniel Arasse, such interpretive enigmas point to a fundamental character of Vermeer's art, and one that helps to explain, if not to justify, his reception as a modern. Unlike the *Allegory of the Catholic Faith*, whose meaning is comparatively public, most of Vermeer's works, Arasse argues, are better understood as "private allegories," in which the artist primarily reflects on the art of painting itself.[74] From this perspective, the various attempts to "read" the map in *The Art of Painting* are finally beside the point: attempting to "force the meaning that Vermeer gave to its presence and that he deliberately left in a state of 'iconographic suspense,'" as Arasse puts it, they overlook its true significance as a form of visual knowledge closely allied with Vermeer's own. Arasse makes much of the fact that two words in the title of the map—"NOVA [. . .] DESCRIPTIO"—stand out as clearly legible, so that they function almost like a subtitle, the motto for what Arasse calls "a new conception of painting." At the same time, Arasse suggests, Vermeer is less interested in realistically reproducing the information the map conveys than in meticulously rendering the accidents of its surface. "And just as what is most precisely seen of the map is its folds and faults revealed by the low-angled light," he writes, "so in painting the knowledge of the object is bedazzled by the very light that allows it to be seen—as would be confirmed several years later by the dazzling map spread out on the table of *The Geographer*." In calling the geographer's map "perfectly visible, but irremediably unreadable," Arasse drives home the argument for a kind of visual knowledge very different from that usually associated with the practice of iconography.[75] (See fig. 1.10.)

Arasse, who subtitles his study of Vermeer *Faith in Painting*, finds evidence of that faith even in works that would appear to have other ends in mind.

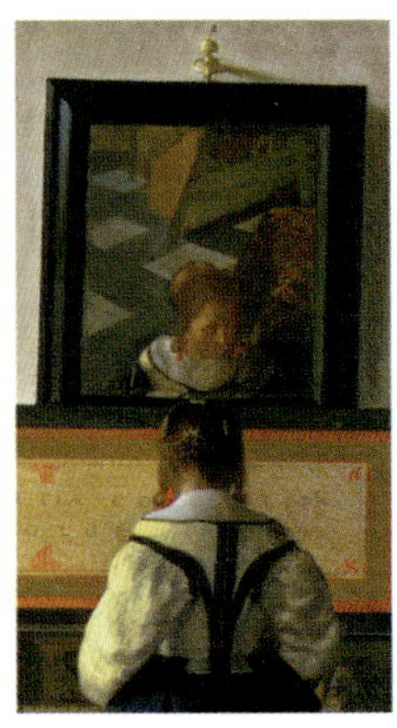

Fig. 3.14. Johannes Vermeer, *The Music Lesson* (detail)

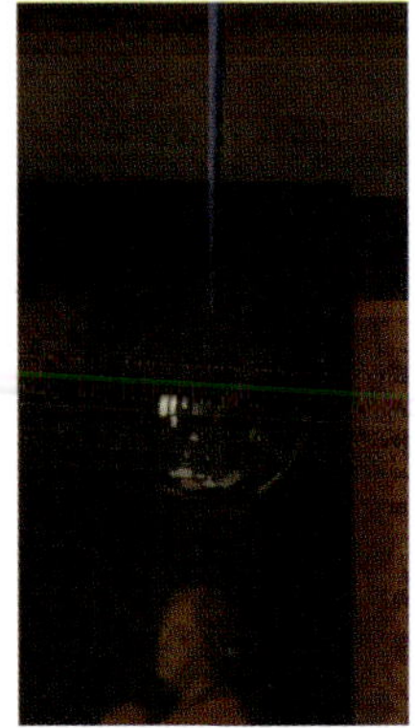

Fig. 3.15. Johannes Vermeer, *Allegory of the Catholic Faith* (detail)

Analyzing *The Music Lesson*, for instance, he argues that the painting comments on itself most significantly neither in the iconography of the *Roman Charity* that hangs on its wall nor in the uncharacteristic text on the virginal, but in the visual conundrum posed by the mirror (fig. 3.14). The only one among the five mirrors painted by Vermeer that actually reflects something, this, too, Arasse suggests, is a picture-within-the-picture, though one that communicates not by narrative allusion, but through the implications of its visual structure.[76] As many others have noted, the woman's face reflected on its surface seems to turn at an angle that doesn't quite accord with the position of her head as seen from the back: an anomaly that Vermeer appears intentionally to have retained when he decided to alter her original pose, and whose effect is to preserve a zone of intimacy for the couple that feels slightly out of reach for the viewer, such that one commentator speaks, for example, of the woman's gazing "secretly" at her companion.[77] Also at once nearby and unreachable, by Arasse's account, is the painter of the picture, who signals his presence with the dimly reflected crossbar and leg of his easel, while keeping his own form completely out of view. Characterizing him as "hidden in the canvas," Arasse suggests that Vermeer thereby sets up an unbridgeable gap between artist and viewer, even as he paradoxically invites us to a kind of intimacy with the making of the picture.[78] Like *The Art of Painting*, which is generally thought to follow a few years later, *The Music Lesson* becomes in this telling a private allegory of the painter's art.

In reflecting on itself by means of a painted reflection, moreover, *The Music Lesson* also anticipates yet another extension of that allegory into what otherwise passes for a very different kind of painting. Focusing his attention on the glass sphere that hangs from the ceiling in the *Allegory of the Catholic Faith*, Arasse argues that what is most salient about this object is how Vermeer altered a key feature of its Jesuit source, transforming the reflected cross depicted in the emblem book into luminous patches of paint that appear to register the light from a partly closed window that is not directly visible to the viewer (fig. 3.15). In doing so, Arasse suggests, Vermeer calls attention to how he has regulated the light in his studio to create the image before us—an image unusual in his work for the intensity of its chiaroscuro—even as he simultaneously chooses not to follow another pictorial convention available to him and incorporate a small image of his own person on the sphere's reflecting surface. Here too, in other words, Arasse sees Vermeer's glass as allegorizing an act of painting in which the painter himself disappears into his work.[79]

Arasse may be unusual among recent scholars in arguing so consistently for Vermeer as an allegorist, but he is far from alone in seeing the paintings as self-consciously commenting on their own medium. Vermeer's solitary women absorbed in their work especially have prompted such associations, as observers register how the artist simultaneously depicts and replicates their careful labor. So Edward Snow, for example, responds to the discovery that the scales of the *Woman Holding a Balance* hold nothing but "gleams of light"

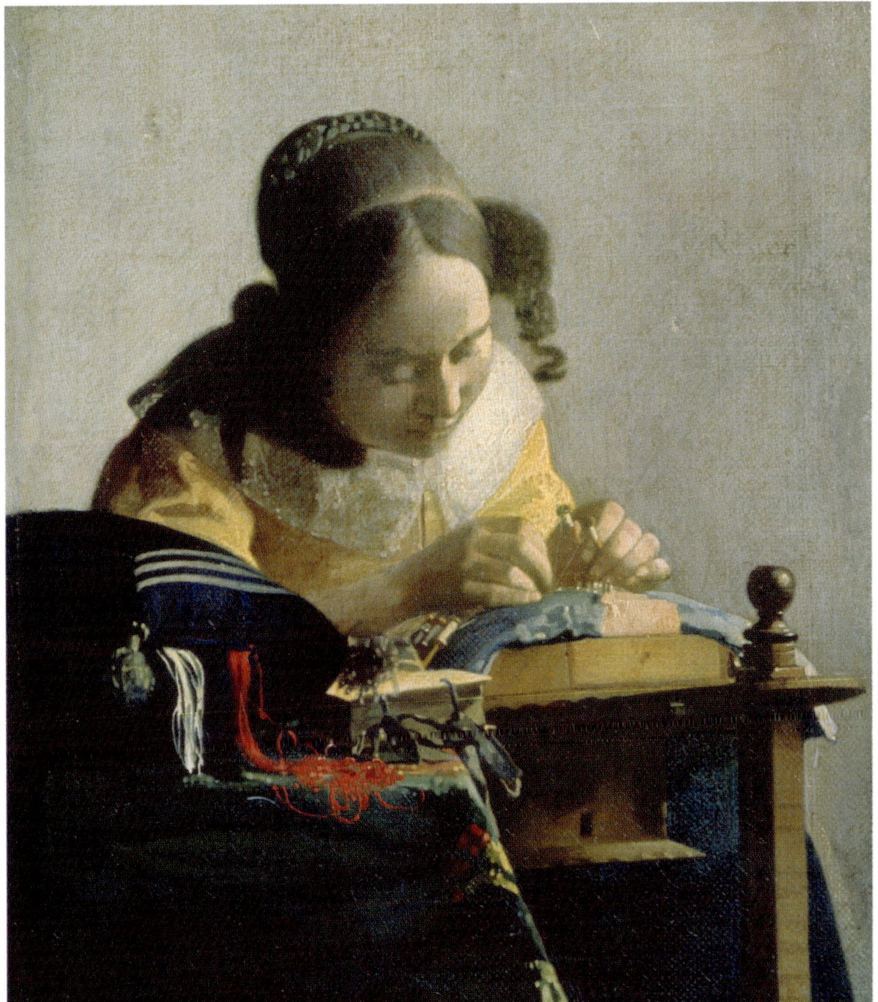

Fig. 3.16. Johannes Vermeer, *The Lacemaker* (ca. 1669–71). Oil on canvas (attached to panel). 24.5 × 21 cm. Musée du Louvre, Paris. Scala / Art Resource, NY

by drawing a direct connection between the woman in the picture and the man who painted her: "how entirely appropriate that a gesture so paradigmatic of Vermeer's art should appear to be concerned with the weighing and balancing of light itself."[80] (See fig. 3.9.) Extending Snow's observation to the artist's women more generally, Lisa Vergara notes how *The Milkmaid*'s "act of directing a stream of liquid straight downward brings to mind one of Vermeer's own most distinctive pictorial habits: the assured, mimetic application of paint [. . .] over carefully plotted straight lines."[81] (See fig. 3.7.) But perhaps the figure who has most inspired observers to associate her with Vermeer himself is *The Lacemaker* (fig. 3.16). As in the other cases, this sense of the painting's self-reflexiveness is partly generated by how it represents the subject's concentrated attention on the task before her. H. Perry Chapman, for instance, acknowledging that she is not the first to suggest that the picture "is as much about painting as it is about lace making," goes on to spell out the identical character of these artistic labors: "[the lacemaker's] integrity, the diligence with which she works, and the precision of her work, are [the painter's]."[82] But as in the other cases, too, the apparent self-reflexiveness of the image also arises from Vermeer's handling of his medium—especially, when it comes to *The Lacemaker*, the blurring of focus in the foreground of the picture, where the red threads "dissolve into light and paint," in the words of Harry Berger. Berger, who playfully offers to retitle the picture *Painter Against Lacemaker*, *The Conflict of Two Crafts*, or *The Stolen Thread*, sees in its composition and texture a potential conflict between Vermeer and his subject: is this finally about her work or his? Rather than directly answer that question, he offers an extended analysis of how the balance between them keeps subtly shifting, even as he concludes by once more identifying the painter with the painting: "At the center of the lacemaker's art, in the distanced dialogue of face with hands, is the mystery of Vermeer's."[83] Svetlana Alpers arrives at a similar conclusion more directly: "Seen at the close distance that the diminutive scale of this painting proposes for the eye, the red pigment is a deposit of *his* paint as much as it is a loop of *her* thread."[84]

Alertness to how Vermeer's art formally comments on its own procedures has not been confined to his pictures of women quietly absorbed in their tasks. In a book-length study of the *Young Woman Standing at a Virginal*, for instance, the art historian and curator Ivan Gaskell has focused especially on the blank card or tablet its Cupid holds aloft: a blank our eyes reach, as Gaskell notes, only after traversing both the plane of the painting itself and that of the picture-within-the-picture. (See fig. 3.3.) The result is what Gaskell terms "a *mise en abîme* of representation," a pictorial contrivance that invites us to witness "the infinite potential, as yet unmarked by realization, of art's power to represent in the hands of Love." Such a reading, of course, still treats the object in Cupid's hands as a kind of allegorical sign, though one that Gaskell explicitly distinguishes from the emblem-book version identified by De Jongh. (That Cupid, as we saw earlier, holds up a numbered card to illustrate the motto "a lover ought to love only one.") Gaskell's approach to the painting is as much formal as iconographical, however, and rather than communicate meaning through emblematic allusion, his Vermeer is more concerned to convey "the conditions under which such an allusion is created." Through a fine-grained analysis of the picture's spatial relations, Gaskell proposes that Vermeer deliberately unsettles the illusion of reality that other artists seek to establish, in order to call attention instead to the painting's status as a painting, even as he blurs features of the picture-within-the-picture and arranges the fall of light on its frame so as "to underline its objecthood at the expense of illusion within the pictorial world of the woman."[85]

Most recent writers who focus like this on the formal self-consciousness of Vermeer's art have hardly abandoned questions of iconography and historical context. But by arguing for a Vermeer who conveys "methodical thought in purely visual form"—the phrase is Gaskell's—rather than through the mediation of language, such accounts can seem to restore a balance that was sometimes lost in the initial reaction against the modernizers that I have been calling counter-histories.[86] Viewed from one perspective, after all, there doesn't appear to be all that much difference between the phrase of Gaskell's I have just quoted and the claim for Vermeer's "purely pictorial vision" that identified a scholar such as P.T.A. Swillens with the generation who first welcomed the artist as a contemporary.[87] Today's art historians may be keenly aware that Vermeer was a seventeenth-century painter, but his distinctiveness still resonates.

4

Camera Tracings

He'd be the ultimate cameraman, the ultimate top-notch cameraman.

WIM WENDERS ON VERMEER (1976)

Vermeer may have died a century and a half before the arrival of the first photograph, but he was reborn into the age of the camera. When Edmond de Goncourt described *The Little Street* as "a daguerreotype brought to life," he inaugurated a way of seeing—and of writing about—the artist that would become increasingly prevalent as cameras themselves increasingly shaped people's view of the world.[1] The journal entry in which Goncourt recorded these words is dated 1861, and though he did not say so explicitly, it seems clear in retrospect that he was thus testifying, yet again, to Vermeer's perceived modernity. The first photograph, generally credited to another Frenchman, Nicéphore Niépce, had only appeared in 1826—four years after Goncourt himself had first seen the light of day; Daguerre's own invention had followed thirteen years later. Yet while commentators have long associated the rise of photography with Vermeer's revival, sometimes even speculating that eyes accustomed to looking at photographs were a necessary condition of the period's receptivity to his work,[2] there's little direct evidence that many of Goncourt's contemporaries consciously made the connection. Though Thoré would report eagerly acquiring photographs of the Delft master's paintings, neither he nor his principal successor in France, Henry Havard, would characterize the work itself as camera-like. Nor, to the best of my knowledge, did the comparison surface in nineteenth-century Britain, apart from Joseph Pennell's brief remarks on the "photographic scale" of the *Officer and Laughing Girl* (see fig. 1.14) in a lecture of 1891 otherwise dedicated to the proposition that "photography is not a fine art, and never can be."[3] Only the frequent tributes to Vermeer's "mastery of the secrets of light"—this particular version comes from an 1885 article by the novelist Mary Augusta Ward—might be read as a tacit acknowledgment of the painter's kinship to the process Niépce had dubbed "heliography": literally, the drawing or writing of the sun.[4]

All that would change in the following century, if perhaps more slowly than one might have expected. For some who ventured it, the analogy seems to have remained purely figurative: a way of characterizing the look of Vermeer's painting by comparison with that of the far more ubiquitous medium. So in 1921 Jean-Louis Vaudoyer, for example, invoked the *View of Delft* by comparing its creator to the camera itself: "Out of doors, the painter has been as faithful as a camera [appareil photographique]. This fidelity is such that it must be said that a reproduction of this picture seems at first nothing other than a proof of a very good negative."[5] In a lecture delivered slightly over a decade later, the French poet and diplomat Paul Claudel similarly deployed the analogy for Vermeer's art as a whole:

> What fascinates me is this pure look, stripped, sterilized, rinsed of all matter, an innocence in a way mathematical or angelic, or let us say simply photographic—but what photography!—in which this painter, confined to the interior of his lens, captures the external world. One can only compare the result to the delicate marvels of the camera obscura and to the first apparitions on the daguerreotype plate of those figures drawn by a more reliable and sharper pencil than that of Holbein: I mean the ray of the sun.[6]

There's no reason to think that Claudel was trying to explain the genesis of Vermeer's art when he offered this comparison. But for most of the twentieth century and well into the twenty-first, accounts of the cameralike effects of the paintings have been difficult to separate from speculations about Vermeer's own use of such a device.

The device in question, the so-called camera obscura, is the predecessor of our modern instrument, and the arguments it has generated have a peculiar place in the story I have been telling. Like the painters and writers who first responded to Vermeer's revival at the turn of the century, many of those who invoke his use of such a camera are seeking to understand, at least in part, why his work particularly appeals to contemporary eyes: what "made him see as we see," to quote again from the 1908 monograph on the painter by the Belgian poet and art critic Gustave Vanzype.[7] But if this is another tale about how Vermeer became modern, it is not one that has been told by removing him from historical context. On the contrary: most of those who have directly engaged with the subject have been scholars who seek to demonstrate—or to question—whether circumstances at the time would have permitted Vermeer to make effective use of such an instrument, and to analyze the paintings themselves for clear evidence that he did so. Much of the discussion is inevitably quite technical—turning on such matters as the quality and focal capacity of seventeenth-century lenses, the extent of window glass in Vermeer's studio, and even the standard size of marble floor tiles in the period. There are exceptions to this rule, but these often come from people who proceed from the assumption that the advocates of the camera obscura have made their case, as when the experimental British film-maker Peter Greenaway repeatedly claims Vermeer as a precursor by invoking an observation he in turn attributes to Jean-Luc Godard: "Vermeer was the first cinematographer because he used the *camera obscura*."[8]

Though scholarly arguments about Vermeer and the camera obscura didn't really take off until the 1960s and 1970s, speculation about his possible use of such an instrument began, strictly speaking, in the late nineteenth century, when Joseph Pennell accompanied his brief remarks on the visual effect of the *Officer and Laughing Girl* with a hypothesis about its origins: "I think it extremely likely that Ver Meer used the camera lucida, if it was invented in his time, for it gives exactly the same photographic scale to objects."[9] No one seems to have followed up Pennell's suggestion, perhaps because it proved a red herring: as subsequent scholars have shown, the camera lucida, which consists of a four-sided prism that appears to superimpose the image of an object or scene on a flat surface for tracing, was virtually unknown until the nineteenth century.[10] As such scholars have also shown, however, knowledge of the camera obscura—or at least the principle behind it—can be traced back to Aristotle (and even earlier in China), and versions of the device in Vermeer's time can be readily documented.[11] Among the accounts most frequently cited in this connection is the eye-witness testimony of the Dutch statesman and polymath Constantijn Huygens, who acquired such a camera in 1622 and wrote ecstatically to his parents of the "admirable effects" it generated: "It is impossible to describe for you the beauty of it in words: all painting is dead in comparison."[12] More recently, Arthur Wheelock has traced a network of individuals in seventeenth-century Delft whose fascination with optics might have influenced Vermeer, while Gregor J. M. Weber, head of fine and decorative arts at the Rijksmuseum in Amsterdam, has uncovered tantalizing evidence that the artist could have learned of the camera obscura from the local Jesuits, whose identification of optical phenomena with the light of divinity may even have prompted them to acquire one for themselves.[13]

But what exactly is a camera obscura, and why should Vermeer's paintings have particularly prompted speculations about its use? In its simplest form, such a camera consists of a pinhole in the wall of a dark room—the literal meaning of "camera obscura"—through which the rays of the sun project images from outside on the opposite wall or other blank surface. To a person standing within the room, the laws of optics dictate that those images will appear upside-down and reversed, left-to-right; under ordinary conditions, of course, they will also be dim and hard to discern. The introduction of a glass lens into the aperture around the middle of the sixteenth century improved things considerably, both sharpening and brightening the projected image. Early experiments with the device had been primarily directed at astronomical phenomena, especially the solar eclipse, but it was around this time, too, that European writers began to remark the camera's potential application for artists. (Leonardo da Vinci seems to have already registered that potential in the late fifteenth century, but the notebook in which he recorded his observations was not published until 1797.)[14] In a manual on perspective published in 1568, for example, the Italian humanist Daniele Barbaro instructed his readers how the device might assist them with their work: "Seeing, therefore, on the paper the outline of things, you can draw with a pencil all the perspective and the shading and colouring, according to nature, holding the paper tightly till you have finished the drawing."[15] The camera in Barbaro's account still requires a dark room, but in the following century portable versions began to be available as well. Whether this is the kind Huygens described to his parents is unclear: an earlier letter in which he had announced his intention to bring one back from London has prompted some to assume that that his was a box-type instrument, but others have argued that the language of the letter in which he reports its marvelous effects indicates that the "carefully-sealed chamber" in question was a room in his house.[16]

Though Huygens himself suspected that at least one Dutch artist of his acquaintance had secretly employed the camera for his illusionistic still lifes, and Vermeer's contemporary Samuel van Hoogstraten (1627–1678) would later include the device in a major treatise on painting, no definitive evidence has emerged to confirm that painters at the time directly relied on it to map out their pictures.[17] In Vermeer's case, skeptics have also noted that no such equipment appears in the inventory of his possessions compiled after his death, though other artist's paraphernalia—easels and palettes, for instance—are duly noted.[18] But even those who doubt that Vermeer actually employed the camera obscura in any significant way acknowledge how his visual style appears to conjure with its effects.

Perhaps the most influential account of that style, Lawrence Gowing's 1952 book on the painter, appears to have set the agenda for much of the discussion that followed. Though Gowing himself largely sidestepped the sort of technical arguments that would occupy later writers, he repeatedly invoked the camera obscura both as a model for Vermeer's art and as a possible aid in composition. For Gowing, the central fact about Vermeer's style is that he registered what light made visible rather than what he knew about the forms he painted. In a frequently cited passage from the opening of the book, he laid out his case:

> Vermeer seems almost not to care, or not even to know, what it is that he is painting. What do men call this wedge of light? A nose? A finger? What do we know of its shape? To Vermeer none of this matters, the conceptual world of names and knowledge is forgotten, nothing concerns him but what is visible, the tone, the wedge of light.

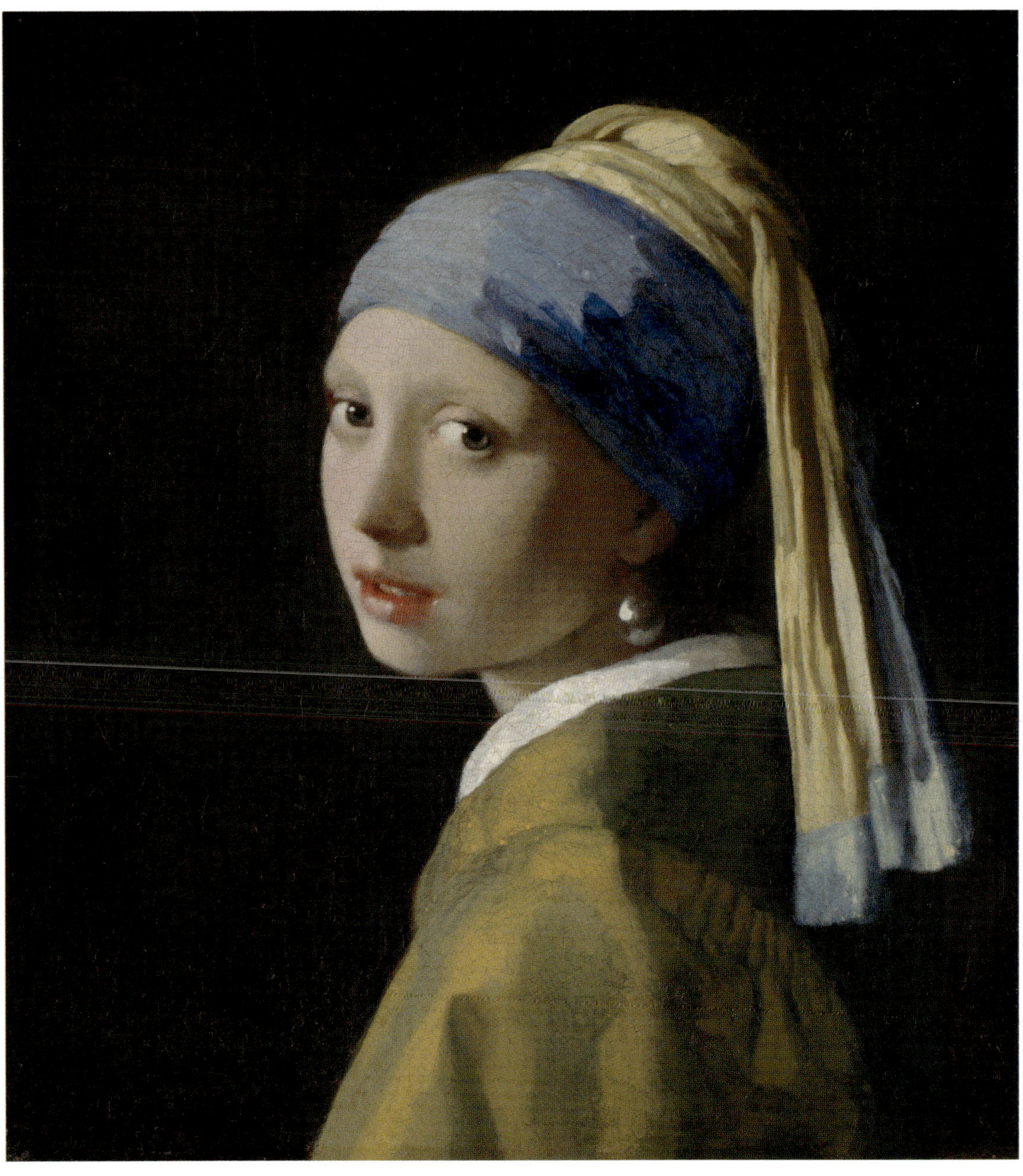

Fig. 4.1. Johannes Vermeer, *Girl with a Pearl Earring* (ca. 1665–67). 44.5 × 39 cm. Oil on canvas. Mauritshuis, The Hague

Such rhetoric may seem extravagant—few people, after all, have been unable to recognize the figures and objects Vermeer depicted—but Gowing's emphasis on the optical character of the painting has been widely accepted. Contending that Vermeer's art "abhors preconception and design and relies entirely on the retina as its guide," Gowing drove home the argument by remarking the absence of any visible drawing or outlines on the canvases—an absence that has only been confirmed, as he noted, by radiographic evidence. As he observed of the layers of paint revealed by a recent radiograph of the *Girl with a Pearl Earring* (figs. 4.1 and 4.2), "nothing is recorded but the oblique fall of light on particular forms." Here and elsewhere in his book, Gowing elaborated upon the observation both by extending the implied analogy to the work of a camera—"we are in the presence of the real world of light, recording, as it seems, its own objective print"—and by speculating that the painting may have originated in Vermeer's actual experiments with the instrument: "Very possibly this first stage in the painting of the *Girl* was a direct transcription of the incidence of light on the screen of the camera obscura."[19]

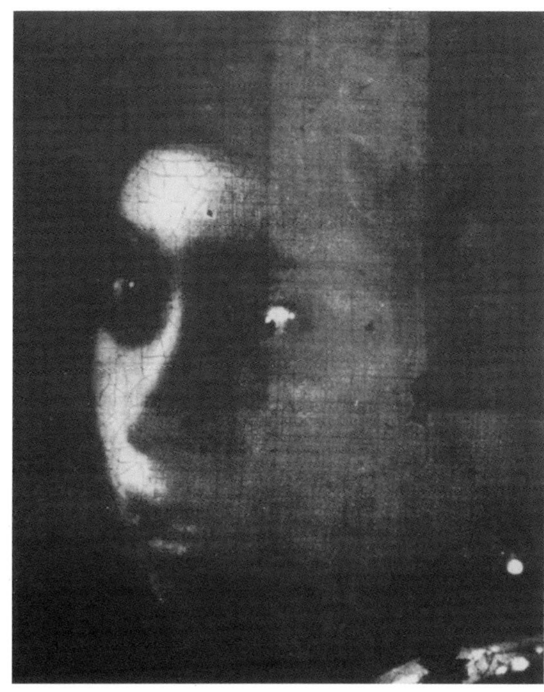

Fig. 4.2. Johannes Vermeer, *Girl with a Pearl Earring* (radiographic detail). Image provided by Dr. P. Cormans of the Central Laboratory of Belgian Museums and published in Lawrence Gowing's *Vermeer*, 3rd edn (University of California Press, 1997)

Unlike others who would develop this line of argument in the decades to come, Gowing didn't spell out all the ways in which Vermeer's effects could be seen to resemble those produced by the camera. Though he termed the *pointillé* highlights with which the artist frequently sprinkled his canvases "the most conspicuous features of his handling of paint," he never explicitly made the connection to the so-called "discs of confusion" that can appear on shiny, brightly lit surfaces when viewed through a camera obscura. Nor did he make much of the intensification of color that some have associated with its images, or the characteristic blurring of focus that results from its limited depth of field: both phenomena that subsequent advocates of Vermeer's camera would invoke in support of the theory. But Gowing found it "easy to think," as he put it, "that an optical projection was a forming influence on [the painter's] mature manner," and he didn't hesitate to spin out an imaginary scenario in which the device enabled Vermeer to fulfill his "deepest fantasy"—"the fantasy, as it seems, that visible things in their integrity were capable of coming together in the community of a perfect plane, [. . .] that on a flat surface the world in essence could become his":

> The germ of it was in him from the first, sought yet hidden, covered by its very contradiction, seeming if ever within the grasp of thought, as it might seem to us, to lead at best to artifice, to abstracted pattern. Yet this was the fantasy which was confirmed in truth, in science, and in the contrivance with which he was equipped, perhaps by a friendly scientist, bodied forth under his eyes: imagining the experience we know the rapture of the camera cabinet. Before him lay the whole depth of the world. There lay the forms of life, disposing themselves in their luminous essence upon the table of his camera, lying in their final amity flatly together, intact.[20]

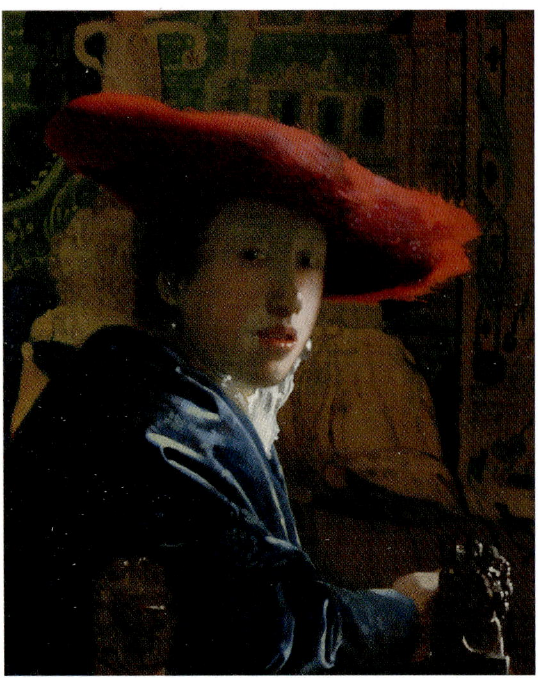

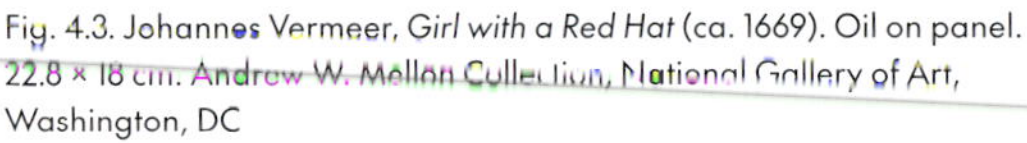

Fig. 4.3. Johannes Vermeer, *Girl with a Red Hat* (ca. 1669). Oil on panel. 22.8 × 18 cm. Andrew W. Mellon Collection, National Gallery of Art, Washington, DC

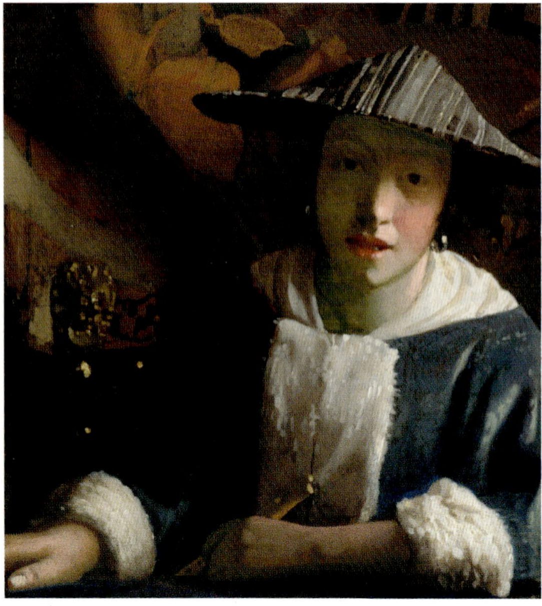

Fig. 4.4. Johannes Vermeer/Studio of Johannes Vermeer (?), *Girl with a Flute* (ca. 1669–75). Oil on panel. 20 × 17.8 cm. Widener Collection, National Gallery of Art, Washington, DC

Most believers in Vermeer's camera have operated in a less imaginative register. Rather than fantasize along with the artist, they have typically tried to demonstrate how he might have used the device, whether by taking photographs that in some way resemble his paintings or by actually attempting to trace the images the device projects. In 1964 the American art historian and curator Charles Seymour Jr. initiated this phase of the debate by performing an experiment in which he sought to replicate some of Vermeer's effects with a nineteenth-century camera obscura he had borrowed from the Smithsonian. Taking as his principal focus—or rather, lack of focus—the "discs of confusion" that appear on the lions-head finials of the chair in the *Girl with a Red Hat* (fig. 4.3), as well as its companion piece, the *Girl with a Flute* (fig. 4.4), Seymour arranged for a similar chair to be photographed both with his nineteenth-century instrument and with a modern camera, the lens of which had been adjusted accordingly. Juxtaposing the blurred photos that resulted with photographic details of their painted equivalents, Seymour suggested not only that the paintings had been produced by tracing mirrored reflections of the camera images, but that the process also explained the distinctive physical format of the two pictures: their unusually small scale, by this account, corresponded to the size of the apparatus's viewing rectangle, while the wooden panels made them easier for the artist to handle while comparing what he was painting with what he could see in his camera. As with many such arguments, one hypothesis generated another in its turn: though most scholars view these panels as late works, Seymour proposed that they represented an "experimental breakthrough" and thus should be dated earlier in Vermeer's career.[21] I have distinguished such accounts from Gowing's attempt to imagine what the painter was thinking, but they too, in other words, entail a form of storytelling.

By comparison with some of its successors, however, Seymour's revision of the standard narrative was relatively minimal. In an article of 1971 Daniel A. Fink followed up Seymour's account by postulating that more than two-thirds of Vermeer's corpus had been painted with the aid of a camera. He arrived at that number by first tabulating the "optical phenomena" visible in the paintings and then setting out to demonstrate that each corresponded to an effect associated with use of the instrument. It's a predictably wide-ranging list—among the phenomena Fink included, for example, are "use of curtains to darken viewing rooms and control subject illumination," as well as the size and shape of Vermeer's canvases[22]—and critics were quick to note that it failed to differentiate between the effects of the camera and the conventions of seventeenth-century Dutch painting more generally. They also called into question other assumptions governing Fink's argument, such as his apparent belief that Vermeer's interiors faithfully represented actual rooms in his house, despite the fact that marble floors such as those depicted in *The Music Lesson*, the *Lady Writing a Letter with Her Maid*, or the *Allegory of the Catholic Faith*, for instance, appear to have been extremely rare in seventeenth-century Delft.[23] (Note, too, the elaborate chandelier hanging above another such marble floor in *The Art of Painting* [see fig. 3.13]: an implausibly elegant set-up for a working studio.) Though circles of confusion figured prominently in Fink's account, his failure to register how often the painter sprinkles his diffused highlights on surfaces where they would not actually be seen with a camera obscura—the nonreflective crust of the bread in *The Milkmaid* (see fig. 3.7), for example, or the tablecloth of *The Lacemaker* (see fig. 3.16)—further weakened his argument in the eyes of the skeptics.[24] Commenting on the former painting, Gowing had explicitly recognized how Vermeer's practice of scattering "granules of light [. . .] irrespective of the textures on which they lie" would henceforth become a mark of artistic style rather than representational accuracy, but ardent proponents of the camera obscura tended to lose sight of that distinction.[25] According to an astronomer who entered the fray in 1998, they also overestimated the quality of the lenses to which Vermeer would have had access when they thought of him as tracing his interior scenes directly from images projected by a room-type camera.[26]

For most scholars of the artist, such reservations continued to predominate, and the debate appeared to have largely settled down before it flared up again in the new century, when two controversial books on the subject appeared almost simultaneously: Philip Steadman's *Vermeer's Camera* (2001) and David Hockney's *Secret Knowledge* (2001). Strictly speaking, Hockney's book had little to say about Vermeer: though it argued excitedly for Renaissance artists' use of optical aids as the key to a revolution in naturalism, the "secret knowledge" it claimed to reveal concerned mirrors and lenses, not the camera obscura, and the bulk of its examples came from the Southern tradition, especially the paintings of Caravaggio. But Hockney, who had been corresponding with Steadman, took Vermeer's use of the camera as a given and in two brief paragraphs on the artist turned that premise into "a starting-point" for the larger project.[27] Given Hockney's fame and the publicity surrounding his work, not to mention the beautiful production values of *Secret Knowledge* itself, the thesis he advanced inevitably helped fuel Steadman's cause: an alliance that was only confirmed when both men participated in a popular film, released in 2013, that further disseminated the argument for Vermeer's camerawork. I shall return to *Tim's Vermeer*, as the film was entitled, shortly, since it too has become part of the painter's afterlife.

Trained as an architect, Steadman built his case on the same assumption about Vermeer's rooms as had guided Fink before him and that both owed to the Dutch art historian P.T.A. Swillens, whose earlier study of the artist had argued strenuously—the emphasis is his—that "*everything he painted he saw immediately in front of him*."[28] Swillens thought Vermeer owed his mastery of perspective to traditional geometric methods rather than the camera obscura, but his belief that he could reason back from the design of Vermeer's painted interiors to the actual rooms on which they were based provided the template for Steadman's more elaborate version of the exercise. In Steadman's case, the point was not so much to demonstrate the consistency of the paintings with a hypothetical reality as to show how reconstructions of that reality, suitably photographed, corresponded to the paintings; and to that end, he concentrated on six canvases that he believed, from patterns of tiles, windows, and other details, all depicted the same room in Vermeer's house. While Swillens had simply drawn diagrams, Steadman also built a miniature model of the room in question, complete with furnishings—and for *The Music Lesson*, even costumed figures—that could then be photographed and compared with the painted originals. But what clinched the argument in his eyes was his calculation that a camera obscura placed at the geometrically established viewpoint for each picture would project a rectangle on the far wall whose size lined up almost exactly with that of the canvas itself. An earlier experiment along these lines had provided the centerpiece for a 1989 BBC documentary, in which costumed figures posed in a full-scale mock-up of *The Music Lesson*, while a camera obscura with a large aperture projected an image of the scene, also at the size of the actual painting, on the opposite wall. "Quite clear and detailed enough to trace," in Steadman's words—"indeed quite bright enough to film"—this *Music Lesson* had proved in more than one sense a piece of camerawork.[29]

Whether it also proved that Vermeer himself had done such tracing is another matter, however. Even Steadman acknowledged that the BBC lighting was "artificial and powerful," though he argued that the human eye would have been sensitive enough to work with a dimmer image.[30] Others have been far more skeptical, their doubts grounded both in the practicalities of the scenario and its governing premises. Questions have been raised not just about the actual illumination that Vermeer would have had available to him—with their side-by-side construction and small windows, seventeenth-century Dutch houses were comparatively dark[31]—but, more importantly, about how the conditions favorable to a camera obscura accorded with the act of reproducing what it projected. "No painter would ever sit with his palette full of bright colors in a dark room painting an upside-down image," Jørgen Wadum had dryly observed of earlier arguments for the device, and versions of that objection continued to bedevil this latest attempt to reconstruct Vermeer's camerawork.[32]

Both in the book and elsewhere, Steadman sought to answer his critics, sometimes by conceding their arguments and at other times by elaborating his theory. Acknowledging the difficulty of discriminating paint colors in a dark room, for instance, he mostly spoke of Vermeer as transcribing "areas of dark tone" or tracing "outlines" from the camera's projection. And while he briefly entertained the possibility that the image might have been reoriented with the help of mirrors, he recognized that this would pose its own problems for the argument: not only would the mirrored reflection have been dimmer than the original, but correcting for the camera's lateral reversals would have meant abandoning his account of how the projections on the back wall coincided with the dimensions of Vermeer's canvases. Steadman was arguably less forthcoming about the various adjustments his scenario required, as when he accounted for differences among the viewpoints of the six pictures by postulating that the artist was somehow able to move the lens of a room-type camera around; but skeptics were ready to add this problem to the list as well. Nor did he seriously question the assumption that guided the entire project: that Vermeer's ultimate aim had been to reproduce what he saw before him. The paintings may have slightly varied in textures and patterns, but Steadman insisted on their "truth to shape and outline": a truth he identified, of course, with reliance on the camera.[33]

That conviction was put to more practical test in the following decade, when two very different experimenters set out to replicate Vermeer's work for themselves. Tim Jenison is an American inventor, art enthusiast, and self-described "computer graphics guy," who attempted to recreate a meticulous version of *The Music Lesson* with the aid of a camera obscura; Jane Jelley is a British painter of still life and landscape who hoped to demonstrate, more modestly, how the artist might have managed to transfer his camera tracings to canvas.[34] Jenison's labors were duly recorded by another kind of camera—in the 2013 film *Tim's Vermeer*, produced and directed by a pair of magicians known as Penn and Teller—while Jelley reported on her own experience in a well-documented book, *Traces of Vermeer*, published four years later. Both were in part responding to Steadman, though Jenison also spoke excitedly of having been inspired by Hockney, but neither in fact followed *Vermeer's Camera* very closely. After building another full-scale model of *The Music Lesson* whose elaborate efforts at historical accuracy far surpassed what the BBC had attempted two decades earlier, Jenison soon abandoned his efforts to paint directly from a projected image and resorted to a rotating mirror that allowed for the continual matching of his colors against the original. (The mirror also served to compensate for the camera's reversals.) Jelley, for her part, worked not from a three-dimensional model, but from a projected image of a reproduction. While Jenison obsessively devoted four months to the painstaking task of replicating a single picture, Jelley was more concerned to show how the artist might have mapped out his tonal underpaintings on oiled paper before transferring them, rightly oriented, to canvas, and her closest attempt at reproducing a complete work was to apply some colors to a print of the *Girl with a Pearl Earring*.

Though both experiments successfully demonstrated how an artist might employ optical aids in the process of painting, neither, of course, proved that Vermeer himself had done so. Not only were both vulnerable to many of the same criticisms that had been leveled at more hypothetical accounts of the painter's camerawork, but each introduced new complications of its own, from Jenison's use of a mirror set-up for which there is no documentation in the seventeenth century to Jelley's working from a flat image rather than a two-dimensional scene. Nor did either really address the principal characteristics of Vermeer's paintings that had first prompted speculations about his use of the camera obscura, such as the areas of blurred focus and the recurrent circles of confusion.[35] While most reviewers of *Tim's Vermeer* found Jenison's obsession with his project endearing, the director's blithe observation at one point that "it doesn't matter who does the brushstrokes" was unlikely to have won over many lovers of painting, let alone any serious art historian. Jenison may have managed to produce what he elsewhere termed "a human-made photograph," but it wasn't hard to see, even on film, that the result fell far short of his claim to have "painted a Vermeer."[36]

Behind the debates about how, if at all, Vermeer might have employed a camera obscura clearly lie deeper feelings about the very nature of art, especially about the implications of the artist's reliance on a mechanical instrument for effects that might otherwise be attributed solely to an expert hand and eye. Those who argue that he literally traced what the camera projected must also cope with the implication that he was engaged in something closer to copying than invention—a charge that has long served to denigrate artists in the Western tradition and that was often leveled against the seventeenth-century Dutch in particular.[37] "Using Tim's device [. . .] isn't easy," Steadman says in the film, "but somehow [. . .] it does turn you into a machine"—a transformation he was willing to imagine Vermeer had contemplated too. ("Maybe Vermeer was strong-minded enough to think, 'I'll become a machine.'") Like others who have argued for painters' use of optical aids, Hockney included, the makers of the film nonetheless insisted that they weren't accusing the artist of "cheating." Hockney himself had begun *Secret Knowledge* by declaring firmly that "optics do not make marks, only the artist's hands can do that, and it requires great skill"—a refrain he would repeat several times in the course of the book.[38] Yet by simultaneously characterizing such aids as to the key to an artistic revolution and a carefully guarded secret, Hockney appeared not only to exaggerate their importance, but to rest his entire case on a conspiracy of silence. Arguments for Vermeer's camerawork have also tended to couch themselves as the revelation of a secret—Steadman's book, for example, is conspicuously subtitled *Uncovering the Truth Behind the Masterpieces*, while the filmmakers have compared their project to a detective story—and one reason the issue has become so fraught may well be how uncannily it appears to resonate with the aura of mystery that has long surrounded the Delft master, as if the discovery of a secret mechanism could finally dispel the obscurities that have otherwise accompanied his life and work. It's not for nothing that Steadman titles a key chapter of his book "The Riddle of the Sphinx of Delft," or that even the more cautious Jelley begins by conjuring with hidden things: "In the solitude of his studio, Vermeer kept his secrets safe, tight behind his door."[39]

At their most extreme, accounts of Vermeer's camerawork can indeed seem reductive, as when Jenison imagines the Delft master as a fellow "geek," or the Japanese biologist Shin-Ichi Fukuoka sums up the painter's achievement by contending, "All he was trying to do was to document [the world], exactly as it appeared to him." For Fukuoka, who says of *The Astronomer*, "It is as if he has pressed the shutter on a camera," Vermeer's modernity is a matter both of photographic appearances and of the artist himself as proto-scientist, one who not only painted two such figures in *The Astronomer* and *The Geographer* (see figs. 3.11 and 1.10), but who belonged to the same intellectual world as his Delft compatriot, the pioneering microscopist Antonie van Leeuwenhoek.[40] Nor is Fukuoka alone in constructing this version of Vermeer's afterlife: though his is an amateur's take on the artist, scholars have also speculated on the possible relations between Van Leeuwenhoek's experiments with the microscope and Vermeer's with the camera obscura, their speculations partly fueled by the knowledge that Van Leeuwenhoek served as the executor of the painter's estate.[41] Some have even gone further, and imagined that Van Leeuwenhoek himself served as the model for Vermeer's painted scientists, a speculation in which Fukuoka, not surprisingly, also indulges.[42] As so often in Vermeer's case, the factual basis for this narrative remains frustratingly thin: Van Leeuwenhoek's executorship appears to have been an official appointment rather than an act of friendship, and no other evidence of a connection between the two men has surfaced.[43]

But most scholars have not needed such evidence in order to conclude that Vermeer must have looked through a camera obscura, nor have they had to believe that he literally traced what it projected in order to observe what they believe to be its impact on his work. The authors of the 1995 Washington, DC, exhibition catalogue, for example, pointed to camera-like effects in a number of the paintings, from the highlights on the boat in the lower right of the *View of Delft* to the saturated colors of the *Girl with a Red Hat*, even as they noted how these often diverge from what the artist could actually have seen when looking at his subject through the instrument. Remarking how Vermeer conveys the impression of "flickering reflections" from the water onto the boat in the *View of Delft* by means of "diffused highlights" that resemble those produced in a camera obscura, for example, they also paused to note that the camera would only produce such highlights if the boat were in bright sunlight rather than shadow, as in the painting. (See fig. 1.1.) A subsequent entry on *The Lacemaker* similarly associated the "diffused, colored threads" that flow from the girl's cushion with the optical effects of a camera, while arguing that the composition as a whole ruled out the possibility that Vermeer painted it directly over an image projected onto the canvas.[44] (See fig. 3.16.)

In a provocative study of the camera's relation to seventeenth-century visual theory, Zirka Z. Filipczak has suggested that it also may help to explain why viewers find his paintings at once so absorbing and so elusive, as they respond to what it taught him about how visual focus and mental focus may diverge. Unlike other seventeenth-century painters, who "met the expectations of viewers as to which parts of a scene would have greatest legibility," Filipczak argues, Vermeer typically scrambles the signals: sharpening our view of a distant nail in *The Milkmaid* or a map on the wall in the *Officer and Laughing Girl*, for instance (see figs. 3.7 and 1.14), while engaging in the "oxymoronic" practice of painting "his iconographic focus as out of focus." The effect is especially pronounced in pictures that otherwise resemble small close-ups, but whose principal figures appear blurred, such as *The Lacemaker* or the *Girl with a Pearl Earring*, so that the center of the viewer's attention remains, paradoxically, "just out of visual reach" (see figs. 3.16 and 4.1). The result, Filipczak suggests, is to keep us subtly off balance—and to keep us looking, as we struggle to reconcile the paintings' conflicting signals.[45]

For all the heated debate the question has provoked, in other words, most scholars seem to agree that looking through the camera left its mark on Vermeer's style. At the same time, most have also insisted that the results were anything but mechanical. The idea that Vermeer "painted the way a camera sees," as the makers of *Tim's Vermeer* put it, is a partial truth at best, though our own familiarity with cameras continues to give it a long afterlife. As Ivan Gaskell has argued, the ubiquity of photographic reproduction has not only made paintings accessible to far more of us than previously, but has shifted the focus of our attention, so that we have learned to see precisely those aspects of a painting that are "compatible with photography as a medium." Gaskell explicitly calls attention to how it allows us to blow up small details, as he himself does in order to study the blank tablet held aloft by the painted Cupid in the *Young Woman Standing at a Virginal*.[46] But he might also have cited the uncanny convergence of brushstrokes with light rays in the radiograph of the *Girl with a Pearl Earring* that Gowing had used to confirm his account of Vermeer's "optical" art, or the way in which cinematic and digital reproductions of the paintings inevitably redouble an effect already documented by Thoré in 1866. As Thoré recounted the story, a naïve viewer had peered behind the *Officer and Laughing Girl* in order to locate the source of its "marvelous radiance." Even as he gently mocked the viewer's confusion, Thoré made clear that it was prompted by a genuine phenomenon: "The light seems to come from the painting itself."[47]

II

Painting Like Vermeer

5

Imitation and Assimilation

I still want to paint something like Vermeer.
—GERHARD RICHTER (2002)

What does it mean to "paint something like Vermeer," centuries after the original? When the German artist Gerhard Richter confessed this aspiration in an interview of 2002, he seems to have taken for granted that the "dream"—the word is his—was "unreachable." Painting like Vermeer meant above all creating pictures as wonderful as those of the old masters at a time and place that made such work no longer possible. "I can't paint as well as Vermeer," he had told the American art critic and curator Robert Storr a minute earlier. "[W]e have lost this beautiful culture, all the Utopias are shattered, everything goes down the drain, the wonderful time of painting is over." He may have been "old-fashioned enough or stupid enough to hang on," as he put it, "but it is the wrong time and I cannot do it."[1]

Whatever one thinks of the historical claim—or of Richter's characteristic modesty—the fact that Vermeer should stand for such an ideal is itself a sign of the exalted place he has come to occupy in the cultural imagination over the century and a half since Thoré first recovered him. In his notebook that same year, Richter referred simply to "Vermeer, the God of painting."[2] But the modern artist's desire to paint "something like" this ideal also has a more specific meaning—one most obviously realized by a well-known work of 1994, in which Richter turned a color photograph of his third wife, Sabine, into a luminous oil painting of a woman reader (fig. 5.1) that has reminded many observers of Vermeer's *Girl Reading a Letter at an Open Window* in particular (see figs. 1.11

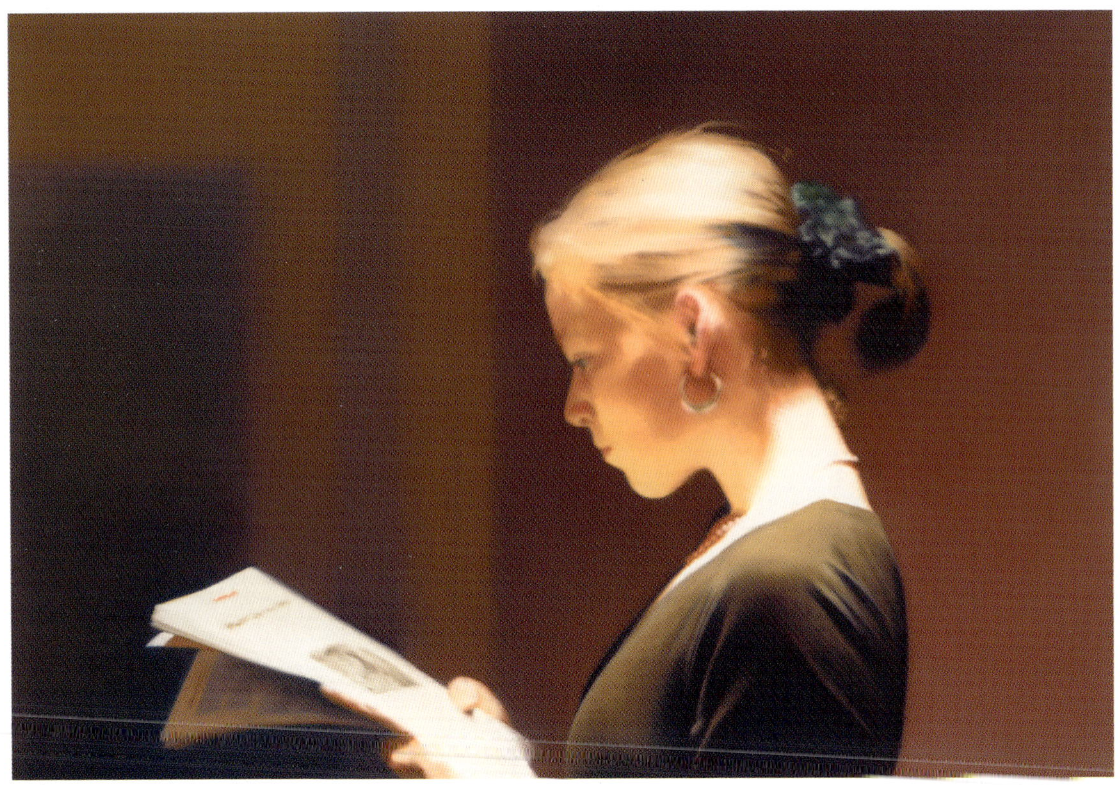

Fig. 5.1. Gerhard Richter, *Lesende* (*Reader*) (1994). Oil on linen. 73.4 × 101.9 cm. San Francisco Museum of Modern Art. Purchase through the gifts of Mimi and Peter Haas and Helen and Charles Schwab, and the Accessions Committee Fund: Barbara and Gerson Bakar, Collectors Forum, Evelyn D. Haas, Elaine McKeon, Byron R. Meyer, Modern Art Council, Christine and Michael Murray, Nancy and Steven Oliver, Leanne B. Roberts, Madeleine H. Russell, Danielle and Brooks Walker Jr., Phyllis C. Wattis, and Pat and Bill Wilson. © Gerhard Richter 2025 (0028). Photograph: Ben Blackwell

and 3.1).[3] Even had Richter himself not joined the chorus—his painting, he told another interviewer, "reminds me of Vermeer"[4]—its kinship with the Dresden picture would have been hard to ignore, especially since Vermeer's canvas, which had been confiscated by the Soviet Union at the end of the Second World War, returned to the city of Richter's birth in 1955, just as the latter was completing his studies at the Dresden Academy of Fine Arts.[5]

I shall come back to Richter's *Reader* and its affinities with Vermeer at the close of this chapter. But before turning to other artists' responses to the Delft master, I should like to pause over the way in which Richter formulates his own understanding of his relation to his admired predecessor. While his claim that the *Reader* "reminds" him of Vermeer might strike some observers as disingenuous, I propose that we take Richter seriously when he denies that he was consciously thinking of the seventeenth-century artist as he set out to paint his picture. "No, never," he replied, when asked by an interviewer whether he had recalled the Vermeer painting at the time. "But, of course, Vermeer's *Girl Reading a Letter* is in my mind or, rather, in my gut," he immediately added, "and that influences the way I perceive things." In response to the same interviewer's previous comparison of *Reader* and his 1988 portrait of his daughter Betty to "great masterpieces, like those of Vermeer," Richter had offered a more general formulation of the same principle: "My relation to such works of art (for instance to the paintings of Vermeer), this love, is natural and part of my flesh and my blood—it's beyond the conscious and the unconscious. It's simply a part of me, and that's why everyone makes references to such paintings."[6] Though one might quibble that no cultural artifact, however familiar, can really be classified as "natural," Richter's understanding of how artworks come to resemble their predecessors will be central to the discussion that follows, even as it inevitably troubles the distinction between what their creators consciously intend us to see and what we end by perceiving.

Most of the images in this chapter were produced by artists who openly acknowledged Vermeer's influence, and all have looked to others as if they in some way belonged to his lineage. But just where the deliberate imitation of Vermeer leaves off and his unconscious assimilation begins is not always easy to determine. In the essay from which I adopt the title of this chapter, the art historian and theorist E. H. Gombrich suggested that family likeness may be a more fruitful way of approaching the problem of imitation than ideas of copying—a metaphor that resonates suggestively with Richter's talk of earlier artworks as part of his "flesh and [. . .] blood."[7] Yet by observing that "everyone makes references to such paintings," Richter also underscored how we perceive a family likeness between images even when no direct line of artistic descent can be traced.[8] The problem is especially acute for work produced in the half century or so after Thoré first restored Vermeer to collective attention, when a sensitivity to the effects of light, on the one hand, and the custom of depicting solitary women in domestic interiors, on the other, were widespread among painters both in Europe and America. If such artistic practices help to account for why Vermeer was so eagerly welcomed as a modern, they also make it particularly difficult to distinguish artists who set out to model their work on his from those who decided, after the fact, to adopt him as their precursor—or simply to see him as the precursor of others. Unlike forgeries or pastiches, each of which will form the subject of a subsequent chapter, the works examined here neither aim to pass themselves off as Vermeer's own nor openly invite the viewer to recognize their transformation of his originals, though all participate, in one way or another, in his afterlife. And so, potentially, do works not included here, but which may also belong to branches of the same extended family. The case studies throughout this book are representative only, and what they represent can sometimes hover ambiguously between one person's deliberate evocation of Vermeer and another's later perception of artistic kinship.

Consider, for instance, the terms in which Mary Cassatt, writing in 1915, urged her wealthy friend Louisine Havemeyer to purchase an unfinished portrait by Edgar Degas (fig. 5.2). "It is much in the style of a Vermeer," she wrote, "and quite as interesting, very quiet and reposeful. It is a beautiful picture."[9] Her judgment was evidently persuasive, and the painting, which depicts Berthe Morisot's elder sister Yves as a married woman, now constitutes part of Havemeyer's bequest to the Metropolitan Museum of Art in New York. Cassatt is not the only one to have sensed an affinity between the two artists: a few years

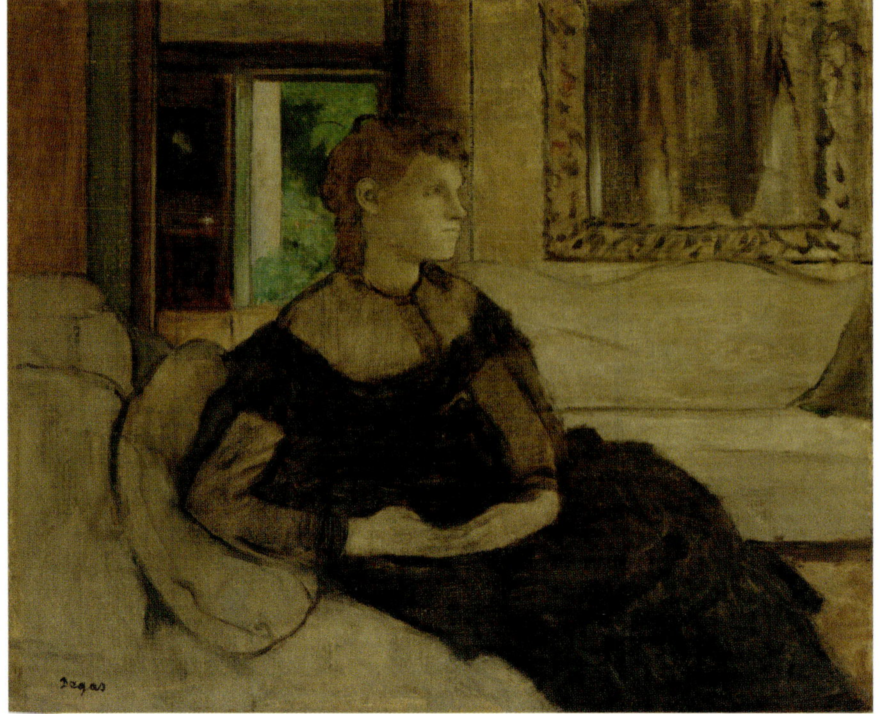

Fig. 5.2. Edgar Degas, *Madame Théodore Gobillard* (1869). Oil on canvas. 55.2 × 65.1 cm. H. O. Havemeyer Collection. Bequest Mrs. H. O. Havemeyer, 1929. Metropolitan Museum of Art, New York

earlier Philip Hale had also invoked Degas's name in connection with Vermeer, and related comparisons would continue to surface from time to time over the century that followed.[10] To the best of my knowledge, however, there is no evidence that Degas was thinking of the Delft master when he undertook the portrait in 1869, nor when he painted any of the other works that have sometimes prompted commentators to reach for the analogy. Apart from the reference to quiet and repose, it's far from obvious, in fact, which features of the portrait Cassatt associated with the style of Vermeer. Presumably she had in mind not only the motif of a solitary woman in a domestic interior, but the juxtaposition of her three-quarter figure against the rectangular geometry of horizontals and verticals that divide up the comparative blankness of the rear wall and doorway. Perhaps Madame Gobillard's apparent absorption also prompted Cassatt to think of the Delft master, though a resistant observer might well remark the absence of any activity to account for that absorption—a difference in turn related to that between the elegant leisure of this portrait and the genre painting in which so many of Vermeer's images originate. Such an observer might also note that neither Degas's palette nor the dark brushstrokes with which he rapidly outlines his principal forms are particularly Vermeer-like. But family resemblance is not identity, and Cassatt evidently felt that the picture looked enough like a Vermeer to be identified as part of his extended lineage.

As we have seen, Hale also argued for a likeness between Vermeer and Whistler, even as he was compelled to acknowledge that influence in this case was

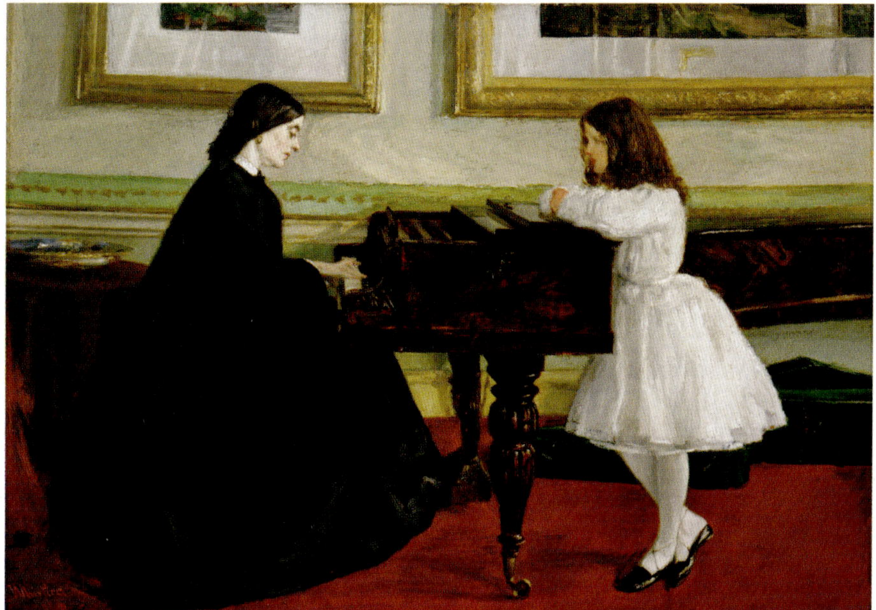

Fig. 5.3. James Abbott McNeill Whistler, *At the Piano* (1858–59). Oil on canvas. 67 × 90.5 cm. Taft Museum, Cincinnati. Erich Lessing / Art Resource, NY

virtually out of the question. (Indeed, it was doubtful, he admitted, "if Whistler was ever very much interested in the Dutchman's work.") The grounds on which Hale offered the comparison were primarily those of pattern and arrangement, such as the practice "of helping out the composition by pictures skillfully placed on the wall," or their shared love for "long simple lines, and large undisturbed surfaces"—similarities that Cassatt might have adduced in support of her case for Degas as well. Whistler's obvious debt to Japanese prints prompted Hale to speculate that Vermeer, too, might have learned from their example; and this is also, of course, an argument that Cassatt could have extended to Degas, whom Hale, not coincidentally, likewise compared to Vermeer.[11] If there was no evidence that Whistler had directly modeled himself on the Delft master, Hale could nonetheless allow himself to wonder whether both could at least be traced to a common ancestor.

Though Hale could not have known it, the affinities he sensed between Vermeer and Whistler had also struck Thoré, who had seen the latter's *At the Piano* (fig. 5.3) at the Paris Salon in 1867 and contacted Édouard Manet in the hope of acquiring it for his collection. Manet was to ask Whistler whether the work was still for sale, and "if the price isn't too shocking," Thoré wrote excitedly, "I will try to give myself this painting which would settle in very well with my Van der Meers of Delft."[12]

As things turned out, the work was no longer available, so Thoré was never able to demonstrate how well it would "settle in" with his collection. But both his admiration for Whistler's work and his impulse to combine it with that of his beloved Vermeer would be shared by a number of painters—especially in North America, but in Europe as well—who would flourish at the turn of the following century.[13] By the time that Hale published his book on the Delft master in 1913, their indebtedness to Vermeer's art had been widely recognized by their contemporaries, for whom the hitherto obscure artist seems to have already become a touchstone of the collective imagination. It is to these painters, several of them clustered around Hale himself, that I now turn.

"Go and have a look at Van der Meer of Delft and give him my love," the Boston-based painter Edmund C. Tarbell wrote to Hale on the latter's journey to France in 1904.[14] This pair of Vermeer enthusiasts had known each other ever since Hale had studied with Tarbell at the school connected to the city's Museum of Fine Arts, and Tarbell surely knew that he was writing at the very time when Hale had first begun to publish on their beloved artist, since it was in 1904 that an anonymous entry on "Vermeer of Delft," later identified as Hale's, appeared in an illustrated series called *Masters in Art* that also originated in Boston. (Each entry combined a selection of reproductions and a description of the plates with a brief account of the artist in question, extracts from previously published commentary on his work, and a bibliography.)[15] More immediately to the point, 1904 was also the year in which Tarbell completed a painting that would effectively inaugurate a new phase in his style and prompt a critic to proclaim him—or at least the canvas—a "modern Ver Meer."[16] Entitled *A Girl Crocheting*, Tarbell's painting depicts a seated young woman absorbed in domestic activity, her figure partly illuminated by light from a window that also partly suffuses a bare expanse of wall behind her (fig. 5.4). And so too, interestingly enough, does another picture painted in London that same year: Laura Alma-Tadema's *Sweet Industry* (fig. 5.5). Though there is no evidence that the two artists were aware of one another's work, there is every reason to believe that they had the same predecessor in mind when they set out to paint their versions of his most characteristic subject.

Nor were these the only artists to produce a Vermeer-like picture that year. The Danish painter Vilhelm Hammershøi was even further removed from Hale and his circle than Alma-Tadema, but his *Interior with Young Woman Seen from Behind* (fig. 5.6) also recalls the art of the Delft master, even as it significantly alters the emotional register of the original. Unlike Tarbell, Hammershøi left no written evidence of his love for his predecessor, though we know that he encountered Vermeer's work in Berlin and the Netherlands, and that contemporaries were quick to remark the two painters' affinity.[17] The catalogue for a 1907 exhibition of Danish art in London specifically singled out another picture of a woman seen from behind for the comparison, declaring *Resting* (fig. 5.7) "a very near approach indeed to Vermeer of Delft"—a judgment echoed by the English critic Arthur Clutton-Brock, who likened its combination of seeming naturalness and "beautiful style" to "Vermeer's finest works," while pointedly

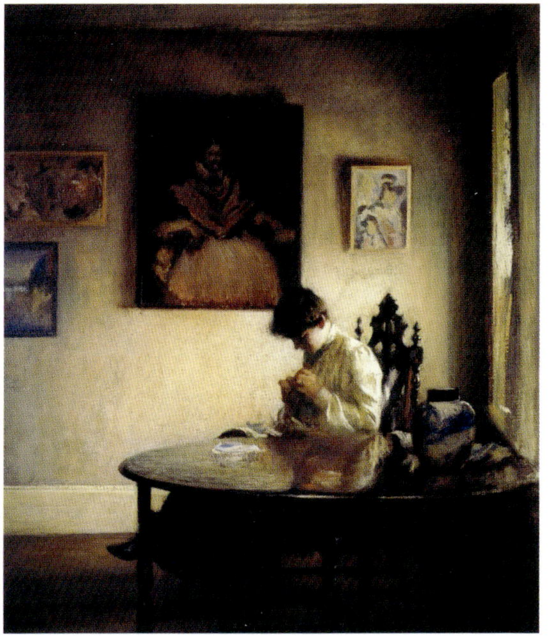

Fig. 5.4. Edmund C. Tarbell, *A Girl Crocheting* (1904). Oil on canvas. 76.2 × 66 cm. The Arkell Museum at Canajoharie, Canajoharie, New York

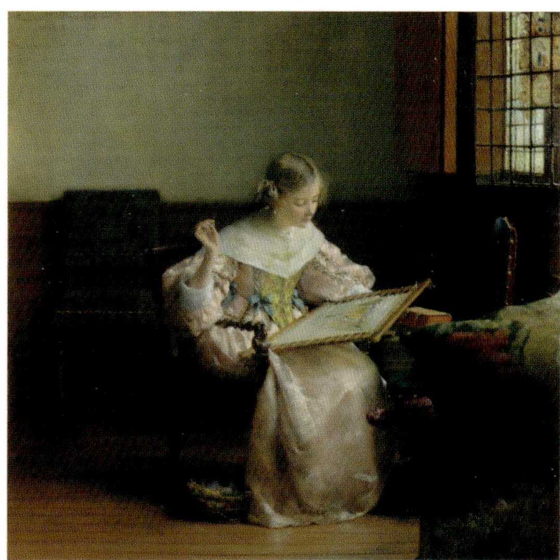

Fig. 5.5. Laura Alma-Tadema, *Sweet Industry* (1904). Oil on canvas. 36 × 35.6 cm. Manchester Art Gallery / Bridgeman Images

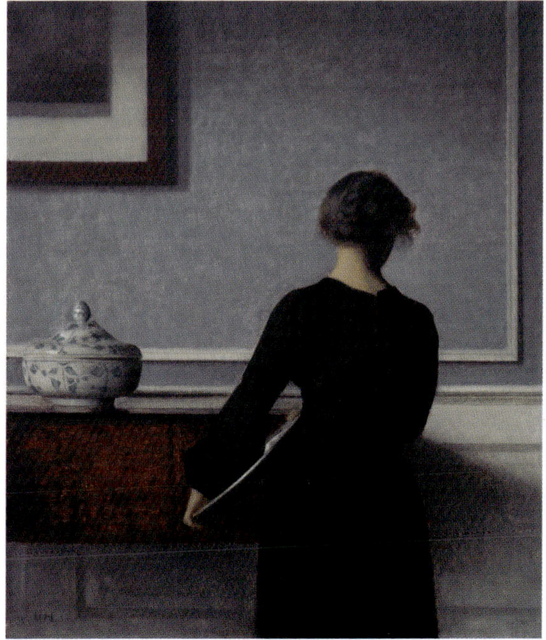

Fig. 5.6. Vilhelm Hammershøi, *Interior with Young Woman Seen from Behind* (ca. 1904). Oil on canvas. 61 × 50.5 cm. Randers Kunstmuseum, Randers, Denmark. Image courtesy of the Art Renewal Center® www.artrenewal.org

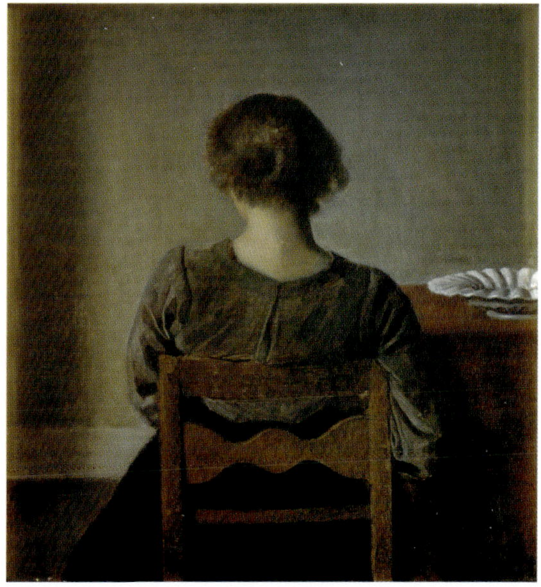

Fig. 5.7. Vilhelm Hammershøi, *Resting* (1905). Oil on canvas. 49.5 × 49.5 cm. Musée d'Orsay, Paris. Erich Lessing / Art Resource, NY

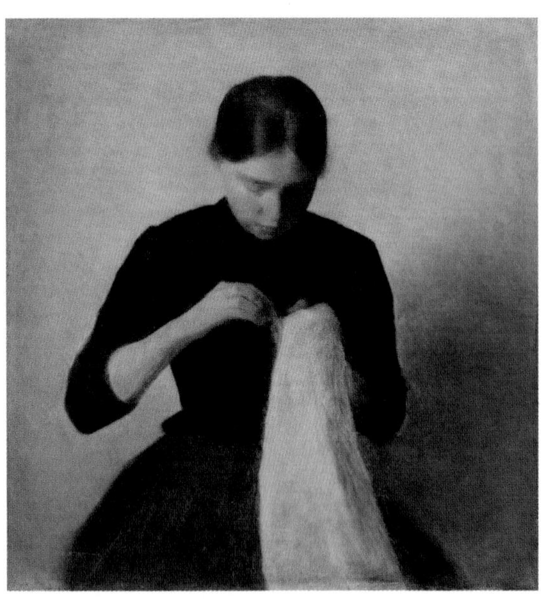

Fig. 5.8. Vilhelm Hammershøi, *Young Girl Sewing* (1887). Oil on canvas. 37 × 35 cm. Ordrupgaard, Copenhagen

seizing the occasion to proclaim the hitherto unknown Hammershøi "a new master."[18]

The near-simultaneity of these paintings—*Resting* dates from 1905—is only in part a coincidence. Their creators' collective response to Vermeer was a generational phenomenon, the product of men and women born within a decade of his recovery, who came of age in the very years when knowledge of his work had begun to take hold among sophisticated members of the art world. John Singer Sargent may not have been a direct imitator of Vermeer himself, but in declaring that "the only *painters* were Velasquez, Frans Hals, Rembrandt, and Van der Meer of Delft, a tremendous man," he clearly spoke for many in his cohort.[19] (Sargent was born in 1856; the dates for Tarbell, Alma-Tadema, and Hammershøi are 1862, 1852, and 1864, respectively.) It was also with the help of Sargent that another Bostonian, Isabella Stewart Gardner, would acquire Vermeer's *The Concert* in 1892—five years before it would first be publicly exhibited, but not nearly so long, in all likelihood, before it could be seen by Tarbell and his colleagues.[20] Indeed, while most of the paintings at which we are about to look come from the first decades of the twentieth century, Hammershøi's engagement with Vermeer's art may have been underway even earlier, when he first traveled to the Netherlands in 1887 and painted the small picture of his sister Anna known as *Young Girl Sewing* (fig. 5.8).[21] Between the motif itself, the expanse of bare wall, and the partial illumination of the whole—not to mention the scale of the nearly square canvas—the picture this one most closely resembles is *The Lacemaker*, though the fact that the latter hung in Paris at the time, where Hammershøi would not travel until 1889, suggests that he'd seen it, if at all, in reproduction. (We know that he eventually collected photographs of paintings that interested him, Vermeer's among them.)[22] But whether or not he was thinking of any work in particular, the quiet absorption of his young woman in domestic activity makes for one of Hammershøi's most straightforwardly Vermeer-like pictures, without the eerie silence conveyed by the motionless figures who occupy—or rather, fail to be occupied in—so many of his other interiors.[23]

Every painter who responded to Vermeer at the turn of the century did so, of course, in their own way, and what each chose to adopt from the earlier artist varied from canvas to canvas.[24] Some generalizations, however, can still be ventured. Virtually all the works in question depict the female figure in a domestic setting, and virtually all exploit the arrangement in order to study the effects of daylight as it is filtered through a window or windows. Many follow

Vermeer, too, in their use of picture frames or other rectangular shapes like doors and paneling, as well as mirrors, to create a geometrically harmonious composition. As my examples have already begun to suggest, painters in this vein typically show the subject engaged in a quiet activity such as sewing or reading; and most downplay, if they do not suppress altogether, the anecdotal implications of the scene, preferring to emphasize its aesthetic rather than its narrative possibilities. With the exception of Alma-Tadema, who betrays a Victorian penchant for moralizing or storytelling when she titles her pictures—in addition to *Sweet Industry*, there is another work of 1904 partly indebted to Vermeer called *Love's Beginning*[25]—most implicitly confirm this emphasis by identifying their works simply by the motifs they depict.[26]

Here are some characteristic titles, their very repetitiveness testifying to the family likeness of the images they designate: *Young Girl Sewing* (1887); *A Young Girl Preparing Chanterelles* (1892); *Interior with a Woman Reading* (1900); *Interior* (1901); *Interior with Woman at Piano* (1901); *The Spinet* (ca. 1901–2); *A Girl Crocheting* (1904); *Interior: Young Woman Seen from Behind* (ca. 1904); *Resting* (1905); *New England Interior* (1906); *The Kitchen Maid* (1907); *The Yellow Jacket* (1907); *The Necklace* (1907); *The Letter* (1908); *Woman Reading* (1908); *The String of Pearls* (1908); *The Guitar Player* (1908); *Girl Reading* (1909); *Girl Combing Her Hair* (1909); *Tea Leaves* (1909); *Girl Mending* (1910); *Woman with a Book* (ca. 1910); *Girl Sweeping* (1912); *Figure in a Room* (1912); *The Seamstress* (1913); *An Interior* (1915); *The Open Window* (1917); *Girl Knitting* (1918); *Woman Sewing* (1919); *Waiting by the Window* (n.d.). I have deliberately given these by date rather than by artist, but the list represents works by eight different painters, including one group mostly clustered around Tarbell in Boston—his fellow-instructors at the Museum School, William McGregor Paxton and Frank W. Benson, as well as two men who also had ties to the city, Joseph DeCamp and Thomas Dewing—and a smaller circle associated with Hammershøi in Copenhagen, consisting of his brother-in-law Peter Ilsted and his friend Carl Holsøe. Ten of the pictures named above are Paxton's, seven Hammershøi's, and four Tarbell's. Benson and Dewing each account for three, while DeCamp, Ilsted, and Holsøe collectively add three more to the total.

From one perspective, the resemblances among these titles are hardly surprising. Close-knit artistic circles have traded motifs back and forth at least since the Dutch genre painters from whom Vermeer himself borrowed liberally; and there had been similar cross-fertilizations among other nineteenth-century painters, from those of the so-called Danish Golden Age, to whom Hammershøi and his friends were also indebted, to the French impressionists. To the best of my knowledge, however, no direct exchange of visual ideas links Hammershøi's *Interior with Woman at Piano* of 1901 (fig. 5.9) with Dewing's *The Spinet* of the following year (fig. 5.10), though each appears to have descended from a branch of Vermeer's *The Music Lesson* (see fig. 3.10). Nor is there any evidence for such a relation between Paxton's *The Letter* (fig. 5.11) of 1908

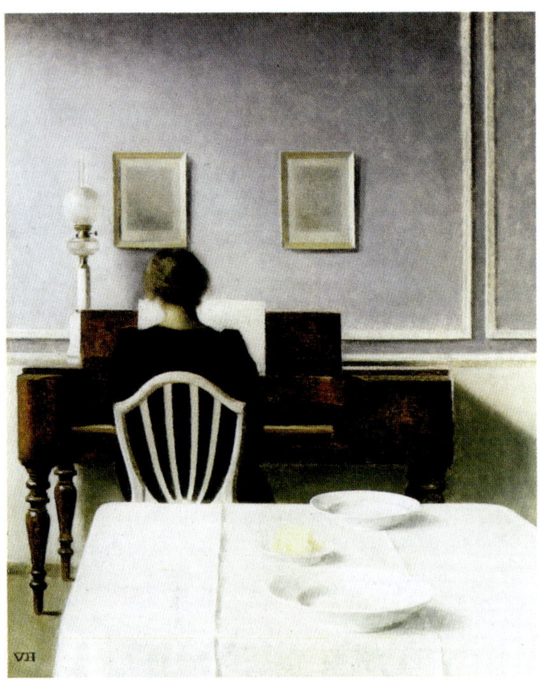

Fig. 5.9. Vilhelm Hammershøi, *Interior with Woman at Piano, Strandegarde 30* (1901). Oil on canvas, 55.2 × 41.8 cm. Private collection. Image courtesy of the Art Renewal Center® www.artrenewal.org

and Hammershøi's contemporaneous *Interior with a Woman Reading* (see fig. 5.21), though their kinship with Vermeer's studies of women reading would be hard to miss, even if we didn't know that Paxton, at least, would soon go on to assist Hale with his book on the Delft master.[27] Analogous connections might be traced for many of the paintings listed above, especially if one does not attempt, as I have just done, to confine the examples to work completed almost simultaneously. The American painters may not have been aware of their Danish counterparts, or the Danes of the Americans, but they clearly looked to a common ancestor.

What such artists saw in Vermeer was by no means limited to subject matter, of course, nor did they all see alike, even when working in close proximity with one another. Hammershøi in particular diverged from his contemporaries in ways that render him at once the most striking and the most memorable of these "modern Vermeers," and I shall return to his case shortly. On the American side, Tarbell appears to have been the first to imitate the Delft master, but Paxton would prove the most technically self-conscious of the group, seeking to adapt not only the earlier artist's motifs and attention to light, but his experiments with vision too. Each of the Americans also arrived at his Vermeer-like work from a somewhat different direction. After studying under the orientalist painter Jean-Léon Gérôme in Paris, the young Paxton traveled to Madrid, where in discovering Velázquez, according to a former pupil, "he fully discovered himself"—a process that would presumably continue when he returned to New England and started to discover himself in Vermeer.[28] DeCamp, too, was strongly influenced by Velázquez, while Dewing began—and remained—a great admirer of Whistler, whose influential patron Charles Freer may have helped spark Dewing's interest in his Dutch predecessor by presenting him with Hofstede de Groot's recent catalogue of Vermeer's work, together with what Freer's assistant called "Van Delft's reproductions," in 1907.[29] Tarbell preceded the Vermeer-like interiors for which he would be primarily known by painting outdoor studies influenced by the French impressionists, while Benson began with domestic scenes lit by fire or oil lamp and then with his own plein-air experiments before briefly following Tarbell into Vermeer territory. When Benson exhibited *The Seamstress* (fig. 5.12) in 1914, a reviewer promptly observed that the painter "has gone into Tarbell's province and shows an admirable 'near-Vermeer.'"[30] The phrase was offered in all sincerity—*The Seamstress*

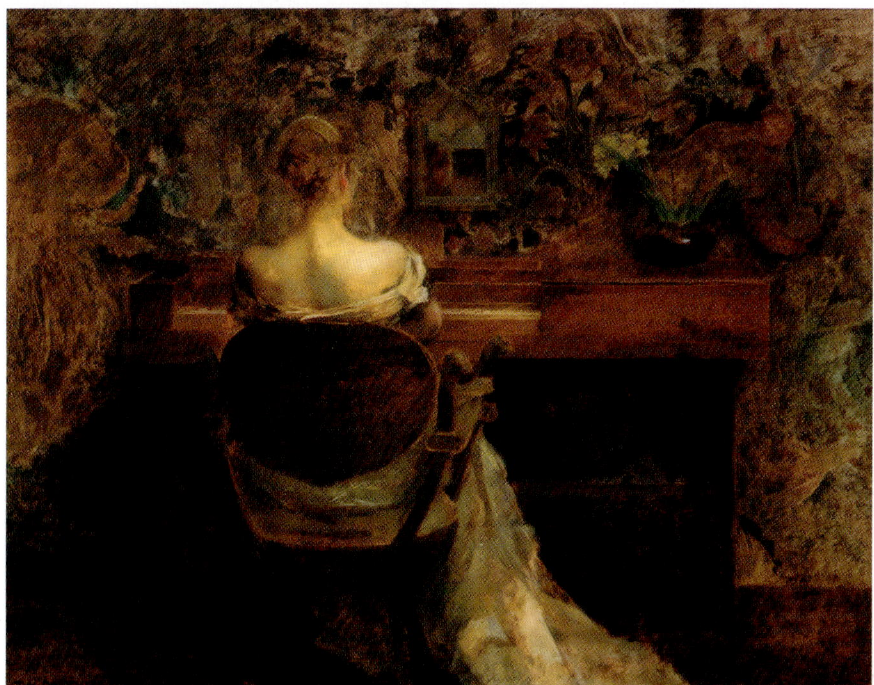

Fig. 5.10. Thomas Dewing, *The Spinet* (ca. 1901–2). Oil on panel. 39.4 × 50.8 cm. National Museum of American Art, Smithsonian Institution, Washington, DC

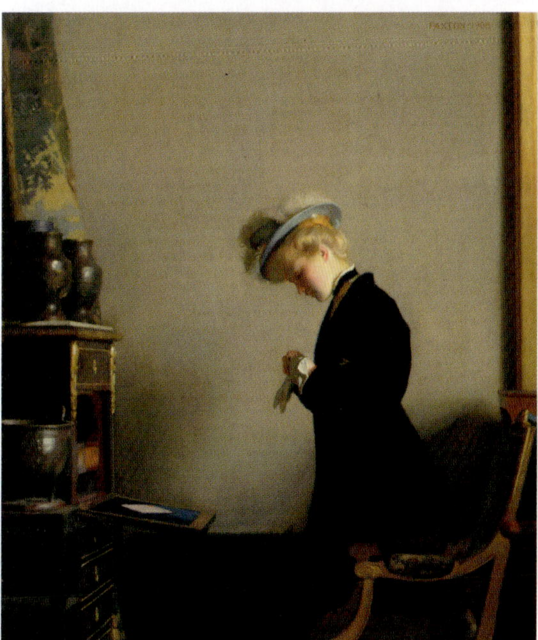

Fig. 5.11. William McGregor Paxton, *The Letter* (1908). Oil on canvas. 76.2 × 63.5 cm. Private collection. Image courtesy of the Art Renewal Center® www.artrenewal.org

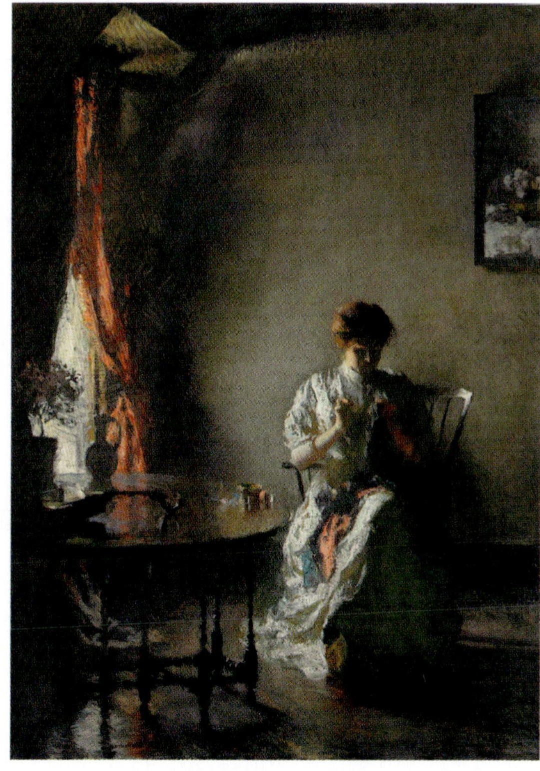

Fig. 5.12. Frank W. Benson, *The Seamstress* (1913). Oil on canvas. 96.4 × 66 cm. Private collection. Image courtesy of the Art Renewal Center® www.artrenewal.org

was said to be "one of those delightful, truthful, interiors with a simple figure and fine painting of reflected light which never tire when done by such skillful hands as those of Tarbell, and now of Benson"—but it would later prove irresistible to those with a less generous view of imitation. "A near Vermeer is a mere veneer" became a popular witticism among circles that wished to consign such work to the dustbin of history.[31]

That is to get ahead of the story, however. For sympathetic observers at the time, there was nothing superficial about the Bostonians' engagement with their model. Among their most enthusiastic champions was the artist, teacher, and writer Kenyon Cox, who combined a deep admiration for the Delft master with a sharp eye for the ways in which modern painters were managing to draw on him. "The analogy of this art to that of Vermeer is apparent at a glance," he declared of Tarbell's recent work in a piece for *The Burlington Magazine* in 1909, before going on to spell out the grounds of his comparison:

> There is the same simplicity of subject, the same reliance on sheer perfection of representation—the same delicate truth of values, the same exquisite sensitiveness to gradations of light. No one since Vermeer himself has made a flat wall so interesting—has so perfectly rendered its surface, its exact distance behind the figure, the play of light upon it and the amount of air in front of it. There is much, too, of Vermeer's accuracy of draughtsmanship without manner or acquired style, and there is the same willingness to use a few elements of composition—a few objects—again and again, in the confidence that slight differences of effect and a fresh observation will ensure sufficient variety. In the *Girl Mending* and in the *New England Interior* we have the same room, with its triple window at the left and its open door beyond, and in both is the same gate-legged table that figured in the *Girl Crocheting*. The sofa of the *New England Interior* appears again in *Preparing for the Matinée*. Yet each is an individual picture—a change in the lighting and in the grouping and distance of the figures has sufficed to give each as great a freshness as if the others had never existed.[32]

For Cox, who would go on the following year to pronounce Vermeer himself "the most perfect painter that ever lived," this was high praise indeed.[33]

In retrospect, Cox's tribute to "accuracy of draughtsmanship" may say more about the academic training of Tarbell's cohort, which still began with traditional instruction in drawing, than about Vermeer's intensely optical style, whose avoidance of sharply delineated contours has been central to our understanding of his art ever since Gowing's influential study.[34] But most of the features Cox chooses to highlight remain familiar features of Vermeer commentary, even if they, too, speak for their time. Consider, for example, how his homage to the visual interest of Tarbell's walls anticipates the enthusiasm with which E. V. Lucas would write in 1922 of the "wonderful" white wall, "beautiful beyond the power of words to express," in Vermeer's *Woman with a Pearl Necklace*, or the far more famous tribute to the "little patch of yellow wall" in the *View of Delft* that would appear in the fifth volume of Proust's masterwork the following year.[35] (Tarbell himself apparently felt strongly on the subject: "Sargent was simply making that wall out of gray paint," he complained disapprovingly, after a studio visit in which he witnessed one of the portraitist's sitters posed against a wall of that color.)[36] Though Proust was steeped in the Vermeer literature, it seems unlikely that he saw Lucas's book before he died, let alone that he'd read Cox on Tarbell. But the latter's account of the two artists' "willingness to use a few elements of composition [. . .] again and again" would also find an echo in the same volume of Proust's novel, when the narrator holds forth on those "fragments of the same world" whose combination and recombination paradoxically distinguish Vermeer's art: "It's always, whatever the genius with which they have been recreated, the same table, the same carpet, the same woman, the same novel and unique beauty."[37]

For all the eloquence Cox devoted to his analogy, he firmly resisted the idea that Tarbell was in any way copying his predecessor. "If the inspiration of Vermeer is evident," he wrote, "there is no trace of imitation":

> Mr. Tarbell is trying to do what Vermeer did, not to do it as Vermeer did it—still less to give the superficial aspect of the Dutchman's pictures. It would never have occurred to him to produce a costume piece and to attempt the reconstruction of a seventeenth-century interior, as Meissonier attempted it. The environment he paints is his own; his models are people of his own day. To find the pictorial elements in what he sees about him is his task, as it was that of the masters of Holland. Neither has he attempted to investigate the technical methods or to reproduce the handling of any painter of the past [. . .].
>
> What Mr. Tarbell has set himself to recover is not the method of the Master of Delft but his point of view, not his technique but his temper. Using his own tools and his own equipment, he sees as Vermeer saw and feels as he felt, and it would be hard to find a better model.[38]

In arguing that Tarbell does not imitate Vermeer but "sees as Vermeer saw," Cox uncannily echoes, even as he reverses, the claim that others were making at the very same time for Vermeer himself—that "we go to him," as the Belgian novelist and critic Gustave Vanzype also wrote in 1908, "because a sort of mysterious prescience made him see as we see."[39] Just which writer arrived at his formula first is impossible to say, but both testify to a moment when the art world was finding more than one way of making Vermeer modern.

Though the avoidance of a costume piece may not have been the most distinctive sign of Tarbell's modernity, Cox was not alone in his appreciation for the familiar setting of the painter's work—a characteristic that distinguished

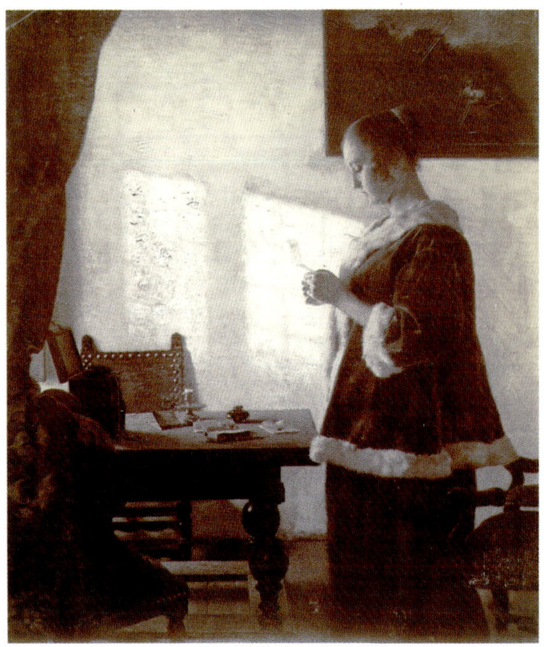

Fig. 5.13. Claus Meyer, *Woman Reading a Letter in an Interior* (1890). Oil on canvas. 65 × 52 cm. Location unknown

Fig. 5.14. William McGregor Paxton, *Girl Sweeping* (1912). Oil on canvas. 102.2 × 77.2 cm. Courtesy of the Pennsylvania Academy of Fine Arts, Philadelphia. Joseph E. Temple Fund 1912.4

Tarbell's pictures not only from the meticulous historical recreations of an Alma-Tadema, but from the work of other artists of the period who are sometimes said to have been influenced by Vermeer. Indeed, the fact that the Boston painters offered serene images of contemporary domestic life constituted a significant part of their appeal. *A Girl Crocheting* may have been hailed as a "modern Ver Meer," but it was also proclaimed a "typically American picture," to quote one reviewer in 1912. "The art of Mr. Tarbell is entitled to be called American in every sense of the word," declared another that same year, "for what have we more truly representative of our own peculiar life and culture than the beautiful American woman in the setting of her refined home?"[40] Both the German painter Claus Meyer (1856–1919) and the American Walter MacEwan (1860–1943), by contrast, not only posed their letter readers in what appeared to be seventeenth century interiors, but duly supplied them with fur-trimmed jackets very like those that often adorn Vermeer's subjects, the *Woman with a Pearl Necklace* and the *Woman Holding a Balance* among them.[41] Usually captioned "after Johannes Vermeer," Meyer's painting in particular so closely resembles its model that it hovers uncertainly between loose copy and pastiche, rather than the kind of imitation by family resemblance we have been examining (fig. 5.13).

Yet if the Boston painters mostly avoided this kind of backdating, they were not averse to gesturing quietly in its direction. The oriental carpet bunched on the table in the foreground of Paxton's *Girl Sweeping* (fig. 5.14), for example, pays tacit homage to the similar placement of such carpets in multiple Vermeer canvases, while the titular garment in the same artist's *Yellow Jacket* (fig. 5.15) more obliquely recalls the fur-trimmed jacket, also a vivid yellow, that reappears in several of the earlier artist's paintings, including *Mistress and Maid* and *A Lady Writing* (fig. 5.16).[42]

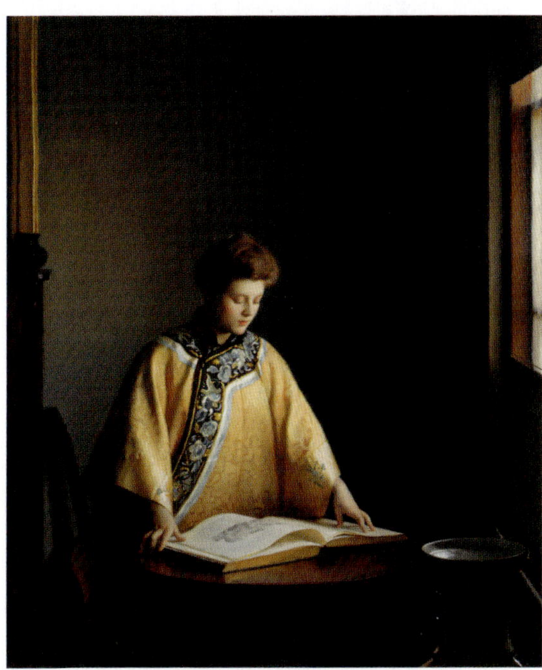

Fig. 5.15. William McGregor Paxton, *The Yellow Jacket* (1907). Oil on canvas. 68 × 56.2 cm. Private collection. Image courtesy of the Art Renewal Center® www.artrenewal.org

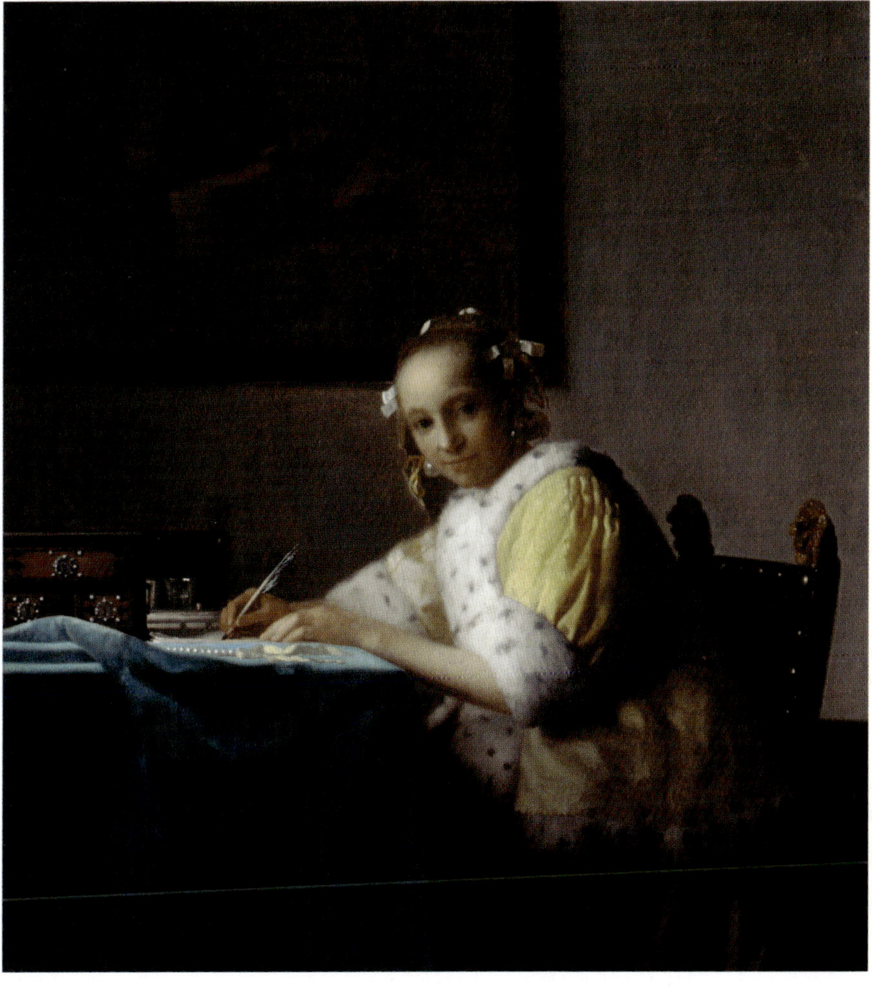

Fig. 5.16. Johannes Vermeer, *A Lady Writing* (ca. 1665). Oil on canvas. 45 × 39.9 cm. Gift of Harry Waldron Havemeyer and Horace Havemeyer Jr. in memory of their father Horace Havemeyer. National Gallery of Art, Washington, DC

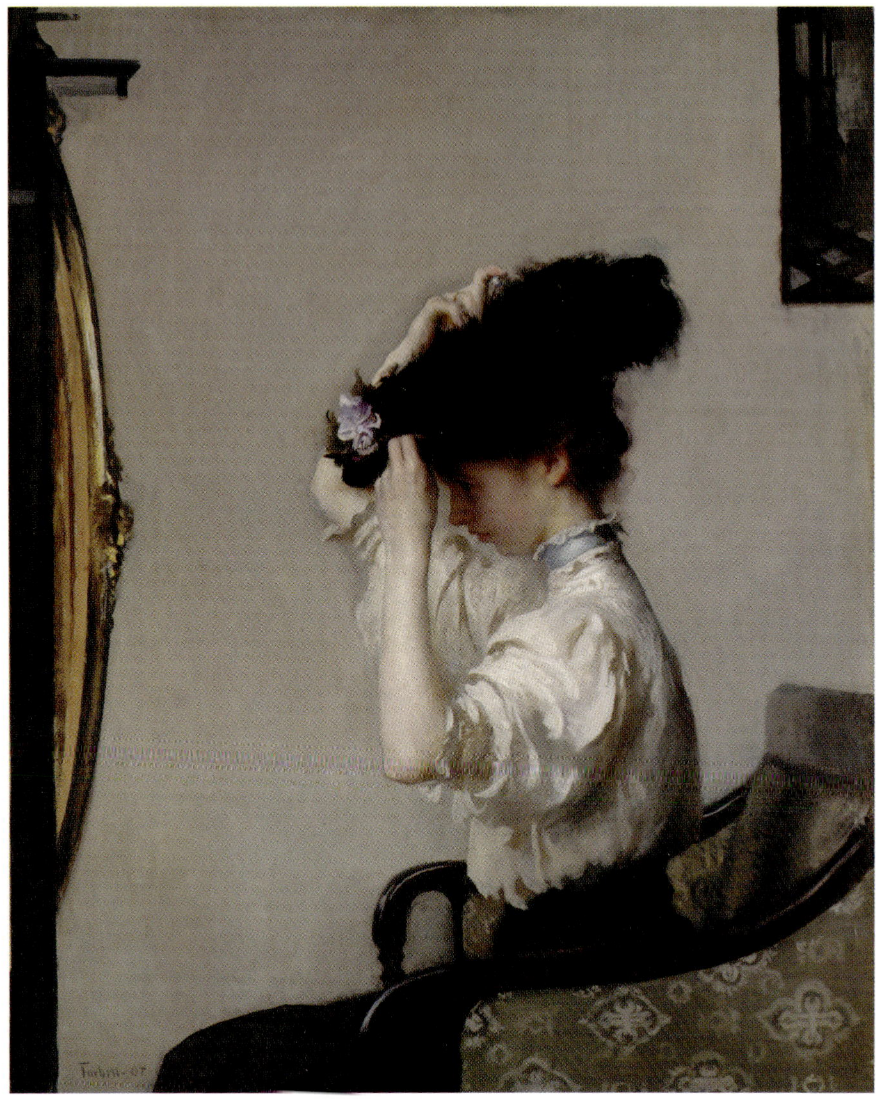

Fig. 5.17. Edmund C. Tarbell, *Preparing for the Matinée* (1907). Oil on canvas. 115.5 × 90.1 cm. Indianapolis Museum of Art, Indianapolis, IN. Image courtesy of the Art Renewal Center® www.artrenewal.org

Benson likewise experimented with a variation on this garment for several pictures—his took the form of a yellow silk robe with embroidered white-and-black trim—and once added to the effect with a chandelier reminiscent of the elegant version that implausibly decorates *The Art of Painting*.[43] Even Dewing, whose style as a whole least resembles that of the Delft master, still seems to have amassed a collection of Vermeer-like props, a chair with lion-head finials most notably among them.[44] In *Preparing for the Matinée* (fig. 5.17), whose "simple empty wall" Cox would single out for particular praise, Tarbell took a different tack, at once updating the mise-en-scène of Vermeer's *Woman with a Pearl Necklace* and placing his fashionable mirror-gazer so that her hat implicitly points toward a bit of tiled floor in a cropped reproduction of *The Music Lesson*.[45]

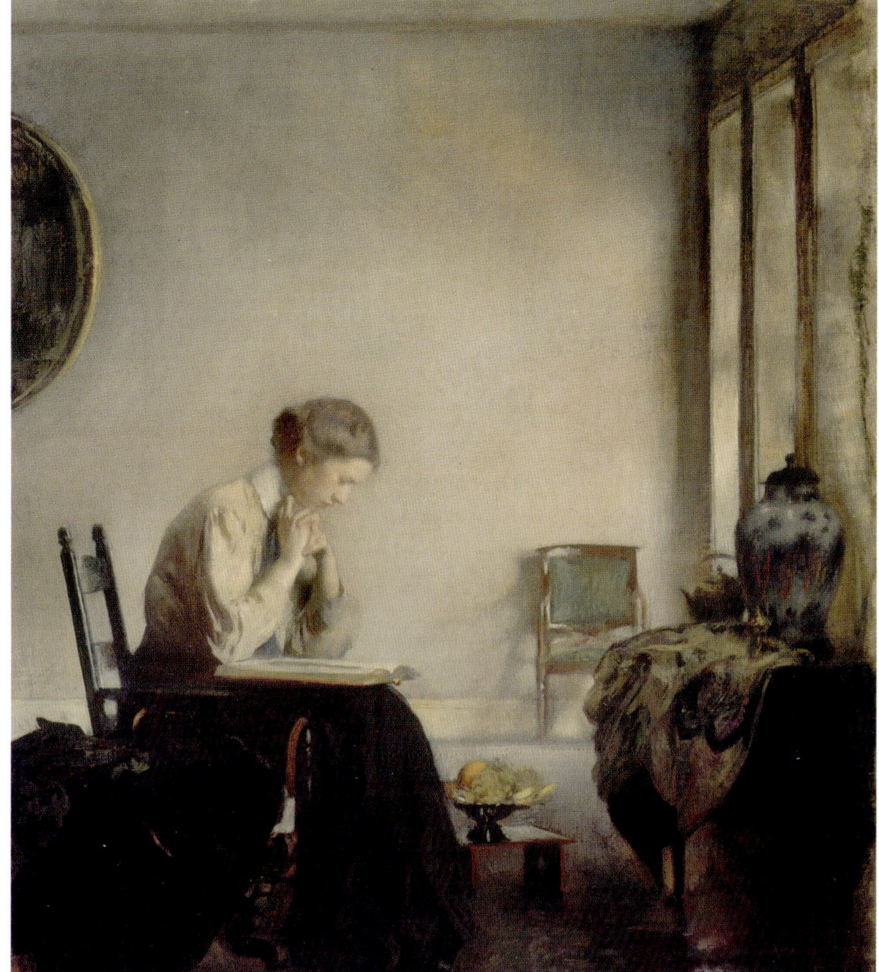

Fig. 5.18. Edmund C. Tarbell, *Girl Reading* (1909). Oil on canvas. 81.9 × 72.4 cm. Museum of Fine Arts, Boston. The Hayden Collection—Charles Henry Hayden Fund 09.209. Photograph © 2026, Museum of Fine Arts, Boston, MA

Such self-conscious echoing of local detail is finally less important, however, than the formal arrangements and visual techniques that the Bostonians adopted from their predecessor. Writing in the same year as Cox, another American critic, James Gibbons Huneker, specifically praised the handling of space in Tarbell's *Girl Reading* (fig. 5.18), even as he attributed such arrangements to the influence of the Delft master. "The spacing is alluring, from the chair to the wall, from the window to the chair," he wrote. "It is the Vermeer gambit, that no one will deny, but who can handle such difficult and lovely problems as Tarbell does?"[46] In a more analytic comparison of the same artist's *A Girl Crocheting* to Vermeer's *Young Woman with a Lute* (see figs. 5.4 and 1.18), Bernice Leader would later elaborate on how the compositional devices they share—"the large table in the dimly lit foreground, the figure in the middleground, the lateral window casting sunlight on the figure and the background wall and the rectangular wall hangings"—"not only structure the space and focus attention on the woman, but lock her permanently into position," thus transforming "an

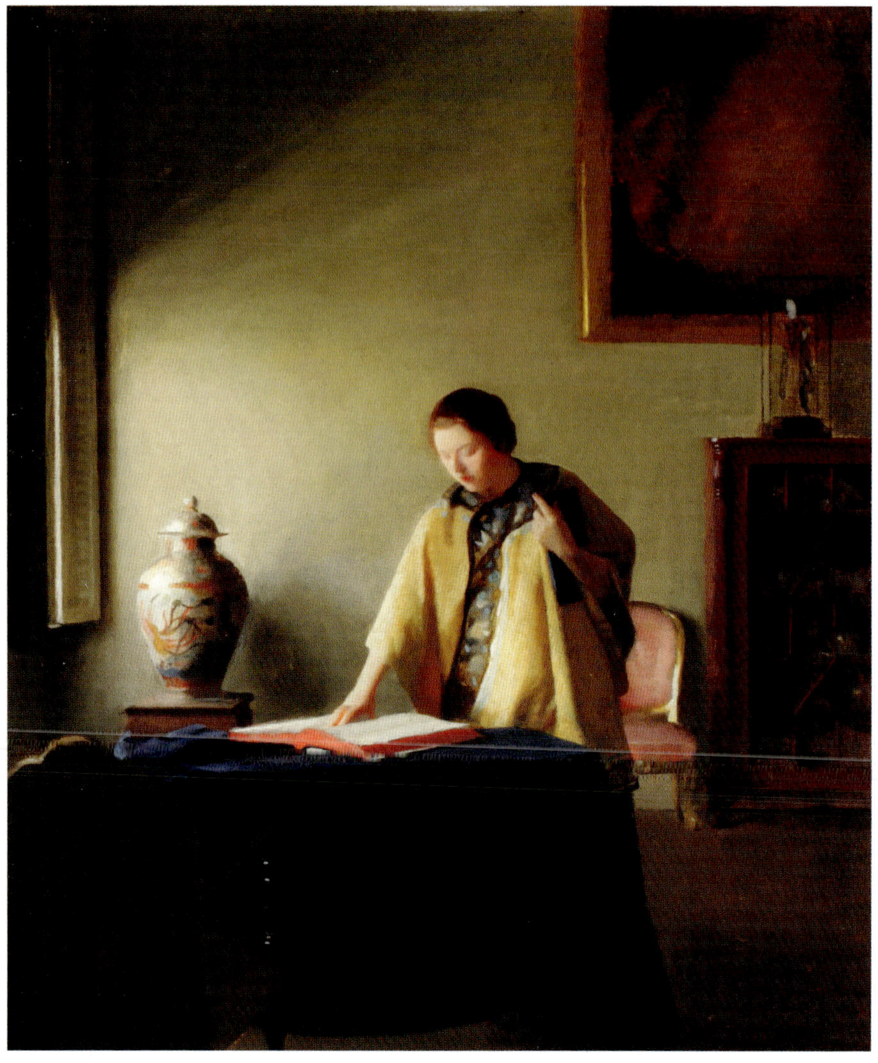

Fig. 5.19. William McGregor Paxton, *Woman Reading a Book* (1910). Oil on canvas on board. 45.7 × 38.1 cm. Gift of Mrs. Wilson Smith. New Britain Museum of American Art, New Britain, CT

ostensibly realistic scene into a poetic, dreamlike vision."[47] Similar observations might be made about the treatment of space in any number of other interiors by Tarbell's colleagues: Paxton's *Yellow Jacket* (see fig. 5.15), for instance, or his *Woman Reading a Book*, a work whose juxtaposition of that same yellow jacket against the deep blue of the tablecloth simultaneously manages to pay vivid homage to Vermeer's characteristic palette (fig. 5.19).

Vermeer's influence can also be felt, of course, in what yet another contemporary critic termed the Bostonians' "exclusive devotion to the gospel of light."[48] Benson, who liked to call himself a "painter of light," apparently kept a small print of the *Young Woman with a Water Pitcher* as a model in this regard; and when his daughter Eleanor, too, began to paint, he duly passed it on to her. "Don't paint anything but the effect of light," he instructed her.[49] From time to time, both Decamp and Dewing seem to have experimented with *pointillé* highlights like those that Vermeer had frequently scattered on his canvases, while Paxton also appears to have registered—and sought to imitate—the earlier artist's use of selective focus.[50] "I have come to depend upon the plain truth, scientifically explicable, that a man looking out through two eyes sees things, within a certain focus, single," he told an interviewer, whereas "outside that focus, [he sees] all vertical lines and vertically inclined spots, double. Hence comes my practice of rendering Japanese jars in the background with double edges and two high-lights, though, as a matter of objective truth, I know well enough there is but one high-light there."[51] We know that Hale experimented with the camera obscura while writing his Vermeer book, and it's possible that Paxton, as his collaborator, did so too; but whatever the impetus for this theory of "binocular vision"—the label is Paxton's—his account of it hardly seems adequate to his own practice, let alone that of his model.[52] Between the blurred surface of the carpet in the foreground of *Girl Sweeping*, for instance (see fig. 5.14), and the similarly blurred forms of various objects in the rear, the evidence suggests that Paxton may have gained more from looking at Vermeer than he did from theorizing, even if he does far less in the end to unsettle the viewer's focus. He was clearly right, however, that a Japanese jar, slightly blurred, was apt to figure in his own inventory.

Just as Hale would argue that Vermeer "anticipated the modern point of view" by caring for "the composition, the aspect and the rendering" of his pictures rather than their potential for anecdote, so the Boston painters confirmed their own modernity by all this attention to arrangement and technique rather than subject matter.[53] Benson's advice to his daughter was unequivocal on this point: "Design is the only thing that matters," he informed her. "Picture making has become to me merely the arrangement of design within the frame. It has nothing to do with the painting of objects or the representation of nature."[54] And these were also the terms on which at least some of Benson's contemporaries chose to receive the Bostonians' work. "They are concerned solely with the things which are proper to painting," the critic Frederick W. Coburn observed of several pictures by Tarbell in 1907,

> for Mr. Tarbell's art is never allegorical [. . .]. A breakfast-room of the well bred, a Venetian blind in one of the houses of the comfortable, a young Canadian nurse doing fancy work at a mahogany table beneath a reproduction from Velasquez—any such motive may furnish Mr. Tarbell with a pretext for a skillful arrangement of color tones.[55]

That "Canadian nurse doing fancy work" presumably refers to *A Girl Crocheting* (see fig. 5.4), whose subject sits beneath a reproduction of Velázquez's *Portrait of Pope Innocent X*, as well as several Japanese prints: pictures-within-the-picture that simultaneously testify to the modern taste of the painter and contribute to what Benson called "the arrangement of design within the frame."[56]

As we have seen, this particular arrangement is also the canvas that had recently been dubbed a "modern Ver Meer."[57] Yet even at the time there was more than one way of understanding that label. For its creator, after all, *A Girl Crocheting* signaled a turn from plein-air impressionism toward a kind of painting that could easily be seen as backward-looking. "Mr. Tarbell's conservatism is the more interesting and the more exemplary because it has been of slow growth," Kenyon Cox wrote in the same piece that went on to elaborate the analogy of the painter's work with that of Vermeer.[58] Cox intended the observation as a compliment, and the Bostonians would probably have taken it as one. By comparison to their peers across the Atlantic, the American impressionists had always remained more devoted to their academic training, as Hale's chapter on "Vermeer and Modern Painting" implicitly acknowledged by characterizing Tarbell and Paxton as "showing the effect of the Impressionistic movement when grafted, so to say, on good old Dutch stock." (Otto Grundmann, Tarbell's teacher, had studied in Antwerp.)[59] The type of picture that Hale championed was already being contested by the so-called Ashcan School, among others, well before his book appeared in 1913, but the fact that its publication happened to coincide with many Americans' first introduction to the European avant-garde at the New York Armory Show only served to drive home how rapidly the art world was changing. Whatever the excitement produced in some quarters by paintings such as Henri Matisse's *Red Turban* (1907) or Marcel Duchamp's *Nude Descending a Staircase, No. 2* (1912), Tarbell and his colleagues thought most of the modernists betrayed a shocking disregard for technical skill, and it's surely no accident that in the following year they founded an institution whose very name—the Boston Guild of Artists—was meant to recall the traditions of an earlier era.[60] Implicitly evoking the painters' guilds of the seventeenth-century Dutch in particular, the Bostonians rededicated themselves to the craftsmanship they associated with Vermeer and his contemporaries, even as they also began to consign their own work to history. In a poignant testament to changing taste, a revised edition of Hale's book published posthumously in 1937 no longer included their names.[61]

Social change, too, has tended to date the Bostonians' peaceful interiors. Images of a leisured feminine world once celebrated as representative of American life at its best have sometimes looked to later eyes both confining and regressive: visual analogues of larger efforts to keep middle-class women in their place, at a time when many were seeking to redefine it. Commenting on the Boston painters in an influential article of 1980, the art historian Bernice Kramer Leader registered her impatience with the social conservatism of their work even more than she did with their aesthetic conservatism: "Either absorbed in quiet reverie or engaged in activities associated with traditional concepts of virtuous womanhood, these women are silent, spiritual, and still."[62] That sweeping judgment notably overlooked the fact that several of the women who modeled for such pictures were simultaneously engaged in painting them:

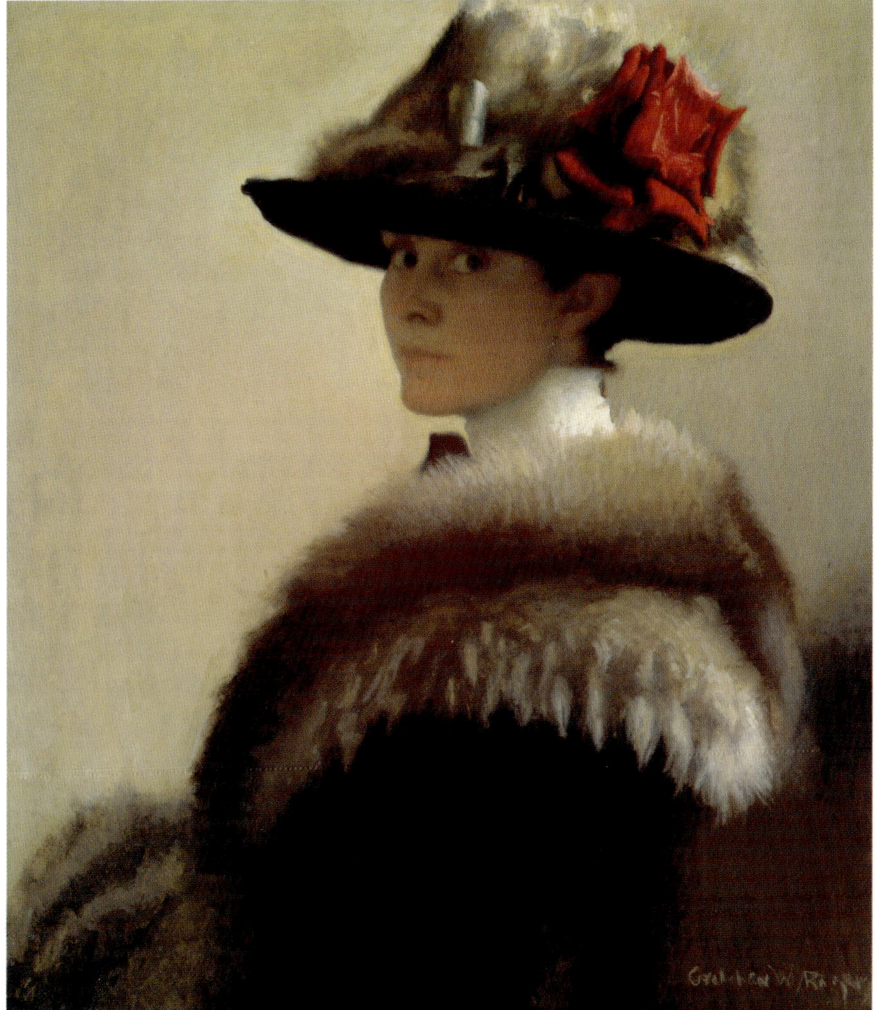

Fig. 5.20. Gretchen Woodman Rogers, *Woman in a Fur Hat* (ca. 1915). Oil on canvas. 76.2 × 64.1 cm. Gift of Miss Anne Winslow. Museum of Fine Arts, Boston. 1972.232. Photograph © 2026, Museum of Fine Arts, Boston, MA

a group that included not only Hale's wife Lilian Westcott Hale (1880–1963), who had once studied with Tarbell, but Paxton's wife and former student Elizabeth Okie Paxton (1877–1971). Working alongside their male colleagues, the women of the Boston School also drew their inspiration from Vermeer—most arrestingly, perhaps, in a self-portrait from around 1915 by another of Tarbell's students, Gretchen Woodman Rogers (1881–1967), whose pose and lighting effects offered a modern take on the *Girl with a Pearl Earring*. That Rogers chose to depict herself as a fashionably dressed woman rather than a working artist may testify to the conservatism that so troubled Kramer, but there is nothing "still" about the dexterity with which the portrait is executed, or the directness of its gaze (fig. 5.20).[63]

Kramer was writing at a moment when feminist critiques like hers were very much in the air, but, as she herself made clear, at least some contemporaries of the artists had already offered similar arguments. In an essay of 1915, the realist painter and art critic Guy Pène du Bois dismissed the work of the Boston group as fundamentally "small and snobbish"—pictures "composed entirely of figures taken from the upper middle class and shown in environments of exceptional taste and refinement":

> These figures when in action or seated, quite idly, in a well-appointed parlor or porch, never do things and are never found in places outside the province of the lady. They sew—not shirts,—read and write letters, finger the finest of grand pianos, ride, or are caught behind Venetian blinds in dainty negligee. They live serene uneventful lives [. . .] amid serene, dignified, tasteful surroundings. There is a complacency in them that may have extinguished the fire of their beauty as it certainly has done away with their passions and impulses. It is the complacency that comes with easy, orderly life, the removal of the evidences of struggle some time after the struggle itself has ceased.[64]

Though a family resemblance could be traced between such critiques and some recent accounts of Vermeer's own work, which likewise emphasize its air of luxury and refinement,[65] Du Bois himself seems to have drawn a firm distinction between the original and his descendants. As "the real leader of this group," Tarbell may have been "much inspired by Vermeer of Delft," but as far as Du Bois was concerned, the modern painter "resembl[ed] that great Dutchman only in language."[66]

It's a harsh verdict, and not everyone since has been prepared to accept it. Later in the century, some scholars chose to look anew at the Boston painters and argue, for example, that Thomas Dewing learned from Vermeer how to "exploit [. . .] spatial relationships to create enigmatic tension between figures," or that Paxton's work resembles the Dutch master's in the elusiveness of its iconography.[67] But the most haunting response to Vermeerian ambiguity at the *fin de siècle* was surely that of Vilhelm Hammershøi. Though many of his female subjects are still more conspicuously idle than those of Tarbell or Paxton, the fact that they "never do things," in Du Bois's phrase, could hardly be taken as a sign of complacency.[68] They, too, inhabit bourgeois spaces, with paintings on the wall and pianos at the ready, but it's not only the relative sparseness of the furnishings by comparison with their American counterparts that renders these interiors so melancholy. If another of the Bostonians' limitations, as Du Bois saw it, was a tendency to treat the human subject as of no more account than the beautiful objects around her, Hammershøi seems to have turned something like this strange equivalence of persons and things into a formal principle of his art.[69] A half century before Gowing would evoke "the zone of emotional neutrality in which Vermeer suspends the human matter in his pictures," Hammershøi had apparently begun to render visible his own, still cooler version of that effect.[70]

Such "emotional neutrality," to adopt Gowing's phrase, is most pronounced in Hammershøi's numerous images of a figure with her back turned to the viewer, but even when she is seen in full-face or profile, the artist takes care to keep her at a distance. Look, for example, at his *Interior with a Woman Reading* of 1908 (fig. 5.21)—a painting that is obviously indebted to Vermeer's *Girl Reading a Letter at an Open Window* (see fig. 1.11) and his *Woman in Blue* (see fig. 2.4)—and notice how Hammershøi adopts his predecessor's characteristic strategy of blocking our access to his human subject by placing a table in the foreground of the picture. (I suggest looking at the unrestored *Girl*, since that would have been the version available in Hammershøi's time.) Between the position of the reader's hands, the lack of a visible window, and the arrangement of the table and chairs, as well as the absence of a curtain, the *Interior* as a whole most closely resembles the *Woman in Blue*, but by simultaneously using the table to occlude more of the woman's figure, as in the *Girl Reading a Letter*, and placing the woman herself further back in space, Hammershøi removes her from the viewer still further than Vermeer does either of his women. Even more to the point, he obscures her face, allowing a shadow to fall on parts of her profile that both of Vermeer's paintings illuminate. While in this picture, at least, the act of reading plausibly absorbs Hammershøi's solitary figure, there is still something unmotivated about her pose: while the *Girl Reading a Letter* appears to have moved close to the window in order to scrutinize her missive, and the *Woman in Blue* to have lifted her letter from the table below her, nothing in the arrangement of Hammershøi's table and chairs explains why his reader stands in the middle of the room with a book in her hands—except the need, perhaps, to balance her dark figure against the brightly lit door that dominates the right half of the canvas. Like the empty coffee cup and the other book on the table, she simply takes her place in the formal design of the picture.

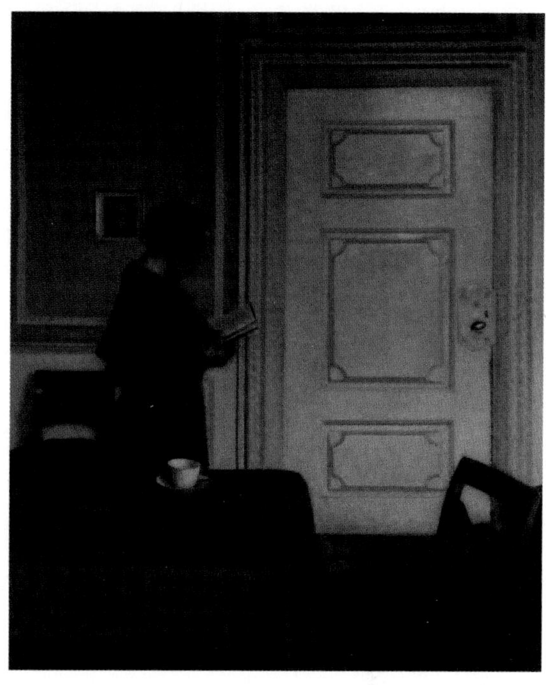

Fig. 5.21. Vilhelm Hammershøi, *Interior with a Woman Reading* (1908). Oil on canvas. 65.6 × 56 cm. Museum Sønderjylland (Denmark)

When Hammershøi turns the woman's back to the viewer, he heightens the mystery, even as he further transforms the Vermeerian paradigm. While turned backs occasionally appear in Vermeer as well, only in three cases—*The Music Lesson*, *Officer and Laughing Girl*, and *The Art of Painting*—does the back in question belong to a principal subject of the picture; and only in the last of these does the artist obscure the subject's features entirely. (The other turned backs appear in *Diana and Her Companions*, *The Concert*, and some tiny figures

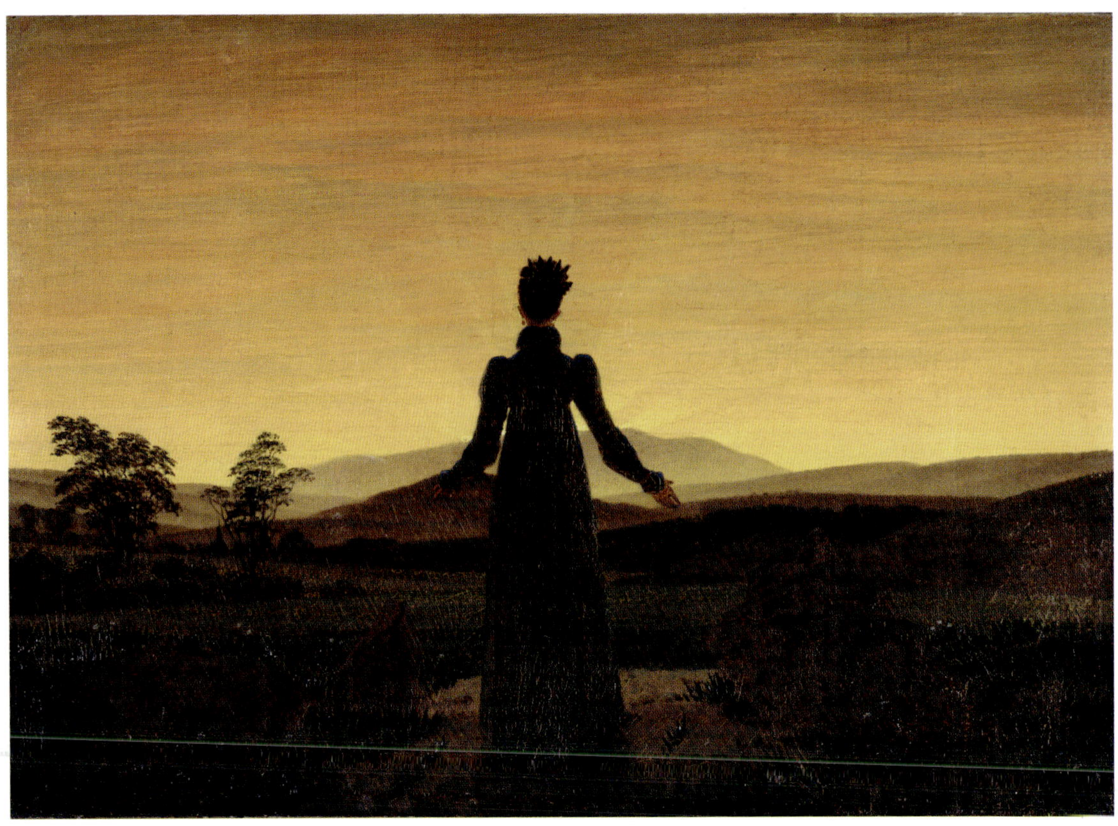

Fig. 5.22. Caspar David Friedrich, *Woman Before the Rising Sun (Woman Before the Setting Sun)* (ca. 1818). Oil on canvas. 22 × 30 cm. Museum Folkwang, Essen. HIP / Art Resource, NY

in *The Little Street*, and *The View of Delft*.) Nor does Vermeer ever exclude us yet further from human interaction by adopting the motif, as Hammershøi so often does, for a solitary figure, while leaving the reason for her turned back so inexplicable. Consider the standing figure in *Interior with Young Woman Seen from Behind* (see fig. 5.6) or the seated one in *Resting* (see fig. 5.7), to choose just two examples among many. In both cases, interestingly, Hammershøi brings the woman much closer to the picture plane than he does in *Interior with a Woman Reading*, but by turning her back to us he also ensures, of course, that she will remain even more inaccessible—a result that effectively intensifies the analogous combination of intimacy and elusiveness that characterizes so many of Vermeer's solitary figures.

Like Vermeer, Hammershøi poses these women against a blank wall, punctuated only, in the case of the *Interior with Young Woman Seen from Behind*, by rectangular molding and a cropped picture frame. But one reason the paintings feel so eerie is that the women themselves face that blankness: a blankness that suggestively extends to the picture-within-the-picture that hangs in the *Interior* as well. In this respect, Hammershøi's frequent use of such backward-looking figures departs radically from the precedent set by the nineteenth century's best-known exploiter of the motif, the German Romantic painter Caspar David Friedrich (1774–1840). Friedrich, who made the so-called *Rückenfigur* into the

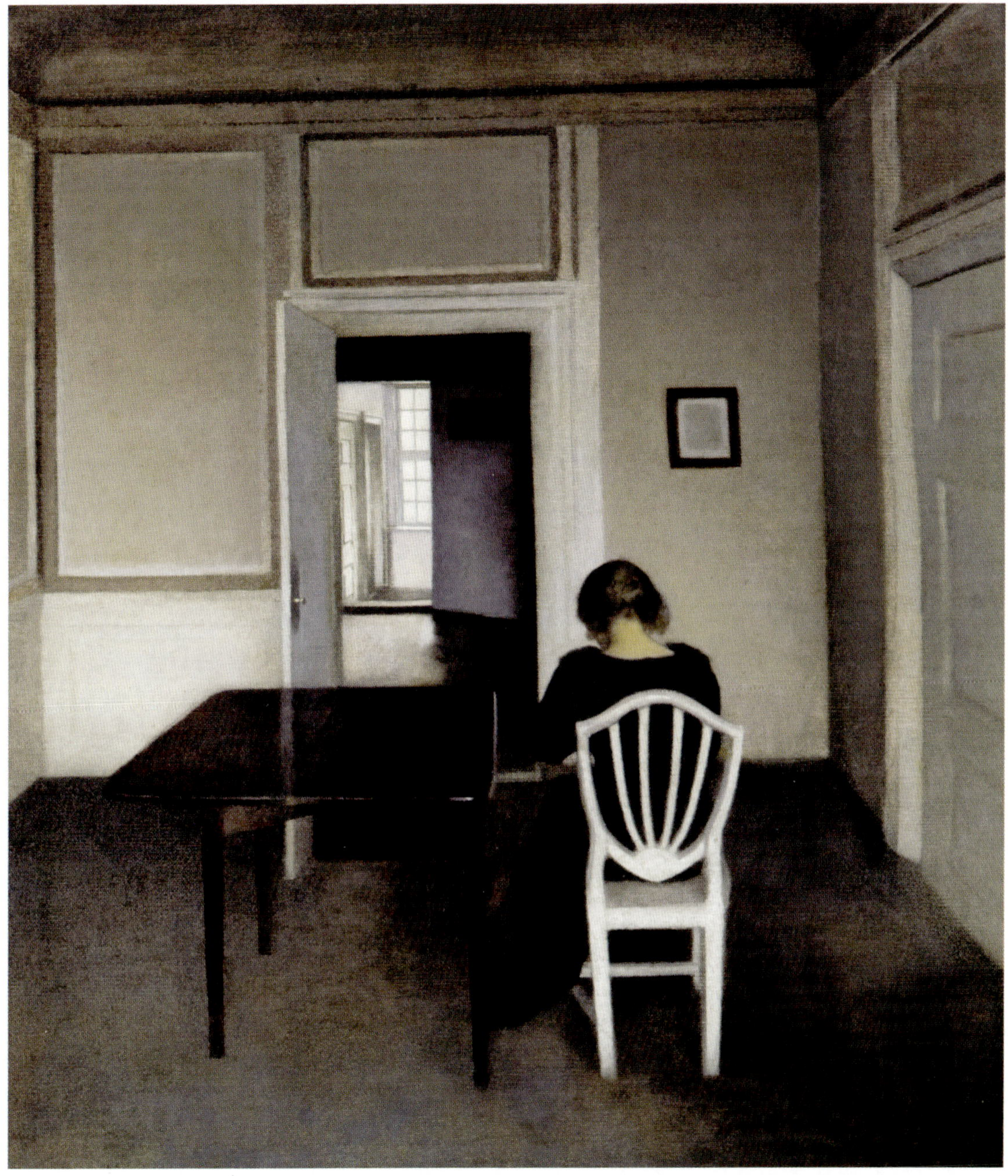

Fig. 5.23. Vilhelm Hammershøi, *Interior with Ida in a White Chair* (1900). Oil on canvas. 57 × 49 cm. Private collection. Image courtesy of the Art Renewal Center® www.artrenewal.org

"visual master-trope" of his art, characteristically posed such figures before an expansive landscape, where they serve as surrogates for the viewer's own encounter with the world—a world that may appear desolate or melancholy but remains, at least, always open (fig. 5.22).[71] Hammershøi, by contrast, routinely closes off the prospect. Even when the rear wall is pierced by a window, the latter is typically "veiled, a blurred lens," in the apt phrase of the Danish art historian Poul Vad (fig. 5.23). And when the scene is lit from the side, as Vad goes on to note, we never see the window through which the light is coming—a marked difference from Vermeer, for whom the presence of the window, both physical and symbolic, so often proves key to the painting. Though Vermeer, too, almost never permits us to see through the glass, it is hard to imagine a critic comparing his interiors, as Vad does Hammershøi's, to "a trap constructed for the purpose of catching the light."[72]

I have said that Hammershøi offers no explanation for these women's turned backs, and an alert reader might object that we have already seen an exception: *Interior with Woman at Piano* (see fig. 5.9). Here, one could argue, the woman faces not so much a blank wall as a musical instrument, and her apparent indifference to the viewer is explained by her absorption in music-making. This *Interior* is, in fact, one of only two in which Hammershøi shows a woman seated at the piano, which elsewhere figures in his paintings simply as another piece of furniture. Yet even here, as Felix Krämer has noted, we cannot see whether the woman is actually playing on the instrument—an effect, he argues, that only "serv[es] to compound the stillness and the sense of loneliness that inform all the artist's works."[73] Though he does not make the comparison, a glance at its closest analogue in Vermeer's oeuvre, *The Music Lesson*, is instructive. (See fig. 3.10.) While the absorption of most of Vermeer's solitary figures is confirmed by the visible activity of their hands, the woman in *The Music Lesson*, like Hammershøi's, is positioned in such a way that we cannot see whether she is actually performing. But between the alert posture of her companion and the mirrored reflection of her face, which appears to turn in his direction, Vermeer conjures up a scene whose atmosphere feels very different from Hammershøi's.

Even if we chose to discount the iconographical cues provided by the inscription on the virginal and the picture-within-the-picture, it would be hard to associate *The Music Lesson* with the kind of loneliness that Krämer sees in Hammershøi—a loneliness oddly intensified, I would like to suggest, by the anomalous character of this *Interior*'s domestic arrangements. The presence of the wine jug in Vermeer's painting hardly calls for explanation, especially if we are inclined to identify the couple as lovers, but what are we to make of those two empty plates and that isolated lump of butter perched so prominently on Hammershøi's table?[74] Like the circular platter that rests on the left hip of the subject in *Interior with Young Woman Seen from Behind* (see fig. 5.6), the simple objects on the table in *Interior with Woman at Piano* clearly have a place in the painting's design, but their lack of other context renders them slightly surreal, as if they had wandered in from a future painting by René Magritte. Rather than transfigure the everyday—as Vermeer does with the bread and milk in *The Milkmaid*, for example, or the basin and pitcher in *Young Woman with a Water Pitcher*—Hammershøi characteristically unsettles it.

There is another respect in which Hammershøi significantly departs from his predecessor, and that is his palette. If "colors, for Vermeer, are at once the words of a material vocabulary and the words of an ideal vocabulary," as the poet and critic Jean-Louis Vaudoyer would put it in 1921, then the painter in Hammershøi speaks a different language altogether.[75] Unlike the brilliant blues and yellows for which Vermeer is famous, Hammershøi typically confines himself to a small range of neutral tones. Another painter who saw him at work thought the daubs on his palette resembled "four oyster shells."[76] Asked about his preference for "a few, muted colours" in an interview of 1907, Hammershøi professed himself at a loss for explanation. "It seems perfectly natural to me, but I can't say why," he declared, before going on to suggest that they might better be termed "neutral and reduced" colors. "I'm utterly convinced," he added, "that a painting has the best effect in terms of its colour the fewer colours there are."[77] Whatever the wisdom of this view, it seems clear that the effect also contributes to the melancholy of Hammershøi's paintings, especially as compared with any Vermeers they might otherwise resemble. Consider, for instance, the difference that color alone makes in a comparison between Vermeer's *Lacemaker* and Hammershøi's *Young Girl Sewing* (see figs. 3.16 and 5.8), or the former's *Girl Reading a Letter at an Open Window*, even in its unrestored version, and Hammershøi's *Interior with a Woman Reading* (see figs. 1.11 and 5.21). Shades of Vermeer's blues and yellows may still haunt the *Interior with Woman at Piano* (see fig. 5.9), but theirs is indeed a "neutral" afterlife.

"When we look at these pictures we sense, as we do with Vermeer's pictures, that time has stopped, the world has been brought to silence, and eternity has commenced—without our having died first," one modern commentator has written; and the observation seems just, with the caveat that the silence of Hammershøi's paintings, like their physical stillness, feels yet more absolute than his predecessor's.[78] The same might be said of what an early supporter of Hammershøi, the pianist Leonard Borwick, called the "underlying mystery" of the painter's work, which likewise heightens, as well as darkens, the mysteriousness of the original.[79] Whether Hammershøi consciously intended these relations is itself a mystery, as is, for that matter, how—if at all—he intended that his paintings be interpreted. "When I choose a motif, I'm thinking first and foremost of the lines," he says in the same interview in which he briefly addresses his color preferences, and though he also acknowledges the importance of the light, he says nothing about the scenarios that light illuminates.[80] "After having seen and spoken with this man for only two minutes," the interviewer adds in conclusion, "one has the profound realization that [. . .] this silent, shimmering, melancholy art [. . .] is not based upon theories or speculation, but has grown from a temperament's deep and peculiar soil."[81]

That does not mean, of course, that subsequent viewers haven't been tempted to speculate in his stead. One prominent scholar of his work has insisted that

> the "emptiness" in the pictures must not be interpreted sentimentally as expressing "a feeling of emptiness," and the solitary woman's presence in

> the oddly bare rooms is not to be regarded as an image of human loneliness, nor as perhaps even expressing the *Zeitgeist* of the middle class around the turn of the century, woman's social situation, and so forth.[82]

Others, however, have understandably ignored such ex cathedra pronouncements. In the past half century, at least, they have also tended to see his work as proto-modernist. "Hammershøi's modernity involves a spiritualizing of spareness and undercutting of the cozy *gemütlichkeit* associated with his domesticated subjects, in favor of something simultaneously more pure and more alienated," Kirk Varnedoe wrote in 1983, a few years before he became chief curator of painting and sculpture at the Museum of Modern Art in New York. The immediate impetus for these remarks was a traveling exhibition on "Realism and Symbolism in Scandinavian Painting, 1880–1910" then touring the United States, but it was Hammershøi in particular whom Varnedoe singled out, in language very like that applied to Vermeer earlier in the century, as "presciently modern."[83] Fifteen years later, a solo exhibition of the painter's work traveled to another venue of modern art, the Solomon R. Guggenheim Museum in New York. Writing in the catalogue for that show, one of the museum's curators, Robert Rosenblum, also associated Hammershøi with the symbolists, among other painters at the time, while identifying him as a forerunner of more recent developments in twentieth-century art, from the abstractions of Piet Mondrian to the paintings of Edward Hopper. In an evocative passage, Rosenblum sought to capture the peculiar effect of Hammershøi's transformation of his predecessors, calling him

> an artist with an uncanny ability to re-create the Dutch realist tradition of immaculate and prosperous domestic interiors in modern spaces so chillingly silent and empty that their lone residents seem to be entombed—as if the women who had once graced the paintings of Jan Vermeer or Pieter de Hooch had become widowed or depressed, never again to leave their four walls.[84]

A more recent piece by the art historian Bridget Alsdorf compares Hammershøi's work to that of the nineteenth-century Danish philosopher and proto-existentialist Søren Kierkegaard, calling the painter's vision of the domestic interior "a profound metaphor for individual subjectivity."[85]

Hammershøi's representational paintings, like those of his North American contemporaries, may have been largely eclipsed by the various forms of abstraction that dominated the art world at mid-century, but such responses suggest a more generous view of what counts as modern: one not wholly distinct, perhaps, from Gerhard Richter's own experiments with representation, which he has conducted even while producing numerous canvases titled simply *Abstraktes Bild*.[86] But there is more continuity in Vermeer's visual afterlife than the history of painting alone might suggest. For at the same time that pictures like those we have been examining were going out of fashion, images that resembled Vermeer's continued to be produced in another medium. And this, too, was a matter of both imitation and assimilation, as some filmmakers consciously modeled their work on his, while others unconsciously assimilated his way of seeing to their own.

The latter process is inevitably diffuse and hard to track. In a wide-ranging study of what she pointedly called "moving pictures," the art historian Anne Hollander traced the development of modern cinema to paintings in the North European tradition, especially their handling of light and their provisional framing of scenes:

> The greatest secret in the engulfing effect of modern cinema is the projection of the film image so that light pours through it onto the screen, and cancels other sources of illumination. In the dark room, the light comes only from the moving picture, so that it alone makes the world. The painters in the Northern tradition often tried for this effect, too, aiming for a jewel-like transparency that made the picture seem to be conducting light.[87]

Unlike their Italian counterparts, Hollander argued, such painters typically minimized the signs of the artist's presence, creating an illusion of unmediated vision that anticipated the cinema by absorbing viewers all the more in an effort to interpret it. By appearing to offer us an arbitrary slice of the visual field rather than a classically arranged composition, they also implicitly invited our eyes to move around within the frame, while simultaneously suggesting that the frame itself might shift at any moment—in this way too, of course, anticipating the moving pictures of cinema.

Hollander's pantheon of "proto-cinematic" painters was by no means limited to the Dutch, let alone to Vermeer: her case extended to work by Velázquez, Chardin, Goya, Turner, and a number of others, including Hammershøi. But it's also not chance, clearly, that Hollander's first example of the kind of art she had in mind was *The Milkmaid*, or that she chose *The Love Letter* (fig. 5.24) for one of her compelling demonstrations of how such artwork could provide templates for the movie camera (fig. 5.25). Her argument was not that filmmakers consciously looked to particular paintings for models, but that the wide circulation of such images, especially through photographs, had accustomed viewers to cinematic ways of seeing even before the cinema itself was invented. Indeed, the very incongruity between the world of Vermeer's pictures and the movies from which Hollander drew her comparison implicitly drove home her point. What connects *The Great Lie* (1941) to a Vermeer painting is neither subject matter nor the tone of the work as a whole, but the emotional effect of a momentary arrangement of bodies in space: an arrangement that paintings like Vermeer's have taught us see as natural.

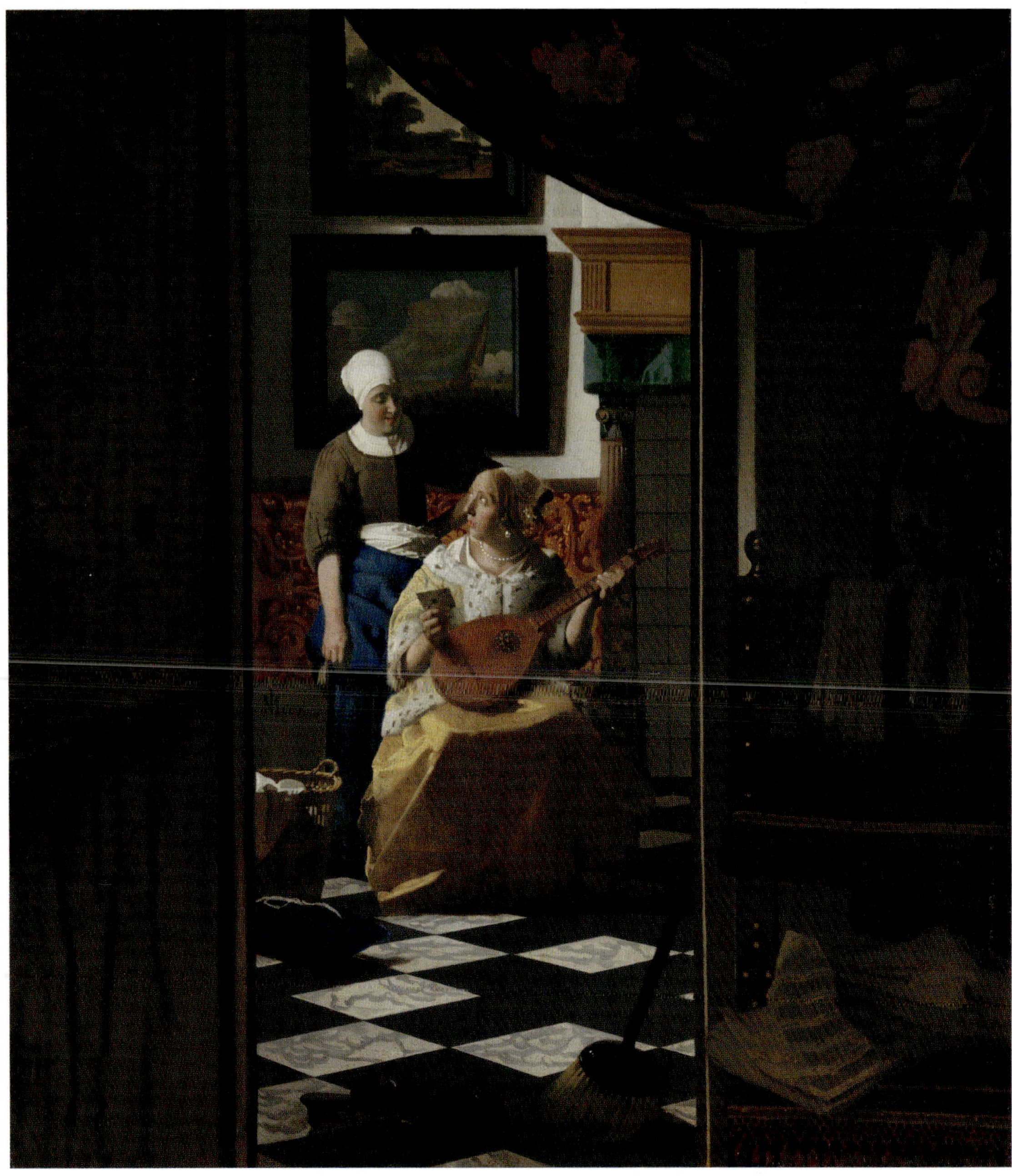

Fig. 5.24. Johannes Vermeer, *The Love Letter* (ca. 1667–70). Oil on canvas. 44 × 38.5 cm. Rijksmuseum, Amsterdam

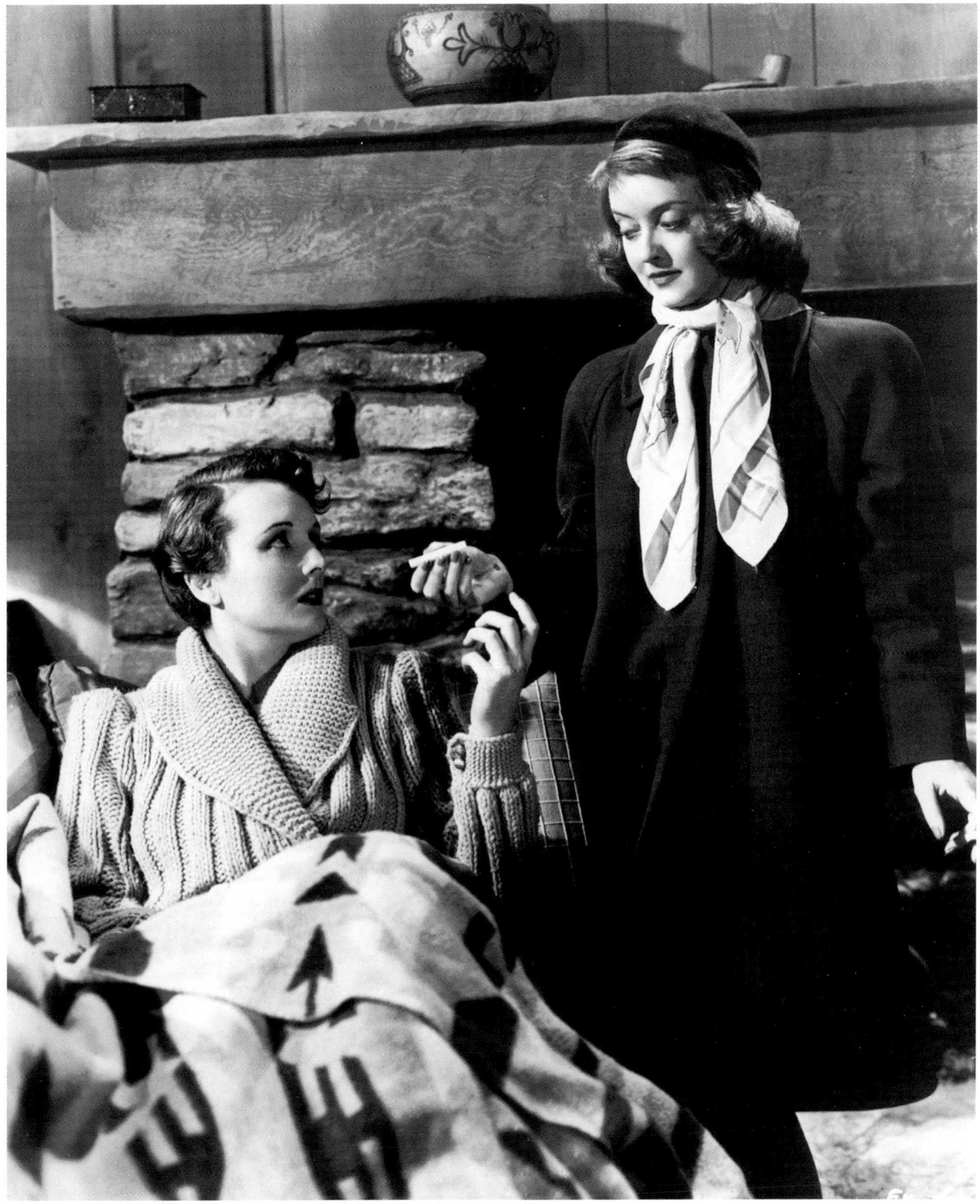

Fig. 5.25. Still from *The Great Lie* (1941), directed by Edmund Goulding (Moviestore Collection Ltd / Alamy Stock Photo). Comparison inspired by Anne Hollander, *Moving Pictures* (Harvard University Press, 1991)

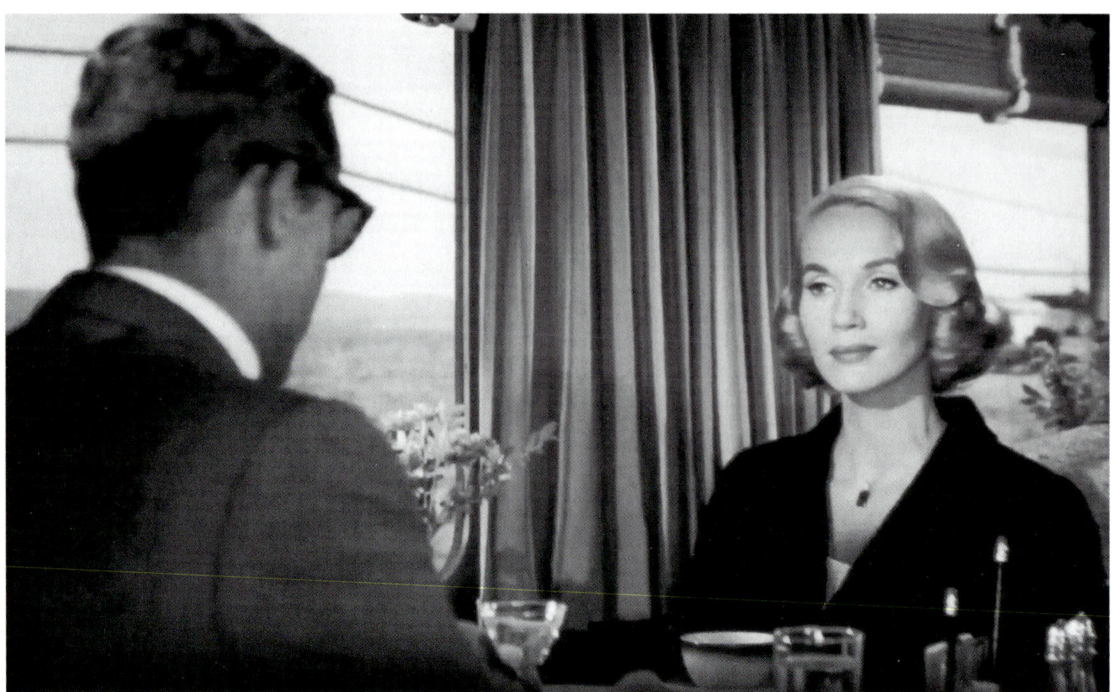

Fig. 5.26. Screenshot from *North by Northwest*, directed and produced by Alfred Hitchcock (Metro-Goldwyn-Mayer, 1959), and Johannes Vermeer, *Officer and Laughing Girl* (ca. 1655–60), Frick Collection, NY. Image © Frick Collection

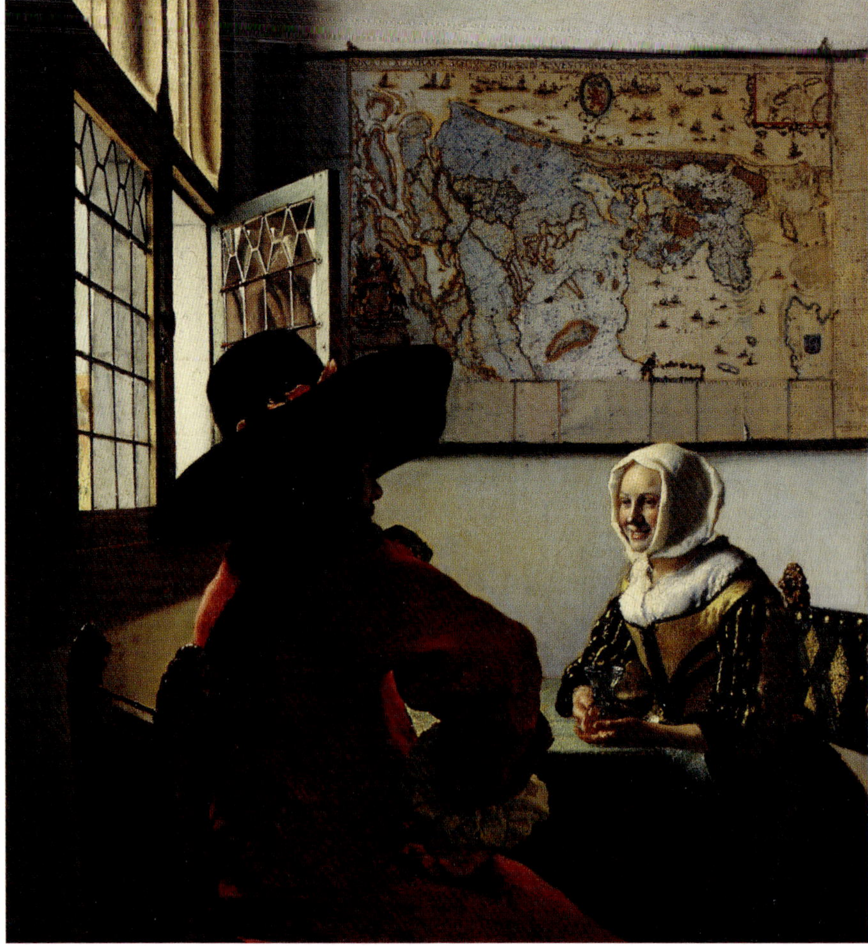

As Hollander herself put it in commenting on the resemblance between an image from *The Man Who Came to Dinner* (1942) and *Officer and Laughing Girl*, one result of "pictorial tradition becoming internalized and naturalized" in this way was that

> a view of a man and woman at a table by a window, facing the woman from behind the man's shoulder, would seem like the most natural, the most effective, the most 'realistic' representational device to use in a movie, chiefly because it would have the support of such mingled generations of illustrative genius behind it—not just current illustrations, but all their great sources.[88]

That particular comparison seems to have been based on a still that didn't make the final cut, but a later shot from Alfred Hitchcock's *North by Northwest* (1959) nicely confirms her point (fig. 5.26).[89] In terms borrowed from Gombrich, quoted at the beginning of this chapter, there is no conscious imitation here, only a family likeness born from generations of picture-making.

Some filmmakers, however, have openly acknowledged Vermeer's paintings as a crucial part of their visual inheritance. It's only to be expected that the cinematographer for the 2003 adaptation of Tracy Chevalier's popular novel about the artist, *Girl with a Pearl Earring* (1999), should have been "obsessed" with Vermeer's use of light,[90] but it's perhaps more surprising that a similar obsession should have governed another film adaptation more than fifty years earlier, whose mise-en-scène was at the farthest remove from a household in seventeenth-century Delft. The man responsible for the look of the filmic *Girl with a Pearl Earring*, Eduardo Serra, is Portuguese, while Jack Cardiff, who won an Oscar for his cinematography in *Black Narcissus* (1947), was British, but when it came to Vermeer, at least, they clearly shared a visual language.

Based on a bestselling novel by Rumer Godden, *Black Narcissus* is a psychological thriller set high in the Indian Himalayas, where a group of Anglican nuns struggle to establish a school and hospital in an abandoned palace formerly occupied by the harem of the local Raja. Between its exotic setting—entirely filmed, as it happens, in England—and its intense, if suppressed, eroticism, *Black Narcissus* is arguably even less Vermeer-like than *The Man Who Came to Dinner* or *The Great Lie*. But according to Cardiff, who drew on a number of painters in the course of his career, it was Vermeer he principally had in mind when he shot the film. As he explained in a late documentary on his work suggestively titled *Painting with Light* (2000), "the light had to be clear and as simple as possible"—a statement that the makers of the documentary immediately illustrated by cutting between a brief scene from the film (fig. 5.27) and an image of *Woman Holding a Balance* (see fig. 3.9).[91]

The comparison works, if only because the religious theme of *Woman Holding a Balance* and the vaguely nun-like headgear of its subject bring the two works of art momentarily into accord. Yet the fact remains that the scene with

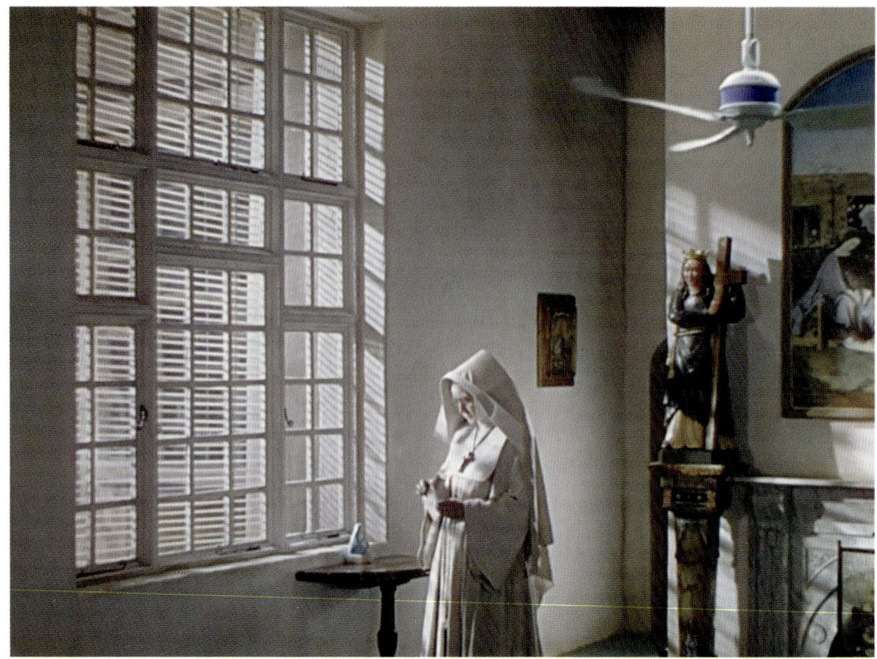

Fig. 5.27. Screenshot from *Black Narcissus*, directed and produced by Michael Powell and Emeric Pressburger, cinematography by Jack Cardiff. The Archers, 1947

which the painting is juxtaposed represents a rare instance in which something like the look of a Vermeer, rather than simply its lighting, figures in *Black Narcissus*. The scene also represents a rare instance when the camera almost holds still long enough to approach the feel of a painted image. "It's easy to say do it like Vermeer," Cardiff himself immediately added after declaring his allegiance to the Dutch artist, "but then people forget that the actors move around."[92] And so, too, as the critic Kent Jones has observed, does the film's camera. "Cardiff may have patterned his lighting after Vermeer," Jones remarks of *Black Narcissus*, "but the breathlessly dynamic pace of the images leaves an altogether different, more unsettled impression in the mind."[93]

Some four decades later, the makers of another thriller also drew on Vermeer to evoke a closed community threatened by violence, but they paid more sustained attention to the stillness of the paintings as well as their lighting. The film in question is Peter Weir's *Witness* (1985), and both the fact that the Amish community on which it focuses is colloquially known as "the Pennsylvania Dutch" and the typical clothing of Amish women doubtless facilitated the association, as the filmmakers implicitly confirmed whenever they posed their white-capped heroine against the "left to right washing in of light" that they deliberately modeled on several Vermeer paintings then on display in Philadelphia (fig. 5.28). For the film as a whole, however, the effect of such images largely depends on their juxtaposition with the fast-paced action that drives the plot: a frenetic sequence that begins when the heroine's young son accidentally witnesses a brutal murder in an urban train station and only concludes after a final shoot-out in which the honorable policeman who has taken

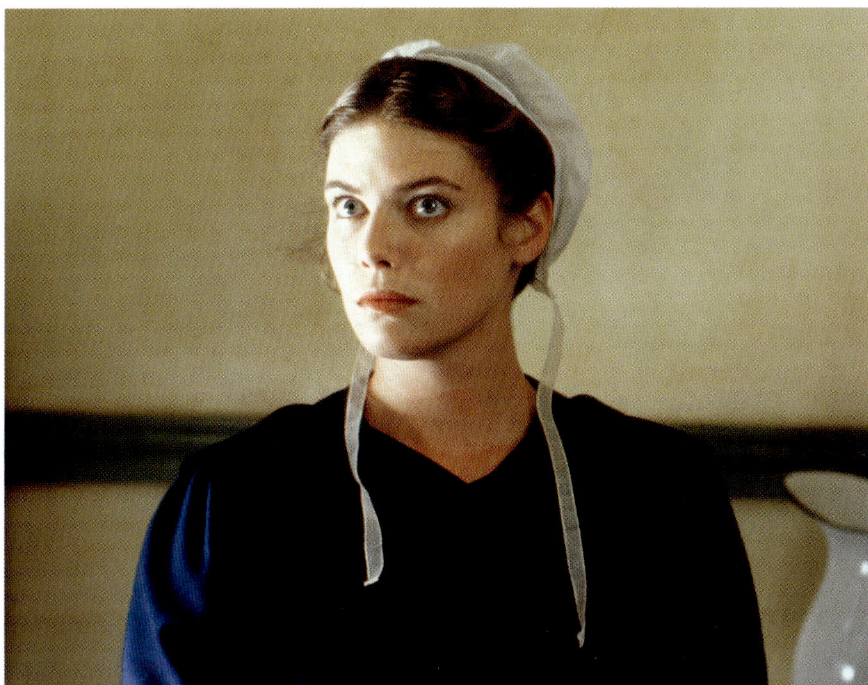

Fig. 5.28. Still from *Witness* (1985), directed by Peter Weir. © Paramount Pictures. All rights reserved

refuge with the family dispatches the corrupt colleagues who have orchestrated the killing. As Weir himself observed in explaining his recourse to Vermeer, "I think you can feel the clock ticking, somehow, more slowly when you look at these paintings."[94]

The motion of motion pictures may be inescapable, but two of the filmmakers most consistently affected by Vermeer's art have found comparable ways to slow it down. The pioneering Danish director Carl Theodor Dreyer (1889–1968) assimilated that art primarily through its afterlife in the work of his countryman Vilhelm Hammershøi, while the late British director Terence Davies (1945–2023) began with a love of Vermeer and seems later on to have discovered Hammershøi as well. But both filmmakers are known for the leisurely pace at which their films unfold, and both, too, are apt to favor what one critic of Davies calls "static, tableau-like compositions."[95] Like the painters from whom they inherit, they also share a tendency to stage those tableaux in domestic interiors, whose rectangular walls, windows, and doors serve to frame and temporarily arrest the human figure. Nearly a century separates Dreyer's first feature film, *Praesidenten* (1919), from Davies's recent biopic of Emily Dickinson, *A Quiet Passion* (2016), but to look at a still from each is to recognize the family resemblance—a resemblance that clearly connects both directors to the extended lineage of the Delft master (figs. 5.29 and 5.30).

The imprint of Hammershøi's art on Dreyer's can be dated quite precisely. We know that in 1916 the filmmaker visited an exhibition in Copenhagen commemorating the painter's death a few months earlier,[96] and that two years

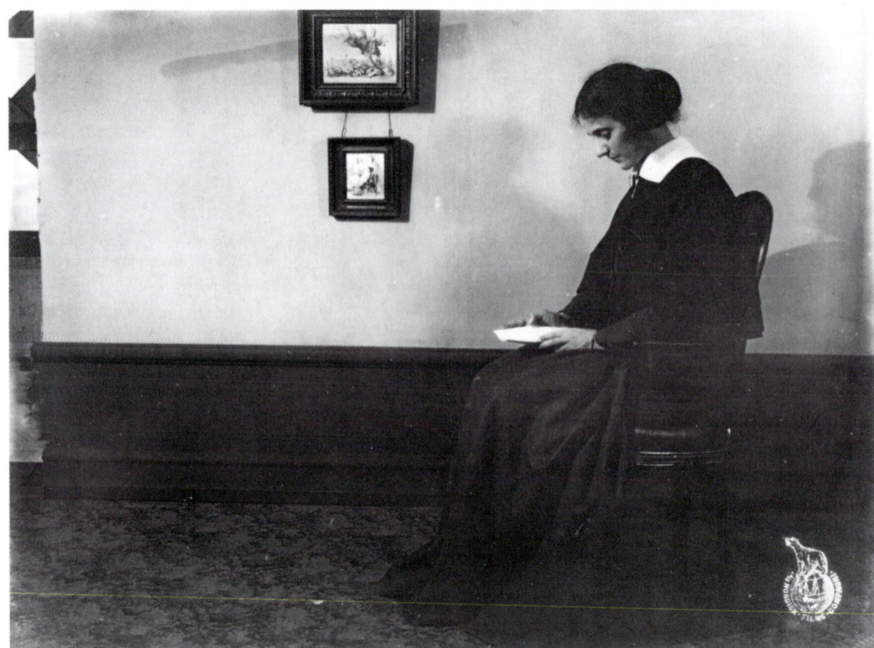

Fig. 5.29. Still from *Praesidenten* (1919), directed by Carl Th. Dreyer. Danish Film Institute / Nordisk Film Production A/S

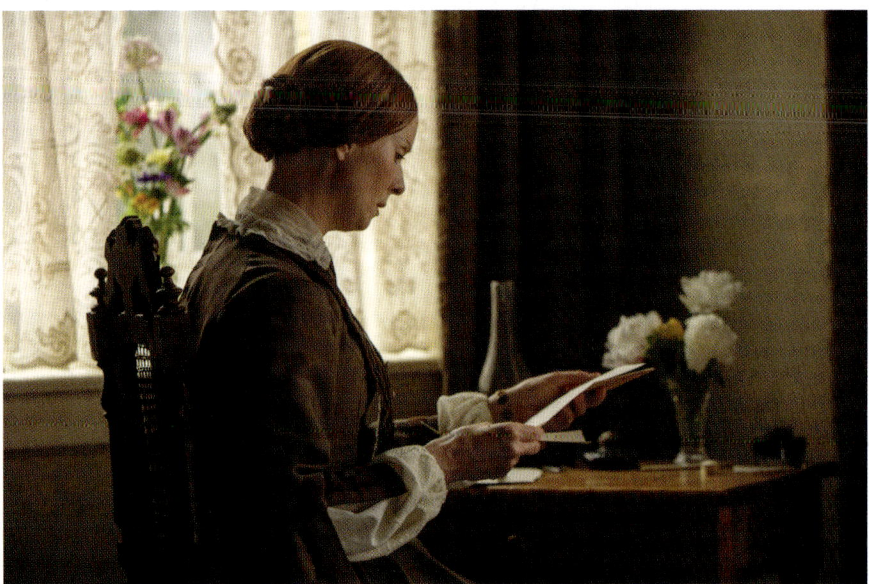

Fig. 5.30. Still from *A Quiet Passion*, directed by Terence Davies. Music Box Films, 2016. Moviestore Collection Ltd / Alamy Stock Photo

before his own death in 1968 he explicitly acknowledged how the look of Hammershøi's still pictures contributed to that of the moving one he began to direct in 1918. "The President's room was built up from very calm walls and very few furnishings," he recalled. "On the walls, a barometer and a few pictures of family groups framed in the black oval frames very commonly used in the old days. For the outfitting of these interiors I was inspired by Vilhelm Hammershøi and to some extent by the American painter James Whistler."[97] There's no evidence that Dreyer was aware of Hammershøi's own admiration for Whistler, which had prompted the Danish painter to travel to London in 1897 in the vain hope of meeting him, though the filmmaker's testimony is one more sign of how Whistler's influence became entangled at the turn of the century with the tradition we have been examining.[98] Nor is there any evidence that Dreyer himself consciously associated his countryman's work with that of Vermeer, though others, of course, have made that association both for Hammershøi and for Dreyer himself. In an extended study of the filmmaker, the theorist David Bordwell, for example, has connected Dreyer's treatment of space to a "chamber tradition" whose "master is undoubtedly Vermeer," while borrowing Gombrich's aphoristic description of the latter's art—"still lifes with human beings"—for Dreyer's as well. "For Dreyer, as for Vermeer and Hammershøi," Bordwell writes, "space is most visible when empty. Neutral white or black walls, stripped bare, act as the ground for patterns that verge on the starkly geometrical." Among the images he uses to illustrate this claim is the still from *Praesidenten* I have already compared to one from Davies's *A Quiet Passion*—another film that belongs, both because of its maker's inclinations and of its subject's, to this chamber tradition.[99]

Just how Davies first discovered the Delft master is not clear, but he was apparently studying reproductions of Vermeer's work, together with Rembrandt's, in preparation for his filmic autobiography *The Long Day Closes* in the early 1990s; and he continued publicly declaring his love in interviews from then on.[100] "I do like to watch someone at a window with the light falling on them," he told the *Chicago Tribune*'s film critic in 2017. "My favorite painter is Vermeer. I could look at Vermeer forever."[101] The immediate occasion of the interview was the American release of *A Quiet Passion*, but the house-bound Dickinson is far from the only Davies subject to be captured in that Vermeerian light. *Sunset Song* (2015) frequently poses its rural Scottish heroine before such a window (fig. 5.31), and so, too—though their urban light is dimmer and more diffused—do *The Long Day Closes* (1992) and *The House of Mirth* (2000).[102] Whether or not it places her before a window, the former's affectionate portrait of Davies's Liverpudlian mother includes several Vermeer-like scenes, in which the camera looks on reverently as she goes about her mundane domestic tasks: a laundry scene that one critic has compared to *The Milkmaid*, for example, or a brief sequence that manages to combine the pleasurable mirror-gazing of *Woman with a Pearl Necklace* with a turban-clad head vaguely reminiscent of *Girl with a Pearl Earring* (fig. 5.32).[103]

Davies's debt to Hammershøi is more subtle than Dreyer's, whose austere settings and melancholic mood make his chamber pieces feel particularly close to those of the Danish painter—as does, for that matter, his consistent refusal of color. (Even Dreyer's last picture, the 1964 *Gertrud*, was filmed in black and white.) But Davies, whose films have their own share of melancholy, seems to have recognized his affinity to this branch of the Vermeer family too. "There's a Danish painter at the end of the 19th and beginning of 20th century called

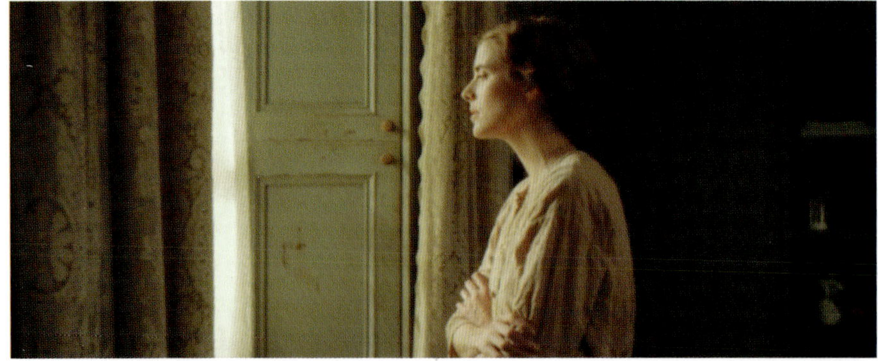

Fig. 5.31. Screenshot from *Sunset Song*, directed by Terence Davies. Iris Productions, Sellout Pictures, and Hurricane Films, 2015

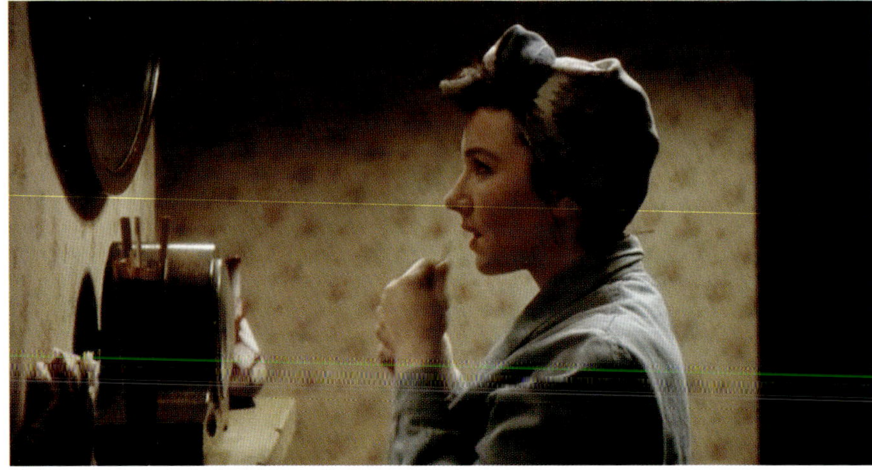

Fig. 5.32. Screenshot from *The Long Day Closes*, directed by Terence Davies. British Film Institute, 1992

Vilhelm Hammershøi, who's like Vermeer but with a kind of northern smudge-light," he told an interviewer in 2016:

> There are open doors or corridors with nobody in them, or if there is someone in them, it's a woman with her back to the viewer. They're wonderful paintings, they're really strange. But it's all about verticals and rectangles. It's almost like Mondrian but it's [. . .] much more [. . .] loveable rather than mathematical.[104]

Davies was responding to a question about the framing of several scenes in *A Quiet Passion*, but what might be called the Hammershøi-effect in his work is visible in *Sunset Song* too, especially when he poses his female figure, as Hammershøi does, with her back to the viewer (fig. 5.33). Not surprisingly, this is a viewpoint that Dreyer occasionally adopts too (fig. 5.34), though Davies characteristically allows more sense of light and air to filter into his painterly interiors.

By Davies's own account, it's with such a scene that *A Quiet Passion* establishes Dickinson's vocation (fig. 5.35). "When she's standing at the window and the light is streaming in," he observed in the interview quoted above,

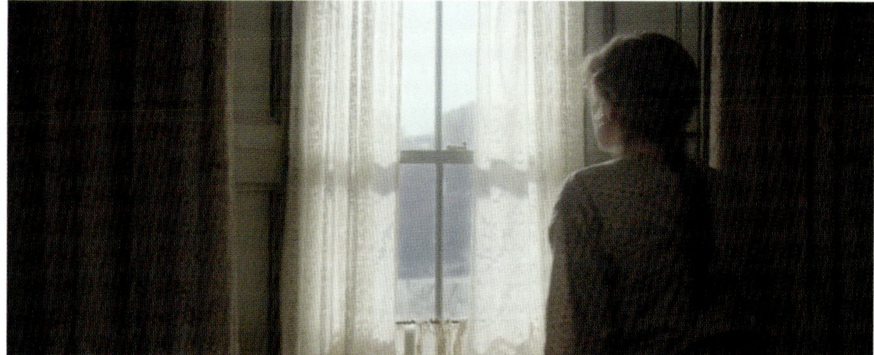

Fig. 5.33. Screenshot from *Sunset Song*, directed by Terence Davies. Iris Productions, Sellout Pictures, and Hurricane Films, 2015

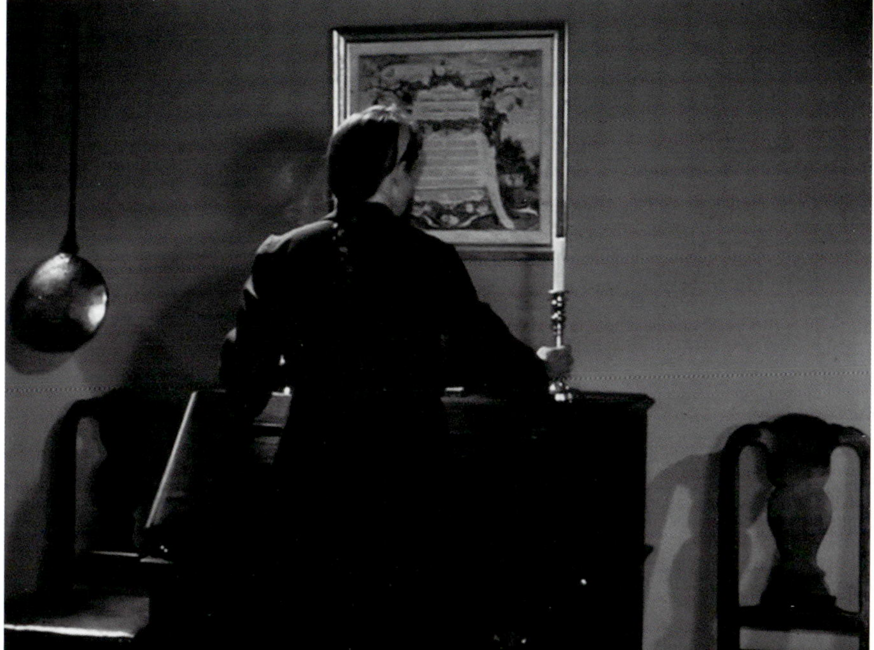

Fig. 5.34. Screenshot from *Ordet*, directed by Carl Th. Dreyer. Palladium Film, 1954

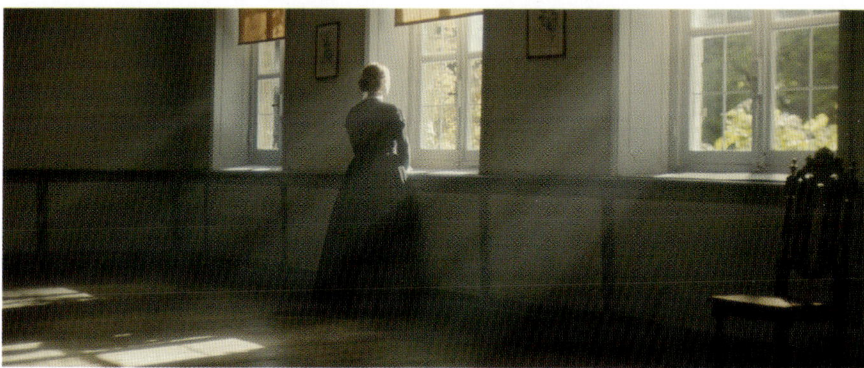

Fig. 5.35. Still from *A Quiet Passion*, directed by Terence Davies. Music Box Films, 2016. Moviestore Collection Ltd. / Alamy Stock Photo

"and most of that was real light, we had it lit but it was the natural light that came through—in that intense moment, it's the first time we know that she's a poet."[105] For Davies, who first fell in love with Dickinson's poetry as an adolescent, and who decades earlier had declared his own commitment to "the poetry of the ordinary," this is clearly one of the film's transcendent moments, its intensity consecrated by that stream of natural light pouring through the window.[106] For those who share his admiration of Vermeer, it also might serve as a vivid reminder of the poetry that others have sensed in the paintings themselves—a poetry, as we shall see, that has itself generated yet more poems in turn.

"The camera does not apprehend objects: it sees them," Gerhard Richter recorded in a notebook early in his career.[107] He was thinking of photography at the time, rather than film, but his point clearly holds for the movie camera too, as Hollander sought to argue when she traced the "unmediated vision" of film to the appearance of a similarly unmediated vision in paintings of the Northern tradition. More specifically, we might also think—as Hollander did—of how Gowing described Vermeer's approach to his art. "Vermeer seems almost not to care, or not even to know, what he is painting," Gowing famously observed. "Nothing concerns him but what is visible, the tone, the wedge of light."[108] If Richter's *Reader* (see fig. 5.1) partly belongs with the other paintings we have examined in this chapter, it also has its place in another branch of the family: one in which Vermeer's canvases generate not only more canvases, but more camerawork. For Richter's portrait of his wife originated not in the painter's direct observation of his model, but in his transformation of a photograph: a photograph that he characteristically chose to treat not as a mere aid to the final version but as a work to be displayed in its own right (fig. 5.36). (Since 1962, Richter has been amassing an encyclopedic collection of photographs, newspaper clippings, and other images, including the photograph for *Reader*, which has been shared with the public both as a multi-volume book called *Atlas* and in various exhibits of the same title, where the images are mounted on panels.)[109] "I use photography to make a painting, just as Rembrandt uses drawing or Vermeer the camera obscura," he wrote in the same notebook, and the evidence suggests that he valued the process precisely because he understood the camera's impersonal vision as liberating.[110] Photography "offered me a new view, free of all the conventional criteria I had always associated with art," he told an interviewer in 1972. "It had no style, no composition, no judgment. It freed me from personal experience. For the first time, there was nothing to it: it was pure picture."[111]

To the degree that Richter openly calls attention to *Reader*'s photographic origins, he can be understood as signaling that a painter, too, can aspire to produce nothing but "pure picture." Yet if he understands himself to share this

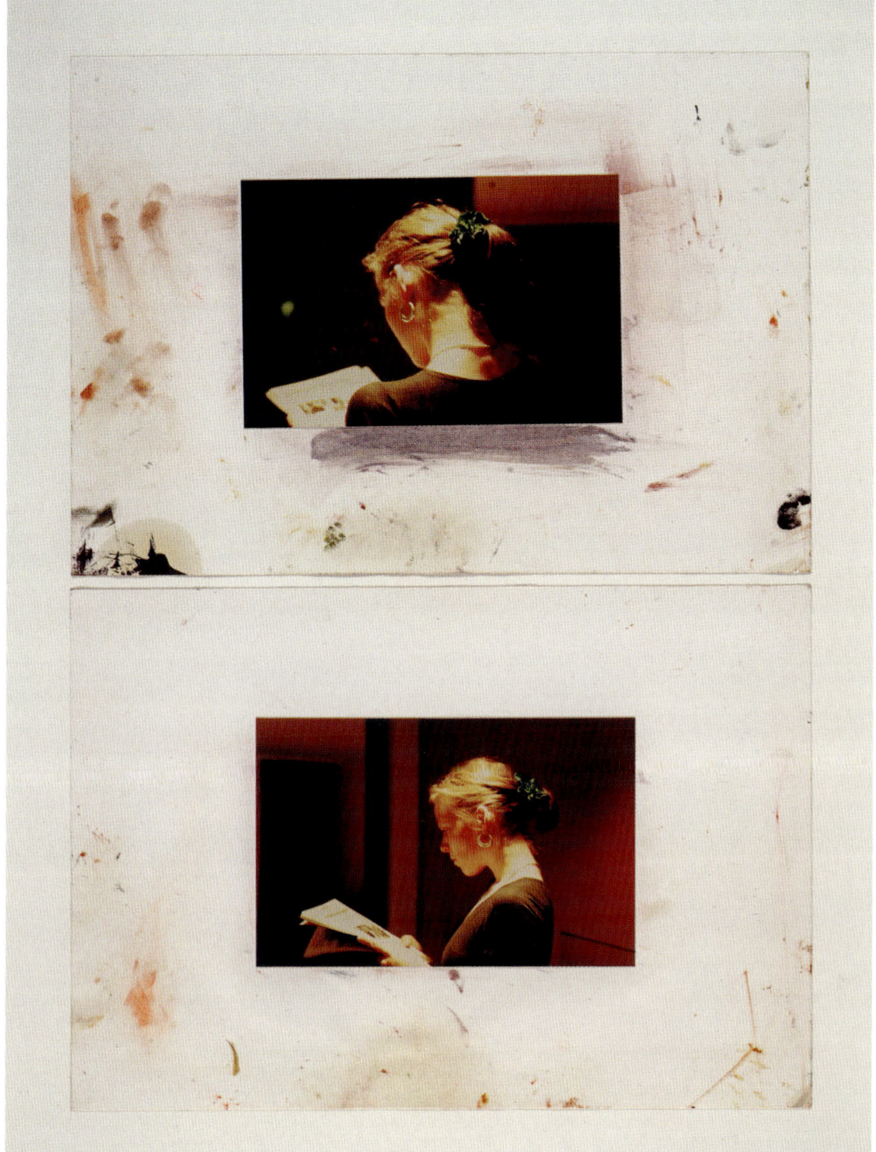

Fig. 5.36. Gerhard Richter, *Sabine* (1993/1995). Atlas Sheet 575. 51.7 × 36.7 cm. Städtische Galerie im Lenbachhaus und Kunstbau, Munich. © Gerhard Richter 2025 (0028)

aspiration with the Delft master, he also knows, of course, that a painter is not a camera—and that Vermeer knew this too. Just as the seventeenth-century artist did not so much replicate what he saw through a camera obscura as gesture toward the instrument's effects, so Richter uses his brush to evoke the effects of a photographic camera, especially its flattening of space and focal blurring. Like his other works in this vein, *Reader* doesn't attempt to pass itself off as a photograph, but only to remind the viewer of its origins.

At the same time, as Darryn Ansted has noted, its "playful, painterly" handling of color corresponds much more closely to the subtleties visible to the human eye than to what the camera can register, as if the modern artist were deliberately paying homage to the medium he shares with his predecessor.[112] Indeed, *Reader* is relatively unusual among Richter's works in appearing to forego what many have taken to be a fundamental skepticism about the possibilities still open to the art of painting. To an interviewer's suggestion that "you have always based your painting on negation, on refusal, and on criticism," Richter immediately cordoned off this exception. "I don't know," he responded. "My *Woman Reading* is not like that."[113] Speaking of the same work a few years earlier, he had offered a possible explanation for that difference, while attributing the motive not to himself, but to his subject: "She is so taken by Vermeer, the artist-god," he explained, "that she tries to represent a similar beauty."[114]

6

Forgery

To Netherlanders who know their Vermeer, it had as much novelty as if it were dated 1938, for a year ago it was not known to exist.

—TIME (1938)

In the autumn of 1937, the eminent Dutch art historian Abraham Bredius announced a momentous discovery: not only had he just identified a new Vermeer, but it was probably the greatest that the artist had ever painted (fig. 6.1). Reporting the find in the pages of *The Burlington Magazine*, he could barely contain his enthusiasm. "It is a wonderful moment in the life of a lover of art when he finds himself suddenly confronted with a hitherto unknown painting by a great master, untouched, on the original canvas, just as it left the painter's studio!" he began excitedly:

> And what a picture! Neither the beautiful signature "I. V. Meer" (I.V.M. in monogram) nor the *pointillé* on the bread which Christ is blessing, is necessary to convince us that we have here a—I am inclined to say—*the* masterpiece of Johannes Vermeer of Delft, and, moreover, one of his largest works (1.29 m. by 1.17 m.), quite different from all his other paintings and yet every inch a Vermeer. The subject is *Christ and the Disciples at Emmaus* and the colours are magnificent—and characteristic: Christ in a splendid blue; the disciple on the left, whose face is barely visible, in a fine grey; the other disciple on the left in yellow—the yellow of the famous Vermeer at Dresden, but subdued so that it remains in perfect harmony with the other colours. The servant is clad in dark brown and dark grey; her expression is

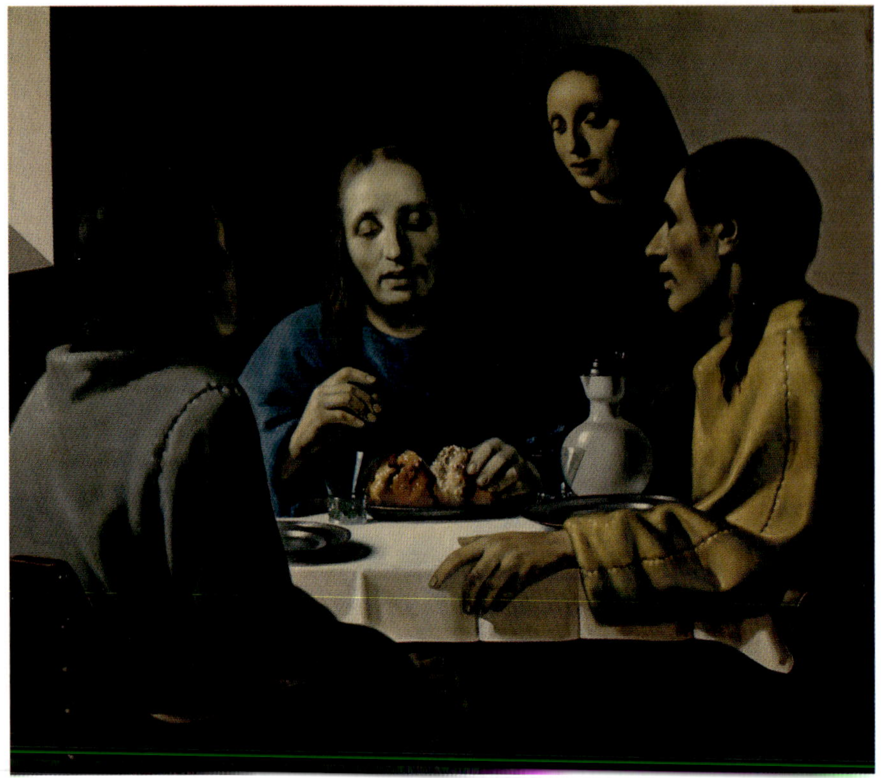

Fig. 6.1. Han van Meegeren, *Supper at Emmaus* (1937). Oil on canvas. 130.5 × 118 cm. Collection Museum Boijmans van Beuningen, Rotterdam. Loan Stichting Museum Boijmans van Beuningen. Photography: Studio Tromp

> wonderful. Expression, indeed, is the most marvellous quality of this unique picture. Outstanding is the head of Christ, serene and sad, as He thinks of all the suffering which He, the Son of God, had to pass through in His life on earth, yet full of goodness [. . .]. Jesus is just about to break the bread at that moment when, as related in the New Testament, the eyes of the Disciples were opened and they recognized Christ risen from the dead and seated before them. The Disciple on the left seen in profile shows his silent adoration, mingled with astonishment, as he stares at Christ.
>
> In no other picture by the great Master of Delft do we find such sentiment, such a profound understanding of the Bible story—a sentiment so nobly human expressed through the medium of the highest art.[1]

Bredius may have been eighty-two at the time—even, by some accounts, "half-blind"[2]—but he had been a formidable presence in the Dutch art world, and his word still registered, especially where Vermeer was concerned.[3] Indeed, spotting work "quite different from all his other paintings yet every inch a Vermeer" had become something of a personal speciality: as the former director of the Mauritshuis, he'd not only been the first to identify the *Allegory of the Catholic Faith* with the Delft master but had been directly involved in the authentication of *Diana and Her Companions* and *Christ in the House of Martha and Mary* as well.[4] Though he'd initially been inclined to explain the style of the

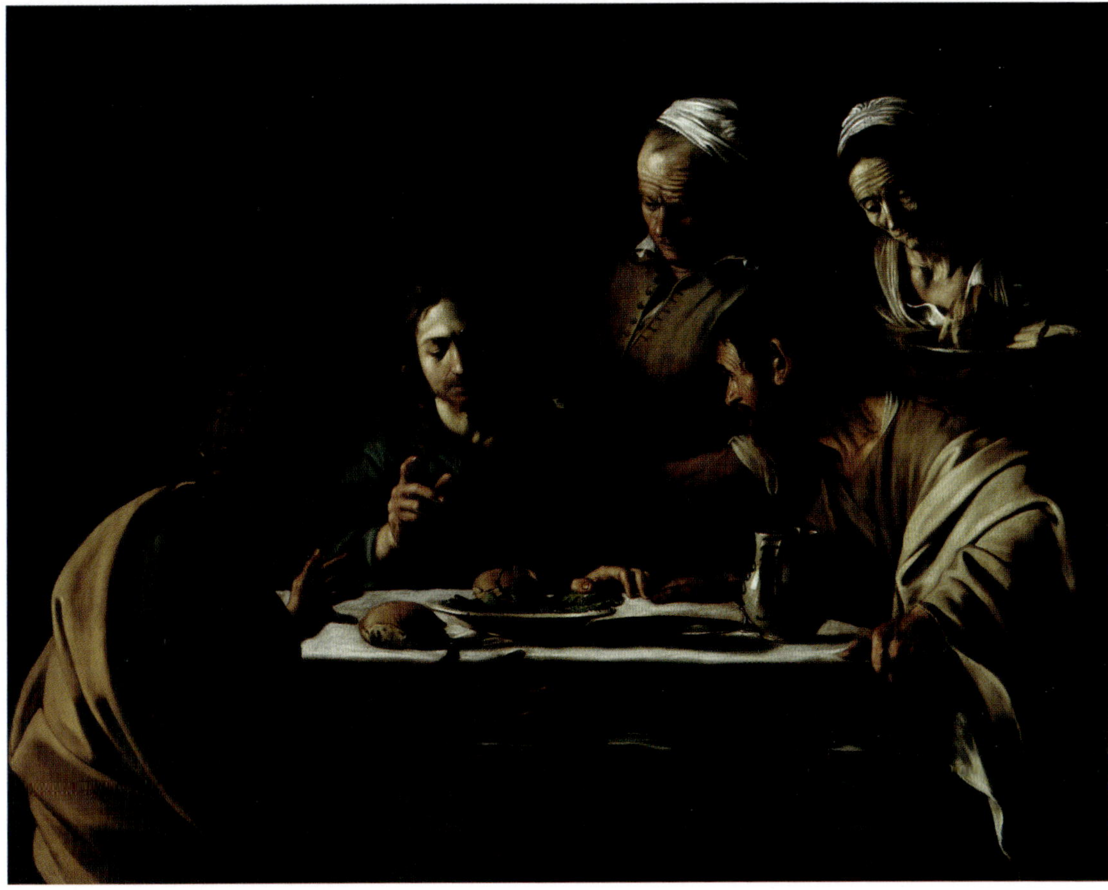

Fig. 6.2. Caravaggio, *Supper at Emmaus* (1606). Oil on canvas. 141 × 175 cm. Pinacoteca di Brera, Milan. © Pinacoteca di Brera, Milan / With permission of the Italian Ministry of Culture / Bridgeman Images

latter two works by attributing them to Van der Meer of Utrecht, Bredius had long since come round to a belief that the Delft artist had also been exposed to Italian influences and that he'd begun his career with these large-scale history paintings before turning to the more intimate—and marketable—art of genre. Both the style and the subject matter of the new picture clearly fit the pattern, as Bredius implicitly confirmed when he dated it to Vermeer's "earlier phase—about the same time (perhaps a little later) as the well-known *Christ in the House of Martha and Mary*"; and after some initial hesitation in this case too, he managed to convince himself that the *Supper at Emmaus* was not just another youthful experiment, but the artist's masterwork.[5]

"I am in an almost overstrained state, in 'ecstasy,'" Bredius had written to his young colleague Dirk Hannema on first seeing what he called this "most important" and "most beautiful" of Vermeer's paintings a few months before going public with his announcement. It was a report that the ambitious director of the Museum Boijmans in Rotterdam was all the more eager to hear because he had already staged a major exhibition on Vermeer—the first ever devoted to him—intended to showcase the Italianate origins of his art.[6] The new painting, evidently inspired by Caravaggio's treatment of the same subject (fig. 6.2), would not only help confirm the argument but provide the museum with its first work by one of the nation's most celebrated artists. By the following summer, Hannema had not only managed to acquire the painting for the Boijmans, but made it the highlight of another big exhibition, this one designed to show off four centuries of masterpieces from Dutch collections. Displayed against a gold leather wall that had been specially erected in a corner of the gallery, the recently discovered *Emmaus* was "the greatest attraction of all," a writer for *Time* reported. "To Netherlanders who know their Vermeer," the writer added, "it had as much novelty as if it were dated 1938, for a year ago it was not known to exist."[7]

There was no date on the canvas—the artist had relied on others to place it chronologically—but *Time*'s hypothetical wasn't far off. The new *Supper at Emmaus* had in fact been painted in 1936–37, and it was, of course, a forgery: the work of a Dutch artist named Han van Meegeren, who resented the lack of enthusiasm with which paintings shown under his own name had been received, and who would go on to produce five more biblical "Vermeers," before he sought to escape other charges by dramatically confessing to his actual crimes at the end of the Second World War. The head of the commission who investigated his case called him "indisputably the greatest forger of all times," and the *Supper at Emmaus* is by general agreement his greatest achievement, even if in retrospect it can be hard to understand why so many sophisticated observers failed to see what an agent for the British art dealer Joseph Duveen immediately recognized when the painting was shown to him in 1937.[8] The telegram he sent to the firm's New York office is partly in code, but there's no mistaking the bottom line: the picture, it reported, was a "ROTTEN FAKE."[9]

Obviously fraudulent as it may now appear, the *Supper at Emmaus* still has a place in Vermeer's afterlife—not just because it is evidence of his reception history, but because it was purposely designed in response to that history. Though Hannema would dismiss those who initially doubted its authenticity by protesting that "the picture speaks for itself," that is precisely, as we shall see, what the picture did not do, having been inspired as much by the scholars who had been studying Vermeer's art—Hannema very much included—as by the art it sought to emulate.[10] Indeed, as Van Meegeren himself surely knew, there were more straightforward ways of forging a Vermeer. For if the *Supper at Emmaus* was by far the most successful of his attempts to pass himself off as the Delft master, it was by no means the first, and a look at those earlier pictures, as well as others whose authorship remains unsettled to this day, may help to clarify what people expected to see—or what forgers thought they expected—when a new "Vermeer" suddenly appeared on the market.

Consider two paintings that the National Gallery of Art in Washington now confines to storage, but which once belonged to the wealthy banker and art collector Andrew Mellon, who had acquired them in the 1920s on the advice of Duveen—the very same dealer, ironically, whose agent would later dismiss the *Emmaus* as a fraud. Unlike the latter, these are small pictures—*The Lacemaker* (fig. 6.3) is precisely the size of the *Study of a Young Woman* in New York, and *The Smiling Girl* (fig. 6.4) somewhat smaller—whose subjects would have seemed immediately familiar to anyone at all acquainted with the master's work.

The Lacemaker, of course, most obviously recalls the painting of the same subject in the Louvre, while *The Smiling Girl* appears to be a variation on the *Girl with a Pearl Earring*, though both also borrow from the *Girl with a Wine Glass* (see fig. 1.7), with the *Lacemaker* adopting her pose and *The Smiling Girl* her expression. Equally to the point, both paintings recycle elements from these and other pictures designed to make us recognize them, to quote Proust again, as "fragments of the same world"[11]: the pearl-drop earrings and yellow jackets worn by both figures; *The Smiling Girl*'s headdress, which loosely evokes both the *Girl with a Pearl Earring* and the *Study of a Young Woman* (see fig. 1.3); *The Lacemaker*'s blue and red cushion; even the latter's metal basin, incongruously lifted not from her fellow lacemaker, who would have had no use for it, but from the *Young Woman with a Water Pitcher* (see fig. 3.8).[12] Welcoming the new *Lacemaker* in an article for the *Gazette des beaux-arts* in 1927, one commentator innocently pointed the moral. "There is not a detail of this painting whose equivalent couldn't easily be found in the other works of Vermeer," Seymour de Ricci remarked—a sign which he took, needless to say, as confirmation of its authenticity.[13]

In a piece on *The Smiling Girl* published the following year, the art historian Wilhelm Valentiner offered a more nuanced take on the phenomenon, even as he ended up in more or less the same place. "To hear almost every year of a newly discovered Vermeer may cause suspicion," he began. "And indeed we can be sure that

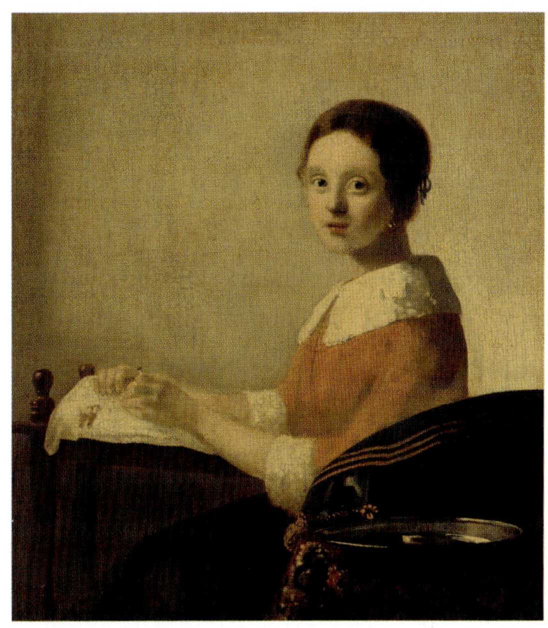

Fig. 6.3. Imitator of Johannes Vermeer, *The Lacemaker* (ca. 1925). Oil on canvas. 44.5 × 40 cm. Andrew W. Mellon Collection, National Gallery of Art, Washington, DC

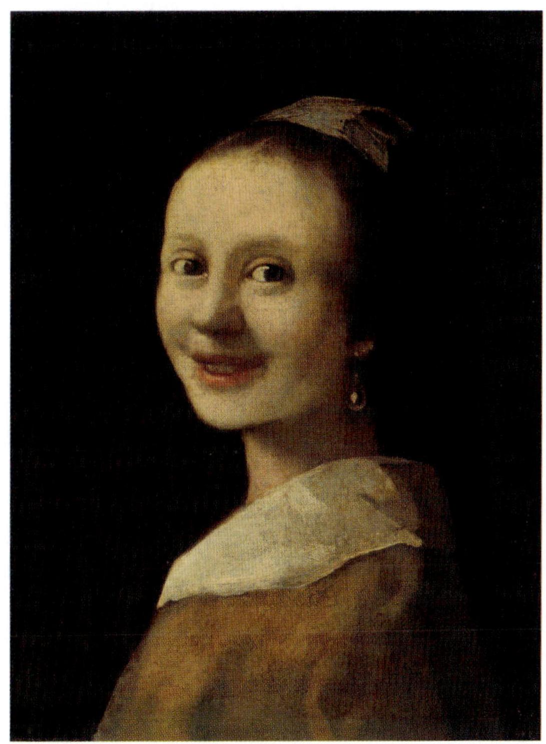

Fig. 6.4. Imitator of Johannes Vermeer, *The Smiling Girl* (ca. 1925). Oil on canvas. 40 × 31.8 cm. Andrew W. Mellon Collection, National Gallery of Art, Washington, DC

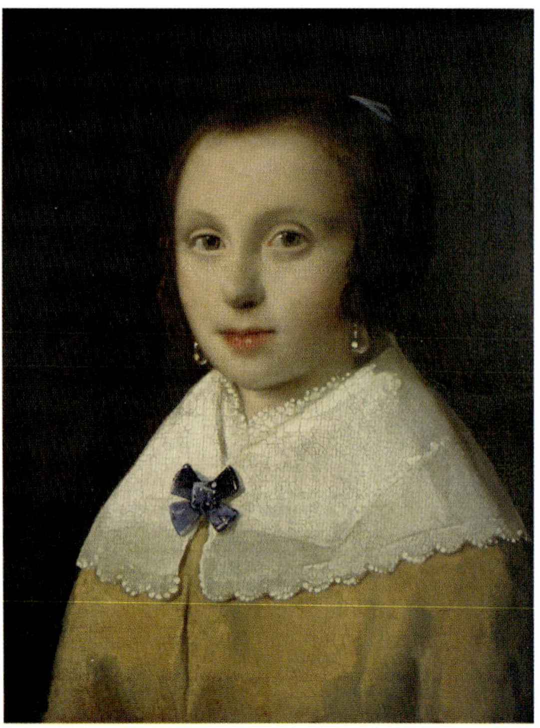

Fig. 6.5. The Hyde Collection source: Henricus Antonium (Han) van Meegeren (Dutch 1889–1947), *Girl with Blue Bow* (ca. 1924). Gelatin-glue medium and pigment over an obscured seventeenth-century painting fragment. 32.7 × 25.1 cm. The Hyde Collection Trust, 1952, 1971.56

in the endeavor to discover unknown works by this rare master in recent times, paintings have often been associated with his name which cannot stand serious criticism." The problem as he saw it, however, was not that such paintings looked too obviously like the rest of the oeuvre, but that they bore only "a faint resemblance either to the subject, composition, or technique of the master." In fact, Valentiner contended, these characteristics varied so little from painting to painting that "after one knows a few works by the master the others are much more easily recognized than is the case with almost any other great artist of the past." Vermeer, he continued, "used a very small number of models, and repeated certain details like costumes, curtains, pillows, windows, mantelpieces, and even the paintings hanging on the wall so often that newly discovered works by him frequently seem like puzzle pictures composed of pieces taken from different groupings in known paintings by him."[14] Like de Ricci, Valentiner failed to grasp that the very patterns he saw as reliable signs of the master's hand could just as easily be taken as blueprints for forgery.

Just who followed the blueprint in the case of these pictures is not entirely clear, though they came under suspicion almost as soon as they arrived at the National Gallery of Art in 1937, and their status as twentieth-century forgeries has been established ever since the museum subjected them to technical analysis in the 1960s. Made with pigments unavailable in Vermeer's time that have been mixed with a glue-like emulsion in order to imitate old paint's resistance to solvents, they also display *craquelure* patterns that correspond only in part to those that ordinarily appear as a painting ages. (Though the forger took care to work with previously used canvases so as to display their old cracks, the rapid-drying glue medium fractures differently.) Both canvases have been deliberately "retouched" in areas that actually incurred no damage in order to further the illusion of aging: one circumstance among several that have led scholars to suspect the hand of a shady picture restorer named Theo van Wijngaarden, who lived and worked in The Hague in the 1920s.[15] The fact that Van Wijngaarden in turn is known to have consorted with Van Meegeren may help to explain how the latter learned many of the same tricks, though at least one of his recent biographers thinks that both forgeries should be attributed to Van Meegeren himself.[16] If so, yet another fake "Vermeer" of the period, the so-called *Girl with Blue Bow* (fig. 6.5), should also be regarded as an early Van Meegeren, since the evidence points to the same hand behind all three pictures.[17] Unsurprisingly, however, this stiff portrait proved harder to pass off as the real thing: Wilhelm von Bode, the former director of the royal museums in Berlin and a specialist in seventeenth-century painting, declined to certify it, though he would go on to authenticate both *The Smiling Girl* and *The Lacemaker*, calling the former "a characteristic, fairly early work of the Delft Master Vermeer."[18]

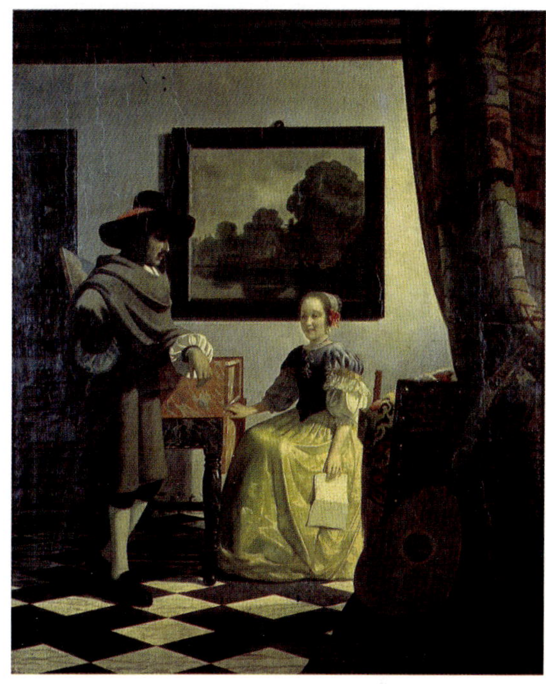

Fig. 6.6. Han van Meegeren (?), *Lady and Gentleman at a Spinet* (ca. 1932). Oil on canvas. 65 × 53 cm. Netherlands Institute for Cultural Heritage, Amersfoort/Amsterdam/Rijswijk

But the history of such verdicts abounds in ironies, and Bode was far from the only expert whose eye for fakes would prove so unfortunately selective. One of the few scholars to buck the initial consensus on *The Smiling Girl* was Abraham Bredius, who wrote dismissively of a "Vermeerish laughing girl [. . .] inspired by the famous girl in the Hague gallery" among the numerous forgeries that had lately been brought to his attention, even as he publicized a new discovery of his own. This was five years before he broke the news about the *Supper at Emmaus*, and the Vermeer he was now proclaiming "one of the finest gems of the master's oeuvre" was not a history painting but a more characteristic genre piece: a work that in retrospect conforms perfectly to the formula for a "puzzle picture" that Valentiner had laid out several years earlier.[19] The painting, which Bredius called *A Conversation Piece*, is now generally known as *Lady and Gentleman at a Spinet* (fig. 6.6), and in the course of describing it, he effectively put the pieces of the puzzle together—remarking on "the true Vermeer lemon colour" of the woman's dress and her telltale pearl earrings, for example, or noting how the curtain on the left was "the same" as the one in the *Allegory of the Catholic Faith* and *The Art of Painting*, while the musical instrument on which the young man was leaning also appeared in one of the Vermeers at the National Gallery in London.[20] It's hard to imagine that the eagerness with which Bredius spotted the curtain from the *Allegory* (see fig. 3.12), whose discovery had once helped make his reputation, was lost on those who had chosen to submit another such curtain for his inspection.[21]

Unlike *The Smiling Girl* and *The Lacemaker*, which won the approval of more than one scholar before being definitively identified as forgeries, this new "Vermeer" was largely ignored by Bredius's fellow specialists, and its creator has never been definitively established. But if Van Meegeren had a hand in it—and there is circumstantial evidence that points in his direction—then he may have learned a valuable lesson both from Bredius's gullibility and from the ultimate

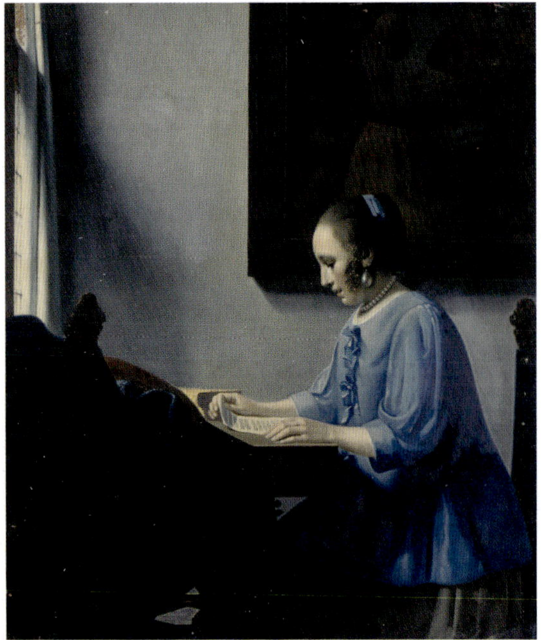

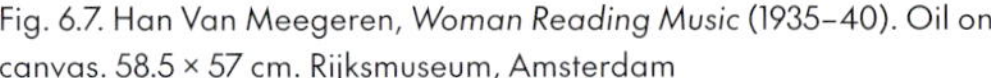

Fig. 6.7. Han Van Meegeren, *Woman Reading Music* (1935–40). Oil on canvas. 58.5 × 57 cm. Rijksmuseum, Amsterdam

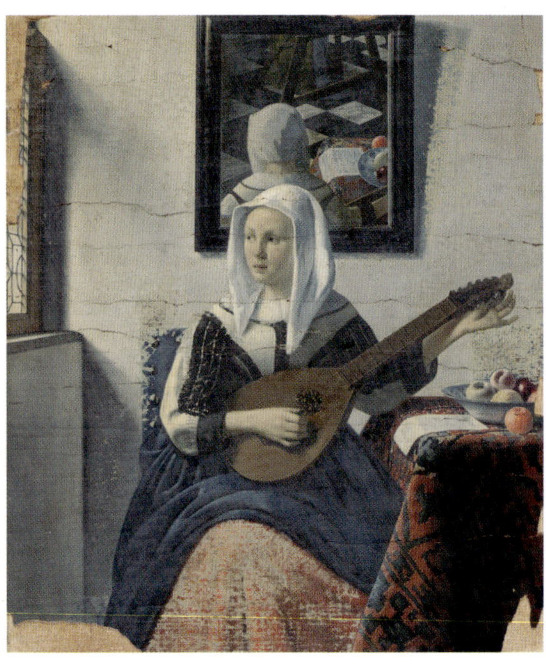

Fig. 6.8. Han van Meegeren, *Woman Playing a Cittern* (1930–40). Oil on canvas. 58 × 47 cm. Rijksmuseum, Amsterdam

failure of the attempt.[22] The type of forgery for which Van Meegeren would later become notorious was also aimed at the presuppositions of the scholars, but it relied on a more subtle form of pastiche: one that flattered the experts precisely by not looking like such an obvious patchwork of other paintings.

Before turning to that project, however, he apparently practiced the art of forging Vermeer by drawing on some of the master's most familiar images. While the *Lady and Gentleman at a Spinet* has never been conclusively traced to his hand, there is no question that *Woman Reading Music* (fig. 6.7) and *Woman Playing a Cittern* (fig. 6.8) are genuine "Vermeergerens," to adopt the term coined by a witty reporter at his trial.[23] Both paintings were found in Van Meegeren's studio in Nice when the police raided it after his arrest in 1947, and both were made using the same techniques that he would soon adopt for the *Supper at Emmaus*.[24] The debt of *Woman Reading Music* to *Woman in Blue Reading a Letter* (see fig. 2.4) is particularly evident, though the position of the figure's hands seems to have been taken from *A Lady Writing* (see fig. 5.16), while the window and the dark form of the chair to the left recall the analogous objects in the *Young Woman with a Lute* (see fig. 1.18). The latter painting is among the obvious inspirations for *Woman Playing a Cittern*, as is the *Guitar Player* (see fig. 2.7), though Van Meegeren has given his performer the head covering of the *Young Woman with a Water Pitcher* (see fig. 3.8) or the *Woman Holding a Balance* (see fig. 3.9), adopted the angle on the window from *Girl Interrupted at Her Music* (see fig. 3.6), and hung a close variation on the mirror from the *Music*

Lesson on the rear wall, its surface still reflecting the floor tiles and artist's easel of the original (see fig. 3.10).

Interestingly, technical analysis of the *Woman Reading Music* suggests that the forger sought to make some of these echoes less blatant: an X-ray shows that the woman's jacket was once trimmed with fur and there are traces of yellow paint, as if he were attempting to deflect from the picture's obvious debt to the *Woman in Blue* by giving his woman the costume worn in later Vermeers such as *A Lady Writing* (see fig. 5.16) or *Mistress and Maid* (see fig. 1.16), only to abandon the effort when he realized that he couldn't match the original yellow. (Though he was relying on the latest research, the problem arose from a misunderstanding of the pigment's chemical composition that was not corrected until after the Second World War.)[25] It's possible that Van Meegeren once intended to market these pictures and they were simply left behind in France when he and his wife were trapped in Amsterdam at the outbreak of the war, but it's more likely that he viewed them, at least retrospectively, as a kind of experiment: a means both of perfecting his technique and of reminding himself of the risks involved in trying to imitate Vermeer's most beloved pictures too closely.[26] As we shall see, one of Van Meegeren's most important breakthroughs as a forger was a chemical discovery that he was already testing on these canvases, even while he was evidently concluding that there were better ways of putting that discovery to use. The *Supper at Emmaus* and the paintings that followed might also be characterized as puzzle pictures, but less because they reassembled the familiar fragments of Vermeer's world than because they appeared to fill the gaps in a current art historical narrative. In a piece otherwise devoted to the material tricks of Van Meegeren's trade, Arie Wallert and Michel van de Laar shrewdly drive home the point: "The forger had to be able to paint well, but he also had to be able to read at least as well."[27]

Among the books Van Meegeren clearly read was not only the scientific treatise that seems to have led him astray where Vermeer's yellow was concerned, but a study of seventeenth-century Netherlandish painting co-authored by Hannema and the future director of the Rijksmuseum, A.F.E. van Schendel, in which the "non-Dutch" character of the artist's early work received considerable emphasis.[28] Published in 1936, a year after Hannema's exhibition at the Boijmans showcased the same argument, the book was representative of a moment when the "modern" Vermeer so celebrated at the turn of the century was beginning to give way to a more historically situated figure, especially, of course, among the very experts whose judgment would be called upon to authenticate any new discoveries. For such commentators, the appearance of *Christ in the House of Martha and Mary* in 1901, combined with the reattribution of the *Diana and Her Companions* formerly ascribed to Nicholas Maes, only deepened the mysteries surrounding the Delft artist. How had he made the transition from such pictures to one like *The Milkmaid*, a painting generally thought to be among the earliest of his representations of ordinary life? After

Christ in the House of Martha and Mary turned up at a London dealer's in 1901, scholars began to speculate that Vermeer had traveled to Italy early in his career, where he came under the influence of Caravaggio, and that more religious paintings from this period would come to light. The exhibition at the Boijmans had in fact offered a candidate for such a missing link in the form of a recently discovered *Mary Magdalene at the Foot of the Cross* that Hannema's catalogue proudly "attributed here, for the first time, to Vermeer," but which was swiftly reassigned to the French Caravaggist Nicolas Tournier after the exhibition closed.[29] Two months later, a Dutch critic named Pieter Koomen continued to speculate about the Caravaggio connection, even as he anticipated the possibility that the gaps in the record might soon be filled. "Perhaps tomorrow we will discover a thus far unknown painting, and next year another one," he wrote hopefully, "which will convincingly show this influence."[30]

It's unlikely that Van Meegeren took his marching orders directly from Koomen, since he seems to have begun work on the *Emmaus* a month or two before the article appeared, but the coincidence of the critic's prediction with the forger's project is still significant.[31] The art world had primed itself for finding not just one missing link, but a chain, and it is just such a chain, each link dependent on those that preceded it, that Van Meegeren would go on to supply. By the time the last of these, *The Footwashing* (fig. 6.9), was acquired by the Dutch state in 1943, even the experts who advised the purchase didn't like it very much, though most of them still believed the painting was a Vermeer. The one serious holdout was a curator named Willy Auping, who called it "a recent forgery" and wrote a scathing account of its flaws in his diary, comparing it, among other things, to a poster for a film or "a piece out of the front wall of a shooting gallery." But like his colleagues, ironically, he was judging the painting according to the standard set by the *Supper at Emmaus*. "A series of photographs ought to be taken and details from both paintings (the Supper at Emmaus and this trash) should be reproduced side by side," he wrote indignantly, "and then every layman would be in no doubt as to the verdict."[32]

Today, it is tempting to add, "every layman" would have no doubt about the fraudulence of the *Emmaus* as well, though virtually everyone agrees that the painting is far and away the strongest of Van Meegeren's forgeries. At the time, however, Duveen's initial disbelief was quickly submerged in the collective enthusiasm, and scholarly excitement about finding another picture from Vermeer's Italianate period was only heightened by the picture's subject: the moment just before the risen Christ reveals himself to his disciples. "Van Meegeren began his biblical series, fittingly, by painting a picture about a miraculous reappearance," Jonathan Lopez has quipped, but the appeal of the painting to the forger's contemporaries transcended even that satisfying conjunction.[33] Despite Vermeer's rising reputation, there were still many art lovers for whom his characteristic genre paintings lacked the emotional seriousness of his great compatriot Rembrandt, but now a work had surfaced that promised to fill that

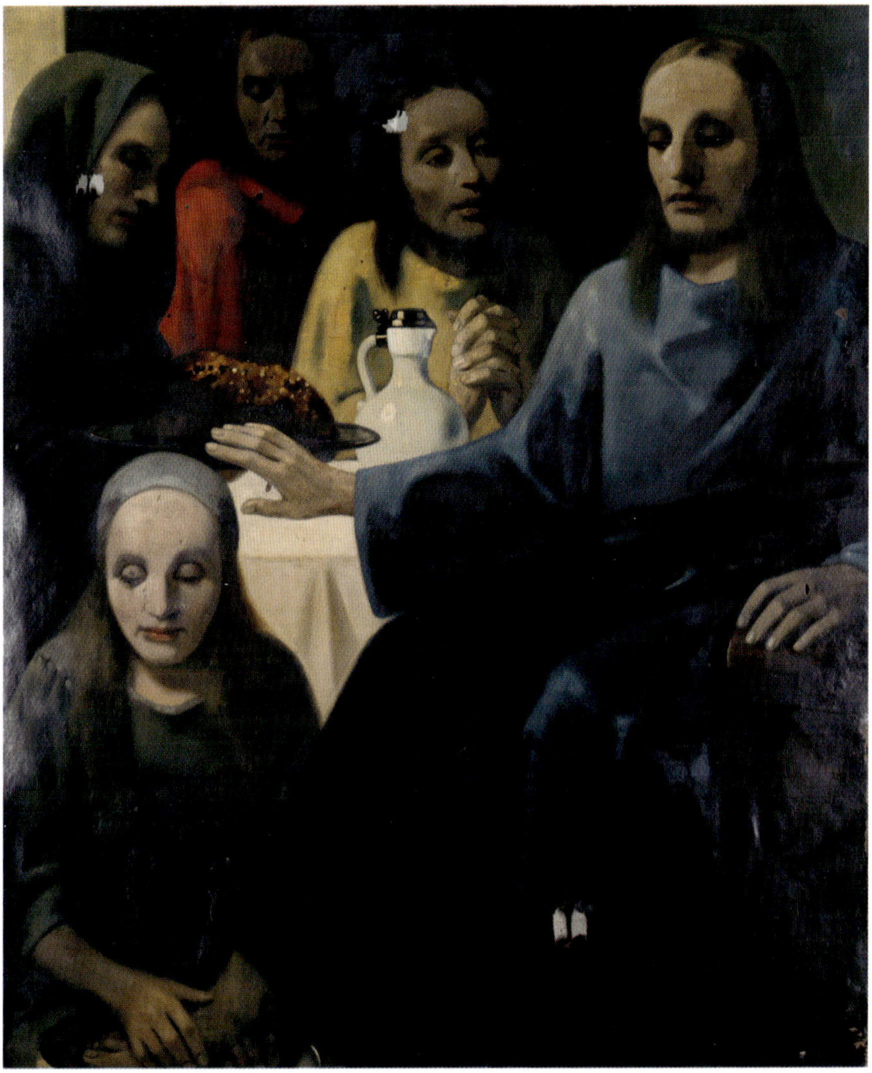

Fig. 6.9. Han van Meegeren, *The Footwashing* (ca. 1943). Oil on canvas. 122 × 102 cm. Rijksmuseum, Amsterdam

gap too. "A depth of feeling springs from it such as is found in no other work of his," Bredius had written on the certificate with which he initially authenticated the picture, and in a private letter to Hannema written several months later he waxed even more emotional:

> How dreadful it is that, for money, and in imitation of Dou and Mieris, who earned a lot of money, the man who COULD make something like this confined himself to miracles of light and colour but without any "spiritual" content—and that this is the man who could paint such a Christ.[34]

By this point, Bredius clearly had a personal stake in the painting, but he was hardly alone in responding to what he saw as the spiritual depth of the *Emmaus*. As Friso Lammertse has shown, both the director of the Rijksmuseum at the time, Frederik Schmidt-Degener, who had hitherto classed Vermeer as "minor" because he revealed "no inner struggle, no wrestling with his subject," and the art historian A. B. de Vries, who had previously contrasted his work with the "deep human tension" of Rembrandt, were similarly moved by the *Emmaus* to revise their views of the Delft painter.[35] What they had been missing—and what Van Meegeren had given them—was evidence not just of Vermeer's stylistic development, but of his soul.

Van Meegeren had also taken great pains to convince them that what they were seeing had really originated in the seventeenth century. One reason most forgers prefer to imitate their contemporaries is that oil paint takes so long to harden: a genuinely old picture will not be affected if its surface comes in contact with alcohol or water, but the pigments on a recently completed painting will begin to soften. The emulsion that had been used for *The Smiling Girl* and *The Lacemaker* would pass the alcohol test, but it was still vulnerable to water. By the time that he painted the *Supper at Emmaus*, however, Van Meegeren had made a crucial discovery: by mixing his oils with a synthetic resin known as Bakelite, invented in 1907, and then heating the canvas in the oven, he could produce a painting as impervious to liquids as one that had been around for centuries.[36] Most commentators think that he learned the trick from another of his shady friends, a British chemist and paint manufacturer named Theodore Ward, but it was clearly Van Meegeren who perfected the technique at his studio in France, where he produced several sophisticated fakes—including not only the two "Vermeers" already mentioned, but a pseudo-Frans Hals and another in the style of Ter Borch—before embarking on the *Emmaus*. The commission that was appointed to investigate his methods after his arrest detected the presence of Bakelite in all these pictures, which also shared the other features that were to characterize his subsequent forgeries, such as the use of seventeenth-century canvases, bent after varnishing to reopen their old cracks, and the filling of those cracks with black ink so as to replicate the dust and dirt that ordinarily accumulate as the painting ages.[37] A later investigation of the *Lady and Gentleman at a Spinet* (see fig. 6.6) turned up Bakelite in that picture too and thus tended to confirm suspicions that it was forged by the same hand, its stiffness possibly explained by Van Meegeren's early experiments with the unfamiliar medium.[38] Both the new "Vermeers" that Bredius greeted so excitedly, in other words, were partly composed of twentieth-century plastic.

As luck would have it, however, no chemical analysis of any kind was performed on the *Emmaus* until after Van Meegeren had confessed. Though it would have passed the standard tests used at the time, the picture's fulfillment of the historians' expectations apparently made even such routine checks seem superfluous, while the subsequent pictures' obvious resemblance to the first in the series meant that these, too, were accepted as genuine. (The only partial exception was *The Footwashing*, whose paints were sampled and said to be consistent with seventeenth-century methods.)[39] Buoyed by his success, Van

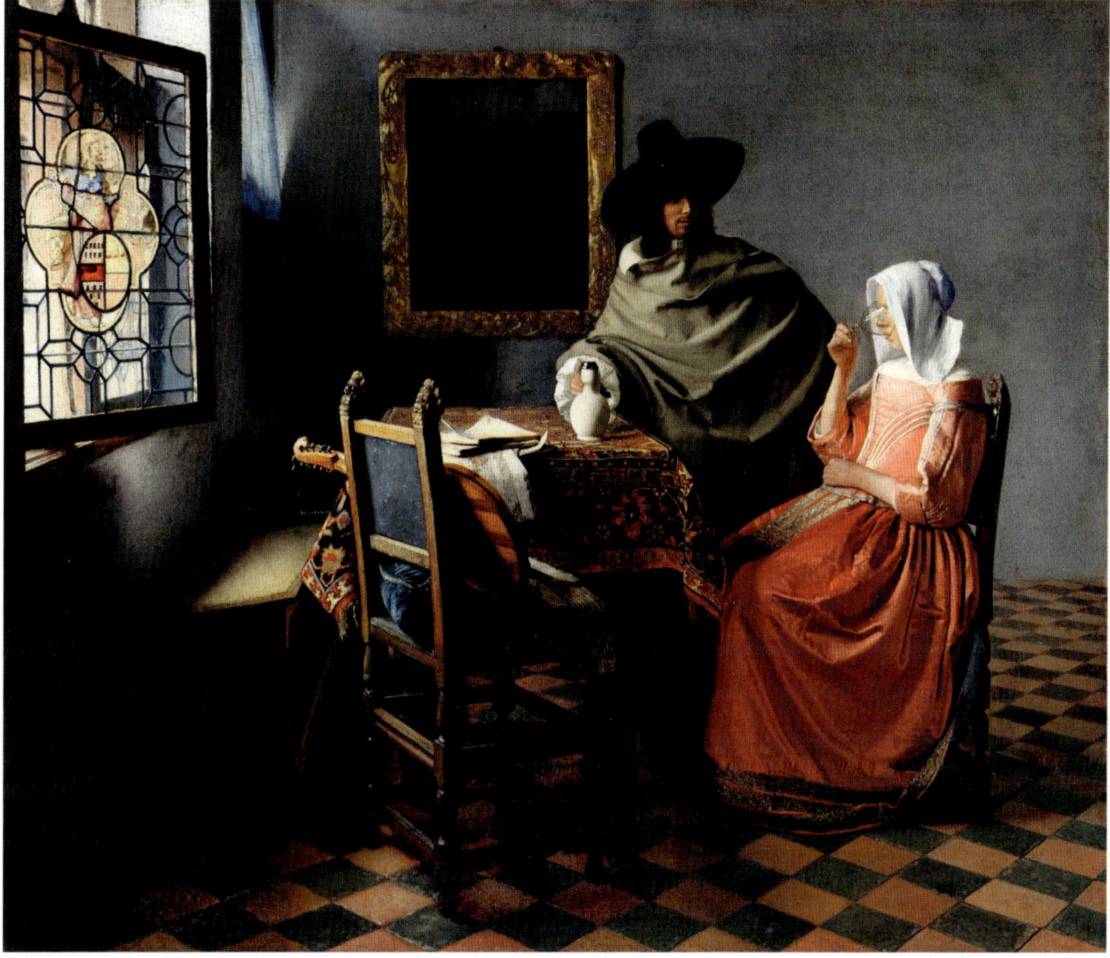

Fig. 6.10. Johannes Vermeer, *The Glass of Wine* (ca. 1658–61). Oil on canvas. 66.3 × 76.5 cm. Gemäldegalerie, Staatliche Museen, Berlin. Photo: Christoph Schmidt. bpk Bildagentur / Art Resource, NY

Meegeren appears to have grown increasingly careless as the series proceeded, and even at the time viewers generally recognized that the later works didn't quite match up to the original "masterpiece."[40]

But if the *Emmaus* was primarily designed to respond to a preexisting narrative, its creator also took some trouble to appeal to the expert eye as well. As several commentators have noted, his version of the biblical episode focuses not on the moment when Christ reveals himself to his disciples—the moment chosen by Rembrandt as well as Caravaggio in his first depiction of the subject—but on the hushed interval that just precedes it: a moment far more in keeping, of course, with the silence and suspended activity characteristic of Vermeer.[41] Though the painting cleverly avoids the kind of obvious pastiche Van Meegeren had attempted with *Woman Reading Music* and *Woman Playing a Cittern*, it still exploits more oblique echoes and allusions, from the blue and yellow robes—the blue concocted, with historical accuracy, from natural ultramarine—to selected fragments of Vermeer's domestic world, such as the white jug that appears in a number of pictures, including *The Glass of Wine* (fig. 6.10) and

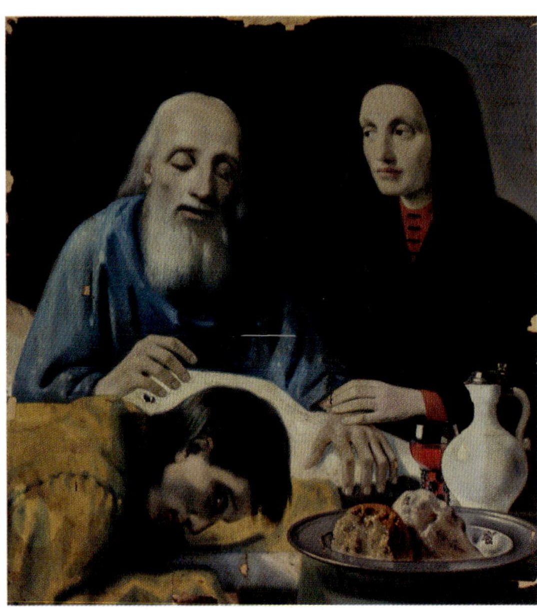

Fig. 6.11. Han van Meegeren, *Isaac Blessing Jacob* (1941). Oil on canvas. 124.5 × 113.5 cm. Collection Museum Boijmans van Beuningen, Rotterdam. Loan Foundation Willem van der Vorm. Photography: Studio Tromp

The Music Lesson (see fig. 3.10), or the *pointillé*-sprinkled bread that links the duller loaf of *Christ in the House of Martha and Mary* (see fig. 1.13) to the more shimmering version in *The Milkmaid* (see fig. 3.7).[42] There is also a notable resemblance between the disciple on the right and *The Astronomer* (see fig. 3.11), while the downcast eyes of Christ and the serving girl recall those in several early pictures, both sacred and secular. (Compare, for instance, the courtesan and her lover in *The Procuress* [see fig. 1.12] or Martha in *Christ in the House of Martha and Mary*). And like virtually all Vermeer's interiors, of course, the scene as a whole is illuminated by a window on the left—a feature significantly absent from the version painted by Caravaggio (see fig. 6.2).[43]

Once the *Supper at Emmaus* was accepted as genuine, Van Meegeren's task became much easier, since he could now worry less about imitating Vermeer and turn instead to replicating what he had just done. Indeed, his next entry in the series was a *Head of Christ* that was taken, as he surely intended, as a study for the *Emmaus*; and when that too passed muster, he followed up with a more ambitious *Last Supper* that reprised the Christ figure from both paintings, while surrounding him with a full complement of twelve disciples awkwardly crowded around the table, including a Saint John whose rounded eyes and parted lips had apparently been borrowed from the *Girl with a Pearl Earring*.[44] Both pictures were purchased by a wealthy Dutch coal baron named Daniel G. van Beuningen, who sold twenty old masters from his collection in order to pay for the *Last Supper* and then housed the precious acquisition in a chapel specially built for the purpose on his estate.[45] The one Old Testament picture in the series, *Isaac Blessing Jacob* (fig. 6.11), went to a rival collector, while *The Footwashing*, as we have seen, was acquired by the Dutch state for the Rijksmuseum. Though Van Meegeren was by now pastiching himself as much—or more than—Vermeer, he continued to include Vermeer-like details from time to time, such as the white jug and *pointillé*-sprinkled loaf of bread that reappear in both the *Isaac* and *The Footwashing* (see fig. 6.9). Such gestures seem to have been well targeted. When the acting director of the Rijksmuseum was debating whether to purchase *The Footwashing*, despite thinking it "less successful" than the *Emmaus*, he cited "the pointillist handling of the bread (almost exactly like the bread in the Milkmaid)" as among the "very fine details" in its favor.[46]

Van Meegeren himself never figured directly in these transactions. His modus operandi was always to enlist the help of a respectable middleman, for

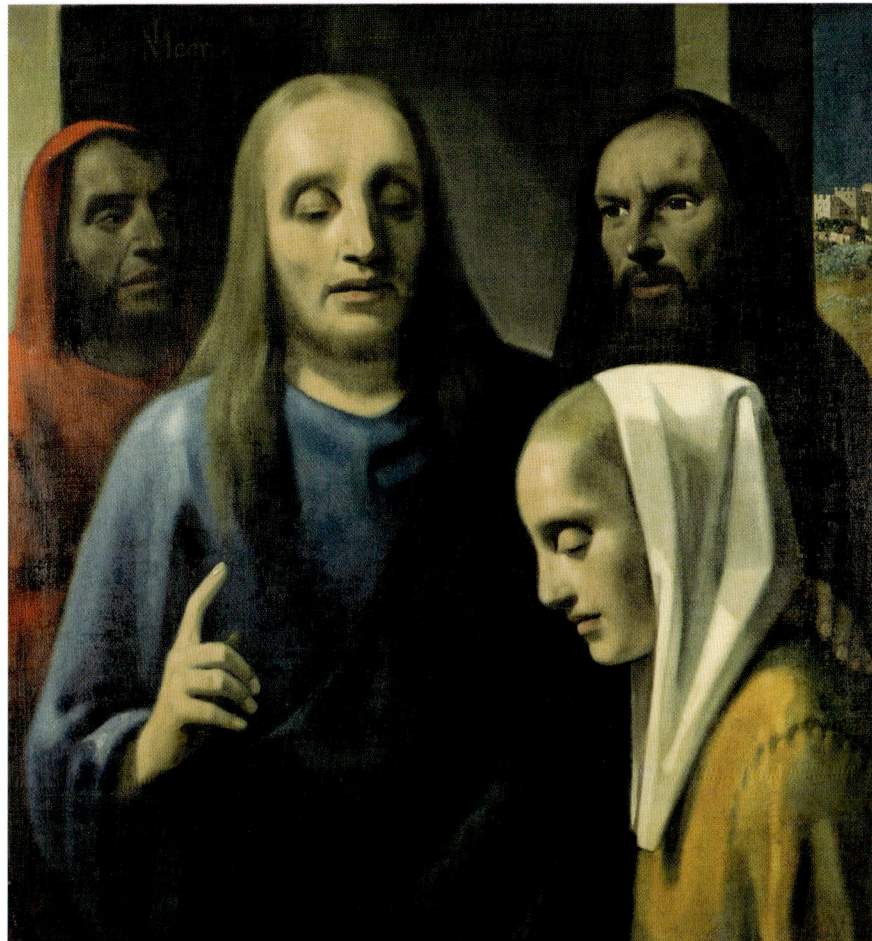

Fig. 6.12. Han van Meegeren, *Christ and the Woman Taken in Adultery* (1942). Oil on canvas. 100 × 90 cm. Rijksdienst Collection, the Netherlands Cultural Heritage Agency. Heritage Images via Getty Images

whom he concocted a vague tale about the painting's provenance that necessarily involved the need for secrecy and that sometimes also required the middleman to invent yet another cover story before he in turn approached a dealer. The fact that much of this business was conducted during wartime not only made the requirement for secrecy more plausible, as many commentators have pointed out, but it also meant that purchasers were unable to compare the forgeries with the Netherlands' genuine Vermeers, which had been hidden away for safekeeping. The patriotic imperative to keep any national treasures from falling into enemy hands—or being shipped off to America, as the sellers sometimes threatened—added to the pressure.[47] But if such conditions helped to account for Van Meegeren's success, they also indirectly led to his downfall. For what prompted his arrest and the confession that followed was not any charge of forgery, but the fact that yet another of his biblical "Vermeers"—*Christ with the Woman Taken in Adultery* (fig. 6.12)—had found its way to the collection of the Nazis' second-in-command, Hermann Goering. After the Netherlands was liberated, the police traced the sale to Van Meegeren; and when he failed to provide a satisfactory provenance for the painting, he was arrested on suspicion of collaborating with the enemy.

Van Meegeren would later claim that he had explicitly forbidden his agents to trade with the Germans, and despite abundant evidence of his own Nazi sympathies, there is good reason to believe that neither he nor his go-between intended to risk this particular move. But the Amsterdam dealer with whom they worked appears to have had no such reservations, and he was already aware that Goering was particularly eager to get his hands on a Vermeer. Having twice lost out to Hitler in a potential competition for the master's work—first when the Führer bought *The Art of Painting* for an advantageous price after the Nazi invasion of Austria, and then when *The Astronomer* was confiscated from the Rothschild collection—Goering was evidently not disposed to question the authenticity of this latest find, though Van Meegeren would later be forced to stonewall when he learned that the Nazi leader had expressed concern about the lack of any paperwork documenting its provenance. There was also some haggling over money, which was eventually settled by Goering's offering about a hundred and fifty paintings from his own collection in exchange for the one he coveted. And it was for this apparent treachery that Van Meegeren now found himself in prison.[48]

When he first blurted out the truth—after two weeks of confinement, Van Meegeren seems to have reached his limits—no one believed him. Only after he undertook to paint yet another "Vermeer" in the presence of court-appointed witnesses did the public learn of the forgeries and its attitude toward the criminal begin to shift. The subject he chose for this last exercise was "the Young Christ Teaching in the Temple," and between the obvious resemblance of the resulting canvas to the rest of the series, the evidence collected from his studio, and the technical analyses performed by the appointed commission, Van Meegeren's boasts of having painted the very "national treasure" he was accused of selling were amply vindicated.[49] The result, in the eyes of the public, was to turn the erstwhile traitor into something of a folk hero: a clever trickster who had managed to hoodwink the nation's experts and its enemies alike. *The Saturday Evening Post* hailed him from the United States as "The Man Who Swindled Goering"; by the time of the trial, his exploits had already inspired a novel, an admiring biography, and a comic book. A newspaper poll conducted in 1947 ranked him second only to the newly elected prime minister as the most popular man in the Netherlands.[50]

Van Meegeren died of a heart attack two months after the trial, before serving the one-year term to which he was sentenced. But the effect of his forgeries continued to resonate, both among those who were forced to reckon with their errors of judgment and a smaller group who persisted in believing that at least one or two of the paintings were genuine. Among the latter were Hannema, whose own shady dealings with the Germans resulted in the loss of his museum directorship after the war, and Van Beuningen, the owner of the *Head of Christ* and *The Last Supper*. Deeply invested in the *Emmaus* and *The Last Supper* in particular, they went to great lengths to convince themselves that Van Meegeren had taken advantage of the rediscovery of these major works to forge the weak imitations that followed and that he was only attempting to boost his reputation by laying claim to the entire series. The argument conspicuously failed to contend with the physical evidence amassed by the commission, including a piece of stretcher found in Van Meegeren's studio that matched the one attached to the *Emmaus*, wormhole to wormhole, and confirmed his report of having cut down the original canvas before beginning to paint. But for the true believers, that only proved that the commissioners, too, were engaged in fraud. Assisted by a Belgian art critic and collector named Jean Decoen, who published an entire book on the subject, they even took their theory to court, where they tried—and failed—to sue the commission for damages. Decoen entitled his book *Back to the Truth: Two Genuine Vermeers* (1951), but despite the conspiratorial narrative he constructed, it's been a long time since any serious scholar has entertained the fantasy that either painting should be ascribed to the Delft master.[51]

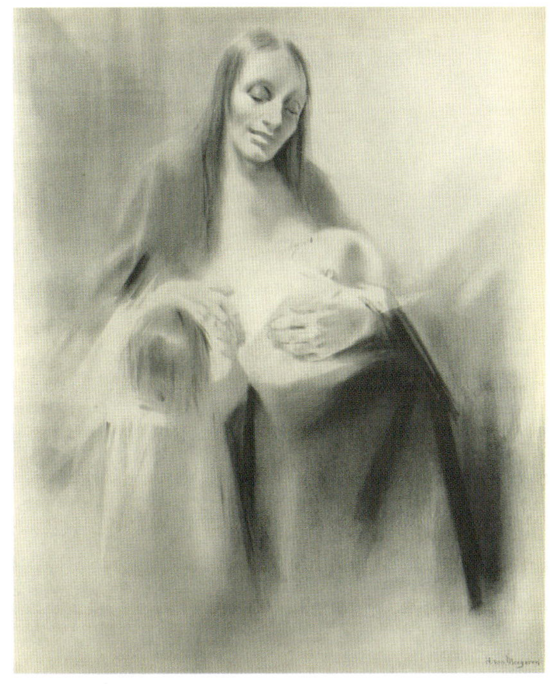

Fig. 6.13. Han van Meegeren, *Mother Breastfeeding her Child* (1932). Drawing. From Han van Meegeren, *Teekeningen* 1, The Hague, 1942. Courtesy of Sterling Memorial Library, Yale University

For most commentators, in fact, the real question is why so many were originally taken in: a question that becomes particularly pointed when the forgeries are juxtaposed not only with genuine Vermeers but with other Van Meegerens. That wasn't, of course, an activity that observers at the time were likely to undertake—the art world's neglect of his work, according to Van Meegeren, had been his chief motive for forgery—but once the comparison is made, the evidence proves hard to overlook. Van Meegeren himself admitted that he had modeled one of the figures in the *Last Supper* on his own drawing of a mother breastfeeding her child (fig. 6.13), and others have seen a strong resemblance between her head and that of Christ as well.[52] Indeed, to place his forgeries in the context of his other work is to recognize that virtually all his people look more or less interchangeable, with the same heavy eyelids—"as good as a second signature," Friso Lammertse observes tartly—elongated faces, and notable absence of musculature.[53] Hindsight also renders embarrassingly visible the spatial and anatomical flaws of these erstwhile masterpieces, and critics have had a field day cataloguing some of the more egregious examples: how the right-hand disciple in the *Emmaus*, for instance, "looks as if he is gripping the

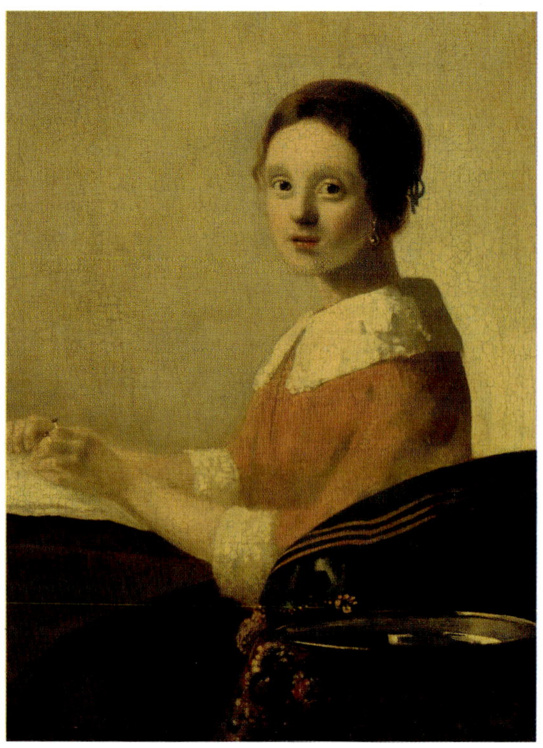

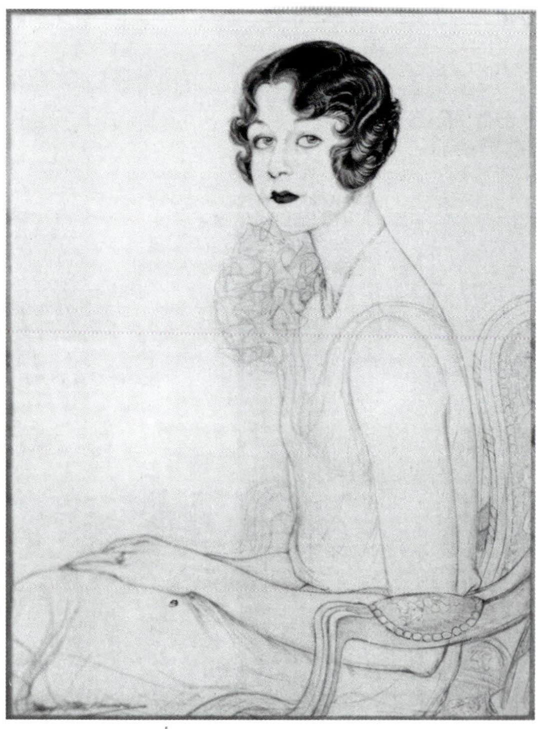

Fig. 6.14. Comparison of detail from twentieth-century imitation of Vermeer (see fig. 6.3) and fashion illustration by Mary MacKinnon for *Harper's Bazaar*, 1927. Comparison courtesy of Arthur K. Wheelock Jr.

table, not in response to the events depicted but simply to avoid falling" (see fig. 6.1); or how the gesture that *The Footwashing* intends as a blessing (see fig. 6.9) "looks disturbingly as though Christ is trying to prevent Martha from bumping her sister with the bread platter."[54] "Jesus looks somewhat healthier than in most Van Meegerens," another critic remarks of *Christ and the Woman Taken in Adultery* (see fig. 6.12), "but a blood transfusion would do no harm."[55]

The resemblance of the women in the forgeries to Van Meegeren's society portraits is another clue that the passage of time makes visible.[56] In a piece on the pseudo-Vermeers in Washington's National Gallery of Art, Arthur Wheelock cleverly juxtaposed a detail from *The Lacemaker*—a face that Valentiner, tellingly, praised as "unusually pretty"—with a contemporary illustration from a fashion magazine (fig. 6.14), in order to drive home a related point: what a previous generation saw as further evidence of Vermeer's modernity now registers only as the signs of a period eye.[57]

In a study of the artist published in 1939, the German scholar Eduard Plietzsch included another painting now widely recognized as a forgery, even as he inadvertently betrayed his own period eye by comparing its "modern female type" to Greta Garbo.[58] Loosely modeled on the *Girl with a Red Hat* (see fig. 4.3), but with headgear implausibly updated for the twentieth century, the picture (fig. 6.15) is sometimes dubbed "the Garbo Vermeer." Jonathan Lopez, who attributes both this work and the forged *Lacemaker* to Van Meegeren, observes that "the face of the sitter bears a striking resemblance to movie posters for *Anna Christie* and *Wild Orchids*," and notes that Plietzsch was not the only authority to be taken in by her "subliminal appeal" to contemporary taste.[59] Responding to a dramatized version of Van Meegeren's story in 1960 that forced them to confront their publication's own responsibility for his success, the editors of *The Burlington Magazine* likewise found themselves reaching for the Garbo analogy. The *Emmaus*, they wrote, "not only reflects the quite false view held about Vermeer shortly before the second war, but is fashioned out of the ephemeral heroes and heroines of the period, the film stars and glamour boys and girls, the heavily lidded eyes of Greta Garbo in the mid- thirties, whom Van Meegeren was unconsciously setting up as his ideal." It's not clear whether they knew of Plietzch's earlier evocation of the film star when they rendered this judgment, but their own eyes had evidently benefited from the perspective afforded by historical distance. "When the next La Tour *Magdalen* emerges out of a 'private collection' and is found to bear a faint resemblance to Brigitte Bardot," they added parenthetically, "we shall be on our guard."[60]

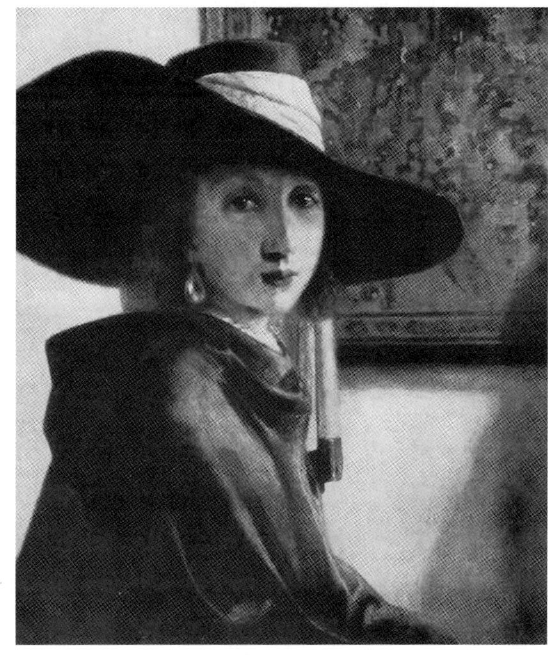

Fig. 6.15. Han van Meegeren (?), *Young Woman with a Blue Hat* (ca. 1930). From a printed reproduction with Van Meegeren's handwritten annotations. Print room, Museum Boijmans van Beuningen, Rotterdam. Photo: Jonathan Lopez.

The quip is well aimed. But if the record suggests that some capacity to identify the visual conventions of one's time is not impossible, it also suggests that any such capacity is distinctly limited. The young curator who likened *The Footwashing* to a film poster at first sight still had complete faith, after all, in the *Emmaus*: the very painting in which the *Burlington* editors saw nothing but "film stars and glamour boys and girls" two decades later.[61] Nor is it only popular culture that thus constrains what we see. Plietzsch may have been taken in by one picture's resemblance to Garbo, but his period eye was equally involved when he enthusiastically pronounced *The Footwashing*, for instance, "almost like a twentieth-century Expressionist work" (see fig. 6.9). Like the dealer who confessed after the war that he'd noticed some anomalies in *Isaac Blessing Jacob* (see fig. 6.11)—"a want of volume" in the figure of Isaac, "something lacking in his hand reaching for Jacob"—but ended up reassuring himself by evoking Picasso's "blue period" and Käthe Kollwitz, Plietzsch welcomed the strange "Vermeer" precisely because it resembled the art he was accustomed to seeing. "I associated the painting with modern art, modern sentiments," the dealer testified, "but at the time that just served to confirm the genius of 'the artist of all times,' of Vermeer's free spirit."[62]

A recent scholarly narrative helped too. Rather than question the sudden appearance of so many biblical paintings in rapid succession, art historians had begun to speculate that the pictures belonged to a series that Vermeer had painted for a clandestine church or ecclesiastical court.[63] The dealer who found himself questioning the anatomical distortions in *Isaac Blessing Jacob* could thus also ascribe them to the picture's "decorative element": a decorative element "which even this painting by Vermeer might have," he explained, "now we were increasingly starting to believe that we were dealing with a series of paintings that must have served to decorate a vestry, for example, or, as Mr. Röell suggested at the time, the room of a secret religious society such as existed in the seventeenth century."[64] "Mr. Röell" was David Röell, who had recently been appointed director of the Rijksmuseum, and the explanation he had constructed was the ironic complement of the narrative that had helped trigger the forgeries in the first place: rather than a story about paintings that were strangely missing, in other words, historians were now composing one to account for their sudden—and still stranger—multiplication.

Whether or not Van Meegeren told the truth when he claimed to have been driven solely by a desire to get revenge on the experts, there were plenty of other reasons why pseudo-Vermeers should have multiplied at the time, and his were not the only such works on the market. The Metropolitan Museum in New York, for example, now consigns to storage two paintings that were purchased as Vermeers by the American banker Jules Bache in the 1920s—a seventeenth-century portrait of a boy that had recently been attributed to the artist by the Dutch scholar Hofstede de Groot, and a small forgery, by an unidentified artist, known as *A Young Woman Reading* (fig. 6.16)—while a *Head of a Girl* closely modeled on the *Study of a Young Woman* at the Met went to the Dutch-born industrialist, Baron Heinrich Thyssen-Bornemisza.[65] Like the fake Vermeers that the National Gallery of Art in Washington has also banished to storage, these forgeries testify to a buying frenzy that first broke out among American industrialists and financiers at the turn of the twentieth century and that seems to have reached a fever pitch in the following decades among Europeans as well.[66] Fueled by new money eager to buy up old masters, the art market as a whole experienced a rapid boom in those years; and Vermeer's increasing fame, heightened by the small size of his output, made him an especially prized commodity. Some observers have also suggested that the political turmoil of the late 1930s led collectors to place an even greater value on the perceived serenity of Vermeer's art—an impulse that Van Meegeren's biblical version of the Delft master was clearly designed to exploit.[67] Jonathan Lopez scarcely exaggerates when he remarks that "discovering a picture—any picture—that might be accepted as a Vermeer was the interwar art world's equivalent of the quest for the Holy Grail."[68]

A century has passed since forged Vermeers began to circulate regularly on the market, and the conditions that gave rise to them seem unlikely to recur, even if the genuine article has lost none of its luster. To the contrary, in fact: while the reverberations of the Van Meegeren scandal and the radical pruning of the corpus that took place in its aftermath did lasting damage to scholarly reputations, "the mystique surrounding Vermeer's name," as Ivan Gaskell has argued, was only enhanced as a consequence. Though Gaskell also contends that the perpetuation of that mystique on the art market requires a continuing belief in the possibility that a hitherto unknown Vermeer might still turn up at any moment, the probability of a forger's exploiting such hopes has considerably diminished since Van Meegeren's day, if only because the technical analysis of old pictures has become far more sophisticated.[69] Forgers are no doubt as thick on the ground as ever—perhaps even more so, given the continuing inflation of the art market—but there are easier targets than the Delft master. New art continues to be generated from the fragments of his world, as we shall see in the next chapter, but rather than seek to deceive, most such work openly flaunts its appropriation of the past, self-consciously inviting the viewer to recognize what has been borrowed and how Vermeer has been remade in the process.

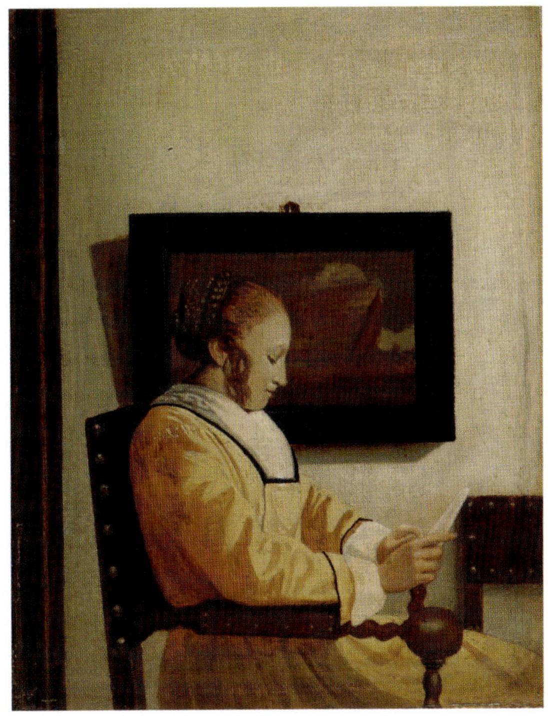

Fig. 6.16. Imitator of Vermeer, *A Young Woman Reading* (ca. 1925–27). Oil on canvas. 19.7 × 14.6 cm. Metropolitan Museum of Art, New York. Image © The Metropolitan Museum of Art. Image source: Art Resource, NY

From time to time, however, contemporary artists do try to pass off new pictures as originals, though the kind of forgery they practice is fundamentally innocent. While some fiction inspired by Vermeer draws on actual work by the Delft master—Tracy Chevalier's bestselling *Girl with a Pearl Earring* (1999) is probably the most familiar example—others choose to invent their "Vermeers," and they typically do so, like many actual forgers, by following the master's habit of recombining familiar elements of his visual world to create new images. Appearing at the same moment as Chevalier's novel, when the cultural atmosphere was still suffused by the afterglow of the international exhibition several years earlier, both Katharine Weber's *The Music Lesson* (1999) and Susan Vreeland's *Girl in Hyacinth Blue* (1999) focus on a single imaginary Vermeer: a fictional object designed to evoke the kind of picture that has long been most closely identified with his name. Despite Weber's potentially misleading title, both invented paintings have a solitary female subject: a seated woman with a lute on her lap and a "smile that isn't quite a smile" in *The Music Lesson*;[70] a young girl in a short blue smock and rust colored skirt, who sits by a table at an open window with her palm gracefully turned upward in *Girl in Hyacinth Blue*. While Weber's subject confronts the viewer directly, Vreeland's appears in profile, and rather than a half-smile, her expression is one of longing.

Partly for plot reasons, Vreeland devotes more space to spelling out the details of her fictional painting than does Weber, but both writers specify the presence of black-and-white tile floors, and both predictably remark the fall of light through a window: a "splash of pale yellow" in Vreeland, and "the rich afternoon light falling [. . .] across the wooden grain of the table" in Weber. "There's no yellow in the world like a Vermeer yellow," Weber's narrator later says of the painting's "sifted light." The fictional *Music Lesson* also displays "the glazed surface of [. . . a] gleaming white pitcher" and "the soft, precise fuzz of [. . .] peaches on the window sill," while a speaker in *Girl in Hyacinth Blue*, who hopes to persuade his companion that the painting is in fact a Vermeer, carefully itemizes a long list of features, from the figures in the tapestry on the table ("same as in nine other paintings") and the "same Spanish chair with lion's head finials that he used in eleven canvases," with the "same brass studs in the leather," to the sewing basket "placed forward on the table, as he often did [. . .] almost as an obstruction between the viewer and the figure." The visual inventory even extends to Vermeer's characteristic variations of focus, as the speaker contrasts the "diffused" weave of the basket with the sharp delineation of the girl's face and the lace edge of her cap, "absolutely precise to a pinprick." Later in the novel, another speaker observes that "the girl's mouth was slightly open, glistening at the corner"—a detail clearly intended to evoke one of the *Girl with a Pearl Earring*'s most celebrated features (see fig. 4.1).[71] Like so many actual forgeries, in other words, the innocent ones at the heart of both fictions are the verbal equivalent of what Valentiner called "puzzle pictures": newly created Vermeers "composed," to quote Valentiner again, "of pieces taken from different groupings in known paintings by him."[72]

And like actual forgers, revealingly, both novelists go out of their way to establish their creations' authenticity. Vreeland deliberately tells *Girl in Hyacinth Blue* backwards, from the late twentieth century to the seventeenth, in order to draw out the mystery introduced in the first chapter as to whether an unsigned canvas possessed by an American teacher of German descent is indeed the genuine Vermeer he believes it to be: a fact that is conclusively proved, within the fiction, when the penultimate chapter allows us to witness the artist himself in the act of painting it.[73] The first chapter even toys with the possibility that the picture might actually be a Van Meegeren by having its owner tremble at the forger's name, only to dispel that alternative—and thus help to confirm the work's authenticity—when a shift in point of view permits us to discover the true cause of his anxiety: not that he possesses a forgery, but that his Nazi father looted the painting from a Jewish family during the German occupation of the Netherlands.

The authenticity of the imaginary *Music Lesson* is also established by contrasting it with a fake, but rather than a work of forgery, the fraudulence in this case is the product of mechanical reproduction. An art historian who works in the research library of the Frick, Weber's narrator never has any cause to doubt that the stolen painting she ends up hiding in an Irish cottage for her lover is a genuine Vermeer: indeed, she herself has helped plan the heist, by suggesting how the thieves, who belong to a splinter group of the IRA, might replace the real thing with a substitute while the shipment is in transit from The Hague to London.[74] But when the plot to ransom the painting goes awry, and the thieves determine to film a video of its burning instead, the narrator performs her own act of substitution: supplying the would-be arsonists with a "deluxe" reproduction purchased from the museum shop and burying the genuine painting in the grave of a woman they have assassinated.[75] "Even the most perfect reproduction of a work of art is lacking in one element: its presence in time and space, its unique existence at the place where it happens to be," the philosopher Walter Benjamin wrote in a famous essay to which the novel alludes more than once.[76] In burying the real painting rather than letting it be burned, Weber's narrator is clearly seeking to preserve that singular presence, and if we allow her novel to work on us, we not only applaud the gesture, but understand it as expressing the same "love of the real" that has earlier been identified with the artist himself. If the fiction succeeds, that is to say, we temporarily succumb to its innocent forgery, even as we remain aware that no actual *Music Lesson* lies buried in the Irish countryside. Unlike the works that have mostly occupied this chapter, after all, this one comes with a partial disclaimer. "The world has never seen this particular painting by Vermeer," says an opening note to the reader, "because it does not quite exist."[77]

7

Homage, Appropriation, Pastiche

When I respond to a painting by Vermeer with a painting of my own, my painting changes how I see the Vermeer.

—GEORGE DEEM (2004)

In 2004 the American painter George Deem published a book called *How to Paint a Vermeer*. Despite its cheeky title, the book was not the confession of a forger. Nor did it set out to tell the story of one, like Frank Wynne's *I Was Vermeer* (2006) or Jonathan Lopez's *The Man Who Made Vermeers* (2008)—two nearly contemporaneous biographies that each took Han van Meegeren as its subject. Quite the contrary, in fact: while Van Meegeren's success at painting a Vermeer depended on a public that failed to perceive what he had done, Deem's numerous variations on the master's work openly court viewers' knowledge of the original. Anyone may admire the technical skill with which the titular objects of *A Stool, A Chair, and a Map* (fig. 7.1), have been rendered, for instance, but only someone who recognizes how those objects have been lifted from Vermeer's *Art of Painting* (see fig. 3.13) will appreciate the visual wit of Deem's transformation. As Deem himself observed to an interviewer in 2004, such work requires of the viewer a kind of double vision: "When you look at a painting of mine, you see two things at the same time—the absent painting I have quoted (or, rather, your memory of it) and the present actuality of my painting as you are looking at it."[1]

"I see no reason ever to stop incorporating Vermeer's paintings in my own work," Deem declared in 1984, and he never did. Though he continued to quote from other previous artists as well, his obsession with Vermeer clearly

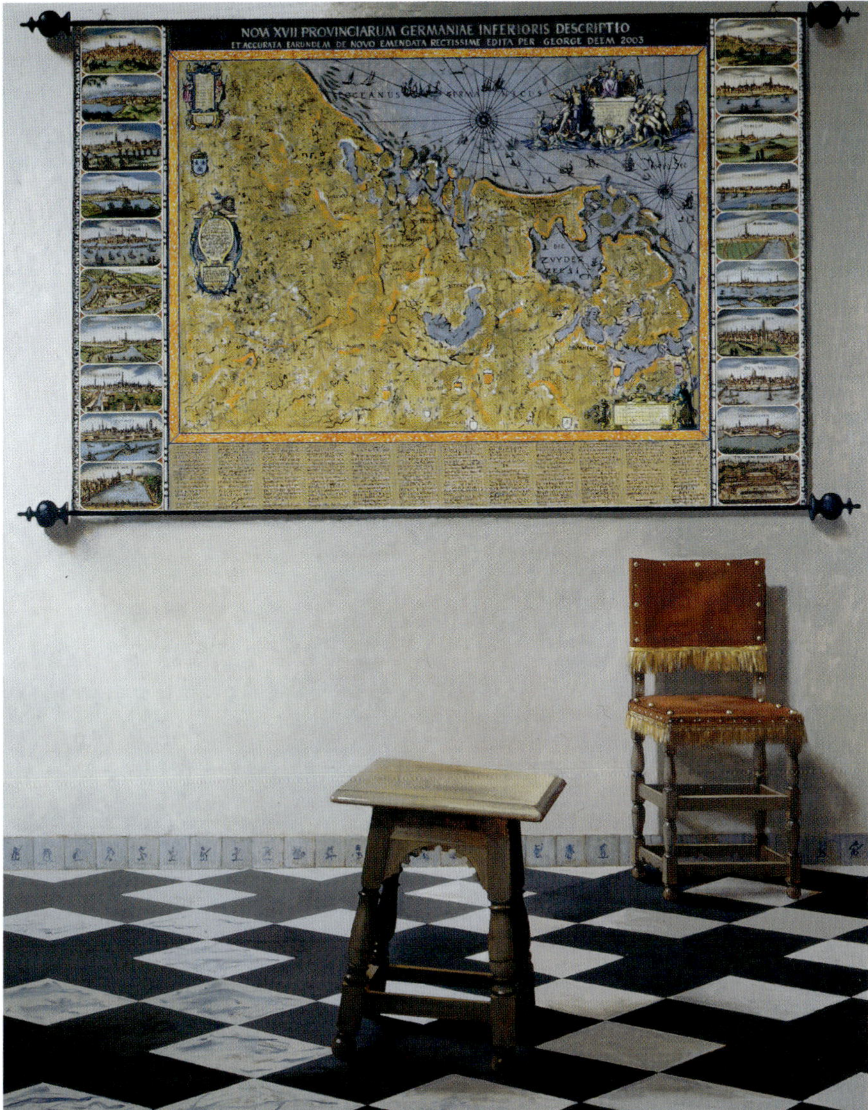

Fig. 7.1. George Deem, *A Stool, A Chair, and a Map* (2003). Oil on canvas. 137.2 × 106.7 cm. Boston Athenaeum. © New Britain Museum of American Art / Artists Rights Society (ARS), NY

overtopped all the rest; and by the time of his death at the age of seventy-five, he would leave behind well over a hundred paintings and drawings variously riffing on the Delft master.[2] But if Deem is probably the most prolific of Vermeer's modern appropriators, he is far, of course, from the only one. As early as 1914 the Dutch photographer Richard Polak produced a transgressive variation on *The Art of Painting*, by staging a tableau in which a naked woman took the place of Vermeer's laurel-wreathed model (fig. 7.2); twenty-four years later, the Spanish surrealist Salvador Dalí paid tribute to two of his favorite artists by creating an optical illusion from their conjunction (fig. 7.3)—a painting that looks from a distance like a portrait of Diego Velázquez, only to dissolve on closer inspection into a version of the *Woman in Blue Reading a Letter* (see

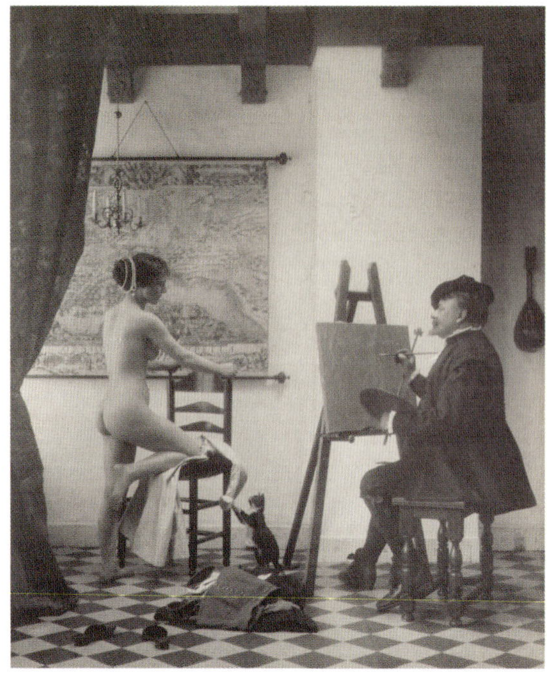

Fig. 7.2. Richard Polak, *The Artist and His Model* (1914). Platinum print. 21.1 × 17 cm. © Royal Photographic Society Collection / Victoria and Albert Museum, London / Art Resource, NY

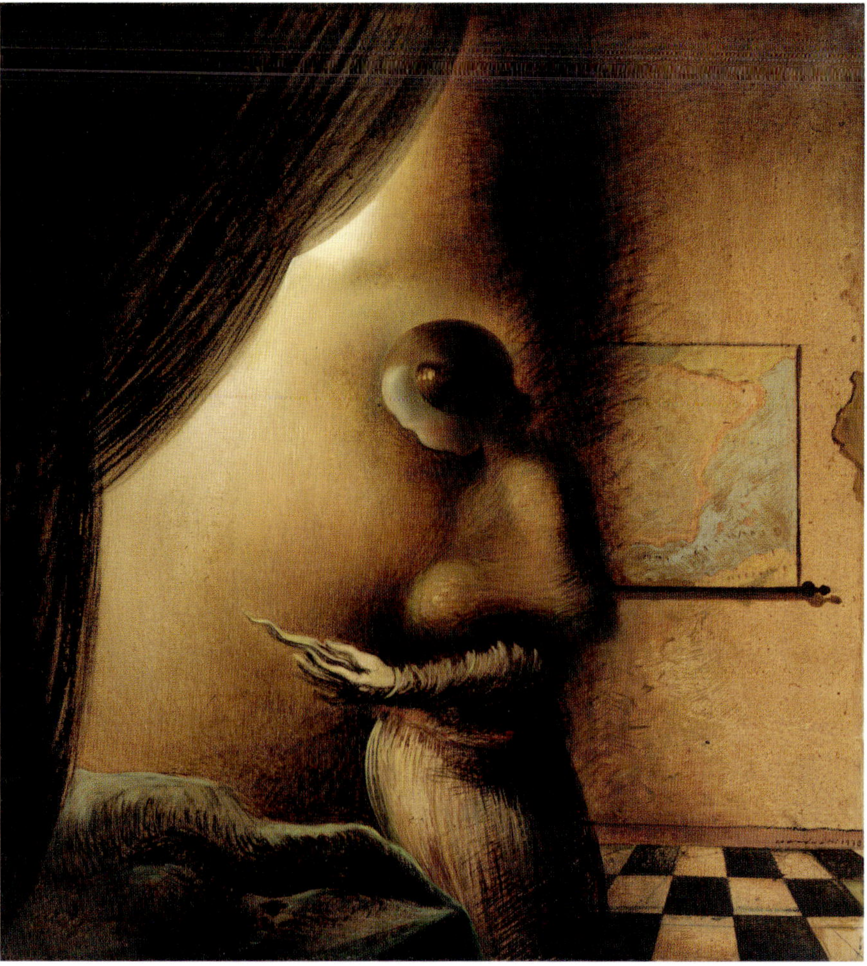

Fig. 7.3. Salvador Dalí, *The Image Disappears* (1938). Oil on canvas. 56.5 × 50.5 cm. Dalí Theatre-Museum, Figueres, Spain. © 2025 Salvador Dalí, Fundació Gala-Salvador Dalí / Artists Rights Society (ARS), NY

fig. 2.4). But it was in the second half of the twentieth century that the practice of quoting Vermeer really took off, as artists increasingly came to view the art-historical record as a horde of material to be freely plundered and recycled. The sheer proliferation of that record, both photographic and digital, has clearly proved crucial to this practice, and so, too, has a general disillusionment with modernist narratives of progress, in which art was understood to move forward by breaking decisively with the past.

While previous generations of Vermeer's admirers sought to translate his subject matter into contemporary terms, or to imitate his handling of light and color, recent artists have been more inclined to approach his work as a collection of images whose very familiarity—and duplicability—is key to their power. And while previous generations felt compelled to visit the paintings themselves, most of the artists to whom we now turn have been content to work from reproductions.[3] Edmund Tarbell sent Philip Hale off to France with the injunction to "go and have a look at Van der Meer of Delft and give him my love";[4] the American sculptor Joseph Cornell, who produced most of his work in his Queens basement and never ventured to Europe, knew the *Girl with a Pearl Earring* only from a photolithograph, which he chose to incorporate in one of his so-called "Hotels": a series of hauntingly spare boxes named after ads in European guidebooks. (Vermeer's girl inhabits—if that is the right word—the *Grand Hôtel Bon Port* [fig. 7.4].)[5] Rather than copy *The Art of Painting* itself, which he'd never seen, the British-American artist Malcolm Morley faithfully modeled his version of Vermeer's masterwork on a museum poster, even down to replicating its off-color printing (see fig. 7.23).[6]

In 2001 the art historian Marguerite Glass reported on interviews with three artists given to quoting Vermeer, each of whom described working from reproductions. One of them, the American painter Terri Priest, told Glass how she liked to buy two copies of books on the artist, so that she could cut one up and begin to fashion her own versions of his images; another, the Greek-born artist Christina Coridou, characterized Arthur Wheelock's 1981 study of Vermeer as her "Bible" and spoke of composing her Vermeer-inspired collages (fig. 7.5) with the aid of photographs and photocopies, despite the fact that she herself now lived in Delft. Even Deem, whose paintings often engage in sophisticated analyses of Vermeer's palette or his use of perspective, nonetheless worked from reproductions, often taken from books that, like Priest, he had purchased in duplicate.[7] "Look at the reproduction carefully and get an idea of how you would copy it," he exhorted himself in a notebook entry of 1978: "Find other reproductions of the same painting. Compare them not only for their differences, but notice which of the reproductions you prefer." Only then did he instruct himself to "visit the painting [. . .] if it is possible," before immediately adding, "but don't let the original intimidate you. Don't attempt copying the original—that is from a different century. It cannot be done anymore." The entry is entitled with characteristic bravura, "How to Paint a Masterpiece."[8]

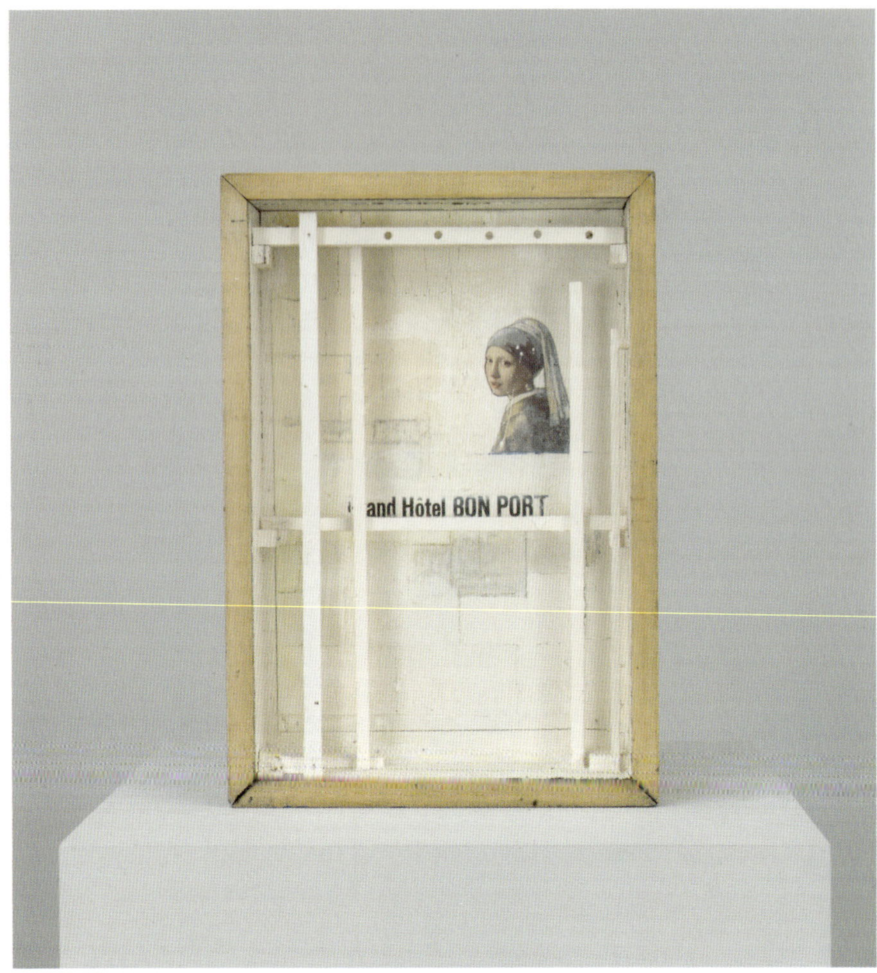

Fig. 7.4. Joseph Cornell, *Grand Hôtel Bon Port* (1952). Painted wood, paper, photolithographs on paper, glass, colored pencil, and metal hardware. 48.3 × 33 × 9.5 cm. Whitney Museum of American Art. Gift of Lindy and Edwin A. Bergman. © 2025 The Joseph and Robert Cornell Memorial Foundation / Licensed by VAGA at Artists Rights Society (ARS), NY. Digital Image © Whitney Museum of American Art / Licensed by Scala / Art Resource, NY

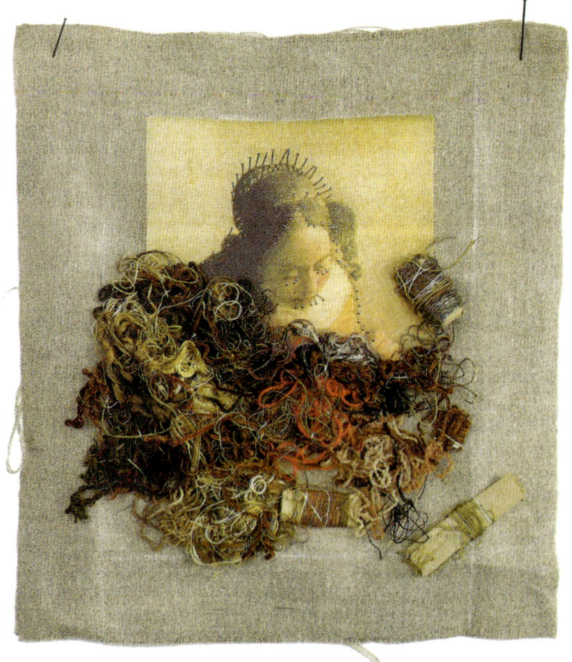

Fig. 7.5. Christina Coridou, *The Lacemaker* (1996). Fabric collage. 24.5 × 21 cm. Private collection. © Christina Coridou

How shall we characterize such a relation to the art of the past? I have already referred to Deem as an "appropriator" of Vermeer's work, and etymologically, as Robert S. Nelson has observed, nothing could be more straightforward: the Latin *appropriare*, from which our word derives, means simply "to make one's own," and that is just what Deem and the other artists I have mentioned are engaged in doing with the art of the Delft master.[9] The connotations of inappropriate taking—I use the adjective deliberately—are still hard to shake, of course; and so too are the negative associations of another term that can also apply to many of the works considered here: "pastiche"—a slippery term that has sometimes meant the imitation of a masterwork and sometimes a mixture of styles or elements (the combination of Velázquez and Vermeer in Dalí's *The Image Disappears*, for instance), with a long history of derogatory uses.[10] Yet both terms are not only necessary in this context, but difficult to separate, I would argue, from the homage that any act of quotation also entails, even when, as in Polak's photograph, such quotation may appear to involve an element of sacrilege or mockery. That is certainly the spirit in which Deem understood his own practice. "Each visual quotation of the figure of the Milkmaid inescapably is a reference to Vermeer's painting [. . .] and adds to the painting's iconographic significance," he wrote, before adding: "We do not have to look beyond painting itself for our gods and goddesses, our heroes and saints."[11]

When the Mauritshuis in The Hague invited the public to respond to the temporary departure of the *Girl with a Pearl Earring* for Amsterdam's Rijksmuseum in 2023 by creating their own versions of the painting, it effectively invited—and received—what might best be termed a flood of pastiche. But it was also, of course, inviting—and receiving—a collective act of homage. "Our world-famous and most beloved masterpiece was on loan to the Rijksmuseum for eight weeks for the Johannes Vermeer exhibition," the museum announced on the painting's return. "But the spirit of the *Girl* did not leave the Vermeer room [. . .]. No fewer than 3,482 Girls from all over the world found their way to The Hague."[12] In the painting's absence, the curators had put a selection of the entries on display, and the fact that one of the winners had been generated by Artificial Intelligence elicited a predictable outcry from the artistic community, especially because the image (fig. 7.6) quickly rose to the top of online searches for "Johannes Vermeer."[13] According to its creator, however, it was meant as "a fun homage" to a work he loved, not any sort of substitute for the original. "I don't want to replace Vermeer, and I don't think it can or will be done with any technology," Julian van Dieken declared. For this digital artist, at least, Vermeer's painting remained the unreachable ideal: "As a photographer, I'll forever chase that kind of detail, mood, and quality of light."[14]

However one chooses to characterize Van Dieken's image, it is clearly not a copy. But as Morley's case may already have begun to suggest, the distinction between appropriation or pastiche, on the one hand, and copying, on the other, is not always so straightforward. If Morley's *Portrait of the Artist in his Studio*

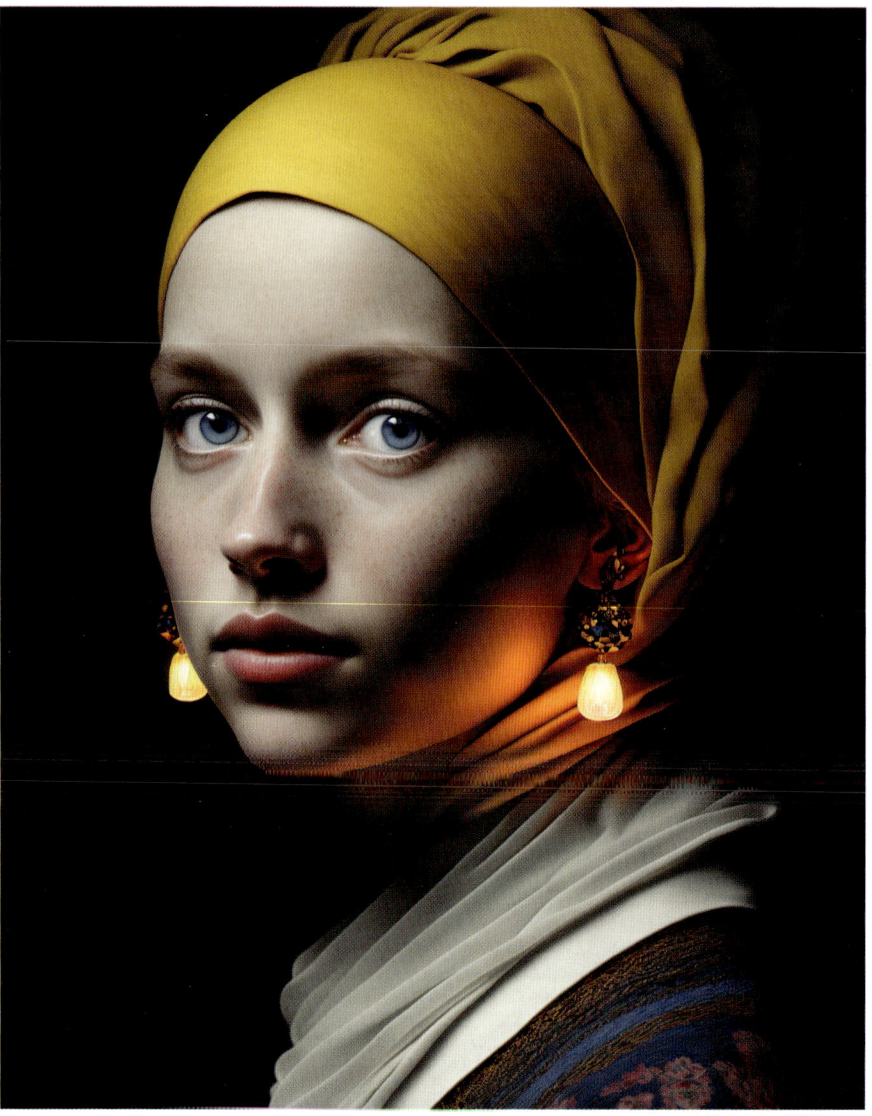

Fig. 7.6. Julian van Dieken, *The Girl with Glowing Earrings*. @julian_ai_art with Midjourney/Photoshop, 2022. © Julian van Dieken

qualifies as pastiche by virtue of having been painted after a poster rather than the original, then does Dalí's dutiful visit to the Louvre make any difference in how we classify his *Lacemaker* (fig. 7.7)?[15] The painting's current owner, the Metropolitan Museum in New York, describes it as a "meticulous copy," yet we might at least pause over the fact that the artist has conspicuously substituted his own signature for Vermeer's, thereby appropriating the latter's work in the most literal sense of the term.[16]

Indeed, this was not the first time that Dalí had seized on *The Lacemaker* for his own purposes—nor would it be the last. He frequently testified to his obsession with the painting, and the evidence of that obsession is recorded in numerous photographs of Dalí at work (fig. 7.8), as well as in the work itself. (He claimed to own some fifty reproductions that he hung all over his olive

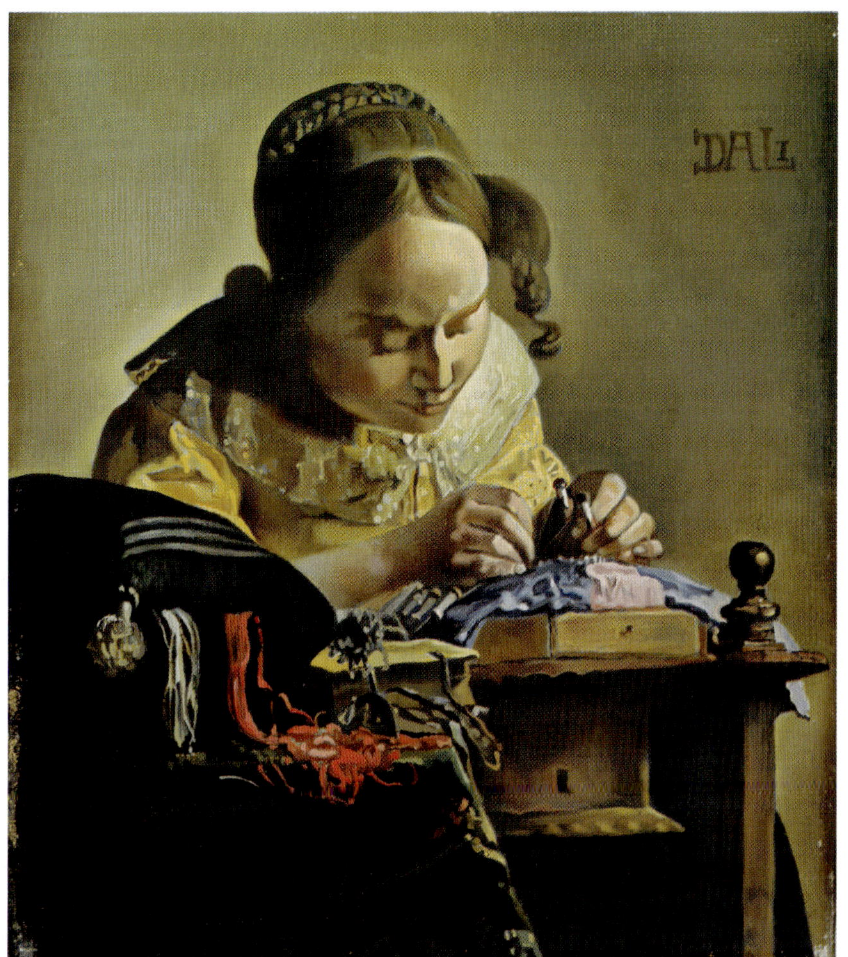

Fig. 7.7. Salvador Dalí, *The Lacemaker (After Vermeer)* (1955). Oil on canvas. 23.5 × 19.7 cm. The Metropolitan Museum of Art, New York, Robert Lehman Collection, 1975. © 2025 Salvador Dalí, Fundació Gala-Salvador Dalí / Artists Rights Society (ARS), NY. Image copyright © The Metropolitan Museum of Art. Image source: Art Resource, NY

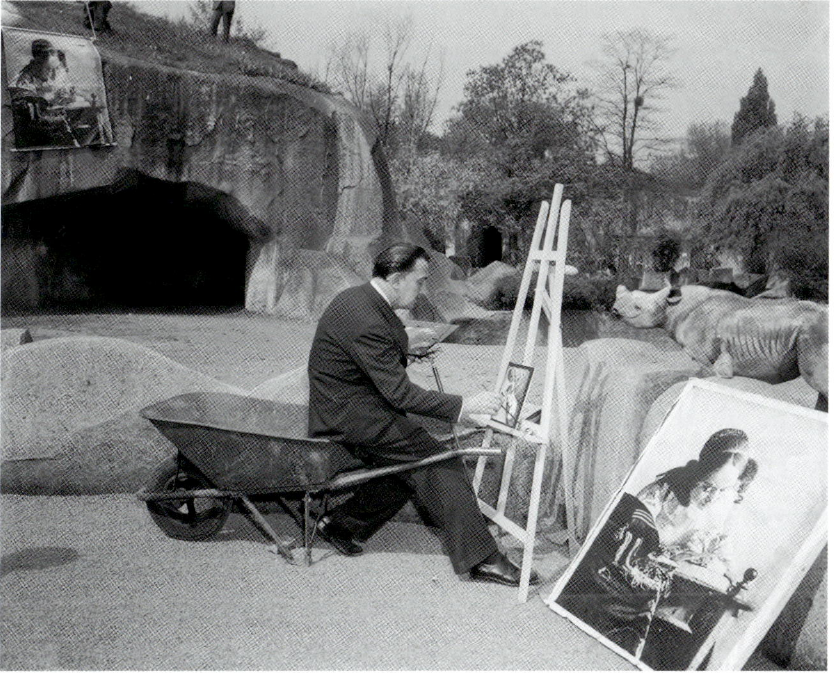

Fig. 7.8. Salvador Dalí Painting in the Zoo. Photograph courtesy of Getty Images. © 2025 Salvador Dalí, Fundació Gala-Salvador Dalí / Artists Rights Society (ARS), NY

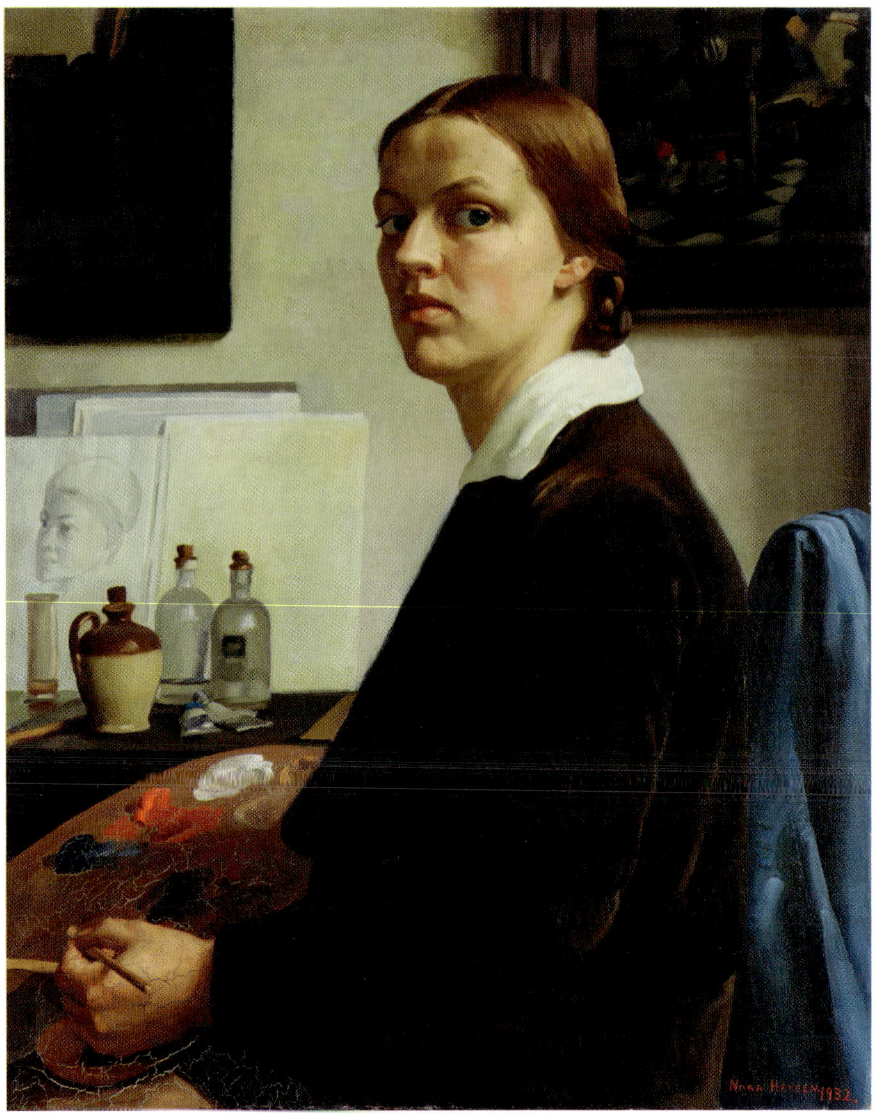

Fig. 7.9. Nora Heysen, *Self Portrait* (1932). Oil on canvas. 76.2 × 61.2 cm. Art Gallery of New South Wales, Sydney, Australia. Gift of Howard Hinton, 1932. © Lou Klepac

grove, even taking one along to the beach where he bathed with his wife.)[17] Before we return to these other uses of the image, however, it's worth noting that what distinguishes this *Lacemaker* is the context in which it was created: the artist had been commissioned to copy Vermeer's painting by a wealthy art collector, the banker Robert Lehman.[18] If this counts as appropriation, in other words, it's of a very traditional kind.

Nor is it the only such historical throwback among modern artists' appropriations of Vermeer. As the Australian painter Nora Heysen (1911–2003) clearly registered, for instance, one can simply quote Vermeer as he himself often quoted others: by incorporating their pictures in a picture of his own. That is the route Heysen chose in one of her best-known paintings, a self-portrait of 1932 that juxtaposes her head against a reproduction of *The Art of*

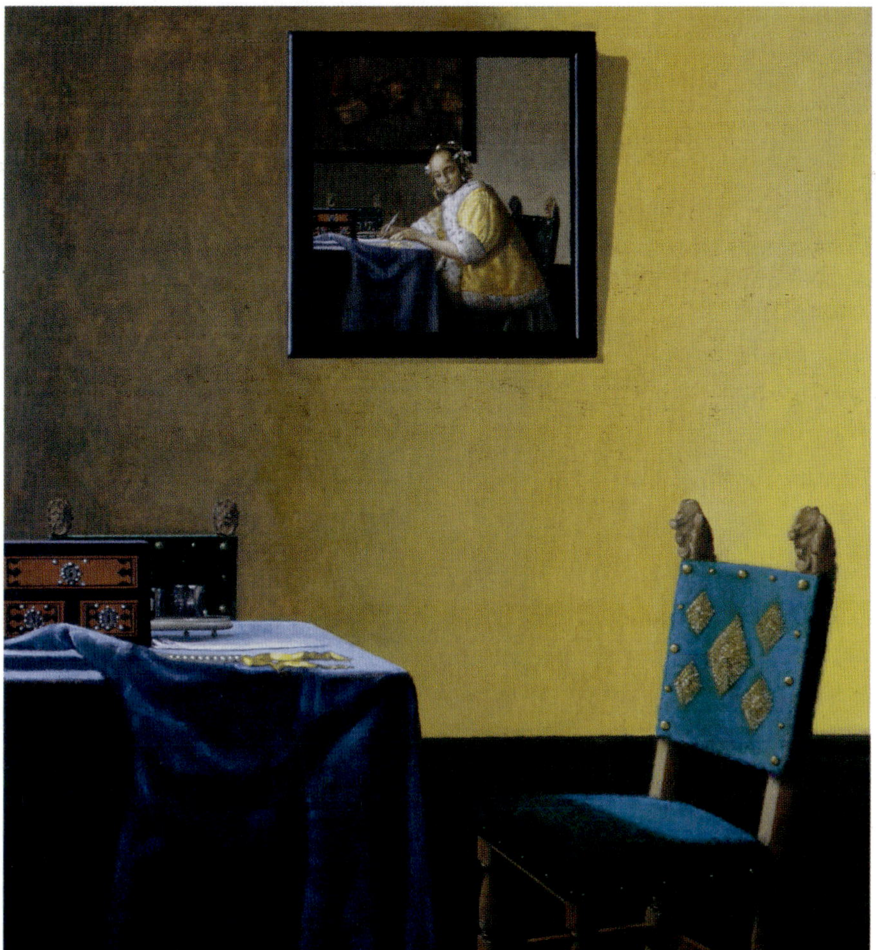

Fig. 7.10. George Deem, *A Lady Writing, Again* (2006). Oil on canvas. 76.2 × 68.6 cm. New Britain Museum of American Art, New Britain, CT. © New Britain Museum of American Art / Artists Rights Society (ARS), NY. Image © Archives of American Art, Smithsonian Institution, Washington, DC

Painting cropped so as eliminate the female model, as if to underscore that the woman who created this canvas prefers to identify with the painter (fig. 7.9; cf. fig. 3.13). (Heysen would later characterize Vermeer as one of her "gods."[19]) At the same time, of course, the fact that any knowledgeable viewer would recognize this picture-within-the-picture *as* a reproduction also marks the modern artist's distance from her predecessor. Like the historically conscious artist herself, such a viewer knows that the actual canvas hangs in a museum.

Though George Deem likes to play more elaborate games with Vermeer quotation, he too sometimes draws on the picture-within-the-picture convention (fig. 7.10). And so, for that matter, do filmmakers, even if we're not ordinarily accustomed to thinking of their use of such images as belonging to the same tradition. As its title suggests, the protagonist of Jan Jost's *All the Vermeers in New York* (1990) is obsessed with the paintings publicly on view in the city, an obsession that soon becomes conflated with his attraction to an aspiring young actress he particularly associates with the Metropolitan's *Study of a Young Woman*. In scenes apparently filmed in the museum itself, we repeatedly observe him observing the painting, together with the other Vermeers that hang in the room (though like most modern admirers of the artist, neither the film's protagonist nor its maker seems to have much interest in the *Allegory of the Catholic Faith*). Presumably because Jost was denied permission to film in the Frick, its three paintings appear only as postcards or book illustrations that the heroine examines early in the film, but these too effectively function as pictures-within-the-moving picture. The heroine is French, and we repeatedly witness her reading extracts from Proust on Vermeer: a pattern that reaches its climax when the protagonist, like Bergotte, dies in the museum, and the camera zooms in on the *Study of a Young Woman*, as we hear in voice-over the passage on Bergotte's burial and possible resurrection, concluding with the phrase, "an artist forever unknown and barely identified under the name of Vermeer."[20] If using a picture-within-a-picture is a form of quotation, then one might call this closing scene a quotation doubled.

Peter Webber's 2003 film of Tracy Chevalier's *Girl with a Pearl Earring* is a more conventional work—though also a more successful one—and its final scene attempts nothing so elaborate. But it, too, necessarily draws on pictures-within-the-picture in this sense, from the reproductions that stand in for the originals on the walls of Vermeer's patron, Van Ruijven, to the unfinished canvases, presumably painted by modern artists, that serve to represent Vermeer's work-in-progress. And it, too, concludes with an extended close-up of its principal picture, though not one filmed, like the *Study of a Young Woman*, on location. Rather than shoot in the Mauritshuis, Webber has explained, the filmmakers used a high-resolution still provided by the museum and relied on a rostrum camera to animate it. "That's a very good rendering of the painting, the one that we used," Webber has said, but it is of course a rendering: an appropriation in another medium that also serves, clearly, as an homage to the original. Noting that people don't ordinarily look at paintings for very long, Webber cheerfully brags that he forced viewers "to sit and stare at a painting for a minute and a half."[21] It's an understandable boast from an artist whose medium depends on such temporal extension, even if it manages to glide over the fact that viewers of the film were not, strictly speaking, looking at a painting. Writing of the visual environment in which Vermeer's modern reception has transpired, Ivan Gaskell argues that it's impossible at this point for commentators to know whether an impression of the painting comes from a direct confrontation with it or from photographic reproductions.[22] The painting he has in mind is the *Young Woman Standing at a Virginal*, rather than the *Girl with a Pearl Earring*, but his point holds for the filmmakers who translated Chevalier's novel to the screen, as well as for the many amateur artists who submitted their versions of the image to the Mauritshuis two decades later.

As it happens, Dalí's first appropriation of Vermeer also involved film—or rather, once again, the film of a reproduction. The brief appearance of *The Lacemaker* in Luis Buñuel's *Un chien andalou* (1929) is undoubtedly less memorable

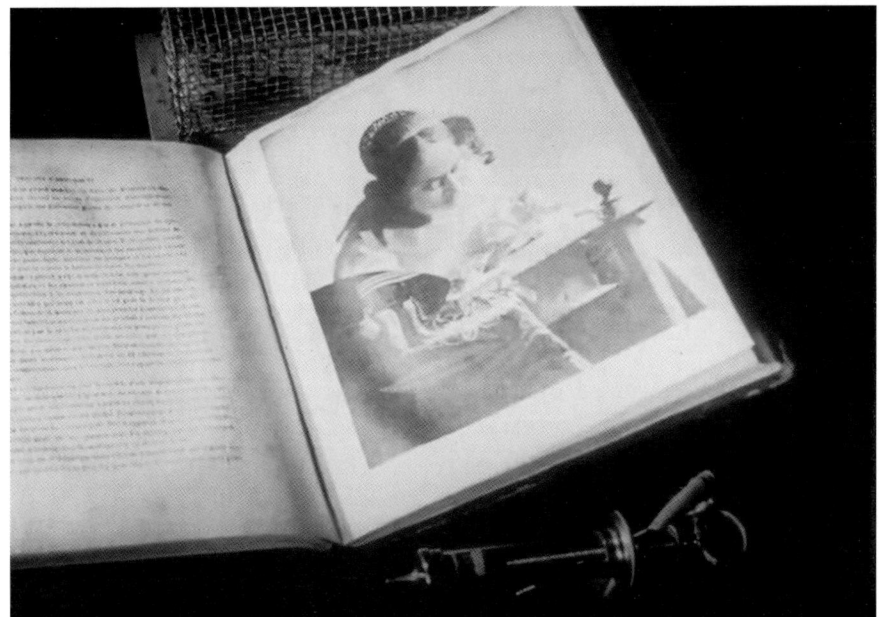

Fig. 7.11. Screenshot from *Un chien andalou*, directed by Luis Buñuel, with screenplay by Luis Buñuel and Salvador Dalí. Les Grandes Films Classiques, 1929

than the notorious scene in which a man slices a woman's eyeball, but both images surface and fade according to the same surrealist logic. Though the screenplay is jointly attributed to Dalí and Buñuel, it seems safe to assume that the painter was primarily responsible for specifying how the opening sequence with the sliced eyeball should be followed "eight years later" by one in which a sudden noise prompts the same young woman to toss aside a book that "remains opened on a reproduction" of Vermeer's painting (fig. 7.11). As an image of absorption, the abandoned *Lacemaker* perhaps symbolizes the woman herself, who is initially said to be "absorbed in reading"—a state in which we will never see her again.[23] But given the meanings that Dalí would subsequently attribute to the painting, it would be foolhardy to try to pin down its significance too closely.

Dalí's most radical appropriation of the painting, which he dubbed *Paranoiac-Critical Study of Vermeer's Lace-Maker* (fig. 7.12), appears to be the surrealist twin of the picture he made for Robert Lehman. Produced around the same time as Lehman's copy, it testifies to a far more complicated relation to the original. By the artist's own account, that relation went back to his childhood, when he began to associate a reproduction of *The Lacemaker* that hung in his father's office with his own burgeoning interest in a servant girl. For some reason, a sharp blow on his elbow decades later prompted "a sharp visualization" of the painting and immediately prompted him—or so he would subsequently claim—to ask the Louvre for permission to copy it. (The account, published in *The Unspeakable Confessions of Salvador Dali* some twenty years after the event, notably elides the commission from Lehman.) But by the time this "highly upsetting picture" was placed before him, copying in the ordinary sense of the

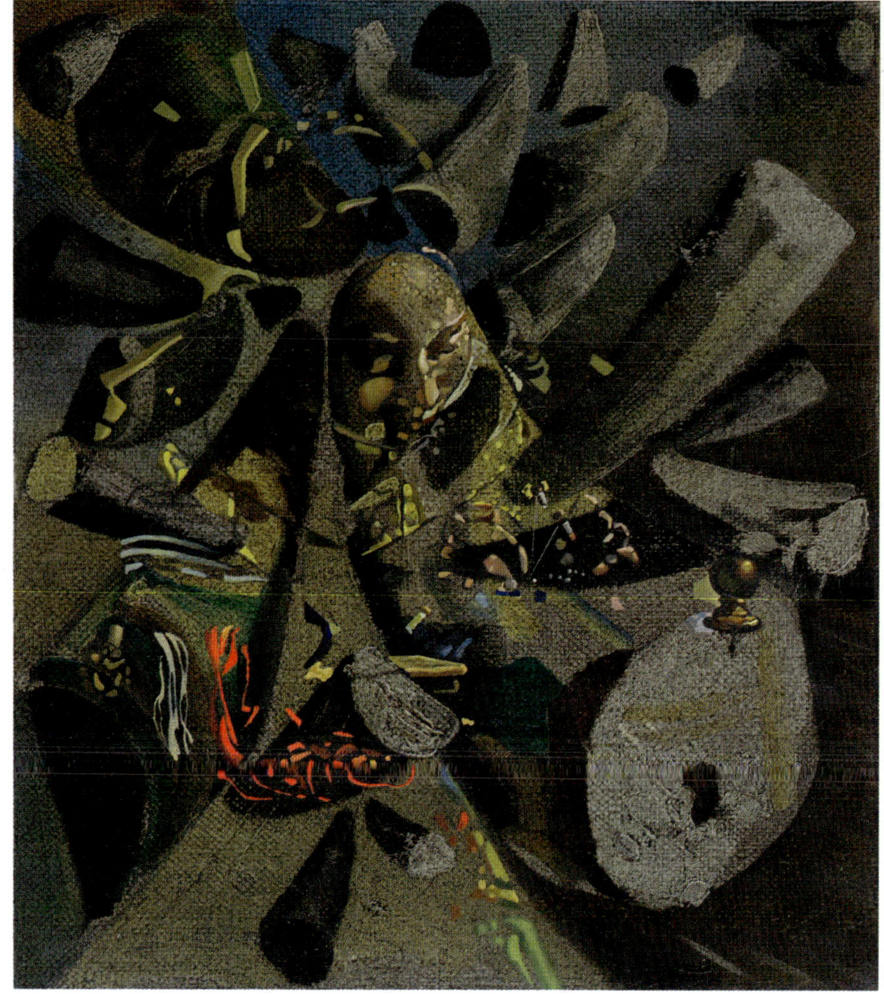

Fig. 7.12. Salvador Dalí, *Paranoiac-Critical Study of Vermeer's "The Lacemaker"* (ca. 1955). Oil on canvas. 27.1 × 22.1 cm. The Solomon R. Guggenheim Museum, New York. Anonymous gift, 1976. 76.2206. © 2025 Salvador Dalí, Fundació Gala-Salvador Dalí / Artists Rights Society (ARS), NY

term had long been rendered irrelevant, as the characteristic perversity of the formula by which his text identifies the original makes evident. Behind the lacemaker's calm appearance, Dalí contended, "was hidden a tremendous ultra-piercing energy": an energy he identified with her invisible needle and that in turn inspired him to begin replacing her figure with rhinoceros horns. The subsequent discovery that the shape of those horns closely matched the "logarithmic curves" of Vermeer's picture, as did the sunflower spirals he adopted for the headdress and cushion, confirmed for Dalí the genius of his transformation. "The lace maker now appeared as the pure symbol of that maximum of spiritual strength that the rhinoceros carried at the end of his nose," the artist exulted, before going on to elucidate that cryptic pronouncement—in a manner of speaking—by noting that "crushed rhinoceros horn is a powerful aphrodisiac." According to this surrealist logic, Dalí had appropriated Vermeer's painting in order to demonstrate a truth latent in the original: "Beauty and Eros are one."[24]

Dalí's obsessions were clearly idiosyncratic—he also fetishized rotting donkeys, for instance[25]—but the combinatory impulse behind his *Paranoiac-Critical Study* is not so different from the impulse that drives many modern appropriators of Vermeer, whether or not we wish to classify the result as pastiche. Cornell's *Grand Hôtel Bon Port* also combines a beloved form with a beloved Vermeer figure, after all, even if his chaste box is a very different sort of object from Dalí's erotic horn. Deem's *Rita Vermeer* (fig. 7.13) partly reverses the formula: the otherwise empty room appears to have been lifted from the *Young Woman Standing at a Virginal* (see fig. 3.3), while the beloved figure has been appropriated from a photograph of the movie star Rita Hayworth—her famously sultry features so positioned that America's "Love Goddess" effectively replaces both Vermeer's young woman and the large Cupid who hangs on the wall behind her. In a related pastiche painted that same year, Deem removed the human figures and several objects from *The Music Lesson* and put Gilbert Stuart's unfinished portrait of America's first president in the space originally occupied by Vermeer's mirror (fig. 7.14; cf. fig. 3.10). According to the artist, the palette of *George Washington Vermeer* alludes to the black-and-white image of the president on the dollar bill, while likewise conjuring up "the black-and-white crispness of historical documents displayed as objects for observation."[26] Though he doesn't say so, it also serves to emphasize the black-and-white tiles that decorate the floors of many Vermeer interiors, *The Music Lesson* included, by extending their palette to take in the entire picture.

It's hard not to sense a certain mischievousness at work when George Washington shows up in *The Music Lesson*, though Deem strenuously resisted the idea that any of his Vermeer-related pictures were intended as visual jokes.[27] But combining quotations from more than one painter is a familiar strategy of postmodern art,

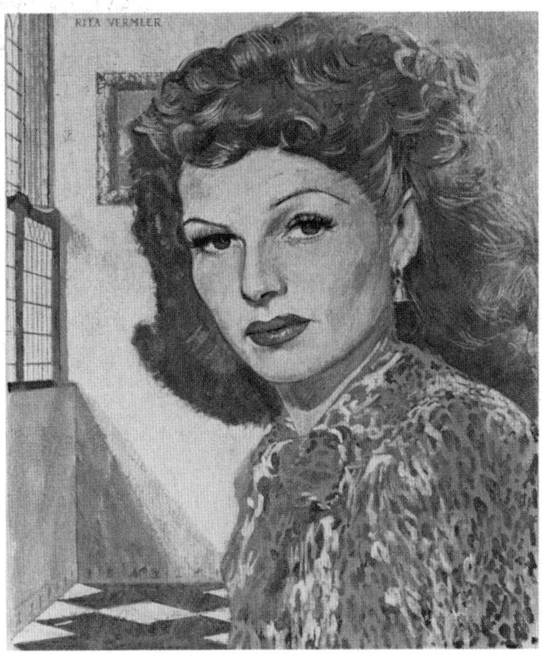

Fig. 7.13. George Deem, *Rita Vermeer* (1974). Pencil, acrylic, and watercolor on paper. 48 × 34.5 cm. Evansville Museum of Arts, History, and Science, Evansville, IN. © New Britain Museum of American Art / Artists Rights Society (ARS), NY. Image © Archives of American Art, Smithsonian Institution, Washington, DC

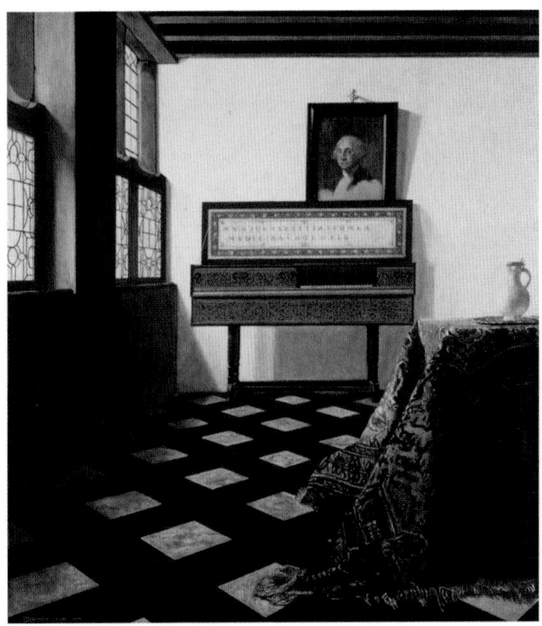

Fig. 7.14. George Deem, *George Washington Vermeer* (1974). Oil on canvas. 80 × 70 cm. New Britain Museum of American Art, New Britain, CT. © New Britain Museum of American Art / Artists Rights Society (ARS), NY. Image © Archives of American Art, Smithsonian Institution, Washington, DC

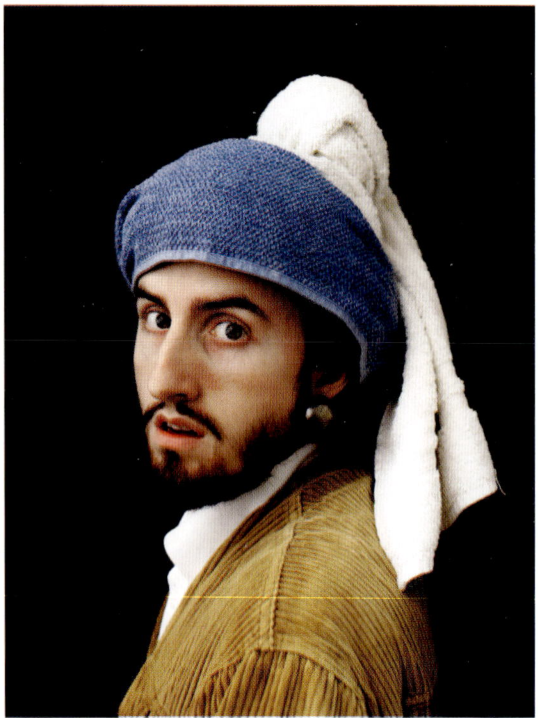

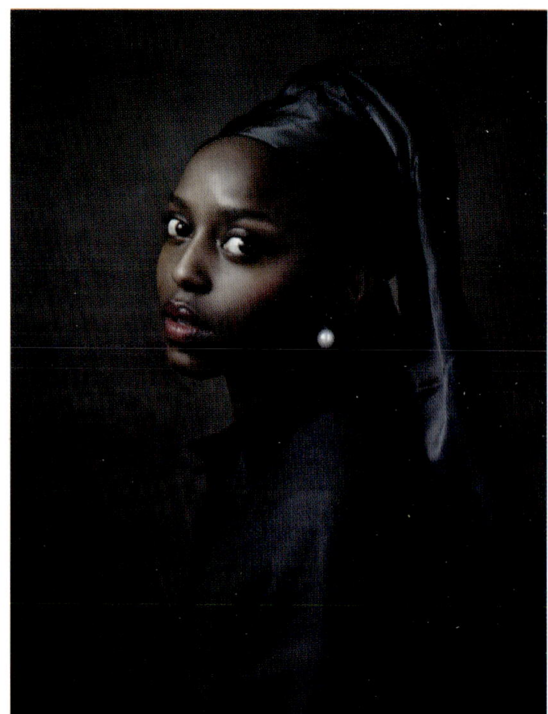

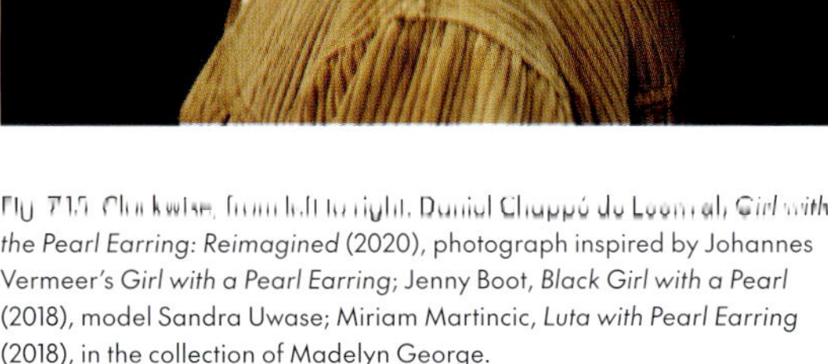

Fig. 7.15. Clockwise, from left to right: Daniel Chappé de Leonval, *Girl with the Pearl Earring: Reimagined* (2020), photograph inspired by Johannes Vermeer's *Girl with a Pearl Earring*; Jenny Boot, *Black Girl with a Pearl* (2018), model Sandra Uwase; Miriam Martincic, *Luta with Pearl Earring* (2018), in the collection of Madelyn George.

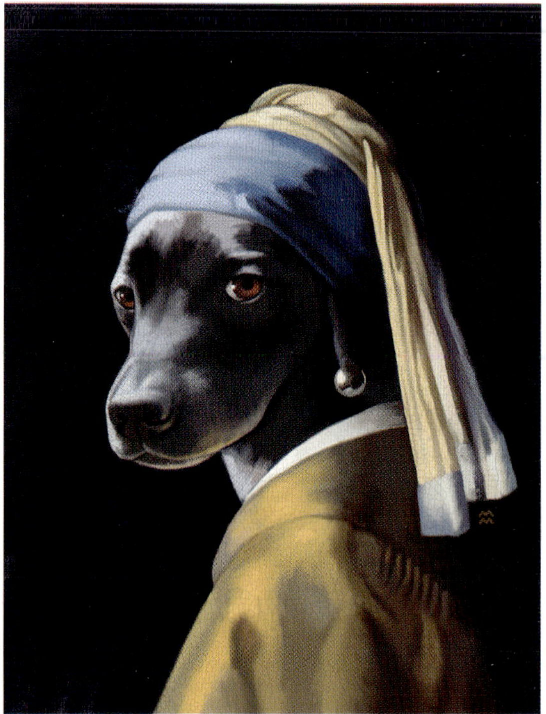

and Gilbert Stuart is by no means the only painter to have been joined with Vermeer in this way. In 1964 the Czech poet and artist Jiří Kolář created an optically challenging image by cutting equally wide strips from reproductions of the *View of Delft* and Rembrandt's *Danaë* (ca. 1636–43) and placing them alternately on a board: a technique he termed "rollage."[28] Several decades later, the American painter Terri Priest produced a number of works in which she combined poster-like images of Vermeer's women—the head of *The Guitar Player* seems to have been a particular favorite—with elements drawn from a range of twentieth-century artists, including Amedeo Modigliani, Georgia O'Keeffe, Joan Miró, Roy Lichtenstein, Tom Wesselmann, and Vija Celmins. In one picture, a flatly painted and truncated version of the model in *The Art of Painting* poses next to Marcel Duchamp's *Bicycle Wheel* (1913)—the stool to which it's fixed presumably substituting for the artist's seat in the original—while clutching what appears to be a small abstract canvas by Priest herself in place of Vermeer's heavy book.

As such substitutions suggest, a fine line separates this form of quotation from the kind in which the seventeenth-century trappings of the original disappear altogether, or remain simply as traces in the updated image. The thousands of entries that the Mauritshuis collected under the rubric "My Girl with a Pearl" begin to convey the range of possibilities. Many attempted to preserve a version of Vermeer's palette; most, but not all, retained the girl's pose and something that resembled her earring, while altering everything from her costume to her race, her gender, and even her species—the *Girl* as dog, for instance, or an ear of corn (fig. 7.15).[29]

This is to treat the painting, of course, less as an arrangement of brushstrokes on canvas than as an icon: an image so familiar that a few marks or gestures suffice to conjure it up in the mind's eye. Indeed, the *Girl* was particularly susceptible to such experiment, as the curators at the Mauritshuis surely knew. Boosted by the fame of Chevalier's bestselling novel, and encouraged by the painting's relative simplicity, at least as compared to Vermeer's multifigure compositions, versions of the *Girl with a Pearl Earring* had proliferated both online and off well before the museum issued its call, while reproductions of the original had served for everything from a magazine cover for the London Underground to posters denouncing gun violence (fig. 7.16). In 2001 the American poet W. S. Di Piero had even produced a mischievous verbal pastiche of the image in which the speaker glimpses "a Netherlandish type" panhandling by an ATM machine in San Francisco and wishfully turns the "pomegranate seed ball / bearings agleam in her nose" into a low-rent version of the iconic earring: "pearls not sea-harvested / but imagined seen put there / by a certain need and fancy."[30] That nose piercings could be spotted on at least one entry to the museum's competition is probably a coincidence, but it was no surprise to see how many participants shared in the demotic spirit of Di Piero's poem.

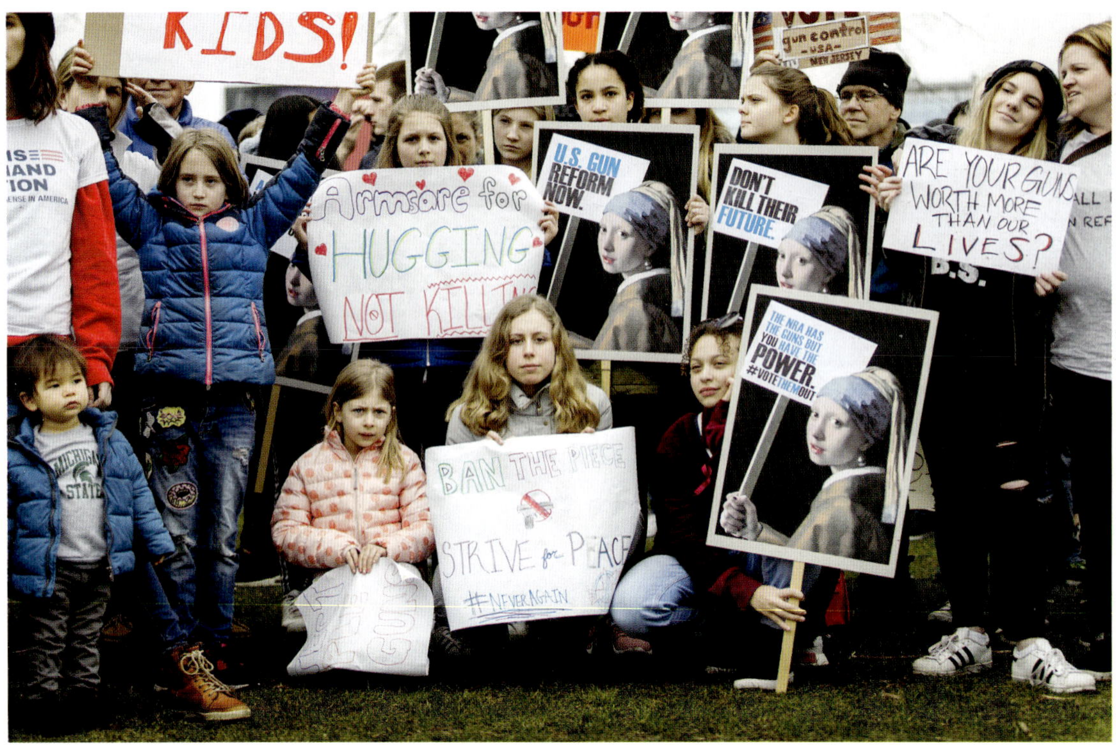

Fig. 7.16. March for Our Lives demonstrators at the Museumplein, Amsterdam, 24 March 2018. Koen van Weel / AFP Via Getty Images

The practice of dressing up and posing as figures in old pictures is a type of performance art with a long history, from the *tableaux vivants* that sometimes accompanied civic processions in the late Middle Ages to the popular versions that continued to flourish on amateur and professional stages alike into the early twentieth century.[31] Unlike the traditional tableau, however, which is necessarily ephemeral, a photograph or film can aspire to a kind of permanence, and some of the energies that once went into staging such tableaux have now clearly migrated to the making of images in which analogous performances are recorded for posterity. By implicitly inviting the public at large to pose as the *Girl* and take out a camera, the Mauritshuis further democratized a practice that was already hovering between high art and low, as a quick comparison between some of the submissions it received and the work of a well-established professional such as the Japanese photographer and performance artist Yasumasa Morimura may serve to illustrate (fig. 7.17).

Morimura has made a career out of playing with gender and racial identity by posing as iconic figures from Western art, but self-portraiture is not the only form such photographed tableaux have taken. In 2019 the Dutch photographer Caroline Sikkenk arranged for models of various races and ages to pose as Vermeer's *Girl* for a photographic series that would later be projected on screens in front of the Mauritshuis and the World Trade Center in Manhattan: an obvious forerunner of the museum's wider call for such images four years later. Nor is the *Girl with a Pearl Earring* the only Vermeer that has lent itself

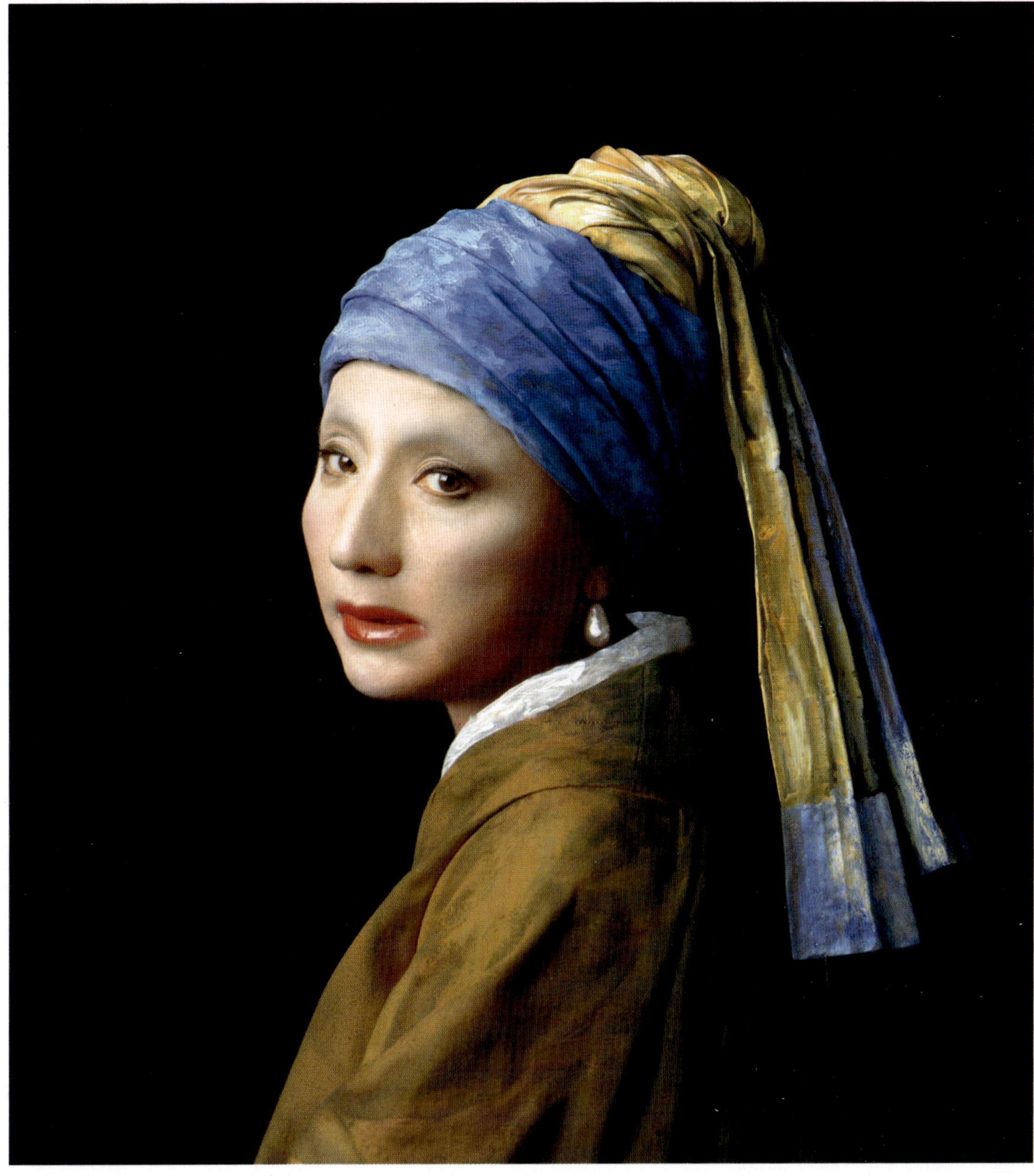

Fig. 7.17. Yasumasa Morimura, *Vermeer Study: Looking Back (Mirror)* (2008). C-print on canvas. 44.5 × 39.1 cm. © Yasumasa Morimura; courtesy of the artist and Luhring Augustine, NY

to the practice. In the 1990s the Norwegian artist Jeannette Christensen took repeated Polaroids over a period of years of the same ordinary people adopting poses derived from Vermeer and assembled them in a series she called *The Passing of Time*.[32] While Christensen confined herself to varying the gender of her subjects—depicting both men and women, for example, as *The Milkmaid* or the *Lady Writing a Letter*—Sikkenk later followed up her *Girls with Pearls* series with an image of a Black model in modern dress posed as the *Woman Holding a Balance* (fig. 7.18).

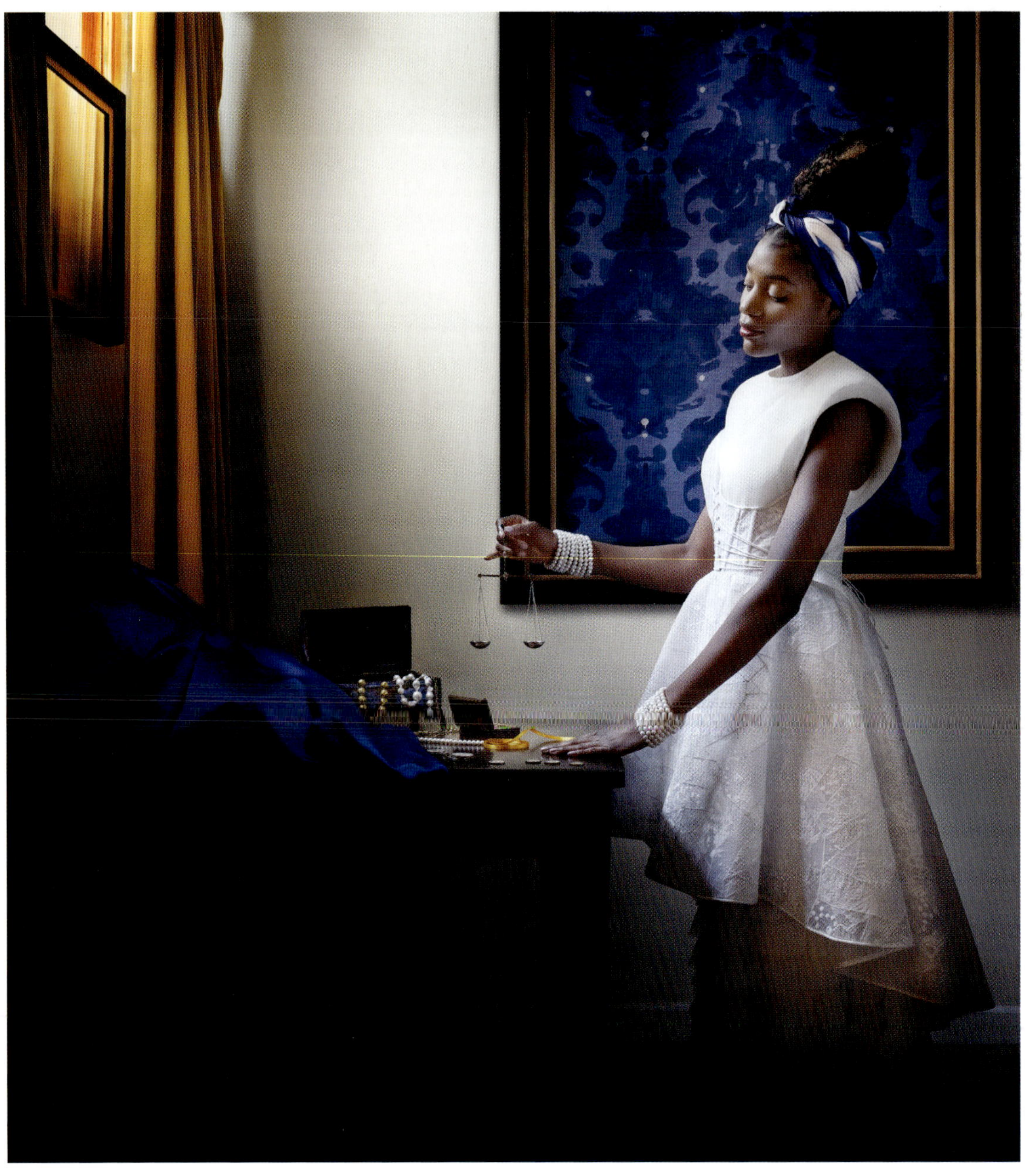

Fig. 7.18. Caroline Sikkenk, *Young Woman Holding a Balance* (2021). Photograph: Caroline Sikkenk—Photoline

But if such experiments with the gender and race of Vermeer's subjects are of relatively recent vintage, photographic tableaux based on his work have a longer history, as Polak's early experiment with *The Art of Painting* has already demonstrated. Though Jan Jost mostly paid homage to the artist by training his camera on actual paintings and reproductions, for example, he also engaged in the practice when he included a scene in *All the Vermeers in New York* that quoted a painting not on view in the city: the *Girl Reading a Letter at an Open Window* (see fig. 1.11), located in Dresden. In Jost's version of the image, the window by

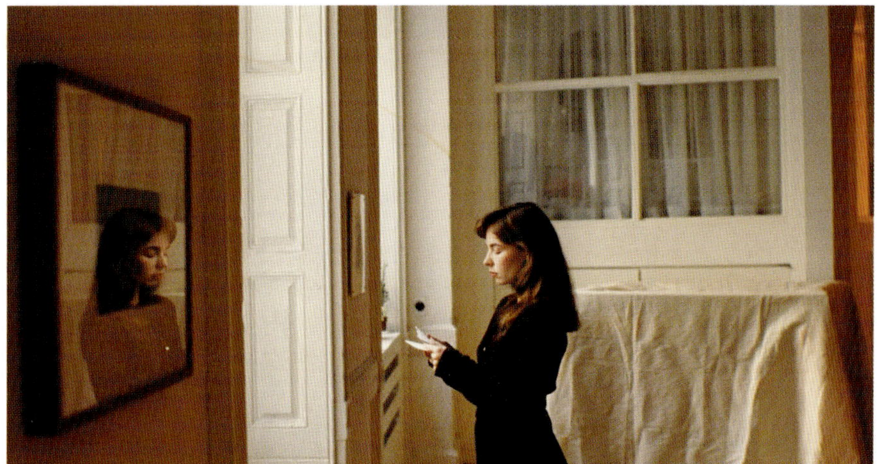

Fig. 7.19. Screenshot from *All the Vermeers in New York*, directed by Jan Jost. American Theatrical Films, 1990

which his heroine reads her letter appears to be closed, but he continues to echo Vermeer's reflection of the young woman's face in its open panes by reflecting his own young woman's face in a glass-covered picture that hangs on the wall (fig. 7.19). No one familiar with the speculation that has often surrounded Vermeer's female readers would be surprised to learn that the letter in the film apparently comes from a distant lover: the boyfriend in France whom the heroine has temporarily abandoned for a potential acting career in New York, and to whom she is returning when the devastated protagonist suffers his fatal aneurism in the Vermeer room at the Metropolitan.

A few years later, the Dresden painting would also provide the template for another piece of camerawork, this one a staged photograph rather than a film shot. Part of a series that the British photographer Tom Hunter collectively titled "Persons Unknown" (1997) after the addressees of the legal notices that he and his fellow squatters had been receiving from the London Borough of Hackney, it deliberately appropriates Vermeer's painting for an act of political protest. Rather than a letter from a possible lover, *Woman Reading a Possession Order* announces that this young woman is reading an eviction notice, while a baby who presumably will share in that eviction replaces the sumptuous still life in the original (fig. 7.20). Touchingly echoing the loose tendrils of the painted woman's hair but otherwise making clear that her contemporary counterpart occupies a very different social stratum from her predecessor, Hunter nonetheless understands his image as a continuation of Vermeer's project: that attentiveness to "the dignity of [. . .] ordinary people involved in their daily lives," as he would later put it, that ends by "lifting the ordinary into the extraordinary."[33]

By his own account, Hunter first came upon Vermeer when some photography instructors responded to the color transparencies he had made for a 3D model of a squatted Hackney street by sending him to the college library to look at the work of the Golden Age painters. "Transfixed" initially by Vermeer's

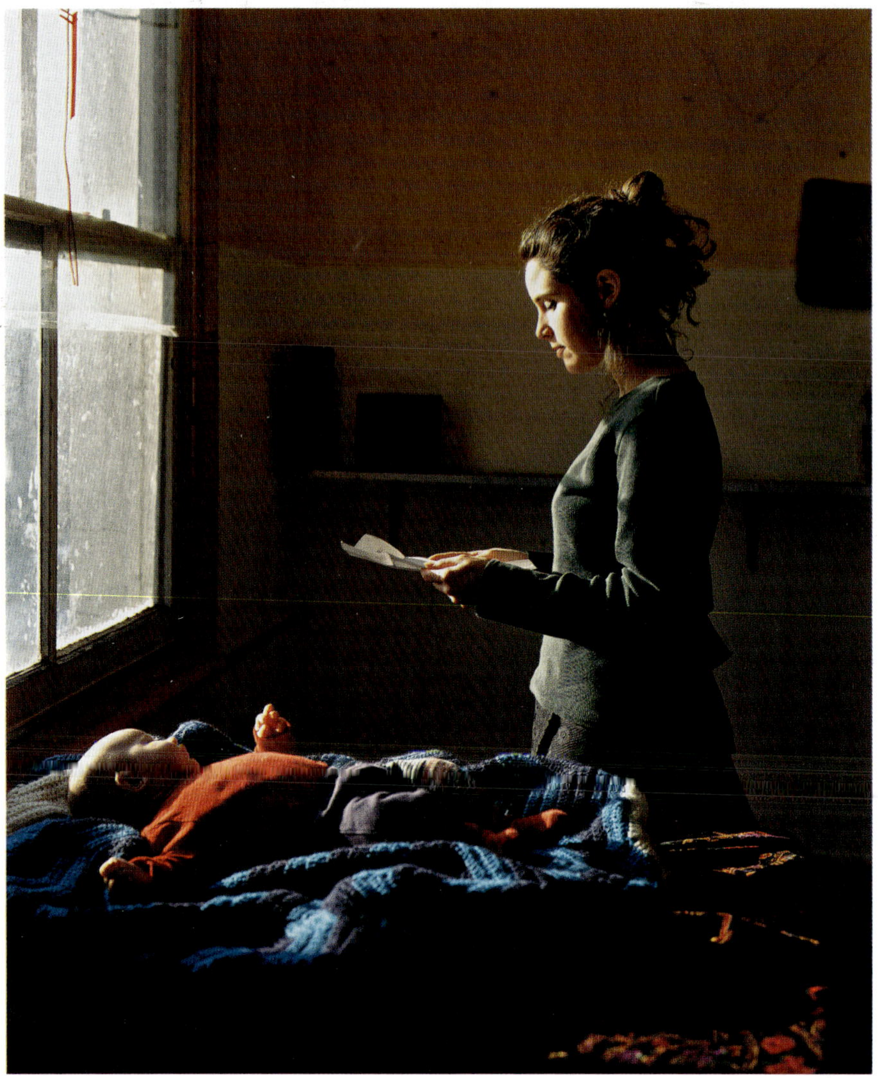

Fig. 7.20. *Woman Reading a Possession Order*, from the series "Persons Unknown" (1997), courtesy of the artist Tom Hunter

color and light, he later came to learn of the artist's possible use of the camera obscura and to associate that camerawork, in a move familiar to us from other users of the instrument, with his own. There are seven photographs in "Persons Unknown," including the prize-winning *Woman Reading a Possession Order,* each of them modeled on a different Vermeer. But it was not until 2001, when a major exhibition on the Delft School drew him to the National Gallery in London, that Hunter ever saw any of the paintings for himself. Like so many of the artists examined here, this modern appropriator of Vermeer based his photographic critique of contemporary social arrangements on the reproductions he had seen in books.[34]

The absence of any seventeenth-century costume or props from Hunter's photographs—or from Jost's filmed version of the Dresden painting, for that matter—raises an interesting question: what distinguishes such appropriations

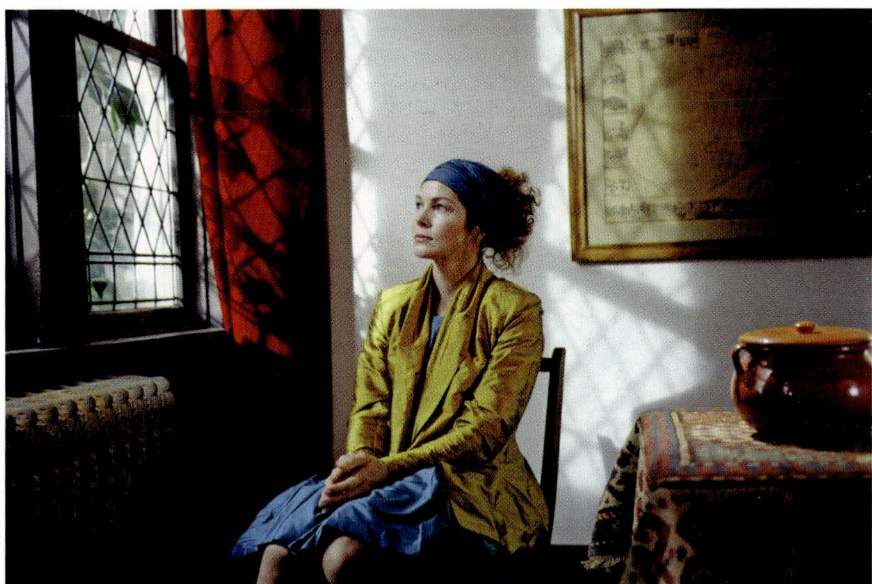

Fig. 7.21. Lois Chiles in *Until the End of the World*, director's cut by Wim Wenders. © 1991 Road Movies—Argos Films. Courtesy of Wim Wenders Stiftung—Argos Films

of Vermeer's work from the imitations we looked at earlier, which also proceeded by updating the artist's images? Clearly the line that separates *Woman Reading a Possession Order* from Richter's *The Reader* (see fig. 5.1), for instance, is a fine one indeed—all the more so, of course, because Richter's work, which appeared only three years before Hunter's, first took shape as a photograph. That Richter professed not to have thought of Vermeer when he composed the image might seem to justify the distinction, though his subsequent acknowledgment that it "remind[ed]" him of his predecessor clearly complicates the issue, as does the fact that Tarbell and the other Boston School painters spoke openly of Vermeer's influence on their work, without prompting later historians to classify that work as appropriation or pastiche.[35]

Hard and fast rules about these matters scarcely seem possible, even if it were obvious—as it's not—that we'd want them. But perhaps the most helpful generalization that can be ventured about the works assembled here is that their creators all intended, to one degree or another, to make art about art: an intention that they visibly signaled in the works themselves. Whether Hunter was primarily concerned with art history when he staged his photographs may be doubted, but he certainly expected viewers to recognize his quotations of Vermeer and to understand those quotations as part of the photographs' meaning. When the German filmmaker Wim Wenders dressed a young woman in a blue turban and gold jacket and posed her before a leaded window, with a map on the wall behind her and an oriental carpet on the table at her side (fig. 7.21), he also made it clear that he was not so much imitating Vermeer as deliberately quoting him—all the more so because the film in question, "an uneasy mix of sci-fi, film noir, and road movie," in the words of one critic, is set in a futuristic world where these particular details have no other obvious purpose.[36]

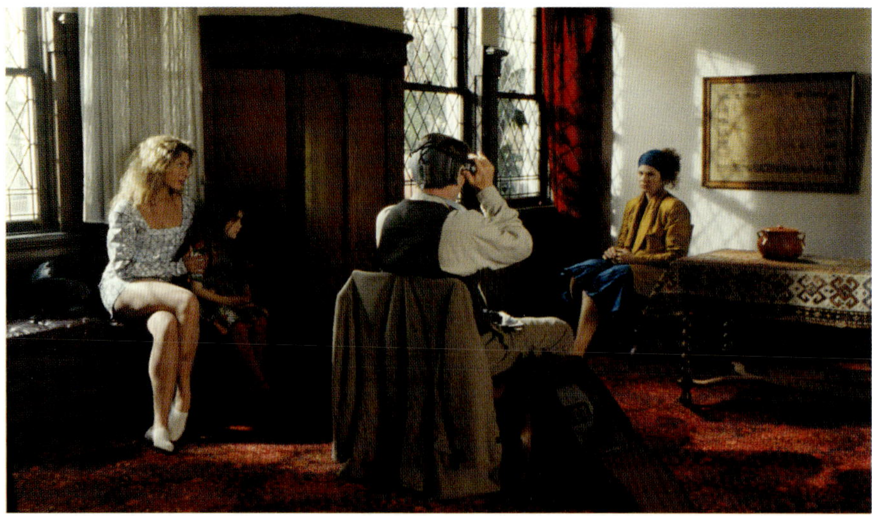

Fig. 7.22. Still from *Until the End of the World*, director's cut by Wim Wenders. © 1991 Road Movies—Argos Films. Courtesy of Wim Wenders Stiftung—Argos Films

Until the End of the World (1991), as the film is titled, is finally less concerned with the history of art than with the dangerous proliferation of images enabled by modern technology. But Wenders, who began as a painter before he took up filmmaking, has often professed his love of painting and of Vermeer in particular, going so far as to tell one interviewer in 1976, "for a film-maker, Vermeer is the only painter there is."[37] Appropriately enough, the scene at issue is itself about picture-taking, though the instrument that will capture the seated woman's image is not a paintbrush but a new kind of camera: one that Wenders's own camera approaches from the back in a shot that manages to combine his pastiche of the *Girl with a Pearl Earring* and several Vermeer interiors with an oblique quotation of *The Art of Painting* (fig. 7.22).[38] The product of a brilliant inventor named Henry Farber, the camera is designed to enable the blind to see, by translating the images processed by the brain of the sighted person wearing the camera to the brain of the sightless person who receives its signals; and in this crucial scene, the film's heroine, Claire, is about to use Farber's fantastic instrument to process an image of his grown daughter, in the hope of eventually transmitting that image to his blind wife, Edith. (Edith, who lost her sight when she was eight, has never seen her children.) According to the film's premise, the effectiveness of the camera partly depends on the visual and emotional sensitivities of the person wearing it, and the fact that Claire is supposed to have great powers of visual concentration is very much to the point. Still more to the point, especially in the context of the scene's Vermeerian resonances, is the fact that "Claire" means light and that "Farber," as Brigitte Peucker has noted, means "'he who colors or dyes'—or in this case, paints."[39] At the ecstatic climax of this sequence, Edith is able to receive Claire's signals and see her daughter for the first time: a daughter whose image comes to her by means of this light-painting, and who is dressed, of course, to resemble another famous light-painting—Vermeer's *Girl with a Pearl Earring*.

Until the End of the World is, however, a film deeply ambivalent about its own medium, and even as Wenders identifies his imaginary camera with the painter he loves, he works to undo that identification. As he himself later told it, he "had always dreamt about a machine that could make a blind person see," and he had originally intended to conclude the film with the Utopian realization of that vision. But the vast explosion of images with which the world had been bombarded in the intervening years threatened to turn that dream into a nightmare, and the film he actually made is one in which the Utopia promised by Farber's invention rapidly devolves into its opposite. Rather than look outward, the film's protagonists begin using the device to stare obsessively at their own dream images, and the heroine is only saved from a final descent into narcissism and madness by a novelist who forces her to abandon her camera for a book.[40] *Until the End of the World* exists in many versions—its initial release in the United States ran to just over half of the five-hour director's cut[41]—but all those available to the viewing public appear to conclude that words alone can provide salvation from our collective addiction to images: a conclusion that seemingly leaves little room for the film's prior gesture toward an older form of image-making.

Yet it is far from clear that Wenders actually meant his homage to Vermeer to be swallowed up by his deep ambivalence toward his medium. In an interview published after the film's release, he described a closing sequence left on the cutting-room floor, in which another of the image-addicted protagonists, Farber's son Sam, achieves his own cure by sitting quietly in the landscape and doing watercolors.[42] It's not looking, but our solipsistic obsession with our screens that the filmmaker appears to find terrifying. Whether or not Wenders was conscious of the fact, he may have been drawn to Vermeer not only for the painter's handling of light, but also for his quiet attentiveness to the independent reality of the women he painted: an independence he appeared to respect rather than attempt to penetrate. As Lawrence Gowing acutely observed of the typical Vermeer subject, "She remains outside him, essentially and perfectly other than he."[43]

The cultural phenomena that inspired Wenders's film have only grown more salient, of course, in the years since its making. But the proliferation of images he found so disquieting is also what enables much of the art we have been examining in this chapter: art that depends for its effects on the public's prior acquaintance with other images. Morley's knowing appropriation of *The Art of Painting*, for instance, obviously gestures to the original, even as it invites us to recognize that what we are seeing is an image not of the painting itself, but of a prior image of it: a fact signaled by everything from Morley's duplication of the poster's border, including the text by which it credits both the painting and the source of its color print, to the chromatic distortions faithfully reproduced from that print and the exaggerated scale of the whole, which more than doubles the size of Vermeer's original (fig. 7.23).[44] The deliberate flatness of Morley's

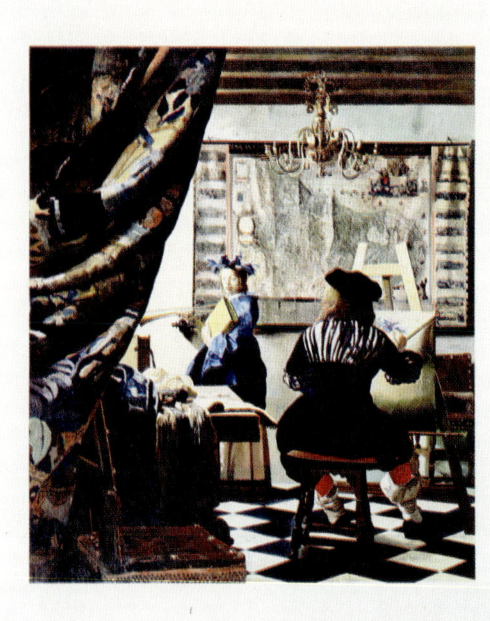

Fig. 7.23. Malcolm Morley, *Vermeer: Portrait of the Artist in His Studio* (1968). Acrylic on canvas. 266.7 × 221 cm. The Broad, Los Angeles. © The Estate of Malcolm Morley

painting, which results from his practice of cutting the reproduction into little squares, fixing them to his canvas one by one, and attempting to duplicate each area of color individually, without regard for the overall illusion, is a further invitation to recognize that this is an image twice removed from the painting it appropriates.[45] As one commentator summarizes the dizzying situation with which the painting confronts us: "*Vermeer: Portrait of the Artist in his Studio* is the painted reproduction of a printed photographic reproduction of a painting in which a painter, with his back turned, reproduces in paint a female model allegorically disguised as Fame—in obvious tribute to the glory of painting."[46]

It may no longer be true that *The Art of Painting* would be surpassed only by the *Mona Lisa* when modern works of art about art were being counted, as the curators of a seminal exhibition on the subject at the Whitney Museum of American Art in 1978 once contended.[47] After the outpouring inspired by the Mauritshuis, it's even possible that the *Girl with a Pearl Earring* has vaulted over both works, especially if the calculation is not limited to art that is likely to end up in a museum. But Morley was one of several painters in the Whitney show who prompted the generalization, and like the others, his self-consciousness about art-making was clearly rooted in the perception that the maker of *The Art of Painting* had been there before him. Vermeer's painting is also art about art, in other words, and one reason it tends to inspire further work in this vein is that subsequent artists can multiply its reflexiveness by quoting it in turn.

Among the other works on display at the Whitney, for instance, was a painting by the American artist James McGarrell (1930–2020) that takes as its premise the fiction that the sketch on which Vermeer's artist was working has been completed and now hangs on the wall of another artist's studio: an effect McGarrell achieves by isolating the portion of the original that shows Vermeer's "real" model standing with her trumpet and book, copying it, and turning it into a framed picture on the wall of his own picture. A different woman holding a book—but no longer furnished with a trumpet or laurel wreath—takes the model's place in front of McGarrell's artist, who sits, as in Vermeer, with his back to the viewer, his striped shirt and baggy socks echoing the costume of his predecessor (fig. 7.24). Though McGarrell may have assumed that he was also following Vermeer in making his artist a self-portrait, it's far from clear that in this respect, at least, he was proving faithful to the original. As many scholars have pointed out, Vermeer's artist is a history painter, who begins—as

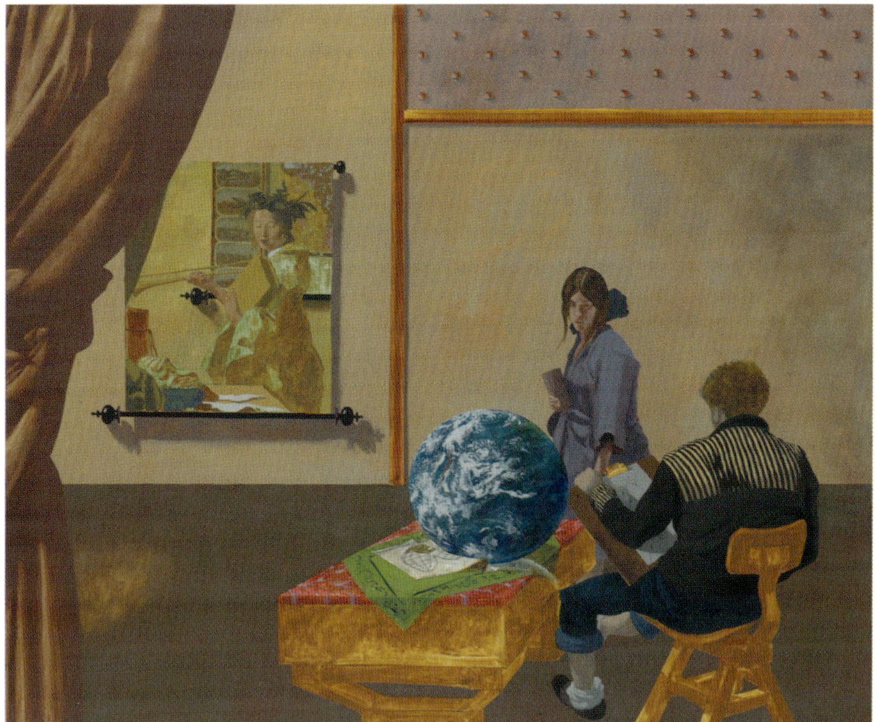

Fig. 7.24. James McGarrell, *Veracity* (1969). Oil and pencil on canvas. 154.9 × 180.6 cm. Gift of Joseph H. Hirshhorn, 1972. © Andrew McGarrell. Image credit: Rich Coulby. Hirshhorn Museum and Sculpture Garden

Vermeer did not—with a preparatory drawing, and whose very costume may be intended to backdate him.[48] But if McGarrell's picture overlooks this dimension of Vermeer's painting, the modern work's relation to its predecessor nonetheless replicates a historical consciousness already present in the original. Though the curators of the Whitney show didn't explicitly recognize the fact, this was another reason so many of their contributors demonstrated their own historical self-consciousness by reference to *The Art of Painting*.

Deem, who had been making his "art of art history," as several commentators have called it,[49] since the 1960s, was an obvious choice for that show, where he was represented both by *George Washington Vermeer* and by another painting of which the curators were thinking when they ventured their generalization: a *Vermeer Interior*, now in a private collection, that widens the space of *The Music Lesson* to accommodate the figures from *The Art of Painting*. Having apparently arrived in this new space accompanied by their chandelier and map, the model joins the couple in the background, her trumpet pointing suggestively at the virginal, as if she were about to join in the music-making, while the artist sits on an elevated platform in the foreground that allows him to survey the entire scene. Creating a new image from a pastiche of two or more Vermeers like this is a favorite Deem technique, and one that he would continue to employ throughout his career, including in other works that take off from *The Art of Painting*. Note, for instance, how he would continue to raid the artist's studio a quarter century later for the titular furnishings of *A Stool, A Chair, and a*

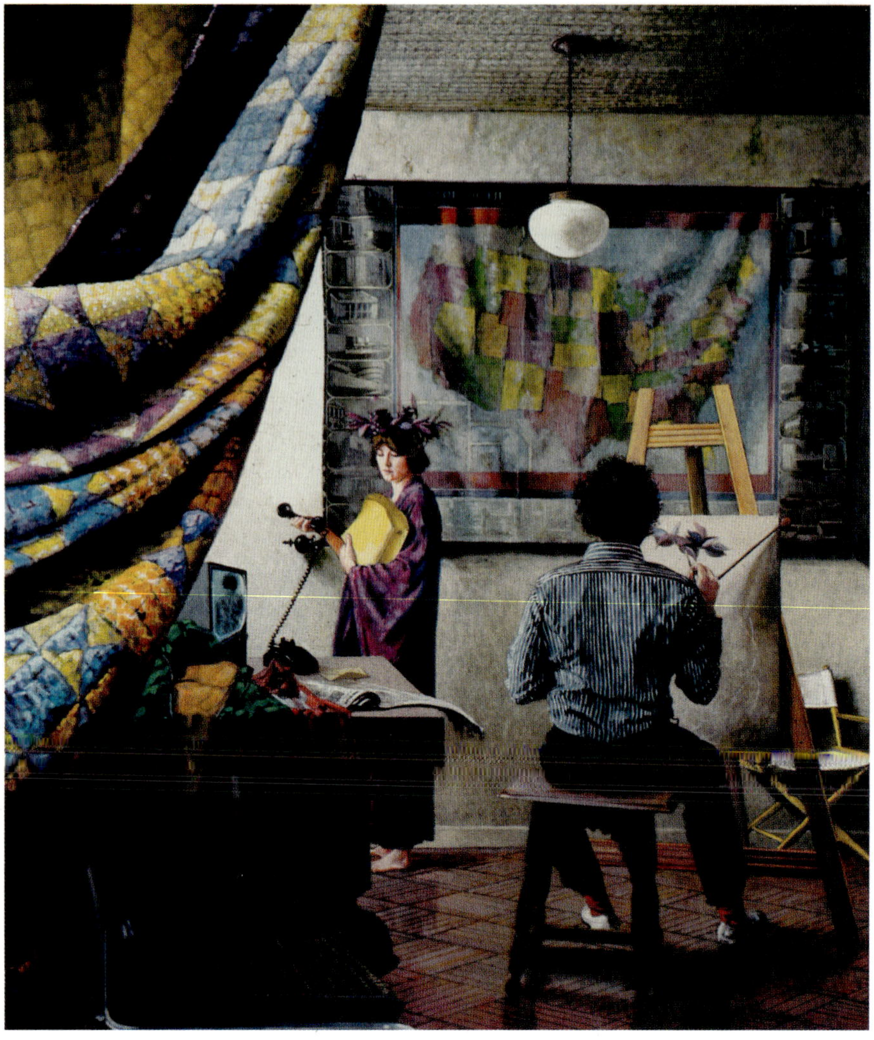

Fig. 7.25. George Deem, *New York Artist in His Studio/Vermeer's "Artist in His Studio"* (1979). Oil on canvas. Each canvas, 134.6 × 111.8 cm. Manney Collection, New York. © New Britain Museum of American Art / Artists Rights Society (ARS), NY. Image © Archives of American Art, Smithsonian Institution, Washington, DC

Map (2003), even as he would quietly vary the formula by importing a border of Delft tiles from the *Young Woman Standing at a Virginal* into the picture (cf. fig. 7.1 and figs. 3.13 and 3.3).

Deem's most thoroughgoing engagement with *The Art of Painting* involved a different kind of doubling, however. A diptych of 1979 entitled *New York Artist in His Studio/Vermeer's "Artist in His Studio,"* it drew on some of the strategies the public had already seen in Morley's and McGarrell's contributions to the Whitney show the previous year: a form of copying, on the one hand, and a lively updating on the other. But rather than highlight his departure from the painting in the copy itself, like Morley, Deem primarily signaled its status *as* a copy by leaving its border unpainted, while saving most of his deviations from Vermeer for the updated image that accompanies it (fig. 7.25). At the same time, by juxtaposing the two canvases, each of which replicates the dimensions of the original, he invited something like the comparison McGarrell

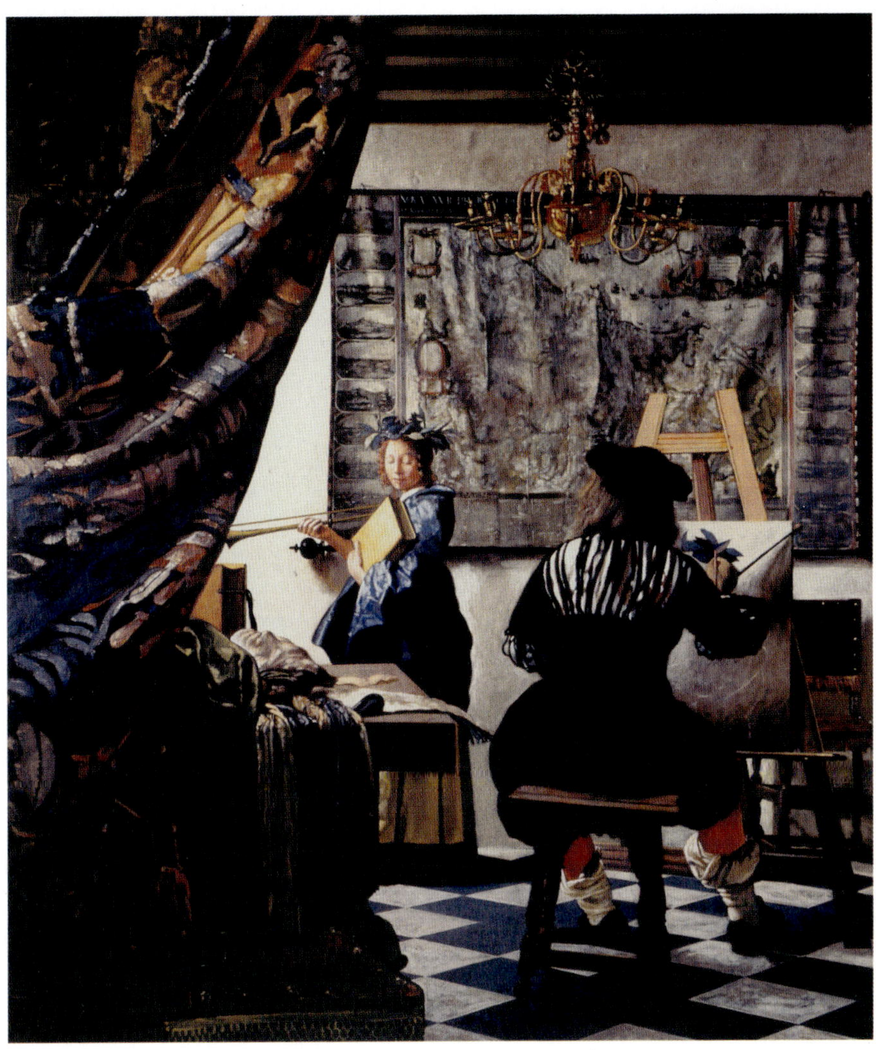

had presumably meant to elicit by incorporating a portion of that original as a picture-within-his-picture. (Note, too, how Deem also settled on a modern version of Vermeer's black-and-white stripes, though he apparently preferred red socks to baggy ones as a means of gesturing at the original's legwear.)

As Deem himself would later anatomize his procedure in detail:

> For my diptych *The Artist in His Studio*, my first step was to make an exact copy of Vermeer's *The Artist in His Studio.* I made it the actual size of Vermeer's painting but placed it within a border of unpainted canvas. The point of the border is to isolate Vermeer's painting as an image which I am "quoting" as part of my diptych [. . .].
>
> The other painting in my diptych, the painting on the left, is *The New York Artist in His Studio*. It is painted the same size as Vermeer's *The Artist in His Studio* and with a matching unpainted border. The elements in

Vermeer's painting are repeated but with a different palette. Vermeer's map is a map of Holland with illustrations of Dutch cities in the ovals of the border. My map is a map of the United States with American art museums depicted in the corresponding ovals. The chair placed against the back wall under the map is a canvas director's chair. The model wears a model's purple kimono. She holds the yellow pages of the New York telephone directory and in her right hand, instead of the horn, a telephone. The New York artist works under an electric light suspended from a pressed tin ceiling. Vermeer's tapestry has been replaced by a down-home American quilt. The artist seated at the easel works with the same tools and equipment used by the artist in Vermeer's painting: the same easel, the same stool, the same brush and mahlstick. These things have not changed. The articles on the table have changed. The bulky manuscript on the table is now the *New York Times*. Instead of fabric piled on the table, there is a green winter downcoat and a red-and-white striped scarf. The book has become a video monitor, on the screen of which the artist, seated with his back to the video camera, sees himself in the act of painting. In this painting, I am the artist in his studio.[50]

One might add yet more items to this catalogue of substitutions, such as the Breuer chair in the foreground or the parquet floor that replaces Vermeer's marble tiles. But if the rotary telephone and the video monitor may primarily look to our eyes like conspicuous reminders that "modern" is a relative term, we can still understand them as signs of the mediated conditions in which Vermeer's twentieth- and twenty-first-century appropriators have increasingly learned to operate. The painter's tools may not have changed, but even the art museums that dot Deem's map testify to the altered circumstances under which his own picture was made. As he clearly knows, he is a long way from the world in which an artist could imagine his fame broadcast with a trumpet.

For all his witty updating, however, Deem continued to insist on the continuity of the painterly tradition. When a BBC interviewer in 2004 noted the video camera that supposedly enables his artist to view himself from the back and asked how Vermeer might have managed the same trick, Deem put a firm end to the inquiry: "There is no reason to assume that the painter depicted in *The Art of Painting* is Vermeer." A subsequent allusion to Vermeer as the "'first studio photographer'" drew an even firmer disclaimer. "Vermeer's compositions are not photographic. They are only painterly. They are a painter's constructions."[51] Yet as we have already seen, artists who work with the camera have not hesitated to appropriate Vermeer—and *The Art of Painting* specifically—for their own purposes. While Polak's *The Artist and His Model* is unmistakably a studio photograph, Wenders's more oblique appropriation of the same work for *Until the End of the World* testified to his view of Vermeer as proto-filmmaker: "really the only one," he told Jan Dawson in 1976, "who gives you the idea that his paintings could start moving."[52]

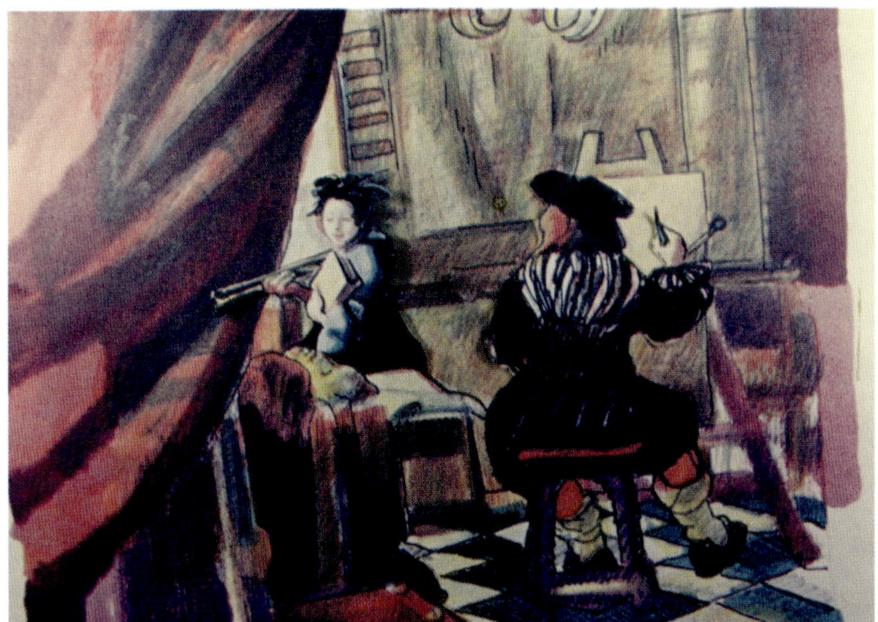

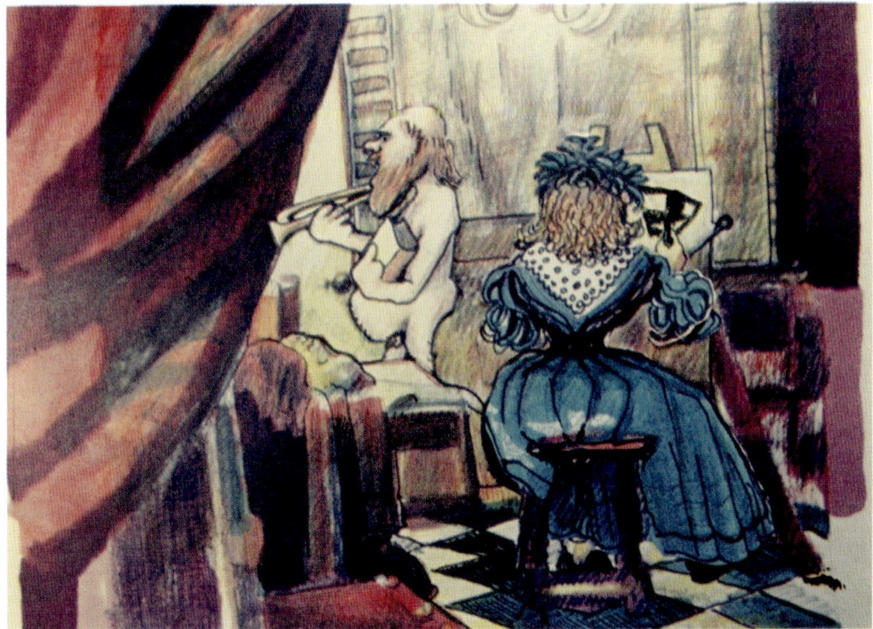

Fig. 7.26. Screenshots from Maria Lassnig, *Art Education* (1976). Animated film, 16 mm.

That same year, as it happens, a short animated film by the Austrian artist Maria Lassnig (1919–2014) did even more to put *The Art of Painting* in motion. Lassnig, who began and ended her career as a painter, once boasted that she "painted better far than any man"; and in *Art Education*, as the film is titled, she took her revenge on the gender hierarchy that governed her profession by at once animating and subverting some canonical paintings. It's the opening sequence that draws on the Vermeer, as Lassnig turns his celebrated image into a feminist critique of the traditional relations between artist and model. In this animated version of the painting, both parties can move as well as speak, though their dialogue begins, tellingly, with the artist's complaint that his model moves too much. (As he confirms when she protests, she is, after all, "an art object.")[53] The whole exchange lasts barely more than a minute, but by its end the artist's demand that the model remove her clothes has backfired, and she has taken his place behind the easel, where she proceeds to paint her now ignominiously bald and paunchy companion (fig. 7.26).

It's tempting to think that Lassnig also had Polak's nude in her sights when she performed this gender reversal, especially since *The Artist and His Model* (see fig. 7.2) had been rendered newly salient by its appearance in Aaron Scharf's influential study of relations between the media, *Art and Photography* (1968), published just eight years before. But Polak's photograph is almost certainly among the images that another experimental filmmaker had assimilated when he, too, set out to make Vermeer's painting move.[54] Like all of his work, Peter Greenaway's *A Zed & Two Noughts* (1985) combines stunning imagery with a convoluted and often mystifying narrative, which in this case weaves together three of his principal obsessions: the phenomenon of twins, the relations of humans to the natural world, and the manipulation of light. Just how these obsessions relate to one another is not always clear, and even Greenaway himself has acknowledged that the work as it stands may be too complicated. What matters for our story, however, is that Greenaway is yet another filmmaker who began as a painter and who still identifies Vermeer in particular with his own light-centered medium.[55] In *A Zed & Two Noughts*, he and his cinematographer, Sacha Vierny, set out to produce a self-reflexive commentary on the art of film partly by reflecting on the art of Vermeer: a commentary poised ambiguously between celebration and critique of both media.

To pastiche another work is necessarily to imitate it, but *A Zed & Two Noughts* makes these two ways of evoking a predecessor particularly hard to disentangle. There are many senses in which Vermeer can be characterized as "the overall visual master-of-ceremonies of the film," in Greenaway's phrase, but insofar as this means that he and Vierny consistently lit their shots from the left in homage to the painter, we are primarily dealing with a kind of imitation—and not one as obvious to the untrained eye as the deliberate echoes of Vermeer's compositions in the films of Terence Davies, for instance.[56] (Indeed, another feature of those shots that Greenaway has understandably emphasized, their formal symmetry, actually weakens the resemblance, since Vermeer's compositions are not especially symmetrical.)[57] The film's quotations of the paintings, however, are inescapable, from an early shot in which a woman dressed as the *Girl with a Red Hat* watches through a window as a doctor operates on a female patient, to extended sequences that pastiche two of Vermeer's most celebrated works: *The Art of Painting* and *The Music Lesson*.

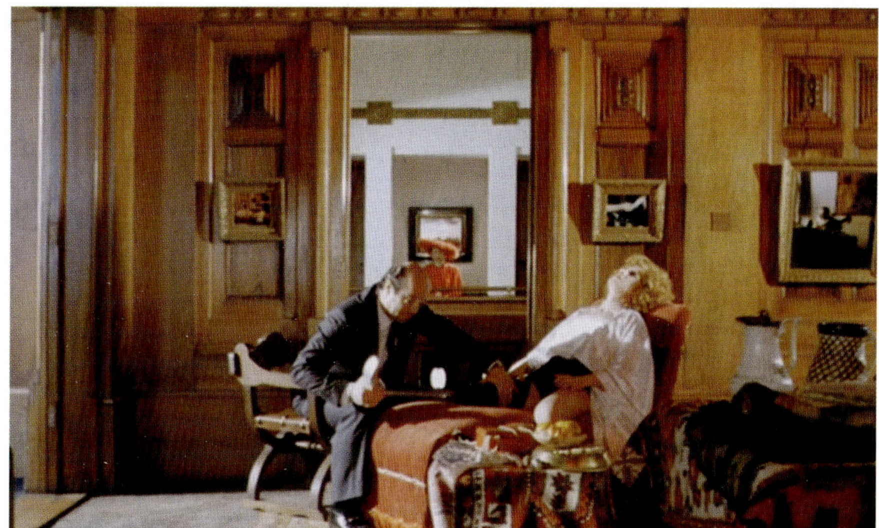

Fig. 7.27. Screenshot from *A Zed & Two Noughts*, written and directed by Peter Greenaway. Channel Four Films, 1985

The figure who presides over these portions of the film is the doctor, a sinister character pointedly named Van Meegeren, and the red hat—an accessory its wearer never removes—belongs to his wife, Catharina Bolnes, who we are told took that name—the maiden name of Vermeer's wife—at the insistence of her husband. Ostensibly a cousin of the forger, this Van Meegeren is a surgeon who specializes in stitching up women, but what he really wants, of course, is to be a painter.[58] More specifically, he wants to be Vermeer; and when we first see his surgery, both the objects with which he has furnished it—a table with a white pitcher and oriental carpet, for instance—and the reproductions that decorate its walls clearly testify to that ambition (fig. 7.27). A dizzying mise-en-abyme of Vermeer references, the surgery even provides an opening in the wall—or is it a mirror?—that allows us to glimpse the red-hatted Catharina framed by a reproduction of the *View of Delft*.

But the film offers its most concerted pastiche of individual paintings—and its most overt commentary on its own art-making—in two scenes staged a few moments apart in the same setting. Much of *A Zed & Two Noughts* takes place, as its title implies, in a zoo, and the first of the scenes in question begins as the camera cuts away from one of its many shots through the bars of the zoo's cages to a close-up of similar bars striping a black-and-white jacket, the visual rhyme doubled by the fact that the previous scene included a zebra pacing back and forth in his cage. Any doubts we might have about the identity of that jacket are rapidly dispelled when the camera pulls back to reveal that it belongs to Van Meegeren, who is in the process of making his own picture from a tableau based on *The Art of Painting* (fig. 7.28). As the camera continues to move, it allows us to see that Clio and her laurel wreath have been replaced by a naked Catharina—the flamboyant color of her omnipresent red hat and her visible pubic hair only exacerbating the shock previously elicited by Polak's comparatively more

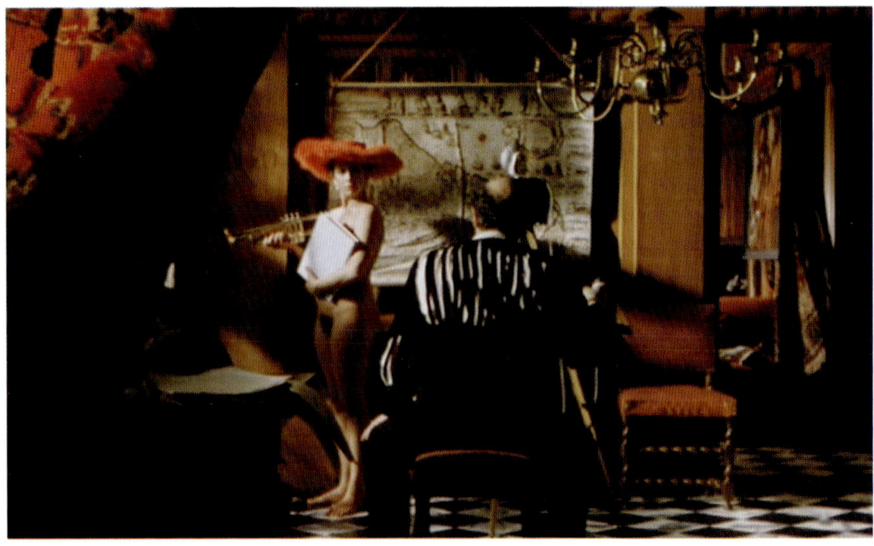

Fig. 7.28. Screenshot from *A Zed & Two Noughts*, written and directed by Peter Greenaway. Channel Four Films, 1985

decorous nude. From the standpoint of the film itself, however, the more salient transformation is that of the instrument with which Van Meegeren is making his picture. What looks at first glance like an easel is in fact a tripod, and the brief burst of light that will soon illuminate the scene is the flash of his camera. If Vermeer anticipated the cinema's "split-second of action" and "drama revealed by light," as Greenaway has claimed, then such camerawork represents the link in the chain by which painting evolved into filmmaking.[59] That Greenaway believes Vermeer's artist is a self-portrait only drives home the logic by which Van Meegeren stands in for both painter and filmmaker.[60]

Yet what kind of avatar of Greenaway's own art is Van Meegeren? The first time we see him, he is amputating the leg of a woman named Alba Bewick, who was injured in the car crash that initially set the film's elaborate plot in motion. But the doctor's designs are not limited to repairing injuries inflicted by accident. According to Alba, Van Meegeren thinks she resembles the *Young Woman Standing at a Virginal*: a resemblance she attributes to the fact that "you never see her legs." When she goes on to observe that Vermeer's figure is "not standing really" because "she's strapped and stitched to her music stool," we may suspect that someone—whether Alba, Van Meegeren, or Greenaway himself is not clear—has confused the standing woman with her seated counterpart, who may at least be plausibly imagined as fixed to the chair that supports her (see figs. 3.3 and 3.5).[61] But for Van Meegeren's purposes, what matters is his determination to replicate this perceived immobility by further experimenting on Alba. In the film's second extended pastiche, he has ordered up a copy of the dress that appears both in *The Concert* and *The Music Lesson* and is attempting to stage a tableau of the latter painting that nonetheless replaces its standing musician with the former's seated one (fig. 7.29; cf. figs. 1.17 and 3.10). Far from a concession to his one-legged patient, the substitution is designed to

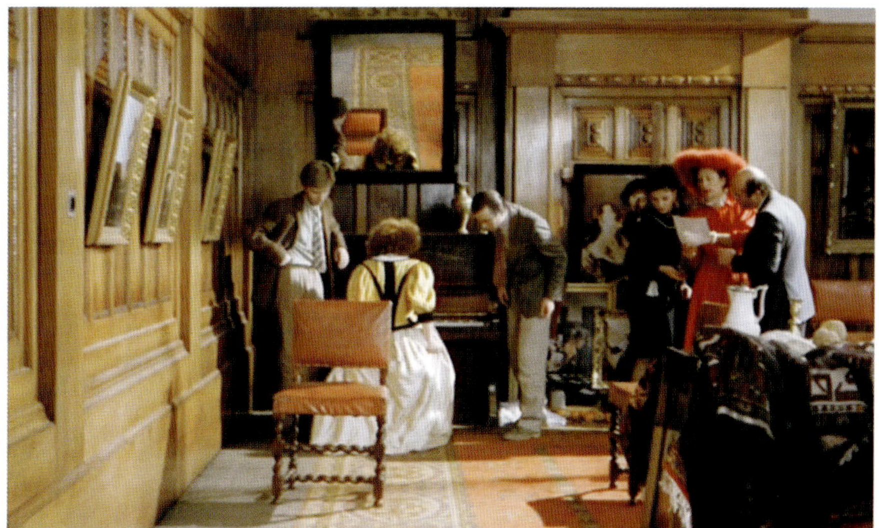

Fig. 7.29. Screenshot from *A Zed & Two Noughts*, written and directed by Peter Greenaway. Channel Four Films, 1985

keep her permanently in place, as Alba, who aptly calls herself "an excuse for medical experiments and art theory," is quick to recognize. "I'm stitched and sewn to the music-stool," she exclaims to the others as the scene closes. "Look. I'm imprisoned"—a word that might remind us of how the camera has already identified Van Meegeren as a kind of jailer when it cut between the bars of the zoo cage and the black-and-white stripes on his jacket.[62]

Nor is this the end of such efforts at imprisonment. Having implicitly compared Van Meegeren to a Nazi doctor as well as Vermeer's most notorious forger, the film arranges for both lines of work to culminate when he determines to cut off Alba's remaining leg, so that she will more completely resemble the apparently legless subjects of his predecessor.[63] After a second operation presided over by multiple reproductions of Vermeer paintings—including a book open at *The Lacemaker* in homage to Buñuel and repeated details of the figure in *Mistress and Maid*—the dying woman pronounces her epitaph: "Here lies a body cut down to fit the picture."[64] Lest we imagine that the picture in question is only Van Meegeren's, a previous bit of dialogue instructs us otherwise. "My body's only half here," Alba says to the twin brothers who have been hoping to probe the mystery of death by setting up a camera to record the decay of her corpse. "Then you'll fit better into the film frame," one of them replies.[65]

Greenaway has long been obsessed with the phenomenon of framing, and there is little question that he includes himself in this critique of what he has elsewhere called its "visual straightjacket [*sic*]."[66] If he wants us to associate Van Meegeren's surgery with "the 'cutting' and 'splicing' that constructs films," as some reviewers have suggested, then the self-reflexiveness of *A Zed & Two Noughts* is even darker.[67] What remains unclear, however, is the degree to which Greenaway means to extend the judgment to the painter whose work both he and Van Meegeren pastiche. Vermeer too, after all, frames his subjects, and the

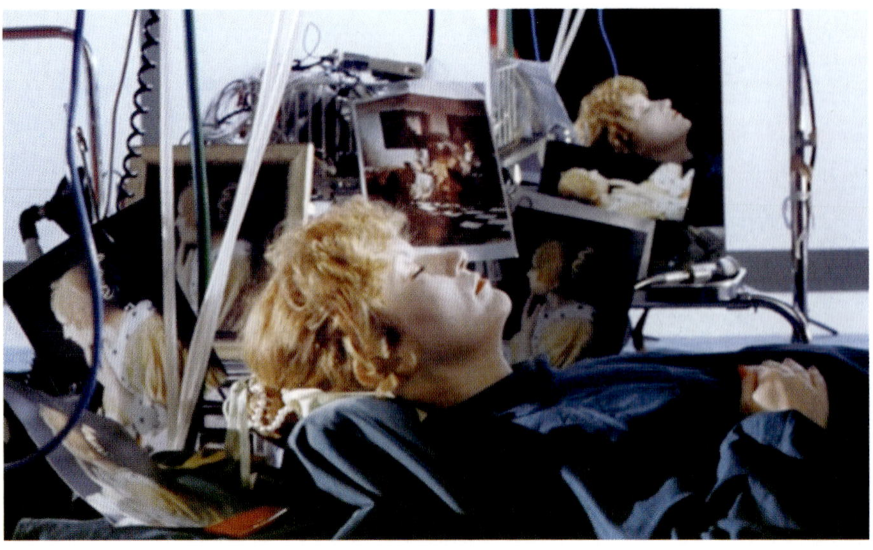

Fig. 7.30. Screenshot from *A Zed & Two Noughts*, written and directed by Peter Greenaway. Channel Four Films, 1985

film isn't wrong to register their apparent leglessness: a visual immobilizing that effectively renders them both monumental and timeless, but which has prompted observers other than Greenaway—or his characters—to speak of them as figurative "prisoners."[68] The most significant exception to the rule, in fact, is the man seated at the easel in *The Art of Painting*: an exception Greenaway does not overtly register, but which would only drive home the argument, at once aesthetic and gendered, he appears to be making.[69]

At the same time, the film takes trouble to distance Van Meegeren from the painter whose work he attempts to appropriate—not least, of course, by naming him after the notorious forger whom Greenaway has called "Vermeer's prime faker."[70] "In a certain sense, all filmmakers are forgers," Greenaway has observed, and *A Zed & Two Noughts* provides abundant evidence that this particular forger thus acts as the filmmaker's dark double, even as he provides the excuse for the film to stage some fake Vermeers of its own.[71] Indeed, by choosing to model "Catharina Bolnes" on the *Girl with a Red Hat*, the film—or is it only Van Meegeren?—implicitly doubles down on the fakery, since Greenaway has repeatedly entertained the idea that the painting may not be genuine.[72] But if both filmmaker and alter ego are only fake Vermeers, where does that leave the real thing? Greenaway himself appears to be torn between indicting all forms of image-making for their lethal artifice and carving out a special place for painting—"still," in his words, "the most essential of the visual arts"—and for a beloved Vermeer in particular.[73] In a sensitive reading of the film's second operation scene, Amy Lawrence calls attention to the way in which Greenaway positions the cropped reproductions of *Mistress and Maid* such that the woman in the painting seems to be looking directly at the patient with an expression of concern, her mouth partly open as if she were about to speak and issue a timely warning (fig. 7.30). Calling this "the warmest, most quietly moving image in the film," Lawrence also pronounces it "no accident" that "Greenaway at this moment yields to Vermeer."[74]

"I began life feeling, and still feel, that painting is the supreme visual image-making process," Greenaway observed to another interviewer in 1990, while suggesting—perhaps counterintuitively—that "cinema is dying as a medium."[75] Whether or not he was right about the comparative staying power of his two media, it does seem right to conclude this account of how visual artists have paid homage to Vermeer by returning to the painter who did more than any other to rethink, by reworking, his images: George Deem.

Over the course of his fifty-year career, Deem approached the problem from many angles, some more compelling than others. In the age of the internet, the kind of updating at issue in *Rita Vermeer*, for instance (see fig. 7.13), can look all too familiar, even if images of the movie star herself have now become a part of visual history. As we already have seen, Deem also liked to experiment by combining Vermeer with other artists: a heterogeneous roster that ranged chronologically from the Italian Renaissance to the twentieth century and included such diverse figures as Andrea Mantegna, Georges de La Tour, Gilbert Stuart, and Hans Hofmann. More typically, however, the elements he chose to put together or disassemble came from Vermeer himself, as Deem continued to experiment not only with his predecessor's subjects and the spaces that contain them, but also with his manipulation of paint. "Vermeer is a colorist because he refined color to an almost gray and white value code," Deem observed at one point.[76] Whatever the truth of that observation, he was clearly interested in how artists handled their pigments, and he often made that interest visually explicit by smearing his Vermeer-related canvases with patches of paint that appear to represent nothing but the medium itself. More than two decades before he published *How to Paint a Vermeer*, Deem produced a painting of the same title that provided a direct visualization of his method. In six equally sized versions of the *Young Woman with a Water Pitcher*, he laid bare both the grid by which he transferred his copies to canvas and the pigments by which he built up an image (fig. 7.31). The result has been called "cinematic," though the suggestion that we are witnessing a chronological sequence is deceptive, as anyone who tries to track what happens to the roughly painted red border in the upper left-hand corner will quickly register.[77] Red does figure in the original (see fig. 3.8), but these swatches of paint are unmoored from any representational function—apart, that is, from signifying the palette that Vermeer has bequeathed to his appropriator. In a related painting a few years later, actually called *Vermeer Palette*, Deem would make that connection explicit, by demonstrating how a version of *The Milkmaid* has materialized from the pigments that thickly daub the right-hand section of the canvas and more thinly streak the wall behind

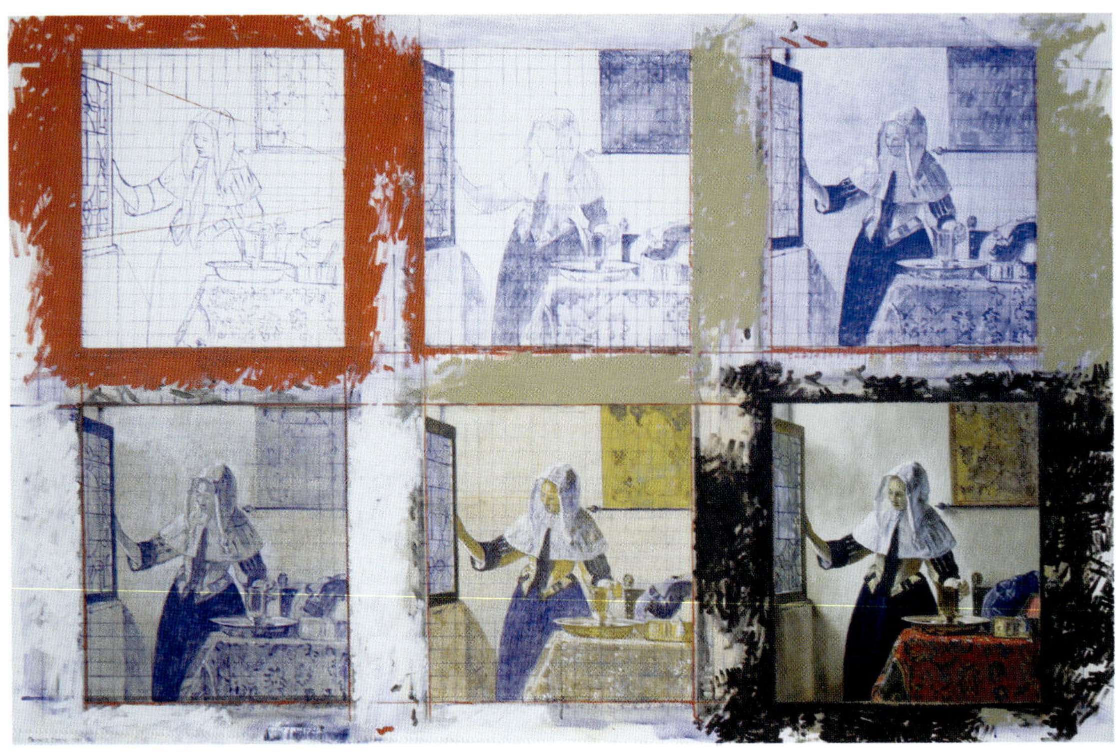

Fig. 7.31. George Deem, *How to Paint a Vermeer* (1981). Oil on canvas. 111.8 × 167.6 cm. Private collection, New York. © New Britain Museum of American Art / Artists Rights Society (ARS), NY. Image © Archives of American Art, Smithsonian Institution, Washington, DC

the subject (fig. 7.32). At the same time, such areas of non-representational color also serve to remind us that these paintings are being made in the aftermath of the abstract expressionists: a more immediate lineage than the one that connects Deem to Vermeer, but which not only colors his response to the earlier artist—I use the verb deliberately—but allows him to claim that artist as their ancestor too. In this sense, at least, Deem does not so much look back at Vermeer as recover him, once again, for modernism.[78]

But perhaps the most evocative of Deem's Vermeer paintings are those in which he eliminates the human figure altogether, as in *A Stool, A Chair, and a Map*, or relegates it to a picture-within-the-picture, like the one that hangs on the wall in *A Lady Writing, Again* (see fig. 7.10). The latter arrangement has a peculiarly ambiguous effect, both recalling Vermeer's original illusion—the woman in *that* picture once was real—and confronting us with its two-dimensional double, a memory preserved only in the form of an obviously inanimate object. *A Lady Writing, Again* is in fact the last in a series of such ghostly doublings of Vermeer, which also includes *A Lady Standing at a Virginal, Again*, *The Love Letter, Again*, and *Young Woman with a Water Pitcher, Again*, all painted the previous year.

More often, however, Deem dispenses with the painted replica, relying on the viewer alone to conjure up a vision of the person or persons who once inhabited these spaces. In an ambitious work called *Seven Vermeer Corners* (fig. 7.33), he extends the practice to seven individual paintings, each of which

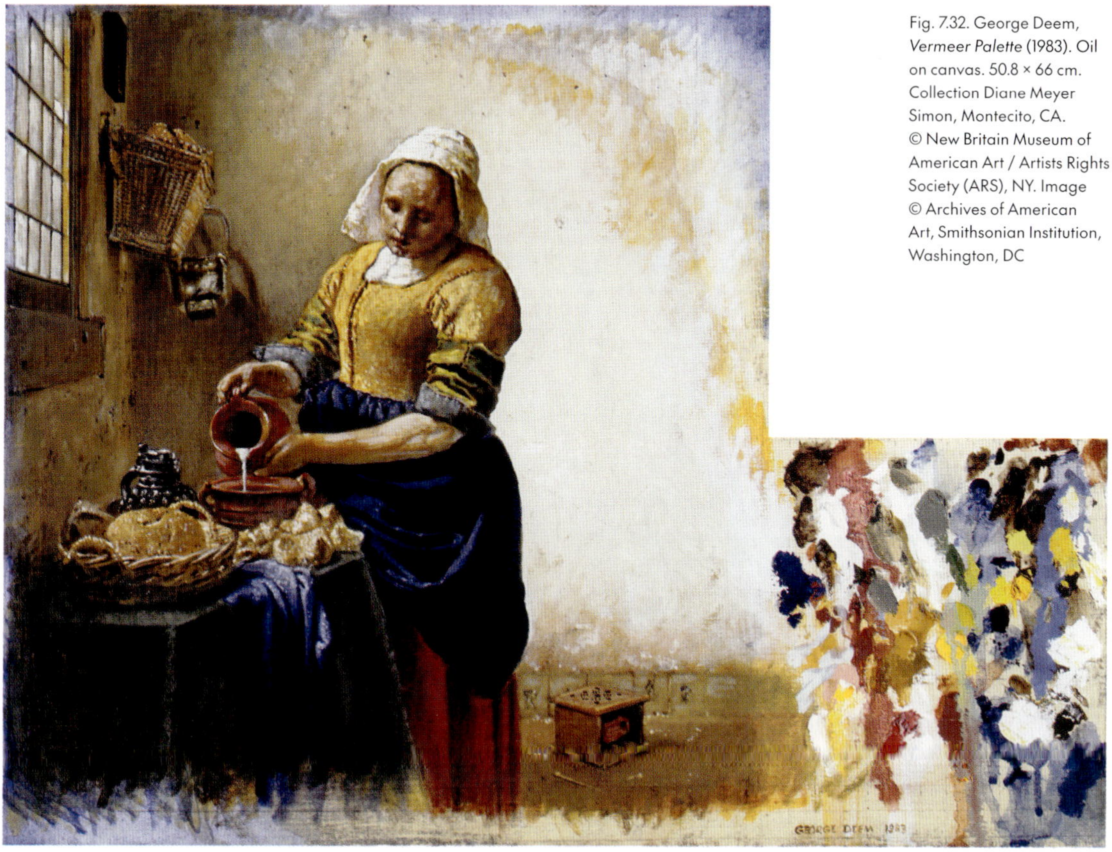

Fig. 7.32. George Deem, *Vermeer Palette* (1983). Oil on canvas. 50.8 × 66 cm. Collection Diane Meyer Simon, Montecito, CA. © New Britain Museum of American Art / Artists Rights Society (ARS), NY. Image © Archives of American Art, Smithsonian Institution, Washington, DC

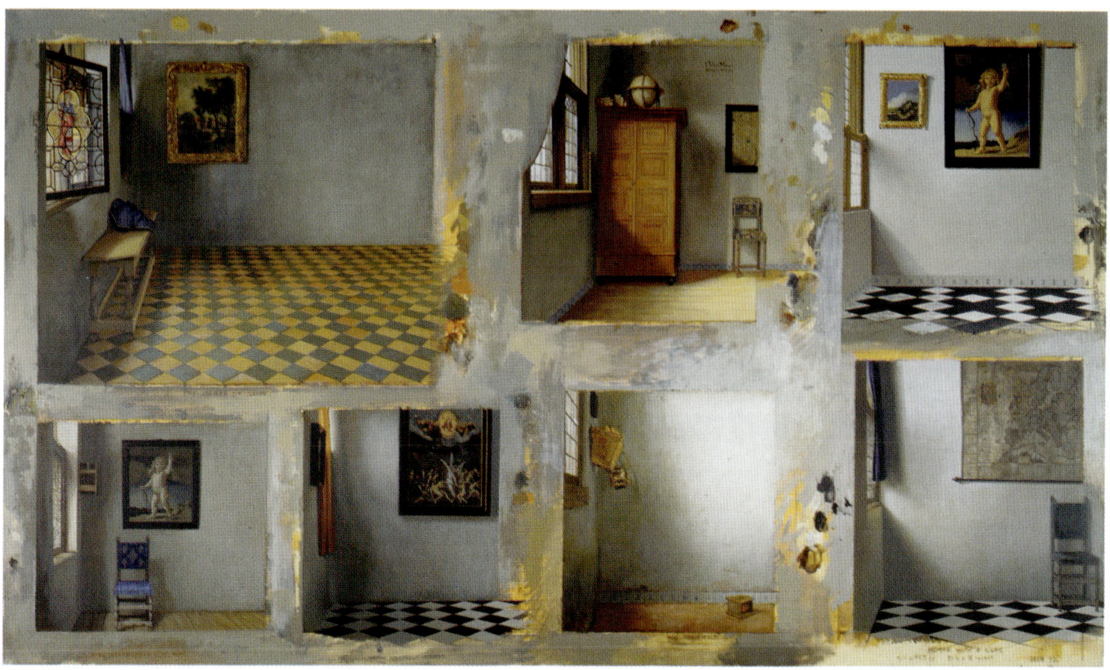

Fig. 7.33. George Deem, *Seven Vermeer Corners* (1999). Oil on canvas. 127 × 218.4 cm. Collection Wellington Management Company, Boston, MA. © New Britain Museum of American Art / Artists Rights Society (ARS), NY. Image © Archives of American Art, Smithsonian Institution, Washington, DC

he reproduces at scale, while evacuating their interiors of everything "except that which touches a wall." (The phrasing is his.)[79] As if he were gently offering an aid to our recollection, the artist hand-letters the titles of the originals directly on the canvas, from upper left to lower right: *The Glass of Wine*, *The Geographer*, *A Lady Standing at a Virginal*, *Girl Interrupted at Her Music*, *Woman Holding a Balance*, *The Milkmaid*, and *Woman with a Lute*. But if every word in these titles names an absence, what remains is just as striking. Deem himself observed that "each corner is a complete statement of its own," and among the things his pared-down versions may help us to see are the rectangular rhythms that punctuate a particular space, or how the arrangement of light and shadow subtly shifts from one wall to another.[80]

The removal of Vermeer's people also renders visible things that their presence partly obscured: the full extent of the cabinet in *The Geographer*, for instance, or the chair whose top can only be glimpsed in *Girl Interrupted at Her Music* (see figs. 1.10 and 3.6).[81] Deem is not just copying what remains, in other words, but reconstructing it. Twenty years before the Dresden restorers would uncover the large Cupid that hangs on the wall of *Girl Reading a Letter at an Open Window*, he thus anticipates them by restoring—figuratively, at least—the badly abraded Cupid in *Girl Interrupted* and placing it diagonally across from the large version of the same picture in the *Young Woman Standing at a Virginal* (see fig. 3.3). The visual rhyme this produces is Deem's, but it also works like an art historical demonstration of Vermeer's iconography—the Dresden restorers would offer similar comparisons—even as it underscores how he kept returning to those "fragments of the same world" that Proust had memorably described at the beginning of the century.[82] That the two Cupids come from very different stages in Vermeer's career just drives home the point: this is not a chronological diagram of his development, like the one that concluded the exhibition at the Rijksmuseum in 2023, but a formal arrangement that seeks to make new art by thinking about—and with—an earlier master of such arrangements. Note, too, how Deem again employs unfinished parts of the canvas to lay bare the process by which his paintings are made—a process which in this case apparently included using the borders of each image as both "a test area for color" and an actual palette.[83]

"I am very much involved with Vermeer these days," Deem wrote to some friends the year before he painted *Seven Vermeer Corners*, before going on to characterize the project as "a series of paintings in which I de-construct paintings by Vermeer. I depict his interiors with their familiar furniture and windows but I have taken away his figures."[84] Though Deem wasn't wrong to speak of "deconstructing" his predecessor, there is a sense in which he was only following the lead of a painter whose art had always depended on leaving things out.[85] Consider, as a final example, another Vermeer from which Deem removed the figure—an act all the more significant because he once told an interviewer that the painting in question, *Woman in Blue Reading a Letter*, was his favorite.[86] That

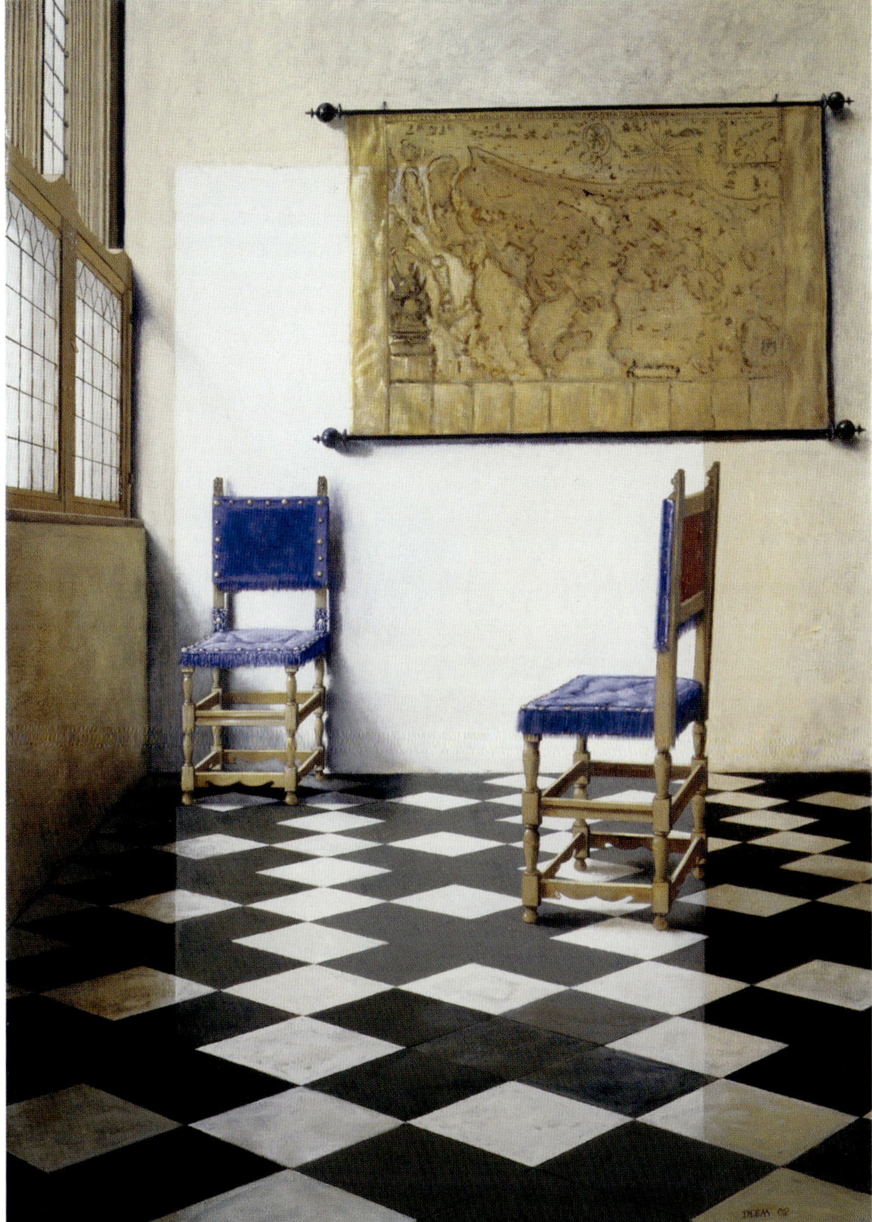

Fig. 7.34. George Deem, *Extended Vermeer, No. 2—The Woman in Blue* (2002). Oil on canvas. 101.6 × 71.1 cm. New Britain Museum of American Art, New Britain, CT. © New Britain Museum of American Art / Artists Rights Society (ARS), NY. Image © Archives of American Art, Smithsonian Institution, Washington, DC

claim notwithstanding, a viewer first confronted with Deem's *Extended Vermeer, No. 2—The Woman In Blue* (fig. 7.34) might well conclude that the artist had simply preferred to leave its titular subject out of the picture. The second in a pair of so-called "extended" Vermeers, the first of which performs a similar magic on the *Lady Writing a Letter with Her Maid*, the painting widens and deepens the space of the original, so that things previously left to our imagination now become visible. At the same time, of course, the principal object of our gaze has disappeared.

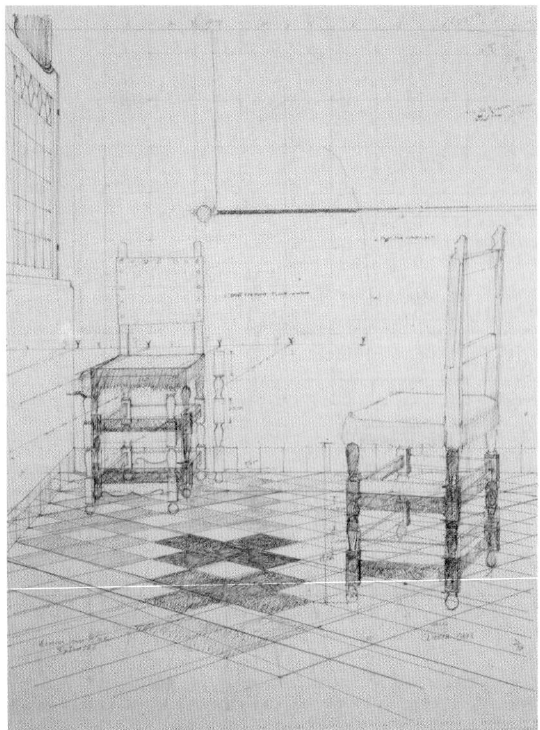

Fig. 7.35. George Deem, *Extended Vermeer, No. 2—Woman in Blue*, Study 1 (2001). Pencil, colored pencil, and ink on paper. 76.2 × 57.2 cm. New Britain Museum of American Art, New Britain, CT. © New Britain Museum of American Art / Artists Rights Society (ARS), NY. Image © Archives of American Art, Smithsonian Institution, Washington, DC

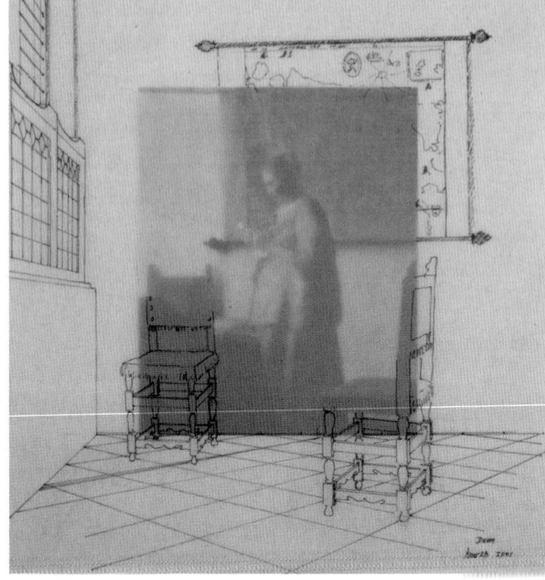

Fig. 7.36. George Deem, *Extended Vermeer: The Woman in Blue*, Study 2 (2001). Pen and ink on vellum over reproduction mounted on paper. 45.7 × 43.2 cm. New Britain Museum of American Art, New Britain, CT. © New Britain Museum of American Art / Artists Rights Society (ARS), NY. Image © Archives of American Art, Smithsonian Institution, Washington, DC

Deem's notes for the extension make clear what he saw—or, rather, didn't see—in his source material, and how he set out to transform it:

> This painting does nothing but present itself. There is no corner of the room, there are no floor patterns, there are no windows, there is no ceiling, there is no beginning and no end to this painting.
>
> You have nothing to do but look at this painting.
>
> Start an extension.
>
> Starting an extension includes extending all four sides of the paintings or it will not read logically. Add a floor, extend the wall to the right, add a window to the left. Continue the chair on the left. Remove the table. Continue the chair on the right and make it sit on the floor. Go slowly and look at what is going on.
>
> Go slowly and realize what is going on.[87]

The preservation of an initial study for the painting means that we too can go slowly and take in these changes (fig. 7.35). But it's the next line in Deem's notes that speaks to the paradox at the heart of the exercise. "Keep the center image dominant," he exhorted himself, even as he plotted to remove it from the picture.[88] A charge ultimately addressed to the mind's eye, the directive nonetheless had a practical corollary: what Deem was telling himself to do was to locate a full-scale reproduction of the *Woman in Blue* at the center of his extended canvas, so that its rectangular shape could be preserved in the final painting. A second study illustrating this stage of the process (fig. 7.36) was not intended as a work in its own right, but the uncanny effect produced by laying the vellum of the drawing over the reproduction is nonetheless a fitting emblem of how Deem will go on to turn the *Woman in Blue* into a ghost of itself.

What we see in the final painting (see fig. 7.34) is not Vermeer's picture, but our memory of it: "a present absence," to quote the critic Charles Molesworth, that Deem conjures in its stead.[89] In place of the *Woman in Blue* there is now only a luminous rectangle, whose uniform radiance defies explanation—no natural light, as Bryan J. Wolf has observed, ever behaves like this—and whose flat surface seems to float free of Vermeer's illusion, as if a piece of abstract painting had wandered into the canvas from a later period in art history.[90] Or perhaps it would be more accurate to say that Deem's rectangle of pure light shows how an early twenty-first-century painter sees Vermeer's art, even as it exemplifies the effect Thoré had already seen in that art more than a century earlier: "The light seems to come from the painting itself."[91] *Extended Vermeer, No. 2* is yet one more demonstration, in other words, of how Vermeer has become modern.

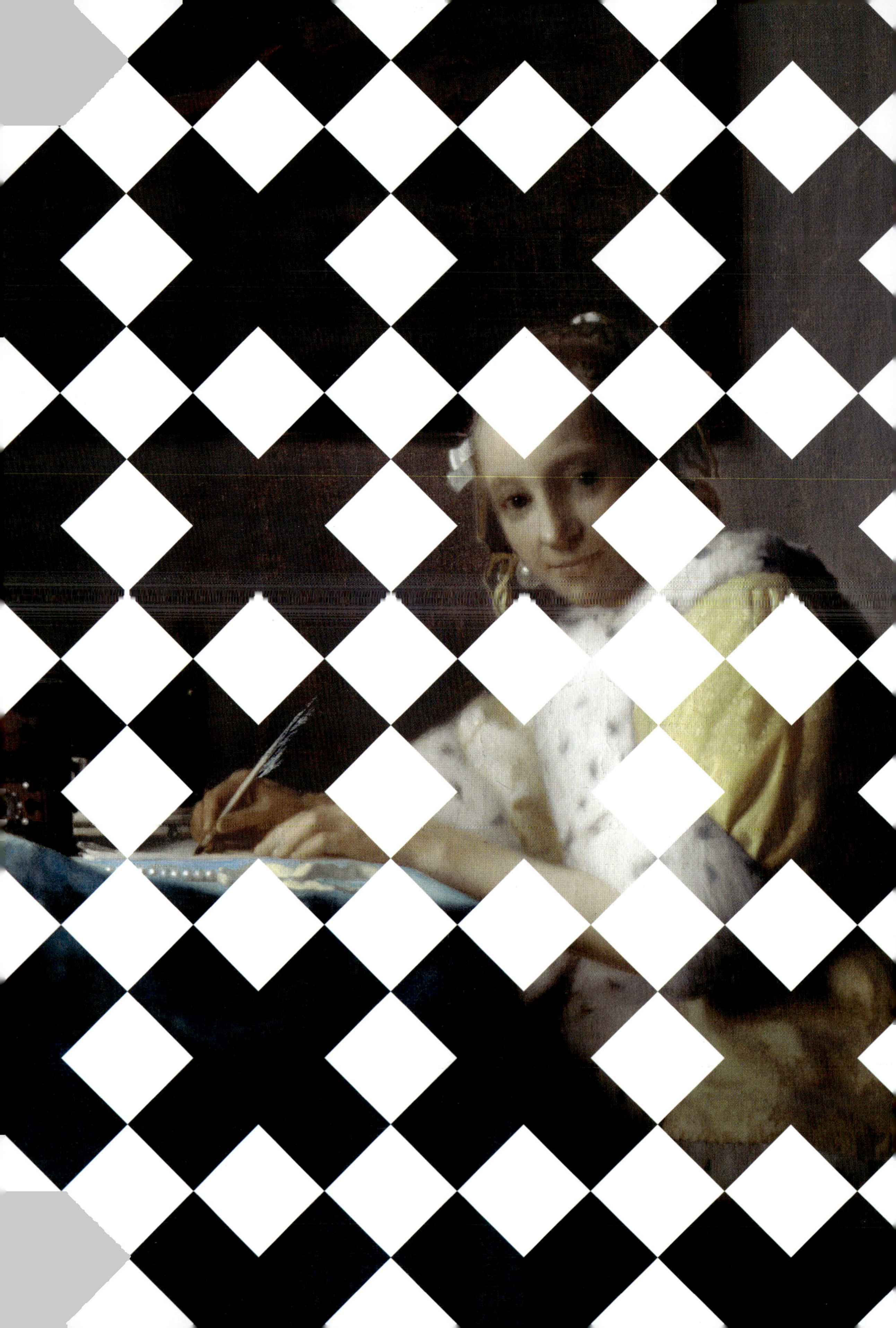

III

Filling the Silences

8

The Language of Poetry

It has been one of my dreams that someday someone would think of Vermeer, without my saying it first.

—ELIZABETH BISHOP TO RANDALL JARRELL (1955)

One of the first references to Vermeer in print took the form of a poem. In 1667 the politician and writer Dirck van Bleyswijck published a history of Delft that included an elegy by the book's publisher, Arnold Bon, for the gifted painter Carel Fabritius, who had died prematurely in the explosion of the city's gunpowder arsenal thirteen years earlier. Like any good elegist, Bon sought not only to mourn the dead but to console the living, and he did so by means of a resonant metaphor: he concluded the poem by comparing the late artist to a phoenix, from whose ashes a new one had miraculously risen to take his place. Though the wording varied somewhat depending on which copy of the book a reader consulted, the identity of the new artist was never in doubt. That reborn phoenix was, of course, Vermeer.

Bon's little poem would prove prescient in more ways than one. There is, to begin with, the metaphor of the phoenix itself. "But happily there rose from his fire / VERMEER, who masterfully trod in his path," the first version of the poem concludes, while the second, which may even have been revised by the hand of the artist, is still more adulatory: "VERMEER, who, masterfully, was able to emulate him."[1] Yet as we have already seen, both these lines and the reputation to which they testified would largely disappear from view after Vermeer's own death in 1675. Though we will never know if Arnold Houbraken's *Great Theater of Dutch Painters* (1718–21) would have helped to keep that reputation alive had its author not accidentally skipped over the lines in question because they were printed on a separate page from the rest of the poem, as Ben Broos has speculated, the fact remains that Houbraken's influential work barely mentioned Vermeer, and subsequent commentators lost track of him altogether.[2] Not until Thoré and others began to publicize his achievement more than two centuries later did Bon's phoenix emerge once again, this time as himself: a rebirth far more spectacular, if also far more delayed, than anything his fellow citizens could have anticipated.

From the perspective of Vermeer's afterlife, however, it seems altogether fitting that his early fate may have been tied to that of a poem, since few painters have been more consistently associated with poetry than the Delft master.[3] In the nineteenth and early twentieth century that association mostly appeared in prose commentary that characterized his work as "poetic"; more recently, it has taken the form of poetry itself, as writers in multiple languages have responded to his paintings in their own medium. The very fact that one such poet felt compelled to begin her 2023 contribution to the genre with the ironic title "I Am Sick of Reading Poems About Paintings by Vermeer" testifies to the phenomenon. Even as she went on to bemoan the loss of aura that has accompanied the artist at least since the crowds "wait[ed] for hours in the snow" at the 1995 exhibition in the nation's capital—a loss she associated with everything from the proliferation of poems about Vermeer to the *Girl with a Pearl Earring* "gaz[ing] up at you / from the bottom of your mug at your last swallow of coffee"—Jane Shore inevitably concluded her own poem, like many before her, by attempting to recapture that aura in words.[4] Subjective and impressionistic as such felt affinities may seem, they also tell us something genuine, I shall argue, about the character of Vermeer's art.

Ideas about painting's relation to poetry go back to antiquity, of course, but the kind of poetry that Vermeer usually brings to mind has little to do with older understandings of the term, by which it often serves as a synonym for literature generally. Indeed, according to most traditional measures Vermeer is a strikingly unliterary painter, especially as compared to his great contemporary Rembrandt. Unlike the latter, who continued to draw on biblical and mythical subjects throughout his career, Vermeer's experiment with history painting, as such work is usually classified, was very brief: of the surviving canvases, only two early works—*Christ in the House of Martha and Mary* and *Diana and Her Companions*—would customarily qualify, unless one counts the recent addition of the yet more anomalous *Saint Praxedis*. Apart from the *Allegory of the Catholic Faith*, a late work whose elaborate iconography also depends on literary sources, though it's not a history painting as such, and the two cityscapes, most of Vermeer's remaining work is usually classified as genre painting, whose representations of everyday life draw on a familiar set of motifs that were passed back and forth among his contemporaries. Women writing and reading letters or absorbed in domestic tasks like lacemaking, couples drinking wine or engaged in music-making: these and similar subjects were among the common stock of seventeenth-century Dutch painters, and Vermeer was hardly original in adopting them. Scenes of daily life rather than evocations of prior texts, such pictures are usually distinguished from the literariness of history painting. But it's a striking fact about Vermeer's art—especially by comparison to his contemporaries'—that his genre paintings also show relatively little interest in narrative. "Unlike De Hooch," as Frederick Wedmore shrewdly observed in one of the first extended discussions of Vermeer in English, "he rarely painted stories."[5]

This is not to say that narratives can't still be teased out of these images. As we shall see in the following chapter, ordinary viewers and novelists alike have been tempted by Vermeer's suppression of narrative cues to fill in the gaps with storytelling, and even poets themselves have sometimes taken the pictures as a provocation to narrative. But it's also no accident, I'd like to suggest, that modern poets have responded most frequently and intensely to paintings in which Vermeer has minimized the potential for action yet further: single-figure works such as *The Milkmaid* and *Woman in Blue Reading a Letter*, for instance, or his celebrated painting of a city "deftly stilled," as the poet Nick Norwood has put it: the *View of Delft*.[6] The question John Ashbery asks himself in his own "View of Delft" speaks for poet and painter alike: "It's all about standing still, isn't it?"[7] The poetry of Vermeer—both the perceived poetry of his paintings and the body of literature inspired by his work—clusters especially around effects that have long been associated with the modern lyric.

Within a few decades of Vermeer's rediscovery, the practice of associating him with the poets had begun. Writing in 1880, the same Frederick Wedmore who distinguished him from the storytelling De Hooch nonetheless grouped both painters, together with Nicholas Maes, as "poets of fine apprehension and quickened sensitiveness"—artists whose appeal to "the meditative pleasure of the cultivated eye" he pointedly contrasted to the "literary or dramatic" interest of Jan Steen and Gabriel Metsu.[8] In 1895 the American art historian and critic John C. Van Dyke likewise pronounced Vermeer "a poet," though "like almost all of the Dutchmen," he hastened to add, "only in the poetry of materials, such as light, color, atmosphere, and values." Despite that anxious concession to old hierarchies, by which the history-painting Italians far outranked the merely mechanical Dutch, Van Dyke went on to defend Vermeer's poetry in terms that call into question his earlier claim that the artist's "concern was for the material and the picturesque, more than for the psychological or the intellectual":

Feeling—the mood of mind that breeds images, and transforms reality into a something beautiful—is the essence of both picture and poem. Mere skill of brush and skill of pen are unable mechanically to effect such transformations. Beautiful thinking must accompany beautiful workmanship. When they go hand in hand the total result is poetry—and poetry is art, and art poetry, whether done with the pen or the brush.[9]

By the following century, commentators appear to have felt less need to qualify—or to defend—Vermeer's poetry. In 1921 the French poet and art critic Jean-Louis Vaudoyer began a discussion of the painter by remarking, perhaps paradoxically, "the vanity" of attempting to translate him into words, while going on to compose a three-part article whose language would echo in the pages of Vaudoyer's good friend Marcel Proust. For Vaudoyer, there was apparently no contradiction between describing Vermeer as "the epitome of painters" and repeatedly invoking his "poetry." What the article calls at one point "the quality of inner poetry with which Vermeer bathes his most beautiful works" is nonetheless thoroughly material: "the power that emanates from his canvases arises uniquely from the way in which colored matter is arranged, treated, worked." Or as he puts it elsewhere in the piece: "colors, for Vermeer, are at once the words of a material vocabulary and the words of an ideal vocabulary."[10]

Similar tributes to Vermeer's "unrivalled poetic intensity"—the phrase is J. H. Huizinga's—appeared in the decades that followed.[11] In 1948 the Dutch art historian Ary Bob de Vries, then director of the Mauritshuis in The Hague, joined forces with René Huyghe, chief curator of paintings and drawings at the Louvre, to publish a revised version of De Vries's 1939 monograph on the artist, *Jan Vermeer de Delft, suivi de La poétique de Vermeer par René Huyghe*. As the French title suggests, the principal account of such poetry was Huyghe's, but De Vries set the tone for his colleague by announcing in his preface that Vermeer's art posed a challenge better met by the language of the poet than that of the scholar.[12] Huyghe himself spoke of Vermeer's "poetry of the real"—an effect he associated variously with the fundamental remoteness of the paintings' seemingly familiar worlds, the "reclusive life" of the young women who typically inhabit them, and above all, perhaps, with "the marvelous immobility" of his images, an immobility that "never signifies an arrest or impoverishment of life, but a patient concentration the better to irradiate it." Like other commentators since the late nineteenth century, Huyghe partly approached the Delft master as a proto-modern, in whom painting was beginning to discover "its autonomous powers"; and he elaborated the point by remarking Vermeer's attention to the sensuous properties of his medium, his handling of light, and the abstract geometry by which he organized his space. But the emphasis of the essay as a whole falls less on technical questions than on subjective responses—the sense, for instance, that "invisible presences" somehow lurk behind the paintings' "visible appearances." Repeatedly, Huyghe links such impressions to an effect of timelessness, writing of Vermeer's capacity to "insinuate [. . .] the perfect and eternal beneath the most faithful appearances of the accidental and the temporary," or to make the moment "accede to that existence in which there is no longer either before or after, where the present no longer has meaning because it coincides with eternity."[13]

Repeatedly, too, if not surprisingly, Huyghe reaches for metaphor, drawing his principal figures—the mirror and the pearl—from objects in the paintings themselves. Mirrors appear in the *Maid Asleep*, *The Music Lesson*, the *Woman with a Pearl Necklace*, the *Woman Holding a Balance*, and, by extension, in the mirror-like effect produced by the open window of the *Girl Reading a Letter* at Dresden; while pearls are virtually ubiquitous in Vermeer's work, figuring not just in the eponymous *Girl with a Pearl Earring* and *Woman with a Pearl Necklace*, but in well over half his canvases centered on the female figure. The mirror is, of course, a conventional trope for realist art, but Huyghe deploys it less to praise Vermeer's illusionism than to conjure with his mystery: the paintings are mirror-like by virtue of evoking a world whose familiar appearance tantalizes us by its silence and inaccessibility. What Huyghe calls at one point "the poetry of the mirror" and at another its "magic" is bound up, counterintuitively, with what can't be seen: "the invisible beyond of the positive aspect of things," a "secret universe [. . .] where man has always dreamed of penetrating." As for the pearl, which also, by Huyghe's account, "attracts and at the same time refuses, impenetrable": opening and closing with extended meditations on its properties, the essay turns Vermeer's favorite gem into a synecdoche for his art itself. "Smooth, luminous, and compact [. . .] a perfect world, self-contained," with an "invisible center" and a surface "radiat[ing . . .] with peace," the pearl that Huyghe imagines himself rolling between his fingers is at once "enclosed hermetically in its mystery and perfection" and the locus of "an infinity [. . .] outside of time and space, an indeterminacy that vexes the taste for definition and to which reverie alone gives access."[14] Such passages amount to a prose poem on the subject of Vermeer's poetry.

Not everyone drawn to the theme is so extravagant. But invocations of Vermeer's poetry have continued to resonate in the scholarship, from Lawrence Gowing's influential study of 1952 to the wall labels provided by the National Gallery of Art in Washington, DC, for the 2017 exhibition "Vermeer and the Masters of Genre Painting: Inspiration and Rivalry." Gowing, who argued for the "deep character of evasiveness, a perpetual withdrawal" that in his view paradoxically accompanied the paintings' "clarity," typically associated such "intangible remoteness" with the poetic effects of Vermeer's art, as when he observed, for instance, that "his very evasiveness is poetic," or wrote that Vermeer's "nature excluded directness; a condition of the investigation for him was that the angle should be oblique. It drew him to the point where he stands, farthest of all from his time, as a poetic illustrator of the subtlest and least expressible meanings of human aspect." In making the formal case for this interpretation, Gowing called particular attention to the way in which Vermeer's intensely optical art tended to dissolve his figures' "tangible substance" in the play of light, as well as to the "immutable barrier of space" that separates those figures from the viewer. He also remarked, like Huyghe before him, on the immobility of such images—what he called the "still-life method" of Vermeer's paintings, even those with multiple human figures. "Eyes never meet in Vermeer, action is stilled. There is no speech, these almost unmoving figures communicate by letter or on the keyboards of the virginals. It is as if they were meditating on the barriers which lie between them."[15]

But perhaps no one has done more to disseminate the idea of Vermeer's poetry than the long-serving curator of Northern European art at the National Gallery of Art in Washington, DC, Arthur K. Wheelock Jr. Beginning with his 1981 monograph on the painter and continuing, presumably, in an unattributed label at the 2017 exhibition on "the timeless and poetic character" of the *Woman with a Pearl Necklace*, Wheelock has used the term to evoke the principal qualities of the artist's work, while implicitly arguing for how it helps to distinguish that work from the painting of his contemporaries. Elaborating on nineteenth-century observations about Vermeer's relative lack of storytelling, especially by comparison with other genre painters, Wheelock has contended that "Vermeer communicates through mood rather than through narrative or anecdote"—a mode of communication whose very resistance to clear definition he associates with "the poetic suggestiveness" of the images. In a related vein, he has tended to resist the temptation to fix a painting's meaning with the aid of iconographical cues: without denying that these are occasionally present, often in the form of pictures-within-the-pictures like the Cupid dimly discernable on the wall of *A Maid Asleep* (see fig. 3.2), or the inscription on the open lid of the instrument in *The Music Lesson* ("Music, companion of joy, balm for sorrow"—see fig 3.10), Wheelock characteristically emphasizes the remaining ambiguities: "Ultimately, however beautiful or sensitive his paintings may be, they continue to appeal because they can never be completely explained."[16]

Indeed, ambiguity is for Wheelock among the chief signs of Vermeer's poetry, as is the effect of "timelessness" that he, like others before him, repeatedly associates with the paintings.[17] As he summed up his argument in another study of the artist, published more than a decade after his first:

> The range of interpretations possible for Vermeer's paintings is part of the poetic quality associated with his work. An even more fundamental aspect of that poetry is his ability to suggest the universal within the realm of the everyday. He conveyed this quality by avoiding the purely incidental and the anecdotal, where actions and gestures become tied to specific events or situations. The emotions of longing and expectation that he so often

incorporated into his work provided a thematic means for suggesting the extension of time, a quality he enhanced with purity of composition, purposefulness of human gaze and gesture, and evocative treatment of light.[18]

Though an extension of time, especially one characterized by expectation or longing, is not quite the same as timelessness, this sense of a moment indefinitely suspended is both a familiar effect of Vermeer's paintings and also, I should like to suggest, a fundamental ground of their association with one kind of poem in particular: the individual lyric. "Timelessness," as Sharon Cameron has observed, "is a generic concern" of the lyric, and insofar as lyric poems "record a history, it is not the history of a life but rather of a moment"—a history typically recorded, by writers of English at least, in what theorists have dubbed "the lyric present."[19] When Cameron characterizes "the shape of the lyric endeavor" as "the collapsing of eternity into immortality in the designated space of the present," she is drawing on spatial metaphors that resonate strongly with the language that critics and poets alike have adopted in writing of Vermeer.[20] I shall turn to some of those poets shortly, but I want to do so while also spelling out a little more fully why certain features of his paintings—and certain of his paintings in particular—seem to call for the language of poetry, especially as that language has been filtered through ideas of the lyric that have crystalized in the century and a half since his recovery.

Literary genres are notoriously resistant to precise definition, and the lyric may be more resistant than most. Lyrics, after all, have been around in one version or another at least since the songs of ancient Greece, and any effort to characterize a form that unites both Sappho and Ashbery, say, is not likely to yield much of interest about either. In an influential study of Emily Dickinson, Virginia Jackson has argued that "lyricization," as she calls it, is a phenomenon originating in the mid-nineteenth century; but despite the seductive coincidence of that timeline with the beginning of Vermeer's modern reception, we need to approach the analogy with caution.[21] Jackson is not claiming, of course, that there was nothing called lyric poetry before the nineteenth century, but only that our modern understanding of the term originated then, and that our habit of conflating all poems with lyric in this sense has continued to distort our account of Dickinson in particular. Jackson's argument has been much disputed, most notably by Jonathan Culler, yet even Culler doesn't question that the nineteenth century had a profound influence on how writers think about the form; and for our purposes what matters is less the truth about Dickinson, or even about "lyricization" as such, than the way a familiar conception of the lyric appears to resonate with the effects of Vermeer's art.[22] "Privacy gone public"; "present-tense immediacy"; "an invitation to interpretation": each of the phrases with which Jackson, for example, sums up received views of the genre have their equivalent in the modern reception of Vermeer.[23] And so, too, does Culler's observation that "the fundamental characteristic of lyric" is "the iterative and iterable performance of an event in the lyric present," though what is iteratively performed in Vermeer is not, of course, conveyed by speech, but by stance and gesture.[24]

The apparent privacy of Vermeer's work is a function of both subject and style. The typical setting of his genre paintings is the private house—a space whose privacy he characteristically intensifies by closing off our view of the outside world.[25] Unlike many of his contemporaries, Vermeer almost never affords us a glimpse through a window or doorway. Windows in his work illuminate domestic interiors, but apart from a hint of clouded sky and a red building just barely visible through the casement of *Officer and Laughing Girl* (see fig. 1.14), the interior is all we see.[26] As Ivan Gaskell has noted, "this effect of self-containment is enhanced by his representation of the world beyond that depicted domestic space exclusively in the form of further representations—paintings-within-paintings," like those barely visible in the *Maid Asleep* or *The Music Lesson*.[27] Though Gaskell doesn't say so explicitly, the maps that frequently hang on Vermeer's walls have a related effect, turning the world outside into still more abstract representations, ones that poets are tempted to identify with the mental states of the figures before them. "Here is heart's cartography / Toying with absence," Eamon Grennan writes of the young woman in *Officer and Laughing Girl*, as he imagines her silently coming to terms with the transience of "this luminous / Mortal minute."[28] "On / the whitewashed wall behind her / hangs a vast, mysterious map of consciousness / itself," says Michael White of the *Woman in Blue Reading a Letter*—a metaphor he extends by associating the map's obscured legibility with "the in-between, / the estuarine wastes of dream."[29] (See fig. 2.4.)

We are tempted to speculate in this way about the interiority of Vermeer's figures because the figures themselves often appear oblivious of the viewer. This is especially true of single-figure canvases such as *The Milkmaid* or the *Woman in Blue*, and the category also includes the *Maid Asleep*, the *Girl Reading a Letter at an Open Window*, the *Woman with a Pearl Necklace*, and five other paintings of solitary women engrossed in a gesture or task, as well as the two surviving pictures of individual male subjects, *The Astronomer* and *The Geographer*. To invoke the language of Michael Fried: while Vermeer's portraits or *tronies* like the *Girl with a Pearl Earring* confront the viewer directly and hence theatrically, his genre paintings are typically images of absorption, a phenomenon that was recognized long before Fried advanced his well-known distinction.[30] "The people in his pictures seem immersed in themselves," Charles Caffin remarked in 1909. "The scene is wrapped in privacy, undisturbed by the suggestion of an outsider."[31] Vermeer's figures "seem to be unaware of the painter and the viewer," Vaudoyer similarly noted in 1921, before going on to associate "the extraordinary poetry of contemplation that flows from the canvases" with "the presence of those figures who, with their backs turned, are busy only with their virginals, their songs."[32] When Northrop Frye observed of the lyric that "the poet, so to speak, turns his back on his listeners," he was elaborating on a famous account of poetry by John Stuart Mill, but the unintended echo of Vaudoyer's metaphor is nonetheless resonant.[33] Paintings, of course, don't have listeners, but neither, for that matter, have turned backs, and Mill's own elaboration of his remarks likewise reaches for a visual metaphor: "no trace of consciousness that any eyes are upon us must be visible in the work itself."[34]

But it's not only the "painted quiet and concentration" of Vermeer's figures that conveys the effect of privacy. (I quote from a translation of a brief tribute to *The Milkmaid* by the Polish poet Wisława Szymborska.)[35] As many commentators on the artist have noted, Vermeer typically places a barrier between the viewer and his subject: the carpet-covered table and still life that, together with the chairback, obstruct our access to the *Maid Asleep* (see fig. 3.2), for instance, or the dark mass of the tablecloth on the left and the obliquely turned chair on the right that form an analogous, if less extreme, barrier in the *Woman in Blue Reading a Letter* (see fig. 2.4). Such blocking objects appear in virtually all the paintings of solitary figures, and the exclusion they create is felt all the more keenly because Vermeer otherwise monumentalizes those figures, bringing them tantalizingly close to the viewer. Writing of a related phenomenon, Daniel Arasse has noted how the artist characteristically combines "a (slight) view from below with regard to his figures and a (slight) raising of the horizon on the surface of the canvas" whose paradoxical effect is "to invite [. . .] the viewer into a proximity that eludes by a minute distancing."[36] Nor is this the only means by which Vermeer's close-ups manage to retain their aura of privacy. Recall Zirka Filipczak's account of how the paintings often frustrate our expectations by presenting their "iconographic focus as out of focus," while rendering minor details with precision: an "oxymoronic" practice that makes the subjects of those paintings seem "just out of visual reach," even as other signals draw us to them. The frequently remarked elusiveness of Vermeer's women, she suggests, derives as much from such optical effects as from their apparent ignorance of the viewer, which helps to explain why we sense that elusiveness not only in images of absorption like *The Milkmaid*, but in the *Girl with a Pearl Earring* as well, despite her appearing to gaze directly at the viewer.[37] In the words of Arasse, Vermeer "made interiority the mystery he celebrated."[38]

By rendering his figures visible, the light that famously suffuses Vermeer's interiors may be understood as the means by which such privacy "goes public," to adapt Jackson's account of the lyric.[39] But it can also feel like a metaphor for that privacy itself, or at least for the inwardness that his images both evoke and conceal from us. The sensation that Vermeer's paintings are somehow lit from within—despite the windows that apparently serve to illuminate them—

has long been a feature of his modern reception. "The light seems to come from the picture itself," to quote Thoré once again: the effect that purportedly prompted one naïve viewer to look behind the easel on which the *Officer and Laughing Girl* was perched for the source of its "marvelous radiance."[40] More technical accounts suggest that the effect may arise from the reflective surfaces that Vermeer incorporates within his images, so that light appears to emanate from the objects and persons occupying the room, as well as the window.[41]

But the very monumentalizing of the human form to which I've already alluded, especially in the single-figure paintings, means that his persons tend to dominate the space they inhabit, such that a private room becomes not only the setting for a private self, but its visible analogue, and the light that fills it a mental or spiritual light as much as a physical phenomenon. "Vermeer really does see us as creatures not merely drawn to light but possessing a light of our own," Arthur Danto wrote after viewing the major exhibition of Vermeer's paintings that traveled between Washington, DC, and The Hague in the winter of 1995–96. Loosely associating that light with the clear glass of Dutch Reformed churches, Danto called it "a metaphor perhaps for truth," and more than one poet has responded in similar terms.[42] "Pray for the grace of accuracy / Vermeer gave to the sun's illumination," Robert Lowell famously exhorts himself in the "Epilogue" to his final book of poems, *Day by Day*.[43] "Who look on Truth with mortal sight / Are blinded in its blaze of light," the painter announces in his own voice at the close of Rosemary Dobson's "The Mirror," a first-person lyric subtitled "Jan Vermeer speaks."[44] Lowell's "accuracy" may lack the metaphysical charge of Dobson's capitalized "Truth," but he, too, speaks a language of spiritual illumination; and it's no accident, I think, that he substituted "vision" for the more mechanical "eye" when he chose to revise and expand a key line in the manuscript: "*The painter's vision is not a lens, / it trembles to caress the light.*"[45]

Others have seen in Vermeer's paintings of solitary women a secularized version of the light that traditionally irradiates the Virgin Mary—an association that seems especially salient for the *Woman Holding a Balance*, where an apparent pregnancy is foregrounded against a picture of the Last Judgment (see fig. 3.9), but one that makes itself felt in less obvious images as well.[46] He "took / The whole Madonna tradition and turned it into light and milk," Robert Hass has written of Vermeer's sturdy *Milkmaid*, for instance.[47] In Eamon Grennan's poetic tribute to the *Woman with a Pearl Necklace*, what begins as an "ordinary room of light" transfigures even a scene that some have been tempted to read as an image of vanity:

> the shaded yellow of it washing
> to pure white where a wall becomes a painted nothing, a figure
> for what he knew but could name no other way: the sheer intensity
> of being this young woman

By the close of the poem, this brilliantly lit wall has become the picture's true "mirror," and what it reflects is "the soul itself": a soul, the syntax manages to suggest, that belongs at once to the painting's subject and its creator.[48] (See fig. 2.5.)

"Since he painted her, she will always be putting this pearl necklace on": the first line of Grennan's poem, with its play on the double meaning of the opening conjunction, both causal and temporal, and its assertion of the continuous present participle, is at once an instance of lyric time and a celebration of its painted equivalent.[49] What Culler terms "the iterative and iterable performance of an event in the lyric present" takes visual shape in Vermeer's paintings of figures engaged in simple gestures or tasks—looking in the mirror, reading a letter, holding a balance—that appear to continue indefinitely in the present of the viewer.[50] Perhaps because a painted stream of liquid both renders motion visible and stills it, *The Milkmaid*'s act of pouring milk seems to have drawn particular attention from the poets. In the insouciantly titled "Seeing All the Vermeers," for instance, Alfred Corn's peripatetic narrator pauses long enough to note "the resonant stillness / centered on movement's figment" that he locates in this "cream paint paying out / a corded rivulet at the cruse's lip."[51] A combination of demotic autobiography and extended catalogue rather than a lyric as such, "Seeing All the Vermeers" is something of an anomaly among the works considered here; and so is its time scheme, with its thirty-year swoop through the poet's personal history. There's a hint of a different temporality in that "paint paying out," but the narrator, intent on moving on to his next encounter, chooses not to linger in it.

For Wisława Szymborska, by contrast, the fate of the entire world depends on the ongoing motion of that paint. Her poem, titled simply "Vermeer," reads in full:

> So long as the woman from the Rijksmuseum
> in painted quiet and concentration
> keeps pouring milk day after day
> from the pitcher to the bowl
> the World hasn't earned
> the world's end.

That capitalized "World" also appears in the Polish original, as if to suggest the metaphysical weight of the painted gesture, how its perpetuation of dailiness allows our merely lowercase world to transcend the limits of time. "So long as the woman [. . .] / keeps pouring," we—like the woman herself—remain indefinitely suspended in the lyric present.[52] (See fig. 3.7.)

A related perception shapes another tribute to the painting, by the German-American poet Lisel Mueller, though, unlike her Polish contemporary, Mueller also amuses herself by briefly contemplating the subjectivity of Vermeer's milkmaid. "No wonder she thinks there's more / where everything came from / a girl as round as the jug / that never runs dry": Mueller's opening lines play on the exasperated question with which parents routinely scold their food-wasting children—"Do you think there's more where that came from?"—wittily transforming the parental cliché into a declaration of art's inexhaustibility. Such wry humor at the milkmaid's expense reappears in the second stanza, even as the emphasis begins to shift from her expectation of plenitude to ours. "She did not ask for this, / three centuries of tilting," the stanza begins, only to pivot on the milkmaid's figurative bondage to the bonds she effectively forges—first "the give-and-take" of "the earthen lip / feeding the earthen bowl" and then that other give-and-take by which art feeds the viewer:

> herself still bound to us
> who watch the milk: it pours
> and keeps on pouring,
> although the paint is dry[.][53]

The paint dries, but what it has brought into being "never runs dry," in a continuous present to which even Mueller's punctuation contributes: despite the period with which I have routinely concluded her final line, no such marks appear in the poem itself.

Not every poet, of course, responds to Vermeer's art with such temporal rigor. At eighteen lines, Mueller's poem is three times as long as Szymborska's, but the relative brevity of both works makes the lyric moment easier to sustain—and even Mueller, for that matter, allows herself a fleeting lapse from consistency, as she imagines what Vermeer's milkmaid "did not ask for" three centuries earlier.[54] Though Robert Hass's own poem on the milkmaid likewise begins with her familiar gesture—"You know that milkmaid in Vermeer? Entirely absorbed / In the act of pouring a small stream of milk"—the restlessness of his speaker quickly unsettles this peaceful ekphrasis. Rather than the continuity of her act, it's the milkmaid's utter absorption that mesmerizes him, especially since that very absorption—the way "her attention, / Turned away from you, is so alive"—renders her at once both profoundly lifelike and inaccessible. From this distinctively male perspective, the artistic triumph of Vermeer's painting arouses a yearning whose frustration is inevitable; and the rest of Hass's poem plays out that scenario, as the speaker's longing for contact is first articulated in an imagined interview with the painting's restorer ("I make the milk milk that flows from the gray-brown paint"), and then in an erotic reverie about the milkmaid herself. In both sequences, the speaker's imagination dwells on the pleasures of touch and the sensuous draw of that flowing milk, even as he implicitly registers how experience necessarily fails to realize what art promises. In the aftermath of lovemaking, "you reach down to feel again / The wetness which is what we have instead of the luminosity / Of paint." Between "Art and Life," as the poem is titled, there is, finally, no contest. "Something stays this way we cannot have," the speaker concludes: "Comes alive because we cannot have it."[55]

Poets may be more inclined to linger in the suspended present of Vermeer's paintings than writers of fiction, but they are clearly not immune from the temptation to narrative, whether that impulse apparently originates in the desires of the observer—Corn's autobiography, Hass's private reverie—or in speculation about the stories that the paintings themselves leave untold. For obvious reasons, the two-figure pictures particularly lend themselves to such storytelling, prompting writers and viewers alike to sense a dramatic potential, however latent, in the relation of painted bodies and gestures. More than one poet has chosen not only to spin a tale of seduction from the *Officer and Laughing Girl*, for instance, but to invent an Othello-like protagonist who in turn woos his companion through narrative.[56] As we shall see in the following chapter, even a solitary figure like the *Woman in Blue Reading a Letter* can serve as a provocation to such tale-spinning. And then there are the stories of the paintings themselves: the record of damage and neglect once visible in the *Girl with a Pearl Earring* that Diana Brebner turns into a figure for other kinds of female injury ("We've all heard / that expression 'damaged goods'"); the pentimenti in the *Maid Asleep* that prompt Marilyn Chandler McEntyre's questions about the now vacant doorway in her collection of poems on Vermeer's women, *Quiet Light* (2000), or that have recently inspired Natasha Trethewey's affecting meditation on our inability to alter the past, as the speaker recalls a painful moment of her own history for which repentance—unlike the painter's pentimento—has inevitably come too late.[57]

Though I've been arguing that poets' affinity for Vermeer can partly be understood through the familiar contrast between narrative time and the suspended moment of painting, Trethewey's observation that "[i]n paint / a story can change   mistakes be   undone" offers an alternative way of thinking about art's relation to time—one in which the emphasis falls on the power to revise what life itself has rendered permanent. This is not a poem that opposes painting to writing, however, even if the initial effect of that enjambement might suggest otherwise. "Story" here means not fiction but history, and despite the implication that the speaker envies Vermeer a capacity she herself lacks, her final lines invite the reader to "[i]magine / [. . .] a moment so / far back" there was "still time" for things to have turned out otherwise. Reminding us that the term for painterly revision "means the same   as remorse," Trethewey's poem ends, that is, with a pentimento of its own.[58]

I want to end, however, with another kind of revision, by looking at two last poems that address, from markedly different perspectives, what I've been calling the suspended moment of Vermeer's art. Both are titled simply "Vermeer," but only one, a poem by Howard Nemerov, from 1962, attempts to gesture at the entire corpus; the other, originally published in Swedish by Tomas Tranströmer in 1986, takes the *Woman in Blue Reading a Letter* as an implicit synecdoche for the whole, though it briefly invokes *The Music Lesson* as well. While Nemerov wistfully imagines the artist's "little rooms" as temporary shelters from life's burdens, Tranströmer refuses even to entertain the possibility of such shelter: "No protected world," the first line of his "Vermeer" baldly announces.[59] But both poets respond to the illusion of such a world that Vermeer's paintings seem to hold out, and both frame that illusion against the inexorable passage of time. If the enigmatic character of Tranströmer's poem makes his final stance toward the painter more difficult to articulate than Nemerov's, this very quality—what Helen Vendler has called "the mysterious inexplicit" in the Swedish writer's work—may also suggest why he is drawn to Vermeer in the first place.[60]

Like others inspired by the painter, Nemerov begins in a continuing present, the ambiguity of his grammar only intensifying the sensation of being suspended without a before or after:

> Taking what is, and seeing it as it is,
> Pretending to no heroic stances or gestures,
> Keeping it simple; being in love with light
> And the marvelous things that light is able to do,
> How beautiful! A modesty which is
> Seductive extremely, the care for daily things.[61]

This is not a claim but an act of conjuring, a sequence of phrases by which the speaker at once invokes and gestures at Vermeer's art. Though it's presumably the painter to whom these lines refer, their syntax manages to efface both doer and deed, turning participles into gerunds and finite acts into ongoing phenomena at which the speaker can only point in wonder. Light alone "is able to do," but merely in a subordinate clause, while "the marvelous things" the light does are themselves the object of a state long associated with the lyric present: "being in love." By the close of the stanza, the gerunds have given way to common nouns, but the incantatory phrase-making continues. To say "Vermeer," these lines suggest, is to name not so much a historical person as a painterly style, a way of "taking" and "seeing" that appears to have no temporal limits.

Translating that style into language is both the work of Nemerov's poem and its subject. Several particularly resonant lines almost produce sonic equivalents of the impressions they evoke: the opening of the second stanza, for instance, with its joyful burst of slant and full rhyme—"At one for once with sunlight"—or the account in the third of "those little rooms / Where the weight of life has been lifted and made light," a line that draws on related sound effects, while playing on the double meaning of its final phrase as illumination and release from burden. But even as the speaker finds words for Vermeer's pictures, he seems to cast doubt on the very possibility of doing so. In the last stanza, he turns to address a second person whose silent presence has hitherto gone unremarked. "If I could say to you, and make it stick," he begins:

A girl in a red hat, a woman in blue,
Reading a letter, a lady weighing gold . . .
If I could say this to you so you saw,
And knew, and agreed that this was how it was
In a lost city across the sea of years,
I think we should be for one moment happy
In the great reckoning of those little rooms
Where the weight of life has been lifted and made light,
Or standing invisible on the shore opposed,
Watching the water in the foreground dream
Reflectively, taking a view of Delft
As it was, under a wide and darkening sky.[62]

This turns to Vermeer's subjects rather than his effects, but what the speaker wishes to say takes form, once again, as a series of nominatives: not a statement about the paintings but a means of translating them into words—words that would "stick" (like paint, perhaps?) and make "you" see. Yet there is a statement here, a syntactical rarity in the poem, and it's the hypothetical that calls the whole exercise into question. "If I could say this to you so you saw [. . .] and agreed [. . .] I think we should be for one moment happy," the speaker declares; but of course putting it so makes that moment no more than a wish—maybe only an illusion conjured up by the power of images. What began in the continuing present—"Taking it as it is"—has become, by the poem's close, the historical past, and even a painting seems to register the threat of time: "Delft / As it was, under a wide and darkening sky."[63] And if there is something willful in this way of invoking an image that happens to depict a city brilliantly illuminated by the light of early morning (see fig. 1.1), that may be the price Nemerov pays for assimilating Vermeer's art to the faint melancholy of his own. While others have taken the dramatic clouds in the *View of Delft* as casting at most a passing shadow on the scene, the poet sees a change both more menacing and more permanent.[64] "Watching the water in the foreground dream / Reflectively," he thus also manages to see in Vermeer's lighting effects the mirror of his mind.[65]

What remains a slight undercurrent in Nemerov's "Vermeer" presses with urgent force in Tranströmer's, which immediately follows through on the implications of its blunt opening with a catalogue of imminent threats, both domestic and political:

No protected world . . . Just behind the wall the noise begins,
the inn
with laughter and bickering, rows of teeth, tears, the din of bells
and the insane brother-in-law,
the death-bringer we all must tremble for.

The big explosion and the tramp of rescue arriving late,
the boats preening themselves on the straits, the money creeping down in the
    wrong man's pocket,
demands stacked on demands
gaping red flowerheads sweating premonitions of war.[66]

The menacing forces that Tranströmer assembles "just behind the wall" derive not from the poet's imagination, but from the facts of history. His poem appeared several years before John Michael Montias's authoritative study of the economic and social milieu from which Vermeer emerged, but any reader of Montias would recognize the disorder and violence to which its opening lines refer. The artist was indeed the son of an innkeeper, and though Montias believes he was no longer living in the paternal household by the time he produced most of the work we now recognize as his, that hardly put a stop to what Montias himself calls "the turbulence of [Vermeer's] daily life."[67] By 1660 he had moved into the home of his wealthy mother-in-law, herself permanently separated from an abusive husband. But even a house that was quite substantial by Delft standards must have been hard pressed to accommodate the eleven children (out of fifteen pregnancies) who eventually arrived—not to mention, of course, the usual roster of servants. The insane brother-in-law was also real enough, and so, too, was his potential for violence: before the family succeeded in locking him up, he had violently attacked both his mother and Vermeer's pregnant wife, following a pattern of domestic brutality he seems to have inherited from his father. If he was not literally "the death-bringer" of Tranströmer's poem, he is nonetheless a fitting avatar of the lethal history with which it directly associates him: the explosion of the gunpowder arsenal in 1654 that destroyed a quarter of the city and numbered Carel Fabritius among its victims; the predatory expansion of empire; the Anglo–Dutch wars of the 1650s and 1660s; and perhaps especially the French invasion of the Netherlands in 1672, which led to the collapse of the art market that Vermeer's widow would blame for the artist's own precipitous death three years later. Tranströmer begins, in other words, not with the paintings themselves, but with a brilliant distillation of what they most appear to leave out: the abundant evidence that there is, in fact, "[n]o protected world."

Only in the third stanza does the poem arrive at the illusion it has begun by denying:

And through the walls into the clear studio
into the second that's allowed to live for centuries.
Pictures that call themselves *The Music Lesson*
or *Woman in Blue Reading a Letter*—
she's in her eighth month, two hearts kicking inside her.
On the wall behind is a wrinkled map of Terra Incognita.

Breathe calmly . . . An unknown blue material is nailed to the chairs.
The gold studs flew in with incredible speed and stopped abruptly
as if they had never been other than stillness.

Ears sing, from depth or height.
It's the pressure from the other side of the wall.
It makes each fact float
and steadies the brush.

Tranströmer's language accords Vermeer even less agency than Nemerov's, but to very different effect. Rather than a way of seeing that appears to perpetuate itself indefinitely, this is an art created by the very forces it attempts to resist: the "incredible speed" whose end is an image of "stillness," "the pressure from the other side of the wall" that "makes each fact float."[68] Yet the result, as Staffan Bergsten has acutely observed, is not so much to oppose speed to stillness as to charge that stillness with a kind of energy.[69] It's as if the ongoing motion that Nemerov and so many others have sensed in Vermeer's art has been displaced from the image itself to the continuing act of its creation.

There's an arrested moment here too—"the second that's allowed to live for centuries"; but unlike so many poets on Vermeer, Tranströmer chooses not to linger in it, any more than he chooses to linger in the imagined space of Vermeer's interiors. With one possible exception, the ekphrasis begins and ends with the lines quoted above. Even the precision with which he specifies the woman's pregnancy—"she's in her eighth month"—drives home its transience.[70] While there's no evidence for such dating (indeed, some scholars have questioned whether she's pregnant at all), Tranströmer draws on the homology that many have sensed between Vermeer's domestic interiors and the enclosure of the womb in order to intimate that their imagined safety will soon be left behind.[71] "Two hearts kicking inside her" yields a lovely synchrony, but the very use of "kicking" for the more obvious "beating"—a use faithful to the Swedish original—is a reminder that one of these creatures, at least, may already be growing restless.[72]

"It hurts to go through walls, it makes you ill/," the next stanza begins, "but is necessary." As if to demonstrate that necessity, the remainder of the poem itself turns away from the painted image, in a refusal of security that mirrors, with a difference, the negation of the poem's opening:

> The world is one. But walls . . .
> And the wall is part of yourself—
> we know or we don't know but it's true for us all
> except for small children. No walls for them.
>
> The clear sky has leaned against the wall.
> It's like a prayer to the emptiness.
> And the emptiness turns its face to us and whispers,
> "I am not empty, I am open."[73]

This is a "Vermeer," in other words, that appears to devote more of its attention to what the artist doesn't depict than to what he does. Yet the poem devotes this attention in a spirit of tribute rather than critique, an imaginative accounting of the very tensions that both characterize Vermeer's work and help to explain its appeal. "If Vermeer executes the pastoral withdrawal from life to art, from subject matter to pure form," Harry Berger has written, "he shows us at the same time what he is withdrawing from. [. . .] The strange stillness of the Vermeer world vibrates with those excluded presences and possibilities." Such "conspicuous exclusion," as Berger has termed it, might well resonate not only for Tranströmer, but for many of the poets examined here, who also turned, however ambivalently, toward a dream of aesthetic autonomy in the aftermath of the Second World War.[74]

It's unclear whether Tranströmer knew that what hangs on the wall in the *Woman in Blue* is not a representation of "Terra Incognita," but an identifiable seventeenth-century map of Holland and West Friesland—the same map, in fact, that also appears in the *Officer and Laughing Girl*.[75] (See figs. 2.4 and 1.14.) But the sense that what is outside Vermeer's room is unknown territory is very much in the spirit of the poem, and so too, of course, is the implication that such territory must be confronted. Yet the change in tone from the poem's opening to its close is also very notable, and I'm tempted to suggest that the difference has everything to do with the painting that's effectively suspended in its middle. From "the death-bringer we all tremble for" and "flowerheads sweating premonitions of war," we have somehow arrived, by the final lines, at a "clear sky" that resembles a prayer: a sky whose principal attribute was already present, however, in the "clear studio" through which we've passed.[76] Whether or not we are meant to associate that sky with the faint blue tones in the upper left corner of the canvas, as Bergsten has suggested, the light that characteristically suffuses Vermeer's empty walls still feels very much present at the close of this poem that bears his name.[77] "I am not empty, I am open," is more cryptic—and less obviously consoling—than Nemerov's "weight of life [. . .] lifted and made light," but it's not so far, perhaps, from Grennan's "pure white where a wall becomes a painted nothing," or from the "intensity / of being" that "nothing" evokes. Though Tranströmer may resist the illusion of safety that Vermeer's art seems to provide, our need "to go through walls" does not necessarily require us to leave that art behind. We have already gone, after all, "through the walls into the clear studio."[78]

9

Stories Not Told

In the eloquence of his silence, we have wiggle room not only to inspect the premises, but to indulge our dreams.

[illegible]

In the winter of 2013, a writer on the staff of the Getty Museum in Los Angeles sought to advertise an upcoming exhibit of Vermeer's *Woman in Blue Reading a Letter* (see fig. 2.4) by inviting the public to engage in a collective act of storytelling. "As we eagerly await the young woman's arrival," Anne Martens wrote on the museum's blog, "we've been actively imagining what this letter might say, and how it might begin": an activity to which viewers were now invited to contribute by composing their own first lines, from one of which Martens would spin out an entire letter.[1] Of the nearly two hundred responses she received, the majority were love letters of one sort or another, many based on the assumption that the woman in the painting was pregnant and that her correspondent was the father of her child, though they differed as to whether the child was legitimate, and whether the man in question was writing to affirm their bond or declare it broken. Other submissions opened with the report of the man's death in battle or at sea, while still others took the form of a business offer or ransom note. One imaginative entrant submitted a letter from Rembrandt declining to paint the woman's portrait; someone else produced an invoice for the painting itself.

Given Martens's position, it's perhaps not surprising that she, too, chose to take the assignment in an art-historical direction: seizing the opportunity offered by one particularly open-ended submission—"Let me tell you of the future"—she composed a narrative in which everything about the woman was forgotten except her "immortal" image, which finally took its rightful place on a museum wall in Amsterdam.[2] But however various the responses, what remained consistent was viewers' eagerness to spin out a tale from the very things the painting left untold. Invited to take Vermeer's silence as a kind of provocation, they rushed to fill it with storytelling.[3]

Theirs was an impulse that others, too, have found hard to resist. Like the visual spin-offs examined previously, many of the stories inspired by Vermeer are a comparatively recent phenomenon: both an outgrowth and a stimulant of the paintings' heightened popularity in an era of blockbuster exhibitions and the easy circulation of images. But well before Tracy Chevalier's *Girl with a Pearl Earring* (1999) became a worldwide bestseller, writers were being tempted to turn Vermeer's pictures into narratives. When it came to the *Woman in Blue*, in fact, even Thoré couldn't resist speculating about what she was reading and what it said about her history. "The Reader in the Hoop Museum is disappointed by bad news," he wrote. "[I]s it her lover who writes her that he's leaving for the West Indies?"[4] Some hundred years later, the Beat poets Allen Ginsberg and Gregory Corso stood in front of the painting, now at the Rijksmuseum, and entertained similar fantasies. Having decided that the woman looked pregnant, they wondered if her lover was a soldier off to war, or perhaps already dead and "gone forever."[5] They also concluded—on what basis is not clear—that she'd read the letter before, thus implicitly introducing a temporal dimension to an act that the painting arrests in a single moment.[6]

Corso's only poem about Vermeer is a short lyric that doesn't follow up on these possibilities. But in 1985 the British poet Rodney Pybus likewise brought a sense of temporality to the picture when he saw—or imagined that he saw—the woman's "knuckles brighten / In apprehension": an anxiety about the future that he immediately identified with his own temptation to narrative. "We will insist / on trying to make up stories," the poem's speaker ruefully acknowledges, before beginning to do just that. Note how he exploits the difficulty of decoding the map on the wall to unsettle what might otherwise seem the peaceful stasis of Vermeer's painting:

That map on the wall behind her
is obscure. *Terra infirma*.
Is it news from the lover she's reading?

Is her dear one out there
somewhere, chasing jagged
masculine glories and money and

fobbing her off with
all my love, darling
and other ardent syrup?

> Her face is so gentle, so trusting,
> the world cannot have raked her yet
> with our dirty claws.

As that ominous "yet" signals, the speaker assumes that it's only a matter of time before her trust will be violated—an expectation of betrayal that the close of the poem makes clear is grounded in his own self-knowledge. He looks at the painting, that is, with the eyes of a man keenly aware of what it means to "write / *all my love, darling,* / *for ever and ever* / from much too far away."[7]

As we shall see, Pybus is not the only writer to weave a narrative of betrayal around a Vermeer painting, though not all such stories so clearly identify the woman in the picture as innocent. But before we turn to these and other fictions, I'd like to pause over one more recent response to the *Woman in Blue*, which also approaches the painting as a stimulus to narrative. In 2023 the Nigerian-American writer and photographer Teju Cole revisited the canvas on the occasion of the major Vermeer exhibition at the Rijksmuseum and began by asking familiar questions about what the woman was reading:

> What has he written to her—for surely it's a he and surely he's the father of her child? Her lips are parted. Vermeer tightens the cord of suggestion around us. The map, the early morning, the letter that has traveled through the night to be delivered: A narrative heaves underneath the silence of the scene. There's drama here, if not melodrama. We imagine someone far away whose awayness is being imagined by this other he has left behind. Perhaps the far away one is a soldier or a sailor. The back of the chair on the left casts soft, bluish shadows on the wall. The window from which the light comes is only implied, not depicted, and the light falls on the woman's forehead and on the gently marine expanse of her beddejak. All of this is done in brushwork that is precise but not fussy, a wedge of light here, a wedge of light there. Our breath as viewers is collectively held because we don't want to interrupt whatever this is. The woman is waiting for her lover to return, she is waiting for her child to be born and the painter is waiting, after working at his easel each morning, for the next morning to arrive, and the next, waiting for those favorable hours, until the work is complete. Lawrence Gowing is right that Vermeer is a painter of light. He is also, exquisitely, a painter of time.[8]

Despite the observation that "a narrative heaves underneath the silence of the scene," Cole doesn't so much tell a story as point to the elements that might inspire one. Or rather—and this is worth noting—he shifts imperceptibly from a narrative about the subject of the picture to a narrative about making it, as Vermeer replaces the woman in blue as the potential protagonist of a story.[9]

That story, insofar as one exists, is remarkably quiet: little more than the act of waiting for a favorable light. But Cole has set out to "look for trouble," as he announces early in the essay, and he soon manages to find it, both in Vermeer's domestic circumstances and in the larger political and economic world that inevitably left its mark on the paintings.[10] Rather than wonder about the woman's distant lover, for example, he begins to ask questions about the miners in Afghanistan who would have supplied the lapis lazuli for the distinctive blue of her jacket and about the conditions under which they labored. Elsewhere in the essay, he similarly speculates about the human costs of supplying the luxuries represented within the pictures, like the pearls that adorn so many of the women, and gestures toward the violence of the wars in which the Netherlands was embroiled for much of the artist's lifetime, as well as the threat of violence closer to home from Vermeer's abusive brother-in-law.

At this point, we seem to have come a long way from what can be seen in the *Woman in Blue*, where war is at most one plausible explanation for the letter writer's absence, and neither Afghan miners nor violent brothers-in-law are anywhere in evidence. But in allowing his mind to wander from the woman and her correspondent to Vermeer himself and the "troubles" in which any or all of them could be implicated, Cole is sketching out a terrain that imaginative writers have increasingly occupied in recent decades. Though he is hardly the first to associate Vermeer's art with imperial plunder—think, for instance, of Timothy Brook, whose popular work of nonfiction *Vermeer's Hat* (2008) traced beaver hats like that worn by the soldier in *Officer and Laughing Girl* to the opening of the fur trade in seventeenth-century North America—no one has yet followed up such leads by weaving a tale that directly connects the painter to the violence of empire.

Stories inspired by Vermeer have hardly lacked for other kinds of conflict, however. A short catalogue of the troubles on which such stories have drawn would include not only various forms of erotic desire and betrayal, but a range of violent acts, from suicide and murder to political terrorism. If we extend the category of Vermeer narratives to *A Zed & Two Noughts*, as I think we should, then Van Meegeren's sinister penchant for cutting up women might be added to the catalogue. Several of these narratives also threaten the physical survival of a painting, whether by stabbing the canvas or burning it outright.

What are we to make of the obvious gap between such material and the paintings themselves? In isolating the most melodramatic aspects of these narratives, I have deliberately exaggerated the phenomenon, but even lesser conflicts raise a related question, especially when we register that Vermeer's images typically minimize what little action they contain. Indeed, with the partial exception of the gruesome activity in which the anomalous *Saint Praxedis* (see fig. 2.3) is engaged—she is collecting the blood of the martyr whose pale corpse lies on the ground behind her—even his rare history paintings are comparatively uneventful. The biblical text Vermeer chooses to illustrate prioritizes silent listening over housekeeping, and in his version of the scene, both women have paused to listen, with the busy Martha differentiated from

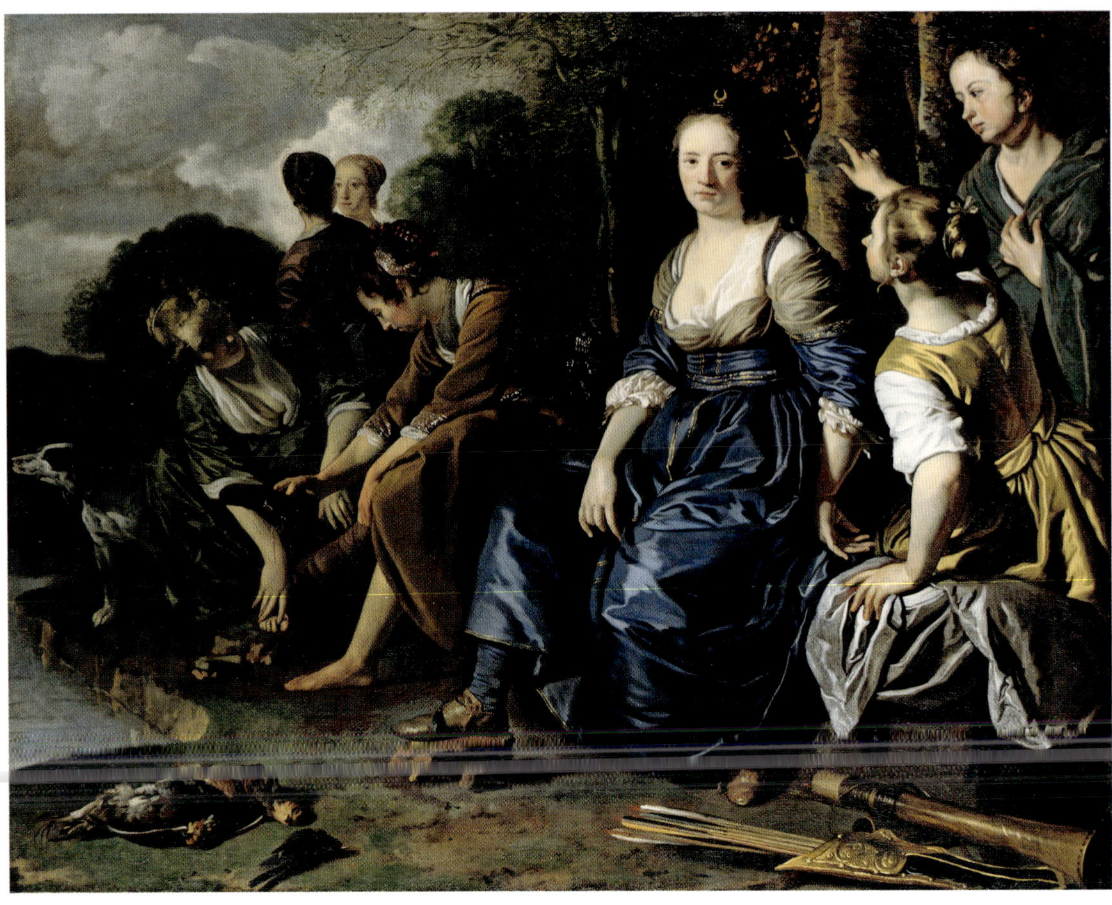

Fig. 9.1. Jacob van Loo, *Diana and Her Nymphs* (1648). Oil on canvas. 136.8 × 170.6 cm. Staatliche Museen, Berlin. bpk Bildagentur / Art Resource, NY

her contemplative sister only by her erect posture and the basket of bread in her hands. (See fig. 1.13.) Vermeer's Diana, too, is represented in repose rather than action, despite the possibilities afforded by her official role as goddess of the hunt. Even more notable, perhaps, is his decision to forgo the most famous episode of that goddess's career, when she punished Actaeon for stumbling upon her bathing naked with her companions by transforming him into a stag. The subject of a celebrated painting by Titian among others, the encounter with Actaeon provides an obvious occasion for visual excitement, both narrative and erotic, but Vermeer chose instead to depict a quiet moment at which one of Diana's companions decorously washes the goddess's feet. (See fig. 2.1.)

Though scholars have identified a probable model for his image in a *Diana and Her Nymphs* by the Utrecht-based painter Jacob van Loo (fig. 9.1), the choice of that model is still significant, especially since other Netherlandish artists hadn't hesitated to exploit the narrative potential of the Actaeon story.[11] The difference between Vermeer's picture and the action-filled composition of a predecessor such as Joachim Wtewael (fig. 9.2) is stark. But its muting of narrative is evident even by comparison to the Van Loo, which scatters reminders of the hunt, including arrows and a dead bird, on the ground, and whose

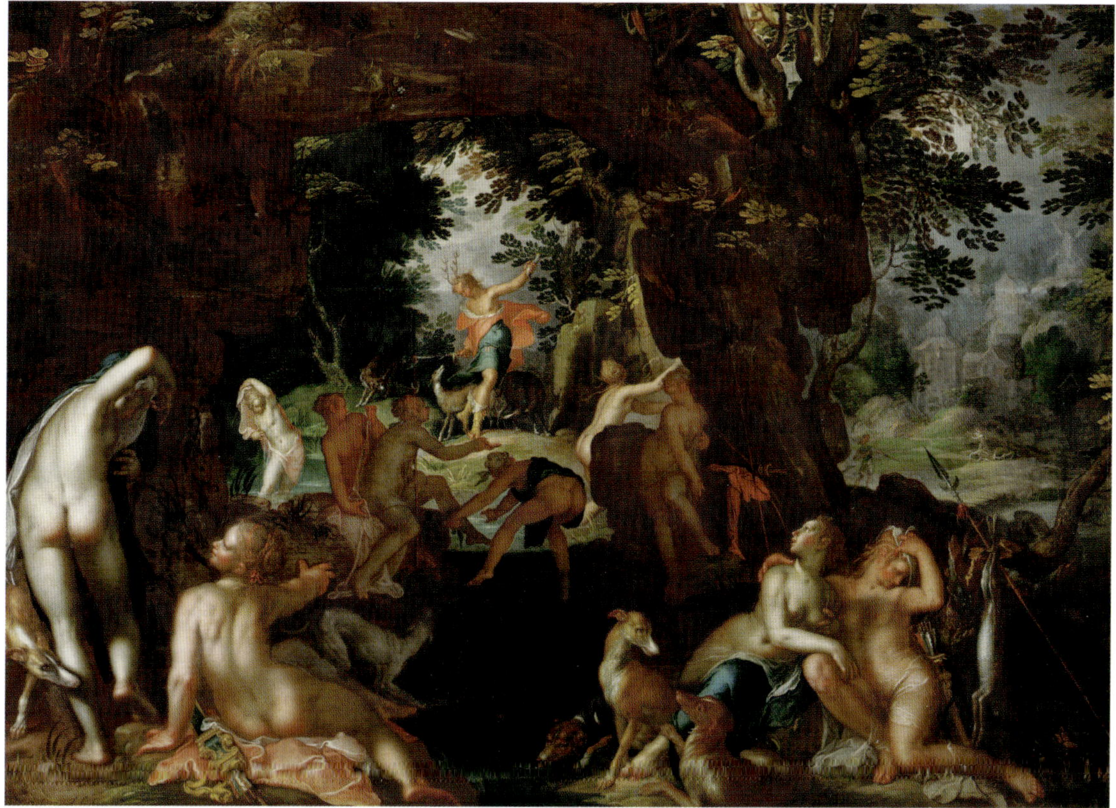

Fig. 9.2. Joachim Wtewael, *Diana and Actaeon* (1607). Oil on oak wood. 57.5 × 78 cm. Kunsthistorisches Museum, Vienna. © KHM-Museumsverband

alert dog, tensed for action, is a very different creature from the animal resting calmly on his haunches in *Diana and Her Companions*.[12]

Much seventeenth-century genre painting is anecdotal, but Vermeer typically suppresses narrative cues, as he once literally did by painting over a man and dog that might have helped account for the ambiguous mood of the early work known as *A Maid Asleep* (see fig. 3.2).[13] In paintings of more than one figure, facial expressions and postures are often equivocal, so that scholars are still divided, for instance, as to whether the upright gentleman in the so-called *Music Lesson* (see fig. 3.10) is the performer's instructor or her lover—an interpretive task not made any easier by the knowledge that Vermeer apparently moved the standing figure further away from the object of his attention in the course of revising the composition.[14] Though virtually everyone agrees on the radiance of the young woman in the *Officer and Laughing Girl*, to cite another much discussed picture, the fact that her companion has his back to us makes his expression unreadable; and opinion is far from settled as to whether there is something sinister in his figure that could soon darken the scene.[15] For a viewer familiar with related images, such as Pieter de Hooch's *The Empty Glass* (fig. 9.3), Vermeer's is all the more notable for what it refuses to show: the threat of drunken seduction—or worse—that is not so much ruled out as indefinitely suspended in the luminous serenity of the young woman's gaze (cf. fig. 1.14).

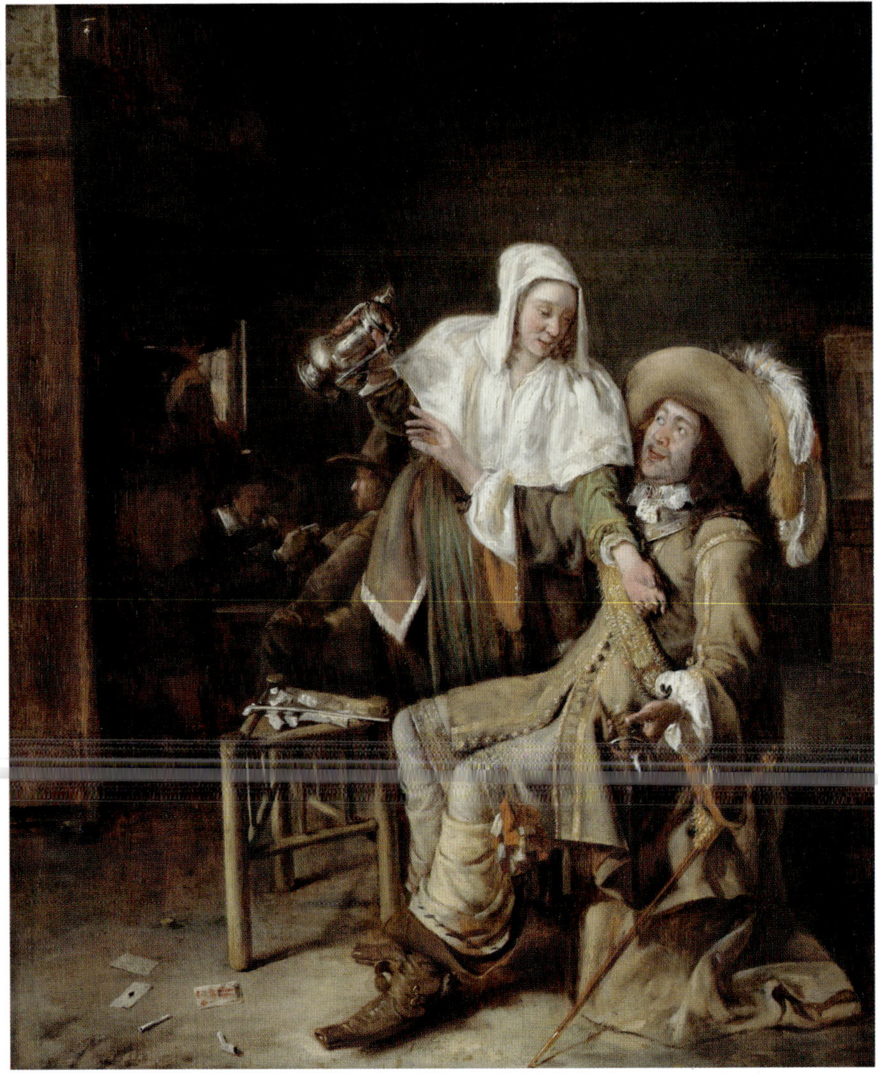

Fig. 9.3. Pieter de Hooch, *The Empty Glass* (ca. 1650–55). Oil on panel. 46 × 37 cm. Collection Museum Boijmans Van Beuningen, Rotterdam. Acquired with the collection of D. G. van Beuningen. Photography: Studio Tromp

"It is one thing for an artist merely to omit, exclude, forget, or ignore something," Harry Berger Jr. has observed of this and other pictures. "But it is another for him to make a point of his omission, directing our attention to it." Berger, who coined the phrase "conspicuous exclusion" to characterize the practice, argued that it was fundamental to Vermeer's art. "If Vermeer has echoed the genre convention of carousing, card-playing, or flirting soldiers," he wrote of *Officer and Laughing Girl*,

> and if he has borrowed a compositional motif—most probably from De Hooch—these are not merely casual sources but conventions and motifs to which the painting conspicuously alludes. Reminded of them, we think perhaps of the possibility of venal or casual love, and this possibility hovers among the others that vaguely threaten or qualify the scene before us. Not

> simply present, not simply excluded, but present-*as*-excluded, it contributes to the precariousness that edges the pastoral stillness and thus adds a delicate poignancy to [. . . the girl's] expression.

Berger would go on to suggest that by making "his shadowy officer's motives" readable only as they are mirrored in the girl's "receptive smile and half-open hand," Vermeer effectively defused the threat, leaving the man's intentions, "at least for the suspended moment of this painting," in Berger's words, "purified of their conventional associations."[16] But the very fact that such conventional associations enter the discussion, if only to be negated, testifies to the peculiar balancing act that commentary on Vermeer's paintings entails.

Just how strongly we attend to what is not there varies, of course, from viewer to viewer, and even the same viewer may find some paintings' exclusions more conspicuous than others.[17] A scholar conscious of the Actaeon myth and the many images it has inspired will be more likely than a casual observer to register its absence from *Diana and Her Companions* and perhaps to speculate, as some have done, that Vermeer nonetheless found means of hinting at the story, whether by identifying his own implicit voyeurism with Actaeon's or by including a prickly plant in the left foreground—a bit of vegetation not adapted from Van Loo—to gesture symbolically at "the male element" missing from the picture.[18] Berger also partly drew on related works of art when he commented on what is conspicuously missing from *Officer and Laughing Girl*, though the touchstones in his case were the genre paintings of Vermeer's contemporaries rather than a pictorial tradition derived from classical myth. But a viewer need not be thinking of any artistic convention in particular in order to sense how Vermeer suppresses narrative cues or to speculate about what he leaves untold. For an imaginative writer, in fact, the more that a painting conspicuously leaves untold, the better. It's no accident that perhaps the most successful fiction to have been inspired by a Vermeer originated with one of his least narrative pictures. "His paintings don't tell stories," observes the heroine of Tracy Chevalier's bestselling novel *Girl with a Pearl Earring* (1999): an observation whose corollary, as Chevalier clearly knew, is that they provoke storytellers like her to fill in the blanks.[19]

Art historians sometimes do speculate about the narrative implications of Vermeer's comparatively more anecdotal paintings, but few imaginative writers have chosen to follow their lead.[20] Commenting on the young woman in *Girl with a Wine Glass* (see fig. 1.7), for example, one scholar has suggested that she is being taught how to hold the glass in question and that the painting thus offers "a comic story wherein a newly arrived ingénue eagerly acquires the skills and attributes commensurate with her station," while her "mate" looks on—or rather, looks away—with "disgust or at least boredom." It's a plausible bit of storytelling, but if the early Vermeer was inclined to tell such comic tales, he is not the artist who has most appealed to modern novelists and poets. Nor have they been tempted by alternative accounts of this particular triangle, which other scholars have read through a seventeenth-century literary convention whereby the offer of wine is a prelude to lovemaking: a scenario in which the figure in the rear, rather than the girl's "mate," becomes either a bystander "overcome by the narcotic effects of smoking" or a "rejected suitor" who has lost her to the other man.[21]

Sexual jealousy remains among the prime motors of plot, but Vermeer-inspired writers seem more inclined to spin out such tales, paradoxically, around his single-figure images. Indeed, it would only be a slight exaggeration to say that the very elusiveness of his solitary women—at once so close and so inaccessible—tends to provoke in male writers especially a kind of creative paranoia. "There is inherent in her being an inviolable status, a separateness," Lawrence Gowing wrote of the prototypical Vermeer woman, and the sense of exclusion this creates, sometimes elicited by reading Gowing himself, has in turn provided the spark for a variety of narratives.[22] If one response to the figure's inaccessibility is to counter it by exploiting the novelist's license to imagine what she is thinking, another is to tell a story focused through the frustrations of the viewer: a story that readily devolves into fantasies of loss and betrayal.

Though it is tempting to divide these responses by the gender of the writer, one of the earliest—and still one of the best—defies such expectations. The first installment of what would become a family saga, Reynolds Price's *A Long and Happy Life* (1962) is set in the author's native North Carolina and centers on a young white woman named Rosacoke Mustian, whose on-and-off-again relation with her elusive lover eventually culminates in a shotgun marriage. By Price's own account, the character of Rosacoke initially came to him when he was still in college and happened to spot a young woman at a local lunch counter. The woman was part of a couple, but her partner, significantly, "left no impression." Price's eyes were solely focused on her, and nearly three decades after the fact she was "still intact in every line—a tall girl, maybe nineteen or twenty, with the strong bones and skull that would carry her beauty undimmed to the grave; long ash-blond hair, a straw church-hat, a white good-dress, and pale blue eyes that alternated looks of grave self-sufficiency and half-smiling bottomless imagined need: all aimed at the boy." After shaving a few years off her age, Price turned this Rosacoke into the heroine of an early short story. But it was only later that his mind suddenly produced the "picture" that would become the germ of *A Long and Happy Life*: a vision of Rosacoke, with a baby in her arms, dressed as Mary for a church Christmas pageant—a vision in turn catalyzed by a color postcard of the *Woman in Blue* he'd propped against the wall near his worktable. Like the girl at the lunch counter, she, too, was a kind of memory picture, since he'd acquired the postcard after seeing the original in Amsterdam the previous summer. As he subsequently described the process, "Vermeer's pregnant girl in blue at a window, absorbed in a one-page letter in her hands, a large map suspended on the plaster behind her [. . .] had silently inserted itself into whatever crowd of motives had brought me my own instant picture, so slowly evolved."[23] The novel he proceeded to write would be designed to fill out this image.

A Long and Happy Life is obviously not a Vermeer novel in the usual sense of the term, and readers unacquainted with this backstory would hardly be apt to think of him when they came upon the scene in question. Price makes no effort to connect rural North Carolina in the mid-twentieth century to the Dutch Golden Age, and neither the painter nor the painting is ever named in the text. But by imagining a heroine who spends most of her time patiently waiting for the man she loves to return home and claim her, Price composes a story that is not all that different, in outline at least, from the tales that other viewers have spun from the *Woman in Blue*; and the fact that much of the couple's relation is conducted by letter after the man heads off to the navy only drives home the resemblance, even if this naval tour amounts to nothing more than a three-year stint fixing radios in Norfolk, Virginia. That he is casually unfaithful and she remains loyal also accords with the familiar scenario that others have projected onto the painting, as does the fact that the lovers are unmarried when the woman becomes pregnant.

The novel opens with the man, whose name is Wesley Beavers, perched astride a motorcycle, while Rosacoke, "who was maybe his girl," clings to him "for dear life," her white blouse "blown out behind her like a banner of defeat." We later learn from one of her letters that she has "sat in silence six whole years waiting for [. . . him] to speak"; but despite the dignity with which she states her case—"it comes a time when you have to speak yourself to prove you are there"—Wesley simply refuses to engage. By the novel's midpoint, Rosacoke has determined that surrendering sexually may be the only way to hold him, and after fending off an earlier attempt at seduction, she partly initiates the encounter that results in her pregnancy—an encounter that concludes with his devastating whisper of thanks to another woman. The implications of that act are driven home when Rosacoke finally tells him that she is "working on a baby," and after making sure that she, by contrast, "don't know nobody but me," as he puts it, Wesley makes what amounts to his first offer of marriage. "Listen here," he says. "We will drive to South Carolina tonight when the show is over. To Dillon. That's where everybody goes—you ain't got to wait for a license there." To which Rosacoke responds, simply but firmly, "I am not *everybody*. I am just the cause of this baby. It is mine and I am having it on my own."[24]

Only in the final scene does Wesley ever appear to see Rosacoke for who she is—"[he] knows me," she thinks—and it is crucial that the moment only arrives after she has issued this declaration of independence.[25] The scene is the one that Price had in mind from the start, and we witness it almost exclusively through his heroine's eyes, as she sits in the church choir, garbed in blue, with another woman's baby, having reluctantly agreed at the last minute to replace her grieving sister-in-law as the Virgin Mary in the Christmas pageant. (The sister-in-law has just suffered a stillbirth, one of two crucial deaths that frame the narrative.) Interweaving bits of the service with Rosacoke's thoughts about the baby—the one who represents the infant Jesus, but also the one growing inside her—Price gives voice to the inwardness that many viewers have sensed in Vermeer's painting, even as he also draws out its potential Marian associations.[26] Though the last paragraph of the novel makes clear that Rosacoke will finally accept Wesley after all, she whispers her "Yes" to the baby in her arms rather than to her future husband; and it is her capacity for love rather than the promise that it will be reciprocated that the ending appears to celebrate.[27] Having begun with a mental picture, Price set out to write a novel that would account for it, but the work that resulted suggests that what most drew him to the picture was not the story it left untold but the occasion it afforded to imagine a state of mind.

Price is not the only writer who has been tempted to translate the mysterious inwardness of Vermeer's women into the stuff of narrative. The painting that inspired perhaps the best-known such fiction leaves still more untold than *Woman in Blue*, but it is precisely in that silence that Tracy Chevalier evidently saw her opportunity. Most of Vermeer's solitary figures are absorbed in some form of action, however minimal, but as a so-called *tronie*, or anonymous head, rather than a pared down genre painting, the *Girl with a Pearl Earring* lacks even such small cues to narrative. Posed against a dark background and visible only from the shoulder up, she challenges the viewer to place her in a social context—a challenge hardly rendered easier by the eponymous earring and fancy headdress. (See fig. 4.1.) Though viewers have occasionally been tempted to identify her as one of the artist's daughters, most scholars rule out the possibility, since his oldest would have been just eleven when the canvas is generally thought to have been painted.[28] Chevalier has traced her decision to imagine the girl instead as his barely literate servant to a feeling that there was something anomalous about that "luxurious" pearl, given the rest of the subject's clothes—hence, the novelist concluded, her heroine wouldn't actually own the ornament in question—and to a sense that the "knowing" directness of her gaze meant that, humble as she was, she nonetheless knew the man who painted her.[29]

As hypotheses about the painting itself, these observations raise all kinds of questions, beginning with the doubtful premise that Vermeer was engaging in a kind of portraiture, whose subject would typically have owned the costume in which he painted her. One might wonder, too, whether what little we can see of the girl's jacket really looks "very plain" when compared with the dress of the artist's other female figures.[30] But Chevalier, of course, was embarking on a work of fiction, not scholarship, and central to her project was an impulse to look for the slightest signs—even to make them up, if need be—that might help generate a narrative from Vermeer's enigmatic painting. Like Price, Chevalier seems to have been motivated above all by the desire to imagine the interior life of her painting's elusive subject: a desire which led her not merely to focalize much of the novel through its heroine, as Price did in *A Long and Happy Life*, but to make her the narrator. If there's a contradiction between that role and the plausible backstory with which the novel provides her—the daughter of a former tile-maker who's been blinded in a kiln explosion, Griet, as we learn to call her, reports at one point that her father taught her to write her name, "but little else"—it's the kind of enabling contradiction that many works of fiction ask us to take as given.[31] Suspending disbelief, we accept the premise that these are Griet's own words we are reading.

Gowing once summed up the subject of Vermeer's art as "the attention that man pays to woman"—an attention that Chevalier, like other writers inspired by the paintings, partly assimilates to the plot of a love story.[32] Though Griet's narrative makes it clearer that she has fallen in love with Vermeer than he with her, the feeling on both sides remains unspoken, sublimated—on her part as well as his—into their shared engagement with the work of art. Even before she is hired to assist the other servants with the household tasks, her account of how she lays out some chopped vegetables for a soup hints at the aesthetic sensitivities that will turn the humble maid into something more like the painter's apprentice, as she explains to an inquisitive Vermeer why she has separated the orange carrot slices from the purple cabbage shreds in her circular arrangement: "The colors fight when they are side by side, sir." Similar impulses will later prompt her to hesitate before cleaning the window of his studio, lest it alter the light filtering into the room, or to tell him that he has made "a better painting" after he has eliminated the map that originally hung on the rear wall of *Woman with a Pearl Necklace* (see fig. 2.5). Later still, after she has learned to grind Vermeer's pigments, she will sense that there is something lacking in the arrangement of *A Lady Writing* (see fig. 5.16) and deliberately introduce "some disorder on the table" by altering the folds of the blue cloth—a change he silently accepts before asking her to explain its visual logic. Toward the end of the novel, it will also be Griet who recognizes even before he does what is missing from her nearly completed portrait, though she carefully refrains from reminding him of "that point of brightness he had used to catch the eye in other paintings" out of a justified fear that borrowing his wife's pearl will mean the end of her stay in the artist's household.[33] It also nearly results in the destruction of the work itself, when Vermeer narrowly prevents a jealous Catharina from plunging a knife into the canvas.

As that final bit of melodrama suggests, Griet has become a tacit rival of the artist's wife, as well as the center of two more erotic triangles, both of them also more implicit than otherwise. In the first, Vermeer figures as the imagined alternative to the man Griet will eventually marry, a young butcher named Pieter; in the second, he opposes his wealthy patron, Van Ruijven, who has previously impregnated another of the painter's models and now lusts after Griet in turn. Chevalier invites us to believe that Van Ruijven seduced his previous victim while they were posing together for the *Girl with a Wine Glass*, and it is his attempt to replicate this scenario with Griet in *The Concert* that precipitates Vermeer's decision to paint the *Girl with a Pearl Earring* instead. Though the artist reluctantly acquiesces in his patron's request for a picture of Griet, in other words, he determines that Van Ruijven will have to settle for a solitary head rather than exploit a scene of decorous lovemaking with its model. As for Pieter, whose bloody hands and "animal smell" are repeatedly counterpointed against Griet's reveries about Vermeer, she finally decides to marry him only after her ejection from the painter's household.[34] There are, in effect, three scenes of sexual intimacy in the novel, but only one act of intercourse: when Griet gives herself to Pieter after she has been rendered figuratively intimate with Vermeer by the accidental fall of her hair from the cap in which she ordinarily conceals it. Deliberately losing her virginity to her future husband, she then reenacts the experience—once again, figuratively—when Vermeer demands that she pierce her ears in order to wear the pearl and follows that up by pushing the earring through her bleeding lobe himself.

Like any historical novelist, Chevalier takes advantage of the novelist's license to alter or invent history as she pleases. Acknowledging her debt to John Michael Montias's *Vermeer and His Milieu* (1989), among other sources, she reconstructs that milieu with some concern for accuracy—assuring, for instance, that all of the paintings invoked in the text correspond to known works by the artist, while appropriately omitting the titles with which their subsequent reception has supplied them. The members of Vermeer's household, including his wife Catharina, his mother-in-law Maria Thins, and even their servant Tanneke, likewise have their real-world counterparts.[35] But if many of these characters actually inhabited seventeenth-century Delft, others belong only to the novel—beginning, of course, with the heroine herself. And even the historical figures are necessarily transformed by the narrative, which requires actions—not to mention thoughts and speeches—notably absent from the historical record. Pieter van Ruijven was indeed a wealthy patron of the artist, for example, but there is no evidence that he exploited that position to abuse the artist's models, plausible as it may be to imagine such a man sexually harassing vulnerable women. Nor is there any evidence that the famous microscopist Antonie van Leeuwenhoek, who can be definitively linked to the artist only as executor of his estate, was the kind of intimate who would have warned Griet, as the fictional Van Leeuwenhoek does, that Vermeer's interest in her is partly driven by competition with his patron. So too, with other partial correlations between fact and fiction, such as Chevalier's use of the religious divide in the Dutch Republic in order to heighten the stakes of her narrative. While tensions between the Catholic minority and their Protestant neighbors were undoubtedly a feature of life in seventeenth-century Delft, Chevalier's decision to exploit such tensions by identifying the model for the *Girl with a*

Pearl Earring as a Protestant outsider in the Vermeer household is purely an artifact of her novelistic imagination.

Among the stories not told by the paintings is an actual history of abuse in the Vermeer family, or rather, in Catharina's; but it only figures briefly in the novel, when Pieter passes on the gossip to Griet. As Montias has shown, both Catharina's father and her brother Willem repeatedly attacked their female relatives, at least twice during pregnancy: a pattern of violence that persisted until Maria Thins, who was legally separated from her husband, arranged for Willem's confinement in a house of correction.[36] When Teju Cole later invoked this violent brother as part of the "narrative" that "heaves underneath the silence" of the *Woman in Blue*, he implicitly identified the gender conflicts in Catharina's family as the kind of material ripe for storytelling.[37] But unless one thinks that Catharina's attempt to plunge a knife into Griet's painted image is a fictional transposition of Willem's documented attempt to use the same instrument on their mother, Chevalier appears to have deliberately sidestepped this history.[38]

To the best of my knowledge, in fact, the only writer to exploit Willem's story for a narrative of his own is not a novelist but an art historian, Benjamin Binstock, whose pointedly titled *Vermeer's Family Secrets: Genius, Discovery, and the Unknown Apprentice* (2009) has more than one impulse in common with *Girl with a Pearl Earring*—including, most prominently, a desire to see in the paintings not just "the attention that man pays to woman," to quote Gowing again, but woman's own capacity for artmaking.[39] But before I turn to Binstock's version of that narrative, I want to take up another novel, published the same year as Chevalier's, that also imagines one of Vermeer's female subjects as a proto-artist.

As we've already seen, the Vermeer at issue in Susan Vreeland's *Girl in Hyacinth Blue* (1999) is not an actual canvas, but what I have called an innocent forgery: an imaginary painting composed, like many less innocent versions of the species, by piecing together motifs from known works by the master. By her own account, Vreeland had never actually seen a Vermeer when she wrote the novel, whose fictional painting derives instead from reproductions in catalogues.[40] While Chevalier confines her narrative to a few years in the artist's life, Vreeland sweeps back over the centuries, as she traces the provenance of her fictive Vermeer from its modern owner to the imagined scene of its making in seventeenth-century Delft. Though she, too, reports having consulted scholarly sources, Vreeland appears to have been less concerned to get her art history right than to exploit the excitement of a narrative in which an initial narrator's skepticism about the painting is repeatedly undermined by scenes that confirm its authenticity. It's one thing for a man whose Nazi father supposedly looted the canvas from a Jewish family during the Second World War to assure himself, "This was a *Vermeer*"; it's another for a dealer in the early eighteenth century, when the artist had all but disappeared from view, to declare with similar confidence, "*That's* Vermeer," even as he enthusiastically pronounces it "a rare find indeed."[41] Both the confidence and the enthusiasm, that is, are a back-formation from the artist's present reputation, rather than a plausible reconstruction of an encounter in eighteenth-century Amsterdam.

One way of generating a plot from Vermeer's stillness, Vreeland's novel suggests, is to make the painting itself the protagonist of the narrative. When the novel opens, its guilty owner, obsessed with his father's Nazi past, is planning to burn the canvas as a form of penance. Though we never know whether he actually carries out his intention, the painting's previous adventures afford Vreeland plenty of occasions to imagine the kinds of trouble that make for narrative. There is, of course, the Jewish family in occupied Amsterdam, whose only daughter, Hannah, contemplates the "quietness" of the girl in the picture, even as she herself is forced to anticipate the oncoming violence, when she voluntarily strangles her brother's beloved carrier pigeons lest they be destroyed by the Nazis. Other episodes entail everything from illicit sex to a young woman's execution for infanticide and witchcraft, an episode narrated by her lover and set during the so-called Christmas Flood of 1717. "You think somewhere girls actually live like that—just sitting so peaceful like?" the woman asks as she gazes on the picture, and even before the terrible sequence of events that ends in her hanging, her lover drives home what her question implies. "There were no words I could give her to diminish the distance between her and the young woman in the painting."[42]

In a piece that first appeared in the *New Yorker* a few years before *Girl in Hyacinth Blue*, Lawrence Wechsler described an exchange with Antonio Cassese, the presiding judge at the Yugoslav War Crimes Tribunal in The Hague, whose litany of the horrors recounted in his court had just concluded with a Muslim prisoner's going mad after being forced to castrate a fellow prisoner with his teeth. Asked how he kept from going mad himself, Cassese replied, "You see, as often as possible I make my way over to the Mauritshuis museum, in the center of town, so as to spend a little time with the Vermeers." For Wechsler, who had also been spending time with the paintings, the judge's words prompted a crucial revelation: what they both saw as the "peacefulness" and "serenity" of Vermeer's art was not just an antidote to pain and suffering but its product—a deliberate effort to counter, by excluding, much of the world the artist inhabited. "When Vermeer was painting those images," Wechsler wrote, "*all Europe was Bosnia* (or had only just recently ceased to be): awash in incredibly vicious wars of religious persecution and proto-nationalist formation, wars of an at-that-time unprecedented violence and cruelty, replete with sieges and famines and massacres and mass rapes, unspeakable tortures and wholesale devastation."[43] Like Katharine Weber, who counterpoints the "tranquillity and timelessness" of her imaginary *Music Lesson* to the ruthlessness of the IRA plotters who end up killing an innocent woman to conceal their theft of the painting, Vreeland exploits her own version of this Vermeer-in Bosnia effect.[44] "No action. So no drama," one of her fictional dealers says dismissively of the

Girl in Hyacinth Blue; but the novel that shares its title is obviously determined to supply plenty of both.[45] As we approach the end, we are even treated to some violent action from Vermeer himself, when he discovers Willem beating Catharina with a stick and knocks him to the ground with a handy pitcher. This is, it should be clear, another story told neither by the paintings nor the documentary records. According to Montias, the eyewitness accounts of Willem's attacks make no mention of the artist's presence.[46]

Yet the final chapters of *Girl in Hyacinth Blue* also have a quieter tale to tell, one at which the novel has been hinting from the start. The protagonist of this subplot is the girl in the picture, a daughter of the painter, whom Vreeland calls Magdalena. Having begun by evoking "the quiet intensity of [. . .] longing" conveyed by the picture, the novel now identifies that longing as its subject's desire to become an artist herself. "She wished to paint," we are told, and pictures not "just [. . .] of women inside cramped little rooms," but of life outdoors: people "bending in the potato fields," for example, or "talking in doorways in the sunlight."[47] She dreams that her father might teach her, but the possibility apparently never occurs to him. Like Griet, who thinks as she poses that "he is looking at the light that falls on my face [. . .] not at my face itself," Magdalena obeys the injunction to sit still, while reflecting that her father looks at her "with the same interest he gave to the glass of milk"—only, that is, as another piece of still life. After his death, she marries "the first man to notice her": a saddlemaker who performs much the same function as Pieter in *Girl with the Pearl Earring*, by confirming that the would-be artist will be swallowed up in the daily routines of marriage and motherhood.[48]

It's perhaps not surprising that two women writing independently of one another at the close of the twentieth century should both fantasize about such unrealized ambitions. Ever since Linda Nochlin began to answer the question posed in her groundbreaking essay "Why Have There Been No Great Women Artists?" (1971), scholars have been pointing to the institutional constraints that have historically limited such achievement, even while continuing to engage in the recovery of the hitherto overlooked or underestimated figures who managed to produce art nonetheless. As Nochlin observed, almost all of the women who did succeed before the nineteenth century were the daughters of artist fathers, and in this respect, at least, Vreeland's premise may be more plausible than Chevalier's.[49] But beyond a general wish to imagine the female potential lost to history, what inspires both novelists, I think, is a response to Vermeer's art in particular: a sense that the mysterious inwardness of his women makes them somehow his secret sharers—and a desire to translate that perception into a story in which one of them yearns for the opportunity to act on her knowledge. In a more light-hearted vein, we also might recall Maria Lassnig's cheeky riff on *The Art of Painting*, in which the model in that picture switches roles with the painter, who is reduced to posing naked for his erstwhile "art object." (See fig. 7.26.)[50]

These are not stories told, of course, by any archive. No such person as Magdalena Vermeer even appears in the genealogical record, though by identifying her as the artist's second oldest daughter and indicating at one point that her full name is Magdalena Elisabeth, Vreeland may have been attempting to graft her fictional heroine onto an actual daughter named Elisabeth, who did in fact occupy that position in the family.[51] But paintings, too, may be regarded as documents, and novelists aren't the only ones to construct narratives from the testimony they provide. Art historians do it all the time, especially when the written evidence is as sparse as it is for Vermeer, most of whose canvases even lack recorded dates.

Few have made such a self-conscious effort to weave a tale from the paintings alone, however, as Benjamin Binstock. Insisting that art history is "a *visual* science" and that Vermeer's art in particular is based in "image rather than text," he nonetheless composes a book whose very title—*Vermeer's Family Secrets*—hints at his penchant for narrative. While most Vermeer scholars have settled on a loose consensus about his artistic development, they are typically content to treat the dating of individual pictures and the order in which he painted them as tentative. Binstock, by contrast, believes that he can reconstruct the timeline precisely—and that he can do so because he has cracked another code that has hitherto eluded his colleagues: the identity of Vermeer's figures. Rather than simply speculate, as many have done, that he may have drawn on his wife and daughters as models, or that he intended *The Art of Painting* as a self-portrait, Binstock sets out to show that Vermeer consistently approached his work as a means by which to reflect on his own family and sexuality. "Family secrets," in this telling, are both Vermeer's subjects and the key to his art—including, most sensationally, the fact that eight of the paintings currently assigned to him are actually the work of his oldest daughter and "secret apprentice," Maria.[52]

Even Binstock admits that the chain of reasoning by which he arrives at his dramatic conclusion can be difficult to follow, and this is not the place to reconstruct it in detail. But before he unspools the "compelling story" of Maria's apprenticeship—the phrase is his—Binstock manages to tell a number of subsidiary tales about the Vermeer household along the way. While most commentators have been struck by the paintings' apparent distance from the domestic turmoil in which Catharina's relatives were embroiled, Binstock contends that Vermeer began his career as a genre painter by placing that turmoil at the center of the picture. Elaborating on the unsubstantiated tradition that the figure to the left of *The Procuress* is a self-portrait (see fig. 1.12), Binstock confidently identifies each of the picture's protagonists with a family member and the work as a whole with Vermeer's self-conscious exploitation of that family's secrets. According to this account, the artist cast his wife as a whore being propositioned by her troublesome brother, while her mother, in the role of procuress, observes the encounter. The whore's apparent contentment "presumably reflects Catharina's feelings for her brother," Binstock declares, while "the soldier handing over his coin corresponds to the fate of Willem's inheritance transferred to his sister (and Vermeer)." As for the painting's internal observers: "the madam looks on with concern, like a mother watching her children," and Vermeer "plays along with the group [. . .] both amused and aroused by them as indicated by the phallic neck of his instrument."[53]

It is impossible, of course, to prove a negative, and something like this imagined scenario might actually correspond to the facts of the artist's biography, even if the idea that his Catholic mother-in-law would have agreed to pose for such a picture in the first place seems rather implausible. For Binstock, however, speculation as to the identity of Vermeer's models quickly hardens into certainty and provides the template for many of the other tales he spins from the paintings. So *Officer and Laughing Girl*, for example, becomes a seduction scene once again featuring Catharina and her brother—the latter ostensibly recognizable from "his shoulder-length dark hair, bright red jacket, and black hat tipped at an angle," as in *The Procuress*—while *The Glass of Wine* shows Willem, now draped in green, likewise posing with his sister for a picture Binstock prefers to call, after its implicit narrative, *The Interrupted Music*. (See figs. 1.14 and 6.10.) Even Vermeer's exclusions are processed through the hypothetical biography: having decided that Catharina also served as the model for *A Maid Asleep* (see fig. 3.2), for instance, Binstock determines that the man painted out of the picture must "logically" be Willem, "who reprised his role in Vermeer's *Procuress* as a real-life counterpart of the randy gentlemen" depicted by Nicholas Maes in his eavesdropper paintings. Not content to identify these real-life originals, Binstock proceeds to spin out the backstory of the picture he chooses to call *Girl*—rather than *Maid—Asleep*, apparently out of deference to Catharina: "The out-turned chair indicates that Willem got up abruptly at the end of the meal, presumably after an altercation, and then checked his appearance in the mirror before going out, presumably in search of 'treats' at a local tavern, such as the Mechelen."[54]

"The Apprenticeship of Maria Vermeer," as Binstock's climactic chapter is entitled, begins with a desire to account for seeming anomalies in the artist's oeuvre, only to morph into an historical fiction that threatens to outdo those of the novelists. The fact that the *Girl with a Red Hat* and *Girl with a Flute* are the only two surviving works to have been painted on wood rather than canvas has long raised questions about their authenticity, especially when combined with their distinctive lighting—both figures are illuminated from the front and right rather than the left, as is typical of Vermeer—as well as the "awkward passages" that some observers have registered in the *Girl with a Flute* in particular. (See figs. 4.3 and 4.4.) At various times, the National Gallery of Art in Washington, DC, which owns both pictures, has itself cast doubts on the latter, most recently by announcing that after extensive technical examination it no longer believes that *Girl with a Flute* should be attributed to the hand of the master. The museum currently labels the painting "Studio of Vermeer," though it acknowledges that "the form of this hypothetical studio remains unclear."[55] Other scholars, most notably the curators of the 2023 exhibition at the Rijksmuseum, reject these conclusions and continue to identify the work with the artist.[56] Neither camp, however, is prepared to make the "leap of faith" Binstock invites when he proposes that the person who really wielded the brush was the artist's eldest daughter—let alone when he extends the claim by contending that it is only one of eight Vermeers that should be reattributed from Johannes to Maria.[57]

Binstock makes no mention of *Girl in Hyacinth Blue*, despite its tale of another Vermeer daughter who dreams of painting, but he does invoke what he calls Chevalier's "curious double of art historical scholarship"—a work that resembles his own, he suggests, insofar as it also responds to the "blind-spots" of that scholarship on the subject of Vermeer's models. He even briefly emphasizes the parallels between Chevalier's narrative and the one he seeks to tell, if only to argue, in effect, that he has composed the more plausible version. "Perhaps," he writes of Maria, "she only helped her father at first, serving as his model, grinding paints, and preparing his canvases, like the 'secret model' in Chevalier's novel, a role more appropriate for the painter's daughter than an unknown maid's assistant." But if this is indeed a more likely scenario, the claim that follows abruptly ditches historical speculation for authorial fiat: "Unlike the fictional Griet, Maria also wanted to try her hand at painting herself." And when Maria tried that hand, as her author tells it, she began with a pair of self-portraits: not only the arguably flawed *Girl with a Flute*, but its companion, the *Girl with a Red Hat*—a work that also betrays some technical weaknesses but still qualifies, in Binstock's words, as a "masterpiece."[58]

Binstock is not the first to suggest that these panels resemble self-portraits, but by contending that they show the same person Vermeer had previously depicted in the *Girl with a Pearl Earring* and by identifying her with Maria, he manages to construct a narrative that outdoes Chevalier, even as he threatens to upend much previous scholarship on the artist.[59] Like the novelist, that is, he turns the subject of Vermeer's famous painting into the heroine of the story, but while Chevalier chooses to imagine her as a barely literate maid with aesthetic sensitivities, he prefers to believe that she arrived on the scene—she was just eighteen at the time of her imagined breakthrough—already prepared to rival her father. And that is in fact the story he proceeds to tell, as he divides up the remaining paintings between Maria's responses to Johannes's work and his to hers. So the *Study of a Young Woman* that once fascinated Thoré becomes Maria's attempt to emulate her father's *Girl with a Pearl Earring*, for instance, while in *Mistress and Maid* she is said to have been responding primarily to his *Lady Writing*, as well as his *Love Letter* and *Lady Writing a Letter with Her Maid*. Before her brief apprenticeship ended, she supposedly also drew inspiration from her father's two paintings of a woman at a virginal, as well as his *Guitar Player* and *Lacemaker*, in order to produce three works that Binstock dubs "uncanny doubles" of the real thing: a rather odd designation, given that only one of the three—the *Young Woman with a Lute*, now at the Metropolitan in New York—has long been regarded as genuine. (The others are the recently attributed *A Young Woman Seated at a Virginal* in the Leiden Collection and the generally discredited *Lady with a Guitar* in Philadelphia.)[60]

But this uneven output is itself part of the story, since Binstock also believes that nothing Maria produced after the *Girl with a Red Hat* equaled its artistry. "As in Goethe's story of the sorcerer's apprentice," he explains, "she was soon employing pictorial strategies derived from her father's art that she found difficult to master": a hypothesis that has the obvious merit of allowing its author to siphon off the ostensibly weaker Vermeers from those of the "misunderstood genius" he sets out to celebrate. In this account of the late Vermeer, we owe his *Guitar Player* to Maria's precedent in *Woman with a Lute* and his *Lacemaker* to "an informal competition" with her *Young Woman Seated at a Virginal* (see fig. 1.20)—another tiny painting whose canvas is cut from the same cloth and is also modeled, according to Binstock, on Vermeer's younger daughter Elisabeth.[61]

Like the fictions it often resembles, *Vermeer's Family Secrets* works to fill the gaps in our knowledge with dramatic incident; and like those fictions, too, it finds itself occasionally forced to twist the historical record in order to make the pieces fit. Among the episodes of Vermeer family history for which we do have written documents, few are more familiar than the account of how the artist's widow was forced to sell two of his paintings after his death in order to settle a large debt to the local baker. The account, which comes down to us from a notarized record of the transaction first published in the nineteenth century, refers to a painting representing "two persons one of whom is sitting and writing a letter and the other with a person playing a cittern"; and Catharina apparently handed over these pictures in exchange for a bread bill that amounted to over six hundred guilders. The parties also agreed that if Catharina managed to repay this and an additional debt owed the baker, he would return the paintings to her or her heirs.[62] Most scholars have assumed that the paintings in question were *Lady Writing a Letter with Her Maid* and *The Guitar Player*, both of which are thought to have been painted late in the artist's career and thus likely still to have been in his studio at the time of his death, though Montias argued from the unfinished appearance of *Mistress and Maid* that it was probably the two-figure picture, while proposing *Woman with a Lute* as an alternate candidate for the musician, partly on the grounds that the Dutch word "cyter" might have referred to a lute rather than a guitar.[63] For Binstock, who notes that a picture of a guitar player eventually turned up in a catalogue of paintings from the estate of Vermeer's principal patron, Van Ruijven, the obvious solution is that both of Montias's alternatives are correct and that Catharina actually handed over two of Maria's paintings in lieu of her husband's. Faced with a large debt and lacking any genuine Vermeers with which to barter, in other words, his widow simply lied. And then she covered over her lie by pretending that she hoped eventually to redeem the pictures, despite the fact that she would never have spent that much on the output of her daughter's apprenticeship. So the plot thickens, as Binstock characteristically piles speculation on speculation: "Rather, she must have insisted on this clause as a means to hoodwink the baker, who would accordingly think he was getting a bargain, or at least not question the deal, and he gullibly believed her."[64]

Whether or not we find Catharina's supposed deception more believable than her notarized testimony, Binstock's version certainly makes for an ingenious bit of storytelling. But it is crucial to note how this final twist in his plot rests on the assumption that has undergirded the entire narrative: that Maria's apprenticeship had been successfully hidden from everyone apart from her immediate relatives—"so well hidden," as Binstock breathlessly emphasizes, "that it has remained a family secret for over three centuries."[65] Like still another Vermeer-inspired narrative, Brian Howell's *The Dance of Geometry* (2002), Binstock's book identifies the artist with a need for concealment, though in the case of Howell's novel this takes the form of an elaborate conspiracy among a group of seventeenth-century artists and scientists to suppress the knowledge of a camera-like device, lest it destroy the art of painting. The report of their clandestine meeting supposedly comes from "The Secret Journal of Balthasar de Monconys," and among those who gather to ponder the question are Gerard Dou, Pieter de Hooch, Samuel van Hoogstraten, Constantijn Huygens, Anthony van Leeuwenhoek, Nicolaes Maes, Gerard Ter Borch, and, of course, Vermeer himself, who finally casts the deciding vote to bury the truth.[66] Employing one's daughter as a hidden apprentice is hardly the same as covertly resorting to a camera obscura, but there is something uncanny about the way accounts of Vermeer keep morphing into stories of secret knowledge.

If the *Girl with a Red Hat* were indeed a self-portrait, then one of Vermeer's women—or at least one we are accustomed to think of as his—would emerge as a subject in her own right, effectively confirming the practice of the novelists and poets who seek to endow his figures with interiority. But not every would-be storyteller shares in that impulse. Some writers, in fact, are goaded into narrative less by the wish to imagine what the artist's women are thinking than by a baffled sense that such access is impossible. As the protagonist of Pascal Lainé's *La Dentellière* (1974) observes of its titular heroine, her power consists precisely in being "other." That protagonist, we will belatedly learn, is the author of the very novel we are reading, but the woman of whom he writes remains, paradoxically, "autre [. . .] que tout ce qu'on a pu dire d'elle"—"other," that is, "than anything one could say about her."[67]

Though *La Dentellière* shares its title with the small canvas that hangs in the Louvre, Lainé's experimental novel is a Vermeer narrative only in an extended sense of the term. The plot takes place in twentieth-century France, not seventeenth-century Delft, and concerns an affair between an aristocratic student named Aimery de Béligné and a lower-class woman called Pomme, whom he first encounters on a seaside vacation in Cabourg. Neither Vermeer nor his painting is ever explicitly discussed in the text, and while the narrator often refers to Pomme as "The Lacemaker," she actually works in a hairdressing salon, where she primarily assists in the cleaning up. Both in its tacit evocation of Vermeer and its humble heroine, the novel may recall *A Long and Happy Life*, but while Price would later explain his relation to the *Woman in Blue*, Lainé leaves the reader to infer the connection from his title and his repeated comparisons of his heroine to a figure in a genre painting.[68] The first such passage begins as a description of her knitting, but the way in which Pomme is absorbed in her work becomes emblematic of her character:

> Her task, no matter what, immediately resolved into this accord, this unity. This time, like the others, she was the subject of one of those genre paintings where the composition, the anecdote give rise to the model as if enshrined in her gesture. That way she had, for example, of pinching the hairpins between her lips when she put up her hair! She was The Laundress, The Water Carrier, or The Lacemaker.[69]

By the time we are introduced to Aimery and learn that he is destined to become the chief curator at an important museum, we have already begun to sense the kind of attraction this woman-turned-artwork will exert on him. As the narrator observes soon after the couple's first meeting,

> The simplicity of the young woman had natural affinities with the most subtle effects of art, just as she had with things, with utensils. And the one perhaps not without the other. The sudden and unconscious beauty that emanated from Pomme at her daily tasks, when she washed up, when she prepared dinner, imbued with the simple majesty of her "Lacemaker" gesture, was, doubtless, even beyond that of a symphony by Mahler.

But this, the narrator goes on to note, Aimery himself wouldn't have been able to admit. For the aspiring student, beauty has its place apart from the rest of the world, "where the banal and ugly reigned," and the same assimilation to ordinary objects and gestures that transforms his simple companion into a figure in a genre painting also acts as an impenetrable barrier. Though he tries to convince himself that observation will somehow provide a key to her thoughts, the Lacemaker remains—like the objects with which she is identified—utterly opaque to him. And that very opacity breeds resentment, especially since her closeness still tantalizes. Even after they finally make love—an act on which he embarks almost arbitrarily—nothing changes. "It was always the same peace, inaccessible, incomprehensible."[70]

The upshot of the affair proves all too predictable. The first act of love-making, Aimery thinks, is "already the end of their story," and the couple have no sooner moved in together than he is anticipating his departure. "The future curator," as the narrator likes to call him, has a history to unfold; it is only the woman in the picture, apparently, who "must live in the present." Indeed, for much of the novel she scarcely has a plot, as if Lainé were implicitly opposing the timelessness of Vermeer's painting to the temporality of narrative. All we know of her subsequent life is that she returns to her mother and more or less fades away, as the once round Pomme—whose name, of course, means "apple"—responds to the breakup by refusing to eat and ends up institutionalized with anorexia. Though one might see this as evidence that she, too, has a history, in Aimery's eyes it hardly signifies. "Her physical appearance was profoundly altered," he concedes when he finally decides to visit her, "but [. . .] the Lacemaker hadn't changed. There was always that same absence of hers facing me [. . .]. She was simply a stranger, other, a prisoner not of the hospital, nor of her 'illness,' but of that distant region where she had never ceased to exist." When he asks what happened before she arrived in the hospital, she replies simply, "Nothing."[71]

The belated revelation that Aimery is not only the protagonist of *La Dentellière* but its author only confirms that narrative is his province—and that making up stories is his way of coping with that ineradicable otherness. "At bottom, what he reproached Pomme for was having dragged him into a world where objects ruled over him," the narrator observes, just before he abruptly abandons the third person for the first. "But then one evening, all of a sudden, he had an illumination":

> He had found the means to settle his quarrel with the things of this world. He would write! He would become a writer (a great writer). Pomme and her objects would finally be at his mercy. He would arrange them as best suited him. He would make of Pomme what he had dreamed about: a work of art.

"And then," he adds, "he would let it be understood, at the end of his story, that he had really met Pomme. He would take pleasure in recognizing that he had not known how to love her. He would transfigure his present shame, and his slight remorse: his weakness would become an *oeuvre*."[72]

With this final twist, Aimery—or is it Lainé?—turns his work into a dizzying metafiction that simultaneously indicts its author and lets him off the hook. The critique of "the future curator" that has long been implicit in the third-person narrative now proves to be a condemnation voiced by the guilty party himself, but this readiness to accuse himself is also, of course, a bid for exoneration: who deserves forgiveness, after all, if not the man who acknowledges his crime? And that crime only requires forgiveness in the first place if we believe in the independent reality of the woman he injures—believe, that is, that Pomme is an actual person and not merely a product of Aimery's newfound skills as a writer. To attribute her to the writer, on the other hand, is to credit him with at least some capacity to bring the woman in the picture to life: to see beyond that "peace" he claims to find "inaccessible, incomprehensible."[73]

Whether we are meant to think of that writer as Aimery or the novelist who has created him is one of the puzzles that this metafiction refuses to solve.[74] But what matters here is what *La Dentellière* suggests about the impulse to turn Vermeer into narrative—especially the kind of narrative that originates in a man's response to the frustrating remoteness of the painter's women. In this novel, that primarily takes the form of treating the heroine as an incomprehensible object and discarding her when she is no longer of use, but the closing pages of *La Dentellière* also hint at another story: one in which the woman's attention is not so much permanently withdrawn as directed elsewhere. Pomme may report that "nothing" happened after Aimery left her, but he insists on filling that absence, especially as a way of countering his own sudden feeling of guilt. "I tried to nullify that," he says, "by making her speak of the men she had known after me. She spoke of several; she told me of other rooms, with them, and then of other walks, and even of voyages she had taken: 'Greece, do you not know Greece? Do you know I have been all the way to Salonika?'" Though we have every reason to regard this as pure fantasy, it works as intended, and Aimery's pain subsides. Just whose fantasy it really is, of course, remains ambiguous, but the novel concludes with the Lacemaker's smile, as she looks at her former lover—or appears to—with "an almost maternal tenderness." Our narrator still has no access to her thoughts, but he chooses to end his own story by imagining otherwise: "it seemed to me," he says, "that she had divined my anguish, and that she pitied me."[75]

Despite its talk of writing as an act of revenge, *La Dentellière* is a comparatively quiet narrative—so quiet, in fact, that a fantasy about the heroine's other lovers serves to console the protagonist rather than spur him to action. But Lainé is not the only writer to chronicle the sense of bafflement and even rage that the elusiveness of a Vermeer woman can sometimes provoke, or to respond to that elusiveness by fantasizing about potential rivals for her attention. Writing in the wake of "a bad divorce"—the phrase is his—the poet Michael White recorded his own frustrated encounter with *The Guitar Player* and thus implicitly testified to the kind of experience that can trigger such a narrative. "She's right here, knees at my fingertips, with nothing in between, and yet she has nothing to do with me," he lamented. "Nor does she play for herself—this creature of darkness—but for another, whom I cannot see."[76]

Given the angle at which Vermeer poses her, one might argue, White has good reason to think of the guitarist's attention as directed elsewhere (see fig. 2.7), but it doesn't take a sideways glance to provoke this kind of reaction in a viewer. Nor does it take a painting of someone engaged in an activity traditionally related to the art of love, like music-making. The idea for J. P. Smith's noir thriller *The Discovery of Light* (1992) first came to the author when viewing the *Woman Holding a Balance* in the National Gallery of Art in Washington, but out of that quietly meditative image Smith managed to weave an elaborate tale of sexual betrayal and revenge—one premised, yet again, on the fundamental inscrutability of the woman in the picture.[77] "For hers is a face that is impossible to look into, her expression indecipherable," the narrator says of the painting in the opening chapter, before adding, revealingly, "The woman is oblivious to you." "Reach out and touch her, go on," he exhorts himself a few chapters later; "but you'll never get close to her. Never." He is speaking this time of the *Girl Reading a Letter at an Open Window*, but he might as well be speaking of any of the Vermeers he invokes in the course of his narrative: all the women, in his eyes, equally unreachable, and all stand-ins, he makes clear, for the young wife whose recent death he is still mourning. Superficially, the narrative that follows will turn on the mysterious circumstances that drove her into the path of an oncoming train, but the mystery that really drives this Vermeer novel, once again, is that of the woman herself.[78]

Smith's narrator, whose name is David Reid, is another writer—a doubling of author and [illegible] that is one of several ways in which this work of genre fiction surprisingly resembles *La Dentellière*—and the wife he is mourning was his British editor, Kate, who also worked as an occasional translator from the French. At the time of her death the couple were already separated, and David was left behind to grapple with the distance that her accident—or suicide—has now rendered permanent. That he associates her remoteness with Vermeer's women is overdetermined, even apart from her purported resemblance to the artist's models, since it was Kate, apparently, whose obsession with the paintings first triggered his. Just as the prints of *Woman Holding a Balance* and *Woman with a Pearl Necklace* that he now thinks of as the "hieroglyphs" of their life together once presided over the beginning of their affair in her London apartment, so a postcard of *Girl Interrupted at Her Music* inevitably turned up in her pocket at the time of her death. A month earlier, she had already sealed the connection by giving him a book on the artist whose reproductions of the paintings now compose the picture album of his memory. But while he initially thinks of these as disconnected images, "still pictures" that lack the coherence and fluidity of narrative, there is nothing static or still about the narratives that he proceeds to weave from them.[79]

"It's bad news. It must be," David characteristically says of the *Girl Reading a Letter at an Open Window*. This is the assumption with which he always looks at the paintings, and the news he expects is always more or less the same—the only question in his mind being what particular sequence of events will result in the outcome he anticipates. In the case of the *Girl Reading a Letter*, he first identifies the news as a warning from the girl's lover that "her husband is onto him," before deciding that something still worse is afoot. "Possibly there has been a death in the family," he speculates. "Or else her lover has been found dead, stabbed behind some squalid public house, lying in a puddle with his only company the rats of Delft with their whiskers and tails and tiny excited voices."

> Or it's something more complicated than that. Her lover must see her immediately. Woven into his phrases is a thread of violence, a sinister subtext that burdens her with guilt and the need for flight. Time is running out; desperation has gripped him: the drama of it is evident in his words, the way his phrases slither rapidly across the page, the splashes of ink here and there betraying his agitation. She must leave: her husband, her children. Now.[80]

Equally dark scenarios play out—or threaten to—in other paintings, from the *Maid Asleep*, in which "our heroine" has "drunk herself into a stupor" over a similar letter, to *Girl Interrupted at Her Music*, where David imagines himself as the husband interrupting his wife's assignation, while her would-be seducer—the same man who was "trying to force a glass of wine on a poor half-drunk woman in another painting"—mutters under his breath, "*Remain calm. Let me handle this.*" Even the "perfect moment" of *Woman with a Pearl Necklace* can only end, as David sees it, in disaster, as the woman prepares to leave her sunlit room to meet her faithless lover. And once again, erotic betrayal spirals into violence:

> In the morning two boys on their way to school will notice something yellow in the Vrouwenregt canal. They will come closer and begin to scream, for what they have seen troubling the reflection of trees and sky is the body of a woman. A woman who has died of disappointment, whose alternatives have run out.[81]

This is not so much a story untold by the painting as the stuff of nightmare. One of Smith's chapters is entitled "Film Noir," and it is tempting to think of such passages as stills from such a film overlaid on Vermeer's images, as if David's rage at his wife's permanent disappearance had radically distorted his visual perception. Yet one of the strangest features of *The Discovery of Light* is the way its own plotting amply confirms its narrator's darkest fantasies.

Not only was Kate apparently pregnant by the French novelist she was translating at the time of her death, but her lover turns out to have been two-timing her with a woman who could pass as her double—a femme fatale who in turn proceeds to seduce David with the hope of persuading him to stage an accident to kill off her husband, so that she can be free to pursue her affair with her French lover. This is, of course, very much the plot of a film noir—think, for example, of Billy Wilder's *Double Indemnity* (1944), with its hapless insurance agent seduced into staging the accidental death of his client's husband—and while David manages to stop short of murder himself, he only does so after nearly killing his rival in a bloody fight. As for the death of his late wife: though the novel strongly hints that Kate committed suicide after discovering the existence of the other woman, it also raises—and leaves open—the possibility that her rival or even her lover might have pushed her onto the tracks instead. "There were a hundred different answers, a multitude of plots that could be woven around these people," David remarks toward the end of his narrative, and it seems clear that he speaks equally for his own feverish imagination and for that of the novelist who created him. Yet he is also forced to acknowledge that none of this desperate plotting has brought him any closer to the "otherness, the mystery" with which he started. The woman he sought to possess remains, as she always was, both unknown and unknowable.[82]

The Discovery of Light is an uneven novel, but it's an exemplary demonstration of the paranoia that Vermeer's women can apparently trigger in some viewers, and of the suspicious narratives that paranoia is all too apt to generate. The more remote and inaccessible the woman, the more frenetically such a viewer seeks to penetrate her secrets, and the more determined he is to imagine the worst. In one particularly strange chapter, David shifts back and forth between speculating that Vermeer himself was consumed with jealousy, his every painting "a crystallization of suspicion," and recalling the accounts of jealous obsession that are woven into the fabric of another novel famously inspired by the artist, Marcel Proust's *À la recherche du temps perdu*.[83] He is right, of course, that both Proust's narrator and his alter ego Charles Swann are fascinated by women whose otherness simultaneously frustrates and baffles them, and that the jealous fantasies to which both men succumb are among the most memorable sequences in the novel. But neither Swann, who is writing a study of Vermeer, nor the narrator, who invokes the "special radiance" of the painter's art, draws any connection between his own erotic experience and the women in the pictures. Nor does either of them attempt to turn those pictures into narrative or to speculate about the personal history of the painter. It's a nice irony, in fact, that the only characters in the novel apt to do so are the very women with whom these admirers of Vermeer are obsessed, neither of whom has the slightest idea what the artist signifies.[84]

For Odette de Crécy, the *demimondaine* with whom Swann falls in love, the artist is a potential rival, who threatens to compete with her for Swann's attention. "This painter who stops you from seeing me," she says, when he declines an early invitation to tea by pleading the pressure of work: "I've never even heard of him; is he alive still? Can I see any of his things in Paris, so I can picture for myself what you love?" This is the first time the artist is named in the novel, but it doesn't take long for Odette to find his story wanting. "As for Ver Meer de Delft," the narrator dryly reports, "she asked whether he had been made to suffer by a woman, if it was a woman who had inspired him, and Swann having told her that we knew nothing about it, she lost all interest in that painter."[85]

The joke at the expense of Albertine, the novel's other female protagonist, is less directly on point, but it, too, turns on her confusion of the paintings with a person:

> "Ah! so you've been in Holland. Do you know the Vermeers?" Mme de Cambremer-Legrandin asked imperiously, in the tone in which she would have said: "You know the Guermantes?"—for snobbishness in changing its object does not change its accent. Albertine replied in the negative, thinking that they were living people. But her mistake was not apparent.[86]

"And still I know almost nothing of Vermeer," Proust himself had confessed to Jean-Louis Vaudoyer in a recent letter, but this was clearly not the kind of knowing he had in mind.[87] For the novelist who had already argued that a writer's true self "is manifested in his books alone," the very gaps in our knowledge of the artist's biography were part of his allure.[88] The only way to know Vermeer in this sense was to look at the paintings.

And the only way to turn this visual knowledge into narrative was to imagine his characters engaged in their own acts of looking. Bergotte's climactic encounter with the *View of Delft* is, of course, the principal example of such a Proustian fiction, but the novelist also flirts with the possibility of allowing Swann, too, to look directly at a painting, when he has that art lover planning to visit The Hague in order to confirm his belief that "a *Toilette of Diana* which had been acquired by the Mauritshuis at the Goldschmidt sale as a Nicolaes Maes was in reality a Vermeer." Swann hopes to "examine the picture on the spot," but his desire to look at the Vermeer is finally outweighed by his obsession with keeping his eyes on Odette, and he ends up merely dreaming of train travel instead.[89] Though Swann never makes it to The Hague, the episode testifies to how closely Proust himself had been tracking recent connoisseurship on the artist, since the painting, now known as *Diana and Her Companions,* wasn't officially reattributed to Vermeer until the beginning of the twentieth century. In arranging for another alter ego to expend his last look on the *View of Delft*, however, the novelist drew directly on his own experience. The unnamed article that prompts the dying Bergotte to leave his sickbed is clearly the same piece that had inspired the ailing Proust to make his own last visit to a museum in the company of its author, whose language is woven, sometimes almost verbatim, into the novel.[90] "Corpse that I am," he had written to Vaudoyer, "would you take me there?"[91] Though the living "corpse" managed to survive the experience, Proust so identified with his creation that he violated the usual rules of first-person narrative and pretended to have access to the thoughts of a dying man.[92] That he was still dictating phrases about that death on his own deathbed more than a year later only confirms the intensity with which he had imagined the episode.[93]

Bergotte, like his creator, is a novelist, but what he sees when he looks at Vermeer's painting has nothing to do with narrative. "Thanks to the critic's article," Proust writes, "he noticed for the first time some small figures in blue, that the sand was pink, and, finally, the precious substance of the tiny patch of yellow wall."[94] It's the blue of the small figures that catches the eye of this fictional novelist, not what they are doing or what story they might tell: he notices them because he has learned to view the painter's colors as a kind of language. "For Vermeer," Vaudoyer had observed, "colors [. . .] are at once words of a physical vocabulary and words of an ideal vocabulary," and the stylistic lesson Bergotte draws for his own work turns on a similar analogy.[95] "That's how I ought to have written," he says, as he fixes his gaze on Vermeer's little patch of yellow. "I ought to have made [. . .] my language precious in itself, like this little patch of yellow wall."[96]

Proust invokes Vermeer for the last time in the extended revelation with which the novel closes, as the narrator once more returns to the analogy between the art of the painter and that of the writer. This time, however, he is concerned with a problem even more fundamental than the need to make his language "precious in itself."[97] The problem is that very inaccessibility of other minds with which he has been grappling throughout the novel, and the solution at which he arrives still turns—if perhaps surprisingly—on the artist's style. "But art, if it means awareness of our own life, means also awareness of the lives of other people," he begins,

> for style for the writer, no less than color for the painter, is a question not of technique but of vision: it is the revelation, which by direct and conscious methods would be impossible, of the qualitative difference, the uniqueness of the fashion in which the world appears to each one of us, a difference which, if there were no art, would remain forever the secret of every individual. Through art alone are we able to emerge from ourselves, to know what another person sees of a universe which is not the same as our own and of which, without art, the landscapes would remain as unknown to us as those that may exist on the moon. Thanks to art, instead of seeing one world only, our own, we see that world multiply itself and we have at our disposal as many worlds as there are original artists, worlds more different one from the other than those which revolve in infinite space, worlds which, centuries after the extinction of the fire from which their light first emanated, whether it is called Rembrandt or Vermeer, send us still each one its special radiance.[98]

For Proust, one might say, the secrets of Vermeer are all on the surface: not in the unknown facts of his life or the inaccessible thoughts of his figures, but in what his distinctive style—his "special radiance"—allows the viewer to see. Rather than tell stories about the paintings, this greatest of all Vermeer-inspired novelists simply invites us to look. That light emanating from a fire long since extinct makes a lovely image of the artist's afterlife.

Acknowledgments

Working on Vermeer's extended family has often felt like extending my own. An early conversation with Elizabeth Prettejohn proved crucial both to the overall design of the book and to the writing of chapter 5 in particular. That we were talking about artistic imitation over lunch at the National Gallery in London seems especially fitting, as does the fact that many of my most productive conversations in the course of writing this book have also taken place in museums. I am grateful to Quentin Buvelot at the Mauritshuis, Adam Eaker at the Metropolitan Museum of Art, and Arthur K. Wheelock Jr. at the National Gallery of Art in Washington, who generously took time out from their own scholarly and curatorial work to answer my inquiries and offer much needed advice. Tracy Chevalier kindly shared her love of Vermeer and some of the thinking that went into her version of his afterlife over tea at the Victoria and Albert. Keith Gervase at the New Britain Museum of American Art arranged for a viewing of several works by George Deem and helped to sort through the late painter's files. Though I have never been in the same room as Jonathan Janson, his website www.essentialvermeer.com has proved a crucial gathering place for material on the artist.

For calling my attention to signs of Vermeer's afterlife I otherwise had missed, I am particularly indebted to Aneta Georgieveksa-Shine, Lanny Hammer, Martha Hollander, Rosalind Parry, Karin Roffman, Colton Valentine, Sarah Weston, and the anonymous readers for Princeton University Press.

Lanny also provided invaluable commentary on the poetry chapter, while Dudley Andrew and John Durham Peters offered helpful feedback on the camera controversies. Exchanges with Gary Haller and Bryan J. Wolf deepened my understanding of George Deem's approach to pastiche. Elizabeth Keto came to my rescue at the last minute by locating transparencies of Deem's work at the Smithsonian Archives of American Art, and Marisa Bourgoin at the Archives graciously responded to an emergency request to digitize them. Jonathan Lopez also helped out at a late stage by generously sharing his photograph of the otherwise elusive "Garbo Vermeer." Tim Noakes provided friendly assistance with tracking down the conversation between Allen Ginsberg and Gregory Corso cited in chapter 9. Thanks also to Jonathan Bumas, Tom Coleman, and R. John Williams for technical assistance with images; to Judith Girardi for help in acquiring them; and to Marta Figlerowicz, Martin Häaglund, and Maurice Samuels for advice on translations.

I first tried out some of this material at the 2017 Victorian Studies Association Conference in Florence and the Symposium on Nineteenth-Century Literature and the Graphic Arts arranged two years later by Deborah Nord and Rebecca Rainoff at Princeton. I am grateful to the organizers of those events, as well as to the editors of *Raritan* for granting me permission to publish a revised version of an essay that originally appeared in volume 41 of that journal. The staff at Princeton University Press saw the final manuscript through the publication process with their customary efficiency. Thanks especially to Anne Savarese for her editorial judgment and to Dimitri Karetnikov for his expertise in all things visual. Emma Wagh and Terri O'Prey answered many frantic queries with unfailing patience and cheerfulness. I couldn't have asked for a better designer than Chris Ferrante, whose sharp eyes and responsiveness to Vermeer are evident on virtually every page.

For various forms of encouragement and support over the years, I am also grateful to Emily Bakemeier, Tim Barringer, Marisa Bass, Claude Bernard, Jordan Brower, Deborah Friedell, Emilie Gordenker, Cora Lazaro-Gredilla, Ellen Kuenstner, Stefanie Markovits, David Quint, Lucy Silbaugh, Caroline Sydney, Katie Trumpener, Doug P. Welsh, Nancy Welsh, Tom Welsh, and Ellen and Marc Zonai. My attachment to Vermeer has become inseparable from the memory of looking together with Deborah, Caroline, Ellen, and Marc.

This book is dedicated to all the scholars and artists who figure in its pages and help to keep Vermeer alive.

Notes

PREFACE

1 Arthur K. Wheelock Jr. and Marguerite Glass, "The Appreciation of Vermeer in Twentieth-Century America," in *The Cambridge Companion to Vermeer*, ed. Wayne E. Franits (Cambridge University Press, 2001), 162.

2 Rachel Donadio, "Louvre Attendants Strike After Vermeer Bottleneck," *New York Times*, 9 March 2017. https://www.nytimes.com/2017/03/09/arts/design/vermeer-louvre.html.

3 Ernst van de Wetering, *A Corpus of Rembrandt Paintings*, vol. 6 (Springer, 2014).

4 Glenn W. Most, "Reflecting Sappho," in *Re-Reading Sappho: Reception and Transmission*, ed. Ellen Greene (University of California Press, 1996), 35.

5 As quoted in interviews with Terri Priest and Christina Linaris-Coridou, respectively, in Marguerite Glass, "Vermeer in Dialogue: From Appropriation to Response" (PhD dissertation, University of Maryland, 2003), 166, 130.

6 Lawrence Gowing, *Vermeer*, 3rd edn (University of California Press, 1997 [1952]), 65.

7 The characterization of Vermeer as "the first cinematographer" has been repeatedly attributed to Jean-Luc Godard by the experimental British filmmaker Peter Greenaway. I have been unable to track down his source, but Greenaway himself clearly finds the idea compelling. See, e.g., Peter Greenaway, interview with Sabine Danek and Torsten Beyer (1994), "Beyond Cinema," in *Peter Greenaway: Interviews*, ed. Vernon Gras and Marguerite Gras (University Press of Mississippi, 2000), 169.

8 Jonathan Janson, "Vermeer's Most Popular Paintings," https://essentialvermeer.com.

9 Marcel Proust, *À la recherche du temps perdu*, ed. Jean-Yves Tadié, 4 vols., Bibliothèque de la Pléiade (Gallimard, 1987–89), 3:879. In what follows, I generally adopt the English translation of C. K. Scott Moncrieff and Terence Kilmartin, as revised by D. J. Enright, *In Search of Lost Time*, 6 vols. (Chatto and Windus, 1992), though I have made some silent alterations from time to time. For the convenience of the reader, volume and page references to this edition appear parenthetically after those to the Pléiade edition in the text. (The reference here is to 5:430.)

10 Proust to Jean-Louis Vaudoyer, 1 May 1921, in Marcel Proust, *Correspondance*, ed. Philip Kolb, 21 vols. (Plon, 1970–93), 20:226.

1. QUESTIONS FOR THE SPHINX

1 W. Bürger [Théophile Thoré], "Van der Meer de Delft," *Gazette des beaux-arts*, vol. 21 (1866), 298, 297, 298.
2 W. Bürger [Théophile Thoré], *Musées de la Hollande*, 2 vols. (Paris, 1858–60), 1:272–73.
3 Bürger, "Van der Meer de Delft," 299.
4 [Théophile Thoré], "Chronique, Documents, Faits Divers," *Revue universelle des arts*, vol. 8 (1858), 454, 456, 454, 455. Though this was published anonymously, it is quoted as an extract from *L'independence belge* in a piece announcing the catalogue of the Arenberg collection that Thoré was then compiling and that would appear under his pseudonym in 1859; the language also corresponds quite closely to the passages on Vermeer in the first volume of Thoré's *Musées de la Hollande* (1858). For the comparison to the *Mona Lisa* (known in France as *La joconde*), see Bürger, "Van der Meer de Delft," 545.
5 Bürger, "Van der Meer de Delft," 298.
6 For first alerting me to this change, I am indebted to Frances Suzman Jowell, "Vermeer and Thoré-Bürger: Recoveries of Reputation," in *Vermeer Studies*, ed. Ivan Gaskell and Michiel Jonkers (National Gallery of Art [Washington, DC], 1998), 45.
7 Bürger, *Musées de la Hollande*, 1:273.
8 Bürger, "Van der Meer de Delft," 298.
9 Proust to the Princess Alexandre de Caraman-Chimay, a little before 28 June 1907, in Marcel Proust, *Correspondance*, ed. Philip Kolb, 21 vols. (Plon, 1970–93), 21:615.
10 Marcel Proust, *À la recherche du temps perdu*, ed. Jean-Yves Tadié, 4 vols., Bibliothèque de la Pléiade (Gallimard, 1987–89), 3:692 (Eng., 5:207 [see Preface, n. 9 above]).
11 Jean-Louis Vaudoyer, "Le mystérieux Vermeer II," *L'opinion*, 7 May 1921, 515. Vaudoyer's article originally appeared in three installments on 30 April, 7 May, and 14 May 1921. An English translation, on which I have partly relied, is given as an appendix in Daniel Arasse, *Vermeer: Faith in Painting*, trans. Terry Grabar (Princeton University Press, 1994), 87–97.
12 Vaudoyer, "Le mystérieux Vermeer I," *L'opinion*, 30 April 1921, 488.
13 [Thoré], "Chronique, Documents," 454.
14 Martin Bailey, *Vermeer*, repr. edn (Phaidon, 2014 [1995]), 60; Arthur K. Wheelock Jr., *Vermeer and the Art of Painting* (Yale University Press, 1995), 74.
15 See especially two articles by Ben Broos: "Un celebre Peijntre nommé Verme[e]r," in *Johannes Vermeer*, ed. Arthur K. Wheelock Jr. (National Gallery of Art [Washington, DC], 1995); and "Vermeer: Malice and Misconception," in *Vermeer Studies*, ed. Ivan Gaskell and Michiel Jonkers (National Gallery of Art [Washington, DC], 1998). See also Albert Blankert, "Vermeer au fil des siècles," trans. Marthe Lory, in Gilles Aillaud, Albert Blankert, and John Michael Montias, *Vermeer*, new edn (Hazen, 2004).
16 Wheelock, *Vermeer and the Art*, 74.
17 John Michael Montias, *Vermeer and His Milieu: A Web of Social History* (Princeton University Press, 1989), esp. 246–62; https://www.essentialvermeer.com/clients_patrons/dissius_auction.html#.XVRanqlRc_U.
18 For a particularly useful discussion of this document, see Blankert, "Vermeer au fil des siècles," 163–65.
19 Broos, "Vermeer," 19.
20 Joshua Reynolds, *A Journey to Flanders and Holland*, ed. Harry Mount (Cambridge University Press, 1996), 106.
21 Jean Baptiste Pierre Lebrun, *Galerie des peintres flamands, hollandais et allemands [. . .]*, 3 vols. (Paris, 1792–96), 2:49. On Lebrun and Vermeer, see also Blankert, "Vermeer au fil des siècles," 166–67; and Peter Wester, "A Mere Pre-Discovery or a Meaningful *découverte*?: The Early Discovery of Johannes Vermeer by Jean-Baptiste Pierre Lebrun" (August 2015), https://www.essentialvermeer.com.
22 Roeland van Eijnden and Adriaan van der Willigen, *Geschiedenis der vaderlandsche schilderkunst*, 4 vols. (Haarlem, 1816), 1:167, as translated in Broos, "Un celebre Peijntre," 59.

23 John Smith, *A Catalogue Raisonné of the Works of the Most Eminent Dutch, Flemish, and French Painters*, 9 vols. (London, 1829–42), 4:110.
24 [Thoré], "Chronique, Documents," 454.
25 Bürger, "Van der Meer de Delft," 557.
26 Provenance of individual paintings from https://www.essentialvermeer.com.
27 Broos, "Un celebre Peijntre," 55, 59.
28 Bürger, "Van der Meer de Delft," 307.
29 Bürger, *Musées de la Hollande*, 2:68, 73, 75. For the 1848 visit to the Six Collection in Amsterdam, see Bürger, "Van der Meer de Delft," 298.
30 Bürger, *Musées de la Hollande*, 2:68.
31 Bürger, "Van der Meer de Delft," 542–75, quotations at 574, 575.
32 Bürger, "Van der Meer de Delft," 300.
33 W. Bürger [Théophile Thoré], *Galerie Suermondt à Aix-la-Chapelle [. . .]* (Brussels, 1860), 34, 37, 38, 34–35.
34 Bürger, "Van der Meer de Delft," 299.
35 Thoré to Barthold Suermondt, 7 January 1867, as excerpted and translated in Frances Suzman Jowell, "Thoré-Bürger's Art Collection: A Rather Unusual Gallery of Bric-à-Brac," *Simiolus* 30.1/2 (2003), 91. The epigraph to this chapter also comes from this letter.
36 See Jowell, "Vermeer and Thoré-Bürger," 35–42, esp. 39.
37 Jowell, "Vermeer and Thoré-Bürger, 42, 54n40.
38 Broos, "Vermeer," 23. Broos also takes up the problem of *The Rustic Cottage* in "Un celebre Peijntre," 60–61.
39 William Harman van Allen, *Travel-Pictures: Two Series* (The Young Churchman Co., 1912), 134.
40 Henry James, *The Outcry*, ed. Jean Chothia (Cambridge University Press, 2016), 32, 19, 32; for the association of Bender with J. P. Morgan, see 161n20. Originally published in 1911, *The Outcry* is a novelization of a play James had written two years earlier.
41 Broos, "Vermeer," 23.
42 Among the thirty-seven paintings that modern scholars have attributed to Vermeer, two have only won widespread—though by no means universal—acceptance in recent decades, while the authenticity of a third remains in some dispute. These are *A Young Woman Seated at a Virginal* in the Leiden Collection in New York, the *Saint Praxedis* in Tokyo, and the *Girl with a Flute* in the National Gallery of Art in Washington, DC. In treating all three as genuine, the curators of the 2023 Rijksmuseum show were explicitly rejecting the argument advanced just a year earlier by colleagues at the National Gallery of Art, who had announced to great fanfare that they were demoting the *Girl with a Flute* to "Studio of Johannes Vermeer." See Marjorie E. Wieseman, Alexandra Libby, E. Melanie Gifford, and Dina Anchin, "Vermeer's Studio and the *Girl with a Flute*: New Findings from the National Gallery of Art," *Journal of Historians of Netherlandish Art* 14.2 (2022), https://doi.org/10.5092/jhna.2022.14.2.3; and Pieter Roelofs, "Vermeer's Tronies: An Outward Gaze of Connection," in *Johannes Vermeer*, ed. Pieter Roelofs and Gregor J. M. Weber (Rijksmuseum [Amsterdam]/Hannibal Books, 2023), 213–14. Though the Rijksmuseum treated the case of the Leiden picture as closed, the curator of the Vermeer website cited above, Jonathan Janson, subsequently posted a detailed critique of the painting's technical and narrative deficiencies, which once more potentially reopened the question of its authenticity. For Janson's article, as well as an earlier critique of the *Saint Praxedis* by Jon Boone, see https://www.essentialvermeer.com.
43 For skeptical accounts of Thoré's contribution, see especially Broos, "Un celebre Peijntre," 47–65, and Broos, "Vermeer," 19–33. For a cogent response, see Jowell, "Vermeer and Thoré-Bürger," 35–57.
44 As cited in Bürger, *Musées de la Hollande*, 1:273n1. DuCamp's article appeared late in 1857; Gautier's in the summer of 1858.
45 Charles Blanc, *Histoire des peintres de toutes les écoles: École hollandaise*, 2 vols. (Paris, 1861), 2:2, 4. (This edition paginates separately for each painter.)
46 Broos, "Vermeer," 19.
47 Paul Mantz, "Collection d'amateurs, 1: Le cabinet de M. A. Dumont, à Cambrai," *Gazette des beaux-arts*, vol. 8 (1860), 304.
48 Edmond and Jules de Goncourt, *Journal: Mémoires de la vie littéraire*, ed. Robert Ricatte, 22 vols. (Éditions de l'Imprimerie nationale de Monaco, 1956–68), 4:238, 236.

49 Bürger, *Musées de la Hollande*, 2:75–76.

50 Bürger, *Musées de la Hollande*, 2:77, 79. (Thoré mistakenly believed Vermeer had died in 1696, the date of the sales catalogue that included twenty-one of his paintings.)

51 Though there is no evidence that Vermeer himself studied with Rembrandt, scholars have traced lines of influence from several of the latter's pupils, including both Maes and Fabritius. For a useful overview, see Walter Liedtke, "Vermeer Teaching Himself," in *The Cambridge Companion to Vermeer*, ed. Wayne E. Franits (Cambridge University Press, 2001).

52 W. Bürger [Théophile Thoré], *Galerie d'Arenberg à Bruxelles, avec le catalogue complet de la collection* (Paris, 1859), 31–32.

53 G[ustav] F. Waagen, *Handbuch der deutschen und niederländischen malerschulen*, 2 vols. (Stuttgart, 1862), 2:110.

54 Bürger, "Van der Meer de Delft," 547. Cf. Broos, "Vermeer," 20.

55 Bürger, "Van der Meer de Delft," 298.

56 Frances Suzman Jowell, *Thoré-Bürger and the Art of the Past* (Garland, 1977), 94–96, viii; [Thoré], "Chronique, Documents," 454; Stanley Meltzoff, "The Recovery of Vermeer," *Marsyas* 2 (1942), 157.

57 "Old Masters at Brussels," *Saturday Review*, 18 September 1886, 387.

58 H[enry] W[allis], "Van der Meer," *Athenaeum*, 12 May 1877, 616.

59 Bürger, *Musées de la Hollande*, 1:326. For more on this aspect of Thoré's career, see Ruth Bernard Yeazell, *Art of the Everyday: Dutch Painting and the Realist Novel* (Princeton University Press, 2008), 47–57.

60 For the effects of Thoré's humanism on his approach to contemporary art, see Francis Haskell, *Rediscoveries in Art: Some Aspects of Taste, Fashion and Collecting in England and France* (Cornell University Press, 1976), 87–90.

61 E. V. Lucas, *Vermeer of Delft*, 2nd edn (Methuen, 1922), 47.

62 [E. and J. de] Goncourt, *Journal*, 4:236.

63 J[oseph] Pennell, "Photography as a Hindrance and a Help to Art," *British Journal of Photography*, vol. 38, no. 1618 (8 May 1891), 295.

64 Proust apparently read a revised and augmented edition of Vanzype's book; see Marcel Proust, *Correspondance*, ed. Philip Kolb, 21 vols. (Plon, 1970–93), 21:292, 293n9.

65 Bürger, "Van der Meer de Delft," 299; Ivan Gaskell, *Vermeer's Wager: Speculations on Art History, Theory and Art Museums* (Reaktion, 2000), 126–28.

66 Bürger, "Van der Meer de Delft," 547.

67 Frances Suzman Jowell, "Thoré-Bürger—A Critical Rôle in the Art Market," *The Burlington Magazine*, vol. 138, no. 1115 (February 1996), 123.

68 Jowell, "Thoré-Bürger," 115–16.

69 Jowell, "Thoré-Bürger's Art Collection," 59, 87.

70 Meltzoff, "Recovery," 145.

71 For a helpful overview, see Arthur K. Wheelock Jr. and Marguerite Glass, "The Appreciation of Vermeer in Twentieth-Century America," in *The Cambridge Companion to Vermeer*, ed. Wayne E. Franits (Cambridge University Press, 2001). On the turn-of-the-century obsession with Holland in particular, see Annette Stott, *Holland Mania: The Unknown Dutch Period in American Art and Culture* (Overlook Press, 1998).

72 The *Saint Praxedis* might be considered a later addition to this list, having first arrived at the National Museum of Western Art in Tokyo only in 2015. But since the museum identifies it as a long-term loan from its current owners, the Kufu Company, Inc., the painting technically remains in private hands.

73 The entry for the painting under "Vermeer Thefts" at https://www.essentialvermeer.com offers a useful summary of these events.

74 Shin-Ichi Fukuoka, *Vermeer: Realm of Light; Travels Through Art and Science in Pursuit of the Greatest Artist of the Golden Age* (Kirakusha, 2015), 252. (The Japanese edition of Fukuoka's book originally appeared in 2011.)

75 Alfred Corn, "Seeing All the Vermeers," *Poetry*, vol. 175 (1999). Corn's title should best be understood as aspirational: by my count, his narrator manages to see a little over half the paintings now generally attributed to the artist.

76 Michael White, *Travels in Vermeer: A Memoir* (Persea Books, 2015), 129.

2. HOW VERMEER BECAME MODERN

1 George Clausen, "Vermeer of Delft and Modern Painting," in Lord Northbourne, George Clausen, and William Norton Howe, *Charlton Lectures on Art* (Oxford University Press, 1925), 74–75.

2 "A Little-Known Dutch Painter," *Saturday Review*, 4 March 1876, 303.

3 Charles H. Caffin, *The Story of Dutch Painting* (The Century Co., 1909), 133.

4 Caffin, *Story of Dutch Painting*, 133–34.

5 Philip L[eslie] Hale, *Jan Vermeer of Delft* (Small, Maynard and Co., 1913), 3, 215–34. For more on Hale and other painters inspired by Vermeer at the turn of the century, see chapter 5 below.

6 Gustave Vanzype, *Vermeer de Delft* (G. van Oest, 1908), 65.

7 Jean-Louis Vaudoyer, "Le mystérieux Vermeer II," *L'opinion*, 7 May 1921, 515.

8 Caffin, *Story of Dutch Painting*, 133.

9 Elizabeth Prettejohn, *Modern Painters, Old Masters: The Art of Imitation from the Pre-Raphaelites to the First World War* (Yale University Press, 2017). Among other artists who underwent a significant revival in the nineteenth century, Prettejohn singles out Piero della Francesca, Mantegna, Crivelli, Carpaccio, El Greco, Zurbarán, the elusive Giorgione—and, of course, Vermeer (38).

10 R.A.M. Stevenson, *Velasquez* (London, 1899), 59. As Prettejohn notes, impressionism in Stevenson's sense differs from that with which we are now most familiar. "By 'impression' Stevenson does not mean the momentary glimpse of something fleeting or transient, but rather the sustained attention given to a large-scale scene when it is viewed *as a whole*, from a distance that is preserved in the composition of the painting itself" (*Modern Painters*, 184).

11 John Singer Sargent to Vernon Lee, undated [1884], Colby College, as quoted in Marc Simpson, with Richard Ormond and Barbara Weinberg, *Uncanny Spectacle: The Public Career of the Young John Singer Sargent* (Yale University Press, 1997), 58.

12 On the modernity of Vermeer's paintings in this sense, see especially Albert Blankert, "Vermeer's Modern Themes and their Tradition," in *Johannes Vermeer*, ed. Arthur K. Wheelock Jr. (National Gallery of Art [Washington, DC], 1995); and Lisa Vergara, "*Antiek* and *Modern* in Vermeer's *Lady Writing a Letter with Her Maid*," in *Vermeer Studies*, ed. Ivan Gaskell and Michiel Jonker (National Gallery of Art [Washington, DC], 1998).

13 As quoted from a letter of Gerard ter Borch the elder to Gerard ter Borch the younger, 3 July 1635, in Vergara, "*Antiek* and *Modern*," 253n28.

14 The exhibition in question traveled from the Louvre in Paris to the National Gallery of Ireland in Dublin and the National Gallery of Art in Washington, DC, from 2017 to 2018. For the specific comparison of the two paintings, see Arthur K. Wheelock Jr., "Private Vanity," in the catalogue of the exhibition: *Vermeer and the Masters of Genre Painting: Inspiration and Rivalry*, ed. Adriaan E. Waiboer (Yale University Press, 2017).

15 See Gerard de Lairesse, "Of Things Antique and Modern," in De Lairesse, *The Art of Painting, in All Its Branches [. . .]*, trans. John Frederick Fritsch (London, 1738), esp. 130. De Lairesse's *Groot Schilderboek* was first published in 1707. For related comments, see Joshua Reynolds, Discourse 4 (10 December 1771), in *Discourses on Art*, ed. Robert R. Wark (Yale University Press, 1997), esp. 69 (on the "Dutch school") and 73.

16 For a thorough account of this phenomenon at the turn of the twentieth century, see Annette Stott, *Holland Mania: The Unknown Dutch Period in American Art and Culture* (Overlook Press, 1998). See also Walter Liedtke, "Dutch Paintings in America: The Collectors and their Ideals," in Ben Broos, Edwin Buijsen, Geerte Broersma et al., *Great Dutch Paintings from America* (Mauritshuis/Waanders Publishers, 1990); M. Elizabeth Boone, "Gilded Age Values and a Golden Age Painter: American Perceptions of Jan Vermeer," *The Rutgers Art Review* 12–13 (1991–92): 47–68; and Arthur K. Wheelock Jr. and Marguerite Glass, "The Appreciation of Vermeer in Twentieth-Century America," in *The Cambridge Companion to Vermeer*, ed. Wayne E. Franits (Cambridge University Press, 2001).

17 On Thoré's relations with Courbet and Manet, including his ownership of works by both artists, see Frances Suzman Jowell, "Thoré-Bürger's Art Collection: A Rather Unusual Gallery of Bric-à-Brac," *Simiolus* 30.1/2 (2003), 102–5.

18 See n. 13 above.

19 See Marten Jan Bok, "Not to Be Confused with the Sphinx of Delft: The Utrecht Painter Johannes van der Meer (Schipluiden 1630-1695/1697 Vreeswijk?)," in *Vermeer Studies*, ed. Ivan Gaskell and Michiel Jonkers (National Gallery of Art [Washington, DC] 1998), 67.

20 Wayne E. Franits, "Johannes Vermeer: An Overview of His Life and Stylistic Development," in *The Cambridge Companion to Vermeer*, ed. Wayne E. Franits (Cambridge University Press, 2001) 12, 184–85n31. Though the controversy over the *Saint Praxedis* appears to have died down of late, at least one *Complete Works* still treated the attribution as "questionable" as recently as 2017. See Karl Shütz, *Vermeer: The Complete Works*, trans. Elizabeth Clegg (Taschen, 2017), 242.

21 W. Bürger [Théophile Thoré] "Van der Meer de Delft," *Gazette des beaux-arts*, vol. 21 (1866), 566. For Bredius's identification of the painting, which he had acquired as an Eglon van der Neer, see Elizabeth E. Gardner, "Thoré's Sphinx," *The Metropolitan Museum of Art Bulletin*, n.s. no. 7 (November 1948), 76.

22 Hale, *Jan Vermeer of Delft*, 3.

23 This discussion of Thoré's humanism, including his critical remarks on Manet, is indebted to Francis Haskell, *Rediscoveries in Art: Some Aspects of Taste, Fashion and Collecting in England and France* (Cornell University Press, 1976), 87–90. For a partial critique of Haskell's argument in this regard that nonetheless acknowledges some of the same tensions in Thoré's approach to modern art, see Charles Rosen and Henri Zerner, *Romanticism and Realism: The Mythology of Nineteenth-Century Art* (Viking, 1984), 192–202.

24 Bürger, "Van der Meer de Delft," 460.

25 Hale, *Jan Vermeer of Delft*, 3.

26 Haskell, *Rediscoveries*, 88–89.

27 W. Bürger [Théophile Thoré], *Galerie Suermondt à Aix-la-Chapelle [. . .]* (Brussels, 1860), 38.

28 Stanley Meltzoff, "The Rediscovery of Vermeer," *Marsyas* 2 (1942), 146; Wayne E. Franits, "Introduction," in *The Cambridge Companion to Vermeer*, ed. Wayne E. Franits (Cambridge University Press, 2001), 6; Camille Pissarro to Lucien Pissarro, November 1898, in Camille Pissarro, *Letters to His Son Lucien*, ed. John Rewald with Lucien Pissarro, trans. Lionel Abel, repr. edn (MFA Publications, 2002 [1943]), 331.

29 Marcel Proust, *À la recherche du temps perdu*, ed. Jean-Yves Tadié, 4 vols., Bibliothèque de la Pléiade (Gallimard, 1987–89), 3:692 (Eng., 5:207 [see Preface, n. 9 above]). For a different account of "The Modern Vermeer" in relation to Proust, see Christiane Hertel, *Vermeer: Reception and Interpretation* (Cambridge University Press, 1996), 103–15.

30 Henry Havard, "Johannes Vermeer (Van der Meer de Delft)," *Gazette des beaux-arts*, vol. 28 (1883), 214, 215.

31 Havard, "Johannes Vermeer," 215, 214. Cf. Thoré, whose enthusiasm for his discoveries didn't prevent him from acknowledging how difficult it was to distinguish Vermeer from De Hooch: "Their inventions, their subjects, the arrangement and shape of their figures, the simplicity of their drawing, the tonality of their coloring, and above all the magic of their light, is nearly identical" (Bürger, "Van der Meer de Delft," 316).

32 See, e.g., Arthur K. Wheelock Jr., "On Balance," in *Vermeer and the Masters of Genre Painting: Inspiration and Rivalry*, ed. Adriaan E. Waiboer (Yale University Press, 2017).

33 William R. Valentiner, "Paintings by Dutch Masters: Preface," in *The Hudson-Fulton Celebration: Catalogue of an Exhibition Held in the Metropolitan Museum of Art*, 2 vols. (Metropolitan Museum [New York], 1909), 1:xxxviii, xl.

34 Valentiner, "Paintings," xxxix, xl, xli.

35 Hale, *Jan Vermeer of Delft*, 169, 219.

36 Hale, *Jan Vermeer of Delft*, 23, 25, 23; Frank Jewett Mather Jr., "Vermeer of Delft," *The Nation*, vol. 99 (1914), 202–3.

37 Hale, *Jan Vermeer of Delft*, 182, 175. See ch. 5 below, pp. 96–98.

38 W. Somerset Maugham, *Of Human Bondage* [1915] (Vintage: 2024), 237. I thank Colton Valentine for alerting me to this passage.

39 Hale, *Jan Vermeer of Delft*, 184–85; Mather, "Vermeer of Delft," 202, 231.

40 René Huyghe, "La poétique de Vermeer," in A[ry] B[ob] de Vries, *Jan Vermeer de Delft, suivi de La poétique de Vermeer par René Huyghe* (P. Tisné, 1948), 95–96, 92, 93.

41 Svetlana Alpers, "The Strangeness of Vermeer," *Art in America*, vol. 84 (May 1996), 64; for comparisons to Mondrian, see 65 and 67.

42 Havard, "Johannes Vermeer," 214.

43 Hale, *Jan Vermeer of Delft*, 220.

44 E. V. Lucas, *Vermeer of Delft*, 2nd edn (Methuen, 1922), 17.

45 Proust, *À la recherche*, 3:692 (5:207). Those who argue for the wall (or walls) to the right include Jean Pavans, *Petit pan de mur jaune* (Éditions de la Différance, 1986), 41–45, and the editors of the Pléiade edition (3:1740). Proponents of the roof include René Huyghe, "Affinités électives: Vermeer et Proust," *L'amour de l'art*, January 1936, 14; Hélène Adhémar, "La vision de Vermeer par Proust, à travers Vaudoyer," *Gazette des beaux-arts*, vol. 68 (1966), 291; Jeffrey Meyers, "Proust and Vermeer," *Art International*, vol. 17, no. 5 (1973), 69; and Arthur K. Wheelock Jr., *Vermeer and the Art of Painting* (Yale University Press, 1995), 76. For an argument close to the one advanced here, which contends that Proust deliberately left the allusion vague, see Lorenzo Renzi, *Proust e Vermeer: Apologia dell'imprecisione* (Il Mulino, 1999).

46 Vaudoyer, "Le mystérieux Vermeer II," 515.

47 Proust, *À la recherche*, 3:692 (5:207).

48 Lucas, *Vermeer of Delft*, 47.

49 See Joseph Leo Koerner's apposite remarks in a review of the 2017 exhibition on "inspiration and rivalry" among Vermeer and the other masters of Dutch genre painting: "No one doubts that Vermeer was of his time. The question is whether his modernity, which has dazzled viewers for more than a century, can and should be denied" (Koerner, "First Among Equals," *The New York Review of Books*, 7 February 2019).

50 Huyghe, "La poétique de Vermeer," 93. In addition to Alpers, see, e.g., Arthur K. Wheelock Jr., *Jan Vermeer* (Harry N. Abrams, 1981), 100. Cf. Albert Blankert, with Rob Ruurs and Willem L. van de Watering, *Vermeer of Delft: Complete Edition of the Paintings* (Phaidon, 1978), 56.

51 Wheelock, *Vermeer and the Art*, 160. In this book, which appeared in 1995, Wheelock also contends that Vermeer's late paintings have been undervalued because they have been mistakenly judged in terms more applicable to the earlier work. For a previous (1981) version of the argument that expresses more ambivalence toward the late work, see Wheelock, *Jan Vermeer*.

3. COUNTER-HISTORIES

1 See https://www.skd.museum/en/besucherservice/press/2019/a-new-vermeer-in-dresden/.

2 Purchased in 1742 for the collection of the Saxon elector Frederick August III, the painting has been on public display since 1816, except for a decade after the Second World War when it was confiscated by the USSR. It was not officially attributed to Vermeer, however, until the middle of the nineteenth century.

3 Lawrence Gowing, *Vermeer*, 3rd edn (University of California Press, 1997 [1952]), 97.

4 Cf. H. Rodney Nevitt Jr., "Vermeer and the Question of Love," in *The Cambridge Companion to Vermeer*, ed. Wayne E. Franits (Cambridge University Press, 2001): "To modern eyes, one aspect of Vermeer's austerity or 'purity' is his white walls, raked by light" (97).

5 Statements to this effect appeared in virtually all scholarly discussions of the painting published between 1979 and the Gemäldegalerie's report. For a brief summary of the relevant history, see Uta Neidhardt and Christoph Schölzel, "The Restoration of 'Young Woman Reading a Letter at an Open Window,' by Johannes Vermeer: Final Report," *The Burlington Magazine*, vol. 163, no. 1423 (October 2021). More detailed accounts are provided in the catalogue that accompanied the museum's display of its findings: *Johannes Vermeer: On Reflection*, ed. Stephan Koja, Uta Neidhardt, and Arthur K. Wheelock Jr., trans. Ian Pepper and Carola Kleinstück-Schulman (Staatliche Kunstsammlungen [Dresden], 2021).

6 For the technical basis of this judgment, see Christoph Schölzel, "On the Restoration and Painterly Technique of *Girl Reading a Letter at an Open Window* by Johannes Vermeer," in *Johannes Vermeer: On Reflection*, ed. Stephan Koja, Uta Neidhardt, and Arthur K. Wheelock Jr., trans. Ian Pepper and Carola Kleinstück-Schulman (Staatliche Kunstsammlungen [Dresden], 2021).

7 Uta Neidhardt and Christoph Schölzel, "The Restoration of 'Young Woman Reading a Letter at an Open Window,' by Johannes Vermeer: An Interim Report," *The Burlington Magazine*, vol. 161, no. 1395 (June 2019), 458.

8 See, e.g., Arthur K. Wheelock Jr., *Vermeer and the Art of Painting* (Yale University Press, 1995), 39–43; Nanette Salomon, "From Sexuality to Civility: Vermeer's Women," in *Vermeer Studies*, ed. Ivan Gaskell and Michiel Jonkers (National Gallery of Art [Washington, DC], 1998);

and Walter Liedtke, "Vermeer Teaching Himself," in *The Cambridge Companion to Vermeer*, ed. Wayne E. Franits (Cambridge University Press, 2001), 37–38. Writing in 2001, Liedtke specifically grouped these changes with those in the Dresden painting, characterizing both "as a kind of editing in which conspicuous cues to meaning are eliminated to enhance a poetic mood" (38).

9 See *Johannes Vermeer*, ed. Arthur K. Wheelock Jr. (National Gallery of Art [Washington, DC], 1995), 104, 148, 108–10, 154; and E. Melanie Gifford and Lisha Deming Glinsman, "Collective Style and Personal Manner: Materials and Techniques of High-Life Genre Painting," in *Vermeer and the Masters of Genre Painting: Inspiration and Rivalry*, ed. Adriaan E. Waiboer (Yale University Press, 2017), 76–77.

10 Jørgen Wadum, "Vermeer in Perspective," in *Johannes Vermeer*, ed. Arthur K. Wheelock Jr. (National Gallery of Art [Washington, DC], 1995), 78.

11 Wadum, "Vermeer in Perspective," 73. According to the Dresden restorers, in fact, the vanishing point is located just where the left edge of the green curtain intersects the middle of the Cupid's lower black frame, thus drawing the viewer's eyes to "the hitherto completely unknown truncated red mask lying on the ground" in front of the figure. See Neidhardt and Schölzel, "Restoration [. . .]: Final Report," 920.

12 E[ddy] de Jongh, *Zinne- en minnebeelden in de schilderkunst van de zeventiende eeuw* ([n.p.] 1967), 49–50; *Johannes Vermeer*, ed. Wheelock, 198. My account of this history is indebted to Ivan Gaskell, *Vermeer's Wager: Speculations on Art History, Theory and Art Museums* (Reaktion, 2000), 45–46.

13 H. Perry Chapman, "Inside Vermeer's Women," in Marjorie E. Wieseman, with H. Perry Chapman and Wayne E. Franits, *Vermeer's Women: Secrets and Silence* (The Fitzwilliam Museum [Cambridge] in association with Yale University Press, 2011), 105.

14 Eddy de Jongh, "On Balance," in *Vermeer Studies*, ed. Ivan Gaskell and Michiel Jonkers (National Gallery of Art [Washington, DC], 1998), 352–55, 357.

15 P. T. A. Swillens, *Johannes Vermeer, Painter of Delft, 1632–1675*, trans. C. M. Breuning-Williamson (Uitgeverij Het Spectrum, 1950), 104–5, and Gowing, *Vermeer*, 50–51.

16 Neidhart and Schölzel, "Restoration [. . .]: Final Report," 922. For further discussion of Vermeer's Cupids and their possible sources, see Gregor J. M. Weber, "Cupid in Vermeer's Paintings," in *Johannes Vermeer: On Reflection*, ed. Stephan Koja, Uta Neidhardt, and Arthur K. Wheelock Jr., trans. Ian Pepper and Carola Kleinstück-Schulman (Staatliche Kunstsammlungen [Dresden], 2021).

17 For a helpful summary, see the entry for the painting in the interactive catalogue at https://www.essentialvermeer.com.

18 See https://www.frick.org/sites/default/files/archivedsite/exhibitions/vermeer/frick.htm.

19 E. V. Lucas, *Vermeer of Delft*, 2nd edn (Methuen, 1922), 32–33.

20 A copy of a work by the Italian artist Felice Ficherelli (1605–1660), the *Saint Praxedis* was first attributed to Vermeer by Michael Kitson in 1969 and subsequently accepted as genuine by the curator of Northern European art at the National Gallery of Art in Washington, DC, Arthur K. Wheelock Jr.—a verdict more recently affirmed by the organizers of the 2023 exhibition at the Rijksmuseum in Amsterdam. For a helpful summary of the controversy initially aroused by the painting, see Jon Boone, "*Saint Praxedis*: Missing the Mark" (2002), https://www.essentialvermeer.com/saint_praxedis.html.

21 Swillens, *Johannes Vermeer*, 165.

22 Arthur K. Wheelock Jr. and Marguerite Glass, "The Appreciation of Vermeer in Twentieth-Century America," in *The Cambridge Companion to Vermeer*, ed. Wayne E. Franits (Cambridge University Press, 2001), 171.

23 For the epigraph to this chapter, see Alfred Blankert, "Vermeer's Modern Themes and Their Tradition," in *Johannes Vermeer*, ed. Arthur K. Wheelock Jr. (National Gallery of Art [Washington, DC], 1995), 42. Though Blankert was more immediately concerned with distinguishing the religious sensibility of the seventeenth century from the rationalism of the one that followed, his words clearly resonate with the impulse to historicize more generally.

24 My count of dated paintings includes the *Saint Praxedis*, but not *The Art of Painting*, where scholars have not been able to decipher the last digits of a Roman numeral first revealed by infrared reflectography in 2009. See Karl Shütz, *Vermeer: The Complete Works* (Taschen, 2017), 234.

25 https://www.essentialvermeer.com/catalogue/diana_and_her_companions.html#top. See the entry under "Special Topics": "A Forged Signature."

26 John Michael Montias, *Vermeer and His Milieu: A Web of Social History* (Princeton University Press, 1989), 57, 105–7, 103–4, 62. See also Wayne E. Franits, "Johannes Vermeer: An Overview of His Life and Stylistic Development," in *The Cambridge Companion to Vermeer*, ed. Wayne E. Franits (Cambridge University Press, 2001), 8–12.

27 Liedtke, "Vermeer Teaching Himself," 32–33. In arguing that the *Christ* is a more accomplished painting than the *Diana* and should thus be dated later, Liedtke provocatively contends that others have been blinded by their investment in a "historical logic" that has "Vermeer proceeding from foreign to domestic, from painterly to precise, from rhetorical to evocative" (33)—a logic, in short, that has the artist becoming more "Vermeer-like" with every picture (32).

28 Wheelock, *Vermeer and the Art*, 71; Nevitt, "Vermeer on the Question of Love," 102.

29 Walter Liedtke, *Vermeer: The Complete Paintings*, repr. edn (Ludion, 2011 [2008]), 76–78, quotation at 76.

30 Chapman, "Inside Vermeer's Women," 121n30; Blaise Ducos, "Maids and Morals," in *Vermeer and the Masters of Genre Painting: Inspiration and Rivalry*, ed. Adriaan E. Waiboer (Yale University Press, 2017), 207.

31 Irene Netta, "The Phenomenon of Time in the Art of Vermeer," in *Vermeer Studies*, ed. Ivan Gaskell and Michiel Jonkers (National Gallery of Art [Washington, DC] 1998), 258.

32 Wheelock, *Vermeer and the Art*, 111; Wayne Franits, *Vermeer* (Phaidon, 2015), 138.

33 For helpful discussions of this history, see especially Daniel Arasse, *Vermeer: Faith in Painting*, trans. Terry Grabar (Princeton University Press, 1994), 26–29; Valerie Hedquist, "Religion in the Art and Life of Vermeer," in *The Cambridge Companion to Vermeer*, ed. Wayne E. Franits (Cambridge University Press, 2001), 122–25; and Franits, *Vermeer*, 152–63.

34 Wheelock, *Vermeer and the Art*, 100; De Jongh, "On Balance," 360–62; Ivan Gaskell, "Vermeer, Judgment and Truth," *The Burlington Magazine*, vol. 126, no. 978 (September 1984); Albert Blankert, "La femme à la balance," in Gilles Aillaud, Albert Blankert, and John Michael Montias, *Vermeer*, new edn (Hazan, 1986), [illegible]

35 Nanette Salomon, "Vermeer and the Balance of Destiny," in *Essays in Northern European Art Presented to Egbert Haverkamp-Begemann on His Sixtieth Birthday*, ed. Anne-Marie Logan (Davaco, 1983). The debate as to whether the woman in the picture is pregnant—a debate that has involved the *Woman in Blue Reading a Letter* as well—also involves a form of counter-history, since those who question it usually argue that such depictions were very rare in the period, apart from images of the Virgin Mary, and that modern eyes are being deceived by the look of seventeenth-century fashion. Though one dress historian has argued that "dress alone provides no substantial evidence either for or against the hypothesis that the women in his paintings are pregnant" (Marieke de Winkel, "The Interpretation of Dress in Vermeer's Paintings," in *Vermeer Studies*, ed. Ivan Gaskell and Michiel Jonkers [National Gallery of Art (Washington, DC), 1998], 332), most recent commentators seem to have decided that Vermeer intended these two women to look different from those in his other paintings and that pregnancy is the most obvious explanation. Exceptions include Blankert, "Vermeer's Modern Themes," 39, and Nevitt, "Vermeer on the Question of Love," 104, 205–6n92.

36 W. Bürger [Théophile Thoré], "Van der Meer de Delft," *Gazette des beaux-arts*, vol. 21 (1866), 460. For a recent interpretation that endorses Thoré's approach to the painting, see Gregor J. M. Weber, *Johannes Vermeer: Faith, Light and Reflection* (Rijksmuseum [Amsterdam], 2022), 121–25.

37 Swillens, *Johannes Vermeer*, 14.

38 Wadum, "Vermeer in Perspective," 78.

39 Arasse, *Vermeer*, 28.

40 Gowing, *Vermeer*, 52, 126n84.

41 Montias, *Vermeer and His Milieu*, 195; Lisa Vergara, "Perspectives on Women in the Art of Vermeer," in *The Cambridge Companion to Vermeer*, ed. Wayne E. Franits (Cambridge University Press, 2001), 66–67.

42 Daniel Arasse, "Vermeer's Private Allegories," in *Vermeer Studies*, ed. Ivan Gaskell and Michiel Jonkers (National Gallery of Art [Washington, DC] 1998).

43 For objects (including paintings) that appeared in the household inventory after Vermeer's death, see Montias, *Vermeer and His Milieu*, 188–95, 339–44.

44 Franits, *Vermeer*, 233–34. The book in question is the second edition of Adriaan Metius's *Institutiones astronomicae geographicae* (1621).

45 Those who question the moralized reading of the *Procuress* in the *Young Woman Seated at a Virginal*—or at least opt for ambiguity—include Arthur K. Wheelock Jr., *Jan Vermeer* (Harry N. Abrams: 1981), 152; Harry Berger Jr., *Second World and Green World: Studies in Renaissance Fiction-Making* (University of California Press, 1990), 491; and Blankert, "Vermeer's Modern Themes," 38.

46 Wheelock, however, is an exception to this interpretive rule. Characterizing the landscape in *The Concert* as "rugged," rather than pastoral or arcadian—and particularly remarking its dead tree—he suggests that it, too, serves as a thematic contrast to the activity of Vermeer's figures (Wheelock, *Vermeer and the Art*, 117).

47 The other inset landscapes appear in the *Young Woman Standing at a Virginal*, *The Guitar Player*, *The Glass of Wine*, and *The Love Letter*, which also includes a seascape that is thought to evoke a familiar comparison of the lover to a ship traversing the sea of love—a comparison that proves to have been the basis of an emblem roughly contemporaneous with the painting. See Elise Goodman, "The Landscape on the Wall in Vermeer," in *The Cambridge Companion to Vermeer*, ed. Wayne E. Franits (Cambridge University Press, 2001); and Nevitt, "Vermeer on the Question of Love," 92–94. On the seascape, see also Wheelock, *Jan Vermeer*, 43, and Arasse, *Vermeer*, 23.

48 Wheelock, *Vermeer and the Art*, 161–62; Lisa Vergara, "*Antiek* and *Modern* in Vermeer's *Lady Writing a Letter with Her Maid*," in *Vermeer Studies*, ed. Ivan Gaskell and Michiel Jonker (National Gallery of Art [Washington, DC], 1998), 238–40.

49 Nevitt, "Vermeer on the Question of Love," 106.

50 Arasse, *Vermeer*, 31. For related statements, see, e.g., Wheelock, *Jan Vermeer*, 152; Netta, "Phenomenon of Time," 258; Zirka Z. Filipczak, "Vermeer, Elusiveness, and Visual Theory," *Simiolus* 32.4 (2006), 271; and Franits, *Vermeer*, 172.

51 Arasse, *Vermeer*, 31; Berger, *Second World*, 506.

52 Philip L[eslie] Hale, *Jan Vermeer of Delft* (Small, Maynard and Co., 1913), 305–6.

53 [illegible]

54 See, e.g., Montias, *Vermeer and His Milieu*, 202; Hedquist, "Religion," 130; Liedtke, *Vermeer*, 165.

55 Ludwig Goldscheider, *Johannes Vermeer: The Paintings, Complete Edition*, 2nd edn (Phaidon, 1967 [1958]), 27.

56 A[ry] B[ob] de Vries, *Jan Vermeer de Delft, suivi de La poétique de Vermeer par René Huyghe*, Fr. trans. Louise Servicen (P. Tisné, 1948), 46.

57 Albert Blankert, with Rob Ruurs and Willem L. van de Watering, *Vermeer of Delft: Complete Edition of the Paintings* (Phaidon, 1978), 59. The first Dutch edition of this work appeared in 1975.

58 Wheelock, *Jan Vermeer*, 148. Others have sought to rescue the painting—and Vermeer's consistent artistry—by ascribing its very incongruities to deliberate parody. Among the proponents of this view are Harry Berger and Edward A. Snow, both originally writing in the 1970s, and Benjamin Binstock, whose idiosyncratic study of the artist, *Vermeer's Family Secrets*, appeared in 2009. Snow thinks the picture best understood as an ironic counterpoint to *The Art of Painting*, while both Berger and Binstock also read it as a subversive commentary on the impulse to commission such a picture in the first place, an impulse Binstock attributes, without any evidence, to Vermeer's Catholic mother-in-law. For all three critics, the ostensible spiritual aim of the painting is deliberately undermined by the intense materiality of its visible world and by the awkwardness of the woman's pose in particular, which appears to call into question the very permanence of the faith she purportedly incarnates. See Edward A. Snow, *A Study of Vermeer* (University of California Press, 1979), 110–12; Berger, *Second World*, 442–50; and Benjamin Binstock, *Vermeer's Family Secrets: Genius, Discovery, and the Unknown Apprentice* (Routledge, 2009), 215–31.

59 Hale, *Jan Vermeer of Delft*, 305–6.

60 A. J. Barnouw, "Vermeers zoogenaamd 'Novum Testamentum,'" *Oud Holland* 32.1 (1914): 49–54.

61 E[ddy] de Jongh, "Pearls of Virtue and Pearls of Vice," *Simiolus* 8.2 (1975–76): 69–97.

62 In addition to De Jongh, "Pearls," see, e.g., Hedquist, "Religion," 125–30; Liedtke, *Vermeer*, 163–65; Franits, *Vermeer*, 257–69; Aneta Georgievska-Shine, "Vermeer, the Art of Meditation, and the Allegory of Faith," in *Personification: Embodying Meaning and Emotion*, ed. Walter S. Melion and Bart Ramakers (Brill, 2016); and Weber, *Johannes Vermeer*, 81–90, 137–43.

63 See, e.g., Jean Lipman and Richard Marshall, *Art About Art* (Dutton, 1978), 80, where *The Art of Painting* is said to be second only to the *Mona Lisa* as a subject to be reworked by modern artists.
64 Montias, *Vermeer and His Milieu*, 339.
65 Bürger, "Van der Meer de Delft," 324.
66 Bürger, "Van der Meer de Delft," 326. On Clio and history painting, see, e.g., Blankert, *Vermeer of Delft*, 48; and Wheelock, *Jan Vermeer*, 128. The argument for the association with honor and fame was advanced most influentially by Eric Jan Sluijter, "Vermeer, Fame, and Female Beauty: The *Art of Painting*," in *Vermeer Studies*, ed. Ivan Gaskell and Michiel Jonker (National Gallery of Art [Washington, DC], 1998), and now seems to be widely accepted. For some representative treatments, see, e.g., Vergara, "Perspectives on Women," 59–60; Liedtke, *Vermeer*, 146; and Franits, *Vermeer*, 213–15.
67 For Pictura as well as Clio, see, e.g., Chapman, "Inside Vermeer's Women," 119. For Pictura alone, see Binstock, *Vermeer's Family Secrets*, 171–83, esp. 172.
68 Swillens, *Johannes Vermeer*, 101.
69 For a variety of takes on the painter's costume, see, e.g., Snow, *Study of Vermeer*, 113, 171n35; Wheelock, *Vermeer and the Art*, 131; Sluijter, "Vermeer, Fame," 269; De Winkel, "Interpretation of Dress," 334; Emilie E. S. Gordenker, "Is the History of Dress Marginal? Some Thoughts on Costume in Seventeenth-Century Painting," *Fashion Theory* 3.2 (1999), 229–35; Vergara, "Perspectives on Women," 59; and Chapman, "Inside Vermeer's Women," 117.
70 Franits, *Vermeer*, 220–22.
71 For different views on this issue, see, e.g., Wadum, "Vermeer in Perspective," 67, and Arasse, *Vermeer*, 52–53.
72 Wheelock, *Vermeer and the Art*, 132–34, provides a useful summary of these interpretations. Cf. also Sluijter, who argues that the map serves to associate Vermeer's art with the glory of the nation as a whole and that its age appropriately corresponds to "the Netherlands as it was still embedded in the minds of his contemporaries" ("Vermeer, Fame," 271).
73 Montias, *Vermeer and His Milieu*, 189, Franits, *Vermeer*, 216–17.
74 Arasse, "Vermeer's Private Allegories."
75 Arasse, *Vermeer*, 46, 51, 50. For a related argument, to which Arasse is partly indebted, see Svetlana Alpers, *The Art of Describing: Dutch Art in the Seventeenth Century* (University of Chicago Press, 1983), 119–22.
76 Arasse, *Vermeer*, 33–39.
77 Wheelock, *Vermeer and the Art*, 95; Snow, *Study of Vermeer*, 93.
78 Arasse, *Vermeer*, 35–36.
79 Arasse, *Vermeer*, 84–86.
80 Snow, *Study of Vermeer*, 133–34.
81 Vergara, "Perspectives on Women," 62.
82 Chapman, "Inside Vermeer's Women," 92.
83 Berger, *Second World*, 472, 473, 475.
84 Svetlana Alpers, *The Vexations of Art: Velázquez and Others* (Yale University Press, 2005), 20.
85 Gaskell, *Vermeer's Wager*, 68, 83, 80.
86 Gaskell, *Vermeer's Wager*, 13. For a related account of the "subtle tension between the descriptive and the purely formal qualities" of Vermeer's art, see Aneta Georgievska-Shine, *Vermeer and the Art of Love* (Lund Humphries, 2022), 77.
87 Swillens, *Johannes Vermeer*, 14.

4. CAMERA TRACINGS

1 Edmond and Jules de Goncourt, *Journal: Mémoires de la vie littéraire*, ed. Robert Ricatte, 22 vols. (Éditions de l'Imprimerie nationale de Monaco, 1956–68), 4:236.
2 A. Hyatt Mayor, "The Photographic Eye," *The Metropolitan Museum of Art Bulletin*, n.s. vol. 5 (1946), 20; Daniel A. Fink, "Vermeer's Use of the Camera Obscura: A Comparative Study," *The Art Bulletin* 53.4 (1971), 505. Cf. also Lawrence Gowing, *Vermeer*, 3rd edn (University of California Press, 1998 [1952]), 65: "No doubt the optical understanding spread by photography contributed to deciding the moment of Vermeer's rediscovery."

3 J[oseph] Pennell, "Photography as a Hindrance and a Help to Art," *British Journal of Photography*, vol. 38, no. 1618 (8 May 1891), 295, 294.

4 [Mary Augusta Ward], "The New National Gallery at Amsterdam," *Macmillan's Magazine*, vol. 52 (1885), 390. On Niépce and heliography, see Helmut Gernsheim, "The 150th Anniversary of Photography," *History of Photography* 1.1 (1977): 3–8.

5 Jean-Louis Vaudoyer, "Le mystérieux Vermeer II," *L'opinion*, 7 May 1921, 515.

6 Paul Claudel, *Oeuvres complètes*, ed. Pierre Claudel and Jacques Petit, 29 vols. (Gallimard, 1960), 17:23–24. Claudel's analogy originally dates from a lecture of 1934 that was published by *La revue de Paris* the following year. It was subsequently reprinted as part of a collection entitled *L'oeil écoute* (the eye listens) in 1946. I am grateful to Heinrich Schwartz, "Vermeer and the Camera Obscura," *Pantheon* 24 (1966), for directing me to this passage (170–72).

7 Gustave Vanzype, *Vermeer de Delft* (G. van Oest, 1908), 65.

8 Peter Greenaway, interview with Sabine Danek and Torsten Beyer (1994), "Beyond Cinema," in *Peter Greenaway: Interviews*, ed. Vernon Gras and Marguerite Gras (University Press of Mississippi, 2000), 169.

9 Pennell, "Photography," 295.

10 Schwartz, "Vermeer and the Camera Obscura," 170; Philip Steadman, *Vermeer's Camera: Uncovering the Truth Behind the Masterpieces* (Oxford University Press, 2001), 24. According to Schwartz, Johannes Kepler had described a type of camera lucida as early as 1611, but the device "fell into almost complete oblivion" until an improved version was patented and publicized by William Hyde Wollaston and Giovanni Battisti Amici at the beginning of the nineteenth century (170, 178nn3–4).

11 For Aristotle in particular, see Jonathan Crary, *Techniques of the Observer: On Vision and Modernity in the Nineteenth Century*, repr. edn (MIT Press, 1999 [1990]), 27; and Steadman, *Vermeer's Camera*, 4. For the dissemination of knowledge about the camera obscura from the sixteenth century onwards, see, e.g., Schwartz, "Vermeer and the Camera Obscura," 176–78; Aaron Scharf, *Art and Photography*, repr. edn (Penguin, 1986 [1968]), 19–23; Arthur K. Wheelock Jr., *Perspective, Optics, and Delft Artists Around 1650* (Garland, [illegible]), [illegible]; and Steadman, *Vermeer's Camera*, 8–24. A useful summary of this material also appears under [Jonathan Janson], "Vermeer and the *Camera Obscura*," at https://www.essentialvermeer.com.

12 I quote from Huygens's letter as translated in Steadman, *Vermeer's Camera*, 18. One scholar has even speculated recently that Huygens might have introduced the camera to Vermeer, who responded to the challenge by demonstrating that painting was hardly "dead by comparison." See Robert Fucci, "Curtains and Perspectives: Vermeer's Optical Realism," in *Johannes Vermeer: On Reflection*, ed. Stephan Koja, Uta Neidhardt, and Arthur K. Wheelock Jr., trans. Ian Pepper and Carola Kleinstück-Schulman (Staatliche Kunstsammlungen [Dresden], 2021), 119.

13 Arthur K. Wheelock Jr., "Exploring the Physical and Spiritual World," in David de Haan, Arthur K. Wheelock Jr., Babs van Eijk, and Ingrid van der Vlis, *Vermeer's Delft*, trans. Mark Baker and Marian van den End (Museum Prinsenhof/Waanders Publishers, 2023); and Gregor J. M. Weber, *Johannes Vermeer: Faith, Light and Reflection* (Rijksmuseum [Amsterdam], 2022), esp. 81–113.

14 [Janson], "Vermeer and the *Camera Obscura*."

15 As quoted (from the English translation of J. Waterhouse) in Steadman, *Vermeer's Camera*, 8. On Barbaro, see also Wheelock, *Perspective, Optics*, 137–47; Schwartz, "Vermeer and the Camera Obscura," 176; and [Janson], "Vermeer and the *Camera Obscura*."

16 Jean-Luc Delsaute, "The Camera Obscura and Painting in the Sixteenth and Seventeenth Centuries," in *Vermeer Studies*, ed. Ivan Gaskell and Michiel Jonker (National Gallery of Art [Washington, DC], 1998), 113; Steadman, *Vermeer's Camera*, 17–19; Walter Liedtke, *Vermeer: The Complete Paintings*, repr. edn (Ludion, 2011 [2008]), 181–82.

17 Steadman, *Vermeer's Camera*, 19–23.

18 Wayne Franits, *Vermeer* (Phaidon, 2015), 71. For the inventory itself, see John Michael Montias, *Vermeer and His Milieu: A Web of Social History* (Princeton University Press, 1989), 339–44.

19 Gowing, *Vermeer*, 19, 20–21, 137–38. Cf. Mayor, "Photographic Eye," 19–20. Though this brief treatment of Vermeer and the camera obscura preceded Gowing by several years, it is not clear whether the latter was building on Mayor's work. A single citation characterizes the article as having reached conclusions similar to his own (*Vermeer*, 70n9).

20 Gowing, *Vermeer*, 22–23, 46.

21 Charles Seymour Jr., "Dark Chamber and Light-Filled Room: Vermeer and the Camera Obscura," *The Art Bulletin* 46.3 (1964), 327, 330.

22 Fink, "Vermeer's Use," 493–94.

23 See, e.g., Wheelock, *Perspective, Optics*, 286–87; and Liedtke, *Vermeer*, 179–80.

24 Wheelock, *Perspective, Optics*, 291–95.

25 Gowing, *Vermeer*, 111.

26 Allan A. Mills, "Vermeer and the Camera Obscura: Some Practical Considerations," *Leonardo* 31.3 (1998): 213–18.

27 David Hockney, *Secret Knowledge: Rediscovering the Lost Techniques of the Old Masters* (Penguin, 2001), 58. Hockney reproduces his correspondence with Steadman, among others, in the last section of the book (226–86).

28 P.T.A. Swillens, *Johannes Vermeer: Painter of Delft, 1632–1675*, trans. C. M. Breuning-Williamson (Uitgeverij Het Spectrum, 1950), 77.

29 Steadman, *Vermeer's Camera*, 133–34.

30 Steadman, *Vermeer's Camera*, 134.

31 Franits, *Vermeer*, 70.

32 Jørgen Wadum, "Contours of Vermeer," in *Vermeer Studies*, ed. Ivan Gaskell and Michiel Jonkers (National Gallery of Art [Washington, DC], 1998), 204.

33 Steadman, *Vermeer's Camera*, 111, 113, 103; Liedtke, *Vermeer*, 188; Steadman, *Vermeer's Camera*, 145. Steadman provides more updated responses to his critics, as well as afterthoughts on his own argument, at https://www.vermeerscamera.co.uk.

34 *Tim's Vermeer*, featuring Tim Jenison, directed by Teller, produced by Penn Jillette, Farley Ziegler, and High Delft Pictures (Sony Pictures Classics, 2014 [2013]), DVD.

35 For these and other criticisms of Jelley in particular, see David G. Stork's review of *Traces of Vermeer*, *Leonardo*, January 2018, https://leonardo.info/review/2018/01/review-of-traces-of-vermeer-by-jane-jelley.

36 Jenison's allusion to a "human made photograph" comes from the filmmakers' Q & A at the Toronto International Film Festival, 7 September 2013, included on the Sony DVD. For an acerbic account of Jenison's "pedantic and laborious imitation," see Jonathan Jones, "Tim's Vermeer," *The Guardian*, 28 January 2014, https://www.theguardian.com/artanddesign/jonathanjonesblog/2014/jan/28/tims-vermeer-fails.

37 On the denigration of Dutch painters as mere copyists, see Ruth Bernard Yeazell, *Art of the Everyday: Dutch Painting and the Realist Novel* (Princeton University Press, 2008), 34–39.

38 Hockney, *Secret Knowledge*, 14; cf. 131. Versions of the observation recur in the correspondence section of the book as well.

39 Jane Jelley, *Traces of Vermeer* (Oxford University Press, 2017), 11.

40 Shin-Ichi Fukuoka, *Vermeer: Realm of Light; Travels Through Art and Science in Pursuit of the Greatest Artist of the Golden Age* (Kirakusha, 2015), 204, 216.

41 See, e.g., Schwartz, "Vermeer and the Camera Obscura," 173–74; Wheelock, *Perspective, Optics*, 284–85; Steadman, *Vermeer's Camera*, 44–53; and esp. Laura J. Snyder, *Eye of the Beholder: Johannes Vermeer, Antoni van Leeuwenhoek, and the Reinvention of Seeing* (W. W. Norton, 2015).

42 Fukuoka, *Vermeer*, 15–17. This speculation apparently goes back at least as far as E. V. Lucas, *Vermeer of Delft*, 2nd edn (Methuen, 1922), 8, 19–20. See also Wheelock, *Jan Vermeer*, 136–38; Steadman, *Vermeer's Camera*, 49–53; Snyder, *Eye of the Beholder*, 160–64. Klaas van Berkel, however, dismisses the identification of the astronomer with Van Leeuwenhoek as "totally unfounded": "Vermeer and the Representation of Science," in *The Cambridge Companion to Vermeer*, ed. Wayne E. Franits (Cambridge University Press, 2001), 134.

43 Montias, *Vermeer and His Milieu*, 225–30.

44 *Johannes Vermeer*, ed. Arthur K. Wheelock Jr. (National Gallery of Art [Washington, DC], 1995), 122, 176–78.

45 Zirka Z. Filipczak, "Vermeer, Elusiveness, and Visual Theory," *Simiolus* 32.4 (2006), 264, 266–67, 268.

46 Ivan Gaskell, *Vermeer's Wager: Speculations on Art History, Theory and Art Museums* (Reaktion, 2000), 160–61.

47 W. Bürger [Théophile Thoré], "Van der Meer de Delft," *Gazette des beaux-arts*, vol. 21 (1866), 462.

5. IMITATION AND ASSIMILATION

1 Gerhard Richter, MoMA interview with Robert Storr (2002), in *Gerhard Richter: Writings, 1961–2007*, ed. Dietmar Elger and Hans Ulrich Obrist (D.A.P., 2009), 417.

2 As quoted by Armin Zweite, *Gerhard Richter: Life and Work; In Painting, Thinking Is Painting* (Prestel, 2020), 444.

3 There also exists a smaller version of Richter's *Reader*, painted that same year from a different photograph, in which the subject's head and neck are viewed from the back. See Dietmar Elger, *Gerhard Richter—Catalogue Raisonné*, 5 vols. (Hatje Cantz, 2011–15), 4:564–65.

4 Gerhard Richter, "I Have Nothing to Say and I'm Saying It": conversation between Gerhard Richter and Nicholas Serota, Spring 2011, in *Gerhard Richter: Panorama*, ed. Mark Godfrey and Nicholas Serota, expanded edn (D.A.P, 2016 [2011]), 17.

5 In 1995 Peter Gidal also reported that Richter had a postcard of what he referred to as Vermeer's "Woman Reading a Letter" tacked up in a corner of the anteroom to his studio, though it is not altogether clear whether this was the Dresden picture or the *Woman in Blue Reading a Letter* at the Rijkmuseum (Peter Gidal, "The Polemics of Paint," *Gerhard Richter: Painting in the Nineties* [Anthony d'Offray Gallery [London], 1995], 26n18). The fact that Richter's reader holds a page of the German newspaper *Der Spiegel* (the mirror) rather than a letter makes it almost tempting to suggest an allusion to Vermeer's mirror paintings as well.

6 Gerhard Richter, interview with Astrid Kasper (2000), in *Gerhard Richter: Writings*, 369, 367–68.

7 Gombrich's immediate focus is the debt that Renaissance artists owed to antiquity. He draws the metaphor of family likeness from a passage in which Petrarch argues that writers who model themselves on other writers should not strive for the kind of resemblance that ideally obtains between a portrait and a sitter, where the aim is identity with the original, but rather for that which obtains between a son and a father. See E. H. Gombrich, "The Style *all'antica*: Imitation and Assimilation," in Gombrich, *Norm and Form: Studies in the Art of the Renaissance* (Phaidon, 1966).

8 Richter, interview with Astrid Kasper, 367–68.

9 As quoted by Frances Weitzenhoffer, *The Havemeyers: Impressionism Comes to America* (Abrams, 1986), 230.

10 Philip L[eslie] Hale, *Jan Vermeer of Delft* (Small, Maynard and Co., 1913), 18–19, 322; Jean-Louis Vaudoyer, "Le mystérieux Vermeer II," *L'opinion*, 7 May 1921, 515; A. Hyatt Mayor, "The Photographic Eye," *The Metropolitan Museum of Art Bulletin*, n.s. vol. 5 (1946), 23; Edward A. Snow, *A Study of Vermeer* (University of California Press, 1979), 25–36; Arthur K. Wheelock Jr., *Jan Vermeer* (Harry N. Abrams: 1981), 140; Anne Hollander, *Moving Pictures* repr. edn (Harvard University Press, 1991 [1986]), 405–6; Michael White, *Travels in Vermeer: A Memoir* (Persea Books, 2015), 133.

11 Hale, *Jan Vermeer of Delft*, 173–78, 139, quotations at 172–73.

12 Frances Suzman Jowell, "Thoré-Bürger's Art Collection: 'A Rather Unusual Gallery of Bric-à-Brac,'" *Simiolus* 30.1/2 (2003), 105.

13 On Whistler's relation to painters treated in this chapter, see Patricia Jobe Pierce, *Edmund C. Tarbell and the Boston School of Painting (1889–1980)*, ed. John Douglas Ingraham (Pierce Galleries [Hingham, MA], 1980), 17; Dean T. Lahikainen, "Redefining Elegance: Benson's Studio Props," in Faith Andrews Bedford, Laurene Buckley, Dean T. Lahikainen, Dan L. Monroe, and Jane M. Winchell, *The Art of Frank W. Benson: American Impressionist* (Peabody Essex Museum [Salem, MA], 1999), 89; Susan A. Hobbs, *The Art of Thomas Wilmer Dewing: Beauty Reconfigured* (The Brooklyn Museum in Association with the Smithsonian Institution Press, 1996), 2, 23, 25–26, 33, 123–24, 132, 177, 199; Poul Vad, *Vilhelm Hammershøi and Danish Art at the Turn of the Century*, trans. Kenneth Tindall (Yale University Press, 1992), 61–62, 162–63, 168–70; and Robert Rosenblum, "Vilhelm Hammershøi at Home and Abroad," in Anne-Birgitte Fonsmark and Mikael Wivel, with Henri Loyrette and Robert Rosenblum, *Vilhelm Hammershøi, 1864–1916: Danish Painter of Solitude and Light* (Ordrupgaard/Guggenheim Museum, 1998), 33.

14 As quoted from the Philip Leslie Hale Papers at the Archives of American Art, in Bernice Kramer Leader, "The Boston School and Vermeer," *Arts Magazine*, vol. 55, no. 3 (November 1980), 174.

15 "Vermeer of Delft," in *Masters in Art: A Series of Illustrated Monographs* (Bates and Guild, 1904), 211–52. The series was issued anonymously; on Hale's responsibility for the entry, see Leader, "Boston School," 174.

16 Royal Cortissoz, "The Galleries: The Exhibition at Philadelphia," *The Scrip*, no. 1 (1906), 192. Hailing it as "The Best Picture in America," a full-page spread in the *Boston Sunday Herald* that December reproduced *Girl Crocheting* next to Vermeer's *Girl Reading a Letter at an Open Window* with the caption "Van Der Meer Interior Suggesting Style of Mr. Tarbell's Picture" (John Fagg, "Near Vermeer: Edmund C. Tarbell's and John Sloan's Dutch Pictures," *Modernist Cultures* 11.1 [2016], https://doi.org/10.3366/mod.2016.0127).

17 According to Poul Vad, Hammershøi saw his first Vermeer on a trip to Berlin in 1885 and followed that up with travels in the Netherlands and Belgium two years later (Vad, *Vilhelm Hammershøi*, 59).

18 A. G. Temple, *Catalogue of the Exhibition of Works by Danish Painters* (Art Gallery of the Corporation of London, 1907), 14; Arthur Clutton-Brock, "Danish Pictures at the Guildhall: A New Master," *Tribune*, 9 April 1907; as excerpted in Vad, *Vilhelm Hammershøi*, 407–8.

19 John Singer Sargent to Vernon Lee, undated [1884], Colby College, as quoted in Marc Simpson, with Richard Ormond and H. Barbara Weinberg, *Uncanny Spectacle: The Public Career of the Young John Singer Sargent* (Yale University Press, 1997), 58.

20 Walter Liedtke, "Dutch Paintings in America: The Collectors and their Ideals," in Ben Broos, Edwin Buijsen, Geerte Broersma et al., *Great Dutch Paintings from America* (Mauritshuis/Waanders Publishers, 1990), 38; Trevor J. Fairbrother, with Theodore E. Stebbins Jr., William L. Vance, and Erica E. Hirshler, *The Bostonians: Painters of an Elegant Age, 1870–1930* (Museum of Fine Arts [Boston, MA], 1986), 76.

21 Vad, *Vilhelm Hammershøi*, 68. See also Marguerite Anne Glass, "Vermeer in Dialogue: From Appropriation to Response" (PhD dissertation, University of Maryland, 2003), which first alerted me to Hammershøi's interest in Vermeer and to this painting in particular (125).

22 Vad, *Vilhelm Hammershøi*, 381. For Hammershøi's trip to Paris, see the chronology appended to Felix Krämer, Naoki Sato, and Anne-Birgitte Fonsmark, *Hammershøi* (Royal Academy of Arts [London], 2008), 162.

23 Both Hammershøi's picture of Anna sewing and its possible connection to *The Lacemaker* may also bring to mind the numerous small paintings that the French *intimiste* Édouard Vuillard (1868–1940) would soon be making of his seamstress mother, especially since in Vuillard's case we have evidence that he himself sensed the affinity to Vermeer. Among the tiny sketches crammed onto a page of his journal for November 1888 are three scenes of women bent over their needlework, presumably inspired by the corset-making business Madame Vuillard ran from their shared apartment, together with a roughly executed copy of *The Lacemaker*. See Francesca Berry and Mathias Chivot, *Maman: Vuillard and Madame Vuillard* (Barber Institute of Fine Arts [Birmingham], 2018), 16, 24n14; and Julia Frey, *Venus Betrayed: The Private World of Édouard Vuillard* (Reaktion, 2019), 355–56. Frey identifies *The Lacemaker* as "the compositional model" for two paintings the artist made of his mother in the 1890s: *Madame Vuillard Sewing* (1893), and *Woman Working by Lamplight* (1895). She also detects the influence of the Delft master in the slightly later *Madame Vuillard Holding a Bowl* (1898), as do Antoine Salomon and Guy Cogeval (with the collaboration of Mathias Chivot) in their catalogue raisonné, *Vuillard: The Inexhaustible Glance; Critical Catalogue of Paintings and Pastels*, 3 vols. (The Wildenstein Institute, 2003), 2:546.

24 Which Vermeers these turn-of-the-century painters knew at first-hand and which only in reproduction is not always easy to determine, and presumably also varied from artist to artist. But even before *The Concert* arrived in Boston, all of the Bostonians except Joseph DeCamp (who went to Munich) studied in Paris, where they could at least have seen *The Lacemaker*, and all would later have been aware of the 1909 Hudson-Fulton Exhibition at the Metropolitan Museum in New York, whose display of Dutch paintings included six Vermeers, five still accepted as genuine—*Young Woman with a Lute*, *A Lady Writing*, *Young Woman with a Water Pitcher*, *A Maid Asleep*, *Girl Interrupted at Her Music*—and one, *Lady with a Guitar*, now generally regarded as a copy. William Paxton may also have encountered Vermeer on an earlier visit to The Hague. See Jessica Todd Smith, "Is Polite Society Polite?: The Genteel Tradition in the Figure Paintings of William McGregor Paxton," 2 vols. (PhD dissertation, Yale University, 2001), 1:106n2.

25 In an exhibition catalogue that focuses on the art of the entire family—and not just the elaborate recreations of the ancient world painted by Laura's more famous husband, Lawrence Alma-Tadema (1836–1912)—Elizabeth Prettejohn specifically calls attention to how "the light catches a woman's pearl earring" in *Love's Beginning* and observes that Laura "was among the first artists to draw inspiration from Johannes Vermeer" (*Lawrence Alma-Tadema: At Home in Antiquity,* ed. Prettejohn and Peter Trippi [Prestel: 2016], 134). An even earlier Vermeer-inflected painting by Laura with a narrative title, *A Knock at the Door* (1897), now belongs to the Currier Museum in New Hampshire. I am grateful to Elizabeth Prettejohn for first introducing me to this body of work.

26 As I've argued elsewhere, titles aren't necessarily a reliable guide to artists' intentions, and it's always possible that some of those listed above were actually the work of middlemen such as dealers, curators, or collectors, rather than the painters themselves. In that case, of course, they would testify more to the pictures' reception than to their creation. At the very least, however, the evidence strongly suggests that most of the painters who worked in this vein had no interest in exploiting the potential of an anecdotal or interpretive title. For a fuller treatment of such issues, see Ruth Bernard Yeazell, *Picture Titles: How and Why Western Paintings Acquired Their Names* (Princeton University Press, 2015).

27 See Ellen Wardwell Lee, R. H. Ives Gammell, and Martin F. Krause, *William McGregor Paxton, 1869–1941* (Indianapolis Museum of Art, 1979), 53n1. The report of Paxton's collaboration with Hale on the Vermeer book comes from their former student, the painter R. H. Ives Gammell, who supplies the biographical chapters of the catalogue.

28 Lee, Gammell, and Krause, *William McGregor Paxton*, 28, 34.

29 R[obert] H[ale] Ives Gammell, *The Boston Painters, 1900–1930*, ed. Elizabeth Ives Hunter (Parnassus Imprints, 1986), 54; Hobbs, *Art of Thomas Wilmer Dewing*, 34–35, 177. Hobbs identifies the book in question as Hofstede de Groot's *Jan Vermeer von Delft and* [*sic*] *Karel Fabritius* (Leipzig, 1905), though this does not appear to be a catalogue raisonné, as she calls it, but a collection of photogravures, and the earliest date I have been able to track down for its publication is 1907. She also suggests that the "reproductions" to which Freer's assistant referred may have been another volume of De Groot (48n159, 197n102).

30 J[ames] B. T[ownsend], "'The Ten's' Annual Show," *American Art News*, vol. 12, no. 24 (21 March 1914), 3.

31 "Oral history interview with S. Morton Vose, 1986 July 24–1987 April 28," Archives of American Art, Smithsonian Institution, https://www.aaa.si.edu/collections/interviews/oral-history-interview-smorton-vose-12367. I thank John Fagg, for directing me to this source (Fagg, "Near Vermeer").

32 Kenyon Cox, "The Recent Work of Edmund C. Tarbell," *The Burlington Magazine for Connoisseurs*, vol. 14, no. 70 (January 1909), 259.

33 Kenyon Cox, "Dutch Pictures in the Hudson-Fulton Exhibition—II," *The Burlington Magazine for Connoisseurs*, vol. 16, no. 82 (January 1910), 246.

34 References to their early training in draftsmanship run through the literature on Tarbell and his colleagues. See, e.g., Gammell, *Boston Painters*, 150; Lee, Gammell, and Krause, *William McGregor Paxton*, 31, 48; Hobbs, *Art of Thomas Wilmer Dewing*, 3. Compare Gowing on Vermeer: "His is an almost solitary indifference to the whole linear convention and its historic function of describing, enclosing, embracing the form it limits, a seemingly involuntary rejection of the way in which the intelligence of painters has operated from the earliest times to our own day": Lawrence Gowing, *Vermeer*, 3rd edn (University of California Press, 1997 [1952]), 20.

35 E. V. Lucas, *Vermeer of Delft*, 2nd edn (Methuen, 1922), 17; Marcel Proust, *À la recherche du temps perdu*, ed. Jean-Yves Tadié, 4 vols., Bibliothèque de la Pléiade (Gallimard, 1987–89), 3:692 (Eng., 5:207 [see Preface, n. 9 above]).

36 Gammell, *Boston Painters*, 5.

37 Cox, "Dutch Pictures," 246; Proust, *À la recherche*, 3:879 (5:430).

38 Cox, "Recent Work," 259.

39 Gustave Vanzype, *Vermeer de Delft* (G. van Oest, 1908), 65.

40 Cortissoz, "Galleries," 192; "Typically American Picture Ranks High: *A Girl Crocheting* Declared to Be a Masterpiece," *Sunday Sun*, 28 April 1912; and "Gossip of the Art Galleries" (review of Tarbell exhibition), Copley Society Boston, 1912—the latter two as quoted from press clippings in Leader, "Boston School," 172.

41 For the suggestion that Claus Meyer belongs among painters at least superficially influenced by Vermeer, see Hale, *Jan Vermeer of Delft*, 217; and A[ry] B[ob] de Vries, *Jan Vermeer de Delft, suivi de La poétique de Vermeer par René Huyghe*, Fr. trans. Louise Servicen (P. Tisné, 1948), 61. On MacEwen and Vermeer, see Annette Stott, *Holland Mania: The Unknown Dutch Period in American Art and Culture* (Overlook Press, 1998), 108–10.

42 Smith, "Is Polite Society Polite?," 1:130; Lee, Gammell, and Krause, *William McGregor Paxton*, 125.

43 Lahikainen, "Redefining Elegance," 91. The combination of yellow robe and chandelier appears in Benson's *Light from a Window* (1912); for a reproduction of the painting, which is now in a private collection, see plate 89 in Faith Andrews Bedford, *Frank W. Benson: American Impressionist* (Rizzoli, 1994), 139.

44 Hobbs, *Art of Thomas Wilmer Dewing*, 35. The other objects Hobbs associates with Vermeer are a spinet, a violoncello, a lute, a framed mirror, and a carved table.

45 Cox, "Recent Work," 260. For the identification of *The Music Lesson* as the picture within Tarbell's picture, see Ivan Gaskell, *Vermeer's Wager: Speculations on Art History, Theory and Art Museums* (Reaktion, 2000), 222.

46 James Gibbons Huneker, "Ten American Painters" (1909), as quoted in Fagg, "Near Vermeer."

47 Leader, "Boston School," 172–73. Cf. Lahikainen, "Redefining Elegance," for a related comparison of Benson's *Figure in a Room* to Vermeer's *Woman with a Pearl Necklace* (88).

48 Joseph Edgar Chamberlain, "The Tenth Year of the 'Ten,'" *Evening Mail*, 19 March 1908, 6, as cited in Laurene Buckley, "A 'Gospel of Light': Frank W. Benson and the Boston School Giants," in Bedford et al., *Art of Frank W. Benson*, 66.

49 Bedford, *Frank W. Benson*, 79, 175; Faith Andrews Bedford, "Frank W. Benson: A Biography," in Faith Andrews Bedford, Susan C. Faxon, and Bruce W. Chambers, *Frank W. Benson: A Retrospective* (Berry-Hill Galleries [New York], 1989), 76.

50 Hobbs, *Art of Thomas Wilmer Dewing*, 37, 177, 188; Leader, "Boston School," 173. Though Hobbs at one point distinguishes Dewing from his predecessor, on the grounds that the modern painter uses his stippling technique "to suggest a shimmering and palpitating atmosphere" rather than "to indicate bright reflected light as it bounces off metal objects," she appears to be unaware that Vermeer, too, scattered *pointillé* on nonreflective surfaces (37).

51 As quoted by R. H. Ives Gammell in Lee, Gammell, and Krause, *William McGregor Paxton*, 37.

52 Leader, "The Boston School and Vermeer," 173. According to Gammell, his former teacher soon abandoned the specific practice described in the interview for "more orthodox methods of studying relative degrees of definition" (Lee, Gammell, and Krause, *William McGregor Paxton*, 38).

53 Hale, *Jan Vermeer of Delft*, 220.

54 Faith Andrews Bedford, "Frank W. Benson: Master of Light," in Bedford et al., *Art of Frank W. Benson*, 30.

55 Frederick W. Coburn, "Edmund C. Tarbell," *The International Studio: An Illustrated Magazine of Fine and Applied Art*, vol. 32, no. 127 (1907), lxxxii.

56 Bedford, "Frank W. Benson: Master of Light," 30.

57 Cortissoz, "Galleries," 192.

58 Cox, "Recent Work," 259.

59 Hale, *Jan Vermeer of Delft*, 230.

60 On the Boston Guild, see, e.g., Gammell, *Boston Painters*, 166; Leader, "Boston School," 175; and Fagg, "Near Vermeer."

61 Philip L. Hale, *Vermeer* (completed and prepared for the press by Frederick W. Coburn and Ralph T. Hale) (Hale, Cushman & Flint, 1937), 89–94. I am grateful to John Fagg for calling this revision of Hale's book to my attention (Fagg, "Near Vermeer").

62 Leader, "Boston School," 176.

63 For a brief account of the Boston School women, see Erica E. Hirshler, *A Studio of Her Own: Women Artists in Boston 1870–1940* (MFA Publications, 2001), 97–105. On *Woman in a Fur Hat* and Vermeer, see also https://customprints.mfa.org/detail/476108/rogers-woman-in-a-fur-hat-about-1915.

64 Guy Pène du Bois, "The Boston Group of Painters: An Essay on Nationalism in Art," *Arts and Decoration*, vol. 5, no. 12 (October 1915), 458, 459.

65 See especially Wayne Franits, whose *Vermeer* (Phaidon, 2015) offers an extended account of the artist as "a purveyor of luxury goods" (119–98), while emphasizing "the evolution of his art [. . .] towards highly refined appearances and the presentation of genteel subject matter" (7). Cf. Leader, who associates the "conservative" taste of seventeenth-century Dutch collectors with that of the industrialists, bankers, and professionals who patronized the Bostonians ("Boston School," 175).

66 Du Bois, "Boston Group," 460.

67 Hobbs, *Art of Thomas Wilmer Dewing*, 32; Smith, "Is Polite Society Polite?," 1:139–42.

68 Du Bois, "Boston Group," 459.

69 Du Bois, "Boston Group," 459. As Poul Vad observes of the solitary figure who often appears in the artist's interiors, "Hammershøi apparently regarded this female figure in the way he regarded a chair or a table"—a mode of regard that Vad characterizes not as "degrading," but rather "a kind of impartiality" (*Vilhelm Hammershøi*, 200–201).

70 Gowing, *Vermeer*, 26.

71 Joseph Leo Koerner, *Caspar David Friedrich and the Subject of Landscape*, 2nd edn (Reaktion, 2009 [1990]), 91. For Hammershøi's possible debt to Friedrich, see Rosenblum, "Vilhelm Hammershøi," 36–39. By offering Friedrich's *Woman at a Window* (1822) as his primary example, Rosenblum partly qualifies my generalization about the earlier artist's expansive spaces, but even this precursor of Hammershøi's interiors gestures at the wider world though its open casement (36–37).

72 Vad, *Vilhelm Hammershøi*, 192, 196. There are occasional exceptions to Vad's claim about the veiling of Hammershøi's windows—see, for instance, *Interior with View Towards the Asiatic Company's Buildings, Strandgade 30* (1901), reproduced on page 184 of his book—but the rule holds far more often than not. The one exception in Vermeer's case is *Officer and Laughing Girl*, in which the closed casement offers a slight glimpse of a clouded sky and reddish building. See Gregor J. M. Weber, "Windows Between Outer and Inner Worlds," in *Vermeer*, ed. Pieter Roelofs and Gregor J. M. Weber (Rijksmuseum [Amsterdam]/Hannibal Books, 2023), 163.

73 Felix Krämer, "Vilhelm Hammershøi: The Poetry of Silence," trans. Michael Foster, in Felix Krämer, Naoki Sato, and Anne-Birgitte Fonsmark, *Hammershøi* (Royal Academy of Arts [London], 2008), 20.

74 According to Krämer, the lump of butter in *Interior with Woman at Piano* is the only food that ever appears in a Hammershøi painting (Krämer, Sato, and Fonsmark, *Hammershøi*, 149).

75 Jean-Louis Vaudoyer, "Le mystérieux Vermeer III," *L'opinion*, 14 May 1921, 543.

76 Thorkild Hansen, "The Black and White Colorist," in Hanne Finsen and Inge Vibeke Raaschou-Nielsen, *Vilhelm Hammershøi: Painter of Stillness and Light; A Retrospective Exhibition*, trans. Henrik Rosenmeier (Danish Government Committee Cultural Exchange, 1983), 14. The painter quoted is Joakim Scovgaard (1856–1933).

77 Vilhem Hammershøi, interview with C. C. Clausen (1907), as quoted in Krämer, "Vilhelm Hammershøi," 21.

78 Hansen, "Black and White Colorist," 16.

79 Leonard Borwick, "Preface" to *An Exhibition of Oil Paintings by the Danish Artist Vilhelm Hammershøi* (E. J. van Wisselingh & Co. Gallery, 1907), as cited in Krämer, "Vilhelm Hammershøi," 17.

80 Vilhem Hammershøi, interview with C. C. Clausen, as quoted in Krämer, "Vilhelm Hammershøi," 23.

81 C. C. Clausen, interview with Vilhelm Hammershøi, as reproduced in the Appendix to Vad, *Vilhelm Hammershøi*, 401. (Though Vad reproduces the entire interview, I have chosen to quote whenever possible from the more felicitous translation provided by Michael Foster in Krämer's text.)

82 Vad, *Vilhelm Hammershøi*, 189.

83 Kirk Varnedoe, "Private Light: Hammershøi," *Art in America*, vol. 71, no. 3 (1983), 111.

84 Rosenblum, "Vilhelm Hammershøi," 42, 32.

85 Bridget Alsdorf, "Hammershøi's Either/Or," *Critical Inquiry* 42.2 (2016), 271.

86 Though "abstract painting" is the usual translation of *abstraktes Bild*, the latter word can also mean "picture" or "image." For the argument that "image" would be more faithful to Richter's

practice, see Peter Osborne, "Abstract Images: Sign, Image, and Aesthetic in Gerhard Richter's Paintings" (1998), in *Gerhard Richter*, ed. Benjamin Buchloh (MIT Press, 1990), 98.

87 Anne Hollander, *Moving Pictures*, repr. edn (Harvard University Press, 1991 [1989]), 15–16.

88 Hollander, *Moving Pictures*, 440–43.

89 I am indebted to Martha Hollander for discovering the shot from *North by Northwest*.

90 David Weddle, "Eduardo Serra: *Girl with a Pearl Earring*," *Daily Variety*, 11 January 2004, A14. Weddle is quoting the film's director, Peter Webber, on the work of its cinematographer.

91 Quotations from *Jack Cardiff: Painting with Light*, directed by Craig McCall (Modus Operandi Films and Smoke and Mirrors Film Production, 2000).

92 From *Jack Cardiff: Painting with Light*.

93 Kent Jones, "Empire of the Senses," pamphlet supplied with the DVD of *Black Narcissus* for the Criterion Collection (2000).

94 Quotations from chapter 2 of "Between Two Worlds: The Making of *Witness*," a documentary included with the 2017 Paramount DVD of the film.

95 Michael Koresky, *Terence Davies* (University of Illinois Press, 2014), 13. The immediate reference is to Davies's *Distant Voices, Still Lives*, but the phrase clearly applies to his other work as well, including what Koretsky later calls Davies's "most painterly film," *The Long Day Closes* (78).

96 Vad, *Vilhelm Hammershøi*, 372.

97 David Bordwell, *The Films of Carl-Theodor Dreyer* (University of California Press, 1981), 232n11. The quoted recollection comes from a documentary film about Dreyer's work directed by Jørgen Roos in 1966.

98 Vad, *Vilhelm Hammershøi*, 162–70.

99 Bordwell, *Films of Carl-Theodor Dreyer*, 42–43, 49. Vad, too, reproduces the still from *Praesidenten* to illustrate Hammershøi's influence on Dreyer (Vad, *Vilhelm Hammershøi*, 440). For another comparison of the filmmaker to Vermeer, see Tag Gallagher, "Chains of Dreams: Carl Th. Dreyer," *Senses of Cinema*, issue 45 (November 2007), https://www.sensesofcinema.com/2007/feature-articles/carl-dreyer/.

100 Wendy Everett, *Terence Davies* (Manchester University Press, 2004), 26.

101 Michael Phillips, "Director Terence Davies Finds a Soul Mate in Emily Dickinson," *Chicago Tribune*, 18 May, 2017, https://www.chicagotribune.com/entertainment/movies/ct-terence-davies-mov-0519-20170518-story.html. For earlier declarations of Vermeer as Davies's "favorite painter" see, e.g., his 2001 interview with Wendy Everett (Everett, *Terence Davies*, 212) and his 2012 interview with Michael Koresky (Koresky, *Terence Davies*, 133).

102 Though Davies's adaptation of Edith Wharton's *House of Mirth* finally owes more to the novelist's contemporary John Singer Sargent than to Vermeer, the filmmaker explicitly evoked the Dutch master when recalling how he chose to light the will-reading scene (Everett, *Terence Davies*, 211–12).

103 For the comparison of the laundry scene in *The Long Day Closes* to *The Milkmaid*, see Koresky, *Terence Davies*, 78–79.

104 Terence Davies, interview with Maximilien Luc Proctor, 23 February 2016, https://photogenie.be/berlinale-2016-terence-davies-it-has-to-be-spontaneous/.

105 Terence Davies, interview with Maximilien Luc Proctor.

106 Everett, *Terence Davies*, 215. Interestingly, Davies told Maximilien Proctor that he first encountered Dickinson's poetry when he heard it recited by Claire Bloom: an experience that he effectively replicates in the scene to which he alludes by having another actress—Cynthia Nixon, who plays Dickinson—recite a poem aloud as she stands by the window.

107 Gerhard Richter, "Notes, 1964–1965," in *Gerhard Richter: Writings*, 32.

108 Hollander, *Moving Pictures*, 28; Gowing, *Vermeer*, 19.

109 Elger, *Gerhard Richter—Catalogue Raisonné*, 2:20–21.

110 Richter, "Notes, 1964–1965," 32.

111 Gerhard Richter, interview with Rolf Schön (1972), in *Gerhard Richter: Writings*, 59.

112 Darryn Ansted, *The Artwork of Gerhard Richter: Painting, Critical Theory and Cultural Transformation* (Routledge, 2017), 87.

113 Gerhard Richter, interview with Benjamin H. D. Buchloh (2004), in *Gerhard Richter: Writings*, 491.

114 Gerhard Richter, interview with Babette Richter (2002), in *Gerhard Richter: Writings*, 443.

6. FORGERY

1 Abraham Bredius, "A New Vermeer," *The Burlington Magazine*, vol. 71, no. 416 (November 1937), 211. Note that Bredius twice describes the right-hand disciple as on the left: a worrying sign for such an authority on the observation of pictures. See Lord Kilbracken [John Raymond Godley], *Van Meegeren: Master Forger* (Charles Scribner's Sons, 1967), 69.

2 Kilbracken, *Van Meegeren*, 56; and Hope B. Werness, "Han van Meegeren *fecit*," in *The Forger's Art: Forgery and the Philosophy of Art*, ed. Denis Dutton (University of California Press, 1983), 30.

3 For a dissenting account of Bredius's influence at this stage of his career, at least among specialists, see Albert Blankert, "The Case of Han van Meegeren's Fake Vermeer *Supper at Emmaus* Reconsidered," in *In His Milieu: Essays on Netherlandish Art in Memory of John Michael Montias*, ed. A. Golahny, M. M. Mochizuki, and L. Vergara (Amsterdam University Press, 2006), 47–57. Though Blankert emphasizes the skepticism with which other scholars had learned to approach Bredius's "discoveries" and implies that only the general public still took him seriously, he fails to explain why the scholarly community largely remained silent until Van Meegeren himself confessed to the forgery.

4 *Johannes Vermeer*, ed. Arthur K. Wheelock Jr. (National Gallery of Art [Washington, DC], 1995), 194, 94, 100. See also Edward Dolnick, *The Forger's Spell: A True Story of Vermeer, Nazis, and the Greatest Art Hoax of the Twentieth Century* (Harper Perennial, 2008), 127–31; and Jonathan Lopez, *The Man Who Made Vermeers: Unvarnishing the Legend of Master Forger Han van Meegeren* (Harcourt, 2008), 135. It was also Bredius who had successfully disputed the authenticity of Thoré's beloved *Rustic Cottage*. See Ben Broos, "Vermeer: Malice and Misconception," in *Vermeer Studies*, ed. Ivan Gaskell and Michiel Jonker (National Gallery of Art [Washington, DC], 1998), 23; and Dolnick, *Forger's Spell*, 99.

5 Bredius, "New Vermeer," 211. For Bredius's early doubts about the picture's authenticity, see Blankert, "Case of Han van Meegeren's Fake Vermeer," 49.

6 A. Bredius to D. Hannema, 13 September 1937, as translated and quoted in Friso Lammertse, "Museum Boymans Buys a Vermeer," in *Van Meegeren's Fake Vermeers: The Connoisseur's Eye and the Forger's Art*, ed. Friso Lammertse and Jonieke van Es (Museum Boijmans Van Beuningen [Rotterdam], 2011), 10. For Hannema's first Vermeer exhibition, see, e.g., Dolnick, *Forger's Spell*, 148–49; and Lammertse, "Museum Boymans," 11–12. Unfortunately for its subsequent reputation, six of the exhibition's fifteen Vermeers have since been discredited.

7 "Art: From a Linen Closet," *Time*, 19 September 1938. I am grateful to Jonathan Lopez (Lopez, *Man Who Made Vermeers*, 208), for directing me to this review: https://content.time.com/time/subscriber/article/0,33009,931727,00.html.

8 P[aul] B. Coremans, *Van Meegeren's Faked Vermeers and De Hooghs: A Scientific Examination*, trans. A. Hardy and C. M. Hutt (J. M. Meulenhoff, 1949), 26.

9 The telegram is reproduced and decoded in Blankert, "Case of Han van Meegeren's Fake Vermeer," 50.

10 As quoted by Lopez, *Man Who Made Vermeers*, 138.

11 Marcel Proust, *À la recherche du temps perdu*, ed. Jean-Yves Tadié, 4 vols., Bibliothèque de la Pléiade (Gallimard, 1987–89), 3:879 (Eng., 5:430 [see Preface, n. 9 above]).

12 Arthur K. Wheelock Jr., "The Story of Two Vermeer Forgeries," in *Shop Talk: Studies in Honor of Seymour Slive*, ed. Cynthia P. Schneider, William W. Robinson, and Alice I. Davies (Harvard University Art Museums, 1995), 273.

13 Seymour de Ricci, "Le quarante-et-unième Vermeer," *Gazette des beaux-arts*, vol. 69 (1927), 309.

14 Wilhelm R. Valentiner, "A Newly Discovered Vermeer," *Art in America*, vol. 16 (April 1928), 101–2. Cf. Hale, who listed several repeating items in Vermeer's paintings—the lion-headed chairs, the little white jug, "the stained glass window of a special design," the characteristically rumpled rugs, "the Vermeer map"—and argued that one of these might not prove very much, but the presence of all five "would go far to make one think one had found a Vermeer" (Philip L[eslie] Hale, *Jan Vermeer of Delft* [Small, Maynard and Co., 1913], 30).

15 Wheelock, "Story of Two Vermeer Forgeries," 271–72. To the best of my knowledge, Wheelock was the first to trace both pictures to Van Wijngaarden.

16 See Lopez, *Man Who Made Vermeers*, esp. 22–24, 54, 64–71, 86. Though Dolnick is more cautious, he too speculates that Van Meegeren may have been the principal hand behind both paintings (*Forger's Spell*, 111).

17 Wheelock, "Story of Two Vermeer Forgeries," 274n4; Lopez, *Man Who Made Vermeers*, 61–64, 85, 239–40; Arie Wallert and Michel van de Laar, "Working Methods, Tricks, Materials and Techniques: Top Quality Forgeries," in *Van Meegeren's Vermeers: The Connoisseur's Eye and the Forger's Art*, ed. Friso Lammertse and Jonieke van Es (Museum Boijmans Van Beuningen [Rotterdam], 2011), 80–81. The painting is also attributed to Van Meegeren by its current owner, The Hyde Collection in Glens Falls, New York.

18 Lopez, *Man Who Made Vermeers*, 61; Wheelock, "Story of Two Vermeer Forgeries," 273–74. For more on Bode's role in this story, see Esmée Quodbach, "Wilhelm Bode and Johannes Vermeer: Creating a Taste and a Market," in *Wilhelm Bode and the Art Market: Connoisseurship, Networking and Control of the Marketplace*, ed. Joanna Smalcerz (Brill, 2023), esp. 87–93.

19 A[braham] Bredius, "An Unpublished Vermeer," *The Burlington Magazine*, vol. 61, no. 355 (October 1932), 145; Valentiner, "Newly Discovered Vermeer," 102.

20 Bredius, "Unpublished Vermeer," 146, 145.

21 On this episode, see esp. Dolnick, *Forger's Spell*, 139–44; and Lopez, *Man Who Made Vermeers*, 107–13. Lopez even suggests that the "overall stiffness and inertia" of the picture may have been a selling point from Bredius's perspective, since a similar awkwardness had not prevented him from authenticating the *Allegory* (111–12).

22 Cf. Dolnick, *Forger's Spell*, 144. In Dolnick's account, this lesson immediately prompted Van Meegeren to begin work on the *Supper at Emmaus*, but the chronology is not that clear. If the Rijksmuseum is correct that *Woman Reading Music* was painted at some time between 1935 and 1940, then it must have been undertaken several years after the publication of Bredius's article on *Lady and Gentleman with a Spinet.*

23 Kilbracken, *Van Meegeren*, 53.

24 Wallert and Van de Laar, "Working Methods," 84–96.

25 Wallert and Van de Laar, "Working Methods," 91, 76.

26 For versions of this argument, see especially Kilbracken, *Van Meegeren*, 33–36 and Dolnick, *Forger's Spell*, 132–36.

27 Wallert and Van de Laar, "Working Methods," 70.

28 M. Kirby Talley Jr., "Van Meegeren's Fake 'Vermeers,'" *Fake?: The Art of Deception*, ed. Mark Jones, with Paul Craddock and Nicolas Barker (British Museum Publications, 1990), 237–38. The treatise from which Van Meegeren drew his knowledge of historical painting methods was Martin de Wild's *The Scientific Examination of Pictures*, first published in Dutch in 1928.

29 Kilbracken, *Van Meegeren*, 39–40; Werness, "Han van Meegeren *fecit*," 24–25; Dolnick, *Forger's Spell*, 148–49; Lammertse, "Museum Boymans," 12.

30 Pieter Koomen, "Vermeer en zijn verwanten" (Vermeer and related artists), *Maandblad voor Beeldende Kunsten*, December 1935, as translated and quoted in Dolnick, *Forger's Spell*, 164. I am particularly grateful to Edward Dolnick for locating this source.

31 Dolnick, *Forger's Spell*, 165.

32 Kilbracken, *Van Meegeren*, 146; Friso Lammertse, "'Vermeer discoveries are coming thick and fast these days,'" in *Van Meegeren's Vermeers: The Connoisseur's Eye and the Forger's Art*, ed. Friso Lammertse and Jonieke van Es (Museum Boijmans Van Beuningen [Rotterdam], 2011), 35, 37–38.

33 Lopez, *Man Who Made Vermeers*, 121.

34 Kilbracken, *Van Meegeren*, 63; Friso Lammertse, "In Conclusion," in *Van Meegeren's Vermeers: The Connoisseur's Eye and the Forger's Art*, ed. Friso Lammertse and Jonieke van Es (Museum Boijmans Van Beuningen [Rotterdam], 2011), 102.

35 Lammertse, "In Conclusion," 102.

36 For helpful accounts of the process, see especially Lopez, *Man Who Made Vermeers*, 107–9, and Wallert and Van de Laar, "Working Methods," 81–82.

37 Coremans, *Van Meegeren's Faked Vermeers*, 20–21; Wallert and Van de Laar, "Working Methods," 80–91.

38 Nadja Garthoff, "A Forger Confesses," in *Van Meegeren's Vermeers: The Connoisseur's Eye and the Forger's Art*, ed. Friso Lammertse and Jonieke van Es (Museum Boijmans Van Beuningen [Rotterdam], 2011), 49–51, 116n53; Lopez, *Man Who Made Vermeers*, 109–10.

39 Lopez, *Man Who Made Vermeers*, 174–75; Lammertse, "'Vermeer discoveries,'" 35. Only after the authorities learned from Van Meegeren about his use of the Bakelite was a test for the

chemical devised and its presence in the paintings confirmed (Lopez, *Man Who Made Vermeers*, 215–16).

40 For a brief history of the other paintings' reception at the time, see Lammertse, "'Vermeer discoveries,'" 24–41.

41 Dolnick, *Forger's Spell*, 166; Garthoff, "Forger Confesses," 53.

42 For Van Meegeren's use of natural ultramarine, which had mostly been replaced at the time by a synthetic version, see Wallert and Van de Laar, "Working Methods," 78–80.

43 The observations above are drawn in part from Werness, "Han van Meegeren *fecit*," 32–35; Dolnick, *Forger's Spell*, 171; and Lopez, *Man Who Made Vermeers*, 121–22.

44 Coremans, *Van Meegeren's Faked Vermeers*, 37. There were actually two versions of the *Last Supper*: the first, which was never sold because it was left behind in Van Meegeren's French studio, was only discovered in 1949. Garthoff speculates that he painted the second either from a photograph or from memory. She also suggests that the *Head of Christ* may actually have been painted after both versions, even though it passed for a preliminary study (Garthoff, "Forger Confesses," 64, 117n93).

45 Lopez, *Man Who Made Vermeers*, 169.

46 Lammertse, "'Vermeer discoveries,'" 34. Max Henkel, the acting director in question, ultimately changed his mind about the painting, but he was overruled by other experts (36).

47 Most of these factors were originally cited by the commission charged with investigating the forgeries and have subsequently been elaborated by historians. For the commission's account, see Coremans, *Van Meegeren's Faked Vermeers*, 34. For the threat to send the *Emmaus* to America, see Lammertse, "Museum Boymans," 18.

48 The fullest account of Van Meegeren's involvement with the Nazis is provided by Lopez, *Man Who Made Vermeers*, esp. 124–85. See also Lammertse, "'Vermeer discoveries,'" 39–41.

49 Kilbracken, *Van Meegeren*, 156.

50 Dolnick, *Forger's Spell*, 288; Lopez, *Man Who Made Vermeers*, 214–15; Kilbracken, *Van Meegeren*, 3.

51 For the most thorough account of Decoen's argument and its weaknesses, see Kilbracken, *Van Meegeren*, esp. 42–46, 111–20, 131–32, and 161–69.

52 Garthoff, "Forger Confesses," 64; Hans Tietze, *Genuine and False: Copies, Imitations, Forgeries* (Max Parrish & Co., 1948), 57; Dolnick, *Forger's Spell*, 267.

53 Lammertse, "In Conclusion," 101.

54 Werness, "Han van Meegeren *fecit*," 35, 41.

55 Talley, "Van Meegeren's Fake 'Vermeers,'" 240.

56 Lopez, *Man Who Made Vermeers*, 6.

57 Valentiner, "Newly Discovered Vermeer," 107; Wheelock, "Story of Two Vermeer Forgeries," 428.

58 Eduard Plietzsch, *Vermeer van Delft* (Bruckmann, 1939), 29–30.

59 Lopez, *Man Who Made Vermeers*, 104, 105, 273–74n104. While the argument for Van Meegeren's involvement with *The Lacemaker* remains circumstantial, his responsibility for the "Garbo Vermeer" is supported both by the testimony of his son and by his signature on a photograph of the painting in a book formerly in his possession, as well as an annotation that reads, "Vermeer? No. Han van Meegeren" (105–6). See fig. 6.15.

60 "Forgery on Television" (editorial), *The Burlington Magazine*, vol. 102, no. 692 (November 1960), 465.

61 "Forgery on Television."

62 Lammertse, "'Vermeer discoveries,'" 38, 30. The quotation from Plietzsch comes from a conversation recorded in the unpublished diary of Willy Auping, the curator who was so quick to dismiss *The Footwashing*.

63 Lammertse, "In Conclusion," 105.

64 Lammertse, "'Vermeer discoveries,'" 30.

65 See the helpful entry under "Erroneous Attributions and Forgeries" at https://www.essentialvermeer.com.

66 See esp. Walter Liedtke, "Dutch Paintings in America: The Collectors and their Ideals," in Ben Broos, Edwin Buijsen, Geerte Broersma et al., *Great Dutch Paintings from America* (Mauritshuis/Waanders Publishers, 1990). As Liedtke notes, between Henry Marquand's purchase of *Young Woman with a Water Pitcher* in 1887 and Frick's acquisition of *Mistress and Maid* in 1919, almost a third of Vermeer's known oeuvre was shipped to America (42).

67 Albert Blankert, "Vermeer au fil des siècles," trans. Marthe Lory, in Gilles Aillaud, Albert Blankert, and John Michael Montias, *Vermeer*, new edn (Hazen, 2004), 179n102; Dolnick, *Forger's Spell*, 218–21.

68 Lopez, *Man Who Made Vermeers*, 53.

69 Ivan Gaskell, *Vermeer's Wager: Speculations on Art History, Theory and Art Museums* (Reaktion, 2000), 39, 32.

70 Katharine Weber, *The Music Lesson* (New York: Picador, 1999), 67.

71 Susan Vreeland, *Girl in Hyacinth Blue* (New York: Penguin, 1999), 6; Weber, *Music Lesson*, 67, 95, 67; Vreeland, *Girl in Hyacinth Blue*, 6, 7, 161. For Vreeland's own catalogue of the paintings on which she drew, see her interview with Jonathan Janson at https://www.essentialvermeer.com.

72 Valentiner, "Newly Discovered Vermeer," 102. The single exception to this rule is Vreeland's inclusion of a slightly out-of-focus glass of milk on the table of *Girl in Hyacinth Blue* (7). To the best of my knowledge, no such object ever appears in a painting by Vermeer, despite the liquid that pours from a jug in one of his most celebrated paintings.

73 See the separately paginated interview with the author appended to the Penguin edition (Vreeland, *Girl in Hyacinth Blue*, 9).

74 Weber's plot draws loosely on an actual heist that took place in 1974, when the British heiress Rose Dugdale and her fellow conspirators stole the *Lady Writing a Letter with Her Maid* and eighteen other paintings from the Irish estate of Sir Afred Beit, in an attempt to liberate four hunger strikers and extort money for the IRA. Though Dugdale was swiftly arrested and the paintings recovered, she first took refuge, like Weber's heroine, in an Irish cottage. See Anthony M. Amore, *The Woman Who Stole Vermeer: The True Story of Rose Dugdale and the Russborough Art Heist* (Pegasus Books, 2020).

75 Weber, *Music Lesson*, 177.

76 Walter Benjamin, "The Work of Art in the Age of Mechanical Reproduction" (1955), in Benjamin, *Illuminations*, trans. Harry Zohn (Harcourt Brace, 1968), as quoted in Weber, *Music Lesson*, 58.

77 Weber, *Music Lesson*, 74, n.p.

7. HOMAGE, APPROPRIATION, PASTICHE

1 George Deem, interview with Susanna Posnett, October 2004, https://georgedeem.org/search/view/Interview-2004-01-01.

2 https://georgedeem.org/writings/view/Chelsea-1984-01-01. A comprehensive record of Deem's work may be found at https://georgedeem.org/.

3 Marguerite Anne Glass, "Vermeer in Dialogue: From Appropriation to Response" (PhD dissertation, University of Maryland, 2003), 35.

4 As quoted from the Philip Leslie Hale Papers at the Archives of American Art in Bernice Kramer Leader, "The Boston School and Vermeer," *Arts Magazine* vol. 55, no. 3 (November 1980), 174.

5 Deborah Solomon, *Utopia Parkway: The Life and Work of Joseph Cornell* (Farrar, Straus and Giroux, 1997), esp. 103–5, 215, 355. Cf. Diane Waldman, who remarks the affinity between Cornell's boxes and Vermeer's tightly structured interiors, two of which—*The Milkmaid* and *A Lady Writing*—the artist might have seen on a visit to the New York World's Fair in 1939 (*Joseph Cornell: Master of Dreams* [Harry Abrams, 2002], 74).

6 Jean-Claude Lebensztejn, *Malcolm Morley: Itineraries*, trans. Lucy McNair (Reaktion, 2001), 43–44, 57.

7 Glass, "Vermeer in Dialogue," 169, 180.

8 https://www.georgedeem.org/search/view/Notebook-1978-1978-01-01.

9 Robert S. Nelson, "Appropriation," in *Critical Terms for Art History*, ed. Robert S. Nelson and Richard Shiff, 2nd edn (University of Chicago Press, 2003 [1996]), 117. Despite Bruce Grenville's claim that "appropriation [. . .] is rooted in an intentional critique of the found object," the term remains too various and contested, I believe, to limit its use in this way. Were he right, however, it would be largely inapplicable to the works examined here—one reason I also choose to speak of "homage." See Bruce Grenville, "Mashup: The Birth of Modern Culture," in *Mashup: The Birth of Modern Culture*, ed. Daina Augaitis, Bruce Grenville, and Stephanie Rebick (Black Dog Publishing, 2016), 31.

10 For a useful summary of this history, see Ingeborg Hoesterey, *Pastiche, Cultural Memory in Art, Film, Literature* (Indiana University Press, 2001).

11 George Deem, *How to Paint a Vermeer: A Painter's History of Art* (Thames & Hudson, 2004), 32.

12 https://www.mauritshuis.nl/en/what-s-on/mauritshuis-at-home/mygirlwithapearl/.

13 https://futurism.com/top-google-result-johannes-vermeer-ai-generated-knockoff.

14 https://www.theartnewspaper.com/2023/03/13/online-storm-erupts-over-ai-work-in-dutch-museums-girl-with-a-pearl-earring-display ; https://art.beopenfuture.com/ai-cant-replace-artists-but-its-already-transformed-the-art-world-forever/. The artist reports that he originally created the image, which predated the museum's call, as a means of self-expression, public learning in a new medium, and generating a discussion about the uses of AI.

15 Salvador Dalí, *The Unspeakable Confessions of Salvador Dali*, as told to André Parinaud, trans. Harold J. Salemson (William Morrow, 1976), 232.

16 https://www.metmuseum.org/art/collection/search/461684.

17 Dalí, *Unspeakable Confessions*, 232.

18 https://www.metmuseum.org/art/collection/search/461684.

19 Jennifer Higgie, *The Mirror and the Palette: Rebellion, Revolution, and Resilience; Five Hundred Years of Women's Self-Portraits* (Pegasus Books, 2021), 176. Heysen also left an unfinished painting of a few years earlier, *Cedars Interior* (ca. 1930), in which a framed reproduction of the *Girl with a Pearl Earring* hangs on the wall. See *Hans and Nora Heysen: Two Generations of Australian Art*, ed. Mark Gomes (National Gallery of Victoria [Melbourne], 2019), 4–5.

20 Marcel Proust, *À la recherche du temps perdu*, ed. Jean-Yves Tadié, 4 vols., Bibliothèque de la Pléiade (Gallimard, 1987–89), 3:693 (Eng., 5:208 [see Preface, n. 9 above]).

21 Carlo Cavagna, "*Girl with a Pearl Earring*: A Profile of the Film Including an Interview with Director Peter Webber," https://www.aboutfilm.com/features/girlwithapearlearring/webber.htm.

22 Ivan Gaskell, *Vermeer's Wager: Speculations on Art History, Theory, and Art Museums* (Reaktion, 2000), 115, 155.

23 Luis Buñuel and Salvador Dalí, *Un chien andalou*, with foreword by Jean Vigo; transcription and introduction by Phillip Drummond (Faber and Faber, 1994), 3.

24 Dalí, *Unspeakable Confessions*, 232–33.

25 Jean-Louis Gaillemin, *Dalí: Master of Fantasies* (Abrams, 2004), 43.

26 Deem, *How to Paint a Vermeer*, 86.

27 I am drawing here on personal conversations with Gary Haller, who organized an exhibition of Deem's work at Jonathan Edwards College, Yale University, in 2003, and on unpublished letters to the artist from Haller and Bryan J. Wolf, concerning the latter's draft of a catalogue essay for the exhibition. Though Deem's side of the correspondence is not available, it is clear from this evidence that he strongly objected to Wolf's use of the word "joke" and related terms, despite Wolf's explanation that he took his jokes seriously. Some revisions were made to accommodate the artist's objections, but the dispute remained unresolved, and the essay never appeared. I am grateful to Haller and to Wolf for permission to recount these events here.

28 As of this writing, a digital image of Kolář's *Rembrandt/Vermeer* is available at https://image.invaluable.com/housePhotos/Karl-Faber/91/676191/H0636-L214336090_original.jpg.

29 https://www.mauritshuis.nl/en/what-s-on/mauritshuis-at-home/mygirlwithapearl/.

30 W. S. Di Piero, "Girl with Pearl Earring by Johannes Vermeer," *Skirts and Slacks: Poems* (Knopf, 2001), 53–54.

31 See, e.g., Johan Huizinga, *The Autumn of the Middle Ages*, trans. Rodney J. Payton and Ulrich Mammitzsch (University of Chicago Press, 1996), 245, 374; and Brenda Assael, "Art or Indecency? *Tableaux Vivants* on the London Stage and the Failure of Late Victorian Moral Reform," *Journal of British Studies* 45.4 (2006): 744–58.

32 See https://khioda.khio.no/khio-xmlui/bitstream/handle/11250/2457025/passing_of_time.pdf?sequence=1&isAllowed=y.

33 Tom Hunter, "Essay: Under the Influence," BBC Radio 3, March 2011, text at http://www.tomhunter.org/essay-under-the-influence/.

34 Hunter, "Essay." The other Vermeers quoted in "Persons Unknown" are *A Maid Asleep*, *Lady Writing a Letter with Her Maid*, *The Art of Painting* (here retitled "The Art of Squatting"), *The Geographer*, *The Glass of Wine*, and *The Milkmaid.*

35 Gerhard Richter, "I Have Nothing to Say and I'm Saying It": conversation between Gerhard Richter and Nicholas Serota, Spring 2011, in *Gerhard Richter: Panorama*, ed. Mark Godfrey and Nicholas Serota, expanded edn (D.A.P., 2016 [2011]), 17.

36 Oliver C. Speck, "Search for the Sublime: The Road Trilogy, or Wenders's *Roam-man*-ticism," in *Wim Wenders: Making Films that Matter*, ed. Olivier Delers and Martin Sulzer-Reichel (Bloomsbury Academic, 2020), 33.

37 Jan Dawson, *Wim Wenders*, trans. Carla Wartenberg (Zoetrope, 1976), 23. For later remarks along the same lines, see Wim Wenders, *The Act of Seeing: Essays and Conversations*, trans. Michael Hofmann (Faber and Faber, 1997), 199–200, 166, 139. The relevant conversations took place in 1988, 1990, and 1991, respectively.

38 Brigitte Peucker, *The Material Image: Art and the Real in Film* (Stanford University Press, 2007), 44. I am grateful to Peucker for first alerting me to Wenders's film and its appropriation of Vermeer.

39 Peucker, *Material Image*, 42.

40 Walter Donohue, "Revelations: An Interview with Wim Wenders," *Sight and Sound*, vol. 1, no. 12 (1 April 1992), 11–12.

41 https://en.wikipedia.org/wiki/Until_the_End_of_the_World.

42 Wim Wenders, "The Truth of Images: Two Conversations with Peter W. Jansen," in Wenders, *Act of Seeing*, 60.

43 Lawrence Gowing, *Vermeer*, 3rd edn (University of California Press, 1997 [1952]), 43.

44 Lebensztejn, *Malcolm Morley*, 43–44.

45 Bonnie Clearwater, *Malcolm Morley: The Art of Painting* (Museum of Contemporary Art [North Miami, FL], 2005), 15–16.

46 Lebensztejn, *Malcolm Morley*, 57.

47 Jean Lipman and Richard Marshall, *Art about Art* (E. P. Dutton, in association with the Whitney Museum of American Art, 1978), 80.

48 Not every scholar agrees that the painter's costume is anachronistic, however, nor do those who see it as such necessarily agree on its implications, with some believing that Vermeer is paying homage to history painting and others that he is gently mocking it. For some representative, if tonally varied, comments on the question, see Edward A. Snow, *A Study of Vermeer* (University of California Press, 1979), 113–14, 171n35; Daniel Arasse, *Vermeer: Faith in Painting*, trans. Terry Grabar (Princeton University Press, 1994), 42–43, 116n40; Eric Jan Sluijter, "Vermeer, Fame, and Female Beauty: The *Art of Painting*," and Marieke de Winkel, "The Interpretation of Dress in Vermeer's Paintings," 332–34, both in *Vermeer Studies*, ed. Ivan Gaskell and Michiel Jonker (National Gallery of Art [Washington, DC], 1998); Lisa Vergara, "Perspectives on Women in the Art of Vermeer," in *The Cambridge Companion to Vermeer*, ed. Wayne E. Franits (Cambridge University Press, 2001), 56–60; Bryan Jay Wolf, *Vermeer and the Invention of Seeing* (University of Chicago Press, 2001), 191–226; and Gaskell, *Vermeer's Wager*, 39–40.

49 Robert Rosenblum, "George Deem: The Art of Art History," in Deem, *How to Paint a Vermeer*, 6–13; and David B. Dearinger, *George Deem: The Art of Art History* (Boston Athenaeum, 2012).

50 George Deem, notes on "The Artist in His Studio," 27 May 1989, https://www.georgedeem.org/search/view/Artist-in-His-Studio-The-diptych-1979-01-01.

51 Deem, interview with Susanna Posnett.

52 Dawson, *Wim Wenders*, 23.

53 I quote from the English subtitles of Lassnig's animated film of 1992, *Maria Lassnig Kantate* (*The Ballad of Maria Lassnig*) and the soundtrack of her 1976 *Art Education*, both on the Index Edition DVD 033, *Maria Lassnig Animation Films*.

54 Alan Woods, *Being Naked—Playing Dead: The Art of Peter Greenaway* (Manchester University Press, 1996), 55. I am grateful to Woods for first alerting me to Polak's photograph, as well as to its probable influence on Greenaway.

55 I draw here on the voiceover commentary by Peter Greenaway that accompanies the 2008 DVD of *A Zed & Two Noughts* from Zeitgeist Video.

56 Peter Greenaway, *A Zed & Two Noughts* (Faber and Faber, 1986), 14. An "Author's Note" indicates that this is the full script used when shooting, though not every line made it into the film.

57 It's clear from the commentary Greenaway supplied for the 2008 DVD of *A Zed & Two Noughts* that these insistently symmetrical arrangements owe more to his obsession with twinning than to his admiration for Vermeer.

58 Here I follow the film's soundtrack rather than the screenplay, which identifies its Van Meegeren as the forger's nephew (Greenaway, *A Zed & Two Noughts*, 46). I have ignored, however, the spelling of Catharina's name as "Caterina" in the film's titles.

59 Greenaway, *Zed & Two Noughts*, 14.

60 Greenaway makes the identification while commenting on the scene for the 2008 DVD of *A Zed & Two Noughts*.

61 Greenaway, *Zed & Two Noughts*, 46.

62 Greenaway, *Zed & Two Noughts*, 77. For further observations about the pastiche of the two Vermeers in this scene, see Amy Lawrence, *The Films of Peter Greenaway* (Cambridge University Press, 1997), 87–88.

63 Greenaway calls Van Meegeren "an ex-Nazi doctor sort of figure" in his commentary for the 2008 DVD.

64 For the quotation of Bueñel, see Anne T. Cieko, "Peter Greenaway's Alpha-Bestiary *Ut Pictura Poesis: A Zed & Two Noughts*," *Post Script* 12.1 (1992), 45.

65 Greenaway, *Zed & Two Noughts*, 107.

66 Leon Steinmetz and Peter Greenaway, *The World of Peter Greenaway* (Journey Editions, 1995), 84.

67 Janet K. Cutler and Thomas E. Benediktsson, review of *A Zed & Two Noughts*, *Film Quarterly* 42.2 (1993–94), 37.

68 Pierre Le Coz and Pierre-Éric Laroche, *Vermeer, ou l'action de voir* (La lettre volée, 2007), 33–35, quotation at 35.

69 Apart from the two cityscapes, the other paintings that include visible legs or feet are *Diana and Her Companions*, *Christ in the House of Martha and Mary*, and the *Allegory of the Catholic Faith*.

70 Greenaway, *Zed & Two Noughts*, 14.

71 Peter Greenaway, interview with Michael Ciment (1985), "*Zed & Two Noughts (Z.O.O.)*," in *Peter Greenaway: Interviews*, ed. Vernon Gras and Marguerite Gras (University Press of Mississippi, 2000), 32.

72 Greenaway, interview with Michael Ciment, 34; Peter Greenaway, interview with Alan Woods (ca. 1989), in Woods, *Being Naked*, 246; and voiceover commentary for the 2008 DVD of *A Zed & Two Noughts*. Though some scholars have indeed questioned the painting's authenticity over the years, most currently accept it as genuine.

73 Greenaway, interview with Hartmut Buchholz and Uwe Kuenzel (1988), "Two Things That Count: Sex and Death," in *Peter Greenaway: Interviews*, ed. Vernon Gras and Marguerite Gras (University Press of Mississippi, 2000), 55.

74 Lawrence, *Films of Peter Greenaway*, 90.

75 Peter Greenaway, interview with Gavin Smith (1990), "Food for Thought," in *Peter Greenaway: Interviews*, ed. Vernon Gras and Marguerite Gras (University Press of Mississippi, 2000), 94.

76 George Deem, "Don't You See?" (2002), https://www.georgedeem.org/search/view/Dont-You-See-2002-01-01.

77 Glass, "Vermeer in Dialogue," 151.

78 I am indebted to Bryan J. Wolf, "First Glance, Second Glance: Deem Paints Vermeer," for clarifying my thinking on this issue. For the genesis of the essay, which remains unpublished, see n. 27 above.

79 I draw here on a notebook entry about the painting that Deem recorded in March 2002. See https://georgedeem.org/works/view/Seven-Vermeer-Corners-1999-01-01.

80 The comment comes from "an undated note page torn from a notebook and inserted with other notes for the painting in [Deem's] studio reference book, Albert Blankert, *Vermeer Every Painting*, 1979." See https://georgedeem.org/works/view/Seven-Vermeer-Corners-1999-01-01.

81 Christiane Hertel, "Seven Vermeers: Collection, Reception, Response," in *The Cambridge Companion to Vermeer*, ed. Wayne E. Franits (Cambridge University Press, 2001), 160.

82 Proust, *À la recherche*, 3:879 (5:430).

83 George Deem, notebook entry, March 2002, https://georgedeem.org/works/view/Seven-Vermeer-Corners-1999-01-01.

84 George Deem to Garland and Suzanne Marshall, 11 May 1998, https://www.georgedeem.org/search/view/Vermeers-Chair-1994-01-01.

85 David Dearinger also notes how Deem's method of "subtraction" intensifies an effect already apparent in the original, as the quiet withdrawal of Vermeer's women becomes literalized by their physical removal from the picture (Dearinger, *George Deem*, 20).

86 Glass, "Vermeer in Dialogue," 145.
87 George Deem, unpublished manuscript, September 2001, https://www.georgedeem.org/search/view/Extended-Vermeer-The-Woman-in-Blue-2002-01-01.
88 Deem, unpublished manuscript, September 2001.
89 Charles Molesworth, "How to Live in an Image World: The Strategies of Memory," *Salmagundi*, no. 139/140 (2003), 22.
90 Wolf, "First Glance."
91 W. Bürger [Théophile Thoré] "Van der Meer de Delft," *Gazette des beaux-arts*, vol. 21 (1866), 462.

8. THE LANGUAGE OF POETRY

1 See Albert Blankert, "Vermeer au fils des siècles," trans. Marthe Lory, in Gilles Aillaud, Albert Blankert, and John Michael Montias, *Vermeer*, new edn (Éditions Hazan, 2004), 163–65. The relevant lines of the poem are quoted in French at 163. Blankert first recorded his discovery of the two versions and the bibliographical evidence for sequencing them as he does in the 1975 Dutch edition of his catalogue raisonnée: Albert Blankert, with contributions by Rob Ruurs and Willem L. van de Watering, *Vermeer of Delft: Complete Edition of the Paintings* (Phaidon, 1978), 147–48. It's also Blankert who suggests that Vermeer himself may be responsible for the more flattering version. Not only was he a neighbor of Bon's, but he had otherwise exhibited a meticulous attention to the written word, twice erasing and revising his signature on a document in order to correct his orthography. If Blankert is right—and like other aspects of the artist's biography, this small act of authorship is admittedly speculative—then the metaphor of Vermeer as a poet is even closer to the truth than subsequent commentators were to imagine. The original poem appears in Dirck van Bleyswijck's *Beschryvinge der stadt Delft* (1667).
2 Ben Broos, "Vermeer: Malice and Misconception," in *Vermeer Studies*, ed. Ivan Gaskell and Michiel Jonkers (National Gallery of Art [Washington, DC], 1998), 19.
3 This is obviously a difficult matter to quantify. But according to one rough measure—the entries in Robert Denham's 2010 bibliography of ekphrastic poetry—Vermeer is marginally surpassed in this respect only by Edward Hopper, Claude Monet, Rembrandt, and Vincent van Gogh, all considerably more prolific painters, whose output affords many more occasions for poetic response than his. See Robert D. Denham, *Poets on Painting: A Bibliography* (McFarland, 2010).
4 Jane Shore, "I Am Sick of Reading Poems About Paintings by Vermeer," *Literary Imagination* 25.3 (2023): 384–85.
5 Frederick Wedmore, *The Masters of Genre Painting: Being an Introductory Handbook to the Study of Genre Painting* (London, 1880), 57.
6 Nick Norwood, "Deftly Stilled," in Norwood, *The Soft Blare: Poems* (River City Publishers, 2003), 46.
7 John Ashbery, "View of Delft," in Ashbery, *Chinese Whispers* (Farrar, Straus and Giroux, 2002), 18. I thank Karin Roffman for calling this poem to my attention.
8 Wedmore, *Masters of Genre Painting*, 53, 46, 51.
9 *Old Dutch and Flemish Masters*, engraved by Timothy Cole, with critical notes by John C. Van Dyke, and comments by the engraver, repr. edn (The Century Co., 1911 [1895]), 117, 115, 117.
10 Jean-Louis Vaudoyer, "Le mystérieux Vermeer I," *L'opinion*, 30 April 1921, 487; "Le mystérieux Vermeer III," 14 May 1921, 543.
11 J[ohan] H. Huizinga, *Dutch Civilization in the Seventeenth Century and Other Essays*, selected by Peter Geyl and F.W.N. Hugenholtz, trans. Arnold Pomerans (Collins, 1968), 85. The Dutch version of Huizinga's book originally appeared in 1941.
12 A[ry] B[ob] de Vries, *Jan Vermeer de Delft, suivi de La poétique de Vermeer par René Huyghe*, Fr. trans. Louise Servicen (P. Tisné, 1948), 7.
13 René Huyghe, "La poétique de Vermeer," in De Vries, *Jan Vermeer de Delft*, 85, 90, 97, 93, 102, 105.
14 Huyghe, "La poétique," 90, 91, 83, 84.
15 Lawrence Gowing, *Vermeer*, 3rd edn (University of California Press, 1997 [1952]), 25, 37, 26, 42, 31, 26.

16 Arthur K. Wheelock Jr., *Jan Vermeer* (Harry N. Abrams, 1981), 11, 124. A revised edition of this book, with the addition of *Saint Praxedis* to the artist's early work, appeared in 1988. Though the pagination differs slightly from the original and a few figures have changed, the introductory text, including the language quoted above, remains unaltered.

17 Wheelock, *Jan Vermeer*, 114; Arthur K. Wheelock Jr., *Vermeer and the Art of Painting* (Yale University Press, 1995), 53; Arthur K. Wheelock Jr. and Ben Broos, "Catalogue," in Arthur K. Wheelock Jr., Ben Broos, Albert Blankert, and Jørgen Wadum, *Johannes Vermeer* (National Gallery of Art [Washington, DC], and the Royal Cabinet of Paintings, Mauritshuis [The Hague]: 1995), 166–68.

18 Wheelock, *Vermeer and the Art*, 166.

19 Sharon Cameron, *Lyric Time: Dickinson and the Limits of Genre* (The Johns Hopkins University Press, 1979), 243, 70; George T. Wright, "The Lyric Present: Simple Present Verbs in English Poems," *PMLA* 89.3 (1974): 563–79.

20 Cameron, *Lyric Time*, 260.

21 Virginia Jackson, *Dickinson's Misery: A Theory of Lyric Reading* (Princeton University Press, 2005), 8, 6.

22 See Jonathan Culler, *Theory of the Lyric* (Harvard University Press, 2015), 83–85, 88. Culler's own history of lyric theory begins with Hegel.

23 Jackson, *Dickinson's Misery*, 53.

24 Culler, *Theory of the Lyric*, 226.

25 This claim might be qualified by the potential ambiguity that hovers over several of Vermeer's canvases with more than one figure, especially the *Officer and Laughing Girl* and perhaps the *Girl with a Wine Glass*, which don't clearly rule out the possibility that the interior in question is an inn or brothel rather than a private house. For a shrewd account of how such ambiguity might function, see Richard Helgerson, *Adulterous Alliances: Home, State, and History in Early Modern European Drama and Painting* (University of Chicago Press, 2000), 79–119.

26 Gregor J. M. Weber, "Windows Between Outer and Inner Worlds," in *Vermeer*, ed. Pieter Roelofs and Gregor J. M. Weber (Rijksmuseum | Amsterdam / Hannibal Books, 2023), 163.

27 Ivan Gaskell, *Vermeer's Wager: Speculations on Art History, Theory and Art Museums* (Reaktion, 2000), 204.

28 Eamon Grennan, "Cavalier and Smiling Girl (Vermeer)," in Grennan, *Relations: New & Selected Poems* (Graywolf Press, 1998), 24.

29 Michael White, "Woman in Blue Reading a Letter," in White, *Vermeer in Hell* (Persea Books, 2014), 29.

30 See Michael Fried, *Absorption and Theatricality: Painting and Beholder in the Age of Diderot* (University of California Press, 1980). There are, of course, some exceptions to this pattern, both among Vermeer's single-figure paintings (*A Lady Writing*, *Young Woman Standing at a Virginal*, *Young Woman Seated at a Virginal*) and those with more than one figure (*Girl Interrupted at Her Music*, *Girl with a Wine Glass*). In these pictures, as well as in his portraits or *tronies* such as the *Girl with the Pearl Earring*, at least one depicted face directly engages the viewer.

31 Charles H. Caffin, *The Story of Dutch Painting* (The Century Co., 1909), 140.

32 Vaudoyer, "Le mystérieux Vermeer III," 543–44.

33 Northrop Frye, *Anatomy of Criticism: Four Essays* (Princeton University Press, 1957), 250.

34 John Stuart Mill, "What is Poetry?" (1833), in Mill, *Literary Essays*, ed. Edward Alexander (Bobbs-Merrill, 1967), 56.

35 Wisława Szymborska, "Vermeer," in Szymborska, *Here*, trans. Clare Cavanagh and Stansiław Barańczak (Houghton Mifflin, 2010), 55.

36 Daniel Arasse, *Vermeer: Faith in Painting*, trans. Terry Grabar (Princeton University Press, 1994), 61. The early *Maid Asleep*, in which we appear to look down on the sleeping figure, is an exception (60). For a discussion of the blocking objects, which in turn follows Gowing, see 65–69.

37 Zirka Z. Filipczak, "Vermeer, Elusiveness, and Visual Theory," *Simiolus* 32.4 (2006), 266–67, 264.

38 Arasse, *Vermeer*, 86.

39 Jackson, *Dickinson's Misery*, 53.

40 W. Bürger [Théophile Thoré] "Van der Meer de Delft," *Gazette des beaux-arts*, vol. 21 (1866), 462.

41 See Jørgen Wadum, "Contours of Vermeer," in *Vermeer Studies*, ed. Ivan Gaskell and Michiel Jonkers (National Gallery of Art [Washington, DC], 1998).

42 Arthur C. Danto, "Vermeer," *The Nation*, 19 February 1996, 33. Danto advances this association of Vermeer's light with Protestant church interiors—and their representations by Vermeer's contemporaries—while acknowledging the artist's conversion to Catholicism.

43 Robert Lowell, "Epilogue," in Lowell, *Day by Day* (Farrar, Straus and Giroux, 1977), 127.

44 Rosemary Dobson, "The Mirror," in Dobson, *Collected Poems*, repr. edn (Angus & Robertson, 1993 [1991]), 67.

45 Lowell, "Epilogue," 127 (emphasis in the original). On the manuscript, see Saskia Hamilton, "Manuscript Study: Robert Lowell's 'Epilogue,'" 5 May 2014, https://poets.org/text/manuscript-study-robert-lowells-epilogue. Hamilton speculates that Lowell may have made the change in order to avoid repeating the word "eye" several lines later, but the repetition would have been semantically as well as sonically problematic: the final version pointedly contrasts "*the painter's vision*" both with photography and with what the later line calls "the threadbare art of my eye."

46 On the *Woman Holding a Balance* as a secularized Virgin Mary, see, e.g., Lisa Vergara, "Perspectives on Women in the Art of Vermeer," and Valerie Hedquist, "Religion in the Art and Life of Vermeer," both in *The Cambridge Companion to Vermeer*, ed. Wayne E. Franits (Cambridge University Press, 2001). For a more extended treatment of the relation between Vermeer's pregnant women and his domestic interiors that also evokes traditional representations of the Virgin, see Karin Leonhard, "Vermeer's Pregnant Women: On Human Generation and Pictorial Representation," *Art History* 25.3 (2002): 293–318. Cf. also Marilyn Chandler McEntyre, *In Quiet Light: Poems on Vermeer's Women* (William B. Eerdmans, 2000), a collection that frequently draws on Marian associations and imagery.

47 Robert Hass, "Art and Life," in Hass, *Time and Materials: Poems 1997–2005* (Ecco, 2007), 28.

48 Eamon Grennan, "Woman with Pearl Necklace (Vermeer)," in Grennan, *Relations: New & Selected Poems* (Graywolf Press, 1998), 191. For Siri Hustvedt, this painting is itself a version of the Annunciation, one "that makes no distinction between the spiritual and the physical world." In concluding her essay by calling the *Woman with a Pearl Necklace* "nothing less than an affirmation of the strangeness and beauty of simply being alive," Hustvedt comes very close to the spirit—and language—of Grennan's poem. See Siri Hustvedt, "Vermeer's Annunciation," in Hustvedt, *Yonder: Essays* (Henry Holt, 1998), 60, 61. On the painting as a possible Vanitas image, see, e.g., John J. Walsh Jr. "Vermeer," *The Metropolitan Museum of Art Bulletin*, n.s. vol. 31 (1973), sec. 8; J. M. Nash, "'To finde the Mindes construction in the Face,'" in *Vermeer Studies*, ed. Ivan Gaskell and Michiel Jonkers (National Gallery of Art [Washington, DC], 1998), 62–63; and Gregor J. M. Weber, "Paths to Inner Values," in *Vermeer*, ed. Pieter Roelofs and Gregor J. M. Weber (Rijksmuseum [Amsterdam]/Hannibal Books, 2023), 254–56.

49 Grennan, "Woman with Pearl Necklace," 191. I owe the observation about the double meaning of the poem's first word to Mary Fitzgerald-Hoyt's illuminating "Vermeer in Verse: Eamon Grennan's Domestic Interiors," *New Hibernia Review/Iris Éireannach Nua* 2.1 (1998), 129.

50 Culler, *Theory of the Lyric*, 226.

51 Alfred Corn, "Seeing All the Vermeers," *Poetry*, vol. 175 (1999), 26. Corn's title should best be understood as aspirational: by my count, his narrator manages to see just about half the paintings now generally attributed to the artist.

52 Szymborska, "Vermeer," 55; 54 (Polish original). I am grateful to Marta Figlerowicz for advice about the translation.

53 Lisel Mueller, "The Cook: After Vermeer," in Mueller, *Alive Together: New and Selected Poems* (Louisiana State University Press, 1996), 129.

54 Mueller, "Cook."

55 Hass, "Art and Life," 27, 29, 30.

56 See, e.g., Ira Sadoff, "Vermeer: The Officer and the Laughing Girl," *The Virginia Quarterly Review* 52.1 (1976), 113–14; Andrew Miller, "Vermeer, The Laughing Girl with her Officer, 1667," *Ekphrasis*, no. 3 (2004), 34–35; and Marilyn Chandler McEntyre, "Officer and Laughing Girl," in MacEntyre, *In Quiet Light*, 47. McEntyre's opening lines make the *Othello*-like character of this scenario explicit: "One more dark soldier, like the Moor, / tells a woman tales."

57 Diana Brebner, "Head of a Girl," in Brebner, *Ishtar Gate: Last and Selected Poems*, ed. Stephanie Bolster (McGill-Queen's University Press, 2005), 47; Marilyn Chandler McEntyre, "A Girl

Asleep," in MacEntyre, *In Quiet Light*, 37; Natasha Trethewey, "Repentance: After Vermeer's *A Maid Asleep*," in Trethewey, *Monument: Poems New and Selected* (Mariner Books. 2019), 165–66.

58 Trethewey, "Repentance," 166, 165.

59 Howard Nemerov, "Vermeer," in Nemerov, *The Next Room of the Dream* (University of Chicago Press, 1962), 37; Tomas Tranströmer, "Vermeer," in Tranströmer, *The Great Enigma: New Collected Poems*, trans. Robin Fulton (New Directions, 2006), 190.

60 Helen Vendler, "The Art of the Inexplicit," *The New Republic*, 2 February 2012, 30.

61 Nemerov, "Vermeer," 37.

62 Nemerov, "Vermeer," 37 (ellipses in original). These lines also draw on an elaborate set of allusions. "In the great reckoning of these little rooms / Where the weight of life is lifted and made light" takes off from Touchstone's remark to Audrey in *As You Like It* 3.3: "When a man's verses cannot be understood, nor a man's good wit seconded with the forward child Understanding, it strikes a man more dead than a great reckoning in a little room"—a phrase widely read as alluding in turn to the death of Christopher Marlowe, which was reputedly occasioned by a brawl over a reckoning, or bill. If death in this sense enters Nemerov's imagination of Vermeer's interiors, it does so primarily to be transfigured "and made light," though there also may be an anticipation here of the "darkening sky" in the *View of Delft* at the poem's end. For another equivocal hint of time and change within the paintings themselves, see the close of the second stanza, which speaks of how "even the inexorable / Domesticates itself and becomes charm" in Vermeer's art (37).

63 Nemerov, "Vermeer," 37.

64 Wayne Franits, *Vermeer* (Phaidon, 2015), for instance, speaks of "passing leaden clouds" (113), while the entry on the painting at https://www.essentialvermeer.com refers to "a momentary shadow." On the time of day, see especially Martin Bailey, *Vermeer*, repr. edn (Phaidon, 2014 [1995]), 60, where Bailey not only remarks the morning light but notes that a tiny clock on the Schiedam Gate indicates that it's just past seven. Interestingly, however, both the nineteenth-century art dealer John Smith and the early twentieth-century critic E. V. Lucas seem to have thought that the painting represented the harbor at sunset. See John Smith, *A Catalogue Raisonné of the Works of the Most Eminent Dutch, Flemish, and French Painters*, 9 vols. (London, 1829–42), 4:110; and E. V. Lucas, *Vermeer of Delft*, 2nd edn (Methuen, 1922), 17.

65 Nemerov, "Vermeer," 37.

66 Tranströmer, "Vermeer," 190 (ellipses in the original).

67 John Michael Montias, *Vermeer and His Milieu: A Web of Social History* (Princeton University Press, 1989), 199. All biographical information is drawn from Montias. For a sensitive reading of the poem, to which I am also indebted, see Staffan Bergsten, "To Go Through Walls: Tomas Tranströmer's 'Vermeer,'" trans. Steven P. Sondrup, *World Literature Today* 64.4 (1990): 582–90. Though he likewise calls attention to the historical context of these lines, Bergsten seems to have been unaware of Montias's findings: he still assumes, as Tranströmer appears to have done, that Vermeer painted in his father's inn.

68 Tranströmer, "Vermeer," 190.

69 Bergsten, "To Go Through Walls," 588.

70 Tranströmer, "Vermeer," 190.

71 For the argument that what looks to our eyes like pregnancy in Vermeer's work may be only an effect of seventeenth-century fashion, see, e.g., Marieke de Winkel, "The Interpretation of Dress in Vermeer's Paintings," in *Vermeer Studies*, ed. Ivan Gaskell and Michiel Jonkers (National Gallery of Art [Washington, DC], 1998), 330–32; and H. Rodney Nevitt Jr., "Vermeer on the Question of Love," in *The Cambridge Companion to Vermeer*, ed. Wayne E. Franits (Cambridge University Press, 2001),104. On the homology between images of pregnancy and Vermeer's domestic interiors, see Leonhard, "Vermeer's Pregnant Women."

72 Tranströmer, "Vermeer," 190. A reproduction of the Swedish manuscript appears in Bergsten, "To Go Through Walls," 582–83. I thank Martin Hägglund for help with the translation.

73 Tranströmer, "Vermeer," 190–91.

74 Harry Berger Jr., "Conspicuous Exclusion in Vermeer: An Essay in Renaissance Pastoral," in Berger, *Second World and Green World: Studies in Renaissance Fiction-Making* (University of California Press, 1990), 447, 450. I am grateful to Langdon Hammer both for the speculation about Vermeer's particular appeal to this postwar generation of poets and for the apt quotation from Elizabeth Bishop that serves as my epigraph. Bishop was responding to Jarrell's review of her

work in a recent issue of *Harper's*: see the letter dated 26 December 1955 in Elizabeth Bishop, *One Art: Letters*, selected and edited by Robert Giroux (Farrar, Straus & Giroux, 1994), 312.

75 Arasse, *Vermeer*, 49. Staffan Bergsten also notes this discrepancy between painting and poem (Bergsten, "To Go Through Walls," 587).

76 Tranströmer, "Vermeer," 190–91.

77 As Bergsten nicely observes, "It is as if the sky had come to the woman in the chamber in the form of an empty blue surface of the wall" ("To Go Through Walls," 590).

78 Tranströmer, "Vermeer," 191; Nemerov, "Vermeer," 37; Grennan, "Woman with Pearl Necklace," 191; Tranströmer, "Vermeer," 191, 190.

9. STORIES NOT TOLD

1 Anne Martens, *Getty: Iris Blog*, "Write the Opening Line to Vermeer's 'Lady in Blue,'" 8 February 2013, https://blogs.getty.edu/iris/write-the-opening-line-to-vermeers-lady-in-blue/.

2 Anne Martens, *Getty: Iris Blog*, "Dear 'Woman in Blue,' Let Me Tell You of the Future," 1 March 2013, https://blogs.getty.edu/iris/dear-woman-in-blue-let-me-tell-you-of/.

3 Cf. Max Kozloff, *Vermeer: A Study* (Contrasto, 2011), 79, including the resonant line that serves as my epigraph.

4 W. Bürger [Théophile Thoré], "Van der Meer de Delft," *Gazette des beaux-arts*, vol. 21 (1866), 460.

5 M0733, Allen Ginsburg Papers, Series 11, box 378 [Untitled], 1979 Nov. 25. This is a transcribed recording of Allen Ginsberg, Gregory Corso, and others at the Rijksmuseum in Amsterdam on 25 November 1979, quoted courtesy of the Department of Special Collections, Stanford University Libraries.

6 In a poem that clearly responds to the *Woman in Blue*, though the painting is never named, Debora Greger also assumes that the subject is "rereading" her letter. See Debora Greger, "Vermeer," *Off-Season at the Edge of the World: Poems* (University of Illinois Press, 1994), 12–13.

7 Rodney Pybus, "Out of the Blue: after Johannes Vermeer" (1985), in Pybus, *Cicadas in Their Summers: New and Selected Poems 1965–1985* (Carcanet, 1988), 55–56.

8 Teju Cole, "Seeing Beyond the Beauty of a Vermeer," *New York Times Magazine*, 25 May 2023, https://www.nytimes.com/2023/05/25/magazine/vermeer-beauty-brutality.html?searchResultPosition=1.

9 For all his sensitivity to the effects of light, Cole makes no mention of the fact that the woman herself casts no shadow—an implicit removal of her from time that may help to explain this subtle shift to the painter as protagonist. On the effect of the shadow's absence from the *Woman in Blue*, see esp. Arthur K. Wheelock Jr., *Vermeer and the Art of Painting* (Yale University Press, 1995), 13; Arthur K. Wheelock Jr., "Vermeer's Craft and Artistry," in *The Cambridge Companion to Vermeer*, ed. Wayne E. Franits (Cambridge University Press, 2001), 48; and Wayne Franits, *Vermeer* (Phaidon, 2015), 145.

10 Cole, "Seeing Beyond the Beauty."

11 On Jacob van Loo's *Diana and Her Nymphs* as a probable model for Vermeer's *Diana and Her Companions*, see, inter alia, John Michael Montias, *Vermeer and His Milieu: A Web of Social History* (Princeton University Press, 1989), 105–6, 143–46; and Franits, *Vermeer*, 25–30. Like others before him, Franits also remarks "the striking affinities" between Vermeer's *Diana* and Rembrandt van Rijn's *Bathsheba at Her Bath* (1654), though it is not clear how Vermeer would have known Rembrandt's painting (26).

12 Montias, *Vermeer and His Milieu*, 143.

13 Wheelock, *Vermeer and the Art*, 39–42.

14 H. Rodney Nevitt Jr., "Vermeer on the Question of Love," in *The Cambridge Companion to Vermeer*, ed. Wayne E. Franits (Cambridge University Press, 2001), 92. As Nevitt goes on to observe, "Few of Vermeer's figures offer clues in facial expression or body language about the nature of their relationship to each other. The markers of love—music, wine, and the interaction among the figures—seem to be deliberately stretched, pulled apart, to precisely the point at which connecting them into a narrative of courtship becomes problematic."

15 While Wheelock invokes "the feeling of warmth and spontaneity conveyed by the informality of the figures' poses and by the joyousness of the girl's expression," Lawrence Gowing speaks

somewhat more equivocally of the picture's "unhappy jocularity," and Edward Snow argues for a subtle dialectic between the soldier's "dark, looming presence, alien and somewhat threatening," and the openness of the young woman, who in his account serves finally to redeem the guilty sexuality of the male viewer's identification with his painted counterpart. See Wheelock, *Vermeer and the Art*, 55; Lawrence Gowing, *Vermeer*, 3rd edn (University of California Press, 1997 [1952]), 89; and Edward A. Snow, *A Study of Vermeer* (University of California Press, 1979), 74.

16 Harry Berger Jr., *Second World and Green World: Studies in Renaissance Fiction-Making* (University of California Press, 1990), 442, 457.

17 Cf. Daniel Arasse, who follows up his own discussion of how Vermeer "excluded two expected motifs" from the hanging globe in the *Allegory of the Catholic Faith*—a reflected image of the painter in the studio, on the one hand, and of a cross, on the other—by contending, contra Berger, that such exclusion is not conspicuous but "discreet" (Arasse, *Vermeer: Faith in Painting*, trans. Terry Grabar [Princeton University Press, 1994], 85, 125n44).

18 Snow, *Study of Vermeer*, 36; Montias, *Vermeer and His Milieu*, 145.

19 Tracy Chevalier, *Girl with a Pearl Earring*, repr. edn (Plume, 2001 [1999]), 91.

20 For a partial exception, see James Ivory's "Two Letters on a Day in the Mid-1660s," a short tale produced by the American film director in response to an invitation from the Frick to comment on the *Mistress and Maid* for its Diptych series. Imagining that one of the letters in the painting comes from the woman's official suitor and the other from the man she prefers, Ivory exploits a writer's license not only to vocalize the thoughts of both mistress and maid but to leap forward chronologically to a time when the woman has been widowed and briefly encounters her former lover on a wintry walk. The Frick series, which pairs an essay by an art historian with a contribution by a writer or artist, might be understood as a less democratic version of the Getty's experiment. See Margaret Iacono and James Ivory, *Vermeer's Mistress and Maid* (The Frick Collection, 2018), esp. 9–15.

21 Nanette Salomon, "From Sexuality to Civility: Vermeer's Women," in *Vermeer Studies*, ed. Ivan Gaskell and Michiel Jonker (National Gallery of Art [Washington, DC], 1998), 321–22; Nevitt, "Vermeer on the Question of Love," 90.

22 Gowing, *Vermeer*, 53. For another eloquent formulation of this inaccessibility, see Svetlana Alpers, *The Art of Describing: Dutch Art in the Seventeenth Century* (University of Chicago Press, 1983), 224: "For all their presence, Vermeer's women are a world apart, inviolate, self-contained, but, more significantly, self-possessed. [. . .] Vermeer recognizes the world present in these women as something other than himself and with a kind of passionate detachment he lets it, through them, be."

23 Reynolds Price, "Preface: A Place to Stand" (1998), in Price, *A Singular Family: Rosacoke and Her Kin* (Simon & Schuster, 1999), 15, 17–18. In addition to *A Long and Happy Life,* this edition includes "A Chain of Love" (1958), the short story in which Rosacoke first appeared, and two further installments of her family's story: a prequel to the novel that Price entitled *A Generous Man* (1966) and a sequel, *Good Hearts* (1988). An earlier version of the preface, including the material on Vermeer, appeared in 1983. I am grateful to Marguerite Anne Glass, "Vermeer in Dialogue: From Appropriation to Response" (PhD dissertation, University of Maryland, 2003), 194, for first directing me to Price's work.

24 Price, *Singular Family*, 251, 297–98, 373, 375.

25 Price, *Singular Family*, 394.

26 Though scholars have been more apt to invoke such associations for the *Woman Holding a Balance* than for the *Woman in Blue*, both paintings resemble traditional images of the Virgin, not only in the apparent pregnancy of their solitary figures but in the women's contemplative aura and the light by which they are illuminated. And blue is, of course, the conventional color of Mary's robe. On traces of the Virgin in one or more of Vermeer's pregnant figures, see, e.g., Nanette Salomon, "Vermeer and the Balance of Destiny," in *Essays in Northern European Art Presented to Egbert Haverkamp-Begemann on His Sixtieth Birthday*, ed. Anne-Marie Logan (Davaco, 1983), 221; Lisa Vergara, "Perspectives on Women in the Art of Vermeer," 61–62, and Valerie Hedquist, "Religion in the Art and Life of Vermeer," 124–25, both in *The Cambridge Companion to Vermeer*, ed. Wayne E. Franits (Cambridge University Press, 2001); and Karin Leonhard, "Vermeer's Pregnant Women: On Human Generation and Pictorial Representation," *Art History* 25.3 (2002), 304, 309–11.

27 Price, *Singular Family*, 394.

28 As we shall see later in this chapter, a notable exception to this rule is the art historian Benjamin Binstock, who dates the picture five years later than others do—ca. 1670 rather than ca. 1665—and confidently identifies its model as Vermeer's eldest daughter, Maria (Binstock, *Vermeer's Family Secrets: Genius, Discovery, and the Unknown Apprentice* [Routledge, 2009], 203–9). Those who raise the possibility that a daughter posed for the picture only to dismiss it on the grounds of dating include Martin Bailey, *Vermeer*, repr. edn (Phaidon, 2014 [1995]), 82; Walter Liedtke, *Vermeer: The Complete Paintings*, repr. edn (Ludion, 2011 [2008]), 132; and Pieter Roelofs, "Vermeer's Tronies: An Outward Gaze of Connection," in *Vermeer*, ed. Pieter Roelofs and Gregor J. M. Weber (Rijksmuseum [Amsterdam]/Hannibal Books, 2023), 211.

29 Tracy Chevalier, interview with Jonathan Janson, 1 August 2003, https://www.essentialvermeer.com/interviews_newsletter/chevalier_interview.html.

30 Chevalier, interview with Jonathan Janson.

31 Chevalier, *Girl with a Pearl Earring*, 131.

32 Gowing, *Vermeer*, 52.

33 Chevalier, *Girl with a Pearl Earring*, 5, 64, 132, 191.

34 Chevalier, *Girl with a Pearl Earring*, 160.

35 On Tanneke, whose last name was Everpoel, see Montias, *Vermeer and His Milieu*, 160–61.

36 Montias, *Vermeer and His Milieu*, esp. 116–20, 126, 154–70.

37 Cole, "Seeing Beyond the Beauty."

38 For the legal deposition in which Tanneke testified to this episode, see Montias, *Vermeer and His Milieu*, 160. In the novel, the attack on the painting is clearly meant to recall the opening scene, when Catharina accidentally knocks the knife with which Griet is cutting vegetables to the floor.

39 Gowing, *Vermeer*, 52.

40 This and other facts about the origins of *Girl in Hyacinth Blue* are drawn from the separately paginated interview with the author that is appended to the 1999 Penguin edition of the novel.

41 Susan Vreeland, *Girl in Hyacinth Blue* (Penguin, 1999), 29, 153, 152 (emphasis in the original).

42 Vreeland, *Girl in Hyacinth Blue*, 51, 163.

43 Lawrence Wechsler, *Vermeer in Bosnia: A Reader* (Pantheon Books, 2004), 13–14. (An earlier version of Wechsler's essay originally appeared in *The New Yorker*, 10 November 1995, under the title "Inventing Peace.")

44 In another work of the same year, Peter Greenaway and Louis Andriessen collaborated on an opera entitled *Writing to Vermeer* (1999) that rendered this Vermeer-in-Bosnia effect both auditory and visual. Interrupting arias in which three women—Vermeer's wife Catharina, his mother-in-law Maria Thins, and a fictional model named Saskia—sing imaginary "letters" to the absent artist about minor details of domestic life with more dissonant passages accompanied by action and video projections evoking the violence and upheaval of the seventeenth-century Netherlands, the opera ends with the stage visually awash in representations of the 1672 flood that the Dutch deliberately triggered in order to thwart the French invasion. Though *Writing to Vermeer* exploits the emotional effects of such juxtapositions, it differs from the other works discussed in this chapter by not really deploying them for narrative purposes, unless one counts Andriessen's claim that the music creates a trajectory in which "what happens, or what could happen outside the home, gradually enters the three women's consciousness." I quote from page 14 of Andriessen's interview with Maja Trochimczyk, "The Music of *Writing to Vermeer*," in the booklet produced for the Nonesuch CD of the opera in 2006.

45 Katharine Weber, *The Music Lesson* (Picador, 1999), 11; Vreeland, *Girl in Hyacinth Blue*, 152.

46 Montias, *Vermeer and His Milieu*, 162.

47 Vreeland, *Girl in Hyacinth Blue*, 26, 228, 230.

48 Chevalier, *Girl with a Pearl Earring*, 180; Vreeland *Girl in Hyacinth Blue*, 234, 237.

49 Linda Nochlin, "Why Have There Been No Great Women Artists?" (1971), in Nochlin, *Women, Art, and Power and Other Essays* (Harper & Row, 1988), 168.

50 Maria Lassnig, *Art Education* (1976), in *Maria Lassnig: Animation Films*, Index Edition DVD 033.

51 In a poem entitled "Catherina Vermeer," the Canadian poet Diana Brebner indulged in a related fantasy, by wishfully conflating one of the artist's daughters with a Dutch painter of the same name that the epigraph implies Brebner spotted in some chronicle. Part of a sequence of poems dedicated to Vermeer, "Catherina Vermeer" is the only one, however, whose epigraph

is neither dated nor sourced, so the evidence that seems to have inspired the fantasy is impossible to confirm. See Diana Brebner, *Ishtar Gate: Last and Selected Poems*, ed. Stephanie Bolster (McGill-Queens University Press, 2005), 46. For the Vermeer family tree, see Montias, *Vermeer and His Milieu*, 370–71.

52 Binstock, *Vermeer's Family Secrets*, 97, 178, 259.

53 Binstock, *Vermeer's Family Secrets*, 259, 81.

54 Binstock, *Vermeer's Family Secrets*, 133, 135–36, 119.

55 Marjorie E. Wieseman, Alexandra Libby, E. Melanie Gifford, and Dina Anchin, "Vermeer's Studio and the *Girl with a Flute*: New Findings from the National Gallery of Art," *Journal of Historians of Netherlandish Art* 14.2 (2022), https://doi.org/10.5092/jhna.2022.14.2.3.

56 Roelofs, "Vermeer's Tronies," 213–14.

57 Binstock, *Vermeer's Family Secrets*, 249.

58 Binstock, *Vermeer's Family Secrets*, 19, 258, 287.

59 For previous comparisons of the two panels to self-portraits, see Binstock, *Vermeer's Family Secrets*, 251–52.

60 Binstock, *Vermeer's Family Secrets*, 257–265, quotation at 265. For clarity's sake, I have chosen not to follow Binstock's occasional retitling of the paintings in question.

61 Binstock, *Vermeer's Family Secrets*, 258, 186, 281.

62 Montias, *Vermeer and His Milieu*, 338.

63 Binstock, *Vermeer's Family Secrets*, 268; Montias, *Vermeer and His Milieu*, 217, 260–61.

64 Binstock, *Vermeer's Family Secrets*, 269.

65 Binstock, *Vermeer's Family Secrets*, 270.

66 Brian Howell, *The Dance of Geometry* (The Toby Press, 2002), esp. 85–151.

67 Pascal Lainé, *La Dentellière* (Gallimard, 1974), 84. All translations are my own, though I have gratefully consulted the one English version currently available: *A Web of Lace*, trans. George Crowther (Abelard-Schuman, 1976).

68 The allusion to Vermeer is explicitly acknowledged, however, in Michael Tilby's introduction and notes to a 19[illegible] reissue of *La Dentellière* for Methuen that also includes a reproduction of the painting. Tilby further elucidates the connection when he comments briefly on the 1977 film adaptation by Claude Goretta: "On the screen, Pomme's existence cannot be doubted. She is also obliged to say more than she does in the novel. As a result, she loses much of her mystery, and Vermeer's painting no longer has a part to play in our appreciation of her distinctiveness" (32–33).

69 Lainé, *La Dentellière*, 17.

70 Lainé, *La Dentellière*, 105, 116.

71 Lainé, *La Dentellière*, 112, 121–22, 173, 172. For other references to Aimery's future as a curator, see 86, 91, 93, 94, 97, 140, 158, and 159.

72 Lainé, *La Dentellière*, 161, 162–63.

73 Lainé, *La Dentellière*, 116.

74 For an analysis of these moves in the context of Postmodernism, see Leroy T. Day, "Pascal Lainé's 'La Dentellière': Adolescent Love and the Postmodern Narrative," *Modern Language Studies* 24.2 (1994): 57–66.

75 Lainé, *La Dentellière*, 172, 176–77.

76 Michael White, *Travels in Vermeer: A Memoir* (Persea Books, 2015), 3, 123.

77 I draw on an author's statement once available on the Amazon website for the novel, but which seems to have since disappeared.

78 J. P. Smith, *The Discovery of Light* (Thomas & Mercer, 1992), 2, 44.

79 Smith, *Discovery of Light*, 21, 37.

80 Smith, *Discovery of Light*, 42–43.

81 Smith, *Discovery of Light*, 78, 121, 122, 139, 141.

82 Smith, *Discovery of Light*, 221, 4.

83 Smith, *Discovery of Light*, 177.

84 Marcel Proust, *À la recherche du temps perdu*, ed. Jean-Yves Tadié, 4 vols., Bibliothèque de la Pléiade (Gallimard, 1987–89), 4:474 (Eng., 6:254 [see Preface, n. 9 above]).

85 Proust, *À la recherche*, 1:195 (1:237). The concluding paragraphs of this chapter partly draw on arguments first advanced in Ruth Bernard Yeazell, *Art of the Everyday: Dutch Painting and the Realist Novel* (Princeton University Press, 2008), 182–94.

86 Proust, *À la recherche*, 3:209 (4:246–47).

87 Proust to Jean-Louis Vaudoyer, 1 May 1921, in Marcel Proust, *Correspondance*, ed. Philip Kolb, 21 vols. (Plon, 1970–93), 20:226.

88 Marcel Proust, "La méthode de Saint-Beuve," in Proust, *Contre Saint-Beuve, précedé de Pastiches et mélanges et suivi de Essais et articles*, ed. Pierre Clarac and Yves Sandre, Bibliothèque de la Pléiade (Gallimard, 1971), 225.

89 Proust, *À la recherche*, 1:347–48 (1:425).

90 For some relevant examples, see the editor's note to the *Pléiade* edition, 3:1740. The occasion of Proust's last visit to the *View of Delft* was an exhibition of Dutch painting at the Jeu de Paume in the spring of 1921.

91 Proust to Jean-Louis Vaudoyer [between 18 and 14 May 1921], in Proust, *Correspondance*, 20:289.

92 Thierry Laget, "Le vernis d'un autre maître: Proust et la peinture ancienne," in *Marcel Proust: L'écriture et les arts*, ed. Jean-Yves Tadié and Florence Callu (Gallimard, 1999), 27.

93 Jean-Yves Tadié, *Marcel Proust: A Life*, trans. Euan Cameron (Penguin, 2001), 776.

94 Proust, *À la recherche*, 3:692 (5:207).

95 Jean-Louis Vaudoyer, "Le mystérieux Vermeer III," *L'opinion*, 14 May 1921, 543.

96 Proust, *À la recherche*, 3:692 (5:207).

97 Proust, *À la recherche*, 3:692 (5:207).

98 Proust, *À la recherche*, 4:474 (6:254).

Index

Locations of images are given in **boldface**.
For the reader's convenience, first notes to all works cited are included in the index.

B

E

F

G

H

I

J

K

M

O

P

T

X

Y

Z

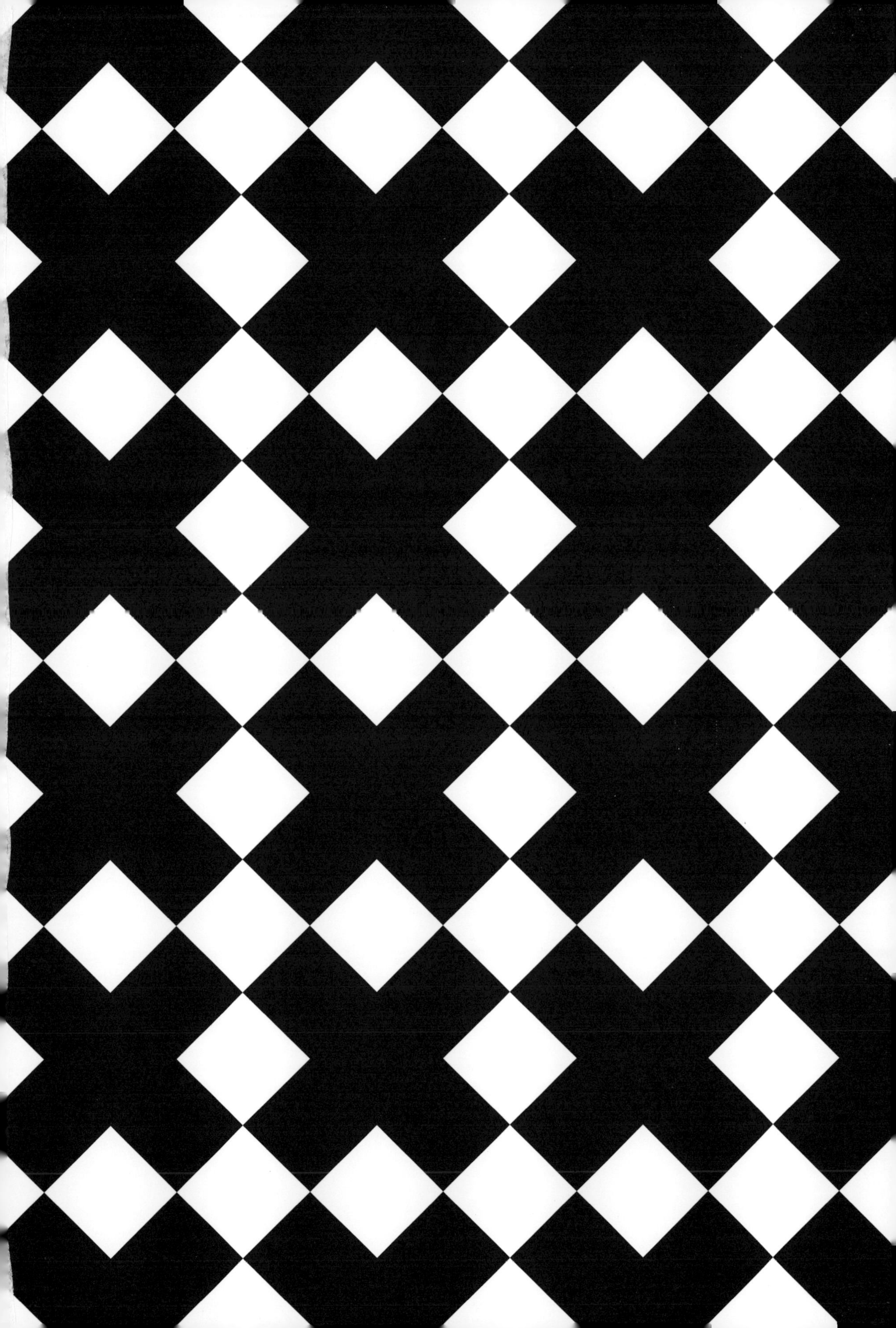

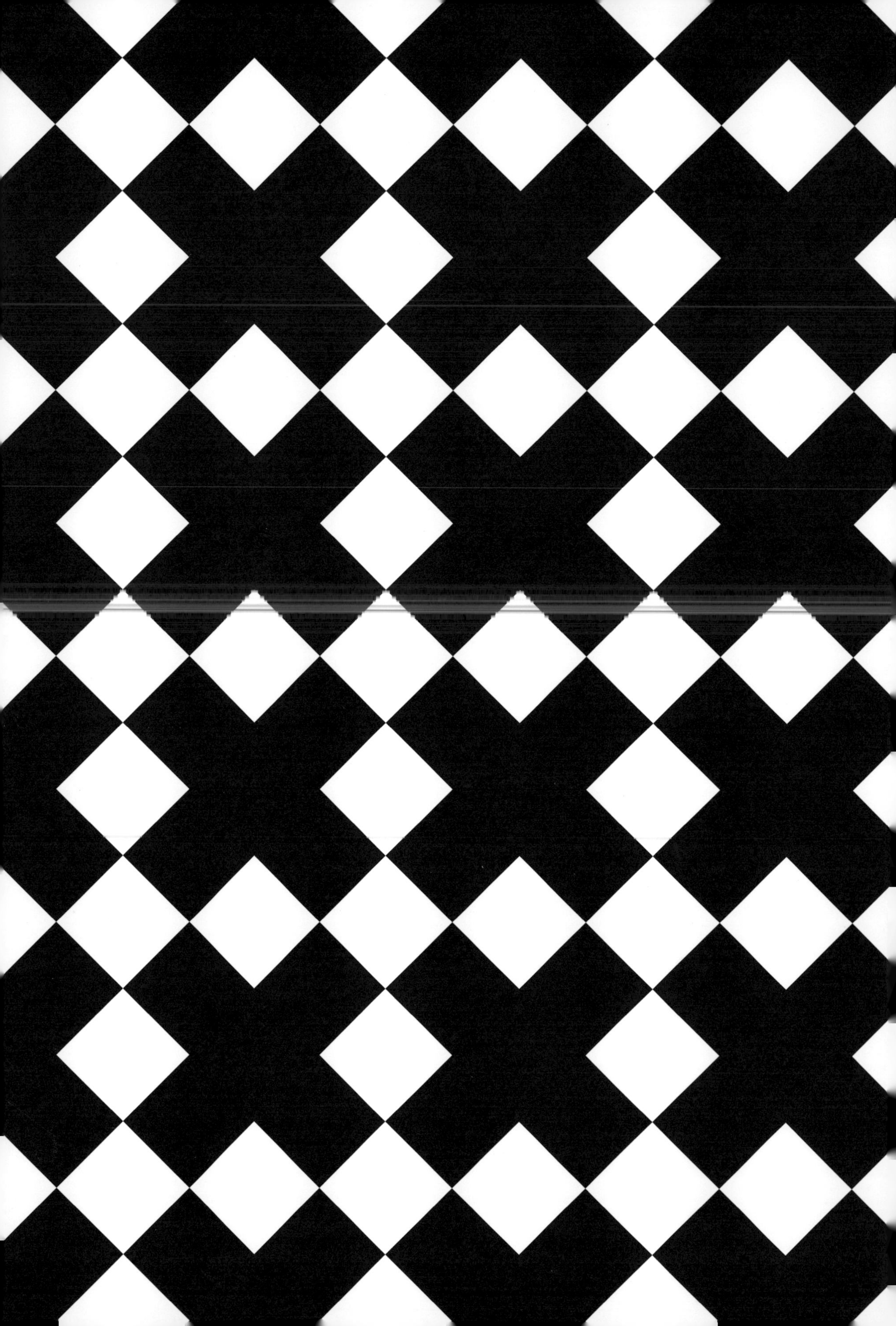